Dreamweaver® 8 All-in-One Desk Reference For Dummies

W9-AYR-927

The Dreamweaver Environment

Document toolbar

Insert bar

Document window

Panels

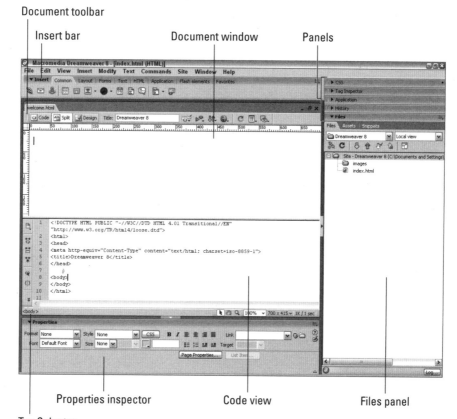

Properties inspector

Code view

Files panel

Tag Selector

Choosing a View

- ✔ **Code:** This view is useful for hand-coding and editing HTML, JavaScript, server-side coding (for example, PHP, ASP, or CFML), and other code. Choose View⇨Code or click the Code button on the Document toolbar.

- ✔ **Design:** This *WYSIWYG* (What You See Is What You Get) editor displays a visual rendering of your Web page. Choose View⇨Design or click the Design button on the Document toolbar.

- ✔ **Split:** The best of both worlds, Split view shows both Design and Code views. Resize the two panes by clicking and dragging the divider bar between them. Choose View⇨Code and Design or click the Split button on the Document toolbar.

BESTSELLING BOOK SERIES

Dreamweaver® 8 All-in-One Desk Reference For Dummies®

Cheat Sheet

Using Panels

Panel	Shortcut	What You Use It For
Assets	F11	Access the components of your Web site, including images, templates, and library items. See Book III.
Behaviors	Shift+F4 (Windows) or Shift+F3 (Mac)	Insert JavaScript behaviors. See Book IV, Chapter 2.
Bindings	Ctrl+F10 (Windows) or ⌘+F10 (Mac)	Create recordsets and datasets. See Book VIII.
Components	Ctrl+F7 (Windows) or ⌘+F7 (Mac)	Add new Web services (with JSP or .NET) or ColdFusion components (if you're using ColdFusion). See Book VIII, Chapter 5.
CSS Styles	Shift+F11	Create internal, external, and embedded Cascading Style Sheets. See Book III, Chapter 1.
Databases	Ctrl+Shift+F10 (Windows) or ⌘+Shift+F10 (Mac)	Review your database connections. See Book VII.
Files	F8	Manage the files in your local, remote, and testing sites. See Book I, Chapter 1.
Frames	Shift+F2	Select and rename frames. See Book IV, Chapter 3.
History	Shift+F10	Undo and redo multiple steps at a time. See Book III, Chapter 4.
Layers	F2	Insert or change a layer on your page. See Book IV, Chapter 1.
Snippets	Shift+F9	Access prewritten snippets of code. See Book III, Chapter 4.
Timelines	Alt+F9 (Windows) or Option+F9 (Mac)	Modify the properties of a layer over time to animate it. See Book IV, Chapter 4.

Web Site Resources

Web Site	Address
Dreamweaver Support Center	www.macromedia.com/support/dreamweaver/
Dreamweaver Exchange	www.macromedia.com/exchange/dreamweaver/
World Wide Web Consortium (W3C)	www.w3.org
Web Accessibility Initiative	www.w3.org/WAI/
W3 Schools	www.w3schools.com
Dynamic Drive DHTML Scripts	www.dynamicdrive.com
JavaScript Source	http://javascript.internet.com

Copyright © 2006 Wiley Publishing, Inc. All rights reserved. Item 8142-8. For more information about Wiley Publishing, call 1-800-762-2974.

For Dummies: Bestselling Book Series for Beginners

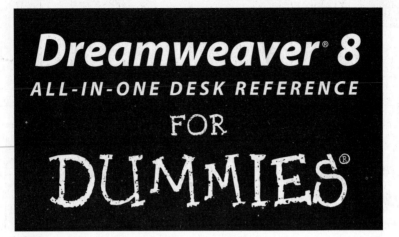

Dreamweaver® 8
ALL-IN-ONE DESK REFERENCE
FOR
DUMMIES®

by
Sue Jenkins
Michele E. Davis
Jon A. Phillips

WILEY

Wiley Publishing, Inc.

Dreamweaver® 8 All-in-One Desk Reference For Dummies®

Published by
Wiley Publishing, Inc.
111 River Street
Hoboken, NJ 07030-5774
www.wiley.com

For general information on our other products and services, please contact our Customer Care Department within the U.S. at 800-762-2974, outside the U.S. at 317-572-3993, or fax 317-572-4002.

For technical support, please visit www.wiley.com/techsupport.

Wiley also publishes its books in a variety of electronic formats. Some content that appears in print may not be available in electronic books.

Library of Congress Control Number: 2006922424

ISBN-13: 978-0-471-78142-4

ISBN-10: 0-471-78142-8

Manufactured in the United States of America

10 9 8 7 6 5 4 3 2 1

1O/QX/QX/QW/IN

WILEY

About the Authors

Sue Jenkins is a Web and graphic designer, illustrator, writer, and teacher. With nearly ten years experience, she provides design services to small and medium-sized businesses, entrepreneurs, consultants, writers, and artists through her company, Luckychair (www.luckychair.com). She ran her own greeting card company from 2002–2005, and continues to license these and other illustrations to manufacturers around the world. Sue is a contributing writer of technical articles for the online e-zine TechTrax. She also teaches courses in Macromedia Dreamweaver, Adobe Photoshop, and Adobe Illustrator at Noble Desktop. Sue lives with her husband and son in New York City.

Michele Davis is a published author and technical writer. She has written trade books for O'Reilly & Associates, Sybex, and Simon & Schuster. Michele has 18 years experience in the technical arena; she breaks down highly technical concepts for end users from an instructional design perspective. Michele has taught technical and creative non-fiction courses at the graduate level and creates custom Web sites. She can be found on the Web at www.kraut grrl.com. Michele lives in Minneapolis with her husband and three children.

Jon Phillips, nicknamed ubergeek, is an open-source programmer with a background in UNIX and databases as well as ERP systems, including Oracle, SQL Server, PHP, and MySQL. Jon creates back-end Web site code including blogs, auction, and Web-based stores. Jon has been programming for 12 years and enjoys building and bug fixing computers on the side. He's co-authored trade books for Sybex and O'Reilly & Associates. Jon lives in Minneapolis with his wife and three children. He promotes his business at www.kraut boy.com.

Dedication

Sue Jenkins: To Phil, for your love, support, patience, and humor.

Jon Phillips and Michele Davis want to thank Simon, Mimi, and Zack for being so patient while their parents write books back to back.

Authors' Acknowledgments

Sue humbly gives thanks to: my agent Matt Wagner for offering me this project and supporting me at every turn; editors Kim Darosett, Rebecca Senninger, Travis Smith, and Nicole Haims at Wiley for carefully reading through every word and offering great suggestions to improve this book; Acquisitions Editor Bob Woerner for his kindness and down-to-earth professionalism; and both Michele Davis and Jon Phillips for their awesome last-minute pinch-hitting. I'd also like to thank my incredible son, Kyle, whose curiosity and humor constantly amaze me.

Jon and Michele want to thank our fantastic agent, Matt Wagner, who has integrity and brings great projects to the table! Kim Darosett and Bob Woerner at Wiley have been fantastic during the writing process as well as incredibly helpful. We want to thank Renee LaPlume for helping out during the writing process and Lori LaChapelle who have been consistent friends in our lives. Both Renee and Lori helped out when we were struggling with content for the book to make it as successful as it can be. Michele wants to thank her eldest son, Simon, for always having cool music to listen to and for helping out with Zack whenever I needed it! I also thank Mimi for being understanding when I've been very busy. Lastly, we want to thank Sue Jenkins for being warm and welcoming when we became co-authors on this project.

Publisher's Acknowledgments

We're proud of this book; please send us your comments through our online registration form located at www.dummies.com/register/.

Some of the people who helped bring this book to market include the following:

Acquisitions, Editorial, and Media Development

Project Editor: Kim Darosett

Acquisitions Editor: Bob Woerner

Copy Editor: Rebecca Senninger

Technical Editor: Travis Smith

Editorial Manager: Leah Cameron

Media Development Manager: Laura VanWinkle

Editorial Assistant: Amanda Foxworth

Sr. Editorial Assistant: Cherie Case

Cartoons: Rich Tennant (www.the5thwave.com)

Composition Services

Project Coordinator: Jennifer Theriot

Layout and Graphics: Claudia Bell, Carl Byers, Denny Hager, Stephanie D. Jumper, Barbara Moore, Barry Offringa, Lynsey Osborn, Heather Ryan, Julie Trippetti,

Proofreaders: Laura L. Bowman, Leeann Harney, Joe Niesen

Indexer: Sherry Massey

Special Help: Nicole Haims, Andy Hollandbeck, Laura Miller, Linda Morris, Nick Rambo

Publishing and Editorial for Technology Dummies

Richard Swadley, Vice President and Executive Group Publisher

Andy Cummings, Vice President and Publisher

Mary Bednarek, Executive Acquisitions Director

Mary C. Corder, Editorial Director

Publishing for Consumer Dummies

Diane Graves Steele, Vice President and Publisher

Joyce Pepple, Acquisitions Director

Composition Services

Gerry Fahey, Vice President of Production Services

Debbie Stailey, Director of Composition Services

Contents at a Glance

Table of Contents

Introduction

*W*hen professional Web designers want to build a Web site, they nearly always pick Dreamweaver. With about 80 percent of all designers using it, Dreamweaver is definitely the top dual-platform (PC and Mac) Web design software application on the market today.

What makes Dreamweaver so great is the combo WYSIWYG *(What You See Is What You Get)* coding interface that allows you to build HTML files containing text, graphics, and other media, all the while seeing the page layout and its code as you create pages in Dreamweaver's Design and Code views.

Dreamweaver accurately generates all the HTML and JavaScript source code needed for Web developers to create HTML- and XHTML-compliant Web pages. No more sweating intricate coding issues such as merging table cells, creating rollover effects, and applying CSS to text. In addition, Dreamweaver integrates well with Fireworks for roundtrip graphic editing and Contribute 3 for Web site maintenance and the publishing of content changes by a non-designer.

Dreamweaver 8 enhancements include a better coding environment, integrated support for JavaScript, CSS, server-side scripting, and accessibility standards-compliant code. You'll also find improved dynamic content creation tools for connecting to databases, such as MySQL, and working with a variety of scripting technologies including PHP, ASP, JSP, ASP.NET, and ColdFusion. The program contains all the tools you need to streamline page development, and many of the tools are customizable through the Preferences dialog box.

Use *Dreamweaver 8 All-in-One Desk Reference For Dummies* as your complete guide to the exciting world of Web design.

About This Book

This is a reference book, which means you can jump around from chapter to chapter reading whatever section you want as the need arises. Don't feel locked into the idea of reading the book from cover to cover. In fact, think of each minibook as its own little reference zone where each zone is split into chapters about performing specific tasks in Dreamweaver 8.

Everything you find in this book is written so you don't have to wade through complicated technical help files or have to commit anything to memory. To keep things simple, you'll find detailed, step-by-step, easy-to-follow instructions. When more technical information is needed to clarify a particular process, it's often set apart from the main text in sidebars or noted in the margins with a Technical Stuff icon.

The bottom line is that we want to make you comfortable with Dreamweaver 8 and hope that you'll continue to use this book frequently and consider it the main resource of your Web-design library.

Conventions Used in This Book

To help with new terms and concepts, the following typographical rules or *conventions* are used in this book:

✦ **New terms:** New terms are set apart with italics. For example:

Dreamweaver 8 comes with the commonly used JavaScripts, which it refers to as *behaviors*, ready to insert into your pages from the Behaviors panel.

✦ **Code samples:** We include short code samples in monospaced text within the paragraph, like this: `<img src="logo.gif">`. We set longer code samples apart from the text, like this:

```
<frameset rows="80,*" cols="*" frameborder="NO"
    border="0" framespacing="0">
  <frame src="top.html" name="topFrame" scrolling="NO"
    noresize title="topFrame">
```

For the times when we want to draw your attention to particular parts of code samples, we indicate the important parts in bold, as in this example: `<div id="`**`Layer1`**`"></div>`.

✦ **Reader entry:** Anything you need to type is in boldface.

✦ **Cross-platform:** Whenever PCs and Macs have different shortcuts, we include both the Windows equivalent (right-click) and the Mac equivalent (Control+click).

✦ **Web addresses:** Web addresses are set apart in monofont, such as `www.macromedia.com`.

What You Don't Have to Read

You don't have to read any part of this book that doesn't interest you. For example, if you never intend to use Fireworks, skip that chapter! And if you see a technical sidebar that covers more technical information than you care to know, pass it by. The main thing is that you know what is available and only read what is useful to you.

Assumptions About You

With only a general idea of the kinds of people who will buy this book, we must make certain broad assumptions about all our readers to write this book with enough specificity for each of you. Therefore, we assume that you're a human being living on planet Earth who knows how to operate a computer and visit Web sites on the Internet, and has a desire to create Web sites using Dreamweaver. Beyond that, we presume no prior knowledge of Web design, HTML, JavaScript, CSS, or Dreamweaver.

How This Book Is Organized

This book is divided into nine minibooks, each of which is further divided into relevant chapters organized by topic. Each minibook relates to the most important concepts in Dreamweaver.

Book I: Getting Started

Begin your trip into the world of Web design with a look around the Dreamweaver workspace and a review of site design. Then find out how to create and manage sites in Dreamweaver — an important step that enables you to take full advantage of Dreamweaver's automated features.

Book II: Mastering the Basics

Book II shows you everything you need to know to create new documents; add and format text on a page; insert graphics and create rollover buttons; convert text and graphics into clickable links to other Web pages; add movies, sound, and other media files to your pages; add tables for organizing content; and build fantastic forms for collecting data from visitors.

Book III: Working Like the Pros

Book III walks you through the process of styling your pages with Cascading Style Sheets (CSS), building sites using Dreamweaver templates, and using Library items. You also find out about using server-side includes, creating and using code snippets, and recording and saving custom commands with the History panel. The final chapter in this minibook contains information on using Dreamweaver with Fireworks for roundtrip image optimization.

Book IV: Energizing Your Site

When you're ready to add more zing and pizzazz to your pages, turn to Book IV. Here you find out how to work with layers instead of tables, create opportunities for visitor interactivity by adding JavaScript behaviors to objects on your pages, and design pages built with frames. The final chapter in this minibook shows you all about the benefits of XHTML and how to configure Dreamweaver to write XHTML-compliant code.

Book V: Publishing Your Site

Book V shows you how to run Dreamweaver's reports and use other tools to test and fix any errors before you publish your site. You also find out how to select and set up a remote connection to your host server and transfer files to the remote site.

Book VI: Working Collaboratively

Macromedia's Contribute 3 is a software program that allows nondesigners to edit and update content on live Web pages through a special interface — all without needing to know any HTML or Dreamweaver. Book VI contains information on setting up, connecting to, and managing a Contribute site.

Book VII: Building Web Applications

This minibook discusses how to select and add Web and application servers along with how to configure, edit, and delete database connections. When working with databases, troubleshooting problems is important, so we also discuss resolving permission problems, database connection issues, and error messages.

Book VIII: Making Pages Dynamic

In this minibook, you find out how to define data sources and make them available for use in your dynamic pages. We also show you how to add simple dynamic data to your Web pages, as well as create HTML tables for your recordsets, navigate through your recordsets, and dynamically control them. In addition, you discover how to test the functionality of your dynamic site by using Dreamweaver's Live Data view. This minibook also includes a chapter on working with ColdFusion components, adding Web services to your site, and putting custom server behaviors to work.

Book IX: Developing Applications Rapidly

Book IX shows you how to build master and detail pages, search and results pages, and record insert, update, and delete pages. We also get into more complicated territory, such as calling ASP command objects, working with JSP prepared statements, and using stored procedures. Finally, you find out how to restrict site access.

Icons Used in This Book

To make your experience with the book easier, you'll find a handful of icons in the margins of the book to indicate particular points of interest.

Tip icons alert you to interesting techniques or hints that can save you time and effort.

The Remember icon is a friendly cue about things to keep in mind when performing certain tasks or important information that can benefit you in understanding how Dreamweaver works.

Any time you see the Warning icon, watch out! Paragraphs marked with this icon include important information that will help you avoid common design mistakes and steer clear of trouble.

Occasionally we include some technical information that, while interesting to some, is not essential reading for everyone. Nevertheless, consider at least glancing at the text marked with the Technical Stuff icon just in case it applies to your situation.

Where to Go from Here

Read through the Table of Contents to find what interests you. Otherwise, consider the following jumping-off topics:

✦ For an overview of Dreamweaver in general and the new features in Dreamweaver 8 in particular, go to Book I.

✦ For information about working with text, graphics, and links, read Book II.

✦ For information on using Cascading Style Sheets, see Book III.

✦ To discover how to work with layers and use JavaScript behaviors, see Book IV.

✦ For information on publishing your site, see Book V.

✦ For details about working collaboratively with a team, see Book VI.

✦ For instructions on building Web applications, go to Book VII.

✦ To build dynamic Web pages, read Book VIII.

✦ For information on rapid application development, see Book IX.

Beyond this book there are loads of valuable Dreamweaver resources on the Internet to help you build Web sites. The following is a sample of some useful sites you'll find out there:

Macromedia Resources

Dreamweaver Support Center www.macromedia.com/support/dreamweaver/

Dreamweaver Exchange www.macromedia.com/exchange/dreamweaver/

Author Resources

Luckychair www.luckychair.com

Standards, Guidelines, and Initiatives

World Wide Web Consortium (W3C) www.w3.org

Web Accessibility Initiative www.w3.org/WAI/

Dreamweaver Extensions

Project Seven www.projectseven.com

Dreamweaver Fever www.dreamweaverfever.com

Web Developer Resources

Web Monkey www.webmonkey.com

W3 Schools www.w3schools.com

JavaScript Resources

Dynamic Drive DHTML Scripts www.dynamicdrive.com

24Fun www.24fun.com

EarthWeb JavaScripts http://webdeveloper.earthweb.com/webjs/

JavaScript Source http://javascript.internet.com

CSS Resources

W3C's CSS www.w3.org/Style/CSS/

CSS Zen Garden www.csszengarden.com

CSS Vault http://cssvault.com

CSS Beauty www.cssbeauty.com

'Glish www.glish.com/css/

Book I

Getting Started

The 5th Wave   By Rich Tennant

"As a Web site designer I never thought I'd say this, but I don't think your site has enough bells and whistles."

Contents at a Glance

Chapter 1: Cruising Around the Dreamweaver 8 Workspace

In This Chapter

✔ **Getting to know the Dreamweaver workspace**

✔ **Understanding the panels and Properties inspector**

✔ **Setting Dreamweaver preferences**

✔ **Finding help in the help files, tutorials, and Reference panel**

A basic understanding of the Dreamweaver workspace can greatly assist you with using the program. If you're familiar with Dreamweaver but new to Dreamweaver 8, use this chapter as a review of the workspace basics.

This chapter provides a general overview of the workspace and Document window, a review of the panels and Properties inspector, a quick look at setting preferences, and tips on how and where to find Dreamweaver help.

Choosing a Workspace Layout

When launching Dreamweaver for the very first time, Windows users are prompted to select a workspace layout, while Macintosh users are automatically brought into the program with the default Mac workspace layout. Once the program is open, however, you can select additional layout options in both platforms from Dreamweaver's Window menu.

Windows workspace layouts

In Windows, the initial Dreamweaver layout choices are Coder or Designer. Both offer an all-in-one-window layout that integrates the windows and panels into one large application window. In both layout styles, you can dock both panel groups to either side of the workspace. Here's a closer look at the two layouts:

✦ **Coder:** Select this layout to have all the panel groups display on the left — similar to Macromedia HomeSite, Macromedia ColdFusion Studio, and other programming software applications — as well as having the Document window display in Code view by default.

✦ **Designer:** Select this layout to have all the panel groups display on the right and have the Document window display in Design view by default.

After selecting a workspace layout, you can change to a different layout at any time by choosing Window➪Workspace Layout.

In addition to the Coder and Designer views, you have the option to select from two additional layout types in Windows when you have a second monitor:

✦ **Dual Screen Left:** Select this layout if you have a secondary monitor to the left of your primary monitor. The panels display in the left monitor and the Document window displays on the right.

✦ **Dual Screen Right:** Select this layout if you have a secondary monitor to the right of your primary monitor. The panels display in the right monitor and the Document window displays on the left.

Macintosh workspace layouts

On a Macintosh, the Dreamweaver workspace automatically opens in the default layout. Similar to the Windows Designer layout, the Mac default layout displays multiple documents in the same Document window with tabs at the top identifying each file. The panel groups are conveniently docked together at startup, but you can easily undock them into separate panels. All the panels snap to the sides of the workspace, to each other, and to the Document window when you resize or drag them.

You can change the layout from Tabbed to Floating Windows, where each document appears in its own window. To show documents as windows, choose Window➪Cascade or Window➪Tile. To switch to the Tabbed layout, choose Window➪Combine as Tabs.

You can also open a tabbed file in a separate window by ⌘+clicking the file or by Control+clicking the document's tab and choosing Move to New Window from the context menu.

To change the default Mac Tabbed setting to a default Floating Windows setting, open the Preferences dialog box by choosing Dreamweaver➪Preferences. In the General category, select or deselect the Open Documents in Tabs setting, and click OK. Changing preferences doesn't affect any currently open documents, but does apply to documents opened after the change.

After initially launching the program, you can choose to display the Dreamweaver workspace as either Default or Dual Screen. Select Dual Screen when using two monitors to maximize workspace.

Getting to Know the Dreamweaver Workspace

The Dreamweaver workspace consists of a Document window and panels, which you use to modify the content in an open document. At minimum, the workspace contains the Insert bar at the top of the screen, the Properties inspector at the bottom of the screen, and the Files panel at the right edge of the screen, as shown in Figure 1-1 for Windows and Figure 1-2 for Macintosh.

Document toolbar

Design view

Insert bar   Document window   Panel groups

Figure 1-1:
The Dream-
weaver 8
Designer
workspace
for
Windows.

Properties inspector   Code view   Files panel

Coding toolbar

Status bar

Insert bar   Document toolbar   Document window   Panel groups

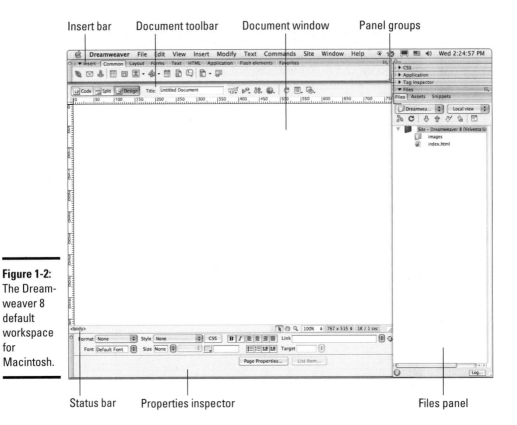

Figure 1-2:
The Dream-
weaver 8
default
workspace
for
Macintosh.

Status bar   Properties inspector   Files panel

You find these elements in the Dreamweaver workspace:

✦ **Start Page:** When you launch Dreamweaver, the Start Page is automatically enabled, and it appears in the open workspace area any time no
files are open. The Start Page (shown in Figure 1-3) contains quick links
to create new documents and open recent files, and provides Web links
to learn more about Dreamweaver, tutorials, and community resources.

Hide and show the Start Page by adjusting the Start Page check box in
the General category of the Preferences dialog box. (See "Setting
Dreamweaver Preferences," later in the chapter, for more on the
Preferences dialog box.)

✦ **Insert bar:** This bar has a variety of buttons for quickly adding objects
such as images and tables into an open file. You can find a more in-depth
description of it in the "Using the Insert bar" section, later in the chapter.

✦ **Document window:** This window shows the active document as you
create and edit it. View the document in Code, Design, or Split (half
code/half design) view.

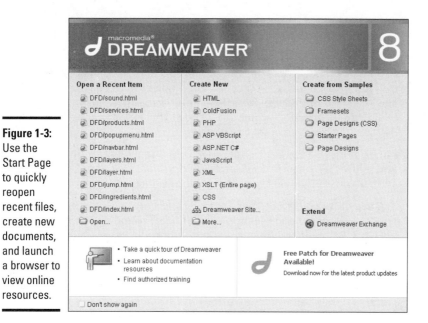

Figure 1-3:
Use the
Start Page
to quickly
reopen
recent files,
create new
documents,
and launch
a browser to
view online
resources.

+ **Document toolbar:** This toolbar is located either at the top of every open document or at the top of the workspace just beneath the Insert bar. The toolbar has buttons for different views of your page as well as quick links for other features. For more on the different buttons and icons, check out the "Document toolbar" section, later in this chapter.

+ **Coding toolbar:** This addition to Dreamweaver 8 adds special quick-coding buttons to the left edge of the Code view area that are particularly useful to programmers. Shortcut buttons include options to collapse and expand lines of code, add or remove line numbers and comment tags, and highlight invalid code, among several others. Toggle this toolbar on and off by choosing View⇨Toolbars⇨Coding. Remember, the Coding toolbar is visible only in Code or Split view.

+ **Standard toolbar:** This toolbar has shortcut links to common tasks from the File and Edit menus such as New, Open, Save, Cut, Copy, Paste, Undo, and Redo. To toggle this toolbar on and off, choose View⇨Toolbars⇨ Standard.

+ **Style Rendering toolbar:** This toolbar has shortcut buttons to show how a design would look using different media types, presuming the page uses CSS (Cascading Style Sheets) specific to those media types. For instance, the <body> tag may have different CSS attributes for handheld devices, such as a BlackBerry, versus screen media, such as a browser. A little button on this toolbar also toggles CSS on and off in Design view. To view this toolbar, which appears in the open Document window above the Document toolbar, choose View⇨Toolbars⇨Style Rendering.

To find out more about CSS in general, see Book III, Chapter 1. To find out more about CSS for media in particular, visit the World Wide Web Consortium at www.w3.org/TR/CSS21/media.html.

✦ **Properties inspector:** The contents of this inspector change according to the object or text selected. Select an object in Design or Code view, and then add or change properties in the Properties inspector. See "Using the Properties inspector," later in this chapter, for a more detailed description of its capabilities.

✦ **Files panel:** Use the Files panel to access and manage all your site files and folders. For a more in-depth description of this panel, page ahead to "Working with the Files panel," later in this chapter.

✦ **Tag selector:** This status bar area is at the bottom of the open Document window. Here you see the hierarchy of tags around a selection or wherever you have placed the insertion point on the page. Click any tag in the Tag selector to quickly select that tag and its contents. This tool is extremely handy when adding CSS to objects in a document.

✦ **Panel groups:** These related panels are combined together into a single panel with tabs. A more in-depth description follows later in the chapter in the section "Accessing other panels and panel groups."

Exploring the Document Window

The Document window is made up of several parts, some of which are always visible, while you can toggle others on and off. The following sections describe features of the Document window including the Document toolbar, the rulers, grids, and guides, and the status bar.

Document toolbar

Located at the top of every open document or at the top of the workspace just beneath the Insert bar, the Document toolbar (shown in Figure 1-4) displays options and details associated with the document currently selected in Design view.

Figure 1-4: The Document toolbar.

Code and Design view   No Browser/Check Errors   File Management   Refresh in Design view

Server Debug   Visual Aids

Code view   Document title   Validate Markup   View Options

Design view   Preview in Browser

The toolbar has buttons that display different views of your page, as well as quick links for other features such as adding a page title and previewing the page in a browser. Click the buttons to select options from their submenus:

✦ **Code view:** Use this setting to hand-code and edit in HTML, JavaScript, server-side coding (for example, PHP, ASP, or CFML), and other code in the open Document window. The default display font for text inside Code view is 9-pt Courier, but you can change it in the Fonts category of Dreamweaver's Preferences.

✦ **Split view:** The best of both worlds, use Split view to simultaneously see both Design and Code views in the open Document window. Resize the two panes by clicking and dragging the divider bar between them. Code view can sit on the top or bottom of the screen. To change the Code view position, click the View Options button on the Document toolbar and select Design View on Top.

✦ **Design view:** This *WYSIWYG* (What You See Is What You Get) editor displays a visual rendering of all the code contained between the <body> tags of the open document. Manipulate text and other objects in this view by selecting, editing, and applying properties to the content. While similar to what you see in a browser window, this view cannot display many interactive code elements, such as links or JavaScript, so be sure to test the page in a browser. You can, however, see dynamic content in Design view by choosing View⇨Live Data. For more information about working with live data and planning dynamic pages, see Book VIII.

If the contents of the document exceed the visible area in any of the three views, scroll bars appear to help you scroll to the hidden areas of the page.

✦ **Server Debug:** Click here to see a report of the page to help with debugging in ColdFusion. This button only appears when a managed site uses a ColdFusion test server.

✦ **Title:** You can enter a title for your page in Design view, which displays in the browser's title bar.

For open documents that have been edited but not saved, Dreamweaver adds an asterisk next to the filename in the document title bar as a visual reminder of the document's unsaved status. Save the document, and the asterisk goes away.

✦ **No Browser/Check Errors:** This tool checks the open file for cross-browser compatibility. The Results panel displays the errors, if any.

✦ **Validate Markup:** Click this button to validate code within the current file, current site, or selected files. You can validate markup against doctypes selected in the Validator category of Dreamweaver's Preferences, and results can include the display of errors, warnings, and messages.

+ **File Management:** Select a function from the file management drop-down list.

+ **Preview in Browser:** Preview or debug the open file in any browser listed in the drop-down list.

+ **Refresh in Design view:** Refresh the document's Design view after making changes in Code view. Code view changes don't automatically appear in Design view unless you save the file or click this button.

+ **View Options:** The View Options menu offers options for turning on and off the grid, rulers, guides, and header bar, among other options. Here you can also flip the position of Design view from top to bottom with the Split view.

+ **Visual Aids:** The Visual Aids menu lets you toggle on and off various tools to assist you with page layout including CSS Layout Outlines, Table Borders, and Invisible Elements, among others.

Rulers

Rulers, which appear along the top and left edges of the Document window, are great tools to assist you with the measurement and placement of objects in your document. Rulers can display in pixels, inches, or centimeters. You can move the ruler's X/Y coordinates, which represent the 0/0 measurement mark for the horizontal and vertical axes, to any location in the open Document window. Modify the X/Y origin coordinates of the ruler by clicking and dragging the origin square at the top-left edge of the rulers, and then release the origin point anywhere on the visible Document window. The X/Y coordinates jump to 0/0 at that position. To reset the X/Y coordinates to the default location at the top-left edge of the Document window, choose View⇨Rulers⇨Reset Origin. Toggle rulers on and off by choosing View⇨Rulers⇨Show.

Grids

Use the grid to assist with laying out content in Design view. Because the grid lines extend in regular intervals through the entire document, from left to right and from top to bottom, you can use them as guides for exact positioning of objects in your document, as shown in Figure 1-5. For best alignment, turn on the Snap to Grid option by choosing View⇨Grid⇨Snap to Grid. Control the grid settings, such as grid coloring and spacing, with the Grid Settings dialog box by choosing View⇨Grid⇨Grid Settings. Hide and show grids by choosing View⇨Grid⇨Show Grid.

Figure 1-5:
Use the
ruler,
guides, and
grids in
Design view
to assist you
with the
placement
of objects.

Guides

Guides are horizontal and vertical guide lines that you can drag in the open Document window to assist you with the measurement and placement of objects. For example, you may want to place the top-left edge of a layer at exactly 150 pixels in from the left edge of the Document window. A guide placed at the 150-pixel mark with the Snap to Guide option enabled would allow you to snap the layer to the guide at that position. Dreamweaver guides work like guides in Adobe Photoshop and Illustrator; they are visible on-screen in the work environment but aren't visible in print or on a Web page.

To create guides, first turn the rulers on (as described in the earlier section "Rulers") and then click and drag guides out from the top and left ruler bars. When the guide is in the desired position, release the guide onto the document. Lock or unlock guides as needed for easy repositioning or quick removal by dragging the guide back onto the ruler bar. Choose View⇨Guides⇨Snap to Guides to have elements snap to guides when positioning objects, such as layers, inside the Document window. Quickly hide and show guides by choosing View⇨Guides⇨Show Guides.

Status bar

Dreamweaver 8 has several new enhancements to the status bar (shown in Figure 1-6). The Tag selector is on the bottom-left edge of the Document window and allows for easy tag and tag content selection. On the bottom-right edge, the status bar shows the current size (in pixels) of the Document window, as well as a file size and estimated file opening time reflecting the file preferences for projected site visitors. For example, an open document may display 760 x 420 and 27K/4 sec, meaning that the current page is optimized for a monitor with a resolution set to 800 x 600, 27K in size, and would take 4 seconds to load in a browser on a computer using a 56K modem.

You can resize the Document window to a predetermined size to approximate the inside of a browser window for testing purposes. On the Window Size drop-down list, select a window size or choose the Edit Sizes option to create and save custom size settings.

New to the status bar in Dreamweaver 8 are a few elements for Design view that Adobe Photoshop and Illustrator users will L-O-V-E (see Figure 1-6):

Figure 1-6:
The status
bar.

Zoom tool

Select tool | Window Size menu

Tag selector | Set magnification

Hand tool

+ **Select tool:** Use the Select tool to select content in the Document window. This tool is the default for selecting objects in your file in Design view. For example, single-click an image to select it with the Select tool.

+ **Hand tool:** Use the Hand tool in conjunction with a Zoom view to move the section of the page you're viewing in the Document window. For example, at 1600% view, the Hand tool allows you to reposition what you see in the Document window at that magnification.

+ **Zoom tool:** The amazing new Zoom tool allows you to zoom in and out of the Design view window. Select the tool and click in the Document window to zoom into the page. Press Alt (Windows) or Option (Mac) and click again to zoom out. Double-click the Zoom tool button to return to 100% view.

+ **Set Magnification menu:** The new Magnification menu displays Zoom settings in percentages from 6% to 6400%. Select a preset magnification view from the drop-down list or type a number in the percentage field and click Enter (Windows) or Return (Mac) to view the page with a custom magnification setting.

Understanding the Panels and Properties Inspector

Dreamweaver uses panels to help you organize, select from, and modify content, as well as provide access to common features and functions. The main panels are the Insert bar, Files panel, and the Properties inspector. You can open, resize, reposition, and close other panels and panel groups as you need to. You can open and close all the panels by selecting them from the Window menu.

All panels have common features making them easy to understand:

✦ **Options menu:** Each panel has an Options menu at the top-right corner of the panel. Use the Options menus to access panel-specific tasks.

✦ **Expand/Collapse:** Click the arrow next to the panel name to collapse and expand the panel or panel group window.

✦ **Repositioning:** Reposition panels by clicking and dragging on the gripper area at the left edge of each panel's title bar.

✦ **Resizing:** To resize the height of docked panels, place your cursor on top of the divider line between two panels. When the cursor turns into a double-sided arrow, click and drag to resize the panels. To resize undocked panels, place your cursor at any edge of the panel window. When the cursor turns into a double-sided arrow, click and drag to resize the panel.

When rearranging panels around the workspace, panels can sometimes get hidden behind each other. If a panel marked as open on the Window menu seems to have disappeared, try choosing Window➪Workspace Layout➪ Designer (Windows) or Window➪Workspace Layout➪Default (Mac) to neatly rearrange the open panels. The Arrange Panels option on a Mac also neatly organizes panels wherever they happen to be on-screen. For example, if you have two undocked panels somewhere in the middle of the screen, the Arrange Panels option stacks those undocked panels neatly to the left of the other docked panels on the page, as shown in Figure 1-7.

Figure 1-7: Mac users can use the Arrange Panels option from the Window menu to organize panels neatly into columns.

Using the Insert bar

The Insert bar (shown in Figure 1-8) has buttons for adding common *objects,* such as tables, images, and media, into an open document. When pressed, each button automatically adds the correct code to your page for the object selected. For instance, to insert an image, you click the image icon, selecting the graphic, and the appropriate HTML code is then added to your page, as in `<img src="logo.gif">`. Though adding objects this way is fast and easy, you can also add the same objects to your page using the Insert menu.

Figure 1-8:
The Insert bar.

By default, the Insert bar displays tabs at the top to give you access to buttons in related categories, such as Forms or Text. You can also choose to display category options in a menu. To change the display from tabs to menu, click the Options menu at the right edge of the Insert bar and select Show as Menu. To return to Tab view, click the down arrow on the Insert bar menu and select Show as Tabs.

Collapse and expand the Insert bar by clicking the expander arrow to the left of the panel's name. The panel also has an Options menu at the top-right edge of the panel. Use the Options menu to maximize or close the panel, among other options.

To add an object or asset to an open document, click one of the tabs (Common, Layout, Forms, and so on) to select a category and then do one of the following:

✦ Click a button to insert the object.

✦ Click the down arrow on a button and select an option from the drop-down menu.

Some of the buttons insert the object automatically while others open object-specific dialog boxes prompting you to select a file or add attributes or parameters to the object. When inserting objects in Code view instead of Design view, you may also encounter the Tag editor. In that case, enter the appropriate information and click OK to add the object to your page.

Using the Properties inspector

The Properties inspector is the panel to use for adding formatting and other attributes or properties to selected objects in your document.

The most versatile of all the panels, the Properties inspector's contents change according to the object or text selected in Code or Design view. For instance, when text is selected on your document, the Properties inspector displays options for adding properties to text; when a graphic is selected, the inspector displays options for adding properties to images, as shown in Figure 1-9. This works for most object selections; the main thing to remember is that you must select the desired object or content before adding properties.

Figure 1-9:
When an image is selected in Design view, the Properties inspector displays options for adding properties.

Working with the Files panel

Use the Files panel to manage all your site files and folders, view both remote and local file listings, access other files on your hard drive, and manage sites within Dreamweaver.

The Files panel displays in its collapsed mode by default, and when displaying a managed site, it lists all the files and folders of the specified directory. You can expand the panel into two panes to show both local and remote site views in one window; see the following list for details.

At the top of the Files panel, two drop-down lists assist you with site management tasks. These two menus, Site Management and Site View, are shown in Figure 1-10. Here's the lowdown on these menus:

Site Management

Site View

Figure 1-10:
The Files
panel.

✦ **Site Management:** This menu lists all the managed sites you've created in Dreamweaver. A site becomes *managed* when you define a folder on your local computer for the HTML files of a specific project, and tell Dreamweaver where to find that file. You need to create a managed site for each project you work on in Dreamweaver. To create a new managed site, scroll down to the bottom of this menu and select Manage Site to open the Manage Sites dialog box. For more information on creating a managed site, see Book I, Chapter 3.

✦ **Site View:** When the Files panel is collapsed, use the Site View menu to toggle among four views:

- **Local:** Select this view to see the file structure of the local site. You may also use this view to see both local and remote sites with the Files panel split into two panes. Use the Expand/Collapse button to toggle between viewing one and two panes. By default, the local site appears in the right pane and the remote site appears in the left, but you can modify this in the Site category of Dreamweaver's Preferences if you're used to having the local pane appear on the left like many older FTP programs do.

- **Remote:** Select this view to see the file structure of the remote site. You must set up a remote site in advance to see the remote site files.

- **Testing:** This view shows a directory listing of both the testing server and local site files. You must set up a testing server in advance to see the testing server site.

- **Map:** This view shows a graphic map of the site based on how the files are linked together. You must specify a home page to see the site in Map view. After selecting this view, you can choose to see the map with or without files.

Beneath the drop-down lists are a series of helpful buttons to aid with transferring files to and from a remote server. Book V, Chapter 4 covers these buttons, which are Connect/Disconnect, Refresh, Get Files, Put Files, Check Out Files, Check In Files, and Expand/Collapse.

Use the Files panel Options menu to create new files and folders by choosing File⇨New File or File⇨New Folder. New files and folders automatically get added to the bottom of the Files panel with the name untitled for easy renaming. To use the Files panel to quickly open a file, double-click a filename or drag and drop a file into the workspace.

In addition to the features-rich Options menu at the top of the panel, the bottom of the Files panel has a Log button to open the background file activity log and a status bar, which displays file data such as title, creation date and time, and file size.

Accessing other panels and panel groups

Dreamweaver has many other panels, windows, and inspectors, most of which you can open via the Window menu.

Panel groups are sets of related panels combined together as separate layers on a single panel. Access each panel by clicking the tab at the top of the panel group. For example, the CSS group displays both the CSS Styles and the Layers panels; to see the Layers panel in that panel group's window, click the Layers tab.

Create, rename, and modify existing groups with the panel Options menu. Expand and collapse panel groups by clicking the expander arrow on the panel title bar. If docked to the right or left side of the Dreamweaver workspace, you can undock them by clicking and dragging on the gripper area where the two columns of dots appear to the left of the panel group title bar.

Customizing the Workspace

The Dreamweaver workspace is highly customizable, so you can create a work environment that best meets your needs and then save the layout for future use. The panels, for instance, are docked to their respective locations, but you can reposition and resize them by clicking and dragging the gripper area on their title bars. When you create and save a custom layout, all the panel locations, groupings, sizes, and expanded/collapsed states are saved along with the Document window and application window sizes and positions.

Here's how to work with a custom layout:

✦ To save a custom layout, choose Window⇨Workspace Layout⇨Save Current. Give your layout a name and click OK.

✦ To open and use a saved layout, choose Window⇨Workspace Layout and then select the layout name.

✦ To rename a saved layout, choose Window⇨Workspace Layout⇨ Manage, select the layout from the listing in the Manage Workspace Layouts dialog box, and click the Rename button.

✦ To delete a selected layout, choose Window⇨Workspace Layout⇨ Manage, select the layout from the listing in the Manage Workspace Layouts dialog box, and click the Delete button.

Setting Dreamweaver Preferences

You can modify many settings in Dreamweaver's Preferences dialog box to further customize your workspace and workflow. To access the Preferences dialog box, choose Edit⇨Preferences (Windows) or Dreamweaver⇨ Preferences (Mac).

The Preferences dialog box offers several categories for customization. Select a category from the list on the left to reveal that category's preference settings on the right side of the dialog box. Figure 1-11 shows the Preferences dialog box with the General category selected.

Figure 1-11: Use the Preferences dialog box to customize Dreamweaver.

Many of the category settings can stay as they are. In some instances, however, you may choose to modify some settings to improve your work experience. You can find entries throughout this book that reference the Preferences settings and suggest ways to customize specific categories.

Finding Help

We all need help from time to time and the best place to find it is through the Help menu. There you find links that open special dialog boxes or browser windows revealing a variety of help topics. We describe these topics in more detail in the following sections.

To find help for a specific Dreamweaver feature, click the Help button, which looks like a little question mark, found in most dialog boxes and panels. Upon clicking the button, the Help window opens to display information for the most closely related topic. For instance, to find out more about setting properties on graphic files, select an image inserted in a document and then click the Help button in the Properties inspector. The Help Index opens automatically to a Setting Image Properties page.

Using the Dreamweaver Help files (F1)

The most resourceful link on the Help menu is Dreamweaver Help. Though the content is identical, the actual layout of the Help window varies significantly between a Mac and a PC. On a PC, the Help window uses a series of tabs and links at the top and left of the panel to assist with navigation, whereas on a Mac the layout uses an index, breadcrumb location identifiers, and a home button. Both platforms allow you to search Help files by asking a question or typing keywords, and both contain quick links to view comments about a particular topic on LiveDocs, the Dreamweaver Web-site area containing the most up-to-date information about Dreamweaver.

To open the Dreamweaver Help window on both Mac and Windows platforms, choose Help⇨Dreamweaver Help or press F1.

Windows Dreamweaver Help

After the Help window opens, as shown in Figure 1-12, review the Help contents by Contents, Index, Search, or Favorites:

✦ **Contents:** The Contents tab organizes all the help files into *books* or categories where specific information is logically grouped for easy, task-oriented access. Use the menu tree to expand and collapse books to reveal helpful information related to each task.

Figure 1-12:
The Dreamweaver Help window.

✦ **Index:** The Index tab has an alphabetical listing of everything in Dreamweaver! For example, to find out more about empty tags, type those keywords in the Find field and a list of results displays. Select a result from the list on the left to reveal the details on the right.

✦ **Search:** If a single keyword isn't enough to narrow your search, try typing several words in the Search field. Results display by topic, title, location, and rank. Select a result from the list on the left of the panel to reveal the details on the right. You can further narrow a search by checking or unchecking the search options at the bottom of the tab.

✦ **Favorites:** Add Help topics to a customized list of favorites to return quickly to favorite or often-used entries. Entries display alphabetically and you may add and remove entries as often as needed.

To assist you in navigating through the Help files, regardless of the category you're in, click these buttons at the top of the window to perform certain tasks and other functions found on the Options menu: Hide/Show Tabs, Go Back, Go Forward, Go Home, and Print.

Macintosh Dreamweaver Help

The Mac version of Dreamweaver's Help files is organized into an index, as shown in Figure 1-13, from which you select a category on the left and drill down to the topic you want on the right. After you select the final topic, details of that topic fill the Help window. Use the navigation buttons and question field to help you find topics:

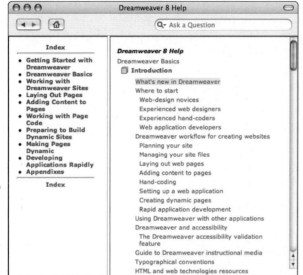

Figure 1-13:
The Dream-
weaver
Help files for
the Mac.

✦ **Index:** Choose a category you want to learn more about. Organized details about each category display on the right. Select a topic to view Help information.

✦ **Breadcrumbs:** When a topic is displayed, it fills the entire Help window. The specific location of that topic is represented in breadcrumbs at the top of the description.

✦ **View comments on LiveDocs:** Click this option to view the most recent comments on this topic on the Macromedia LiveDocs Web page.

✦ **Navigation buttons:** Click the Forward, Backward, and Home buttons at the top of the Help window to assist you with navigating.

✦ **Ask a Question:** Type a question or keywords in this field to find details on a specific topic.

Working with the Reference panel

The main Reference panel displays reference information for all the markup languages, programming languages, and CSS you can use when building your Web site.

Open this panel by choosing Help⇨Reference and then pick a book from the panel's drop-down list to display information from that reference book, as shown in Figure 1-14. Each entry contains descriptions and examples of the styles, tags, and objects in your code.

Figure 1-14: Select a reference book.

To reference a specific tag, keyword, or attribute in Code view, do one of the following:

✦ Right-click (Windows) or Control+click (Mac) the item and choose Reference from the context menu.

✦ Place the insertion point in a tag, keyword, or attribute and press F1.

If the reference contains an example you want to copy and paste into another document, select it from the Reference panel and copy it using the context or Options menu in the panel.

Other reference links on the Help menu launch special dialog boxes:

✦ **Using Dreamweaver:** Click this option to open the default Help (F1) window, which has information about all the features in Dreamweaver.

✦ **Extending Dreamweaver:** This option opens a special Extending Dreamweaver dialog box with information on the Document Object Model (DOM).

✦ **Dreamweaver API Reference:** Click this link to open the Dreamweaver API Reference dialog box with information about APIs (Application Programming Interfaces) that let JavaScript and C developers make Dreamweaver extensions.

✦ **Using ColdFusion:** This option launches the ColdFusion Documentation dialog box.

Visiting the Dreamweaver Support Center

Several of the Help menu links launch browser windows for online Macromedia Support for Dreamweaver users. The entire Macromedia Web site gets updated regularly and includes tips, updates, examples, and detailed information on advanced topics, so check the site often.

To help you find specific destinations within the online Support Center, Dreamweaver provides quick access to the following locations through the Help menu:

✦ **Dreamweaver Support Center:** Open a page for searching the Macromedia Dreamweaver Knowledge Base, which is at `www.macromedia.com/support/dreamweaver/`.

✦ **Dreamweaver Developer Center:** Open the Developer Center page (`www.macromedia.com/devnet/dreamweaver/`), where you can find tutorials, tools, and other Macromedia information.

✦ **Dreamweaver Documentation Resource Center:** Open the Dreamweaver 8 Documentation Web page (`www.macromedia.com/support/documentation/en/dreamweaver/`), which includes links to search for tutorials, product manuals, and errata. You can view the files online or in downloadable PDF format.

✦ **Macromedia Online Forums:** Open a page providing access to several Macromedia Web-based and newsreader-based online forums. Use the forums at `www.macromedia.com/go/dreamweaver_newsgroup/` to talk about technical issues with other Dreamweaver users.

✦ **Macromedia Training:** Launch the Macromedia page detailing authorized training and certification programs. Macromedia offers self-paced and instructor-led courses, books, links to authorized continued learning facilities, and details about professional certification programs.

✦ **Dreamweaver Exchange:** Go to the Dreamweaver Exchange page where you can search for, download, and purchase Dreamweaver extensions.

✦ **Manage Extensions:** Launch the Dreamweaver Extension Manager for installing, removing, and submitting extensions to/from the Macromedia Exchange.

If you're using a Mac, you see a slightly different order along with links to two additional resources:

✦ **Online Registration:** Connect to the Internet and register your product online.

✦ **Print Registration:** Print a registration form, which you can complete and mail to Macromedia to register your product.

Chapter 2: Planning and Designing Your Site

In This Chapter

✔ Figuring out who your audience is

✔ Taking a look at the site design

✔ Adding graphics to your design

*P*utting a Web site on the Internet involves more than learning how to build Web pages. Creating a site that people will actually use requires careful planning and design, based on site visitors' expectations and your (or your client's) Web site goals.

Planning a good Web site involves conducting market research, defining client needs, making decisions about Web-based technology, discussing search engine optimization and accessibility, gathering and organizing content, setting a budget and signing contracts, purchasing a hosting plan, and designing and optimizing graphics. Discussing all these topics in detail is beyond the scope of this book; instead, this chapter focuses on a few key aspects of Web design that you need to think about. If you want more in-depth information on Web design, check out *Web Design For Dummies,* 2nd Edition by Lisa Lopuck (Wiley).

Whether designing a site for yourself, your company, or freelance clients, the overall planning and design process is relatively the same. This chapter discusses knowing your audience, reviewing design considerations, and designing a successful site.

Understanding the Web Design Workflow

Building a Web site has a logical workflow. The different stages of the Web design workflow are as follows:

Define > Design > Build > Test > Launch

Each stage requires cooperation from all parties involved — including the client, designers, and programmers — because each is responsible for different parts of the process. Table 2-1 shows who should be involved with each step of the workflow process.

Table 2-1		Web Design Workflow		
Define	*Design*	*Build*	*Test*	*Launch*
Client, Designer	Designer	Designer, Programmer	Client, Designer, Programmer	Designer, Programmer

The client typically provides content, the designer (you) creates the design and builds the site, the programmer adds dynamic functionality, everyone gets involved in testing, and finally, the site gets published to the Internet.

Knowing Your Audience

The ultimate aim of a Web site is to meet the audience's needs and, at the same time, achieve the client's mission. Both the client and you (the designer) need to have knowledge of the target market, an understanding of the demographics of the target audience, and a good overview of the existing online competition.

Defining the client's expectations

Use the client's mission statement as a starting point to define its goals for the Web site. If the client doesn't have a mission statement, you need to ask some questions to help define the goals. For example, what does the client hope to achieve with the Web site? Here are some goals the client may have for the site:

✦ Provide information to current and potential customers

✦ Generate leads

✦ Sell products and services

✦ Provide information to the general public

When defining the Web site goals, consider the three most important aspects about the business that make it unique and beneficial to customers. The look of the site should be largely determined by the industry and Web site needs, and the organization of the site should be defined by the content being delivered.

Exploring the audience's expectations

Market research is one of the best ways to determine site visitors' expectations. Here's the information you need to assemble:

✦ The target demographic.

✦ The visitors' Web browsing habits. Determine whether they are seeking products, information, or a consultation, or have information to share with others.

✦ The amount of money they have to spend.

✦ Whether they prefer to purchase online or shop in a bricks-and-mortar store.

Collecting this information can help you determine the design direction, layout, and structure of the site. For instance, if the site is aimed at a worldwide audience, you may need to consider language and cultural issues.

You can find Web sites for every conceivable industry in the world, and a good place to start when creating a new Web site is to review what's already on the Internet. Do a general online search for companies in the same industry world- or country-wide. Then do additional searches for competition in the same general geographic region, such as statewide, countywide, and citywide. Think about design, usability, budget, timeframe, and technical issues. Look at the competitors' sites and take notes about what works and what doesn't with regard to content and layout.

After gathering data about competitors' sites, draw diagrams and design ideas, write copy, and make a list of key points that the site should address. A clear understanding of the target audience helps define the site's organization and structure.

Examining Issues That Impact the Site Design

When you're designing a Web site for yourself or for a client, keep in mind the three main components to any Web project:

✦ **Time:** Decide when you can deliver the job.

✦ **Cost:** Determine how much the project is going to cost.

✦ **Scope:** Determine what you hope to achieve.

Most projects begin with some kind of specific limitations with regard to these project components. One frequent limitation has to do with budget; a client may specify that they hope to pay a particular fee for a new Web site that achieves the defined scope and is delivered by a specific time. While that may be an ideal goal, achieving all three components of the Web project may not be feasible. For example, if a project needs to be delivered in a short time frame, the project fee may need to increase, or if the client only has X dollars to pay for the project, then only parts of the scope may be met. Obviously, the three Web project components have a strong dependency between them; if the project fee, time frame, and scope are in synch, then all three can be achieved. However, if limits are placed on any one of the components, a compromise may need to be reached.

When you're considering the best way to transmit a message on a Web site, you need to take into account several site design considerations, including design, usability, accessibility, copyright, budget, and technicality. For instance, is the new site selling a product or service, is it a nonprofit organization, or is it a personal Web site? Decide whether the new site will be a *brochureware* site (a print brochure in Web format), or if it will have any dynamic functionality for gathering information, selling products, or providing password-protected content.

Before beginning any Web project, spend some time reflecting on the following site concepts:

✦ **Design:** The visual design of the page is the most important aspect of the site. Not only does the look convey the information contained on the page, but it also says a lot about the client, the product or service being sold, and the level of professionalism and competence.

The design itself should be simple with a clear navigation plan. The navigation scheme and company logo or other identifying icon should appear on every page in the same general location, allowing easy access to the home page at all times. You want visitors to move through the site easily and find what they're looking for as quickly as possible.

✦ **Usability:** Consider in advance how users will interact with the pages and the Web site as a whole. Is the site easy to understand and navigate? Can users access information quickly and is it formatted logically in an easy-to-read way? You need to clearly define the main idea of each page. Keep text short and to the point and include links and graphics relevant to the rest of the site. Above all, proofread the site for spelling errors and double-check links.

✦ **Accessibility:** Making a site accessible to people with visual, auditory, motor, and other disabilities has implications for a site's design. Consider adding text navigation links in addition to graphical links for visitors with browsers that don't support graphics or visitors using disability software such as speech readers and text viewers. Dreamweaver has tools that let you author accessible content. See the "Designing Web sites with accessibility" sidebar in this chapter for more information about accessibility issues.

✦ **Copyright:** Make sure that any graphics, text, music, video, and other media you add to the site is original or legally licensed to avoid copyright infringement. In other words, assume everything online is copyrighted unless otherwise stated.

✦ **Budget:** You need to know the budget defined for the project so you can appropriately allocate time to designing and building, and possibly even maintaining, the site. Extra costs may also be incurred for hosting, training, and other Web site needs.

✦ **Technical:** You have many technical considerations when designing and building a Web site that affect how visitors experience the site, including the browsers and operating systems the site supports, if the site uses any dynamic functionality, and whether the site requires a secure server for data protection. For instance, information collected from visitors needs to be kept secure and protected.

Before building the site, you need to decide upon other issues that affect the overall design of the site, including monitor resolution, browser optimization, and breadth of content. We discuss these issues in detail in the sections that follow.

Monitor resolution

When visitors come to your Web site, how much of the Web site design they see in their browsers is somewhat determined by the monitor resolution setting. Monitor resolutions can be set anywhere from 600 x 400 to 1920 x 1440. The smaller the numbers, the larger the site appears in the monitor display; the larger the numbers, the smaller the site appears.

Currently, most monitors come with a factory preset resolution of 1024 x 768 or larger. Nevertheless, because you have no control over what monitor resolutions visitors will have, consider doing some advanced market research to find out who your audience will be, and what monitor resolution they're likely to have. This information helps you determine the ultimate size of your Web site design. For a few years the standard was to design a Web site for a monitor set to 800 x 600 resolution. That standard, however, is starting to shift because new designs are being optimized for 1024 x 768 and larger resolution settings.

For a great discussion about designing for multiple screen sizes, check out the whitepaper titled "Screen Size Matters" by Catalyst Group Design at www. catalystgroupdesign.com/cofactors/upload/catalyst_resolution_ whitepaper.pdf.

Designing Web sites with accessibility

When designing Web sites, you need to consider whether the audience will include people with visual and other disabilities. If so, you should add accessibility features, such as image labels and keyboard shortcuts, to your site. Dreamweaver has the tools that let you author accessible content that complies with government guidelines. In addition, Dreamweaver supports designers who need accessibility features themselves to create accessible sites.

To turn on Accessibility features in Dreamweaver, which prompts you to add Accessibility tags and attributes to objects when they are inserted onto a page, follow these steps:

1. **Choose Edit⇨Preferences (Windows) or Dreamweaver⇨Preferences (Mac).**

   The Preferences dialog box opens.

2. **Choose the Accessibility category on the left to reveal the accessibility options on the right.**

3. **Next to the Show Attributes When Insertion option, choose the objects that you want to be prompted for.**

   For example, to always be prompted to add accessibility tags or attributes to images inserted on a page, select the Images option.

4. **For Web designers with disabilities who are using Dreamweaver to create Web pages, consider the following options:**

Choose the Keep Focus option to access an accessibility panel after you open it. This is a good option for Web designers using screen readers who need accessibility settings to create Web pages in Dreamweaver.

Consider disabling the Off-Screen Rendering option if using a screen reader. This option is turned on by default but may cause conflicts for designers using screen readers.

5. **Click OK to accept the new preferences.**

In addition to these accessibility features, Dreamweaver comes with several sample Web page designs that comply to accessibility standards. To access these sample designs, choose File⇨New to open the New Document window, and choose an accessible page design from the Page Designs category. Accessible sample Web page designs are identified by the word ACCESSIBLE in the Description box.

If you do use accessibility settings on your Web pages, be sure to run an accessibility report to test your page or site against the government's Section 508 guidelines as part of the testing process prior to publishing your site. See Book V, Chapter 1 for more about testing.

To find out more about Accessibility initiatives, visit the Web sites for both the World Wide Web Consortium Web Accessibility Initiative (www.w3.org/wai) and Section 508 of the Federal Rehabilitation Act (www.section 508.gov).

Browser optimization

Another issue to consider is browser optimization. Taking a look at browser trends can give you insight into important design considerations, such as layout size and CSS (Cascading Style Sheets) support. For example, currently the most popular browser is Internet Explorer (IE) 6, the most used operating system is Windows XP, and the most common monitor display setting is 1024 x 768.

The W3 Schools Web site lists browser and operating system usage statistics on a monthly basis dating back to 2003. Examples are shown in Tables 2-2 and 2-3. For the most current browser optimization statistics, visit www.w3 schools.com/browsers/browsers_stats.asp.

Table 2-2			Browser Usage Statistics				
2006	*IE 6*	*IE 5*	*Firefox*	*Mozilla*	*Netscape Navigator 7*	*Opera 8*	*Opera 7*
January	61.3%	5.5%	25.0%	3.1%	0.4%	1.4%	0.2%

Table 2-3			Operating System Usage Statistics				
2006	*Windows XP*	*Windows 2000*	*Windows 98*	*Windows NT*	*Windows .NET*	*Linux*	*Mac*
January	72.3%	13.1%	2.4%	0.3%	1.7%	3.3%	3.5%

Content

Before building the Web site, you need to create and gather content and other site assets. Content gathering includes writing text and creating or licensing image, sound, and video files. It's important to gather these assets in advance so that you don't have to stop site development repeatedly to create or find any missing content.

Gathering content is a big undertaking, even for the smallest sites, so unless you're also being compensated as the project/content manager, this process should be the client's sole responsibility. After you've gathered the content, organize everything electronically in a place that's easily accessible when it comes time to build the site. For example, you may decide to create a folder on your computer called Websites, and in that folder create a subfolder for the client. Inside the client's folder, you may create several additional subfolders for all the different assets, as shown in Figure 2-1.

Figure 2-1:
File assets
into folders.

Planning the Site Layout

You can save time by planning and designing the site layout before working in Dreamweaver. A consistent layout and design helps create a good user experience. Site layout applies to the look of all the pages on the site, as well as how the pages are logically arranged and interact with each other. This phase is where you're creating the site's *architecture,* or structure.

With regard to the layout of the pages themselves, consider designing a mock-up that has fixed as well as editable areas. Dreamweaver allows you to create templates and library items for page layouts and elements that are consistent on every page. For instance, the navigation element may be at the top of every page, with an area for subnavigation on the left margin, and page-specific content in the center of the page below the navigation.

As you create the design, think about the experience the visitors to the site will have:

✦ Visitors should be able to move from page to page with ease. Therefore, navigation should be consistent throughout the site.

✦ Visitors should know where they are in your site and how to return to the home page. Use indexes and subnavigation to assist visitors with finding information. Also provide a method for contacting the company in case a visitor wants to communicate with the company.

After you gather and organize your data, you may want to create HTML *wireframe* pages to help organize the site's structure. A wireframe is a tree diagram or flowchart of a Web site that includes all its pages. The wireframe shows links between pages but doesn't typically include any reference to the design of the site or the content on any of the individual pages. You can create additional wireframes for the individual pages to assist with the layout of the content on the page, in advance of having real content.

To create a page-based wireframe, consider using Dreamweaver's Site Map Layout mode (see Book VI, Chapter 1). Figure 2-2 shows an example of a wireframe created with Dreamweaver Site Map Layout.

Should you need, however, to create a graphics-based Web site wireframe, consider using a graphics program such as Adobe Illustrator or Adobe Photoshop, or a diagramming program such as Microsoft Visio. In addition to labeling each page on the wireframe, these programs have the tools you need to customize the diagram with graphic elements, color, text, specific fonts, and other information.

To find out more about wireframes, check out the SitePoint article by Matt Beach at www.sitepoint.com/article/wire-frame-your-site.

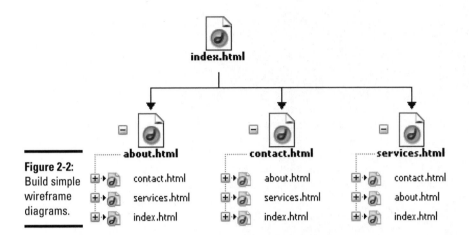

Figure 2-2:
Build simple
wireframe
diagrams.

After creating a wireframe and prior to building the site in Dreamweaver,
you may also want to create a mock-up or *comp* of the site design on paper
or in a graphics program such as Adobe Photoshop, Adobe Illustrator, or
Macromedia Fireworks. A key benefit to designing a mock-up in a graphics
program is that after the client approves the mock-up, you can use it to generate many if not all of the graphics.

A mock-up differs from a wireframe in that the mock-up is a design of the site
that contains all the graphical information for the Web site layout including
company identity, navigation, headers, text, and other graphics. In other
words, the mock-up should have all the elements the client has requested
for the site. For instance, clients may tell you that they "want the logo on the
top of the page, the navigation below that, an area for links to frequently
accessed pages, and a section for a photo gallery." In response to these
needs, you plan the layout of the page and the site. Then you show the
mock-up to the client to make sure the design meets their needs.

Designing and Optimizing Graphics

After the design is finalized, the next step is to slice and optimize graphics.
Slicing and *optimizing* describe the process of dividing a large flat mock-up
into individual pieces, or *graphics,* that are then compressed into GIF or JPEG
graphics.

The number of graphics overall should be limited to ensure the page loads
quickly in a browser. If you're considering rollover button functionality and
other interactive features on the site, create the graphics for these elements
at this stage of the process, in advance of optimization.

Before adding graphics to Web pages, you need to compress them, because in their native format (PSD, PDF, TIFF), the file sizes are much too large to download over the Internet.

For compressing images for the Web, you can choose from three graphics formats: GIF, JPEG, and PNG, as shown in Table 2-4. Web browsers widely support GIF (Graphics Interchange Format) and JPEG (Joint Photographic Experts Group). Each uses a different compression format to crunch data and create smaller file sizes. With both formats, the compression goal is to achieve the best image quality possible while reducing the file size. Fortunately, because the Web displays images at low resolution (72 ppi or *pixels per inch*), most of the loss in image quality from the compression is hard to see. Only the most current browsers support the third graphic format, PNG (Portable Network Graphics), which creates good quality images at smaller file sizes. Therefore, for now, use PNG files on your Web pages only if your target audience will be using the most current browsers to view your site.

Table 2-4	Graphics File Formats	
Format	*Is Best For*	*What It Supports*
GIF	Images with large flat areas of color	Maximum of 256 colors (8-bit); both animation and background transparency
JPEG	Photographs and graphics with lots of color and gradient blends	Millions of colors (24-bit), but not animation or transparency
PNG	Not as widely supported by browsers, although it has been recommended for replacing GIFs by the W3C	Millions of colors (48-bit); background transparency, but not animation

Use an image-compression program such as Adobe ImageReady to optimize the images. ImageReady, which comes bundled with Adobe Photoshop, allows you to slice, optimize, and export graphic files and HTML. Other compression programs and plug-ins are also available, such as Spinwave (www.spinwave.com), Boxtop (www.boxtopsoft.com), Fireworks (www.macromedia.com/software/fireworks), and Equilibrium's Debabelizer (www.equilibrium.com).

Whichever program you choose, be sure to consult the program's Help files for further instruction on image sizing and optimization.

Chapter 3: Creating and Managing Sites

In This Chapter

✔ Understanding how Web sites are put together

✔ Setting up a managed site the basic way

✔ Setting up a managed site with the advanced method

✔ Keeping track of multiple sites

A *Web site* is a group of pages that are linked together and share common features such as design, content, and purpose. Dreamweaver enables you to organize all the pages and assets of your site in one convenient location. To take advantage of Dreamweaver's great site-management features, such as uploading files and managing links among many others, first you need to create or *manage* your site in Dreamweaver. When creating your site, you'll likely adopt a general Web site structure and opt for either a root-level or document-level organization for your files.

In this chapter, you find out how to create and manage a Web site, gain an understanding of root-level and document-level site organization, review the settings in the Site Definition dialog box, and discover how easy it is to manage multiple sites in Dreamweaver.

Understanding General Web Site Structure

Before you create a Dreamweaver Web site, you need to be familiar with the general Web site structure and have a basic understanding of the different types of root level organization, as discussed in the sections that follow.

Web site structure

Web sites typically consist of two or three basic parts:

✦ **The local folder:** This folder, also called the *local root folder*, holds all the files, images, and other assets of a managed site. The root level, simply put, is the top level or starting point a browser uses for finding objects within a Web site. The local folder typically sits somewhere on your computer's hard drive, though it may also be on a mapped or network server drive. Wherever it resides, you must specify the location of the local root folder in the Site Definition dialog box (see Book V, Chapter 3).

✦ **The remote folder:** This folder is where you publish your site, typically on a remote Web server. You'll be transferring files to the remote folder from the local folder to ensure the published Web site is functional and up to date. You can choose from a lot of options when you're setting up the remote folder. See Book V, Chapter 3 for more info on setting up a remote folder.

✦ **The testing server folder:** This folder is where Dreamweaver processes dynamic data to create dynamic content and connect with a database while you create and test your site. Your testing server can be on the local computer, a development or staging server, or a production server. We don't recommend that you use the remote folder for the testing server folder because you can run into some problems. See Book VII, Chapter 1 to set up your testing server.

Root-level organization

After deciding on the general Web site structure for your site, the next step is to determine how to organize and link the files to one another relative to the *root* (top-level) folder.

Each page on a Web site has its own unique address or URL (Uniform Resource Locator), such as `http://www.macromedia.com/software/ dreamweaver/index.html`. When you make a *local link* (a link from one file to another on the same site), however, you don't generally need to specify the entire URL of the file you're linking to. Instead, you just need to set the *relative path,* which is the path from the current file or the site's root folder to the linked file. For instance, to link from an `about.html` page to a `contact.html` page, both of which sit at the root level of a URL, the local link code would look like this: `<a href="contact.html">Contact Us</a>`.

You can use three types of link paths:

✦ **Document-relative paths:** This type of link specifies the path and name of the document being linked to, such as `about.html` or `photogallery/ MollySurfing.html`. The general idea behind document-relative paths is that you don't need to add the *absolute* (full) URL including http:// for them to work because all the files being linked to reside either at the root level or inside a subfolder of the local root folder.

Using the Pacific Surf site structure shown in Figure 3-1 to create a document-relative path to a file inside a subfolder at the root level, add a forward slash after the folder name containing the file you want to link to, as in the path

```
photogallery/MollySurfing.html
```

This path tells the browser to move down a level in the folder hierarchy, from the root level into the `photogallery` folder to find a file called `MollySurfing.html`. If you were then to add a text link from the `MollySurfing.html` page to the `about.html` page, you'd add a `../` before the filename, as in `../about.html`. The `..` tells the browser to move up a level in the folder hierarchy.

Figure 3-1:
This site uses document-relative paths.

Be sure to save new files before creating document-relative paths to ensure that the path is saved correctly. Otherwise, you may see a temporary path starting with `file://` in the code until the file gets saved and Dreamweaver can update all the temporary paths to relative paths.

✦ **Site root-relative paths:** Links using site root-relative paths display the path and name of the document being linked to, but they direct the browser to begin searching for the path by starting at the root level of the site. To indicate this, you include a forward slash before the first folder or filename in the link code, as in the following two examples:

```
/contact.html
/services/widgets.html
```

The forward slash stands for the site's root folder. Use these paths for large sites sitting on several servers, a site that has multiple hosts, or sites that use server-side includes (SSIs), as described in Book III, Chapter 3.

✦ **Absolute paths:** An absolute path is the full URL to the linked document, as in

```
http://www.example.com/services/widgets.html
```

You must use absolute paths for files that sit on other servers, such as a link to purchase a specific *For Dummies* book from Amazon or a link that takes you to a particular page on a blog site. Using absolute paths is somewhat discouraged for local site pages because links on files moved from one domain name or folder location to another get broken. So unless you have a particular reason for using absolute paths, try to use document-relative paths for local links whenever possible.

Setting Up a Site with a Wizard

Setting up a managed site simply means defining a local site on your computer so that Dreamweaver knows where to save documents and find files related to that site. You'll want to create a managed site for each project that you work on. Always try to define or manage a site before you start development to ensure the site takes advantage of Dreamweaver's great site management features, such as sitewide filename change support.

Dreamweaver provides you with two easy ways to create a managed site. The Basic method uses a wizard with step-by-step prompts, and the Advanced method lets you manually set all the local, remote, and testing folder settings as well as other category options. If you're new to Dreamweaver, we encourage you to use the wizard. If you'd rather go the advanced route, check out the later section, "Setting Up a Site Using the Advanced Method," for details.

To set up a Dreamweaver site using the wizard, follow these steps:

1. **Choose Site⇨Manage Sites.**

   You can also launch the wizard by selecting Manage Sites from the Files panel drop-down list.

   The Manage Sites dialog box opens, as shown in Figure 3-2.

Figure 3-2: The Manage Sites dialog box.

2. **Click New, and then from the drop-down list that appears, select Site.**

   The Site Definition dialog box opens.

3. **Select the Basic tab.**

   Figure 3-3 shows the Basic Wizard. The wizard walks you through the steps for setting up a new site.

4. Provide a name for your site and enter the site's HTTP Address (URL); then click the Next button.

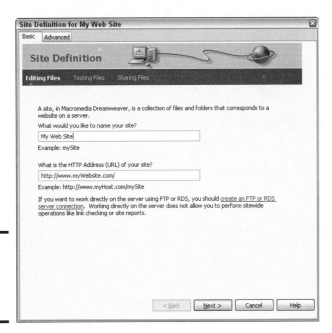

Figure 3-3:
The first
screen of
the Basic
Wizard.

5. Decide whether you want to work with a server technology:

- **No, I do not want to use a server technology:** Select this option and click Next.

- **Yes, I want to use a server technology:** Select a server technology from the drop-down list and click Next.

6. Choose whether to edit local copies of your files before uploading or work directly on the server using a local network. In addition, specify the location on your computer where the files for this site will be stored (this site's *local root folder*). Click Next.

7. Select a method of connection to your remote server. The bottom half of this screen changes to match the method you select. Click Next.

For example, if you plan on connecting using Local/Network settings, enter the path to the folder on the server where the files will be stored.

8. If you selected a remote server option, choose whether to enable the Check In/Out feature for this site. Click Next.

When this option is enabled, only one person at a time can check files out. You must also select a method for how Dreamweaver handles files upon check-out, and enter your name and e-mail address.

9. **A summary of the site settings appears, for your review, as shown in Figure 3-4.**

    Use the Back button to return to a previous screen if you need to make any changes.

Figure 3-4:
Review your settings and click Done to accept them.

10. **Click the Done button to accept the settings and close the Basic Wizard.**

11. **Click the Done button in the Manage Sites dialog box.**

    The Manage Sites dialog box closes, and the newly defined site in Dreamweaver opens, displaying all the existing files, if any, in the root folder in the Files panel.

If your server or work computer is not backed up regularly, seriously consider making a local backup copy of your site before you modify it. Having backups is a great practice, one that can serve you well when mistakes are made, data gets lost, or you need to revert to a previous version.

Setting Up a Site Using the Advanced Method

If you're an experienced designer, you'll probably want to use the Advanced tab of the Site Definition dialog box to specify managed-site settings. To start

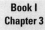

working quickly, you can set up just the local folder for now; you can return to the Site Definition dialog box at any time to add remote and testing folder information. That said, if you already have all the information you need to set up your site, entering everything at once may be easier.

Technically, it's only necessary to fill out the Local Info category to begin building a site and the Remote Info category if you also intend to use Dreamweaver to upload your site to a remote server. You can complete the remaining categories as needed. We discuss how to set up a remote server in Book V, Chapter 3.

To get your site up and running locally, follow these steps:

1. **Choose Site⇨Manage Sites.**

   The Manage Sites dialog box opens (refer to Figure 3-2).

2. **Click New, and from the drop-down list, select Site.**

   The Site Definition dialog box opens.

3. **Select the Advanced tab.**

   The Advanced tab of the Site Definition dialog box appears, as shown in Figure 3-5.

Figure 3-5:
The
Advanced
Site
Definition
options.

Changing the link path

By default, Dreamweaver uses the document-relative path for links. If you would rather use site root-relative paths for links, you need to modify the Local Info settings during the site-management process. To change from the default document-relative path setting to site root-relative paths, follow these steps:

1. **Choose Site⇨Manage Sites.**

   The Manage Sites dialog box opens.

2. **Double-click the site you want to modify from the list.**

   The Site Definition dialog box opens.

3. **Click the Advanced tab at the top of the dialog box.**

4. **In the Local Info category, change the relative path of new links from Document to Site Root.**

This step doesn't change the paths of existing links but does apply to any new links created in Dreamweaver.

When using site root-relative paths, the pages don't appear when you preview the files in a browser. Browsers don't recognize site roots — servers do. To preview the paths in a browser while working in Dreamweaver, choose Edit⇨Preferences (Windows) or Dreamweaver⇨Preferences (Mac) to open the Preferences dialog box. Then select the Preview Using Temporary File option in the Preview in Browser category.

4. **In the Site Name field, enter the name of your site.**

   Picking a name that indicates your site's purpose is best, such as Recipe if you're building a site to store recipes.

5. **Verify that the Local Root Folder field points to a directory in your local Web root directory.**

   To keep your files organized, add the recipe folder (\recipe\), for example, onto the end of your Web root so that all files related to this site are in their own Web-accessible folder. This isn't required, but it keeps you from having a mess of unrelated files in your Web root.

6. **Leave the Default Images Folder field blank.**

   Type a folder name, such as **images**, at this prompt if you want to keep all your site's images in a separate folder.

7. **Select Document from the Links Relative To options.**

   This option builds links in your sites that reference other files by their positions relative to the active file. It allows you to easily move your site to a different directory.

8. **In the HTTP Address field, type** http://localhost/*directoryname*, **where** *directoryname* **is the directory in your local Web root directory from Step 5.**

   For example, if you're using the directory `recipe` under your Web root, enter **http://localhost/recipe**.

9. **Leave the Case-sensitive Links check box unchecked.**

   This option tells Dreamweaver not to worry about the case of names in links.

10. **Leave the Enable Cache check box selected.**

    This option speeds up working with files in Dreamweaver.

11. **Click OK in the Site Definition dialog box.**

12. **Click the Done button in the Manage Sites dialog box.**

    Your site opens, displaying all the existing files in the root folder in the Files panel.

The following sections describe the other categories, in case you're filling them in.

Remote Info

After specifying the local folder, fill in the Remote Info category information. The remote folder is the place to store files for collaboration, testing, production, and deployment. If the Web server is running on your local computer, you don't need to set up the remote folder as long as the specified local folder points to the same file. See Book V, Chapter 3 for more info on setting up a remote folder.

Testing Server

In the Testing Server category, specify the location where you want your dynamic pages processed. In other words, this folder is an alternative location where you can test your files on a server with an identical database setup, without having to deploy the files to the live site while they're still under development. The testing server can be on your local computer, or on a staging, development, or production server. Check out Book VII, Chapter 1 if you need to set up a testing server.

Cloaking

Cloaking prevents specified files and folders from being included in a variety of site operations, such as site file synchronization between local and remote servers. For example, you may want to cloak large movie files or Design Notes folders from being uploaded each time you update site files to the remote server. For more details on how to enable site cloaking, see Book V, Chapter 3.

Design Notes

Dreamweaver lets you create and share Design Notes about site files, which are then stored in a separate location. Enable this feature when communicating within a design team or workgroup about a shared managed site. You can attach Design Notes to documents, templates, images, Flash movies, ActiveX controls, and applets. Refer to Book VI, Chapter 1 for details on Design Notes.

Site Map Layout

Dreamweaver lets you view the files in the local folder as a visual map of linked file icons. You can customize the look of the site map in the Site Map category. For details about using the Site Map Layout mode, including how to modify the site map settings, turn to Book VI, Chapter 1.

File View Columns

In the expanded Files panel, Dreamweaver displays file and folder details in columns next to the filenames. You can customize which file and folder details show up there by making changes to the File View Columns category. For instance, you can hide and show, add and delete, reorder, share, and rename column settings. You can find out more about defining File View Columns in Book VI, Chapter 1.

Contribute

When creating a site for use with Macromedia Contribute software, you must enable Contribute compatibility before administering the site in Dreamweaver. The Contribute category allows you to enter Administration settings. See Book VI, Chapters 2 and 3 for the lowdown on using Dreamweaver with Macromedia Contribute.

Managing Multiple Sites

Because you create a new managed site for each project you work on in Dreamweaver, keeping track of all your sites is relatively easy. You can view a list of all your managed sites as follows:

+ **Files panel:** The Files panel lists the files from a selected managed site. To change from viewing one site's files to another site's files, select the desired site by choosing it from the list of managed sites.

✦ **Manage Sites dialog box:** Choose Site⇨Manage Sites to open the Manage Sites dialog box. Select your desired site from the list and click the Done button to switch to the selected site. You may briefly see the Opening Site and Uploading Site Cache dialog boxes as Dreamweaver opens the selected site.

Duplicating sites

Create exact duplicate copies of any existing defined site by clicking the Duplicate button in the Manage Sites dialog box. Dreamweaver copies all the settings and creates the new site with the same filename appended with the word `copy`. For example, if duplicating a site called Company ABC, the name of the new duplicate managed site would be `Company ABC copy` until you rename it.

This doesn't copy the actual files. It just creates a new site setting within Dreamweaver, which you can then modify. Often, you'll also want to duplicate the local folder and all its files so you have a new copy to work on in Dreamweaver.

Exporting and importing sites

Dreamweaver allows you to save and reopen sites as XML files using the Import and Export buttons. In other words, you'll export a site with all its settings as an XML file and then import the site with the same settings later, either on the same machine or on another machine. This way is handy to get a new computer up and running with all the sites you're currently managing.

Exporting sites

To save a site as an XML file, follow these steps:

1. **Choose Site⇨Manage Sites to open the Manage Sites dialog box.**

2. **Select one or more sites and click the Export button.**

   Use Control+click (Windows) or ⌘+click (Mac) to select multiple files.

3. **Browse to, select, and save the location for the export of each site.**

   The exported file gets saved as an XML file with the `.ste` file extension.

Importing sites

To import previously exported XML files into Dreamweaver, follow these steps:

1. **Choose Site⇨Manage Sites to open the Manage Sites dialog box.**

2. **Click the Import button.**

3. **Browse to and select one or more sites with the `.ste` file extension for importing.**

   Use Control+click (Windows) or ⌘+click (Mac) to select multiple files.

4. **Click Open to begin the importing process.**

   The Manage Sites dialog box lists the site name when the import process is complete.

Removing sites from the managed-sites list

When removing sites, keep in mind that sites listed in the Manage Sites dialog box are merely pointers to the location of files on the specified computer and not the actual files and folders themselves. Therefore, removing a site from the managed-sites list removes only the location information Dreamweaver needs to work on the files in the specified site.

To remove your site from Dreamweaver, select your site from the Manage Sites dialog box and click the Remove button. Dreamweaver gives you the `You cannot undo this action` message. Don't be unnerved; if you accidentally delete a managed site from the list, you can just re-create it.

Book II

Mastering the Basics

The 5th Wave   By Rich Tennant

"Look into my Web site, Ms. Carruthers. Look deep into its rotating, nicely animated spiral, spinning, spinning, pulling you in, deeper... deeper..."

Contents at a Glance

Chapter 1: Creating Documents

In This Chapter

✔ **Creating a new document**

✔ **Saving files**

✔ **Setting page properties**

✔ **Importing data**

*C*reating documents is the basis for everything you'll do for the Web. Dreamweaver provides several ways to create them, several types of new documents to choose from, and even several premade "design files" to use as starting points for your own designs.

This chapter explores document types, document creation, document saving, and document opening. You also discover how to set page properties, work with invisible page elements, and import Word and Excel files (Windows only).

Creating a New Document

In Dreamweaver 8, as in Dreamweaver MX and MX 2004, the default Start Page appears in the workspace when you launch the program. The Start Page allows you to open existing files from a list of the ten most recent documents, create new files by type such as HTML or PHP, and create new files with CSS (Cascading Style Sheets) or framesets from sample Dreamweaver design files. If you don't see the Start Page when you launch the program, you can enable it by following the steps in the nearby sidebar.

When the Start Page is visible (shown in Figure 1-1), the quickest way to create a new blank document is to click one of the file types in the Create New column. Click the HTML link, for instance, and a new untitled Document window opens, ready for adding content and saving with a filename and extension.

Enabling the Start Page

You can enable and disable the Start Page through Dreamweaver's Preferences. To turn on the Start Page, follow these steps:

1. **Choose Edit⇨Preferences (Windows) or Dreamweaver⇨Preferences (Mac).**

   The Preferences dialog box opens.

2. **Select the General Category to reveal general category options.**

3. **Select the Show Start Page check box in the Document Options area on the right. Then click OK.**

   Dreamweaver displays the Start Page in the center of the workspace beneath the Insert bar.

Figure 1-1: Use the Start Page to quickly create new documents.

To create a new document, follow these steps:

1. **Choose File⇨New to launch the New Document window, shown in Figure 1-2.**

   This dialog box has two tabs at the top of the panel, one for general documents and one for templates. In this chapter, we discuss the General tab; Book III, Chapter 2 shows you how to work with templates.

2. **In the Category list on the General tab, select the category of document you want to create.**

3. **In the center list, select the type of document you want to create.**

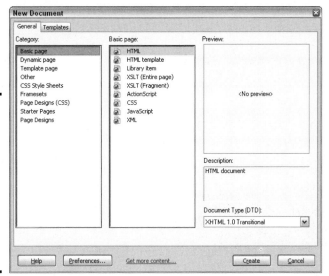

Book II
Chapter 1

Creating Documents

Figure 1-2:
Select a category, page type, and document type definition (DTD) from the General tab.

Take some time to explore the different file options in each category. Dreamweaver supplies you with a nice group of blank documents or sample design files in each category as a starting point. For example, the Starter Pages category has documents with the general Web layout already created, the Framesets category has premade frames, and the CSS Style Sheets category is filled with preset colors, fonts, and sizes for you to use as is or as a starting point for further development.

4. **At the bottom of the New Document window, click the Preferences button to set default document preferences such as document type, file extension, and encoding.**

The Get More Content link takes you to Macromedia's Dreamweaver Exchange where, once registered, you can download more design files. (See Book IV, Chapter 2 for more on the Dreamweaver Exchange.)

5. **Select an option from the Document Type (DTD) drop-down list.**

For example, when creating a basic, dynamic, or template page, you can make the page XHTML compliant by choosing an XHTML document type definition from the Document Type (DTD) drop-down list. Dreamweaver automatically writes the DTD code at the top of your new document above the opening <html> tag and at times may append the <html> tag itself, like this:

```
<!DOCTYPE html PUBLIC "-//W3C//DTD XHTML 1.0 Transitional//EN"
    "http://www.w3.org/TR/xhtml1/DTD/xhtml1-transitional.dtd">
<html xmlns="http://www.w3.org/1999/xhtml">
```

The default document type for HTML is HTML 4.01 Transitional and the default document type for XHTML is XHTML 1.0 Transitional, but you can also choose from any of the other options available in the drop-down list. For a more detailed discussion of XHTML, turn to Book IV, Chapter 4.

6. After you make all your selections from the New Document window, click the Create button.

The new file opens in the Document window.

Saving Documents

When saving a document, give the file a unique name with the appropriate file extension and save it to the root level of the managed site folder.

To save a new file, follow these steps:

1. Choose File⇨Save.

The Save As dialog box opens.

2. In the Save As dialog box, navigate to the folder where you want to save the new file.

Remember to save your file in a managed Dreamweaver site. If you haven't managed your site yet, turn to Book I, Chapter 3.

3. Type the name of your file in the File Name text box.

When naming the file, consider using all lowercase letters and avoid using special characters such as ñ or ö, spaces, or punctuation, such as periods or slashes. Though filenames can be any length in Windows, keep filenames under 29 characters in length to avoid Mac OS issues (31 characters is the published Mac character length recommendation).

By default, Dreamweaver assigns a default file extension to your untitled document, which for HTML files can be either .html or .htm. Regardless of which extension you choose to work with, be consistent and use the same extension throughout your entire Web site. The extension on the file-name ensures the files display correctly in a browser window. If needed, choose a different file type from the Save as Type drop-down list.

4. Click Save.

After the file has been named and saved, you can continue saving new changes to the file by choosing File⇨Save.

Book II
Chapter 1

Creating Documents

Changing the default file extensions

In previous versions of Dreamweaver, the default extensions for all document types were listed in an external XML file. To change the default extension, you had to manually open the XML file and edit the code by hand. Thankfully, Dreamweaver 8 now allows you to change the default HTML file extension right in the Preferences dialog box. (To change any of the other document type file extensions — though you'll probably never need to do so — you still open the XML file.)

To edit the default document type and preferences, follow these steps:

1. **Choose Edit➪Preferences (Windows) or Dreamweaver➪Preferences (Mac) to launch the Preferences dialog box.**

2. **Click the New Document category on the left.**

3. **On the right, change the preferences as needed for default document, extension, document type definition (DTD), and encoding.**

4. **Click OK when you're done.**

The new default file extensions work immediately for all newly created documents.

After you initially save your document, you have some additional options when saving it in the future. For instance, you can save a copy of the file, save several files at once, or revert to a previous version of the file, as described in the following sections.

Saving a copy of a file

You can save changes to documents after the initial save with their existing name and location, thereby overwriting the previous version of that file. You can also save a file as a copy using the Save As command.

To save a copy of the file using Save As, follow these steps:

1. **Choose File➪Save As.**

   The Save As dialog box opens.

2. **In the Save As dialog box, navigate to the folder where you want to save a copy of the file.**

   You can save a copy of the file with the same or different filename in a new folder, or save a copy of the file with a different filename in the same folder.

3. **Enter a different filename in the File Name text box.**

4. **Click Save.**

Saving multiple documents at once

Another saving command that can often come in handy is Save All. This command saves all the open documents in the workspace with one command.

To save all the open files at once, choose File➪Save All. If any open documents are unsaved, the Save As dialog box opens for each unsaved file. For each unsaved file, enter filenames with file extensions and navigate to the folder you want to save the file to. Then click the Save button.

If Save All is a function you intend to perform often, create a custom keyboard shortcut for the Save All command! See Book III, Chapter 4 for details.

Reverting to a previous version of a file

Inevitably, a time comes when you need to revert to the last saved version of a file. During each work session, Dreamweaver allows you to revert to the previously saved version.

Follow these steps to refer to the previous version of a file:

1. **Choose File➪Revert.**

   A dialog box opens and asks if you want to discard any changes you've made to the current file and revert to the previous version.

2. **Click Yes to revert; click No to cancel.**

This function works only during the current Dreamweaver session. When you close Dreamweaver and restart it, you can no longer revert to a previous version of a file.

Opening Existing Files

After creating, saving, and closing a file, you can reopen it at any time for editing in Dreamweaver. Furthermore, you can open any existing Web page or text-based file in Dreamweaver, even when it was created in another program. Other file types you can open in Dreamweaver include JavaScript (`.js`), CSS (`.css`), XML (`.xml`), and text files (`.txt`). You can't, however, open Word (`.doc`) files directly in Dreamweaver.

Here's how to open an existing file:

1. **Choose File➪Open.**

   The Open dialog box appears.

2. **Navigate to and click the file you want to open.**

3. Click Open.

The file opens in the Document window. With HTML files, you can choose Code, Split, or Design view for editing purposes. However by default, JavaScript, CSS, and text files open in Code view. (See Book I, Chapter 1 for more on these views.)

You can also open files by double-clicking the file in the Files panel or by pressing Ctrl+O (Windows) or ⌘+O (Mac) to launch the Open dialog box where you can navigate to and open a file.

If the file you open is a Microsoft Word file that's been saved as a Microsoft Word HTML file, you need to clean up the Microsoft markup. Choose Commands⇨Clean Up Word HTML to have Dreamweaver remove all the unnecessary Microsoft markup. For more information, check out Book V, Chapter 2.

Book II Chapter 1

Creating Documents

Setting Page Properties

Dreamweaver lets you set the page formatting properties in the Page Properties dialog box (see Figure 1-3). Formatting options include setting the page's default font family, font color, font size, background color, background image, link styles, page title, and page margins. Each page can have its own property settings, and you can modify these settings at any time.

In Dreamweaver 8, all the page properties settings are added as a Cascading Style Sheet in the head area of the page. To find out more about CSS, turn to Book III, Chapter 1.

Figure 1-3:
Set the appearance and other properties of a page.

To access the Page Properties dialog box from any open document, use any of the following methods:

✦ Click the Page Properties button in the Properties inspector.

✦ Press Ctrl+J (Windows) or ⌘+J (Mac).

✦ Choose Modify⇨Page Properties.

After you open the Page Properties dialog box, select the layout and formatting properties that you need from the Appearance, Links, Headings, Title/Encoding, and Tracing Image categories.

Understanding Invisible Page Elements

When certain HTML code, such as JavaScript or comment tags, needs to be in the body of the page but won't be displayed in the browser, Dreamweaver hides that code in Design view with little yellow icons called *invisible elements*. That way, rather than seeing an entire swatch of JavaScript code, Dreamweaver inserts the invisible element to show where the code sits in Code view. Grab the invisibles by their icons if you need to move, edit, or delete them.

By default, about half the available invisible elements are enabled and appear in Design view when you choose View⇨Visual Aids⇨Invisible Elements. A check mark next to Invisible Elements means it's turned on; without the check, the Visual Aid is turned off.

You may notice that content in Design view shifts slightly when the invisible elements appear. Therefore, for precision with layout, you may need to toggle the invisibles on and off; if you prefer to leave them on, preview your page in a browser often to test the accuracy of the layout.

Use the settings in the Preferences dialog box to further control which invisible elements appear in Design view. For instance, you may want to show an invisible icon for named anchors but not line breaks. Table 1-1 provides a brief description of all the invisible elements.

To change the Invisible Elements preferences, follow these steps:

1. **Choose Edit⇨Preferences (Windows) or Dreamweaver⇨ Preferences (Mac).**

   The Preferences dialog box opens.

2. **Click the Invisible Elements category.**

   On the right side of the dialog box, as shown in Figure 1-4, you see a list of invisible elements.

3. Place a check mark next to the name of each invisible you want to show on your pages in Design view.

4. Click OK.

Your changes take effect immediately. Modify these settings at any time by reopening the Preferences dialog box.

Figure 1-4:
The Preferences dialog box with the Invisible Elements options.

You can add some invisibles, like comments or named anchors, to your document with the buttons on the Common tab of the Insert bar. With the invisible element selected in Design view, you can edit its contents in the Properties inspector.

Table 1-1	Invisible Elements
Invisible Element	*What Its Yellow Icon Hides in the Code*
Named Anchors	Marks the spot where each named anchor (`a name=""`) sits in the code.
Scripts	Marks the spot where JavaScript or VBScript sits in the body part of the file. The invisible element spans from the opening to closing `<script>` tags and includes the entire contents of the script. Edit the content of the script in Code view and change the language, source, and type in the Properties inspector by selecting the invisible element icon in Design view. ***Note:*** Script invisibles don't appear for inline JavaScript or JavaScript URLs.
Comments	Marks where you find HTML comments. Edit the comments in the Properties inspector by selecting the invisible element icon in Design view.

(continued)

Table 1-1 *(continued)*

Invisible Element	What Its Yellow Icon Hides in the Code
Line Breaks	Shows icons for every line break (` ` or ` `) in the code. Select the invisible element icon to move or delete the break.
Client-Side Image Maps	Marks the spot of each client-side image map in the code.
Embedded Styles	Marks the spot where CSS is embedded in the body of the file rather than in the head of the file or in an external CSS. Technically, `<style>` tags should only be in the head, though Dreamweaver lets you manually put them in the body.
Hidden Form Fields	Shows an icon for every instance of a hidden form field with the type attribute `"hidden"`.
Form Delimiter	This invisible element appears as part of the `<form>` tag and displays in Design view as a red dotted border to show where you can insert form elements. This feature is a good one to leave on. You must insert form fields inside the dotted line to work properly.
Anchor Points for Layers	Shows an icon to visually represent each layer in the file. You can position the layer itself anywhere on the page, while the icon typically sit at the top-left corner. Click the layer icon to see the layer's contents.
Anchor Points for Aligned Elements	Marks the spot where code can have the `align` attribute, including tables, images, plug-ins, and applets.
Visual Server Markup Tags and Non-Visual Server Markup Tags	These invisibles mark the spot where server markup tags, such ASP and ColdFusion, sit in the code even though they don't display in the Document window.

Importing Tabular Data Files

Tabular data files are delimited text files containing records that are separated or *delimited* by a specified character, such as a tab or comma, that doesn't appear in the data. You can create delimited text files with most spreadsheet and database programs such as Microsoft Excel and Access.

After you convert an Excel or database file into a delimited text file, you can import it into a Web page. During the import process, you select the delimiter type that you originally used to separate the data. The delimiter is used to separate data into individual table cells. This gives you a new level of control over your imported data that wasn't available before!

To import a tabular data file, follow these steps:

1. **Choose File⇨Import⇨Import Tabular Data.**

   The Import Tabular Data dialog box opens, shown in Figure 1-5.

2. **Browse to and select the file to import.**

3. **From the Delimiter drop-down list, choose the delimiter type used when the file was saved.**

   Select from Colon, Comma, Semicolon, Tab, and Other. If Other, enter the character that was used as the delimiter.

4. **(Optional) Enter other options to format the table that will hold the imported data.**

5. **Click OK.**

After importing, save your page and edit the imported data as you need.

Figure 1-5:
The Import
Tabular
Data dialog
box.

Importing Word and Excel Files (Windows Only)

Windows users can import Word and Excel files right into any new or existing Dreamweaver page. During the import process, Dreamweaver automatically strips the Microsoft files of unnecessary code including style formatting and converts the content into HTML code. The only cautionary restriction is that the file must be smaller than 300K after importing.

Follow these steps to import the entire contents of a Word or Excel file:

1. **Choose File⇨Import and then choose either Word or Excel.**

2. **In the Import File dialog box, browse for and select the file to open and click Open to begin the import.**

   Figure 1-6 shows the Import Word Document dialog box.

Figure 1-6:
Import a
Word file
with the
Import Word
Document
dialog box.

If your computer alerts you that the server is busy and that the action cannot be completed because another program is busy, click the Switch To or Retry button to correct the problem and import the file.

3. Edit the imported data as you need.

You're making changes in the new document and not altering the original Microsoft file.

4. Choose File➪Save.

To include only part of a Microsoft file and preserve formatting, paste the portion of the file you want directly in the Web document.

Chapter 2: Working with Text

In This Chapter

✔ **Adding, editing, and removing text**

✔ **Inserting text with the Paste and Paste Special commands**

✔ **Using the Properties inspector**

✔ **Creating inline style sheets**

✔ **Creating bulleted and numbered lists**

✔ **Searching with Find and Replace**

*A*dding text to your pages in HTML is as easy as typing in a word processing document or text editor. You can insert, change, or delete text, as well style, order, and structure it. You can even paste text from another file into an open Dreamweaver Document window.

Text is the keystone of all Web pages. In fact, a Web page is simply a text file (that may also contain other objects, such as images and tables) that uses a set of HTML tags to describe to a browser how to format and display the text. Use text to describe a company's products or services, provide contact information, make important facts and figures available to visitors, tell stories, and more. In addition, text on a Web page is searchable by search engines, which means what you add to a page should not only be easy to read and understand, but it should look good too.

This chapter covers everything you need to know about working with text including adding, editing, and removing copy; using the Properties inspector to create inline CSS; making lists; and using the Find and Replace tool for robust text and code editing.

Adding Text

You can type text directly into the Document window in either Design or Code view. To begin adding text in Design view, open any new or existing document and place your cursor at the point where you want to add the text; then, begin typing. In Code view, you can add text straight to the code anywhere inside the opening and closing `<body>` tags, including inside table cells, `<div>` tags, and `<span>` tags.

In Design view, when you select a word, sentence, or paragraph, the code also gets selected in Code view, and when you select content in Code view, that content also gets selected in Design view. Switch freely between typing text in Design and Code views.

Editing Text

To edit text, select the text you want to edit and start typing. By selecting the text first, you automatically overwrite the text in the selection when you type. Make a selection by double-clicking a word to select the whole word, or triple-clicking a word to select an entire block of text.

When selecting with a triple-click in Design view, only the copy gets selected. However, when triple-clicking in Code view, both the content and the content container tags get selected.

If, however, the content between any two tags includes any unnecessary breaks in the text (not including <br> or <p> breaks), the triple-click in Code view only selects a single line rather than the entire content block between the two tags. If that happens, clean up the code by removing any unnecessary spacing between characters and try the triple-click again.

Text containers include <body>, <p>, <div>, <span>, <td>, and <li> among others. If a paragraph of text is contained inside a paragraph tag, the opening and closing <p> tags aren't selected along with the text in Design view, but they are selected in Code view, as shown in the following examples.

When triple-clicking a word inside a paragraph in Design view:

```
Hot cross buns! Hot cross buns! One a penny two a penny - Hot cross buns!
```

When triple-clicking a word inside a paragraph in Code view with no unnecessary breaks in the content:

```
<p>Hot cross buns! Hot cross buns! One a penny two a penny - Hot cross buns!</p>
```

When triple-clicking a word inside a paragraph in Code view with an unnecessary break in the content, in this case the break is after the second instance of the word *buns!*:

```
<p>Hot cross buns! Hot cross buns!
```

Removing Text

To remove text, select it and delete it by pressing Delete or Backspace on the keyboard or by choosing Edit⇨Clear or Edit⇨Cut from the main menu to clear or cut the selection.

Pasting Text from Another File

When pasting data into Dreamweaver from a Word document, Web site, or other word processing file, Dreamweaver often preserves that document's formatting when you use the regular Paste command. Formatting, including font face, size, and alignment, transfers to the file with the copied text. If you want to preserve formatting, choose Copy⇨Paste.

On the other hand, if you want to have some control over how the pasted copy gets formatted, follow these steps:

1. **Copy the text you want to paste and then choose Copy⇨Paste Special.**

    The Paste Special dialog box opens, as shown in Figure 2-1.

Figure 2-1:
Set
formatting
preferences
for pasted
text.

2. **Select one of the following paste options:**

    - **Text only:** Paste the copied text as unformatted text. Any formatting attributes copied from the original source file, including line and paragraph breaks, bold or italics, font size, and font color, is stripped.

    - **Text with structure:** Paste the copied text with its existing paragraph structure, including line and paragraph breaks, lists, and tables. Its formatting attributes, such as bold or italics, are not included.

    - **Text with structure plus basic formatting:** Paste the copied text with pre-existing structure and HTML formatting, including paragraphs, line breaks, and tables, and basic text formatting using tags such as `<b>`, `<i>`, `<strong>`, `<em>`, and `<hr>`.

• **Text with structure plus full formatting:** Paste the copied text into Dreamweaver with all its original structure, HTML formatting, and pre-existing internal CSS data. This option does not include the copying of styles that come from sources external to the copied file, such as an external CSS file, or from any programs that don't allow style information to be copied to the Clipboard.

3. **Check the Retain Line Breaks option.**

   Enable this option to keep pre-existing line breaks, or disable this option to remove the unwanted line breaks that some applications add at the ends of each line of text. This option is not available for the Text Only option.

4. **Check the Clean Up Word Paragraph Spacing option.**

   Enable this option when using the Text with Structure and Text with Structure plus Basic Formatting options to remove extra spaces between paragraphs in the pasted text.

5. **Click OK.**

   The copied text is pasted into your document with the selected settings.

Setting Text Properties in the Properties Inspector

The Properties inspector is context specific, so when you're adding text to the page, it displays options for formatting and linking text, as shown in Figure 2-2. From the Properties inspector, you can specify font face, size, style, alignment, and color, select formats such as Paragraph or H1, create and format lists, indent or outdent text, and enter hyperlink information. These settings, or *styles*, are applied immediately to selected content, and you can change them at any time.

Figure 2-2:
The Properties inspector displays formatting options for selected text.

When you add Bold or Italic formatting by clicking the B or I button in the Properties inspector, Dreamweaver writes the newer `<strong>` and `<em>` (for emphasis) tags into the code instead of the former `<b>` and `<i>` tags. This is because `<b>` and `<i>` are formatting tags whereas `<strong>` and `<em>` are structural tags. Both tags format text, but structural tags can also provide cues about the text's importance that can help improve search engine rankings by emphasizing important keywords or phrases as well as complying with Web Accessibility guidelines to improve the way screen readers interpret text on a page with speech inflections. You can continue using the `<b>` and `<i>` tags if you want to, but the newer tags are strongly preferred.

You can find these text options in the Properties inspector, as shown in Figure 2-2:

Book II
Chapter 2

Working with Text

✦ **Format** lets you choose the paragraph style that's applied to the selected text. Styles include none, paragraph `<p>`, preformatted `<pre>`, or headings `<h1>` through `<h6>`.

✦ **Style** shows a list of custom styles on the inline and/or attached external CSS, if any. Select and apply a style by name, remove a style attribute by selecting None, or launch dialog boxes to rename or manage styles. When no style is applied, the drop-down list appears blank or says None, and when multiple styles are applied, the drop-down list is blank.

✦ **CSS** launches the CSS panel, which displays the current CSS properties, if any, applied to a selection or to the page. If, however, the CSS panel is already open, the CSS button in the Properties inspector may be greyed out.

✦ **Bold** adds the `<strong>` tags around selected text to emphasize the selection with boldness.

✦ **Italic** adds the `<em>` tags around selected text to emphasize the selection with italics.

✦ **Left, Center, Right,** and **Justify Align** are the choices you have for the alignment of your content relative to the browser window or to the tags the content is placed inside of, such as a table cell or layer.

✦ **Link** adds hypertext links to selected text or graphics. To add a link, do one of the following:

  • Select the text or graphic in Design view. Type the URL or filename of the link in the Link text field.

  • Click the folder button to browse for and select a file by name.

  • Click and drag the Point to File button onto the name of the file in the Files panel. Release the button, and Dreamweaver writes the filename in the text field for you.

  • Drag and drop a file from the Files panel into the Link text box.

To create a link before you know what the URL or filename is, enter # or `javascript:;` in the Link text box.

✦ **Font** shows a list of font sets to choose from to apply to the selected text. If the first font is unavailable, the second font is used, and so on.

✦ **Size** applies a font size to selected text in pixels (px), points (pt), inches (in), centimeters (cm), millimeters (mm), picas (pc), ems (em), exs (ex), or percentages (%). Because fonts render uniformly on both platforms when specified in pixels, pixels are currently the preferred measure for specifying font size.

Table 2-1 lists descriptions for all the acceptable units of measure. If you've specified HTML instead of CSS as the default option, you can choose from font sizes ranging from 1 through 7 and + or –1 through + or –7 relative to the base font size (default set to 3).

✦ **Text Color** turns the selected text to the color specified. In the text field next to the Text Color box, type a color name, such as **aqua**, or enter a hexadecimal number, such as **#000000** for black. Click the Text Color box to pick a color from the Web-safe color palette or the color picker (it's the rainbow colored circle button at the top of the Web-safe color palette).

✦ **Unordered List** converts the selected text into a bulleted list.

✦ **Ordered List** converts the selected text into a numbered list.

Table 2-1	Units of Measure
Unit of Measure	*Description*
px	Pixels.
pt	Points. One point is equal to ½₂ of an inch.
pc	Picas. A pica is equal to 12 points.
%	Percentage.
in	Inches.
cm	Centimeters.
mm	Millimeters.
em	A proportional unit of measure that equals the point size of the current font. For example, if the current font is 10 point, 1.2 em is equal to 12 points.
ex	A proportional unit of measure that equals half the point size of the current font. For example, if the current font is 10 point, 1.2 ex is equal to 6 points.

TECHNICAL STUFF

Hexadecimal numbers and the Web-safe palette

Colors on a Web page, whether used to format page properties, text, table cells, or other objects, display in a browser by using special color codes called hexadecimal numbers. These numbers are actually a set of three hexadecimal number pairs where each digit in a pair represents a value for red, green, and blue, as in #RRGGBB. A number symbol (#) always precedes the six digits when they appear in the HTML or CSS code, and each digit can have a value from 0–F (0–9 and A–F), as in #CC33FF. On the 0–F scale, 0 has a null value and F has the highest value of 15. The biggest value for any of the RGB pairs is FF, which is equal to 255 in the normal decimal system. This means, for example, that a value of #00FF00 yields the highest amount of green possible.

Web-safe colors refer to the 216 colors that can accurately display in Web browsers on both

Mac and PC computers. These browser-safe colors use only the following hexadecimal values: 00, 33, 66, 99, CC, and FF. In addition to using the hexadecimal values, you can also specify Web-safe colors using a color name, such as **cornflowerblue, crimson,** or **plum**.

To make specifying a color in Dreamweaver easy, click in the Text Color box in the Properties inspector to choose a color from the Web-safe palette or the color picker, or if you happen to know it, type the hex value or color name of the color.

You can find a listing of all the acceptable color names along with a swatch with their color and hexadecimal equivalents at www.w3schools. com/html/html_colornames.asp.

**Book II
Chapter 2**

Working with Text

✦ **Target** specifies where the linked page opens, whether in the same browser window, another browser window, or a frame inside a frameset. Without adding a target, the default setting is to open the linked page in the same browser window. Choose _blank to display the linked page in a new browser window, _self to open it in the same browser window, _parent to open the file in the parent frameset or the same frame as the link, or _top to open the file in the full browser, breaking any pre-existing frames. This option appears greyed out until you activate it by entering a link in the Link field.

✦ **Text Outdent** and **Indent** uniformly apply indenting and outdenting to lists and blocks of text inside container tags such as <p>. Click the Indent and Outdent buttons in the Properties inspector to add and remove margin spacing evenly around the selected text. You can also apply indents and outdents from the main menu or the context menu. Indenting regular text adds the <blockquote> tag around a selection, while outdenting removes the tag. By contrast, clicking the Indent and Outdent buttons with list text creates sublists using <ol> or <ul> and <li> list tags. You format multitiered lists by nesting indents inside other indents. Indenting with the `<blockquote>` tag typically adds about 40 pixels of padding on the left and right margins and a little extra white space above and below. To override this default display, consider using CSS to create a custom style that indents your content without the need for `<blockquote>` tags.

✦ **List Item** allows you to specify a list type from a dialog box. For unordered lists, choose a list style of circle, disc, or square. For ordered lists, choose from numbers (1, 2, 3), upper (I, II, III) or lowercase (i, ii, iii) roman numerals, and upper (A, B, C) or lowercase (a, b, c) letters. The list item button remains greyed out until you create a list on your page and place your cursor anywhere inside, but not selecting, part of the list.

✦ **Page Properties** opens the Page Properties dialog box, from which you can modify the properties of the currently open page, including the default font face, size, and color, background color, and margin spacing. (See Book II, Chapter 1 for details on the Page Properties dialog box.)

Creating Inline Style Sheets

By default, Dreamweaver uses CSS instead of HTML to write some tags for text formatting. Use the Properties inspector's format, bold, italic, list, indent, align, link, and target fields to add inline formatting to the page (as described in the preceding section). For example, bold linked text looks like this:

```
<a href="http://www.google.com"><strong>Google</strong></a>
```

By contrast, when using the Font, Style, Size, or Color settings in the Properties inspector, Dreamweaver writes inline CSS in the head of the open document. New styles are given unique style names, such as `style1`, and you can use them to style any of the other text on the same page.

When choosing a font, select one that is available for any site visitor (whether using Mac OS or Windows). Here's an acceptable list of fonts to choose from when specifying the font face for your HTML text:

Arial	Verdana	Helvetica	Times
Times New Roman	Courier	Courier New	Georgia
Geneva	Trebuchet	Serif	Sans-serif

For additional information about browser-safe fonts in general and a thorough list of fonts that come preinstalled in Windows and Macintosh computers, check out `www.websitenotes.com/websitenotes-37-20041220Browser SafeFonts.html` or `www.ampsoft.net/webdesign-1/Windows MacFonts.html`.

To help further with font selection, Dreamweaver allows you to select *font sets* to style your text. Font sets are lists of fonts that browsers read and use to display text. The browser looks for the first font listed in the set and renders the page using that font face. If the first font listed is unavailable, the browser searches for the next font in the list, and so on. Most font sets end with either serif or sans-serif, which are standard to all computers. A typical font set is `Arial, Helvetica, Sans-serif`. The benefit of using font sets instead of a single font is that if a single font is not found on the computer viewing the page, the text on that page displays with the browser's default font face. With a font set, you have more control over which fonts are tried — and hopefully used — to display the text on the page.

To set the entire page's default font face, size, and color, use the Page Properties dialog box, as described in Book II, Chapter 1.

Book II
Chapter 2

Working with Text

Inserting Special Characters

From time to time you may need to access special characters such as © or ® or ñ when typing text in the Document window. Though you could look up the HTML code for the appropriate character and then type it in Code view, Dreamweaver lets you choose many of the commonly used symbols found in other programs. All special characters are represented in HTML with a name or number. Dreamweaver calls each of these an entity. For instance, you can code the copyright symbol with `&copy;` or `&#169;`.

If you need to use the greater- and less-than brackets in your text and don't want HTML to interpret them as tags, use the entity symbols: `&gt;` for greater than (>) and `&lt;` for less than (<).

To add a special character to an open file, follow these steps:

1. **Place your cursor in the position you want to add the special character.**

   Single-click in Design view or Code view to place the insertion point in the right position.

2. **Choose Insert⇨HTML⇨Special Characters. Then from the flyout menu, choose from the list of commonly used special characters.**

3. **If you don't see the character you want to use, choose Other at the bottom of the flyout menu.**

   The Insert Other Character dialog box, shown in Figure 2-3, appears.

4. **Select the character you want and click OK to insert that character.**

   You can also copy and paste the HTML code from the Insert field at the top of the dialog box. For instance, the HTML code for the British pound symbol is `&pound;`.

Figure 2-3:
Add special
characters
to your
page.

For a great list of commonly used unicode symbols, see `www.w3schools.com/tags/ref_entities.asp`.

Creating Lists

Lists are classified as either *unordered* or *ordered:*

✦ **Unordered:** A bullet precedes all the list items. The style of the bullet can be a bullet (a solid circle), a circle (a hollow disc), or a small square. Dreamweaver only lets you choose a bullet or a square, however, so to use the circle style you need to modify the code.

```
<ul type="disc|circle|square">
```

✦ **Ordered:** The list type can be Numbered (1, 2, 3), Roman Uppercase (I, II, III), Roman Lowercase (i, ii, iii), Alphabet Uppercase (A, B, C), or Alphabet Lowercase (a, b, c).

```
<ol type="A|a|I|i|1">
```

In addition to the number type, ordered lists can have a starting value different than 1. For example, to start an ordered list using Alphabet uppercase at the letter J, add the start value of 10 (J is the 10th letter) to the `<ol>` tag:

```
<ol type="A" start="10">
```

To add a start value to a list item `<li>` tag instead of the ordered list `<ol>` tag, use the value attribute instead of the start attribute:

```
<li value="10">
```

If you don't specify a list type, the default unordered list is bulleted with a solid circle, and the default ordered list is numbered (1, 2, 3).

To convert selected text into list format, follow these steps:

1. **Select the text you want to convert to a list.**

   You can also type your first entry, convert it to a list format, and then continue adding items. Dreamweaver automatically continues to format your list.

2. **Click the Unordered or Ordered List button in the Properties inspector.**

   The Unordered List button looks like a bulleted list, and the Ordered List button looks like a numbered list (refer to Figure 2-2).

3. **Deselect the text by clicking the cursor inside any of the list items.**

   When the list is deselected, the List Item button becomes active in the Properties inspector.

4. **Click the List Item button in the Properties inspector.**

   The List Properties dialog box opens.

5. **Select a list type.**

6. **Click OK to close the List Properties dialog box.**

To change the list type of an existing list, place your cursor anywhere inside the list and choose another list type from the List Properties dialog box. You can also convert unordered lists into ordered lists and vice versa. The list buttons in the Properties inspector are toggle buttons allowing you to add and remove list formatting to selected text as needed.

Editing with the Find and Replace Tool

The Find and Replace feature is a powerful editing tool. Use this feature to find and replace text or source code in a selection, in an open document, for a specified folder, or for the currently managed site. This is a great tool for replacing filenames, stripping out unnecessary tags, adding or removing site root-relative path formatting, and replacing entire blocks of code with other content.

The following sections explain how to search for specific tags and attributes, search for text in specific tags, save and reuse search strings, and search using regular expressions.

Searching for tags and attributes

The most common use of the Find and Replace tool is to search for and modify specific tags and attributes. For instance, you may need to find all instances of the old `<font>` tag and strip them from the code, or you may want to find all instances of the attribute `valign="center"` and change them to `valign="left"`, or find all occurrences of the word *Principle* and replace them with the word *Principal*. Whatever your need, the general find and replace method is the same. The differences are where you're searching, what you're searching for, and what you want to do with the results when you find them.

Follow these steps to search for specific tags or attributes:

1. **Open the file you want to search in, or select the document or folder you want to search in the Files panel.**

2. **Choose Edit⇨Find and Replace.**

   The Find and Replace dialog box opens, as shown in Figure 2-4.

Figure 2-4: Find and replace items including text, source code, and specific tags.

3. **Select the files to be searched from the Find In drop-down list. These are your options:**

   • **Current Document** searches the open file.

   • **Open Documents** searches any file that's open in the workspace.

   • **Entire Current Local Site** searches an entire local or remote site.

   • **Selected Files in Site** searches only the files and folders selected in the Files panel.

   • **Folder** searches only in the specified folder.

   • **Selected Text** searches only in text selected in the open document.

4. **Select a search type from the Search drop-down list.**

   • **Source Code** searches for specific HTML code or tags.

   • **Text** searches for specific words or word combinations ignoring HTML. For example, searching for *the perfect car* would match both *the perfect car* and *the perfectcar*.

- **Text (Advanced)** searches for specific text inside or outside of tags. For instance, searching for *apple pie* and specifying Inside Tag and the <b> tag would only find the first instance of the words *apple pie:* I wanted to eat *<b>apple pie</b>* for breakfast but my mother told me I had to wait until dinner. Who made her the apple pie rule queen?

- **Specific Tag** searches for specific tags, their attributes, and those attribute values, such as all <td> tags with align set to bottom: *<td align="bottom">*.

To search for a Return character, add line breaks in the search query by pressing Shift+Enter (Win) or Shift+Return (Mac). Just be sure to turn off the Ignore White Space option if regular expressions are not part of the search. Doing so ensures the search finds a Return and not a <br> or <p> tag.

Book II
Chapter 2

Working with Text

5. **Enter additional options as needed to further define the search:**

- **Match Case** matches upper and lowercase letters as defined. For example, if you search for *Chocolate Cake* you won't find *chocolate cake.*

- **Ignore Whitespace** reads any white space except <p> and <br> tags as a single space for the purposes of matching items in your search. With the option turned on, *me and you* would match *me and you* and *me   and you,* but not *meandyou.* This option is not available when using regular expressions, so if you use them you need to write the expression to ignore white space.

- **Match Whole Word** searches for text matching a whole word or phrase, similar to the regular expression search for strings starting and ending with *\b.*

- **Use Regular Expression** forces specific characters and strings like *\b* or *?* to be interpreted as regular expression *operators.* See the upcoming section "Using regular expressions in your searches" for more information on regular expressions.

When starting a search from within Code view, Dreamweaver may let you know that it's synchronizing views before beginning the search. If that happens, click OK to continue.

6. **Search for your text by clicking the appropriate button:**

- **Find Next** jumps from each found instance to the next, and if searching in multiple documents, jumps from one document to the next.

- **Find All** opens the Results panel and displays search results.

- **Replace** replaces your search criteria with your replacement text in the To field. Click Find Next to move to the next instance.

- **Replace All** finds all instances of your search criteria and replaces them with your replacement text in the To field.

You can't undo these commands, so be sure to perform a backup of your files prior to replacing all, or just be really, really careful that you're replacing what you want to be replacing.

7. Click the Close button when finished.

Press F3 (Windows) or ⌘+G (Mac) to search for the same criteria again without launching the Find and Replace dialog box.

Searching for text in specific tags

When searching in code for specific tags, you may find including attributes is helpful as a way to narrow the search. Dreamweaver lets you search not only for specific tags, but also for the attributes of those tags and the attribute values, as shown in Figure 2-5.

Figure 2-5: Search for attributes in specific tags.

For instance, to ensure all your images have `alt` attributes for W3 accessibility compliance, you may need to search for all the `<img>` tags without `alt` attributes. You can set parameters to add the attribute with an empty value (`alt=""`) by leaving the To field blank.

To search for text in specific tags, follow Steps 1 through 3 from the previous section and continue with these steps:

1. From the Search drop-down list, select Specific Tag.

2. Click the plus (+) button to add a tag modifier (optional):

- **With Attribute** lets you specify the attribute type and attribute value of the tag to be a match.

- **Without Attribute** lets you specify that a particular attribute is not in the search to be considered a match.

- **Containing** lets you specify either text or a tag that must be present in the specific tag to be a match.

- **Not Containing** lets you specify that certain text or a tag must not be in the first tag to be a match.
- **Inside Tag** lets you specify that a tag must be found inside the first tag to be a match.
- **Not Inside Tag** lets you specify that a tag must not be found inside the first tag to be a match.

Note: When the search does not need any tag modifiers, click the minus (–) button to remove any pre-existing tag modifiers.

3. **To further limit the search, repeat Step 2.**

4. **If replacing content, choose an action from the Action menu and input additional information as prompted:**

- **Replace Tag** prompts you to enter Replace With information.
- **Remove Tag** removes the selected tag.
- **Change Tag** prompts you to select another tag type from a drop-down list.
- **Set Attribute** lets you select a tag and specify its attribute, if any.
- **Remove Attribute** prompts you to select an attribute to be removed from the specified tag.
- **Add Before** lets you enter data to add before the specified tag.
- **Add After** lets you enter data to add after the specified tag.

5. **Search for your text by clicking the appropriate button:**

- **Find All** opens the Results panel and displays search results.
- **Find Next** jumps from each found instance to the next, and if searching in multiple documents, jumps from one document to the next.
- **Replace** replaces your search criteria with your replacement text in the To field. Click Find Next to move to the next instance.
- **Replace All** finds all instances of your search criteria and replaces them with your replacement text in the To field.

6. **Click the Close button to exit the Find and Replace dialog box.**

Saving and reusing searches

When creating complex search parameters, you may need to reuse a search in the future. To save a search to reuse later, click the Save Query button, which looks like a disk, after entering search options. When prompted, name the search with the `.dwr` file extension, browse to the location where you want to save the search, and click Save.

To use a saved search, launch the Find and Replace dialog box and click the Load Query button, which looks like a folder button. Navigate to the folder where you saved the search, select it, and click Open. Once loaded, click any of the Find or Replace buttons.

Using regular expressions in your searches

Regular expressions are patterns made up of letter, symbol, and number combinations used in searches to help narrow search terms. Dreamweaver allows for use of regular expressions in your searches if you want to use them. Common regular expression characters include the following:

✦ **/d:** Matches a single digit between 0 and 9.

✦ **^:** Matches at the start of the line.

✦ **/b:** Matches at a word boundary.

For example, to compile a search for a specific e-mail address (info@companyname.com) in the entire Web site, your search criteria is the following:

✦ Look for the specific tag, in this case <a>.

✦ The tag must contain text including the regular expression, in this case ^info.

✦ Replace the text with the e-mail address.

Take a look at Figure 2-6 to see this search.

Figure 2-6:
Search using regular expressions.

To find out more information about regular expressions visit www.regular-expressions.info/ or see the "Introduction to Regular Expressions in Dreamweaver" article on the Dreamweaver Developer Center Web site at www.macromedia.com/devnet/dreamweaver/articles/regular_expressions.html.

Chapter 3: Inserting Graphics

In This Chapter

✔ **Inserting, editing, deleting, and moving images**

✔ **Setting image attributes**

✔ **Adding interactive elements, such as rollover images and image maps**

Graphics give a Web page personality. They help create the look and feel that represents the product, service, company, or person the Web site is for. Graphics are great for navigation buttons, logos, photographs, icons, buttons, background images, illustrations, and more.

For Web sites, you're limited to certain types of graphics. The two main types of graphics supported by most browsers are GIF (pronounced JIF, like the peanut butter, though some people say GIF with a hard G as in *gate*), and JPEG or JPG (pronounced J-peg). Both formats take high-resolution images and compress the data to keep file sizes smaller than their high-resolution counterparts. Because most browsers can only support 72 pixels per inch for on-screen display, you need to reduce your Web graphics to 72 pixels per inch. Fortunately, what is lost in resolution is made up for in reduced file sizes.

When optimizing your images for the Web, GIF files are best used for graphics with large, flat areas of color with a maximum of 256 colors, while JPEGs support millions of colors and are best used for photographs and images with gradients.

This chapter presumes your graphics are optimized in the GIF or JPG format and are ready to insert into your Web page. Besides inserting images, you find out how to edit, delete, and move graphics, set image attributes such as borders, create rollover buttons and image maps, build an image-based navigation bar, and work with graphics and HTML generated in Fireworks.

Inserting Images in Your Web Page

As with many features of Dreamweaver, you have several ways to add images to a Web page. Oftentimes, the insertion method you choose is simply determined by where the mouse happens to be on-screen. For instance, if your mouse is closest to the Files panel, you'll probably insert the image from there.

Before you begin adding images to your Web page, be sure you save all your graphics into an images folder at the root level of your managed Web site. If the folder doesn't exist yet, create it so you can place all your graphic files inside it. Organizing your graphics into a common folder can help you keep track of files as the site grows.

When inserting your images, whatever method you choose, Dreamweaver automatically writes the code for you, including the path where the image is. If the image is outside the managed site folder, Dreamweaver may prompt you to copy the graphic file into the current site. Furthermore, whenever the Select Image Source dialog box appears, you can select File System to pick a graphic from a folder, or choose Data Source to specify a dynamic image source.

Using the Insert bar

The easiest way to insert images is by using the Images pull-down menu on the Common tab of the Insert bar. The pull-down menu remembers the last button selected, but by default, the Image button appears.

To insert an image, follow these steps:

1. **Click the Image button on the Common tab of the Insert bar.**

   The button looks like a little tree in a grassy field.

   The Select Image Source dialog box opens (shown in Figure 3-1) where you can navigate to and select the graphic you want to insert. The dialog box has a panel to display the files by name and a preview area including an image preview, image dimensions, format, size, and probable loading time.

2. **Select the image you want to insert and click OK.**

   The image appears on the page.

Figure 3-1:
Use the
Select
Image
Source
dialog box
to select an
image to
insert.

If you have Accessibility options activated in Preferences, the Image Tag Accessibility Attribute dialog box appears to add accessibility attributes. Enter one or both accessibility attributes. At the minimum, it's highly recommended that you add Alternate text to describe the image in 50 characters or less. Alt attributes are read by screen-reader software used by the visually impaired. Enter a filename or URL to a page that has a longer description of that image. Then click OK. To bypass Accessibility options and insert the image, click Cancel. To discover more about designing Web sites with accessibility, see Book I, Chapter 2.

You can also drag and drop the Image button from the Insert bar into the open file in either Design or Code view. Believe it or not, you can even drag and drop an image from the desktop into an open Dreamweaver document.

When working in an unsaved file, Dreamweaver writes a `file://` reference to the image, but converts that reference to the document-relative path upon saving the file. For instance, before saving your file, the image path may look like this:

```
<img src="file:///C|/Documents and Settings/Administrator/My Documents/
    Clients/ClientX_HTML/images/logo.gif" width="200" height="200" alt="logo" />
```

But after saving the file, the path may look like this:

```
<img src="images/logo.gif" width="200" height="200" alt="logo" />
```

Using the Insert menu

Use the Insert menu as an alternate method of inserting images. Choose Insert⇨Image to insert an image. As with the Insert bar method described in the preceding section, navigate to and pick the image to insert from the Select Image Source dialog box.

Using the Assets panel

To use the Assets panel to insert images, you must define your site first (see Book 1, Chapter 3 for details). After defining the site, click the Images button located at the top-left corner of the Assets panel (as shown in Figure 3-2) to see a list of images. The Assets panel has a preview window that shows a thumbnail of any selected graphic file in the managed site. Beneath the preview window, graphics are listed alphabetically by name and also show file dimensions in pixels, file size in KB, file type (GIF, JPG, and so on), and the full path and filename of the image.

Images button   Preview window

Figure 3-2:
The Assets panel displays images.

Insert button

To insert an image from the Assets panel, select the image and do one of the following:

✦ Click the Insert button at the bottom of the panel.

✦ Drag and drop the image into the page at the desired location.

Using the Files panel

To add images to an open document from the Files panel, simply select, drag, and drop the chosen image into the desired location on the page. If you have Accessibility preferences enabled, the Image Tag Accessibility Attribute dialog box opens and prompts you to enter accessibility attributes for the image. Enter those values and click OK, or click Cancel to bypass accessibility options and insert the image without the Alt and Long Description attributes.

Editing, Deleting, and Moving Inserted Images

After you insert the image, you can do many things with it:

✦ **Edit:** Select the image to modify any of the image attributes or replace the image with another image in the Properties inspector. For the lowdown on modifying image attributes, see the section "Setting Image Attributes with the Properties Inspector," later in the chapter.

✦ **Delete:** Select the image and press Delete or Backspace, or choose Edit⇨Clear or Edit⇨Cut.

✦ **Move:** In Design view, drag the image to its new location and release the mouse button. You can also cut and paste the image in both Design and Code views.

Using an Image Placeholder When a Graphic Isn't Ready

Placeholder images are great to use if you know you need graphics in parts of your layout but the graphics aren't ready yet. Placeholder images can be any size in pixels, and the width and height attributes display in the center of the placeholder image itself.

Image placeholders don't display in browser windows and are intended for use in the Dreamweaver environment only. Therefore, before launching a Web page or site, be sure to replace any image placeholders with the desired GIF or JPEG files.

To insert a placeholder image, follow these steps:

1. **Click the Image Placeholder button on the Common tab of the Insert bar.**

   The button has an image of two tiny squares overlapping; one has a picture of a tree on it and the other has a big greyed out X.

   You can also choose Insert⇨Image Objects⇨Image Placeholder.

   The Image Placeholder dialog box opens, as shown in Figure 3-3.

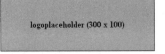

Figure 3-3:
Set Image
Placeholder
attributes.

2. **Enter the placeholder image attributes: Name, Width, Height, and Color. Also, fill in the Alternate Text box to describe the image to visitors who are visually impaired or are using a text-only browser.**

   To choose a color, click the button to the right of Color and choose your color from the pop-up palette. The hexadecimal number then appears in the text box to the right. You can also type a color name, such as **green**, or enter a hexadecimal number, such as **#FF9933.** (See Book II, Chapter 2 for more about using hexadecimal numbers.)

   In Figure 3-3, the placeholder name is `logoplaceholder`, the width is `300`, the height is `100`, the color is `#66CCCC`, and the Alternate text is `Company Logo Goes Here`.

3. **Click OK.**

   The placeholder image is inserted on the page.

   In Code view, you see the following HTML for the example:

   ```
   <img src="" alt="Company Logo Goes Here" name="logoplaceholder"
       width="300" height="100" id="logoplaceholder" style="background-
       color: #66CCCC" />
   ```

   Figure 3-4 shows how the image looks in Design view. The image placeholder uses a hex number of `#66CCCC`, which is a turquoise blue.

Figure 3-4:
A place-
holder
image.

logoplaceholder (300 x 100)

Setting Image Attributes with the Properties Inspector

After you insert an image into your document, you can format it with various style attributes. Because you can create these styles in either an internal or an external style sheet, pay attention to the code when adding attributes. You can assign many of the image attributes in the Properties inspector, but you can also apply these attributes by creating custom styles in an external style sheet. (See Book III, Chapter 1 for the lowdown on creating style sheets.)

Suppose, for example, you insert an image called `logo.gif` into a Web page. Select the image to apply attributes. As shown in Figure 3-5, a thumbnail of the image displays in the top left of the Properties inspector, along with the file size in K, width and height sizes, image source, and Alternate text.

If you can't see all the image properties shown in Figure 3-5, click the expander arrow in the bottom-right corner of the Properties inspector.

Figure 3-5:
The Properties inspector displays fields to add image attributes.

Naming your images

First and foremost, it's a good idea to name all your images so you can quickly apply Dreamweaver behaviors, JavaScript, and/or VBScript to them later. To name your images, select the graphic and enter a name in the Name field of the Properties inspector (refer to Figure 3-5).

Specifying the width and height of images

By default, Dreamweaver reads image dimensions, writes them into the code in pixels, and displays them in the W and H fields of the Properties inspector. While Dreamweaver inserts dimensions in pixels, you can also insert dimensions as percentages. When specifying sizes in percentages, be sure to add the % symbol after the number, as in 80%. In the example image, the logo graphic is 192 x 201 pixels. If the image gets resized, the new image dimensions appear in the W and H fields.

Resizing and resetting images

Resize images by either dragging the resize handles located on the left, bottom, and bottom-left corners of the image or by entering new image dimensions in the W and H fields on the Properties inspector. Once an image is stretched or scrunched beyond its normal size, the Reset Size button appears between the W and H fields in the Properties inspector and the W and H values appear in bold. To revert to an image's normal size, click the Reset Size button.

It's a good idea — especially if you're scaling up — to create new graphics with an external image-editing program rather than resize them in Dreamweaver. Inserting correctly sized images reduces browser download time as well as helps to maintain the integrity of the image as it appears elsewhere on the site.

Adding vertical or horizontal padding

To push the edges of a graphic away from surrounding text, you may want to add padding to your images. Use the V Space and H Space fields to add uniform vertical or horizontal padding. For vertical padding above and below the image, enter pixels in the V Space field. For horizontal padding on the left and right sides of the image, enter pixels in the H Space field.

If you want to add non-uniform padding around an image, such as padding on just the top and left sides, or just have better control over the image padding, use CSS instead of these HTML attributes.

Adding image links

The Properties inspector has a Link field to enter the filename or full path of a document. To add a link to an image, select the image and enter the filename and/or path, including file extension, in the Link field. For alternate link options and detailed instructions on linking, see Book II, Chapter 4.

Adjusting targets

When an image contains a link, the Target field becomes active to set the browser frame or browser window into which the linked file should load. When unspecified, the default target for all links is _self. In other words, when you click a link in a browser window, the linked document opens in the same browser window. If that's what you want to happen when clicking the link, leave the Target field blank. Otherwise, to specify that the link opens a new window for displaying the linked page, select _blank from the Target drop-down list. (You can read more on setting link targets in Book II, Chapter 4.)

Specifying a low resolution image to appear first

The Low Src field allows you to specify a low resolution image by filename. If you have an image that's particularly large in file size and are concerned that it may take a while to view it, create a low resolution version of that file and enter the low res filename in the Low Src field. That way, when the browser displays the page, the low resolution image appears on the page first until the high resolution image is fully loaded and ready to display in its place. The low source image can even be as simple as a 2-bit black-and-white version of the original. That said, using the Low Src field is rarely done anymore due to faster Internet connections. Furthermore, if a low source image is really needed, JavaScript can replicate the process.

Adding image borders

By default, images with no links have no borders, but they can have black borders of any pixel width. Images with links have a border that takes on the properties of text links. For example, if the default text link color is blue, a linked image has a blue border.

While adding a border may seem like a great advantage, the major drawback to it is that you can't choose a different border color through the Properties inspector. (Similar to Henry Ford and his Model-T: "You can buy it in any color, as long as it's black.") Technically, the border color can be the same color as surrounding text color, so you could control the border color with the old `<font>` tag if for some reason you don't want to use CSS, as in the following example:

```
<p><font color="#CC0066">This text is pink, which means the image will have the
    same border color. <img src="images/logo.gif" width="192" height="201"
    border="1"></font></p>
```

The major browsers don't consistently support this method, so be sure to test it if you intend to use it.

Therefore, to make a simple black border on your images, enter a number for the width of the border in the Border field in the Properties inspector. To make your border a different color, either redefine the `<img>` tag or create a custom style in an internal or external CSS to apply border attributes to your images. Turn to Book III, Chapter 1 to redefine tags and create custom styles in Cascading Style Sheets.

Providing Alternate text

Another thing you can do with images is provide them with Alternate text. Alternate text, or *Alt text,* is useful for site visitors who use text-only browsers, have their browsers set to manually download images, or use speech synthesizer software to read the descriptions of the image. In some browsers, Alt text appears when images are downloading and when the mouse pointer hovers over an image. Furthermore, some search engines use Alt text to help determine site ranking by presuming the words used in Alt text are more relevant and important than text found in <meta> tags.

You can make Alt text as brief as one word or as long as a paragraph, though you should enter a complete, meaningful sentence rather than a list of keywords. If you want to provide a longer description for your images, you can also include a Long Description attribute that links to a separate Web page containing the longer description. The code for an image with both Alternate text and a Long Description looks something like this:

```
<img src="images/logo.gif" alt="Company Logo" width="200" height="200"
    border="10" longdesc="logohistory.html" />
```

When adding images to your page, the Image Tag Accessibility Attributes dialog box appears when you've enabled accessibility features in Dreamweaver's Preferences. The dialog box has fields to enter both Alt and Long Description text.

Aligning images

You can align images in two different ways, and each way does something slightly different to the image and any surrounding text:

✦ **Align the image as part of the text block:** Click the Left, Center, or Right Align buttons in the Properties inspector, just to the right of the Border field (refer to Figure 3-5).

Specifying alignment in this way adds the align attribute to the opening <p> tag.

✦ **Wrap elements — such as text — around the image:** Select an option from the Align drop-down list (shown in Figure 3-6). The default alignment is Left.

This alignment method adds the align attribute to the <img> tag.

Figure 3-6:
Image
alignment
options.

Additionally, you can also control image alignment through CSS. For example, you can create a style that adds a 1-pixel border, 5 pixels of padding, and right alignment to an image:

```
<style type="text/css">
<!--
.alignright {
   padding: 5px;
   border: 1px solid #000033;
   clear: right;
   float: right;
}
-->
</style>
```

Using the image-editing buttons

Dreamweaver has six tools for editing images without the need to launch an external image editor. You can use these editing tools on any GIF or JPEG file inserted on a page. The following six image-editing tools are located under the Alt field in the Properties inspector whenever you select an image on a page in Design or Code view (refer to Figure 3-5):

✦ **Edit:** Launches the default image-editing program. Specify an image editor in the File Types/Editors category of the Preferences dialog box. Choose Edit⇨Preferences (Windows) or Dreamweaver⇨Preferences (Mac).

✦ **Optimize in Fireworks:** Launches the Fireworks Optimization dialog box. Check out Book III, Chapter 5 for more info about working with Fireworks in conjunction with Dreamweaver.

✦ **Crop:** Allows you to crop the graphic. Clicking this button opens an alert dialog box that warns you about the permanence of any changes you make. Click OK in the alert dialog box to continue. Cropping handles then appear around the image that allow you to crop the image. Press Enter (Windows) or Return (Mac) to accept the cropping.

✦ **Resample:** Allows you to resample a resized image to improve the quality of the image at the new size. This feature appears only after you resize an image. Try, though, to keep resampling to a minimum (especially resampling up) as this process can degrade the quality of the image. If you really need a graphic at a different size, create a new graphic in an image-editing program.

✦ **Brightness/Contrast:** Allows you to adjust the brightness and contrast of the image. Like the Crop tool, clicking the Brightness/Contrast button opens an alert dialog box that warns you about the permanence of any changes you make to the image. Click OK in the dialog box to continue and a Brightness/Contrast dialog box appears. Move the sliders in the dialog box to the left or the right to increase or decrease the brightness and contrast. Click OK to accept the new settings or Cancel to close the Brightness/Contrast dialog box without changes.

✦ **Sharpen:** Adjusts the overall image contrast and edge pixel clarity. The Sharpening dialog box uses a sliding scale of 0–10 to adjust the image sharpness; the higher the number, the more intense the image's definition or sharpness.

Creating Interactive Images

Besides inserting the occasional static graphic here and there on a Web page, Dreamweaver greatly simplifies the process of adding interactive image options on a Web page, including creating rollover images, image maps, and navigation bars, and adding Fireworks HTML to an existing Web page.

The following sections discuss these interactive techniques. All the interactive image buttons are accessible from the Common tab of the Insert bar as shown in Figure 3-7.

Image button

Figure 3-7:
Choose
an image
option.

Adding rollover images

Rollover images are graphics that change to a different image in a browser window when a visitor moves the mouse over the image. To make a rollover button, you need two graphics — one for the normal state and one for the over state — that are exactly the same pixel width and height but that look different enough that a visitor will notice the rollover effect.

Dreamweaver lets you create rollover images by inserting JavaScript into the code that tells a browser to display one image for the normal state and another image for the mouseover state.

Before creating your rollover images in Dreamweaver, optimize the graphics for both normal and rollover states and place them in an images folder at the root level of your managed site. Make sure both images have the same image dimensions in pixels so that the over state image does not get distorted during mouseover.

To create rollover images, follow these steps:

1. **Place the insertion point in the Document window where you want the rollover image to go.**

   The spot you click in the Document window is where the rollover image will appear on the page.

2. **Click the Image button on the Common tab of the Insert bar and choose Rollover Image from its drop-down list (refer to Figure 3-7).**

   Or choose Insert⇨Image Objects⇨Rollover Image.

   The Insert Rollover Image dialog box opens, as shown in Figure 3-8.

3. **Enter an image name, browse to and select the graphics to use for both the original and rollover images, add Alternate text, and a filename or URL for a link.**

   By default, the Preload Rollover Image option is enabled. This option adds JavaScript to the page that tells the browser to preload this graphic into the browser's cache as the page is loading. When this happens, the over state graphic is ready to appear by the time a visitor places the mouse on the rollover graphic's normal state.

4. **Click OK.**

   Dreamweaver inserts the original image and writes all the JavaScript necessary to perform the rollover function. JavaScript is attached to the `<img>`, `<head>`, and `<body>` tags.

Because you can't preview or test JavaScript behaviors in Design view, choose File⇨Preview in Browser to test the rollover effect in a browser window by positioning the mouse over the rollover button.

Figure 3-8:
Specify a
rollover
image.

Creating image maps

An image map is an image that has shaped regions or *hotspots* defined by pixel coordinates in the code that can have a behavior (such as a hyperlink) assigned to it. When a visitor clicks the hotspot, an action occurs (for example, another page opens). Hotspots can be rectangular, oval, or polygonal in shape. The following example shows how image maps are defined in the code for a hotspot in the shape of a circle:

```
<img src="images/logo.gif" width="192" height="201" border="1"
    usemap="#Map1"><map name="Map1" id="Map1"><area shape="circle"
    coords="97,98,75" href="#">
```

Images can have multiple hotspots as well as multiple behaviors assigned to a hotspot. For instance, you may have a photograph of a map of the United States and want to turn each state's shape into a unique hotspot linking to information elsewhere on the site specific to that state. (See Book IV, Chapter 2 for more on behaviors.)

You can draw hotspots using the Rectangular Hotspot, Oval Hotspot, and Polygon Hotspot tools in the Properties inspector beneath the image thumbnail (refer to Figure 3-5). You can adjust the hotspot border with another tool, the Pointer Hotspot.

Here's how to create a hotspot on a graphic:

1. **Select the image in Design view.**

    By selecting the image in Design view, you activate the image hotspot options in the Properties inspector.

2. **In the Properties inspector, enter a name for the image map in the Map field.**

    If unspecified, image maps get assigned a default name such as Map1, Map2, Map3, and so on. If creating multiple image maps in the same document, definitely use separate map names for each.

3. **Select a hotspot tool and draw a hotspot shape on the image:**

    • **Rectangular:** Drag and release the mouse to create an enclosed rectangular shape.

    • **Oval:** Drag and release the mouse to create an enclosed oval shape.

    • **Polygon:** Create a non-uniform polygonal shape by selecting this tool and clicking the image multiple times to insert anchor points for the hotspot shape. Click the pointer tool to finish the shape.

    To select these hotspot tools, click one of the buttons in the bottom-left corner of the Properties inspector (see Figure 3-9).

4. **Use the Pointer Hotspot tool to select the hotspot and assign `link`, `target`, and `alt` attributes.**

   When the hotspot is selected, the Properties inspector displays fields for assigning a link, link target, and Alternate text to the hotspot. You can also adjust the anchor points of the hotspot shape with the Pointer Hotspot tool.

5. **Deselect the hotspot and/or image by clicking away from the image in Design view.**

   Figure 3-9 shows an image with a hotspot.

6. **To continue adding hotspots on the same image, select another hotspot tool and repeat Steps 2 through 5.**

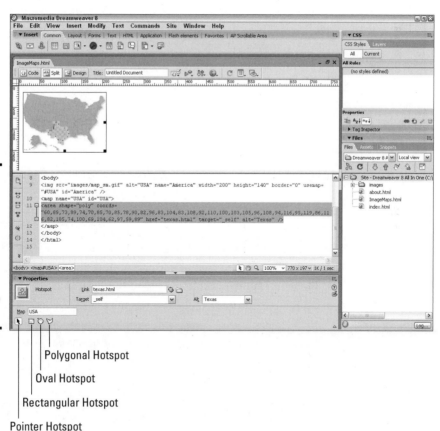

Figure 3-9:
Create image map hotspots with the hotspot tools and assign behaviors to hotspots.

Polygonal Hotspot

Oval Hotspot

Rectangular Hotspot

Pointer Hotspot

Inserting a navigation bar with images

Creating a simple vertical or horizontal navigation bar in Dreamweaver has never been easier. From the Insert Navigation Bar dialog box (Insert⇨ Image Objects⇨Navigation Bar), you can specify and organize all the nav bar elements at the same time.

Follow these steps to create and insert a navigation bar with images:

1. **Click the Image button on the Common tab of the Insert bar and choose Navigation Bar from its drop-down list (refer to Figure 3-7).**

   Or choose Insert⇨Image Objects⇨Navigation Bar.

   The Insert Navigation Bar dialog box opens, as shown in Figure 3-10.

Figure 3-10:
Create a custom graphic navigation bar with the Insert Navigation Bar dialog box.

2. **For the first rollover graphic on the navigation bar, enter the following information:**

   • **Element Name:** Enter the name of the button.

   • **Up Image:** Select an image for the button's normal *up* (nonclicked) state.

   • **Over Image:** Select an image for the button's mouseover state.

   • **Down Image (optional):** Select an image for the button's *down* state, which appears when a visitor clicks the button.

   • **Alternate Text:** Enter a text description for the button, such as **About Us** or **Contact us for more information**. Alternate text displays as the images are downloading and is read aloud by any screen-reader software used by the visually impaired. It may also appear in some browsers as pop-up text when the cursor is placed over the graphic.

   • **When Clicked, Go to URL:** Select the page that is the target of the button.

3. **Select any other options you need.**

4. **To add additional rollover buttons to the navigation bar, click the plus (+) button and repeat Steps 1 through 3.**

5. **To remove a button from the navigation bar, click the minus (–) button.**

6. **To reorder the navigation bar elements, select a button name and click the Up and Down arrows to reposition the element in the list.**

7. **When you're satisfied with the navigation bar, click OK.**

   Dreamweaver inserts the new navigation bar (see Figure 3-11) and all attending JavaScript. The navigation bar, essentially, is a single row or column table with a series of hyperlinking rollover buttons in each cell.

Only one navigation bar can exist at a time on any one page, but it can be modified if you need to add, edit, or remove a rollover button. To make adjustments to an existing navigation bar, do one of the following to open the Modify Navigation Bar dialog box:

✦ Click the Navigation Bar button on the Common tab of the Insert bar.

✦ Select the navigation bar in the Document window and choose Modify⇨ Navigation Bar.

Book II Chapter 3

Inserting Graphics

Navigation bar

Figure 3-11: Create horizontal or vertical navigation bars with your own custom graphics.

Inserting Fireworks HTML

Fireworks lets you create, slice, and optimize images for the Web, and because it's Macromedia, it integrates nicely with Dreamweaver. One of the main things you can do with Fireworks is create a page layout and then export the file as an HTML page including images and rollover effects. After you export the file, you can import it into Dreamweaver. Dreamweaver lets you quickly add design elements, such as animated rollovers, pop-up menus, and other images, generated by Fireworks into an open document. Fireworks has an export command that lets you specify which Dreamweaver folder to place the code so you can import the code in Dreamweaver when you're ready.

To import Fireworks content into an open document, follow these steps:

1. **Click in the page to place the insertion point where you want to add the Fireworks HTML.**

2. **Click the Image button on the Common tab of the Insert bar and choose Fireworks HTML from its drop-down list (refer to Figure 3-7).**

   You can also choose Insert➪Interactive Images➪Fireworks HTML.

   The Insert Fireworks HTML dialog box opens, as shown in Figure 3-12.

3. **Browse to and select the Fireworks HTML file that you want to import.**

   To have Dreamweaver delete the Fireworks HTML after inserting it on your page, click the Delete File After Insertion check box.

4. **Click OK.**

   Dreamweaver imports the HTML, graphics, and any associated JavaScript to support rollover effects and other interactivity.

For more on using Dreamweaver with Fireworks, see Book III, Chapter 5.

Figure 3-12:
Insert
Fireworks
HTML.

Chapter 4: Making Links with Text and Images

*W*eb pages become a Web site when they are joined together by hyperlinks. Hyperlinks (often called just *links*) convert nearly any content — including text or graphics — into clickable pointers and lead the site visitor through other pages on a site, winding through text and graphics along the way.

Links can point to another Web page on the same site, another page on a different Web site, a section of the same or another page, PDF, Word or PowerPoint document, graphic, sound file, movie, or downloadable software. They can open a blank e-mail message with the recipient's address already in place, or they can be temporary placeholders for behaviors and scripts to attach to.

You can add, edit, or remove links from a page at any stage of the site building process. Though they look like links inside of the Dreamweaver Document window, they don't work when you click them there, so be sure to launch a browser window (press F12) to test the functionality and accuracy of your links.

This chapter takes an in-depth look at the different kinds of links that you can create in Dreamweaver.

Understanding Hyperlinks

You can create four types of hyperlinks in Dreamweaver:

✦ **Regular:** Links pages together by converting content, including text and graphics, into hyperlinks.

✦ **E-mail:** Launches a computer's default e-mail program and prompts the site visitor to send e-mail to the e-mail address in the link.

✦ **Named anchor:** Takes the site visitor to a link location embedded on the same page as the link or to an anchor link location embedded on another page.

✦ **Temporary:** There are two kinds of temporary links, called *null* and *script* links, that convert selected content into undefined links for adding detailed link information or behaviors at a later time.

Before adding links, be sure you understand the difference between document-relative, absolute, and site root-relative paths as the link syntax varies slightly depending on the path type. Turn to Book I, Chapter 3 for a general discussion about paths.

One of the fastest ways to add links to your page is to select some text, graphic, or object on the page and enter the link information in the Link field in the Properties inspector. Type the link by filename or full URL, including http:// and the file extension. After you enter the link, the Target field becomes activated. Then, you can select a target for the link (see the "Setting Link Targets" section in this chapter).

To the right of the Link text are two buttons (shown in Figure 4-1) that also allow you to add links to any selected text, graphic, or object on the page:

✦ **Folder:** Click the folder button to open the Select File dialog box. Browse to and select the file you want to link to, and then click OK and Dreamweaver writes the link of the filename into the Link field. Enter any target information in the Target field.

✦ **Point to File:** Click this button to click and point to a file listed in the Files panel. Release the mouse when the cursor is on top of the file and Dreamweaver writes the link of the filename into the Link field. Enter your target information in the Target field. The Point to File button also works for selecting named anchors on a page.

Point to File

Figure 4-1:
The
Properties
inspector
helps you
add links.

Link field

Folder

Link
Target

Target field

To test a link, you must launch a browser window. Here's how to open a browser to test your link:

✦ To preview an open page, press F12 or Shift+F12 to launch your primary or secondary browser (see Book V, Chapter 1 to specify a primary and secondary browser). The currently open document opens in a browser window.

✦ To preview a file listed in the Files panel, right-click (Windows) or Control+click (Mac) the file, choose Preview in Browser, and choose the browser type from the list.

To open a locally linked file inside Dreamweaver, either highlight the link and choose Modify⇨Open Linked Page, or press Ctrl (Windows) or ⌘ (Mac) and double-click the link to open the document in Dreamweaver's Document window.

All links use the <a> tag plus one or two different attributes to convert selected text or graphics into links. The next few sections give separate descriptions and examples of the four link types.

Book II Chapter 4

Making Links with Text and Images

Creating Text Links

You can create text links from a word, phrase, sentence, paragraph, or even an entire page worth of text. The link code surrounds a selection of text and converts it into a clickable hyperlink. Text links use the <a> tag with the href attribute. The href attribute stands for *Hypertext REFerence,* and the attribute points to a file at the root level of the defined site or to an external Web page including the http:// and full path to that page. The target attributes, which tell the browser whether to open the link in the same or another browser window, also go inside the opening <a> tag.

This example opens the Google page in a new window:

```
<a href="http://www.google.com" target="_blank">Search on Google</a>
```

This example opens the About page in the same browser window:

```
<a href="about.html" target="_self">About Us</a>
```

To create a text link, follow these steps:

1. **Choose Insert⇨Hyperlink or click the Hyperlink button on the Common tab of the Insert bar, which looks like a chain link.**

   The Hyperlink dialog box opens, as shown in Figure 4-2.

Figure 4-2:
Complete
these fields
to create a
text
hyperlink.

2. Enter the following information in the dialog box:

- **Text:** Enter the text you want to make into a link, such as **Learn More** or **Contact Us.**

- **Link:** Type the path and filename of the linked page. If the linked page is on the same site, enter only the filename, such as **contact. html**. However, if the linked page is external to the current site, enter the full URL including the http://, as in **http://www.dummies.com**.

- **Target:** By default, pages automatically open in the same browser window. To override this setting, enter **_blank** to have the link open in a different browser window. See the "Setting Link Targets" section for more about other target settings.

- **Title:** Add a description for the link. The title appears as a tool tip in a browser when a visitor mouses over the link, and comes in handy to improve search engine rankings.

- **Access Key:** A one-letter keyboard equivalent that the visitor can use in combination with the Tab key to select the link in the browser. Once selected, the visitor can press Enter (Windows) or Return (Mac) to visit that linked page.

- **Tab Index:** Add a number for the tab order of this link, relative to other links on the page. The tab order, which defines the order of accessible elements on a page using the Tab key, begins at the top of the browser window and moves downward from left to right, as when reading a book.

3. Click OK.

Dreamweaver adds the link to the page.

Making Image Links

Image links work the same way text links do, but instead of surrounding text, the link code surrounds an image.

Here's an example of a link to visit Google using a GIF file:

```
<a href="http://www.google.com" target="_blank"><img
    src="images/googlelogo.gif"></a>
```

Here's an example of a link to a page at the root level of a defined site using an About Us graphic:

```
<a href="about.html"><img src="images/aboutus.gif"></a>
```

To create an image link, select the image on the page in Design view and type the filename or path of the linked page in the Link field in the Properties inspector. You can also add a link target.

You can also create an image link the same way you create a text link. See the previous section to find out how to do so.

Inserting E-Mail Links

E-mail links, when clicked in a browser window, tell the computer to launch the default e-mail program and populate the Send To field with the e-mail address in the link. E-mail links use the `<a>` tag with the `href` attribute just like text links do, but instead of listing the `//` before the filename, an e-mail link uses the `mailto:` attribute before the e-mail address (`mailto:` is a URL just like `http://` is), like this:

```
<a href="mailto:me@example.com">me@example.com</a>
```

To create a standard HTML e-mail link, follow these steps:

1. **Type the e-mail address into the Web page and then select it.**

2. **Choose Insert⇨Email Link to launch the Email Link dialog box.**

   Or, on the Common tab of the Insert bar, click the Email Link button, which looks like an envelope.

3. **In the Text field, enter the text that will appear in the browser window as linked text. In the E-Mail field, enter the e-mail address for the link.**

4. **Click OK.**

   Dreamweaver writes the e-mail link code into the page.

Adding an e-mail address to a Web page using this type of HTML e-mail link makes the e-mail address vulnerable to spam bots and spam spiders that crawl the Web in search of anything that has the `me@example.com` format or for links containing the `mailto:` attribute. For encryption ideas, check out the nearby sidebar "Encrypting e-mail addresses" or search online to find more about e-mail encryption.

Encrypting e-mail addresses

E-mail addresses are very vulnerable to being harvested by spam-gathering software and then sold to zillions of spam lists. To better protect your e-mail address, encrypt your e-mail address or use some other form of hiding the e-mail address so it can't be harvested or easily obtained.

Try these suggestions for hiding or encrypting e-mail links on Web pages:

✦ Encrypt your e-mail address with a JavaScript encryption software application. Several freeware and shareware versions are available, including Email Riddler at `www.dynamicdrive.com/emailriddler/;` do a search for **Email Address Encryptor** to find others.

✦ Enter your e-mail address in Code view using URL code entities for all the special characters. For example, `me@example.com` becomes `me%40example%2Ecom`.

Visit the W3Schools Web site (`www.w3schools.com/tags/ref_url encode.asp`) to convert your e-mail address into URL unicode.

✦ Include your e-mail address on the page but don't turn it into a link. Your e-mail address is still vulnerable, but less so than as a standard e-mail link.

For a great article about e-mail harvesters and the countermeasures you can take to fight them, read Tim Williams's take on e-mail at `www.u.arizona.edu/~trw/spam/`.

Creating Named Anchor Links

Named anchor links are great for creating links that jump to another location on the same page. Use named anchor links for FAQ lists, Table of Contents, Indexes, Back to Top links, and other page elements where internal linking would be useful.

Creating a named anchor requires two steps:

1. **Lay down and name the anchor in the spot you want to link to.**

2. **Make a link that points to the named anchor you just laid down.**

Say you have a page with two FAQs and you want to list the questions at the top of the page and the answers in sequence below the questions. The text on your page may look something like this:

1. Question
2. Question

1st Question Answer
Answer to question. Answer to question. Answer to question. Answer to question. Answer to question.

2nd Question Answer
Answer to question. Answer to question. Answer to question. Answer to question. Answer to question.

To link each question to its answer, you create a named anchor right before each answer and then link it. This type of link is called a named anchor because it uses the `name` attribute of the `<a>` tag. You'll notice, however, that the code for named anchors includes both `name` and `id` attributes:

```
<a name="Q1" id="Q1"></a>
```

The `name` and `id` attributes have the same values so that they share the same domain value space, which means you could use either one when specifying the link. For example, you can create an anchor using the `name` attribute, as the following example shows:

```
<a name="Q1">1st Question Answer</a>
```

or turn another element into an anchor using the `id` attribute, as this example shows:

```
<h1 id="Q1">1st Question Answer</h1>
```

Once the anchor is laid down, the link to the anchor is the same:

```
<a href="#Q1">Go to question 1 answer </a>
```

Dreamweaver tries to simplify the process by including both `name` and `id` attributes in the code whenever you create a named anchor.

The following sections cover the two-step process for creating a named anchor.

Step 1: Lay down the named anchor

Remember to create your page with all the text before creating the named anchors. Then lay down your anchors at each of the destination points. For example, in a FAQ list, you want to place the anchors right before the text for each answer in the list.

To lay down a named anchor, follow these steps:

1. **Click the Named Anchor button, which looks like a golden anchor, on the Common tab of the Insert bar or choose Insert⇨Named Anchor.**

   The Named Anchor dialog box appears, as shown in Figure 4-3.

Figure 4-3:
The Named
Anchor
dialog box.

2. **Enter a name for your anchor and click OK.**

Try not to use any spaces or funny characters in your anchor names, and do not put any anchors inside a layer.

In Design view, your named anchor displays as a little yellow invisible element to mark where the named anchor sits in the code.

If you don't see the invisible element in Design view, be sure the Invisible Elements Visual Aids option is enabled in the Document window and that the invisible elements in the Preferences dialog box are set to show named anchors. To see visual aids, choose View➪Visual Aids➪Invisible Elements.

Step 2: Link to the named anchor

Creating the link to the named anchor uses the `href` attribute just like standard text and image links, but it has one unique twist: Instead of linking to a filename or URL, the `link` attribute is preceded by a number symbol (#) to tell the browser to look for the named anchor on the same page, like this:

```
<p><a href="#Q1">1. Question</a></p>
```

To create a link to a named anchor, do one of the following:

✦ Select the text, and in the Link field of the Properties inspector, type the number symbol (#) followed by the anchor name, as in **#Q1.**

✦ Select the text and choose Insert➪Hyperlink, which opens the Hyperlink dialog box (refer to Figure 4-2), from which you can select the named anchor from the Link drop-down list. (See the previous section "Creating Text Links" for details.)

You can also use named anchor links when linking from one page to another by typing the number symbol (#) followed by the anchor name after the name of the file being linked to. For example, if you want a visitor to click a link in one page and go right to a particular section of another page, your link may look something like this:

```
<a href="contact.html#wholesale">Learn more about Wholesale Pricing</a>
```

In this example, the visitor is taken to a named anchor destination called `wholesale` within the page called `contact.html`.

Creating Temporary Links

The most common types of links are the links you create to other files and named anchors, but you can add other link types to a page:

✦ **Script:** These links call JavaScript functions or run JavaScript code to provide information to the site visitor without having to leave the page, such as when a JavaScript alert box opens. These types of links can also do other page processing duties, such as form validation, when the visitor interacts in some way with the page, like clicking a particular button.

✦ **Null:** These empty links don't go anywhere but still treat the text or object like a link. Once created, you can use null links to attach behaviors to the text and objects on the page. (You can find more about behaviors in Book IV, Chapter 2.)

To create a script link, follow these steps:

1. **Select the text, graphic, or object in Design view.**

2. **Enter** `javascript:` **(the word *javascript* followed by a colon) into the Link field in the Properties inspector, followed by a JavaScript or function call.**

   For instance, to create a script link that closes the currently open browser window, type the following text in the Link field:

   ```
   javaScript:parent.close();
   ```

   The script for the link appears in the code like this:

   ```
   This is a <a href="JavaScript:parent.close();">script</a> link.
   ```

   where the JavaScript code appears between double quote marks as a value of the `href` attribute. If you need to include double quote marks as part of your script, be sure to add escape marks before your double quotes, as `\"This link goes to the home page\"`.

To create a null link, do one of the following:

✦ Select the text, graphic, or object in Design view and enter **javascript:;** (the word *javascript* followed by a colon, followed by a semicolon) into the Link field in the Properties inspector.

✦ Select the text or graphics and enter a number symbol (#) in the Link field in the Properties inspector.

Some browsers jump to the top of the page when a number sign is used as a null link. Therefore the JavaScript null link is preferred.

Whenever you're ready to convert the temporary link into a permanent link, replace the temporary link with the appropriate filename or URL.

Setting Link Targets

After adding a link to text or a graphic, you can assign a *target* in the Target field of the Properties inspector. The target defines where the linked file opens, whether in a specific frame of a frameset, the same browser window, or a new browser window.

When unspecified, the linked page typically opens in the same browser window. Other options from the Target drop-down list include the following:

✦ _blank tells the browser to load the linked page into a new, unnamed browser window.

✦ _self is the same as the default and tells the browser to open the linked page in the same browser window as the link.

✦ _parent tells the browser to display the linked page in the parent frame-set or frame containing the link. When the link is in a non-nested frame, the linked page loads into the main browser window.

You can also specify the target by frame name so that the linked file opens into a specified frame of the browser window. To find out more about framesets, see Book IV, Chapter 3.

✦ _top tells the browser to break and remove any frames in a frameset and display the linked page in the main browser window.

Editing and Deleting Links

Links aren't set in stone after you create them; you can edit and even delete them at any time you see fit. You can edit a link used on several pages of your site at the same time.

Editing links

To edit a link after inserting it into your page, select the link — whether it's a text, graphic, or object link — and then do either of the following:

✦ Edit or replace the link text using the Property inspector.

✦ Choose Modify⇨Change Link. The Select File dialog box opens, allowing you to search for and select another file for the link.

Dreamweaver has a great feature that allows you to change a link throughout an entire managed site (for instance, change the August newsletter link to a September newsletter link). To do this, follow these steps:

1. **Select a file in the Files panel and then choose Site⇨Change Link Sitewide.**

   The Change Link Sitewide dialog box opens, as shown in Figure 4-4, with the filename you selected in the Change All Links To box.

Figure 4-4:
The Change Link Sitewide dialog box.

2. **Enter the new filename in the Into Links To box and click OK.**

   The Update Files dialog box appears showing a list of files that will be changed.

3. **Click the Update button to convert all those links in the site. Click the Don't Update button if you change your mind.**

Deleting links

To delete an existing link, do one of the following:

✦ Select the link text, graphic, or object and remove the `link` attributes from the Link field in the Properties inspector.

✦ Select the link text, graphic, or object and choose Modify⇨Remove Link.

✦ Delete the opening and closing link tag code by hand in Code view.

Using the Tag Chooser

The Tag Chooser is a special place you can go to find and insert tags on your page. The Tag Chooser bills itself as "A collection of Markup Language Tags." That's because, in addition to all the HTML tags, the Tag Chooser contains tags for several other markup languages including CFML, ASP, JSP, ASP.NET, PHP, and WML.

What's more, each language is housed in its own tag library folder and has its tags categorized into logical subfolders to help you find the right tag. For example, if you're looking for a tag to add an iframe to your page, you'd open the HTML Tags Language folder, and search for the tag in the Page Elements category, as shown in Figure 4-5. When you select a tag in the panel on the right side of the dialog box, the Tag Info panel at the bottom of the dialog box reveals tag reference information such as syntax and tag usage.

To use the Tag Chooser, follow these steps:

1. **Choose Insert⇨Tag.**

   The Tag Chooser dialog box opens, as shown in Figure 4-5. This dialog box provides access to all the tags in a variety of markup languages.

Figure 4-5:
Find and insert specific markup language tags with the Tag Chooser dialog box.

2. **Select the language folder you want to use in the left pane of the dialog box and navigate to that folder's subcategories to find the type of tag to insert.**

   Expand folders as needed to narrow down the tag search.

3. **Search the right pane for the specific tag you want to insert.**

   Tags in each subcategory are listed in the right pane of the dialog box, and descriptions for each tag appear in the bottom panel of the dialog box.

4. **To insert a tag on your page, select the tag and click the Insert button.**

   If the tag is listed in the right pane with angle brackets surrounding it (such as <u></u>), it's inserted in your document. All other tags, however, need additional information.

If the tag needs more information, the Tag Editor dialog box opens. Figure 4-6 shows an example of the Tag editor set to insert properties for the `<iframe>` tag.

Figure 4-6: Enter tag details in the Tag editor.

5. **Enter the tag and attribute details.**

   The Tag editor is context specific, meaning it displays all the property fields available for the selected tag. If you're unsure of what to add in any field, leave it blank for now because you can always edit the tag through the Properties inspector at a later time.

   If the Tag editor displays multiple categories, such as General, Browser Specific, and Style Sheet/Accessibility, look at those category options and add tag attributes.

6. **Click OK in the Tag editor.**

   The selected tag is inserted onto your page.

7. **To add more tags to your page, repeat Steps 2 through 6. Otherwise, click the Close button to close the Tag Chooser.**

Coding Links by Hand

If you happen to know the syntax, by all means feel free to hand-code your links. Simply go right into Code view and type away. Just be sure you remember to close your link tags with the closing `</a>` tag. Table 4-1 shows examples of the link types.

Table 4-1	Sample Links
Link Type	*Link Example*
Hyperlink with text, including `target` attribute and link to file on same site	`<a href="about.html" target="_self">` `About Us</a>`
Hyperlink with text, including `target` attribute and full path of link	`<a href="http://www.google.com"` `target="_blank">Google</a>`
Hyperlink with graphic, including `target` attribute and link to file on same site	`<a href="about.html" target="_self">` `<img src="images/about.gif"></a>`
Hyperlink with graphic, including `target` attribute and full path of link	`<a href="http://www.google.com"` `target="_blank"> "><img src=` `"images/google.jpg"></a>`
E-mail link	`<a href="mailto:me@example.com">` `me@example.com</a>`
Named anchor	`<a name="anchor1" id="anchor1"></a>` (Anchor laid down) `<a href="#anchor1">` `Go to Anchor 1</a>` (Link to anchor)
Named anchor laid down that includes a `target` attribute and the full path to a link	`<a name="anchor1" id="anchor1" href=` `"http://www.example.com">Link to the` `home page</a>`

Chapter 5: Adding Flash, Movies, Sound, and More

In This Chapter

✔ Adding Flash, movies, buttons, and text

✔ Adding FlashPaper and Flash video

✔ Inserting Shockwave movies, Java applets, and ActiveX controls

✔ Working with Netscape Navigator plug-ins

✔ Adding other video and sound

You've probably seen Web sites that include Flash intros, MPEG videos, MP3 songs, QuickTime movies, and other various kinds of sound and video plug-ins. Dreamweaver makes it easy to insert these media clips along with attributes that determine how the media displays on a Web page and, if applicable, how the user can interact with it.

This chapter shows you how to add Flash, movies, sound, and other media types to a Web page. You also find a brief discussion about acceptable sound file formats and the differences between linking and embedding video and sounds.

Flash Elements You Can Add to Your Web Site

Your basic Flash movie uses the most common SWF file format, but you can add other Flash elements to your Web pages. Before you begin adding them, however, you need to understand the subtle differences between the different Flash file formats:

✦ **.fla,** or *Flash files,* are Flash movies. These are the original, editable source files for creating SWF files.

✦ **.swf** files (pronounced *swiff*) are compressed, portable versions of .fla files that you can preview in Dreamweaver and play in browsers. Flash buttons and Flash text also use SWF files. These files are not editable as the original FLA files are.

✦ **.swt** are Flash template files that allow you to change information in SWF files. For example, Flash buttons use SWT files to let you create multiple buttons with different text.

TIP

Macromedia's Dreamweaver Exchange has many button templates available for download at www.macromedia.com/exchange/dreamweaver/. After downloading, save the templates into the Dreamweaver/ Configuration/Flash Objects/Flash Buttons folder.

✦ **.swc** are Flash element files or special SWF files that make customizable Rich Internet applications.

✦ **.flv,** or *Flash video files,* play movies that have encoded audio and video data that allows the free Flash player to play them. For example, a Windows Media or QuickTime video could be encoded with special software into FLV files for viewing in a Flash player. Flash 8 Video Encoder (www.macromedia.com) and Sorensen Squeeze (www.sorensonmedia. com) are two recommended encoders. To discover more about this process, visit www.macromedia.com/go/flv_devcenter.

To add Flash movies to your site, you must first create the SWF files in Flash. However, to add Flash buttons, Flash text, FlashPaper, or Flash video to a page, all the creation and editing is done right in Dreamweaver, regardless of whether or not you have Flash installed on your computer!

Inserting Flash Movies (SWFs)

Inserting Flash movies into your Web page in Dreamweaver is a simple two-step process. Before you can insert a Flash movie in Dreamweaver, however, you must first create the movie in the Flash program and save it as a SWF file. Check out *Macromedia Flash 8 For Dummies* (Wiley) if you need help preparing your Flash movie.

Adding a Flash movie to your page

To add a Flash movie (SWF) to a Web page, follow these steps:

1. **Place your cursor where you want the Flash movie to appear on your Web page.**

2. **Choose Insert⇨Media⇨Flash.**

   You can also click the Media button on the Common tab of the Insert bar and select Flash from its drop-down list.

   The Select File dialog box opens.

3. **Select the Flash movie file you want to insert on the page and click OK.**

   Note: If you enabled Accessibility options in Preferences, the Object Tag Accessibility Attributes dialog box appears prompting you to add a title, access (shortcut) key, and tab index number to the SWF file. Enter those attributes and click OK; click Cancel to add the SWF file without the Accessibility attributes.

Dreamweaver embeds the movie with all the Flash HTML code needed for the movie to play in most major browsers by including the `<embed>` tag for Netscape Navigator plug-ins and the `<object>` tag for Microsoft ActiveX controls. The code, as in the following example, shows how a SWF file called `flashsample.swf` would be embedded on a page:

```
<object classid="clsid:D27CDB6E-AE6D-11cf-96B8-444553540000"
    codebase="http://download.macromedia.com/pub/shockwave/cabs/flash/swflash.ca
    b#version=6,0,29,0" width="320" height="240" accesskey="x" tabindex="1"
    title="Flash Sample">
    <param name="movie" value="flashsample.swf" />
    <param name="quality" value="high" />
    <embed src="flashsample.swf" quality="high"
    pluginspage="http://www.macromedia.com/go/getflashplayer"
    type="application/x-shockwave-flash" width="320" height="240"></embed>
  </object>
```

Dreamweaver displays the embedded Flash movie on the page in Design view as a grey box (see Figure 5-1). The Document window doesn't automatically preview the Flash movie.

Book II
Chapter 5

Adding Flash,
Movies, Sound,
and More

Figure 5-1:
The Flash movie appears as a grey box in Design view.

To preview the Flash movie, select the Flash movie and do one of the following:

◆ Click the Play button in the Properties inspector. Click Stop to stop the preview.

◆ Press F12 to preview the movie in a browser window.

Setting Flash movie attributes

After inserting the movie onto the page, select the Flash placeholder in Design view and use the Properties inspector to set the movie attributes. If you don't see all the movie properties, click the expander arrow in the bottom-right corner of the Properties inspector.

◆ **Flash ID/Name:** Input the movie ID or name.

◆ **Loop:** If you check this option, your embedded movie plays continuously; leave it unchecked, and your movie plays once.

◆ **Autoplay:** Plays the movie automatically when the page loads in a browser window.

◆ **W** and **H:** Set the size of the movie in pixels.

◆ **V Space** and **H Space:** Set white space in pixels above and below, and on both sides, left and right, of the movie.

◆ **File:** Specifies the path of the Flash `.swf` file. Browse for and select the file using the folder button or type the path.

◆ **Quality:** This setting deals with *anti-aliasing,* or smoothing, of the movie during playback. The higher the setting, the smoother the movie, but also the potentially slower the movie displays. By contrast, low settings load faster but look less crisp. Auto Low and High options improve appearance or emphasize quality, respectively.

◆ **Scale:** Determines how the movie fits into the pixel sizes displayed in the W and H text boxes:

  • **Default (Show all):** The entire movie displays at 100 percent.

  • **No Border:** Maintains the original movie dimension aspect ratio but fits the movie, without borders, into the sizes set in the W and H text boxes, which means that any parts of the movie that extend beyond the W and H settings are cut off.

  • **Exact Fit:** Squishes the movie into the specified dimensions, regardless of the original size of the movie.

◆ **Align:** Sets the alignment of the movie relative to the page.

✦ **Bg Color:** Adds a background color behind the movie. This color displays only if and when the movie is not playing.

✦ **Edit:** Updates FLA files when Flash is loaded on the same computer. If no Flash application is detected, this button is disabled.

✦ **Reset Size:** Reverts a file to its original movie size.

✦ **Play/Stop:** Starts and stops movie previews within Design view.

✦ **Parameters:** Opens a dialog box where you can enter more parameters for the movie if the movie has been created to accept these parameters.

✦ **Class:** Applies CSS to a movie, such as styles with border or alignment attributes.

**Book II
Chapter 5**

Adding Flash,
Movies, Sound,
and More

Creating Flash Buttons

Flash buttons are special Flash-generated buttons that act like graphic rollover buttons but are created directly in Dreamweaver with preinstalled Flash templates. When you use Flash buttons, you eliminate the need for creating special graphics for a regular rollover button's normal and over states.

You can create, insert, and update Flash buttons as often as you need — all within Dreamweaver. Flash buttons can have up to four views, or *button states* (up, down, over, active), to which you can add text, choose a background color, and add a link to another file. Dreamweaver includes over 40 flash button templates for you to choose from as starting points for creating your custom Flash buttons, and additional button templates are available on the Macromedia Web site.

Inserting a Flash button on your page

You can insert Flash buttons into any saved document; if you try to add a Flash button to an unsaved page, Dreamweaver displays an alert message requesting you to save the file before creating the button.

To insert a Flash button on a saved page in either Design or Code view, follow these steps:

1. **Place the insertion point where you want the Flash button to appear.**

2. **Choose Insert⇨Media⇨Flash Button.**

   You can also click the Media button on the Common tab of the Insert bar and choose Flash Button from its drop-down list.

   The Insert Flash Button dialog box appears, as shown in Figure 5-2.

Figure 5-2:
The Insert
Flash Button
dialog box.

3. From the Style list, select a style for the button you want to create.

When you select a button type, a preview of the button appears in the Sample box.

You can select from nearly 45 preinstalled styles or click the Get More Styles button to visit Macromedia's Dreamweaver Exchange to download more button styles.

4. In the Button Text field, enter the text (max 14 characters) that you want to appear on the face of the button. Select a font and size for the button text by filling in the appropriate fields.

Because the Flash button is a SWF movie file, you can select any font you have installed on your computer!

Pay careful attention to the amount of text you add to your button; you may need to change it if it exceeds the dimensions of the button.

5. Select the link, target, and background color in the appropriate fields:

- **Link:** Type the path and filename of the linked page for the button. If the linked page is on the same site, enter only the filename, such as **contact.html**. However, if the linked page is external to the current site, enter the full URL including the http://, as in **http://www.dummies.com**.

- **Target:** By default, pages automatically open in the same browser window. To override this setting, enter **_blank** to have the link open in a different browser window. See Book II, Chapter 4 for more about other target settings.

- **Bg color:** Sets the background color of the rectangular area *behind* the button. Choose a color by clicking the Text color box and selecting a color from the Web-safe palette, or enter the hexadecimal number preceded with a # (number sign) in the Bg Color text field.

6. **In the Save As field, enter a filename for the resulting .swf file.**

7. **If you want to see a preview of the Flash button in your open file before committing to the options selected, click the Apply button.**

8. **Click OK to insert the Flash button on your page.**

To preview the Flash button effects, such as rollover or on-click states, select the button in Design view and click the Play button in the Properties inspector. Click Stop to stop the preview. You can also press F12 to preview the button in a browser window.

Editing a Flash button

In Design view, you can resize the Flash button using the resize handles. Because the button is vector based, it should look crisp and clean at any size; just be sure to hold Shift while resizing to maintain the button's width-to-height aspect ratio.

To return the button to its original W and H dimensions, click the Reset Size button in the Properties inspector. The button is located between the Edit and Play buttons.

In addition to resizing the button, you can edit the Flash button attributes in the Insert Flash Button dialog box. To open this dialog box, do one of the following:

✦ Select the Flash button and click the Edit button in the Properties inspector.

✦ Double-click the Flash Button object in Design view.

After making your changes, click OK to update the Flash button.

Inserting Flash Text

A *Flash Text object* is a small text-only vector graphic Flash movie. You generally display text in only a few font styles, because you have no control over what fonts are installed on a visitor's computer. With a Flash Text object, however, you can add text to a page using any font installed on your computer, in any size and color, on any background color, and the text can contain a single link with `target` and `rollover color` attributes.

Flash text is not a button; it is simply another way of displaying text on a page using a "fancy" font without the need for creating a GIF or JPEG graphic. That said, because Flash text is technically an object, you can assign a link to it.

Because you can't specify the size of the Flash Text object in pixels, pay special attention to how your text flows and apply paragraph or line breaks as necessary to achieve the look you need.

To insert a Flash Text object into a page, follow these steps:

1. **Open a document and place the insertion point at the spot where you want the Flash text to appear.**

2. **Choose Insert⇨Media⇨Flash Text.**

   You can also click the Media button on the Common tab of the Insert bar and choose Flash Text from its drop-down list.

   The Insert Flash Text dialog box appears, as shown in Figure 5-3.

Figure 5-3: The Insert Flash Text dialog box.

3. **Enter text and select font, size, color, and other attributes:**

   • **Font and Size:** Select a font and size for the Flash text.

   • **Color:** Select the color of the text.

   • **Rollover Color:** Select a color for the text when the user moves the mouse over the text.

   • **Text:** Type the text you want to appear on the Flash Text object. This can be a word, phrase, or paragraph of text. For longer text entries,

apply paragraph or line breaks as necessary to achieve the look
you need.

- **Link:** Type the path and filename of the linked page for the Flash Text
  object. If the linked page is on the same site, enter only the filename,
  such as **contact.html**. However, if the linked page is external to the
  current site, enter the full URL including the http://, as in **http://www.
  dummies.com**.

- **Target:** By default, pages automatically open in the same browser
  window. To override this setting, enter **_blank** to have the link open
  in a different browser window.

- **Bg Color:** Select a background color for the area behind the text.

- **Save As:** Enter a filename for the resulting .swf file, such as **aboutus
  heading.swf**.

4. **If you want to see a preview of the text, click the Apply button.**

5. **Click OK to insert the Flash text on your page.**

To edit the Flash text after it's been added to your page, select it and click
the Edit button in the Properties inspector, or double-click the Flash Text
object in Design view to open the Insert Flash Text dialog box. After applying
changes, click OK to update the Flash text.

Figure 5-4 compares the appearance of regular HTML text with Flash text,
and a regular GIF button graphic with a Flash button.

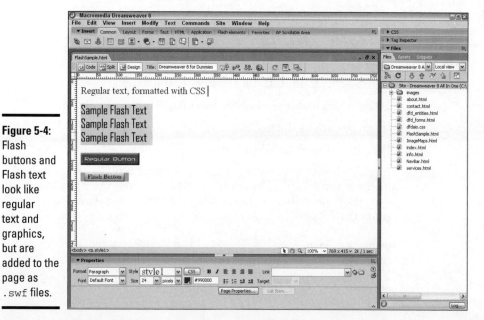

Figure 5-4:
Flash
buttons and
Flash text
look like
regular
text and
graphics,
but are
added to the
page as
.swf files.

Inserting FlashPaper

Macromedia's FlashPaper software converts any printable document, such as a Word or Excel file, into either a FlashPaper SWF file or PDF (Portable Document Format) file. Like PDFs, anyone can open FlashPaper SWFs in a browser; unlike PDFs, anyone can view FlashPaper online without needing to link to another file or open another browser window. FlashPaper also allows a user to see all the pages in the document, as well as zoom in and out, search, and print.

For more information on FlashPaper, see the Macromedia Web site at www.macromedia.com/go/flashpaper.

To insert a FlashPaper document in your Web page, follow these steps:

1. **Open a document and place the insertion point where you want the FlashPaper to appear.**

2. **Choose Insert⇨Media⇨FlashPaper.**

   You can also choose the FlashPaper button from the Media drop-down list on the Common tab of the Insert bar.

   The Insert FlashPaper dialog box appears, as shown in Figure 5-5.

Figure 5-5:
The Insert
FlashPaper
dialog box.

3. **In the Source field, select a FlashPaper document.**

4. **Set the width and height of the FlashPaper object in pixels.**

   FlashPaper scales the document to fit the width and height.

5. **Click OK to insert the FlashPaper on your page.**

   The Flash object appears on the page as a grey box. To set additional attributes for the FlashPaper object (which are the same as other Flash elements as described earlier in this chapter), select it and enter attributes in the Properties inspector.

To preview the FlashPaper object, select the FlashPaper placeholder and click the Play button in the Properties inspector. Click Stop to stop the preview. You can also press F12 to preview the document in a browser window and test the functionality of the FlashPaper toolbar.

Inserting Flash Video

Flash video is different than a regular Flash movie in that a Flash video uses the FLV file format and allows you to add prerecorded video to a Web page in a format that most visitors can view. A Flash movie, by comparison, is more of a limited animation clip delivered on the Web using the SWF file format.

Flash videos start as captured video, which can be in many formats, including Avid Xpress DV, Adobe After Effects, Apple QuickTimePro, and Apple Final Cut Pro. Once captured, the video gets encoded into the Flash Video format (FLV). You can then decide on a delivery mechanism and add the video to your Web site.

You need to acquire the video and encode it into the FLV format, or at least obtain the FLV files prior to adding them to your site. Once a Flash video has been encoded, you can add it to your page using the Dreamweaver Insert Flash Video command. This tool enables you to add Flash video to your pages without using the Flash program, and it enables browsers to play the inserted Flash video with playback controls.

Find out more about Flash video from the Macromedia Learning Guide, including tips on encoding video with Flash 8 and other programs, at `www.macromedia.com/devnet/flash/articles/video_guide.html`.

You can select two options for the video type: Progressive Download and Streaming. The decisions you make for inserting Flash video vary slightly depending on which type you choose:

✦ **Progressive Download Video** downloads the FLV file to the user's computer and plays it there. The benefit of FLV is that the video starts to play during the download.

✦ **Streaming Video** streams the Flash video and plays it in the browser window. Streaming video typically buffers for a few seconds before playback to help the playback be smooth rather than bumpy. Streaming also requires the file to be served by your own Flash Media Server or a hosted server running Flash Video Streaming Services.

To insert Flash video using the Progressive Download Video type, follow these steps:

1. **Open a document and place the insertion point where you want the Flash video to appear.**

2. **Choose Insert⇨Media⇨Flash Video.**

   You can also click the Insert Flash Video button on the Common tab of the Insert bar.

   The Insert Flash Video dialog box appears, as shown in Figure 5-6.

Book II
Chapter 5

Adding Flash, Movies, Sound, and More

Figure 5-6:
The Insert
Flash Video
dialog
box for
progressive
download
video.

3. Select Progressive Download Video as the video type.

4. Set the following options:

- **URL:** Enter the relative or absolute path of the FLV file. Or click the
  Browse button to choose a FLV file. For absolute paths, type the complete URL including http://, as in **http://www.mySampleSite.com/
  video.flv**. If you're using a Mac, you must use an absolute path when
  FLV files sit more than two levels up from the HTML file the video is
  inserted on.

  Note: The FLV files must contain metadata in order to work properly
  as a video player. Many encoders automatically add metadata to the
  FLV files, but some do not.

- **Skin:** Select an appearance for the video player from the Skin drop-
  down list. A preview window displays an approximation of how each
  option looks.

- **Width** and **Height:** Enter a dimension in pixels for both the width
  and height of the FLV file. Click the Detect Size button to have
  Dreamweaver attempt to automatically read the FLV file dimensions;
  if the dimensions are unreadable, manually enter W and H sizes. The
  Total with Skin dimensions represent the total W and H of the FLV file
  plus the W and H of the chosen skin.

- **Constrain:** This option is enabled by default and ensures that the
  aspect ratio between the width and height of the FLV movie is
  maintained.

- **Auto Play:** Enable this option to have the video begin playing as soon as the Web page loads in the browser window.

- **Auto Rewind:** Enable this option to have the video playback return to the start position when the video reaches the end.

- **Prompt Users to Download Flash Player:** This option, enabled by default, inserts Flash player version-detection code into the page. If visitors need to download a newer version of the player, this code prompts them to do so.

- **Message:** When visitors do need to download a newer version of the Flash player to see the Flash video, you can customize the message they see. Use the suggested text or add your own.

5. **Click OK to close the dialog box and insert the Flash video on your page.**

A video SWF file and SWF skin are created to play the video in a browser. These files are added to the same directory as the HTML file the video has been inserted in. In the example shown in Figure 5-7, these files are called `Clear_Skin_3.swf` and `FLVPLayer_Progressive.swf`.

You must also upload these files to your server for the video to play properly. Dreamweaver automatically uploads these files as dependents as long as you agree to upload dependent files during the upload process.

You can also modify some of the Flash video settings, such as Auto Play, Auto Rewind, and the Skin, in the Properties inspector (see Figure 5-7).

Figure 5-7:
The Properties inspector for progressive download video.

To insert Flash video using the Streaming Video type, follow these steps:

1. **Open a document and place the insertion point where you want the Flash video to appear.**

2. **Choose Insert⇨Media⇨Flash Video.**

   You can also click the Insert Flash Video button on the Common tab of the Insert bar.

   The Insert Flash Video dialog box appears, as shown in Figure 5-8.

Figure 5-8:
The Insert Flash Video dialog box for streaming video.

3. **Select Streaming Video as the video type.**

4. **Set the following options:**

   • **Server URI:** Enter the server, application, and instance names in the form, as in **rtmp://www.mySite.com/application_name/ instance_name**.

   • **Stream Name:** Enter the name of the FLV file (either with or without the `.flv` extension), as in **video3.flv** or **video3**.

   Note: The FLV files must contain metadata in order to work properly as a video player. Many encoders automatically add metadata to the FLV files, but some do not.

- **Skin:** Select an appearance for the video player from the Skin drop-down list. A preview window displays an approximation of how each option looks.

- **Width** and **Height:** Enter a dimension in pixels for both the width and height of the FLV file. Click the Detect Size button to have Dreamweaver attempt to automatically read the FLV file dimensions; if the dimensions are unreadable, manually enter W and H sizes. The Total with Skin dimensions represent the total W and H of the FLV file plus the W and H of the chosen skin.

- **Constrain:** This option is enabled by default and ensures that the aspect ratio between the width and height of the FLV movie is maintained.

- **Live Video Feed:** Enable this option only when the video feed is live. When live, the player plays a live video streamed from the server. The name in the Stream Name text box is the name of the live video feed. Because a viewer can't manipulate live video, only the volume control appears on the skin. Furthermore, the Auto Play and Auto Rewind options are also inoperable with live video.

- **Auto Play:** Enable this option to have the video begin playing as soon as the Web page loads in the browser window.

- **Auto Rewind:** Enable this option to have the video playback return to the start position when the video reaches the end.

- **Buffer Time:** This is the time it takes, in seconds, before the video begins to play in a browser. By default, the buffer is set to 0, but you can increase the number of seconds to have the player pause before the video begins to play, which may be helpful for sites that have occasional bandwidth issues when visitor traffic is high. When Auto Play is enabled, however, the buffer time is ignored.

- **Prompt Users to Download Flash Player:** This option, enabled by default, inserts Flash player version-detection code into the page. If visitors need to download a newer version of the player, this code prompts them to do so.

- **Message:** When visitors do need to download a newer version of the Flash player to see the Flash video, you can customize the message they see. Use the suggested text or add your own.

5. **Click OK to close the dialog box and insert the Flash video on your page.**

    A video SWF file and SWF skin are also created to play the video in a browser. You must upload the SWF files to your Web server and the ASC file to the Flash Communication Server for the video to play properly. Dreamweaver automatically uploads these files as dependents as long as you agree to upload dependent files during the upload process.

To upload all the required files quickly, select the Flash video on the page, and click the Upload Media button in the Properties inspector. Use the Properties inspector to modify other Flash video settings too.

Flash videos may require different players depending on which codec the video was created with. For more information about Flash video, visit the Flash Video Developer Center at `www.macromedia.com/go/flv_devcenter` and read the Flash Video with Dreamweaver 8 tutorial by Jen deHaan at `www.macromedia.com/devnet/flash/articles/flv_tutorial.html`.

Adding Shockwave Movies, Java Applets, and ActiveX Controls

In Dreamweaver, you can add Shockwave movies, Java applets, ActiveX controls, and other sound and video files to any open, saved file. If the object you want to add is not one of these types, use a Netscape Navigator plug-in instead (as described in the section "Adding Netscape Navigator Plug-ins," later in the chapter). You need to prepare these objects in advance before inserting them on your page. Table 5-1 describes the type of objects you can add to your Web page.

Table 5-1	Media Types
Media Type	*Description*
Shockwave Movie	Macromedia's standard for interactive multimedia files on the Web, typically created from compressed Macromedia Director files. Shockwave movies download fast and can display in browsers with the appropriate free Shockwave player.
Java Applet	Lightweight applications *(applets)* generated with the Java programming language that are inserted onto Web pages.
ActiveX Control	Formerly called OLE controls, these media files are reusable components that behave like Netscape browser plug-ins. They run only in Windows versions of Internet Explorer. You can assign these controls additional attributes and parameters in Dreamweaver.
QuickTime Movie	A movie format created with Apple's QuickTime program that can include video, audio, and other bitstreams, such as images and animations.
Netscape Navigator Plug-In	A plug-in, or helper application, that allows a Netscape Navigator browser to display multimedia content (audio, video, animation, virtual reality, and 3D objects) in a range of file formats. Plug-ins include RealPlayer, QuickTime, and MP3 files, among many others.

Follow these steps to insert a media object:

1. **Choose Insert➪Media and select the media type (Shockwave, Applet, ActiveX, or Plug-in).**

   Or click the Media button on the Common tab of the Insert bar and choosing the media type from its drop-down list.

   The Select File dialog box appears.

2. **Browse to and select a source file, and set any parameters for the media file.**

   For the lowdown on adding parameters for media files, see the nearby sidebar "Controlling media objects with parameters."

    To insert a media placeholder and bypass having to select a source file or set any preferences (though the Tag Accessibility dialog box may still pop up when Accessibility features are enabled), press and hold Control (Windows) or Option (Mac) while inserting the media object. For example, to insert a placeholder for a plug-in without selecting the plug-in file, press and hold Control or Option and choose Insert➪Media➪Plug-in, or click the Plug-in button in the Media drop-down list on the Common tab of the Insert bar.

3. **Click OK to insert the media.**

   If you've enabled Accessibility options in Preferences, the object's Tag Accessibility Attributes dialog box appears prompting you to add a title, shortcut *(access)* key, and tab index options to the media file. Enter those attributes and click OK; or click Cancel to add the media file or placeholder without the Accessibility attributes.

Setting Shockwave movie properties

Shockwave movies, which are compressed multimedia files created with Macromedia Director, are embedded into a page in a similar fashion and have the same options as Flash files.

To specify the properties for Shockwave movies, select the movie in Design view and apply attributes from the Properties inspector. See the earlier section "Setting Flash movie attributes" for a description of each property.

Setting Java applet properties

You can also add Java applets to HTML files with Dreamweaver. Java is a programming language that creates *applets,* or little applications.

After inserting the applet on the page, select the applet placeholder and set the applet attributes in the Properties inspector (see Figure 5-9):

Figure 5-9:
Set prop-
erties for
the Java
applet.

✦ **Applet Name:** Enter the applet name in the text box.

✦ **W** and **H:** Set the width and height of the applet in pixels.

✦ **V Space** and **H Space:** Set white space in pixels above and below, and on both sides, of the applet.

✦ **Code:** When you select the applet, this field gets filled in automatically. To change the Java file, click the folder button or type a different filename.

✦ **Base:** If you selected a file in the Code field, the location or path of the applet displays in this box.

✦ **Align:** Set the alignment on the applet relative to the page.

✦ **Alt:** Set alternative content and specify a graphic file that displays if the user's browser doesn't support Java applets or has Java disabled. You can also insert Alt text instead of a graphic. When you add an image, the `<img>` tag gets inserted between the opening and closing `<applet>` tags. To specify both an image and Alt text, insert the image first, and then add the `alt` attribute to the `<img>` tag in Code view:

```
<applet code="myapplet.class" codebase="applet/" width="32" height="32">
  <img src="applet/ myapplet.gif" width="32" height="32" alt="Spinning
    Counter" />
</applet>
```

✦ **Class:** Apply CSS to an applet.

✦ **Parameters:** Enter more parameters for the applet. See the upcoming sidebar "Controlling media objects with parameters" for more info about setting parameters.

If you don't see all these properties, click the expander arrow in the bottom-right corner of the Properties inspector.

Setting ActiveX control properties

Formerly known as OLE controls, *ActiveX controls* are mini-applications that behave like browser plug-ins and can be reused as often as you need. The ActiveX object lets you add attributes and parameters for an ActiveX control in a user's browser.

Controlling media objects with parameters

With most media objects, the Properties inspector includes a Parameters button when you're specifying properties for that media object. Parameters are special values for Shockwave movies, Java applets, ActiveX controls, Netscape Navigator plug-ins, and Flash SWF files. These values are attached to the `<object>`, `<embed>`, and `<applet>` tags in the code, and usually set specific attributes for the type of media object being added to the page. For instance, a Shockwave movie can have a URL parameter that is part of the `<embed>` tag as the following line of code shows (where `swURL` is the name and `file-name.html` is the value of the parameter):

```
<embed src="swmovie.dcr" height="100"
       width="100"
       swURL="filename.html">
```

To find out what attributes you can add to an object, see the documentation for the media object you're inserting. Whatever parameters you do add, the procedure for adding them is the same.

To add parameters to media objects, follow these steps:

1. Select the media file in Design view.

2. Click the Parameters button in the Properties inspector.

The Parameters dialog box opens, shown in the following figure.

3. Enter a value for the parameter. Click the plus (+) button to add a parameter or the minus (–) button to remove a parameter.

4. Enter the parameter name in the Parameter column and the value in the Value column.

5. To reorder the parameters, click the up and down arrow buttons.

6. Click OK when you're done setting all the parameters.

You can also view the assigned attributes to any selected media object by viewing the Attributes tab of the Tag panel. There you can add, edit, and delete attributes like `src`, `width`, and `height`.

ActiveX controls run on Windows with Internet Explorer but not on Macs or in Netscape, so use them with consideration.

Select the ActiveX control in Design view, and set the attributes of the `<object>` tag and the parameters of the ActiveX control in the Properties inspector (see Figure 5-10).

Figure 5-10:
Set
properties
for the
ActiveX
control.

✦ **ActiveX:** Enter the name in the ActiveX text box in the top-left corner of the Properties inspector. The name assists with scripting the object.

✦ **W** and **H:** Set the width and height of the object in pixels.

✦ **V Space** and **H Space:** Set white space in pixels above and below, and on both sides, of the object.

✦ **ClassID:** Select a value from the drop-down list or type a value for the ClassID, such as RealPlayer or Shockwave for Flash. This field identifies the control to the browser. If the browser can't find the ActiveX control specified, it tries to download it from the URL listed in the Base field.

✦ **Embed:** Activate the Netscape Navigator plug-in equivalent of the ActiveX control using the `<embed>` tag within the `<object>` tag. ActiveX property values assigned in Dreamweaver are applied to their Netscape Navigator plug-in equivalents.

✦ **Src:** If you enabled the Embed option, type or browse to and select the data file for a Netscape Navigator plug-in. If you don't specify a filename, Dreamweaver attempts to find the value using the other ActiveX properties.

✦ **Base:** Identify the URL with the ActiveX control. If the control is not already installed on the user's computer, IE downloads it. Without the proper ActiveX control installed, the browser can't display the object.

✦ **ID:** Set the ID for the ActiveX control to load. If you don't have information for this parameter, leave this field blank.

✦ **Data:** Set the data file for the object to load in the browser. Some ActiveX controls, such as RealPlayer, don't use this parameter. Leave the field blank if you don't have information for this parameter.

✦ **Alt Img:** Specify a graphic file that displays if the user's browser doesn't support the `<object>` tag. The Embed option must be unchecked to use this feature.

✦ **Align:** Set the alignment of the object relative to the page.

✦ **Class:** Apply CSS to an object.

✦ **Parameters:** Enter more parameters for the ActiveX control. See the sidebar "Controlling media objects with parameters" for more info about setting parameters.

Adding Netscape Navigator Plug-ins

Typical plug-ins for Netscape Navigator include QuickTime movies, RealPlayer content, and MP3s. If you want to insert an object that is *not* a Flash, Shockwave, applet, or ActiveX object, try inserting it on your page with the Netscape Navigator plug-in. You can create your own content or get it from another source, and then use Dreamweaver to insert the file into your HTML page. To insert a Netscape Navigator plug-in, follow the steps in the earlier section "Adding Shockwave Movies, Java Applets, and ActiveX Controls" and choose the Plug-in option in Step 1.

Setting Netscape Navigator plug-in properties

After adding the Netscape Navigator plug-in object, select it in Design view and set the plug-in properties in the Properties inspector (see Figure 5-11). Here are your options:

Book II
Chapter 5

Figure 5-11:
Set
properties
for the
plug-in.

Adding Flash,
Movies, Sound,
and More

+ **Plugin ID/Name:** Enter the name in the Plugin text box in the top-left corner of the Properties inspector.

+ **W** and **H:** Set the width and height of the plug-in object in pixels.

+ **V space** and **H space:** Set white space in pixels above and below, and on both sides, of the plug-in object.

+ **Plg URL:** Specify the URL where users can download this plug-in. If the user's computer doesn't have the plug-in, the browser downloads it from this URL.

+ **Src:** If you selected a source file for the plug-in when you inserted it, this field is already filled in. If not, identify the source data file of the plug-in by typing the filename or click the folder button to browse to and select the file.

+ **Border:** Add a black border, in pixels, around the entire plug-in.

+ **Align:** Set the alignment of the object relative to the page.

+ **Class:** Apply CSS to an object.

+ **Parameters:** Enter more parameters for the Netscape Navigator plug-in. See the sidebar "Controlling media objects with parameters" for more info about setting parameters.

Playing Netscape Navigator plug-ins

Dreamweaver lets you preview movies and animations that use Netscape Navigator plug-ins (but not ActiveX controls) in Design view. As long as you've installed the appropriate plug-ins, you can play previews of all the plug-ins at once or play them separately.

Be sure to also test the plug-ins in as many browsers as possible to ensure your site visitors have the most consistent experience viewing them.

Here's how to preview movies and animations with Netscape Navigator plug-ins:

+ **To preview a single movie or animation:** Select a media file inserted on the page and click the Play button in the Properties inspector. The media file plays in Design view.

   Or choose View⇨Plugins⇨Play.

+ **To preview all the media files on a single document:** Choose View⇨ Plugins⇨Play All. All the media files on the same page play.

+ **To stop playing the media files:** Click the Stop button in the Properties inspector. For multiple media files, you can also choose View⇨Plugins⇨ Stop All.

If for some reason the plug-in content does not play in the Document window, try the following troubleshooting tips:

+ Be sure the plug-in is installed on the test computer and that the plug-in content is compatible with the plug-in version installed. For instance, if a movie runs with QuickTime V7, but only the QuickTime V5 player is installed, the movie won't play.

+ Open the `Configuration/Plugins/UnsupportedPlugins.txt` file in a text editor to see if the plug-in is listed. This file automatically adds problematic plug-ins to the list.

+ Check the computer to see if enough memory is allocated to run the file. Many plug-ins need an extra 2 to 5MB of memory just to run! That said, most modern operating systems don't use memory allocation, so this issue may be more applicable for Mac OS9, Windows 95, and earlier operating systems.

Acceptable Sound File Formats

There are several common sound file formats, each with their own set of benefits and drawbacks. Here are the most common file formats:

✦ **.mp3 (Motion Picture Experts Group Audio, or MPEG-Audio Layer-3):** This sound file compresses files so they are much smaller in size. The quality is very good — even close to CD quality if recorded and compressed in the right way. One of the great things about this format is the ability to stream data so the user doesn't have to wait for the entire file to download before listening to it. Most podcasts are MP3 or ACC.

One possible drawback is the overall file size, which can get pretty big, making download times on a dialup connection seem impossible. The user's computer must have helper applications, such as QuickTime, RealPlayer, or Windows Media Player, to play MP3 files.

✦ **.qt, .qtm, .mov, or QuickTime:** This format is great because it can contain both sound and video. Developed by Apple, it's the default sound/video player for Macintosh computers. PCs can play QuickTime files too, but the user needs to download and install the QuickTime player first. The encoding formats supported by QuickTime include JPEG, MPEG, and Cinepak.

✦ **.ra, .ram, .rpm, or Real Audio:** Like MP3s, this format allows for streaming audio data. It also compresses files, but into even smaller file sizes than MP3s. Visitors need to download and install the RealPlayer application to play these files.

✦ **.wav (Waveform Extension):** These files have good sound, are widely supported by browsers, and don't need any special plug-ins to play. They tend to have very large file sizes, so sound clips need to be small enough to add to Web pages. Most computers allow you to record your own WAV files in some way with a microphone.

✦ **.midi or .mid (Musical Instrument Digital Interface):** These files are intended for instrumental music only. Small files can provide long sound clips, too. The sound quality, however, is dependent on the sound card on the user's computer. Like WAV files, most browsers support MIDI files and they don't require special plug-ins. The biggest drawback to MIDI files is that you can't easily record with them; they must be synthesized using specific software and hardware.

✦ **.aif (Audio Interchange File Format, or AIFF):** Like the WAV format, these sound files have good sound, are supported by most browsers, and don't need plug-ins to play. AIFF files can be recorded to CDs and tapes using a microphone through your computer, but because of their large file sizes, sound clips need to be small enough to add to Web pages.

If you come across another file format that you want to use on your Web page, check with the format creator's technical help files to find out about browser support.

Book II
Chapter 5

Adding Flash, Movies, Sound, and More

Adding Other Video and Sound to a Page

Dreamweaver supports adding sound to a Web page. There are many types of sound files and formats, such as `.wav`, RealPlayer, and `.mp3`, as described in the preceding section.

Before you decide on a format and how to add the sound to your page, consider the audience, the file size, the sound quality, and the different ways browsers support these files because different browsers handle sound files very differently. If you're trying to create a consistent experience for your visitors — regardless of their browser type — consider adding the sound to a Flash SWF file rather than have it linked or embedded to the page. Ultimately, testing the sound and video files in multiple browsers is the best way to decide what to add and how to add it.

Linking versus embedding video

You can link or embed your prepared video files (non-Flash) to a Web page, depending on the video format and preferred method of display. That means you can set up the video to download to the user's desktop, or embed it in the page so it streams in the browser while downloading.

Follow these steps to link or embed a short video in your page:

1. **Add the video clip to your site folder.**

   Video clips often use the MPEG or AVI file format.

2. **Link or embed the clip to your page.**

   - **Linking:** Type the text you want to appear on your page (such as **Download Video**), select that text, and in the File text field in the Properties inspector, type the video filename with extension, or click the folder button to browse for and select the video file.

   - **Embedding:** Follow the steps in the earlier section, "Adding Shockwave Movies, Java Applets, and ActiveX Controls."

      Streaming video requires that the user's computer has a helper application, such as RealMedia, Windows Media, or QuickTime, for the video to play.

Be sure to upload the video file to the server along with the file it's linked to so the site visitor can download or watch the video.

Linking versus embedding sound

Linking to a sound file is the best way to add sound to a Web page because it allows users to decide for themselves whether they want to listen to the file in advance of hearing it.

Embedding sound, by contrast, adds the sound directly into a Web page so it plays automatically, as long as the user has the right plug-in. Embedded files can play background music, for instance. Sound plug-ins often embed volume control as well as On/Mute control.

Linking to a sound file

To add a link to a sound file on a Web page, follow these steps:

1. **Select the image or text you want to use as the link to the audio file.**

2. **In the Properties inspector, type the filename in the Link text box, or click the folder button to browse for and select the audio file you want to use.**

Be sure to upload the sound file to the server along with the file it's linked to so the site visitor can access the sound file. This method makes the sound file available to the widest audience.

Embedding a sound file

To embed a sound file on a Web page, follow these steps:

1. **In Design view, place the insertion point on the page where you want to embed the file.**

2. **Choose Insert⇨Media⇨Plug-in.**

   Or click the Media button on the Common tab of the Insert bar and choose Plug-in from its drop-down list.

   The Select File dialog box appears.

3. **Browse to and select the sound file you want to insert.**

4. **Click OK to insert the sound file.**

After inserting the sound object, select the sound placeholder object in Design view and enter values in the attribute fields in the Properties inspector. The Width and Height values, for example, determine the size of the audio controls displayed in the browser window.

Be sure to upload the sound file to the server along with the file it's embedded in so the site visitor can hear and play the sound file.

Launching a Media External Editor

Dreamweaver allows you to launch many external editors for a variety of media types should you need to edit those media files while working within

Dreamweaver. For example, you can launch Fireworks to modify GIF files, Photoshop to modify JPG files, and oXygen to modify XML files. Launching an external editor from within Dreamweaver to edit most media types is a simple process that requires only a few simple steps.

First, you need to associate the media file type with the editor on your computer. To so do, follow these steps:

1. **Choose Edit⇨Preferences (Windows) or Dreamweaver⇨Preferences (Mac) and then choose the File Types/Editors category in the Preferences dialog box, as shown in Figure 5-12.**

2. **Select the file extension in the Extensions panel to see any associated editors in the Editors panel.**

   For example, in Figure 5-12, the .png extension is associated with the Fireworks editor, which is also the primary editor.

3. **If needed, add or change extension types by clicking the plus (+) or minus (–) button. To make an editor the primary editor, click the Make Primary button.**

4. **When you finish, click OK to save your changes.**

Figure 5-12: The File Types/ Editors preferences.

After you establish the file types/editor preferences, double-click the media file in the Files panel to start the external media editor. The primary editor associated with that media type opens.

If you'd prefer to occasionally not use the primary editor to edit the media file, right-click (Windows) or Control+click (Mac) the media file from the Files panel or from within Design view and choose Open With or Edit With from the context menu.

Chapter 6: Creating Tables for Layout

In This Chapter

✔ **Creating tables**

✔ **Using table visual aids**

✔ **Formatting tables and table cells**

✔ **Adding content to table cells**

✔ **Importing tabular data**

*T*ables are a great way to organize tabular data and other content in a visually pleasing way. HTML tables can have as many rows and columns as needed, and additional tables can be nested inside other table cells ad infinitum for more complex layouts. Tables are made up of one or more rows, and each row has one or more cells. The cells make up columns, and though the columns are not explicitly defined in HTML, Dreamweaver allows you to manipulate rows, columns, and cells.

As far as styling goes, tables can have borders, background colors, background images, and be aligned relative to the page. Their individual table cells can also have similar attributes. Furthermore, table content can include text, graphics, links, movies, sound, and other plug-ins, and each of those can have their own formatting or style attributes.

This chapter guides you through the process of inserting, editing, and deleting tables, formatting and adding content to them, plus some general tips for using tables to improve the overall look and feel of a page.

Creating Tables

If you want to add your own table for layout, simply create the table in an open file in the Dreamweaver Document window and format the table and content inside the cells according to a predetermined design or your own personal aesthetic. For instance, you can create a page with an information bar at the top containing a logo and other general information and have navigation below with graphics and content areas. Both the content and navigation areas sit inside nested tables in the main table (see Figure 6-1).

When your page contains a lot of text, it's best to fix the width of the text to a readable size, usually 600 pixels wide or less. To contain text inside a fixed area of the page, insert a fixed-width table with one row and one column and paste the content inside the table cell. When opened in a browser window, the text then wraps inside the cell boundaries instead of expanding and collapsing with the edges of the browser window.

On the Layout tab of the Insert bar, shown in Figure 6-2, you can choose from three layout modes when working with tables:

✦ **Standard:** By default, Dreamweaver uses Standard mode, which shows tables as a grid of rows and columns.

✦ **Expanded:** For even easier editing, try using the Expanded mode, which adds temporary cell padding and cell spacing for more precise selections.

✦ **Layout:** If you plan on doing more complex Web page layouts — which admittedly can be difficult — work in Layout mode. In Layout mode, you can draw, resize, and even move "boxes" around in Design view while still using tables for the overall page structure.

Figure 6-2:
The Insert
bar.

To switch layout modes, click the Layout mode buttons on the Layout tab of the Insert bar. You can also switch modes by choosing View➪Table Mode and then a layout mode.

In the following sections, you find out how to insert a basic table in your Web page and how to draw a table in Layout view.

Inserting a basic table in your page

To create a basic table in Dreamweaver, follow these steps:

1. **Place your cursor where you want the table to appear on the page.**

2. **Choose Insert➪Table.**

You can also click the Table button on the Layout tab of the Insert bar when using Standard mode or Expanded mode.

The Table dialog box appears, as shown in Figure 6-3.

**Book II
Chapter 6**

Creating Tables
for Layout

Figure 6-3:
Set table options before adding a table to the page.

3. **Specify the following attributes for the new table:**

- **Rows** and **Columns:** Enter the number of rows and columns for your table.

- **Table Width:** Enter a fixed width in pixels or a percentage width between 1 and 100 percent.

- **Border Thickness:** Enter the size, in pixels, for the table border. If left blank, the border displays as if it was set to 1 pixel. To remove a border completely, set the thickness to 0.

- **Cell Padding:** Enter a number in pixels to increase the space between the cell's walls and its contents. If left blank, the cell padding displays as if it was set to 1 pixel. To remove cell padding completely, set the size to 0.

- **Cell Spacing:** Enter a number in pixels to increase the walls of the table between the cells. If left blank, the cell spacing displays as if it was set to 2 pixels. To remove cell spacing completely, set the size to 0.

4. Choose a header for the table.

The content in header rows or columns format differently than content in other table cells. In addition, screen readers identify the content in header rows or columns differently to assist visually impaired visitors in understanding the content in the table.

5. In the Accessibility area, fill in the following fields:

- **Caption:** This is a title for the table, which appears outside of the table.

- **Align Caption:** Select top, bottom, left, or right alignment. By default, if no alignment option is selected, the caption is centered on top of the table, using the `<caption>` tag.

- **Summary:** Add a description for your table. This information is hidden from view in a browser, but is read by screen readers.

6. When you finish, click OK to create your table.

Dreamweaver adds the table to your page with the specified settings.

7. Add content to your table cells.

You can insert text, graphics, media, and other files in a table cell — anything that can exist on a page can also be placed and formatted in a table cell. For details, see the "Inserting Text and Images in Table Cells" and "Formatting Individual Table Cells" sections.

After inserting the table, you can also nest tables inside the table. To nest a table inside a table cell, place your cursor inside the table cell and repeat Steps 2 through 7.

Drawing a table in Layout view

If you plan on doing more complex Web page layouts, work in Layout mode. In Layout mode, you use the Draw Layout Cell and Layout Table buttons on the Layout tab of the Insert bar to create the layout of your page. To do so, open your document and follow these steps:

1. Select the Layout mode option on the Layout tab of the Insert bar.

The words *Layout mode* appear above the ruler in the Document window. You also see a pale grey bar with diagonal lines across it at the top of the document.

2. Click the Layout Table button on the Layout tab of the Insert bar.

Once selected, the cursor changes to a crosshair when you move it to the Document window. This indicates that you're ready to draw the table.

3. **In the Document window, click and drag to draw a rectangular shape in the appropriate size for the outer border of your table.**

The new layout table appears on the page, as shown in Figure 6-4.

4. **Click the Draw Layout Cell button and then draw cells anywhere inside the table, as shown in Figure 6-5.**

5. **Click the Layout Table and Draw Layout Cell buttons to continue defining the layout and insert nested regions where necessary.**

To continue drawing cells or tables without having to click the button each time, hold Ctrl (Windows) or ⌘ (Mac) when drawing them.

Cells automatically snap to the edges of the table to help improve layout formatting. If, however, you want to disable snapping temporarily while drawing the cells, press Alt (Windows) or Option (Mac) while dragging.

6. **When the layout looks good, continue working in Layout mode or switch to Standard mode to add content and finish building your Web page.**

To switch to another mode from Layout mode, click the layout buttons on the Layout tab of the Insert bar, or click the Exit link next to the words Layout Mode in the grey striped bar at the top of the Document window, right beneath the Document toolbar.

Figure 6-4:
The layout table appears in the Document window with a green tab at its top-left border.

Figure 6-5:
Cells have light blue borders and lie within the bounds of the table.

Turning On Table Visual Aids

Creating tables can sometimes be a tricky business, so Dreamweaver created some interesting visual aids. They help you select table cells, columns, and rows, edit the tables themselves, and view table attributes such as cell widths in pixels or percentages.

To use the Table Visual Aids, choose View⇨Visual Aids⇨Table Visual Aids. You see a check mark if the aids are enabled, and no check mark when they're turned off. You can also turn on Visual Aids through the Options menu of any open Document window. Figure 6-6 shows an example of a table with and without Table Visual Aids.

When Table Visual Aids are turned on, Dreamweaver shows a table header menu, which displays table widths and column widths when the table is selected or the cursor is somewhere inside the table. Next to the widths you see tiny green arrows that, when clicked, quickly access a few of the table-related commands.

If two numbers are specified for the width dimensions, check the HTML code to ensure that the column widths add up to the total table width. For instance, one column's width may be set to 100 pixels, but after adding a long sentence or large graphic, the cell stretches to 300 pixels. The first number is the HTML-specified cell width, and the (300) is the visual width as displayed on-screen. Fix the table dimensions in the code by clicking the table header menu and selecting Make All Widths Consistent. Then preview the page in a browser window (press F12) to test for visual accuracy.

Visual Aids

**Book II
Chapter 6**

**Creating Tables
for Layout**

Figure 6-6:
A table with and without Table Visual Aids enabled.

Formatting Tables with the Properties Inspector

After creating a table, you can set formatting options for the whole table or for specified rows, columns, or cells in the Properties inspector.

To select a table to format it, do one of the following:

✦ Click on the table's outer edge.

✦ Click the table tag on the Quick Tag Editor bar at the bottom of the Document window.

When a table is selected, selection handles appear on the right-center, bottom-center, and bottom-right corners of the table, and the Properties inspector displays table formatting options, as shown in Figure 6-7.

Figure 6-7:
The
Properties
inspector
shows table
formatting
options
when a
table is
selected.

Selection handles

Table formatting attributes are totally optional. Use them in any combination to format tables in harmony with the data contained in them and the overall look of the Web site design. When adding formatting to a table, keep in mind that cell formatting takes precedence over row formatting, which takes precedence over table formatting. In other words, a cell with a background color displays that color in the browser even if the row or entire table has a different color attribute.

The Properties inspector includes these table formatting options:

✦ **Table ID:** Input the table name. IDs are now used instead of name attributes for easier assignment of CSS, Dreamweaver behaviors, and JavaScript events. You don't need to name all your tables, but a Table ID helps keep better track of them when you do.

✦ **Rows** and **Cols:** Change the numbers in the Rows and Cols fields to adjust the table rows and columns accordingly (see the "Adding Rows and Columns to a Table" section).

✦ **W** and **H:** Adjust the size of the table in pixels or percentages. Widths are generally specified for tables automatically, while the height field is typically left blank so that the overall height is determined by the contents of the table. When specifying dimensions in percentages, the width and height are relative to the open browser window or containing cell. For instance, `W=80%` means the table expands to 80 percent of the open browser window, or 80 percent of a containing cell if the table is nested inside another table.

✦ **Border:** Add a border to the outer edges of a table. By default, the Border field is blank. Enter any number from 0 to 750. Borders without a `border color` attribute appear beveled.

✦ **Brdr Color:** Add flat areas of color to both the outer edges and inner walls of a table.

✦ **Bg Color:** Add a background color to the entire table.

✦ **Bg Image:** Specify an image of any size to tile vertically and horizontally. Background images sit on top of background colors, if any.

✦ **Class:** Apply a custom style from an internal or external CSS.

To gain further control over the look of your tables, consider adding cell padding, cell spacing, and cell alignment attributes:

✦ The **CellPad** field adds uniform spacing in pixels inside all the cells in a table, padding cell contents away from the cell walls.

✦ The **CellSpace** field adds uniform spacing in pixels to the walls of the cells in the table.

✦ The **Align** field determines where the table sits relative to other content on the page. The browser determines the default alignment, but most browsers have the default set to Left. To ensure the table aligns properly, select Left, Center, and Right from the drop-down list.

By default, the CellPad and CellSpace fields are blank, which has the equivalent of 2 pixels, respectively. To remove the default spacing attributes, enter **0** in both fields.

Using Preformatted Table Designs

After converting your table into HTML, you can format and customize it by using Dreamweaver's preset table designs. Use them as is or as a starting point for creating your own formatting options to be consistent with the design of your Web page or Web site.

To customize a table, select the table and then follow these steps:

1. **Choose Commands⇨Format Table.**

The Format Table dialog box appears, as shown in Figure 6-8.

Figure 6-8:
Select table formatting options in the Format Table dialog box.

2. **Select one of the preformatted table designs from the list in the upper-left corner of the dialog box.**

   Each time you select a design a preview appears to the right of the list.

3. **If you want to customize the preset design, edit the options that appear below the list.**

4. **Click the Apply button to see how your data will appear with the new formatting attributes.**

   You can modify the formatting as often as you need before committing to it.

5. **When you're satisfied with your table design settings, click OK to add formatting to your table or click Cancel to exit without formatting.**

By default, formatting attributes are applied to the table's `<tr>` tags to produce cleaner HTML code. However, for more consistent rendering of these formatting attributes in multiple browsers, select the Apply All Attributes to TD Tags Instead of TR Tags check box in the Format Table dialog box. For the best formatting, however, use CSS (see Book III, Chapter 1).

Merging and Splitting Rows and Columns

Editing rows and columns in Dreamweaver is a dream come true! Macromedia has made splitting and merging cells so easy that you'll never go back to hand-coding your tables.

It's important to understand what's happening to the code when you split or merge cells. For example, when merging two cells in a row into one cell, the two cells are combined by making the first cell span across two columns, using the colspan attribute in the <td> tag:

```
<table width="300" border="1">
   <tr>
     <td colspan="2">Merged Cells</td>
   </tr>
   <tr>
     <td>Bottom Left</td>
     <td>Bottom Right</td>
   </tr>
 </table>
```

By contrast, when merging two cells in a column, those cells actually span across two rows, this time using the rowspan attribute in the <td> tag:

```
<table width="300" border="1">
   <tr>
     <td rowspan="2">Merged Cells</td>
     <td>Right Top</td>
   </tr>
   <tr>
     <td>Right Bottom</td>
   </tr>
</table>
```

Figure 6-9 shows examples of what a merged row and a merged column look like in Design view, compared to normal tables with no merged cells.

Figure 6-9:
Before and
after views
of a merged
row and a
merged
column.

Seems simple enough, but this process can get very confusing the more complex your tables get. Imagine having to figure it out and code it by hand! Thankfully Dreamweaver handles all this merging and splitting with ease. The following sections explore ways to split and merge cells and add rows and columns.

You can merge or split any number of cells. For instance, you may want to select all the cells in a particular row and merge them into one wide cell, or take one cell somewhere in the table and split it into three cells.

If you forget which button is which (merge or split) in the Properties inspector, hover your cursor over the button to read the tool tip description. Merge says `Merges selected cells using spans` and Split says `Splits cell into rows or columns`.

Merging cells

To perform a merge, follow these steps:

1. **Select the cells that you want to combine by clicking and dragging across several cells.**

Selected cells must be *contiguous,* or touching, as well as evenly matched horizontally and vertically (in the shape of a rectangle) for the merge to work. If the selection is unbalanced in some way, the merge button is grayed out. As long as the merge button is active, the merge can take place with the selection.

2. **Click the Merge Selected Cells button in the lower-left corner of the Properties inspector.**

Dreamweaver merges the selected cells into a single cell.

To remove a merge, place your cursor inside a single cell and do one of the following:

✦ Choose Modify⇨Table⇨Decrease Row Span to merge the selected cell into the cell below it.

✦ Choose Modify⇨Table⇨Decrease Column Span to merge the selected cell into the cell to the right of it.

Splitting a cell

To split a cell, follow these steps:

1. **Place the cursor inside the cell you want to split.**

2. **Click the Split button in the Properties inspector.**

You can also choose Modify⇨Table⇨Split Cell.

The Split Cell dialog box opens, shown in Figure 6-10.

Figure 6-10:
The Split
Cell dialog
box.

3. **Select Rows or Columns as the split type and enter a number for the split in the Number Of field.**

4. **When you're finished, click OK.**

   Dreamweaver splits the cell.

Setting Table Width and Heights

When first creating a table, the overall size of the table is determined by the pixels or percentages settings in the width and height fields. Both pixels and percentage settings split cells and rows evenly but without adding exact pixel dimensions into the W and H fields for each row or column. The reason for this is that most table cells use their contents to determine their size. However, sometimes you need to fix one or both dimensions.

When the need arises, select an entire row or column, or place your cursor inside any cell to modify the dimensions of the cells, and then enter W and H attributes in pixels or percentages in the Properties inspector.

Take care when manually entering W and H cell sizes to your cells because if the math doesn't add up right, the table may not display accurately in a browser window. Therefore, be sure each row or column adds up to 100 percent or the total amount of pixels specified for the table. The same holds true for column cell heights and table height attributes. For example, in a table with two columns that is 200 pixels wide, check to see that the total cell width equals 200 (100 pixels wide each). Unequal columns can be any size as long as they equal 200, as in the following code where 85 is the width for the first column and 115 is the width for the second column:

```
<table width="200" border="1" cellpadding="5">
  <tr>
    <td width="85" rowspan="2">Coffee</td>
    <td width="115">Regular</td>
  </tr>
  <tr>
    <td>Decaffeinated</td>
  </tr>
</table>
```

Adding Rows and Columns to a Table

When adding rows and columns, all the contents in each of the cells are duplicated right along with the new row or column.

Adding a row

To quickly add a row to a table:

✦ To add a row above a certain row, place your cursor inside a cell and choose Insert⇨Table Objects⇨Insert Row Above.

✦ To add a row below a certain row, place your cursor inside a cell and choose Insert⇨Table Objects⇨Insert Row Below.

Adding a column

To quickly add a column to a table:

✦ To add a column to the left of a certain column, place your cursor inside a cell and choose Insert⇨Table Objects⇨Insert Column to the Left.

✦ To add a column to the right of a certain column, place your cursor inside a cell and choose Insert⇨Table Objects⇨Insert Column to the Right.

Adding multiple rows or columns

When adding columns, the rightmost column gets duplicated and added to the right edge of the table. When adding rows, the bottom row gets duplicated and added to the bottom of the table.

To add multiple rows or columns, place your cursor inside the cell where you want to add the rows or columns, and follow these steps:

1. **Choose Modify⇨Table⇨Insert Rows or Columns.**

The Insert Rows or Columns dialog box opens, shown in Figure 6-11.

Figure 6-11:
The Insert Rows or Columns dialog box.

2. **Select either the Rows or Columns option button, enter the number of rows or columns that you want to insert, and select either the Above the Selection or the Below the Selection option button.**

3. **When you finish, click OK.**

   Dreamweaver inserts the specified number of rows or columns into your table.

Deleting rows and columns

Delete rows and columns quickly with any of these methods:

✦ Place your cursor inside a cell of the row or column to be deleted and choose Modify⇨Table⇨Delete Column or Delete Row.

✦ Select an entire row or column and click the Delete or Backspace key.

Inserting Text and Images in Table Cells

Add text and graphics to table cells just as you'd add them to a page. Click inside the cell and begin typing to add text or use the Insert bar to add an image (see Book II, Chapter 3). Insert other media to table cells in the same way by browsing for and selecting the media that you want to insert.

You can also paste contents from other sources — such as a word processing document — into a cell. Apply text and graphics formatting attributes with the Properties inspector or with the help of CSS. (See Book III, Chapter 1 for more on CSS.)

Formatting Individual Table Cells

In addition to standard text formatting options, the cells themselves can have specific formatting attributes, which are slightly different from formatting options for an entire table. If you don't see cell formatting options in the Properties inspector, click the down expander arrow in the bottom-right corner to reveal the cell's formatting area.

Format several cells at once or one at a time depending on your needs using any of these formatting options in the Properties inspector (see Figure 6-12):

✦ **Horz** and **Vert:** Stands for Horizontal and Vertical alignment options for any cell, row, or column. The default horizontal alignment is Left for regular cells and Center for header cells. Horizontal alignment options include Left, Center, and Right. Vertical alignment options include Top,

Middle, Bottom, and Baseline. Both dimensions also have a Default option, which aligns the contents of the cells left and center.

✦ **W** and **H:** Set the width and height for an entire selection. Enter dimensions in pixels or percentages.

✦ **No Wrap:** Forces text or other content in that cell to not wrap, thereby pushing out the cell walls and adjusting the cell sizes if the content extends beyond the cell's specified size. Use this feature for addresses or other information that needs to be all on one line.

✦ **Header:** Turns any regular cell into a header cell by converting the `<td>` tag into a `<th>` tag. Table headers have preset formatting attributes to help set their content apart from the rest of the content in the table. Headers are typically only used on the top row or left column of a table.

✦ **Bg Image:** Enter the path and filename for any image used as a tiling background for a cell. If you prefer, click the folder button to browse and select a file by name, or use the Point to File button to point to the image you want to insert as the background image.

✦ **Bg Color:** Sets the background color of a cell or set of selected cells. Background cell colors sit on top, or *hide,* a table background color. To specify a background color, click the color picker icon and select a color or enter the hexadecimal number preceded with a # (number sign) in the Bg Color field.

✦ **Brdr Color:** Sets the internal border color of a cell or set of selected cells. Most browsers inconsistently support this browser so be sure you preview this setting in multiple browsers to ensure it appears accurately. To specify a border color, click the color picker icon and select a color or enter the hexadecimal number preceded with a # (number sign) in the Brdr Color field.

Figure 6-12:
Set cell
properties.

Changing Table Measurements from Pixels to Percentages

Another great feature Dreamweaver provides when working with tables is the ability to convert a table's measurements from pixels to percentages and vice versa. This is especially useful when you want the flexibility of adjusting a table with percentages but need to convert to fixed pixel widths before publishing.

To change table measurements from pixels to percentages (or vice versa), select the entire table and choose Modify➪Table. Or, for faster access, use the table property conversion buttons located in the Properties inspector, as shown in Figure 6-13.

Convert Table Widths to Pixels

Clear Column Widths | Convert Table Widths to Percent

Figure 6-13:
The table property conversion buttons.

Clear Row Heights | Convert Table Heights to Percent

Convert Table Heights to Pixels

A description of each is provided in the following list:

✦ **Clear Column Widths:** Completely removes any width attributes from column cells in the entire table.

✦ **Convert Table Widths to Pixels:** Converts all table widths from percentages to fixed pixels.

✦ **Convert Table Widths to Percent:** Converts all table widths from fixed pixels to percentages.

✦ **Clear Row Heights:** Completely removes any width attributes from row cells in the entire table.

✦ **Convert Table Heights to Pixels:** Converts all table heights from percentages to fixed pixels.

✦ **Convert Table Heights to Percent:** Converts all table heights from fixed pixels to percentages.

Importing Tabular Data

Dreamweaver now swiftly imports tabular data saved as tab delimited `.txt` files and converts it into HTML tables! This is great news to anyone who's ever tried to paste table data from Microsoft Excel or Access into an HTML page.

To insert tabular data, choose File⇨Import⇨Tabular Data. The Import Tabular data dialog box opens, where you can enter the filename of the tab delimited data file, set the delimiter type, and perform other table formatting. Turn to Book II, Chapter 1 for more info about importing tables.

Sorting Information in a Table

Another great Dreamweaver table tool is the Sort Table command. Though normally you'd sort your data prior to inputting it in a table in Dreamweaver, you may want to improve the order of the information in your table. Use this sort command to sort your alphabetical or numerical table data in either an ascending or descending order, such as alphabetizing a list of client names or store addresses, or ordering a list of items by their unique ID numbers.

Because Dreamweaver can only sort data along a single column of data, this feature does not work on tables with `colspan` or `rowspan` attributes. Therefore, you should perform this task before you merge or split any cells in your table. The sorting command physically changes the order of the content in your tables.

With the table filled with data selected, follow these steps to sort the information in the table:

1. **Choose Commands⇨Sort Table.**

The Sort Table dialog box, shown in Figure 6-14, opens.

Figure 6-14:
Select table sorting options.

2. **In the Sort By drop-down list, select which column you want to sort by.**

For example, if your table has two columns, select either Column 1 or Column 2.

3. **In the two Order drop-down lists, choose whether you want to sort the column alphabetically or numerically and in ascending (A to Z or 1 to 100) or descending (Z to A or 100 to 1) order.**

   To alphabetize a list, select Alphabetically and Ascending to sort your data from A to Z.

4. **In the Then By list, choose another column number for a secondary sort, or leave the field blank.**

   This option offers a second level of organization for your sort. For example, you may want to sort a list of names by last name and then by first name.

5. **In the Options area, further refine your results:**

   - **Sort Includes the First Row:** Select this option if your table doesn't include headings, so the first row of data gets included in the sort. If your table does include headings, leave this option disabled.

   - **Sort Header Rows:** This option sorts all the rows in the table's `thead`, separate from the sorting of the data in the rest of the table. To find out about the `<thead>` tag, open the Reference panel by choosing Help⇨Reference.

   - **Sort Footer Rows:** This option sorts all the rows in the table's `tfoot`, separate from the sorting of the data in the rest of the table. To find out about the `<tfoot>` tag, open the Reference panel by choosing Help⇨Reference.

   - **Keep All Row Colors the Same After the Sort Has Been Completed:** Select this option to have any row attributes stay with the data after the sort. This option doesn't work well with tables formatted with alternating row colors; rather, this feature is best for tables that have row attributes specific to the content in each row.

6. **To see the sorting results before committing to them, click the Apply button. If you're satisfied with the result, click OK. Or to exit without sorting, click Cancel.**

   If you like the new ordering, save the changes to the table.

If you want to revert the table contents to the order it was in prior to the sort command, choose Edit⇨Undo Sort Table.

Working with Tables Created by Other Programs

If you want to harness the power of another program to do much of the table organization for you — especially with regard to graphics — several Web optimization programs can help you convert your graphic layouts from flattened artwork or layered files to a tables-based HTML file with sliced graphic images in each of the table cells. Most notable are ImageReady and Fireworks, but other programs do essentially the same thing.

Inside the optimization program, you'll probably use a slice tool to cut the graphic into slices, which in turn get converted into individual GIF or JPEG files upon optimization. Many of these programs also allow you to add JavaScript behaviors to the slices including rollover button behavior, animation, and graphical styles or effects. After all these extras have been applied to the slices in the optimization program, all the slices (or selected slices) can be optimized and converted into HTML-ready files. Typical options for exporting optimized graphics from an optimization program include HTML and Images, Images only, or HTML only. Once the optimization process is complete, you can bring the HTML files with table and graphics into Dreamweaver for further editing.

For ImageReady-generated HTML files, which typically include an `index.html` page and an attending images folder, move these files to a logical location on the local computer. Many Web designers organize their Web files into one master folder containing separate HTML folders for each Web site, as in the following example:

> Hard Drive/Clients/ClientA/A_HTML
> Hard Drive/Clients/ClientB/B_HTML
> Hard Drive/Clients/ClientC/C_HTML

Once the ImageReady files are in the appropriate folder on your computer, define a new Dreamweaver site, as described in Book I, Chapter 3. Taking this step is essential to ensuring that you have access to all of Dreamweaver's managed-site tools. From within the managed site, open the individual ImageReady-generated HTML files and apply further formatting, links, and so on.

Using Fireworks-generated HTML is slightly different than ImageReady and other optimization programs. For more about Fireworks HTML and how to use it in Dreamweaver, see Book III, Chapter 5.

Chapter 7: Building Fabulous Forms

In This Chapter

✔ Putting together a form

✔ Adding fields to your form

✔ Performing form validation

*F*orms are a great tool for collecting information from site visitors. Forms allow users to request information, send comments and questions, sign up for services or newsletters, fill out an online application, or enter payment information for purchasing products or services.

Before building a form for your Web page, spend some time figuring out what data you need to collect and consider how to organize that data logically so your form is easy to understand and navigate.

Forms, by default, are not secure documents. If you need your forms to be secure — a must if you're collecting confidential personal information such as a credit card or password — speak to your host provider about purchasing an SSL (Secure Sockets Layer) digital security certificate of some kind. SSL encrypts data and provides secure connections for e-commerce and communication so your site visitors can feel confident that their personal information is protected and safe. VeriSign (www.verisign.com), GeoTrust (www.geotrust.com), and Thawte (www.thawte.com) are the most popular SSL encryption certificates.

You can do many other things to make your forms secure, such as creating a secure login script, using cookies, and creating XForms with XML, but that falls a little beyond the scope of this book. To find out more about security in general, visit the VeriSign, GeoTrust, and Thawte Web sites. For more on XForms, visit the W3C (www.w3.org/TR/xforms) and W3Schools (www.w3schools.com/xforms/default.asp) Web sites.

In this chapter, you find out how to create fabulous forms, validate them with JavaScript, and submit them to your server for processing.

Organizing Data in Your Form

Though you can't nest forms inside other forms, you can have multiple forms on a page, if needed. To organize your form data, use tables, line breaks, paragraph breaks, and other formatting, just as you would anywhere else on the page to make the form data look good.

One of the best ways to organize your form is to use a table. (See Book II, Chapter 6 for the lowdown on creating tables.) Though you can build your form in any order, adding all your form labels is often useful before adding form fields. For instance, in a two column, multi-row table, enter form labels for name, address, city, state, zip, phone, e-mail, and so on down the left column, and then add all the form fields down the right column. By labeling all the form fields, the users know what information to input or select from. Figure 7-1 shows a simple form requesting billing information to make a purchase.

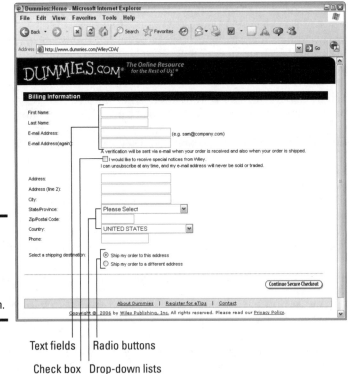

Figure 7-1:
A simple form requesting billing information.

Text fields   Radio buttons

Check box   Drop-down lists

For more complex data collection needs, feel free to nest tables within tables to further help with organization. For instance, you may have a section of the form that describes an event as well as listing the event's location and date. If the data needs to be broken up into categories, it may benefit from being organized inside a nested table.

Creating a Fabulous HTML Form

This section describes how to create an HTML form. If you want to use Dreamweaver to make dynamic Web forms, turn to Book VIII, Chapter 4 for more information.

When creating a form, you start by adding the `<form>` tag to an open document. If you forget the `<form>` tag, Dreamweaver prompts you to add it when you insert your first form field. Nevertheless, inserting the `<form>` tag yourself before you build your form is a good habit to get into.

When a visitor enters information into your form and clicks the Submit button, the data needs to go somewhere for processing. In most cases, that somewhere is a server-side script or program. Forms are often processed with ASP, PHP, CGI, and ColdFusion scripts. The script or program then processes the data and responds by returning information back to the user, performing an action based on the form's instruction (like sending the user to a Thank You page), or sending an e-mail directly to a specified e-mail recipient. Host providers often have a forms processing method available as part of your hosting package, so be sure to check with your provider for details and instructions.

To create a form and link it to a script, follow these steps:

1. **Place the cursor where you want the form to appear on the page.**

2. **Choose Insert⇨Form⇨Form.**

   You can also click the Form button (which looks like a little square with a dotted red outline) on the Forms tab of the Insert bar.

   In Design view, the `<form>` tag appears on your page as a dotted red line in the shape of a large rectangle. In Code view, the inserted form tag looks like this:

   ```
   <form name="form1" method="post" action=""></form>
   ```

   If you don't see the dotted red line, which Dreamweaver considers an *invisible element* that appears in Design view but doesn't show up in the browser, choose View⇨Visual Aids and check that invisible elements are enabled.

After you create the `<form>` tag, the Properties inspector displays the form formatting options, as shown in Figure 7-2.

3. **Give your form a unique name by typing it in the Form Name text box in the Properties inspector.**

Names are important if you plan on adding JavaScript or VBScript to control the form in some way. If you forget to name the form, or don't need to add scripting, Dreamweaver uses the form*n* syntax to name your forms, where *n* is equal to the number of each form that gets added to a page, such as `name=form2`.

4. **In the Action field, click the folder button to browse to and select the script or file that will process the collected data in the form.**

If the script is on the server, type the path to that script. For example, many forms use CGI scripts located inside a CGI folder on the server, like this script where the name *email.pl* should be replaced with the actual name of your script filename:

```
<form name="form1" method="post" action="cgi-bin/email.pl"></form>
```

Figure 7-2: Add form-processing details to your form tag, which appears as a dotted rectangular line.

By default, the form field gets inserted with the following information:

```
<form name="form1" method="post" action=""></form>
```

The CGI script is something that your host provider or system administrator provides you.

5. **Choose a method for transmitting collected form data to the server from the Method drop-down list:**

   • **Default** uses the browser's default setting to send the data. Because the default is usually — but not always — the GET method, it's better to specify GET or POST rather than using the default.

   • **GET** adds the value of the collected data to the URL requesting the page, making this URL bookmarkable, and therefore vulnerable to hackers. Also, because URLs can only have a maximum of 8192 characters, this method is not useful for long forms. GET is best for repeatable, stateless form applications.

   • **POST** hides the form data inside the HTTP request, preventing the collected data page from being bookmarked. The data, however, is not encrypted (it's also vulnerable to hackers), so be sure to use a secure connection to a secure server, especially if you're collecting personal information such as credit cards, usernames, and password information.

6. **(Optional) In the Enctype drop-down list, choose the MIME encoding type of the data being sent to the server.**

   By default, this field is blank. Select application/x-www-form-urlencode as the default type for the POST method, or when adding a file-upload field to a form, select the multipart/form-data MIME type.

   If you're unsure of what to select here, leave the field blank and check with your host provider or system administrator for assistance.

7. **Set the target browser location for any returned data or documents in the Target drop-down list:**

   • **_blank:** Display the returned document or data in a new browser window.

   • **_self:** Display the returned data in the same window.

   • **_top:** Use the current open window even if other windows are open.

   • **_parent:** Use the parent window of the current file.

You have now completed the preliminary steps for adding a form to your page. The dotted red line marks the boundaries of your form. Within this border, you can add *form objects,* such as check boxes, radio buttons, lists,

Book II
Chapter 7

Building Fabulous Forms

menus, and so on, as described in the next section. If you plan on organizing your form objects inside a table, now is the time to add the table to your page. (See Book II, Chapter 6 for details on creating tables.)

Adding and Labeling Form Fields

Dreamweaver calls all the form input fields *form objects*. These are what you use to collect data from the site visitor. The following sections provide descriptions for adding each of the form objects to your form and customizing them with their respective property setting options.

Text fields

Use text fields to collect text or numerical data, such as a name, address, telephone number, e-mail address, or password.

Inserting a text field

To insert a text field in your page, follow these steps:

1. **Place your cursor inside the form area on your page where you want to insert a text field.**

   For example, if you've already inserted form tags and created a table inside the form tags with labels to indicate the data you will be collecting in the form, place your cursor in the table cell (next to the cell containing the first form label) where you intend to insert the first text field.

   If you haven't yet created a form, see the earlier section, "Creating a Fabulous HTML Form."

2. **Choose Insert⇨Form⇨Text Field.**

   You can also click the Text Field button on the Forms tab of the Insert bar.

3. **In the TextField box in the Properties inspector, enter a name or label for the text box.**

   All text fields need a unique name for the form to work properly. Names can contain numbers and letters as well as the underscore character, but can't include any spaces or special characters. Figure 7-3 shows an example of a form layout including the form tag (red dotted outline), form labels (Name, Address, Phone, and so on), and form fields to collect data. The Properties inspector shows the properties for the Address field, as shown in Figure 7-3.

   This text field name is the variable that stores the value of the field (which is the data the user inputs), and is sent to the server for processing. For example, a text field with the name `Address` and corresponding input by a user of `123 Main St.` may be returned to you as `Address=123 Main St.`

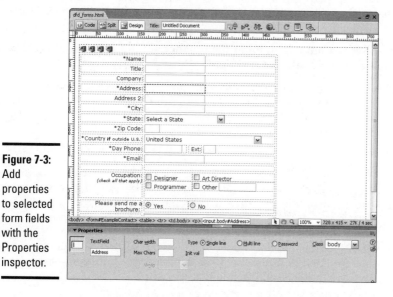

Figure 7-3:
Add
properties
to selected
form fields
with the
Properties
inspector.

4. **In the Type area, indicate whether you want the text field to be a single-line, multi-line, or password field:**

   - **Single Line** uses the `<input>` tag with the `type=text` attribute.

   - **Multi Line** creates multi-line text input fields. Multi-line fields use the `<textarea>` tag with the `cols` attribute for character width and the `rows` attribute for number of lines.

   - **Password,** which uses the `<input>` tag with the `type=password` attribute, makes asterisks or bullets appear when typing inside the form field in a browser. The data, however, is not encrypted. To provide encryption, talk to your host provider about buying an SSL certificate.

   Figure 7-4 shows examples of the three types of text fields.

Figure 7-4:
Three types
of text
fields.

5. **In the Char Width box, enter the maximum number of characters that you want displayed in the text field.**

This determines the width of the text input field. Additional characters may be accepted, but not displayed, depending on the value entered in the Max Chars field. Controlling the width of an input field with CSS is better because different browsers interpret this attribute in different ways.

6. **In the Max Chars field, enter the maximum number of characters that can be entered into the text field.**

This is especially useful for limiting phone numbers to ten digits, zip codes to five digits, or other data that requires a limited number of characters. If a visitor enters more characters than defined by this field, the form makes an alert sound.

7. **In the Num Lines box (for multi-line only), set the height, in lines, of a multi-line text field.**

8. **In the Wrap drop-down list (for multi-line only), select how you want input exceeding the specified text area to display.**

You can choose from the following options:

- **Off/Default** is the equivalent to a no-wrap setting. Text continues to flow from left to right unless the user enters a Return to move the insertion point to the next line down.

- **Virtual** forces text to wrap within the specified text area even though the data is still submitted to the server as a single string.

- **Physical** forces text to wrap within the specified text area and those wrap breaks are applied to the data being submitted to the server.

9. **(Optional) In the Init Val box, enter any text that should appear inside the form object when the page loads.**

This text can then be replaced with information from the user.

10. **(Optional) From the Class drop-down list, choose a CSS to apply to the form object.**

For example, you may have created a custom CSS for all your text input fields. Choose the style from the menu to apply it.

Inserting a text area

A text area object is exactly the same as a text field object set to multi-line, only you don't need to set the Multi-line type in the Properties inspector yourself. Like the text field object, the text area object has fields for you to specify character width and number of lines as well as entering any initial value text to appear inside the field when the page loads and setting the wrap preferences, as described in the preceding section.

Hidden fields

For times when you need to hide information from the site visitor while providing information about the form to the server during form processing, or for when you want to store information entered by a user, add hidden fields to your form. For example, you can use a hidden field to specify an e-mail address or subject with an input name and value such as the following:

```
<input name="recipient" type="hidden" id="recipient" value="contact@example.com">
<input name="subject" type="hidden" id="subject" value="usercomments">
```

To insert a hidden field in your form, open your document and follow these steps:

Book II
Chapter 7

Building Fabulous
Forms

1. **Place your cursor inside the form area on your page where you want to insert a hidden field.**

   Hidden fields are typically placed right after the opening `<form>` tag.

   If you haven't yet created a form, see the earlier section, "Creating a Fabulous HTML Form."

2. **Choose Insert⇨Form⇨Hidden Field.**

   You can also click the Hidden Field button on the Forms tab of the Insert bar.

   The Properties inspector, shown in Figure 7-5, shows the properties for the hidden field.

Figure 7-5: Use the Properties inspector to set the name and value of hidden fields.

3. **In the HiddenField box in the Properties inspector, enter a name for the field.**

The name labels the hidden field, such as Redirect, Recipient, Subject, or Title.

4. **In the Value field, enter a sentence, e-mail address, URL, or other information.**

The following are examples of hidden fields, including type (hidden) name, and value:

```
<input type="hidden" name="Redirect" value="http://www.example.com/
    thankyou.html">
<input type="hidden" name="Recipient" value="info@example.com">
<input type="hidden" name="Subject" value="Brochure Request">
```

Check boxes

Check box fields allow users to specify multiple responses when presented with a single question. You can add as many check boxes to the form as you want to support the question being asked. Figure 7-6 shows an example with four check boxes.

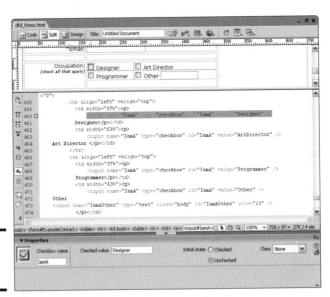

Figure 7-6: Four check boxes.

To insert a check box in your form, follow these steps:

1. **Place your cursor inside the form area on your page where you want to insert a check box.**

If you haven't yet created a form, see the earlier section, "Creating a Fabulous HTML Form."

2. Choose Insert⇨Form⇨Checkbox.

You can also click the Checkbox button on the Forms tab of the Insert bar.

3. In the Properties inspector, enter a name for the check box in the Checkbox Name field and a value in the Checked Value field.

When listing multiple check boxes, be sure to give each check box a unique name to identify it within the form. The name must not have any spaces or special characters in it, but the checked value can contain letters, numbers, and spaces, as in the following:

```
<input name="chkGrapes" type="checkbox" value="Likes grapes" checked=
    "checked"> Grapes
<input name="chkBanana" type="checkbox" value="Likes bananas" checked=
    "checked"> Bananas
<input name="chkApple" type="checkbox" value="Likes apples"> Apples
```

4. Select the appropriate option button to set the initial state of the check box to either checked or unchecked.

5. Repeat Steps 2 through 4 to insert additional check boxes.

Radio buttons

Radio button fields allow users to specify either/or choices when presented with a question. You can have as many radio buttons as you want for any question, but the user can only select one answer.

Inserting radio buttons one at a time

To insert a radio button in your form, follow these steps:

1. Place your cursor inside the form area on your page where you want to insert a radio button.

If you haven't yet created a form, see the earlier section, "Creating a Fabulous HTML Form."

2. Choose Insert⇨Form⇨Radio Button.

You can also click the Radio Button button on the Forms tab of the Insert bar.

3. In the Properties inspector, enter a name for the radio button in the Radio Button field and enter a value in the Checked Value field.

A group of radio buttons must have the same name but different values to make the selection mutually exclusive. Therefore, provide the same name to each radio button in your list and add a word in the Checked Value field to match the question being asked. You should also set one of the radio button's initial state value to checked. For instance, if asking people to choose their preference for beef, chicken, or vegetarian, the name for each radio button would be `meal` and the value for each is equal to the individual meal choice, and if they fail to make a selection on their own, they'll get beef, as in the following example:

```
<input type="radio" name="meal" value="beef" checked="checked">
<input type="radio" name="meal" value="chicken">
<input type="radio" name="meal" value="vegetarian">
```

Figure 7-7 shows how to configure the radio buttons using the Properties inspector.

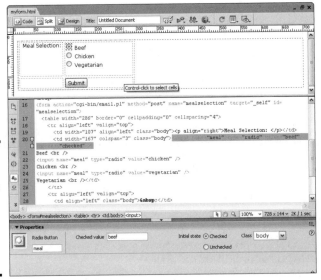

Figure 7-7: Set radio button name and value attributes with the Properties inspector.

4. **Select an option to set the initial state of the radio button to checked or unchecked.**

   The radio button doesn't actually show a check mark; rather it displays with a small dot in the center to indicate that it's been *checked* (selected).

5. **Repeat Steps 2 through 4 to insert additional radio buttons.**

   Make sure that radio buttons are always used in sets of two or more. Then be sure to only check one radio button as checked by default; if

you specify more than one button with a checked value, it can create
problems with data collection.

Inserting a group of radio buttons

The Radio Group button launches a helpful dialog box to help build an entire
radio group all at once rather than creating a group of buttons one button at
a time. All the same rules apply to radio groups as to radio buttons with the
added benefit of having Dreamweaver write `<label>` tags for you to identify
the text associated with the radio button. When you launch the Radio Group
dialog box, simply enter labels and values for each button, name the group,
and select a layout type.

To insert a radio group in your form, follow these steps:

1. **Place your cursor inside the form area on your page where you want
to insert a radio group.**

If you haven't yet created a form, see the earlier section, "Creating a
Fabulous HTML Form."

2. **Choose Insert➪Form➪Radio Group.**

You can also click the Radio Group button on the Forms tab of the
Insert bar.

The Radio Group dialog box opens (see Figure 7-8).

Figure 7-8:
Create a
group of
radio
buttons all
at once.

3. **In the Radio Group dialog box, enter a name for the radio button
Group.**

The group name identifies all the buttons as belonging to the same
group and adds the same `name` attribute (such as `name="dessert"`)
to each button.

4. **In the Label column, type a label for each radio button in the group.**

   Each item in the list represents a radio button in the radio group.

   To add new buttons, click the plus (+) button. To remove any buttons, select the item to be removed from the list and click the minus (–) button.

   To reorder the buttons listed in the group, select a button from the list and click the up or down arrows.

5. **In the Value column, type a checked value for each radio button in the group.**

   The checked value represents the value that is submitted as the selected choice for this radio group.

6. **Choose Line Breaks or Table as the layout option for the radio group.**

   The buttons can be separated by line breaks or by table cells.

7. **Click OK to insert the radio group on the page.**

8. **Select one of the buttons in the group to be checked by default by entering the initial state as checked in the Properties inspector.**

   Use the Properties inspector to make further adjustments to the radio buttons in the group.

Lists and menus

The List/Menu form object creates both list and menu type form fields. Use this object to provide a list or menu that allows users to make a selection, such as a state or country.

To insert a list or menu in your form, follow these steps:

1. **Place your cursor inside the form area on your page where you want to insert a List/Menu object.**

   If you haven't yet created a form, see the earlier section, "Creating a Fabulous HTML Form."

2. **Choose Insert⇨Form⇨List/Menu.**

   You can also click the List/Menu button on the Forms tab of the Insert bar.

3. **Click the List Values button in the Properties inspector.**

   The List Values dialog box opens. You use this dialog box to add labels and values to your list or menu (see Figure 7-9).

Book II
Chapter 7

Building Fabulous
Forms

Figure 7-9:
Add labels
and values
to lists and
menus.

- **Item Label:** This text appears as a selection in the list.

  To add new list items, click the plus (+) button. To remove any items from the list, select the item to be removed and click the minus (–) button. To sort items, select an item from the list and click the up or down arrow.

- **Value:** This value gets returned with the collected data when the item is selected, as in CA for California.

  After you add all the items to your list, click OK to close the List Values dialog box.

4. **With the list/menu object selected, select a type in the Properties inspector.**

   Choose List to make a drop-down list or Menu to make a box that displays the options to choose from.

5. **In the Height box (for List type only), enter a number to represent the number of lines to be displayed in the list.**

   If the contents of the box exceed the box height, scroll bars appear.

6. **(Optional) Click the Allow Multiple Selections option to allow users to Shift-click for making multiple selections from the list or menu.**

7. **Select any item in the list/menu to display as the initial item, such as** *Select a State.*

Jump menus

Use jump menus to create a list of items that a visitor can select from, and once selected tell the browser to jump to another page or URL. Jump menus automatically add the necessary JavaScript behaviors required to instruct the browser to go to another page. This type of menu can be a useful tool for quick navigation on a Web site.

To find out how to set up a jump menu, see Book IV, Chapter 2.

Image fields

The Image Field option inserts an image into the form, for times you may prefer to use your own graphic for a Submit button or other form input field.

Images in forms become clickable Submit buttons by default, unless you apply a different JavaScript to the image.

To add an image field to your form, follow these steps:

1. Place your cursor inside the form area on your page where you want to insert an image field.

If you haven't yet created a form, see the earlier section, "Creating a Fabulous HTML Form."

2. Choose Insert➪Form➪Image Field.

You can also click the Image Field button on the Forms tab of the Insert bar.

The Select Image Source dialog box appears.

3. Browse to and select the image you want to add to the form.

If you enabled Accessibility features, the Input Tag Accessibility Attributes dialog box opens. Complete the dialog box and click OK to insert the image or press Cancel to insert the field without accessibility attributes.

The image is inserted onto your page, as shown in Figure 7-10.

4. In the Alt field in the Properties inspector, enter Alternate text for the image.

Typically, though not required, the text in the Alt field mirrors the text on the button graphic.

5. (Optional) From the Align drop-down list, select an alignment option for the graphic.

Alignment options include Default, Top, Middle, Bottom, Left, and Right.

Figure 7-10:
With the
Image Field
form object,
you can use
your own
graphics.

6. **(Optional) From the Class drop-down list, choose a CSS to apply to the form object.**

   For example, you may have created a custom CSS for all your text input fields. Choose the style from the menu to apply it.

7. **In the ImageField field, enter Submit or Reset to use the image as a Submit or Reset button.**

   Alternatively, you can give your button a unique name to use the button with a JavaScript behavior. For example, you can create a button that, when a visitor presses it, runs a script to launch a pop-up window.

File upload fields

Add a file field to your form when you want to allow visitors to search for a file on their own computers and upload it to the server. When adding a file field, Dreamweaver inserts a text field with a Browse button next to it.

To use a file field on a Web page, you must make sure your server has a server-side script that can accept this type of data submission. File fields require the POST method for transmitting files from the browser to the server. Select enctype="multipart/form-data" as the encryption type for the form. The data is posted to the address in the form's action field; you can use a regular HTTP URL as the value so long as your application has the right server permissions to be able to write files accepted this way.

Be sure to test this feature in your target browsers before publishing the page, as the file field displays very differently in different browsers: Safari, Internet Explorer, and Firefox all have very unique ideas about how to handle this field, including how much space they take up and what words are displayed.

To insert a file field in your form, follow these steps:

1. **Place your cursor inside the form area on your page where you want to insert a file field.**

   If you haven't yet created a form, see the earlier section, "Creating a Fabulous HTML Form."

2. **Choose Insert➪Form➪File Field.**

   You can also click the File Field button on the Forms tab of the Insert bar.

   The file field is inserted onto the page.

3. **In the Properties inspector, enter the following attributes:**

   - **FileField Name:** Enter the name for the file field.

   - **Char Width:** Enter a number of characters to set the width of the file field.

   - **Max Chars:** Enter the maximum number of characters that a visitor can enter into the file field.

   - **Class:** If you've created a custom CSS to format this field, select it by name from the Class drop-down list.

Buttons

Add a form button to your form for visitors to click when they're ready to submit data or trigger other form processing operations. Typical form buttons are labeled as Submit, Reset, or Send, but you can create buttons with other labels that perform other tasks such as calculating shipping charges based on a user's geographical zone.

To create a button, follow these steps:

1. **Place your cursor inside the form area on your page where you want to insert a form button.**

   If you haven't yet created a form, see the earlier section, "Creating a Fabulous HTML Form."

2. **Choose Insert➪Form➪Button.**

   You can also click the Button button on the Forms tab of the Insert bar.

The Properties inspector shows the properties for the button, as shown in Figure 7-11.

Book II
Chapter 7

Building Fabulous
Forms

Figure 7-11: Add a button to your form so visitors can submit data or trigger other operations.

3. **In the Button Name field in the Properties inspector, enter a name for your button.**

4. **In the Value field, enter the text to appear on the button face.**

   For instance, if you want a button that says Join Mailing List, type **Join Mailing List**.

5. **(Optional) From the Class drop-down list, select a CSS to apply to the button.**

6. **Choose an action from the Action field:**

   • **Submit:** This default form button type submits the collected data to a script or processing application on the server. Submit buttons can have any label as long as the Action type in the Properties inspector is set to Submit.

   • **Reset:** A Reset form button clears the form fields by returning the form to its original state. You can label reset buttons with any text. Choose the Action type in the Properties inspector to reset the form.

   • **None:** A third option creates a button with customized text that you can attach a behavior to, such as a Go button for a jump menu.

Select None as the Action type in the Properties inspector and apply a JavaScript behavior using the Behaviors panel (see Book IV, Chapter 2 for more about behaviors).

Label tags

The `<label>` tag is used for enhancing accessibility attributes. When the `<label>` tag wraps around another form item, not only can screen-reader software read the label, but a *focus rectangle* surrounds both the label and form field in some browsers, which allows the user to click anywhere inside the text and form field area to select it. This grouping is especially helpful when using radio buttons and check boxes!

If you label your objects without the `<label>` tags, the label isn't associated with the form object, as in the following sample code:

```
<input name="Dessert" type="radio" value="Apple" checked="checked" />Apple
    Crumble
```

With the `<label>` tags, however, the label is associated with the form object, as in the following:

```
<label><input name="Dessert" type="radio" value="Apple" checked="checked" />Apple
    Crumble</label>
```

If you've enabled Accessibility preferences, the Input Tag Accessibility Attributes dialog box automatically appears any time you insert a form object on your page. There you can wrap your object with the `<label>` tag.

To insert a `<label>` tag in your form after you add objects to your form, follow these steps:

1. **Place your cursor inside the form area on your page where you want to insert a `<label>` tag.**

   If you haven't yet created a form, see the earlier section, "Creating a Fabulous HTML Form."

2. **Choose Insert➪Form➪Label Field.**

   You can also click the Label Field button on the Forms tab of the Insert bar.

   The `<label>` tag is inserted into your page code, as shown in Figure 7-12.

If you're adding a `<label>` tag to an existing form object, such as a check box or radio button, check the code to ensure that the label for the form object sits between the opening and closing `<label>` tags.

Figure 7-12:
Use the
`<label>`
tag to group
form objects
and their
labels
together.

Fieldset tags

A `<fieldset>` tag is used as a container for other form objects. Use fieldsets to
define multiple fields into logical groups within the form. For instance, one fieldset may include text input fields for name and e-mail information, and another
fieldset may include username and password information (see Figure 7-13).

Figure 7-13:
Use the
`<field
set>` tag to
group form
objects
together.

You can use the `<legend>` tag with the `<fieldset>` tag to label each field set, as in the following example:

```
<form method="post" action="...">
<fieldset>
<h2>
  <legend>Contact Information</legend>
</h2>
<label>
Name:
<input name="name" type="text" id="name" />
</label>
<br />
<label>Email:
<input name="email" type="text" id="email" />
</label>
</fieldset></form>
```

These tags create a very interesting look in a browser. Figure 7-14 shows how the example appears with Internet Explorer on a PC.

Figure 7-14:
The
`<field
set>` and
`<legend>`
tags format
form data in
a unique
way.

To insert `<fieldset>` and `<legend>` tags, follow these steps:

1. **Open a file containing a form in which you want to insert `<fieldset>` and `<legend>` tags.**

If you haven't yet created a form, see the earlier section, "Creating a Fabulous HTML Form."

2. **Select all the form elements that you want to group inside the `<fieldset>` tags.**

3. **Choose Insert➪Form➪Fieldset.**

   You can also click the Fieldset button on the Forms tab of the Insert bar.

   The Fieldset dialog box opens.

4. **In the Fieldset dialog box, enter a name for the legend and click OK.**

   The legend is like a heading for the objects grouped inside the `<fieldset>` tags.

   Dreamweaver wraps the selected content with `<fieldset>` and `<legend>` tags. Once applied to your code, you can style the content with CSS.

Validating a Form with JavaScript

If you've ever filled out a form and gotten a pop-up message back from your browser that says you filled out the form incorrectly or that you missed entering data in a field, you've witnessed form validation in action. Validation can be performed dynamically with PHP, ASP, JSP, or ColdFusion code. However, for most non-dynamic sites, a simple JavaScript Validate Form action does the trick.

The Validate Form action cross-checks all the fields against the validation rules you specify to ensure that the user entered the data correctly. This way, you can check the form on the client side for completion and accuracy before the server collects the data.

You can attach validation events to as many fields in the form as you want. A couple of validation events are

✦ **onBlur:** Validates individual fields as the form is being completed

✦ **onSubmit:** Reviews the entire form input data all at once

To validate a form with the Validate Form action, follow these steps:

1. **To validate the entire form, select the form's `<form>` tag, or to validate an individual field, select that form object.**

2. **Open the Behaviors panel by choosing Window➪Behaviors.**

3. **Click the plus (+) button in the Behaviors panel and then choose Validate Form from the Add Behavior pop-up menu.**

   The Validate Form dialog box opens, as shown in Figure 7-15, showing a list of all the named fields in your form.

Figure 7-15:
The Validate
Form dialog
box.

4. **Select a form input field from the Named Fields listing, and then choose a setting for it:**

   - **Value Required:** Enable this option when the field must contain data of some kind, rather than stay blank.

   - **Accept Anything:** If this option is selected, the selected field must also be set to Required so that a user can input any type of data into the form field.

   - **Accept Email Address:** Select this option to have the validation script verify that the field contains the @ symbol.

   - **Accept Number:** Select this option to have the validation script check that this field contains numbers only.

   - **Accept Number From/To:** When this option is selected, you can specify a range for acceptable numbers.

   When validating the entire form, you must set a value and accept option for each field in the form.

5. **Repeat Step 4 for every form imput field in your form.**

6. **Click OK.**

   Dreamweaver adds the Form Validation JavaScript code to the `<form>` and `<head>` tags. When validating an entire form, the `onSubmit` validation event automatically displays next to the Validate Form Events menu in the Behaviors panel. If validating only a single field, the default validation event is either `onBlur` or `onChange`.

Book III

Working Like the Pros

The 5th Wave   By Rich Tennant

"What you want to do is balance the image of the pick-up truck sittin' behind your home page, with a busted washing machine in the foreground."

Contents at a Glance

Chapter 1: Looking Good with Cascading Style Sheets (CSS)

In This Chapter

✔ Understanding Cascading Style Sheets

✔ Creating internal and external style sheets

✔ Creating new CSS styles

✔ Editing, renaming, and deleting styles

✔ Attaching Design Time Sheets

Cascading Style Sheets (CSS) are a recommended standard from the World Wide Web Consortium (W3C) to provide Web designers with more control over the layout and appearance of HTML and XML files. Cascading Style Sheets perform a similar function as formatted text in a word processor. You can set default formatting for particular styles such as paragraphs and headings. You can also create your own custom styles for text, graphics, tables, and more, plus create styles that control the format and position of block-level assets like margins and borders.

With CSS you can control

✦ Fonts, font sizes, font styles, and font colors

✦ Line spacing and letter spacing

✦ Margins, indenting, and outdenting

✦ Background images and colors

✦ List and link formatting

Dreamweaver 8 formats text with Cascading Style Sheets (CSS) as the default text styling method (instead of HTML tags), as CSS has been implemented in all modern browsers including Microsoft Internet Explorer, Netscape Navigator, Safari, Firefox, Opera, and Mozilla.

You'll enjoy these benefits with CSS:

✦ Style sheets separate content from the style and formatting information.

✦ Style sheets simplify HTML code and file size (because all the styling information is contained in one location — either the head of the file or in an external style sheet — rather than inline with the text) without compromising the structure of the content.

✦ Style sheets give you more control over the presentation of your pages.

✦ Using style sheets means your HTML files have faster download times across multiple browsers.

✦ You have a centralized location for the Web site design, so you can change an entire site's look by changing just one file.

✦ Site visitors with disabilities have better access to CSS pages.

✦ Older browsers can still view pages.

This chapter presents an overview of Cascading Style Sheets, including the difference between internal, external, and inline style sheets. You discover the three general types of styles and how to create, edit, rename, and delete your own CSS using the Dreamweaver CSS Styles panel. You also find a full explanation of the categories of the CSS Rule Definition dialog box, plus when and how to use Design Time CSS.

Understanding Cascading Style Sheets (CSS)

In the early days of the Internet, how the content looked was largely the work of specialized formatting tags used inside the HTML code, such as `<font face="Arial" size="2">`, which would instruct a browser to display the text in a specific font (Arial) and size (2). With the advent of HTML 4 in late 1997, however — which began supporting Cascading Style Sheets and scripting, among other great enhancements — most formatting can now be written with style sheets, either inside the HTML document itself or outside the document in an external style sheet file.

Cascading Style Sheets (CSS) separate form from content by taking control over the appearance of the text through specification of font style, font size, text color, and alignment, as well as positioning and additional formatting attributes for other elements such as images, tables, and forms. HTML can now primarily be used for organizing content while the external CSS typically has all the formatting and positioning instructions.

One of the great benefits of separating form from content with style sheets is that when you need to make formatting changes, rather than modifying the style attributes inside the HTML code for every page, you need to adjust only the style sheet.

For example, a sentence using the old `<font>` tag with face, size, and color attributes looks like this:

```
<p><font="Verdana, Arial, Helvetica" size="2" color="#990000">Do an Internet
    search to find the best restaurants in your neighborhood.</font></p>
```

In comparison, using a style sheet that defines a custom style called `.restaurants` with attributes of Verdana, 12px, #990000 looks like this:

```
<style type="text/css">
<!--
.restaurants {
    font-family: Verdana, Arial, Helvetica, sans-serif;
    font-size: 12px;
    color: #990000;
}
-->
</style>
```

the same sentence simply looks like this:

```
<p class="restaurants">Do an Internet search to find the best restaurants in your
    neighborhood.</p>
```

When you place the CSS in an external file, you can simply upload the revised CSS to the hosting server to change the look of your entire site. By contrast, HTML styles require that you change all the pages on a site before uploading to the server.

Another great feature about CSS is that style sheets allow you to somewhat control what site visitors see when they visit your page regardless of the platform they are browsing in. Like the old tags, styles override default browser font face and font size settings, but in a much cleaner way.

Exploring Different Style Sheet Types

Dreamweaver 8 uses CSS, rather than HTML tags, as the default method for editing text. If you like, you can still use HTML tags for styling your text by unchecking the Use CSS Instead of HTML Tags box in the Editing Options area of the General category in the Preferences dialog box. Choose Edit⇨ Preferences (Windows) or Dreamweaver⇨Edit (Mac) to get to the Preferences dialog box. The trend, however, is to use CSS.

You can place your style sheet information in three different locations, relative to the HTML code that allow it to work properly:

✦ **Inside the document.** You can create an internal style sheet through the CSS Styles panel and automatically add styles inside the `<head>` tags of the document through the Properties inspector.

✦ **Outside the file in a separate CSS file.** You can create an external style sheet through the CSS Styles panel.

✦ **Inline, right next to the HTML code that is being styled.** You need to know the proper syntax to add inline CSS so you can manually type the style code in the HTML.

You can use all three style sheet types (internal, external, and inline) in combination with one another. For instance, you may have some internal styles and an external style sheet linked to the same document, plus an inline style or two throughout the code. You may even use multiple style sheets on a page or in an entire site, if it suits your needs. Just remember that whatever styles are closest to the content typically (though not always) take precedence over styles that are farther away.

Internal styles

After adding text to a Web document, you can apply certain styling attributes to your text with the Properties inspector. The text properties are, to some extent, divided into two types: Type A adds HTML markup to your code; Type B adds internal style sheet markup to the head area of your document. Figure 1-1 shows which attributes on the Text Properties inspector are Type A and which are Type B.

Figure 1-1:
Create automatic internal styles for styling selected content.

These Properties inspector settings add formatting tags to the HTML code (Type A):

Bold (Strong)	Italic (Em)
List/Bullet	Align (Left/Center/Right/Justified)
List Item	Indent/Outdent
Link	Target

These Properties inspector settings add internal style sheets to your page (Type B):

Format	Font
Style	Size
Color	Bg Color

Any time you use the Type B properties, Dreamweaver automatically writes the style sheet code to your HTML, right before the closing `<head>` tag of the page. For example, if you select the Arial font from the Font drop-down list in the Properties inspector, the following style sheet code is added to your HTML:

```
<style type="text/css">
<!--
.style1 {font-family: Arial, Helvetica, sans-serif}
-->
</style>
```

The style sheet markup begins and ends with the `<style>` tag. Nested between those are opening and closing comment tags (`<!--` and `-->`), which *comment out* (hide) the style attributes so that older browsers don't display them as text in the body of the page. Comment tags are used to insert text in your code that isn't displayed in a browser. Between the comment tags is where the style attributes go.

Styles you apply with the Properties inspector are automatically given unique names, such as `.style1` and `.style2`. Between the comment tags, you can list as many styles as you need to style the page. Each time you style the text with the Properties inspector, a new custom style is created and added to the internal style sheet. After new custom styles are added to the internal style sheet, the Style menu in the Properties inspector (refer to Figure 1-1) displays those styles by name and preview.

Because the style sheet code sits inside the page, it only styles the contents on that page. To use the same style sheet for multiple pages on a Web site, you must create an external style sheet, described next.

External styles

External styles refer to style descriptions saved in a separate, external file, often with the `.css` file extension. One exception for using a different file extension, for example, is when PHP code is used. Then as long as the link to the external file contains the `type="text/css"` attribute, the filename for the style sheet data could have a `.php` extension, as in the following:

```
<link rel="StyleSheet" href="abc_styles.php" type="text/css" />
```

External style sheets are often named after the company or project they're used with, or with some acronym or abbreviation relative to the Web site, such as `monkey.css` for a site about monkeys.

The external style sheet needs to link to the HTML pages using a special line of code. When the link is present and the page is displayed in a browser window, the browser interprets and displays the page's contents using the external style sheet information. You place the link to the external style sheet inside the `<head>` tag of the document with the `href` attribute referencing the location and filename of the CSS, as in this example:

```
<link href="monkey.css" rel="stylesheet" type="text/css" />
```

External style sheet styles use the same syntax and formatting as internal style sheets to define styles with one tiny exception: The styles in an external style sheet do not need to be surrounded by the `<style>` and `<!--comment-->` tags that internal styles require. Furthermore — and this is what makes external style sheets so powerful — external style sheets are best when working with a multipage Web site, because a single external style sheet can control the formatting for all the pages on the site. For example, if you need to change the style attributes of all the Heading 1s sitewide, you only need to modify the one external style sheet to make all the pages conform to the new style definitions!

Inline styles

You may need to add an inline style to a document rather than using internal or external style sheets. For example, if you're creating an HTML e-mail, you might use an inline style because many e-mail programs prefer to interpret HTML tags over CSS for formatting text. When the style data is inline with the content, a visitor can also read the mail offline and view it styled as you intended.

Inline style descriptions are written inside the code, surrounding the selected text, oftentimes appending whatever existing tag is closest to the content to be styled, or by adding a `<span>` tag with the `style` attribute, as in the following two examples:

```
<p style="font-size: 12px; color: #990000;">Inline styles are "in line" with the
    text.</p>
<p>This example uses the span tag to selectively apply a <span style="font-size:
    12px; color: #990000;">custom style</span> to selected text.</p>
```

Working with the CSS Styles Panel

Use the CSS Styles panel to create internal and external styles. If it's not visible, open the panel by choosing Window⇨CSS. We recommend using the CSS Styles panel instead of the Properties inspector for creating and editing all your CSS.

The Dreamweaver 8 CSS Styles panel has many enhancements from previous versions, including multiple panes. Resize panes by clicking and dragging a pane up or down until it's the size you want.

Two buttons appear at the top of the panel: All and Current, as shown in Figure 1-2, which display different views of the CSS Styles panel. The following sections discuss these views in detail.

All mode   Current mode

Figure 1-2:
The CSS
Styles
panel.

**Book III
Chapter 1**

**Looking Good with
Cascading Style
Sheets (CSS)**

All mode

Click the All button and the CSS Styles panel splits into two parts:

✦ **All Rules:** The top pane displays a list of all the styles attached to, or contained inside of, the currently selected open document.

✦ **Properties:** Select a style in the top pane, and the bottom pane displays its specific attributes. You can quickly make a change to an existing property or add more properties by clicking the Add Property link.

Current mode

Click the Current button and the CSS Styles panel divides into three panes:

✦ **Summary for Selection:** The top pane shows an attributes summary of the currently selected style. Properties display in order of specificity. Class styles have higher specificity than tag selectors.

✦ **Rules:** The second pane displays the style name and the tag in the code the selected style is applied to, such as the <p> tag. You can toggle this area to display data in two views by clicking the buttons on the top-right edge of the section's title bar. The left About button displays location and name information about a selected property while the right Rules button shows cascading style rules for the selected tag.

✦ **Properties:** The bottom pane displays the attributes of the selected style in an editable format. Make a change to a property or add more properties by clicking the Add Property link.

CSS Styles panel viewing buttons

The bottom edge of the CSS Styles panel (as shown in Figure 1-3) displays buttons that are shared by both All and Current views and allow you to select from different viewing and editing options.

Figure 1-3:
These buttons display viewing and editing options.

Attach Style Sheet

Show List View   Edit Style Sheet

Delete CSS Rule

Show Category View   New CSS Rule

Show Only Set Properties

The panel's bottom right edge displays four buttons:

✦ **Attach Style Sheet** launches the Link External Style Sheet dialog box to select an external style sheet to link to or import to the current file.

✦ **New CSS Rule** opens the New CSS Rule dialog box for naming, choosing a selector type, and specifying the location for the new style.

✦ **Edit Style Sheet** opens the CSS Rule definition dialog box when a style is selected in the CSS Styles panel.

✦ **Delete CSS Rule** permanently removes a selected rule from the CSS Styles panel, as well as any formatting from elements to which it was applied. It doesn't, however, delete references to that style.

The panel's bottom left edge displays three buttons that change the listing view for the properties:

✦ **Show Category View** splits CSS properties into nine categories: Font, Background, Block, Border, Box, List, Positioning, Extensions, and Tables, Content, Quotes. Each category's properties are displayed in expandable list format. You can expand and collapse the list by clicking the plus (+) or minus (−) button next to the category name. Properties in each category are listed alphabetically with set properties sorted on top in blue text.

✦ **Show List View** shows CSS properties in descending alphabetical order with set properties in blue text at the top of the list.

✦ **Show Only Set Properties** shows only set properties. This is the default view.

In all the CSS Styles panel views, any set properties display in blue text while irrelevant properties display with a red strikethrough line. In addition, irrelevant rules contain explanatory pop-up messages that you can see when you hover your mouse over the rule.

Looking at What Styles You Can Create

Cascading Style Sheet rules are written in two-part syntax consisting of the selector and the declaration:

✦ The *selector* is the name of the style, which could be a tag like <p> or <h1>, or a custom name, such as .tableheader.

✦ The *declaration* specifies all the style's elements, such as font face, size, color, and so on.

Here's an example of a CSS rule where p is the selector and everything inside the curly brackets ({}) is the declaration:

```
p {
font-family: Verdana, Arial, Helvetica, sans-serif;
font-size: 12px;
color: #993300;
}
```

Notice that the declarations themselves have two parts: the property (such as color) and the value (such as #993300). In the rule for p in the preceding example, a style has been defined for all <p> tags, meaning that all content in the document between the opening and closing <p> tags displays as Verdana, 12px, and #993300 (which is the hexadecimal code for a deep brick red color). (To find out more about hex colors, see Book II, Chapter 2.)

The *cascading* part of Cascading Style Sheets refers to the capability of adding multiple style declarations to the same rule as well as applying multiple rules to the same elements. For instance, you can have one rule define the style of text and another rule define the margin and line spacing around it. In a greater sense, however, the term refers to the ability to use multiple style sheets and multiple style inheritances in a cascading way that determines which styles take precedence over the others. To find out more about

**Book III
Chapter 1**

**Looking Good with
Cascading Style
Sheets (CSS)**

CSS cascading rules, see the About.com article on CSS types at `http://webdesign.about.com/od/css/f/blcssfaqcascade.htm`.

In addition to hand coding, Dreamweaver provides you with two different ways to create CSS styles for your documents:

✦ The first way automatically adds internal style sheets to your page when styling content using the Properties inspector.

✦ The second way, using the CSS panel (as described in the section "Adding a Style to a New or Existing Style Sheet") lets you add internal or external styles to your files.

Before you begin creating your styles, you need to be familiar with the different style types. You can create three general types of styles using the CSS panel: Custom styles, Tag redefines, and Advanced CSS selectors. Each type modifies different parts of the HTML, as described in the following sections.

Custom styles (Class)

If you want to selectively style content, use custom styles. For instance, in the sentence, "When collecting seashells, remember to bring a bucket or other container with you," you could create a custom style for the word *seashells*. That custom style might look something like this:

```
.seashells {
    font-family: Verdana, Arial, Helvetica, sans-serif;
    font-size: 12px;
    color: #3366CC;
    font-style: italic;
}
```

Custom style names, whether placed on internal or external style sheets, must have a period (.) before the style name to display properly in a browser window. Dreamweaver lists, in preview form, all custom styles in the Styles or Class drop-down lists in the Properties inspector.

To apply the custom style to a document, select the content in Design view, and select the custom style from the Styles or Class drop-down lists in the Properties inspector. Dreamweaver modifies the text by adding the <span> tag with the designated `class` attribute as the following example shows:

```
<p>When collecting <span class="seashells">seashells</span> remember to bring a
    bucket or other container with you.</p>
```

Figure 1-4 shows how this sentence looks in Design and Code views.

Book III
Chapter 1

Looking Good with
Cascading Style
Sheets (CSS)

Figure 1-4:
Selectively
apply
custom
styles to
content on
your page
with the
`<span>`
tag.

CSS tag redefines

Use tag redefine CSS styles, created with the CSS Styles panel, to modify the preformatted look of existing HTML tags, such as the `<p>`, `<h1>`, and `<td>` tags. For example, the Heading 1 tag (`<h1>`) is preformatted to be large and bold, using whatever font styles the browser's default H1 setting are set to display it in. By redefining the tag in the CSS, you can force content styled with the `<h1>` tag to display with your chosen style attributes, such as 36 pixels, Verdana, navy blue, and bold:

```
h1 {
    font-family: Verdana, Arial, Helvetica, sans-serif;
    font-size: 36px;
    color: #000033;
    font-weight: bold;
}
```

Whatever properties or tags you don't redefine in the CSS, however, remain set at the browser defaults.

Advanced: IDs and CSS selectors

Advanced selectors are like the muscles of CSS where you can create some really amazing layout and formatting styles. The only drawback is that advanced CSS can seem a bit complicated for the beginner. The W3C (www. w3.org/TR/REC-CSS1) has technical definitions of all the things you can achieve with CSS and advanced selectors, but if you're new to CSS, these instructions may be difficult to understand. For a more basic breakdown, try reading the Advanced Selectors article by Ross Shannon on the HTMLSource Web site at www.yourhtmlsource.com/stylesheets/advancedselectors. html.

The most common use of the Advanced selector type is to modify the color of links. The default link color for browsers is royal blue, and the default visited link color is purple. If those colors don't blend well with the colors of your Web site, create custom link colors with the Advanced style type.

In addition to changing the link and visited link colors, style sheets allow you to add two additional link states to your links:

◆ The hover state, for when you mouse over the link.

◆ The active state, for when you actually click the link.

The order in which you create these link states is important. Create the normal link state first, then the visited state, and then the hover and active states. A different order may cause the links to not work properly. If you have trouble remembering the order, try using the mnemonic "LoVe HAte" for Link, Visited, Hover, Active.

When added to a style sheet, the following code changes the link color for each of the states:

```
a:link {
    color: #990000;
}
a:visited {
    color: #FF0000;
}
a:hover {
    color: #6600CC;
}
a:active {
    color: #000000;
}
```

Use any hexadecimal color needed to match your design. In addition to the text color, you can also modify the text decoration (the type of underline attribute the link has), background color (behind the text), and other style attributes in the CSS Styles panel.

You can also use the Advanced selector type for creating styles for combinations of tags and tags with specific id attributes. Tag combinations are for times when you need to create a style that you'll apply to multiple tags, such as the <body>, <th>, and <td> tags:

```
body,th,td {
    margin: 0px;
    padding: 0px;
    font-family: Verdana, Arial, Helvetica, sans-serif;
    font-size: 10px;
    color: #99FFFF;
    font-weight: bold;
}
```

When using layers or when you want to apply a style to a tag's `id`, use the Advanced selector to create special styles using the #*n* syntax, where *n* is equal to the tag's `id`, as in this example that would automatically apply to a layer on the page with an `id` of `footer`:

```
#footer {
    background-image: url(images/background.gif);
    background-repeat: repeat-x;
    background-position: left top;
    background-color: #CCCCFF;
    height: 10px;
    width: 100%;
    position: absolute;
    z-index: auto;
    left: 0px;
    right: auto;
    bottom: auto;
}
```

Other great resources for finding more about CSS and advanced selectors include the following:

```
www.w3schools.com/css/
http://glish.com/css/
www.csszengarden.com/
www.meyerweb.com/eric/css/
www.htmlhelp.com/reference/css/
www.bluerobot.com/web/layouts/
```

Adding a Style to a New or Existing Style Sheet

To create an internal or external style sheet, you start by defining a style. You can create a custom style, tag redefine, or advanced style (all of which are described in the preceding section) using the CSS Styles panel.

Open your HTML document and follow these steps to add a style to a new or existing style sheet:

1. **Click the New CSS Rule button at the bottom of the CSS Styles panel.**

You can also choose Text⇨CSS Styles⇨New.

The New CSS Rule dialog box opens, as shown in Figure 1-5.

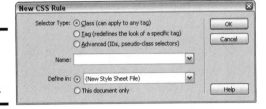

Figure 1-5:
Create a
new CSS
rule (style).

2. **Choose a selector type from the following options:**

- **Class** creates a custom style that can be applied to any content such as a word, phrase, sentence, graphic, or layer.

- **Tag** redefines the look of an existing tag, such as `<p>` and `<h1>`.

- **Advanced** selectors style links, combinations of tags, and tags with specific `id` attributes. They can also be used to create styles using combinators, attribute selectors, pseudoclasses, and pseudoelements.

3. **Depending on the selector type you choose in Step 3, do the following:**

- **Class:** Enter a name for your new style in the Name text box with a period (.) before the style name, as in **.biggreen.**

  Class names must begin with a period and can have any combination of numbers and letters but no spaces or other special characters. Fortunately, if you forget to enter the period before the style name, Dreamweaver automatically enters it for you. This, however, is not foolproof; if your style doesn't display in a browser, check the CSS to see if the period is missing before the class name.

- **Tag:** Enter an HTML tag in the Tag text box or select the tag that your style redefines from the Tag drop-down list, such as `<h1>`, `<table>`, or `<p>`.

- **Advanced:** Select a pseudoclass selector for redefining link styles from the Selector drop-down list, or type the HTML tag, the combination of tags separated by commas, or the `id` attribute of the new style in the Selector text box.

  For example, typing **#redlayer** creates a style that could apply to an asset ID, typing **body,th,td** creates a style that automatically applies to multiple tags, and typing or selecting **a:link**, **a:visited**, **a:active**, or **a:hover** creates a style that redefines one of four link state styles. If you know how to create the more advanced selector styles, type the proper syntax for that advanced selector style into the Style text box.

4. **Next to Define In, choose one of the following options to specify the location of the new style information:**

- Choose (**New Style Sheet File)** to create a new external style sheet.

- Choose **This Document Only** to create an internal style sheet.

- Choose the filename of any existing CSS file, if available, from the drop-down list.

5. **If you chose to add the new style to a new style sheet in Step 4, the Save Style Sheet File As dialog box appears. Enter a name for your new CSS and click OK to save it to the specified directory. Then skip ahead to Step 7.**

Be sure to name your new CSS with the .css file extension and save it to the root level of your currently managed site. Upon closing this dialog box, Dreamweaver automatically opens the CSS Rule Definition dialog box for defining the new style.

6. **Click OK to close the New CSS Rule dialog box.**

The CSS Rule Definition dialog box appears, as shown in Figure 1-6.

Figure 1-6:
Choose
style
attributes
when
creating a
new style.

**Book III
Chapter 1**

Looking Good with
Cascading Style
Sheets (CSS)

Depending on your selection in Step 3, the title bar in the CSS Rule Definition dialog box may display slightly different text. For instance, if adding a style to an existing CSS, the title bar reads CSS Rule Definition for *.example* in *example.css*.

7. **Enter the style information for the new style, in any combination of categories.**

When you select a category from the listing on the left, the right side of the panel changes to support that category's options. The upcoming section "Exploring the CSS Rule Definition Dialog Box" covers all the category options in this dialog box.

To preview before committing to the style settings, click the Apply button. Don't feel pressured to get the style to look exactly right during the creation process, as you can easily edit the styles at any time (see the "Editing a CSS Style" section, later in this chapter).

8. **Click OK.**

The new style is added to the style sheet and displays in the CSS Styles panel. To cancel out of the New CSS Rule dialog box without adding a style, click the Cancel button.

9. **Repeat Steps 1 through 8 to create additional styles in the same CSS.**

You can add as many styles as you want to the CSS.

Attaching a Style Sheet to Your Document

You can attach an existing style sheet to your document at any stage of development. It can be a fully realized style sheet or a blank one that you build as you style your document; for the purposes of attaching the style sheet, its contents don't matter so long as the file is created and saved in advance with the .css file extension.

If you have an existing external style sheet (perhaps a copy of one used on another project or one provided by another member of your team) or want to use one of Dreamweaver's sample style sheets, save it to the local root folder of your currently managed site or in a folder at the root level of that site. Then follow these steps:

1. **Open the CSS Styles panel and click the Attach Style Sheet button at the bottom of the panel (refer to Figure 1-3).**

The Attach External Style Sheet dialog box opens, as shown in Figure 1-7.

Figure 1-7:
Attach an external CSS to a page.

2. **In the File/URL field, enter the name of the existing style sheet or click the Browse button to navigate to and select the existing style sheet.**

Dreamweaver has several sample style sheets you can use either as-is or as a starting point for customizing your own style sheet. To use one of the existing style sheets, click the Sample Style Sheets link in the dialog box. The Sample Style Sheets dialog box opens from which you can preview and select a style sheet from the listing. Click OK and Dreamweaver instantly attaches the style sheet to your page.

3. In the Add As field, choose the Link or Import radio button.

Choose the Link option to add the CSS as an external file, where a line of link code containing the CSS file you specified gets inserted into the head of the page:

```
<link href="example.css" rel="stylesheet" type="text/css">
```

Choose the Import option to add a link to the CSS internally, in the head area of the page:

```
<style type="text/css">
<!--
@import url("example.css");
-->
</style>
```

Both options link to external CSS files; however, the second method is less reliable with older browsers than the first, so when linking, choose the Link radio button.

4. In the Media field, either select an option from the drop-down list or leave this field blank.

Media types refer to the different types of devices or media a user can view your page with — such as a screen device (like a browser), a handheld device (like a BlackBerry), or a printer. Choose a media type from the drop-down list to identify the linked CSS as being the one to use when that device is used to view the page.

To enter multiple media types at once, separate each type with a comma, as in **screen, printer, handheld**.

To find out more about CSS for media, visit the World Wide Web Consortium at `www.w3.org/TR/CSS21/media.html`.

5. Click the Preview button to see how the CSS will change the appearance of your document.

6. Click OK to attach the CSS to your document.

The CSS Styles panel displays the newly attached style sheet. Internal styles display in a list below a `<style>` tag, while external style sheets display below the CSS filename.

Applying a Custom Class Style

You can apply custom styles you've created in your internal or external style sheets to any selected asset in an open document. For example, you may want certain words in a sentence to stand out from the rest of the text or style graphics with uniform styling attributes. Before applying a custom style, create the style with the CSS Styles panel (see the preceding section).

To apply a custom style to your document, follow these steps:

1. **Select the content to be styled in either Design or Code view.**

   To assist in selecting an exact tag, select the tag in the tag selector bar at the bottom left edge of the Document window.

2. **Using the Properties inspector, select the custom style from the Style or Class drop-down list.**

   The Style or Class menu not only lists the custom styles by name, but the style names themselves display in a preview of their respective styles (as shown in Figure 1-8).

Figure 1-8:
Apply
custom
styles.

Dreamweaver styles your selection by either adding the `<span>` tag with your custom class around your selection, or by appending an existing tag with the new custom class:

```
<p>Applying <span class="special">custom</span> styles is easy!</p>
<p class="special">Applying custom styles is easy!</p>
```

To remove a custom style from a selection, select the text or object in Design view and choose None from the Style drop-down list in the Properties inspector.

Editing a CSS Style

Editing styles in the CSS Styles panel is as easy as creating a new style. Essentially you're changing the style attributes in the same dialog box you used to initially create the style in. You can use either Current or All mode to enter the style changes.

Editing in All mode

To edit a CSS style with the CSS Styles panel in All mode, open your HTML document and follow these steps:

1. Click the All button at the top of the panel.

A list of style rules used on the entire document displays, whether internal or external.

2. Select the style that needs editing.

3. Click the Edit Style Sheet button at the bottom of the panel (refer to Figure 1-3).

The CSS Rule Definition dialog box opens, identifying the style and location by name, such as CSS Rule Definition for *.example* in *example.css*.

You can also open the CSS Rule Definition dialog box by right-clicking (Windows) or Control+clicking (Mac) the style name and selecting Edit from the context menu.

4. Edit the style information as needed in any of the style categories.

The upcoming section "Exploring the CSS Rule Definition Dialog Box" covers the different options in this dialog box.

To preview before committing to the edited style settings, click the Apply button.

5. Click OK.

The edited style with its new style attributes displays in the CSS Styles panel. To cancel out of the New CSS Rule Definition dialog box without modifying the style, click the Cancel button.

Editing in Current mode

To edit a CSS style with the CSS Styles panel in Current mode, follow these steps:

1. Click the Current button at the top of the panel.

A summary of style properties for any currently selected style displays.

2. Select a text element or other asset on the page to view its style properties.

The CSS Styles panel shows the summary for the current selection including detailed information about the style location and editable style properties.

3. **To edit any of the style's properties, select a rule in the Summary pane and edit those properties directly in the Properties pane at the bottom of the panel.**

   Or you can double-click the rule in the Summary pane to enter changes in the CSS Rule Definition dialog box. This option is only available if you've enabled the Edit Using CSS Dialog setting in the CSS Styles category of Dreamweaver's Preferences.

   The upcoming section "Exploring the CSS Rule Definition Dialog Box" covers the different options in this dialog box.

   To preview before committing to the settings, click the Apply button.

4. **Click OK.**

   The edited style with its new style attributes displays in the CSS Styles panel. To cancel out of the New CSS Rule Definition dialog box without modifying the style, click the Cancel button.

You can also edit your styles by hand in Code view.

Adding properties to a CSS style

Add properties to any existing CSS style at any time by following these steps:

1. **Choose a rule in the All Rules pane in All mode or pick a property in the Summary section of Current mode.**

2. **Do one of the following:**

   - Click the Show Only Set Properties button and then click the Add Properties link in the Properties pane.

   - Click either the Show Category View or Show List View button, and fill in the new property value next to the property you want to add.

Deleting a CSS Style

Sometimes you create a style and then never use it. To help clear the CSS file of unnecessary style information — which also keeps the overall file size low — delete any unused styles from your style sheet before publishing your site.

To delete a style from a style sheet listed in the CSS Styles panel, follow these steps:

1. **Click the All button at the top of the panel.**

   A list of style rules used on the entire document displays, whether internal or external.

2. **Select the style you want to delete.**

3. **Click the Delete CSS Rule button at the bottom of the panel (refer to Figure 1-3).**

   You can also right-click (Windows) or Control+click (Mac) the style name and choose Delete from the context menu.

   If you feel comfortable doing so, you can also delete internal styles from your document or external styles from an external CSS file in Code view.

Removing styles by either method only removes the style from the CSS, not from within the HTML code. To remove the application of a removed style from HTML, use the Find and Replace dialog box to search the entire site for that style attribute. For details about using the Find and Replace dialog box to remove specified content, see Book II, Chapter 2.

Exploring the CSS Rule Definition Dialog Box

With the CSS Rule Definition dialog box, Macromedia has created a simple user interface to create, test, and apply styles. The dialog box includes several categories of style rules that you can add in any combination, including style rules for type, background, block, box, border, list, positioning, and extensions.

To use the dialog box, first select a category from the left side of the panel. Then choose styling options from the right side of the panel. The right side of the panel's options are determined by the category you select on the left.

As a general rule, when entering individual values to rules with Top, Bottom, Left, and Right fields, enter **0** or **None** for sides that should not contain values. Doing so improves the chances of different browsers rendering your styles consistently.

Type properties

Use the Type category (shown in Figure 1-9) to create specific font attributes and type styles. In addition to the font face, you can customize the font size, line height, style, decoration, and weight, among other settings.

Not all browsers support all the type properties so be sure to test the CSS styles in all your target browsers before publishing your site. This gives you the opportunity to select different style attributes for your styles if needed.

The following rules are available in the Type category:

✦ **Font:** Select a font family from the drop-down list or type the name of the font or font set you want to use. Default sets include cross-platform–compatible fonts such as "Verdana, Arial, Helvetica, Sans-serif".

Figure 1-9:
Create text
styles with
the Type
category
settings.

To create your own custom font sets, select the Edit Font List option
from the bottom of the drop-down list. The Edit Font List dialog box
opens, wherein you create new lists from available system fonts. (For
more of a discussion on font sets, see Book II, Chapter 2.)

✦ **Size:** Choose from preset font sizes ranging from 9 to 36 from the drop-
down list or type a number in the size field. Specify font size in px (pixels),
pc (picas), pt (points), in (inches), mm (millimeters), cm (centimeters),
(ems), (exs), or % (percentage). Though using pixels is generally recommended over points (the primary unit for print design) to ensure uniform
display on both Macs and PCs, due to a resizing issue in Internet Explorer,
many CSS tutorials now suggest you use ems for font sizes instead.

✦ **Style:** Select normal (the default), italic, or oblique as the font style. The
oblique style is similar to italic, only it typically refers to a sans-serif font
that's tilted about 12 degrees before being adjusted to improve the font's
appearance.

✦ **Line Height:** This setting, also called *leading,* sets the text line height.
Choose Normal to use the automatically calculated standard ratio of
font size to line height, or enter a number value in pixels, points, in, cm,
mm, picas, ems, exs, or %.

✦ **Decoration:** The following options are available for text decoration:

 • **underline:** Adds an underline to the selected text. This setting is the
 default for links.

 • **overline:** Adds an overline to the selected text. The overline looks
 just like an underline, only it's above the characters rather than
 below them. It's a strange-looking style, to be sure, so try not to use
 it for styling links unless you know your audience is sharp enough to
 figure it out.

- **line-through:** Adds a line-through, or *strikethrough,* effect to the selected text.

- **blink:** Makes the text blink, or *flash,* in the browser window.

- **none:** Removes all decorative formatting. This setting is the default for normal text.

✦ **Weight:** The default font weight is normal, but you may specify the amount of boldness using other font weight options including bold, bolder, lighter, and bold settings in increments of 100 from 100 to 900, where normal is equal to 400 and bold is equal to 700.

✦ **Variant:** Select normal or small caps. Normal refers to the default font variance of upper and lowercase figures. A small caps setting converts text to display in small caps.

✦ **Case:** Options include capitalize, uppercase, lowercase, and none. For example, selecting uppercase changes the display from normal upper and lowercase lettering to all uppercase letters.

✦ **Color:** Select a color from the Web-safe palette or system color picker. You can also type the hexadecimal code; just remember to include the number symbol (#) before the hex number, as in **#990033**, so the color renders properly in the browser.

Background properties

The Background category's rules (see Figure 1-10) define the background settings of various elements on a document. For example, you can add a background color to a page, a table cell, a layer, or selected text.

Figure 1-10:
Add custom
background
properties
to your
styles.

The following rules are available in the Background category:

✦ **Background Color:** Apply a background color to the body of the page, text, tables, table cells, layers, and more. Select a background color from the Web-safe palette or system color picker, or type the hexadecimal code along with the number symbol (#) before the hex number (as in **#990033**), so the color renders properly in the browser.

✦ **Background Image:** Type a filename or browse to and select the location and filename of an image. You can apply background images to the body of the page, a table, table cell, or layer.

✦ **Repeat:** Instruct the browser how to display the background image. By default, background images automatically repeat, or *tile*, both vertically and horizontally unless otherwise specified:

  • **no-repeat:** Displays the background image once, without any horizontal or vertical repeating.

  • **repeat:** Mirrors the default setting of continuous horizontal and vertical repeating of a normal background image.

  • **repeat-x:** Forces the specified background image to tile horizontally only. Images are cut off at the borders to fit the element's dimensions.

  • **repeat-y:** Forces the specified background image to tile vertically only. Images are cut off at the borders to fit the element's dimensions.

✦ **Attachment:** Choose how the background image interacts with content above it:

  • **fixed:** Treats the background image as if it is immovably fixed to the background of the browser, while text and other assets on the page scroll past or over it.

  • **scroll:** Adds the background image to the page so that text and other assets on the page scroll along with it.

  • **inherit:** Inherits the fixed or scroll rule from a parent asset, such as a table cell inside a table. This option doesn't display in the attachment field in Dreamweaver, but you can type it in the text box. (In fact, the inherit option can be ascribed to every property, including the repeat and font-size properties.)

Browsers inconsistently support these features, so use them with caution.

✦ **Horizontal Position:** Determine where in the browser window the background image begins its horizontal display or repeat. Enter positioning settings for Left, Center, or Right, or type your own value in pixels, points, in, cm, mm, picas, ems, exs, or %.

✦ **Vertical Position:** Determine where in the browser window the background image begins its vertical display or repeat. Add positioning settings for Top, Center, or Bottom, or type your own value in pixels, points, in, cm, mm, picas, ems, exs, or %.

To center a single image inside the browser window, create a style for the `<body>` tag and set the Horizontal and Vertical alignment to center in conjunction with a Fixed attachment. In the following example, a file called `logo.gif` is used as the single, centered image:

```
<style type="text/css">
<!--
body {
   background-image: url(images/logo.gif);
   background-position: center;
   background-repeat: no-repeat;
   background-attachment: fixed;
}
-->
</style>
```

Block properties

The Block rules (shown in Figure 1-11) control the space and alignment of styled tags and attributes. Elements that Dreamweaver treats as CSS layout blocks include:

✦ `<Div>` tags assigned with absolute or relative positions

✦ `<Form>` and `<table>` tags

✦ Images assigned with absolute or relative positions

✦ Tags using the `display:block` style

✦ Paragraphs assigned with absolute or relative positions

Figure 1-11:
Add style properties to set spacing and alignment.

Book III
Chapter 1

Looking Good with
Cascading Style
Sheets (CSS)

You can view CSS layout block properties such as layout outlines, back-grounds, and box models with Dreamweaver's Visual Aids. To toggle the visibility of these properties on and off, choose View⇨Visual Aids and then the visual aid you want.

The following rules are available in the Block category:

✦ **Word Spacing:** Select or enter a numerical value in pixels, points, in, cm, mm, picas, ems, exs, or % to control the space between individual words. Both positive and negative values are acceptable.

✦ **Letter Spacing:** Increase or decrease space between letters and characters by adding positive or negative numerical values in pixels, points, in, cm, mm, picas, ems, exs, or %. Be aware that these settings override text justification. Internet Explorer 4 and up and Netscape Navigator 6 and up support this rule.

✦ **Vertical Alignment:** Choose Baseline, Sub, Super, Top, Text-top, Middle, Bottom, Text-bottom, and Value in pixels, points, in, cm, mm, picas, ems, exs, or %. Preview these alignments in a browser window (except for any in an <img> tag) to see their effect (press F12).

✦ **Text Align:** Choose Left, Right, Center, or Justify.

✦ **Text Indent:** Enter a text indent numerical value in pixels, points, in, cm, mm, picas, ems, exs, or % to set the rule for indenting the first line of text. Indent sizes may be positive or negative values.

✦ **Whitespace:** Determine how white space inside an element displays:

  • **Normal:** Collapses any white space.

  • **Pre:** Leaves the white space as it was coded.

  • **Nowrap:** Wraps text only when the code contains the line break <br> tags. Netscape Navigator and Internet Explorer 5.5 and later support this rule.

✦ **Display:** Determines whether the element displays in the browser at all, and if so, how. You may, for instance, want to use one of these settings to turn off a style attribute in a CSS for print media:

  • **none:** Completely turns off the display of the styled element.

  • **inline:** Displays the element inline with other elements, typically inside the current block.

  • **block:** Forces an element to display as a block.

  • **list-item:** Displays elements as a list item with bullets, similar to the <ul> and <ol> tags.

  • **run-in:** Forces a block box following a run-in box to become an inline box of the block box. Only Opera 5 and later and Internet Explorer 5 for Macs currently support this feature.

- **compact:** Styles a box of content in such a way that subsequent block boxes display to its left side when room permits. Though a bit buggy, this feature is currently supported by Opera 5 and 7. (For a visual illustration of this feature, see `www.quirksmode.org/css/display.html#compact`.)

- **marker:** Add a marker setting to format content inside a marker box, such as adding numbers or graphics to a list or special notations to styled content.

- **table:** Displays elements as a table. Nested elements display as `table-row` and `table-cell`, as they appear if contained in typical `<tr>` and `<td>` tags. Other table display settings include: `inline-table`, `table-row-group`, `table-header-group`, `table-footer-group`, `table-row`, `table-column-group`, `table-column`, `table-cell`, and `table-caption`.

For more details regarding display properties, visit the W3C Web site at

```
www.w3.org/TR/REC-CSS2/visuren.html#display-prop
www.w3.org/TR/REC-CSS2/generate.html#markers
www.w3.org/TR/REC-CSS2/tables.html#value-def-table-column
```

Box properties

The Box rules (shown in Figure 1-12) define tags and attributes that control the position of assets in the document. Box rules apply to individual sides of the styled asset when adding margin and padding values.

Check the Same for All check box to have uniform box settings.

Book III
Chapter 1

Looking Good with
Cascading Style
Sheets (CSS)

Figure 1-12:
Create styles to set the position of page content.

Unless you have other rules for other sides of an asset, when entering individual values to rules with Top, Bottom, Left, and Right fields, enter **0** or **None** for sides that don't contain values.

The following rules are available in the Box category:

✦ **Width/Height:** Select Auto or enter a value in pixels, points, in, cm, mm, picas, ems, exs, or %. Auto adjusts the layer's size to fit the area of the layer's contents, while a fixed value expands the layer to a fixed size. Note that the width refers to the space inside the padding, except in Internet Explorer, which is buggy.

✦ **Float:** Choose Left, Right, or None to control the direction in which other objects float around an object.

✦ **Clear:** Choose Left, Right, Both, or None to control the side of an asset that does not allow layers. Thus, when a layer appears on the specified side, the asset with the clear setting gets bumped to the area below it.

✦ **Padding:** Adds space between the content of an element and its border or inner margin, such as a word inside of a table cell. Enter individual padding values in pixels, points, in, cm, mm, picas, ems, exs, or % to the Top, Right, Bottom, and Left sides of the styled element.

✦ **Margin:** Adds space between the border of an asset and other nearby assets, as with the area surrounding a sentence or the margin space on the outer edge of the browser window. Add individual margin values in pixels, points, in, cm, mm, picas, ems, exs, or % to the Top, Right, Bottom, and Left sides of the styled asset.

Border properties

Use the Border rules (shown in Figure 1-13) to define the style, width, and color for border features around styled content.

Check the Same for All check box to include uniform border settings.

The following rules are available in the Border category:

✦ **Style:** Add border styles to your assets using the following settings: None, Dotted, Dashed, Solid, Double, Groove, Ridge, Inset, or Outset. Preview the styles in a browser window (press F12) as Dreamweaver does not display this attribute in the Document window.

✦ **Width:** Enter border thickness as Thin, Medium, or Thick, or enter a value in pixels, points, in, cm, mm, picas, ems, exs, or % to the Top, Right, Bottom, and Left fields.

Figure 1-13:
Create
custom
border
styles with
the Border
category.

✦ **Color:** Select a border color from the Web-safe palette or system color picker, or type the hexadecimal code along with the number symbol (#) before the hex number, as in **#990033**, so the color renders properly in the browser.

List properties

Lists in HTML can be numbered or bulleted, and when styling lists with CSS, both list types can have different style options. Use a custom designed image in place of the default bullet types. Figure 1-14 shows the List category. You can also set the position of the bullet image relative to the list item text.

Figure 1-14:
Create
custom list
styles with
the List
category.

The following rules are available in the List category:

✦ **Type:** If creating bulleted lists, select from Disc, Circle, or Square as the list type. If creating numbered lists, choose from Decimal, Lower-roman, Upper-roman, Lower-alpha, Upper, Alpha, or None.

✦ **Bullet image:** Type the filename and location of the graphic, or browse to and select the graphic to be used as the bullet image.

✦ **Position:** Determine how the list item text interacts with the list item's bullet or number.

- **Outside:** Forces the text to indent and wrap around the bullet/number.
- **Inside:** Wraps the text along the left margin.

Positioning properties

Use the Positioning rules (shown in Figure 1-15) to modify the tag or selected text into a layer. For example, you can control a layer or an image's position within the browser window using positioning rules.

Figure 1-15: Choose options for setting the position of a layer or image.

The following rules are available in the Positioning category:

✦ **Type:** Using the coordinates entered in the Placement boxes, determine positioning of the layer or tag relative to the browser window:

- **Absolute:** Positioning is relative to the top-left corner of the browser.
- **Relative:** Positioning is relative to the styled object's position in the text flow of the file. You must preview this effect in a browser (press F12).

- **Static:** Similar to Relative, Static positioning puts the styled object at its location in the text flow, causing elements to stack vertically. This option is the default position of elements when no type is selected.

✦ **Width:** Select Auto or enter a value in pixels, points, in, cm, mm, picas, ems, exs, or %. Auto sets the layer's size to fit the width of the layer's contents, while a fixed value holds the width open to a fixed size.

✦ **Height:** Select Auto or enter a value in pixels, points, in, cm, mm, picas, ems, exs, or %. Auto sets the layer's size to fit the height of the layer's contents, while a fixed value holds the height open to a fixed size.

✦ **Visibility:** Choose Inherit, Visible, or Hidden to set the initial display settings of the layer:

- **Inherit:** Forces the layer to inherit the visibility property of the layer's parent. If no parent exists, the layer is visible.

- **Visible:** Displays the layer's contents, regardless of a parent's visibility value.

- **Hidden:** Hides the layer's contents, regardless of a parent's visibility value.

✦ **Z-Index:** The z-index determines the styled layer's stacking order relative to the browser window:

- **Auto:** Gets the next available z-index number

- **Inherit:** Inherits a parent's z-index

You can also manually enter a specific number. The lower the number, the closer to the background; the higher the number, the closer to the viewer. Layers can have both positive and negative values.

You can also change the z-index number quickly through the Layers panel.

✦ **Overflow:** Specify how the browser handles the content in a CSS layer that exceed the boundaries of the box the layer sits in:

- **Visible:** Increase the layer's size (usually its `height` attribute first, then its `width`) so that all the layer's contents are visible.

- **Hidden:** Maintain the width and height settings of the layer's original size and cuts off, or clips from view, any content that exceeds this size.

- **Scroll:** Add scroll bars to the layer regardless of whether the content fits or exceeds the layer's size. You must preview this option in a browser window (press F12), as it doesn't display in the Dreamweaver workspace. Furthermore, this feature only works in browsers that support the feature, such as Internet Explorer and Netscape Navigator 6.0 and up.

Book III
Chapter 1

Looking Good with
Cascading Style
Sheets (CSS)

- **Auto:** Add scroll bars automatically if the contents of the layer exceed the layer's width and height. You must also preview this option in a browser window (press F12), as it doesn't display in the Dreamweaver workspace.

✦ **Placement:** Set the exact size and position of the layer. Browsers then rely on the Type setting for interpreting the location. Be aware that sizes may be overridden if content exceeds the layer's size. The default units for size and position are pixels, but for CSS layers you can also use points, in, cm, mm, picas, ems, exs, or % to the Top, Right, Bottom, and Left sides of the layer.

✦ **Clip:** Set the visible area of the layer relative to the layer's top-left edge. Besides clipping content, the clipped area can be accessed with JavaScript to manipulate the values and thereby create special effects like *wipes* that hide or reveal content on absolutely positioned layers. Enter clip region dimensions in pixels, points, in, cm, mm, picas, ems, exs, or % to the Top, Right, Bottom, and Left sides of the layer.

Extensions properties

Extensions apply forced page breaks and unusual visual effects including pointer styles to your documents. Most browsers don't support many of these extensions, so be sure to test extensively before publishing them on your site. Figure 1-16 shows the Extensions category.

Figure 1-16:
Add visual effects and page breaks to your files.

The following style attributes are available in the Extensions category:

✦ **Page Break (Before/After):** Forces a page break during the printing process before or after an asset styled with this option. For instance, you may want to force a page break after every instance of a particular image on the Web page styled with this feature. Enter **auto**, **always**, **left**, or **right** in the Before and After fields. Though this feature is not supported by any 4.0 browser, most 6.0 and 8.0 browsers do support this feature.

✦ **Cursor:** Select a different cursor that displays when the pointer mouses over an object controlled by the style. Cool effects include crosshair, text, wait, default, help, e-resize, ne-resize, n-resize, nw-resize, w-resize, sw-resize, s-resize, se-resize, and auto. Internet Explorer 4.0 and up and Netscape Navigator 6 and up support these effects.

✦ **Filter:** Apply several special-effect filters, such as drop shadow and glow, to styled asset. Remember to test the setting in multiple browsers before publishing (press F12).

Renaming CSS Styles

Dreamweaver 8 streamlines the process of renaming custom styles. In previous versions, you'd have to change the name in the style sheet and update all the instances of the style name on all the pages of the site for the name change to be complete. Now, you can edit the name in one location and Dreamweaver handles all the sitewide updates.

To rename a custom (class) CSS style, follow these steps:

1. **From the Properties inspector, choose Rename from the Style drop-down list.**

Or, in the CSS Styles panel, select the style name and choose Rename from the Options menu.

The Rename Style dialog box opens, as shown in Figure 1-17.

**Book III
Chapter 1**

Looking Good with
Cascading Style
Sheets (CSS)

Figure 1-17:
Rename
custom
styles.

2. **Select the style you want to rename from the list of available styles in the Rename Style drop-down list and enter the new name in the New Name field.**

Be sure not to use any spaces or special characters in the new filename.

3. Click OK.

Dreamweaver recognizes when the style is defined in an external style sheet and offers to fix the name change in all documents sitewide.

4. Click the Yes button to change the name in all documents, the No button to change the name on the style sheet only without updating the site, or the Cancel button to stop the name change process.

When you click Yes, the Find and Replace dialog box appears.

5. If you clicked Yes in Step 4, select an action in the Find In field of the Find and Replace dialog box.

Dreamweaver auto-populates the Find and Replace dialog box with the appropriate settings to fix the name change, but you must decide where the updates should occur. Select Current Document, Open Documents, Folder, Selected Files in Site, or Entire Current Local Site.

6. Click the Replace All button.

The Results panel opens to display the results.

Exporting Internal Styles to an External Style Sheet

You can export internal styles to an external style sheet in Dreamweaver in a couple of ways. The first way is to cut the styles from the internal style sheet in Code view, and then paste them into an external style sheet. The second way uses the CSS Styles panel, requires no hand coding, and is as fast as clicking a few buttons.

To export internal styles to an external style sheet, follow these steps:

1. Click the All button at the top of the CSS Styles panel.

A list of all the style rules used on the entire document displays, including internal and external styles.

2. Below the All button, click the `<style>` tag in the All Rules section.

All the contents of the internal style sheet are selected.

3. Choose Text⇨CSS Styles⇨Export from the main menu.

The Export Styles as CSS File dialog box appears.

4. Enter a filename for the new, exported CSS file. Click OK to save the exported file.

Name the file and save it into the existing managed site or navigate to and select another folder to save the new CSS file into.

5. Remove the internal style information from the page.

With the `<style>` tag still selected in the CSS Styles panel, click the Delete Embedded Style Sheet button at the bottom of the panel (refer to Figure 1-3).

6. Click the Attach Style Sheet button at the bottom of the panel to add a link to the new external CSS.

Enter the File/URL of the new CSS, click the Add as: Link radio button, enter a media type, and click OK. Dreamweaver adds the link code to attach the selected CSS to the open document.

The CSS Styles panel now lists the name of the newly linked external CSS. Continue using the new external CSS by adding new styles and editing existing styles as needed.

Using Design Time Style Sheets

Design Time Style Sheets allow you to view, edit, and hide multiple style sheets while working on a document in Design view. Though less necessary these days, you may need multiple style sheets if you're developing two different versions of the same Web site — one for Windows and one for Macintosh-only site visitors.

This multiple style sheet option is only enabled within Dreamweaver's Design view to assist you with editing style sheets. In a browser window, however, only the style sheet that is actually attached inside the document appears to style the page.

Follow these steps to set up Design Time Style Sheets:

1. Choose Text⇨CSS Styles⇨Design-time from the main menu.

The Design Time Style Sheets dialog box appears, as shown in Figure 1-18.

Book III
Chapter 1

Looking Good with
Cascading Style
Sheets (CSS)

Design Time Style Sheets

⊞ ⊟

Show only at design time:

OK
Cancel
Help

⊞ ⊟

Hide at design time:

Figure 1-18:
Add multiple
CSS to the
workspace.

2. **In the dialog box, add the settings to hide or show selected style sheets:**

- **Show a style sheet:** Click the plus (+) button above the Show Only at Design Time field. Browse to and select the style sheet from the Select File dialog box. Repeat to add additional style sheets as you need.

- **Hide a style sheet:** Click the plus (+) button above the Hide at Design Time field. Browse to and select the style sheet from the Select File dialog box. Repeat to add additional style sheets as you need.

- **Remove a style sheet:** Select the style sheet you want to remove and click the minus (–) button above that category.

3. **Click OK to close the dialog box.**

The CSS Styles panel updates to reflect the new style sheet settings, with hidden or design indicators to show each style sheet's design-time status.

Chapter 2: Building Sites with Templates

In This Chapter

✔ **Creating a template**

✔ **Creating editable template regions**

✔ **Nesting templates**

✔ **Creating a template-based document**

✔ **Editing templates and the pages that use them**

*D*reamweaver has created a quick and easy way to manage the look of your Web site with a master file process called Templates. You can unify the overall design of your Web site into one file, called a *template,* and then use that file as the basis for creating all the other pages on your site.

Templates enable you to control which parts of the pages can be edited and which parts remain fixed across all the pages on a site:

✦ The *editable areas* on a template are defined areas for specific parts of a Web document that have different content on each page of the site, such as the page header, the body of the page, or a subnavigation element. You need to define and name each editable area in the template. This helps you keep track of the content that should be placed inside it when you create template-based documents.

For example, the body editable area on the template-based Contact page would display detailed contact information and the body editable area on the template-based About page would display detailed information about the company.

✦ The *uneditable areas* of a template, by contrast, are the parts of the layout and design that are constant throughout the Web site. You don't need to define uneditable areas in the template as you do with editable areas; only editable areas in template-based pages are editable.

For example, your navigation and company logo placement should be in the same location from page to page throughout the site; these areas would be uneditable on any template-based pages. Uneditable areas are a particularly useful tool when you work in a team with other designers, writers, and Web developers.

You discover the true beauty and power of Dreamweaver templates when you need to update part of your master layout or design (that means changing any of the uneditable areas of the template). Instead of having to individually modify those elements on each of the pages on your managed site, you need to update only the template, and Dreamweaver automatically updates those elements on all the pages that utilize that template!

You can apply templates to blank or existing documents, and if you change your mind after applying a template to a page, you can simply detach it. You can also remove template markup or export a page without template markup. After editing a template, Dreamweaver can selectively update pages that use the template or update code inside the entire managed site. Furthermore, from within a page created from a template, you can modify editable tag attributes such as image source or width. One of the most amazing functions of templates, however, is that you can completely modify the entire look of a Web site without having to redo the content, just by attaching a different template to the page!

When you publish your site, you don't need to upload templates to the remote server because they do not affect site functionality. Rather, Dreamweaver uses them as a local tool to help you control the code for common areas on all the pages that use the template file. What you do need to upload to the remote server are all the pages created from the template.

This chapter gives you the lowdown on templates and why they're such a powerful tool, especially for small-to-medium–sized Web sites. You also find detailed instructions for creating, using, editing, and deleting templates.

If you have a larger site and or a site that uses dynamic functionality, other solutions may work better, such as server-side includes (see Book III, Chapter 3) or PHP Advanced SQL Smarties.

Creating a Template

You can create a template from an existing HTML, Macromedia ColdFusion, or Microsoft ASP document, or you can build a template from scratch with a new, untitled, blank template file. After creating the file, you can add editable regions to the template, as described in the later section "Working with Editable Regions." You can also add Design Notes to the file (see Book VI,

Chapter 1 for details), as well as modify the default highlighting and code colors in the Preferences dialog box (skip ahead to the "Creating editable regions" section).

In the process of creating a template, Dreamweaver marks up the document code with special Dreamweaver template comment tags that identify the document as a template and define the various areas of the template. The first template comment tag gets inserted right after the opening HTML tag, as in the following example:

```
<!-- InstanceBegin template="/Templates/mytemplate.dwt" -->
```

Additional template comment tags, such as the ones that mark the beginning and ending of editable regions, are inserted throughout the file to assist Dreamweaver with sitewide editing.

Understanding template markup

Dreamweaver templates use a series of comment tag markup code to define areas of the template as editable or uneditable. While it's not necessary that you know what these tags mean or even how they work to use templates, you may find the following information interesting. On the other hand, for those of you who are less inclined to know more about template markup, feel free to skip ahead to the next section.

The template tag syntax rules are not too strict, but you still need to pay attention to things like case sensitivity and proper use of quote marks:

+ Comment and attribute names are case sensitive.

+ Attributes need to be inside quotation marks, and you can use either single or double quotes.

+ Attributes can come in any order.

+ White space is allowed using spaces, line breaks, and tabs, except at the beginning or end of a comment.

The following lists all the Dreamweaver template and instance tags. Dreamweaver automatically inserts these tags when you add template objects to the page, such as creating an optional editable region.

Here are the template tags:

```
<!-- TemplateBeginEditable name="..." -->
<!-- TemplateEndEditable -->

<!-- TemplateParam name="..." type="..." value="..." -->
```

```
<!-- TemplateBeginRepeat name="..." -->
<!-- TemplateEndRepeat -->

<!-- TemplateBeginIf cond="..." -->
<!-- TemplateEndIf -->

<!-- TemplateBeginPassthroughIf cond="..." -->
<!-- TemplateEndPassthroughIf -->

<!-- TemplateBeginMultipleIf -->
<!-- TemplateEndMultipleIf -->

<!-- TemplateBeginPassthroughMultipleIf -->
<!-- TemplateEndPassthroughMultipleIf -->

<!-- TemplateBeginIfClause cond="..." -->
<!-- TemplateEndIfClause -->

<!-- TemplateBeginPassthroughIfClause cond="..." -->
<!-- TemplateEndPassthroughIfClause -->

<!-- TemplateExpr expr="..." --> (equivalent to @@...@@)

<!-- TemplatePassthroughExpr expr="..." -->

<!-- TemplateInfo codeOutsideHTMLIsLocked="..." -->
```

These are the instance tags:

```
<!-- InstanceBegin template="..." codeOutsideHTMLIsLocked="..." -->
<!-- InstanceEnd -->
<!-- InstanceBeginEditable name="..." -->
<!-- InstanceEndEditable -->
<!-- InstanceParam name="..." type="..." value="..." passthrough="..." -->
<!-- InstanceBeginRepeat name="..." -->
<!-- InstanceEndRepeat -->
<!-- InstanceBeginRepeatEntry -->
<!-- InstanceEndRepeatEntry -->
```

Converting an HTML page into a template

You can convert any existing HTML page into a template. However, we suggest taking the time to create a page with the design layout you want to use for the entire Web site. Design a master HTML page: Add the text and graphics, enter alternate text tags to images, create hyperlinks where needed, assign JavaScript rollover button behaviors, add text formatting with Cascading Style Sheets, check for spelling mistakes, and include any other media and dynamic settings necessary on the page.

Test this master HTML page in multiple browsers for link accuracy, layout consistency, and dynamic functionality to ensure the new template you create from this master page doesn't contain any errors.

Using server scripts in templates

Of necessity, some server scripts must be added to the document code above and below the opening and closing `<html>` tags. When server scripts are placed inside templates, however, Dreamweaver may not always copy the script code — or subsequent changes made to it — to pages generated using a particular template, and that could cause significant server errors when scripts in the body of a template-based document depend on these "outside HTML" scripts.

Though Dreamweaver warns you about changing outside HTML scripts, you can avoid the problem altogether by adding the following code to the `<head>` area of the template:

```
<!-- TemplateInfo codeOutsideHTMLIsLocked=
        "true" -->
```

The addition of this line of code to the head of the template forces Dreamweaver to copy any changes to scripts outside the `<html>` tags to documents based on that template.

Keep in mind that adding this code removes the ability to edit these scripts in the template-based documents. Therefore, you can either edit the scripts in the template or edit them individually in the template-based documents, but not both.

After you're sure the master HTML page is fully functional, open the page in the Dreamweaver workspace window and follow these steps to convert the file into a Dreamweaver template:

1. **Choose File⇨Save as Template.**

Be sure to choose *Save as Template* rather than *Save* from the File menu.

You can also click the Templates button on the Common tab of the Insert bar and select Make Template from the Templates drop-down list to begin the conversion process.

The Save as Template dialog box appears (see Figure 2-1).

**Book III
Chapter 2**

**Building Sites with
Templates**

Figure 2-1:
Save your
template file
with a
unique
name.

2. From the Site menu, select a site from the list of all your managed sites into which the new template will be saved.

When creating a template in a managed site, that site's name should automatically be selected.

3. In the Description field, enter a short description.

The description displays in the Description field of the New from Template dialog box when creating a new template-based page.

4. In the Save As field, enter a name for the template.

For simplicity, name the template after the project or client and use all lowercase letters with no spaces or special characters, as in `xyzcompany`.

5. Click the Save button. When prompted to update links, click the Yes button.

If you click the No button, the links and paths no longer function properly.

Dreamweaver creates a Templates folder in the Files panel and places the newly created template file inside that folder, which means the template's location relative to the other files on the site has changed; it's now inside a folder at the root level.

Leave the template files inside the Templates folder and do not store any non-template files there. This helps you avoid causing errors to template paths.

6. To create an editable region, select the content on the template and choose Insert⇨Template Objects⇨Editable Region. Enter a name for the editable region and click OK.

Each editable area can contain any asset or combination of items such as a word or block of text, a graphic, a table cell, or even an entire table. Dreamweaver prompts you to name each editable area. Name them using a descriptive term to define their purpose, such as `header`, `bodytext`, or `storephoto`. When naming editable regions, use single or conjoined words written in all lowercase letters without spaces or any special characters.

For a more in-depth discussion of editable regions, see "Working with Editable Regions," later in this chapter.

7. Save and close the template.

Template files automatically get saved in the Templates folder with the `.dwt` file extension; when opened in the Dreamweaver workspace, they display the word `<<Template>>` in the title bar.

Creating a new template from scratch

To create a new, blank template into which you add all the necessary content, follow these steps:

1. **Choose File⇨New to open the New Document window, which is shown in Figure 2-2.**

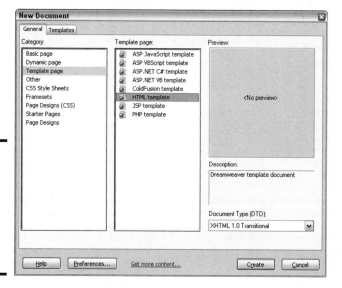

Figure 2-2:
Create a
new
template
using the
Template
Page
category.

2. **To create a new, untitled template page, select Template Page from the Category list and a template type, such as HTML Template, from the Template Page list.**

3. **Click the Create button.**

The new template page opens as an untitled, unsaved template file inside the Dreamweaver workspace.

4. **Add content to the new template.**

When adding content to the template, pay attention to the document-relative links and paths in the Properties inspector (see Book I, Chapter 3 for details). A correct path includes code that points from the Templates folder to the linked document and appends the link with the appropriate document-relative code, such as `../contact.html` instead of `contact.html`. For best results, use the Point to File or Folder buttons in the Properties inspector to ensure the links are correct.

5. **To create an editable region, select the content in the template and then choose Insert➪Template Objects➪Editable Region. Enter a name for the editable region and click OK.**

   Read the upcoming section "Working with Editable Regions" for instructions on all the editable template region types.

6. **Choose File➪Save As Template.**

   The Save As Template dialog box opens (see Figure 2-3).

Figure 2-3: Enter template details in this dialog box.

7. **From the Site drop-down list, select a managed site to save the new file into.**

8. **(Optional) Add a description for the template.**

   The description displays in the Preview area of the New Document window.

9. **In the Save As field, provide the template with an appropriate filename. Then click Save.**

   Use all lowercase letters with no spaces or special characters for the template name, as in `abcwidgets`.

   Template files automatically get saved in the Templates folder with the `.dwt` file extension; when opened in the Dreamweaver workspace window, they display the word `<<Template>>` in the title bar.

Working with Editable Regions

The *editable regions* are the parts of a template that are unlocked, or editable, in a template-based page. These editable regions are perfect for areas that are specific to the page's purpose. For instance, each page has its own header graphic, text, and subnavigation areas.

Each editable area can contain any elements or combination of elements such as a block of text, a graphic, a table cell, or even an entire table. Though you may create as many editable regions as you want, each template should have at least one editable region.

Editable regions are the most basic form of editable areas on a template. In addition to these, you can also create optional editable regions, repeating regions and repeating tables, and editable tag attributes, as described later in this chapter.

Creating editable regions

To create an editable region on a template, follow these steps:

1. Select the contents in the template file that you want to set as an editable region.

For example, select a header graphic that displays the name of the page in a special font (as shown in Figure 2-4). In addition, rather than selecting content, place the insertion point at the point on the page where you want to insert an editable area.

Turn this header into an editable region.

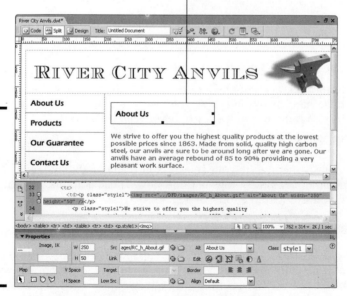

Figure 2-4:
Select template content, such as a header graphic, to convert it into an editable region.

When creating editable regions that include tables and layers, pay attention to the source code of your selection. For example, when you select the `<td>` tag and convert it into an editable region, that editable region includes both the table cell and its contents. By contrast, when you make only the contents of a cell into an editable region, only the contents of the cell become editable and any formatting associated with the table cell itself remains uneditable. Likewise, when creating editable areas with layers, when you select a `<layer>` tag along with the layer's contents, the layer's positioning and contents are editable. But if you select and convert only the contents of a layer into an editable region, only the contents are editable and the layer's position remains fixed.

2. Choose Insert⇨Template Objects⇨Editable Region.

You can also click the Templates button on the Common tab of the Insert bar and choose Editable Region from the drop-down list.

The New Editable Region dialog box opens, as shown in Figure 2-5.

Figure 2-5:
Name
editable
template
regions.

New Editable Region

Name: EditRegion3

This region will be editable in documents based on this template.

OK

Cancel

Help

3. Enter a name for the new editable region.

Name editable areas using a descriptive term such as `header`, `phone`, or `headshot`, using single or conjoined words written in all lowercase letters without any spaces or other special characters.

4. Click OK.

Dreamweaver converts your selection into an editable region by adding template markup comment tags in Code view. These editable content regions begin and end with the following code:

```
<!-- TemplateBeginEditable> ... <!-- TemplateEndEditable -->
```

The space between the template markup indicates areas that remain editable in template-based documents. Take care, however, not to modify the template markup when working in Code view, as Dreamweaver uses this markup to manage template updates.

In Design view, editable regions on a template are defined by a blue rectangular outline, topped by a tab labeled with the name you just provided, surrounding the selection for the new editable region (see Figure 2-6). The blue color is Dreamweaver's preset editable region color, which you can change in the Highlighting category of the Preferences dialog box. Choose Edit⇨Preferences (Windows) or Dreamweaver⇨Preferences (Mac).

Editable region

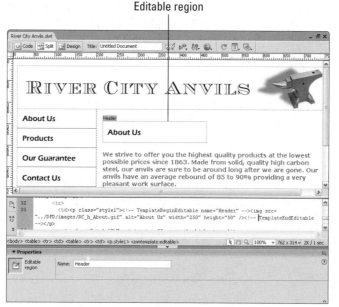

Figure 2-6:
Editable regions are defined by a blue outline and tab label.

Book III
Chapter 2

Building Sites with Templates

Editable regions in pages created from templates are shown with the same blue label and outline, clearly marking where content can be edited.

Removing editable regions

From time to time you may need to remove an editable region from your template. For example, because nested editable regions are not allowed in Dreamweaver, you may decide to enlarge or reduce the size of an existing editable region to better define the editable areas on the template, which requires you to delete an existing region before defining a new area.

To remove an editable region from a template, follow these steps:

1. **Open the template in the Dreamweaver workspace window.**

2. **Select the region by clicking the blue tab in the upper-left corner of the editable region.**

Or place your cursor inside the editable region you want to delete so Dreamweaver knows which code you want to remove.

3. Choose Modify⇨Templates⇨Remove Template Markup.

Dreamweaver instantly removes the template markup for that editable region, including the code in Code view and the blue outlines in Design view. The content in that region isn't deleted on the template. However, for template-based files, you need to resolve the issue of where to place any content that used to be in the removed region, which we talk about in the next section.

Renaming editable regions

If you accidentally misspell an editable region label, you can remove and then reapply the editable region with the correct spelling. But for simple name changes to an editable region, Dreamweaver has an even better solution:

1. Open the template in the Dreamweaver workspace window.

2. Select the region you want to rename by clicking the blue tab in the upper-left corner of the editable region.

For example, suppose you have an editable region called *email* that you want to rename as *address*.

3. Choose Modify⇨Quick Tag Editor.

The Quick Tag Editor opens, shown in Figure 2-7, where you adjust the code.

If you prefer, you can also modify the code directly in Code view.

Figure 2-7:
Use the
Quick Tag
Editor to edit
code.

The code in the Quick Tag Editor looks something like this:

```
<!-- TemplateBeginEditable name="email" -->
```

4. Type the new editable region name in the area in quotes.

Using the same example, change `email` to `address`:

```
<!-- TemplateBeginEditable name="address" -->
```

An even quicker method for renaming the editable template region on a template is to select the editable region by clicking the editable region's blue tab and changing the name in the Properties inspector.

5. **Choose File⇨Save to save the template.**

   Dreamweaver opens the Update Template Files dialog box.

6. **Click the Update button to update all the template-based files in the managed site.**

   We don't recommend clicking the Don't Update button as it updates only the template file, but not any of the template-based files.

   Dreamweaver launches the Inconsistent Region Names dialog box, shown in Figure 2-8, to map any new region names to any old region locations. If you fail to map the regions, content in the old region name area may be discarded on pages using the template.

Figure 2-8:
Use the Inconsistent Region Names dialog box to map old editable region names to new editable regions.

7. **In the Name column under Editable Regions, select the old editable region name. Then choose the new region name from the Move Content to New Region drop-down list.**

   After selecting the new region name, you see the new region name listed under the Resolved column of the dialog box.

8. **Continue mapping remaining regions, if you need.**

9. **Click OK.**

   Dreamweaver automatically closes the Inconsistent Region Names dialog box and finishes the region renaming process by updating all the pages on the site that use the template you just modified.

10. **Click the Close button on the Update Pages dialog box.**

The process of changing the region name is complete. If you have any files open that use the template you just modified, save the files before closing them to accept the most recent changes.

Exporting a site without any template markup

In addition to removing or renaming editable regions, Dreamweaver can export an entire Web site full of template-based files to another folder without any template markup. The exported file can even be in XML format if you like. One benefit of removing the markup is that the file sizes may be slightly smaller. Furthermore, when you export an XML version, the XML file is transportable as well as easily importable back into Dreamweaver and other applications.

To export a site without any template code, follow these steps:

1. **Choose Modify⇔Templates⇔Export without Markup.**

The Export Site without Template Markup dialog box opens, as shown in Figure 2-9.

2. **In the Folder field, choose a destination folder outside of the current managed site.**

Figure 2-9:
Export template-based Web files without template markup.

3. **To save an XML version of exported template-based documents, check the Keep Template Data Files check box. To update changes to files that have already been exported, check the Extract Only Changed Files check box.**

XML (eXtensible Markup Language) is a simple text format that is used to describe data for electronic publishing and exchanging data on the Web. Visit the W3.org (`www.w3.org/XML`) and W3Schools (`www.w3schools.com/xml/xml_whatis.asp`) Web sites to discover more about XML.

4. **Click OK.**

Creating Optional and Optional Editable Regions

Use *optional regions* on a template for content such as graphics or text that may or may not be needed on every template-based page. For example, you can create an optional region for a Back to Top link that can be either visible or hidden, depending on the length of the text placed on the page above it. By using optional regions, you let the users of template-based files decide whether they want to include the optional region in the pages they're adding content to.

Within optional regions, you can also set values for template parameters (such as true/false operations) and make conditional statements (such as if . . . else statements) that can later be edited in the template-based file. Dreamweaver adds template comment tags to the page code for the new optional region in two locations. In the head, you see something like this:

```
<!-- TemplateParam name="saleImage" type="boolean" value="true" -->
```

Then in the code, where the optional region appears, you see additional comment tags like this:

```
<!-- TemplateBeginIf cond="saleImage" -->
<p><img src="/images/onsale.gif" width="100" height="23"> </p>
<!-- TemplateEndIf -->
```

Similar to regular optional regions, *optional editable regions* are also controlled by the template user from within the template-based page, but have the added feature of allowing the template user to edit the optional region's contents.

Creating optional regions

To create an optional region, follow these steps:

1. **Open the template in the Dreamweaver workspace window.**

2. **Select the content that you want to set as the optional region.**

3. **Choose Insert⇨Template Objects⇨Optional Region.**

You can also click the Templates button on the Common tab of the Insert bar and choose Optional Region from the drop-down list.

The New Optional Region dialog box opens, as shown in Figure 2-10.

4. **On the Basic tab, enter a name for the new optional region and enable or disable the Show by Default option.**

When Show by Default is enabled, the new optional region appears on the template-based page; when disabled, the optional region is hidden on the template-based page.

Figure 2-10:
Use this dialog box to specify optional regions within a template.

5. (Optional) On the Advanced tab, enter additional parameters or expressions for the region:

• **Use Parameter:** Select this option to choose an existing parameter from the drop-down list that the selected content should be linked to.

• **Enter Expression:** Choose this option to write your own template expressions for controlling whether the region is visible or hidden by default, such as the expression COUNTRY=='United States'.

Use parameters to control the display of the optional region or expressions to define conditional statements, such as if . . . else statements or true/false operations. Regions can have a default setting of either show or hide.

6. Click OK.

The new optional region is inserted onto the template.

Creating optional editable regions

To create an optional editable region, follow these steps:

1. Open the template in the Dreamweaver workspace window.

2. Click your cursor inside the template file where you want to insert the optional editable region.

Insert the optional editable region before inserting the content into the region, as you can't wrap an editable region around a selection.

3. Choose Insert➪Template Objects➪Editable Optional Region.

You can also click the Templates button on the Common tab of the Insert bar and choose Editable Optional Region from the drop-down list.

The New Optional Editable Region dialog box opens.

4. On the Basic tab, enter a name for the new optional editable region.

5. (Optional) Click the Advanced tab (shown in Figure 2-11) to add other options such as parameters for conditional statements or expressions.

Figure 2-11:
Specify optional editable regions within a template.

See Step 5 in the preceding section for details on setting parameters and entering expressions.

6. Click OK.

Modifying optional regions

After you add an optional editable region to a template, you can modify its settings, including whether the region is hidden or showing.

To modify an optional region, follow these steps:

1. Open a template-based document in the workspace window.

2. Inside the Document window, do one of the following to open the Optional Region dialog box:

- **Design view:** Click the template tab of the optional region you want to edit.

- **Code view:** Click the comment tag of the optional region you want to edit.

3. Click the Edit button in the Properties inspector.

The New Optional Region dialog box opens (refer to Figure 2-10).

4. Make any desired changes to the optional region.

5. Click OK when you finish making changes.

Book III
Chapter 2

Building Sites with
Templates

Creating Repeating Regions

Repeating regions in a template are wonderful to use when you have consistent content areas that repeat, such as rows in a table, but are unsure as to how many sections any particular page may need. With a repeating region, the number of sections can be controlled from within the template-based page, while the overall layout and design is still controlled by the template.

For example, Figure 2-12 shows a repeating table that lists all of ABC Company's store locations by name, phone number, and address. From inside the template-based page, the template user can add, delete, and reorder table rows by clicking the repeating region buttons.

Figure 2-12:
Click these buttons to manage the content inside the repeating region.

Adjust table rows with the repeating region buttons:

✦ **Add a new row:** Click the plus (+) button.

✦ **Delete a row:** Place your cursor inside an editable area in the row you want to remove and click the minus (–) button at the top of the table.

✦ **Move an entry up or down:** Place your cursor inside an editable area on the row you want to adjust and click the Up or Down arrow buttons at the top of the table.

You can also choose Modify⊅Templates and choose a repeating entry or move position option from the submenu.

You can add two kinds of repeating regions to a template file: *repeating regions* and *repeating tables*. Though repeating regions are mostly used for tables, you can use them for other things as well, such as a product detail layout including text and graphics. If you need a region's contents to be editable, create a regular editable region from that content, as the repeating regions themselves are not editable.

Creating repeating regions

To create a repeating region, follow these steps:

1. **Open the template in the Dreamweaver workspace window.**

2. **Place the cursor where you want to insert the new repeating region.**

3. **To add the repeating region, choose Insert⇨Template Objects⇨ Repeating Region.**

You can also click the Templates button on the Common tab of the Insert bar and choose Repeating Region from the drop-down list.

The New Repeating Region dialog box opens.

4. **Enter a name for the new repeating template region.**

When naming repeating template regions, use single or conjoined words written in all lowercase letters without spaces or any special characters.

5. **Click OK.**

Dreamweaver inserts the new repeating region into the template.

Creating repeating tables

Use a repeating table for making editable areas with repeating rows. You can also set table attributes and pick which consecutive rows within the table repeat.

Follow these steps to create a repeating table:

1. **Open the template in the Dreamweaver workspace window.**

2. **Place your cursor inside the file where you want to insert the table.**

3. **Choose Insert⇨Template Objects⇨Repeating Table.**

You can also click the Templates button on the Common tab of the Insert bar and choose Repeating Table from the drop-down list to open the dialog box.

The Insert Repeating Table dialog box opens, shown in Figure 2-13.

Figure 2-13:
Add a
repeating
table to your
template.

4. **Specify the following attributes for the new repeating table:**

   - **Rows** and **Columns:** Enter the number of rows and columns for the repeating table.

   - **Cell Padding:** Enter a number in pixels to increase the space between the cell's walls and its contents. If left blank, the cell padding displays as if it were set to 1 pixel. To remove cell padding completely, set the size to 0.

   - **Cell Spacing:** Enter a number in pixels to increase the walls of the repeating table between the cells. If left blank, the cell spacing displays as if it were set to 2 pixels. To remove cell spacing completely, set the size to 0.

   - **Width:** Enter a number to set the fixed width of the repeating table in pixels or enter a percentage width between 1 and 100 percent.

   - **Border:** Enter the number in pixels for the table border. If left blank, the border displays as if it were set to 1 pixel. To remove a border completely, set the border size to 0.

   - **Starting Row:** Enter the row number that begins the repeating region within the repeating table.

   - **Ending Row:** Enter the row number that marks the end of the repeating region within the repeating table.

   - **Region Name:** Specify a name for the repeating region within the repeating table.

5. **Click OK.**

   The repeating table is inserted into your template.

TIP

Add alternating row background colors

After you insert a repeating table to your template, you can add some template markup to create alternate table row background colors in your template-based pages. The markup gets added to the first repeating region `<tr>` tag in Code view:

```
<tr bgcolor="@@(_index & 1) ? '#FFFFFF' : '#FFFFCC'@@">
```

You can change the #FFFFFF (white) and #FFFFCC (pale yellow) hexadecimal values of the alternating rows in the sample code to any other colors to match your particular Web design color scheme. The main thing is that the syntax is correct and the code gets placed in the right part of your template.

The following example shows repeating table code with repeating regions and alternating background row colors (see the figure):

```
<table width="600" border="1" cellpadding="3" cellspacing="0" bordercolor="#666666">
<tr><th>First Name</th><th>Last Name</th><th>Telephone</th></tr>

<!-- TemplateBeginRepeat name="contacts" -->
<tr bgcolor="@@(_index & 1 ? '#FFFFFF' : '#FFFFCC')@@">
<td> <!-- TemplateBeginEditable name="firstname" --> firstname <!--
        TemplateEndEditable -->
</td>
<td> <!-- TemplateBeginEditable name="lastname" --> lastname <!-- TemplateEndEditable -->
</td>
<td> <!-- TemplateBeginEditable name="telephone" --> telephone <!-- TemplateEndEditable -->
</td>
</tr>
  <!-- TemplateEndRepeat -->

</table>
```

After you add this line of code to the repeating table on your template, any new rows added to the repeating region on the table in the template-based page use the alternating row colors you specified in the code.

Repeat: contacts [+][-][▼][▲]	Last Name	Telephone
firstname Billy	lastname Jones	telephone 212-555-1212
firstname Mary	lastname Lee	telephone 213-555-2121
firstname Jack	lastname Baker	telephone 214-555-1313
firstname Helen	lastname Smith	telephone 215-555-3131

**Book III
Chapter 2**

**Building Sites with
Templates**

Creating Editable Tag Attributes

Editable tag attributes let you create unlocked tag attributes in a template, which can be modified from within the template-based page. For instance, a table may be locked into the page design, but with editable tag attributes, its width or border thickness may be set by the template user. Set as many editable tag attributes in the template as you want. Attributes can include text, Boolean (true/false), URL, and color data types.

To create an editable tag attribute, follow these steps:

1. **Open the template in the Dreamweaver workspace window.**

2. **Select the tag of the object you want to add an editable tag attribute to.**

3. **Choose Modify⇨Templates⇨Make Attribute Editable.**

The Editable Tag Attributes dialog box opens, as shown in Figure 2-14.

Figure 2-14:
Specify editable tag attributes in your templates.

4. **Enter details for the attribute you want to make editable:**

- **Attribute:** If the attribute you want to make editable is listed in the drop-down list, select it. If the attribute is not listed, click the Add button to enter the name of the new attribute.

- **Make Attribute Editable:** Enable this feature to make the attribute editable. After you enable this field, the remaining fields in the dialog box become active.

- **Label:** Type a unique name for the attribute to help identify its purpose, such as **tableBorder** or **buttonSrc**.

- **Type:** Choose a value from the drop-down list that helps set the attribute's editability. Your options include the following:

- **Text:** Text values allow you to type a text value to edit the tag attribute. For example, you can use text to define the value (*left*, *right*, or *center*) of the `align` attribute.

- **URL:** Select this option to add a link to an object, such as the path to the source file of a graphic.

- **Color:** Choose this option to select a color from the color palette.

- **True/False:** Select this option to change the value of an attribute from true to false or vice versa.

- **Number:** Select this option if you want to type a number for the value of an attribute, such as when you want to change the `border` attribute of an image.

- **Default:** This field shows the value of the selected object's current attribute. Type a new initial value for the parameter in the template-based file.

5. **If creating multiple editable tag attributes for the selected tag, repeat Steps 2 through 4 until you've set all the editable tag attributes.**

6. **Click OK to accept the settings.**

   Each editable tag attribute adds template parameters to the code whereby the initial value of the attribute is set in the template and the parameter can be changed from within the template-based document.

Changing editable tag attributes in template-based files

To modify an editable tag attribute from within a template-based document, open the file in the Dreamweaver workspace window and do the following:

1. **Choose Modify➪Template Properties.**

   The Template Properties dialog box opens, as shown in Figure 2-15.

**Book III
Chapter 2**

Building Sites with Templates

Figure 2-15:
Editable tag attributes can be modified in template-based files.

Template Properties

Name	Value
src	images/nav_01.gif
width	400

OK
Cancel
Help

src: ges/nav_01.gif
☐ Allow nested templates to control this

2. **Select the editable tag attribute to modify from the Name column.**

   The bottom half of the dialog box updates to display the corresponding attribute editing options.

3. **Modify the selected editable tag attribute.**

   For instance, if one of the attributes allowed the value of the background color of the page to be modified, the bottom of the dialog box displays a Background Color Picker field for selecting a new background color.

4. **If modifying multiple editable tag attributes at once, repeat Steps 2 and 3.**

5. **Click OK.**

Resetting an editable tag attribute to uneditable

To change an editable tag attribute to an uneditable one, open the template and follow these steps:

1. **Select the editable tag in Code view.**

   Selecting the tag makes the editable attribute for this tag automatically display in the Attribute field of the Editable Tag Attributes dialog box.

2. **Choose Modify⇨Templates⇨Make Attribute Editable.**

   The Editable Tag Attributes dialog box opens (refer to Figure 2-14).

3. **Deselect the Make Attribute Editable check box next to the attributes you want to disable, and click OK.**

4. **Save the template and update all the template-based files.**

Building Nested Templates

Nested templates are templates whose design layouts and editable areas are based on another template file. A nested template is created when a template-based file is modified and then resaved as a new template file with new editable regions. For example, you can create a nested template that contains specific layout elements, such as a real-estate listing Web site where the detail information for each listing shares the same layout yet the overall page layout and design instructions come from the original template.

To make nested templates quickly, begin the creation process with a new template-based document that uses the base template you intend to modify.

Creating nested templates

To create a nested template, follow these steps:

1. **Create a template-based document from the base (original) template.**

Choose File⇨New and click the Templates tab at the top of the New Document dialog box. Select the managed site and template that you want to use and click the Create button in the dialog box. A new template-based document opens in the workspace window.

The nesting feature doesn't work if you attempt to create a new template from an existing template file. You must create the nested template from a template-based document.

2. **Choose File⇨Save as Template.**

You can also click the Templates button on the Common tab of the Insert bar and choose Make Nested Template from the drop-down list.

The Save As Template dialog box opens.

3. **Name the new nested template and click OK.**

4. **Add content and new editable regions to the nested template.**

For example, a new nested area can contain a table layout with an image, a header graphic, and a nested table for displaying content. For details on creating an editable region, see "Working with Editable Regions," earlier in the chapter.

5. **When you finish making changes, save the file before creating template-based pages from the new nested template.**

Modifying nested templates

By default, the base template passes along any editable regions to the nested template. To convert an editable region passed through from a base template to a nested template into an uneditable region, you need to add some markup to the nested template.

To prevent an editable region from getting passed to the nested template, follow these steps:

1. **Open the nested template in the Dreamweaver workspace.**

2. **In Code view, add the following code to the editable region code:**

```
@@(" ")@@
```

Add this code anywhere between the template markup tags:

```
<!-- InstanceBeginEditable --> <!-- InstanceEndEditable -->
```

For example, code would change from:

```
<td><!-- InstanceBeginEditable name="Address" -->
Address 1
<!-- InstanceEndEditable --></td>
```

to this:

```
<td><!-- InstanceBeginEditable name="Address" -->
@@(" ")@@ Address 1
<!-- InstanceEndEditable --></td>
```

Blocked editable regions inside nested templates display with a little expression marker inside their boundaries, as shown in Figure 2-16. In Design view, they also display with an orange highlighting color around the region, compared to the blue used to identify regular editable regions.

Expression icon

Figure 2-16:
In Design view, uneditable regions in nested templates display a small expression icon.

Though nested templates look nearly identical to base templates, they do not necessarily share common areas when edits are made to the base template. For example, if you add a sentence to a noneditable region on the base template, that content doesn't pass through or appear on the nested template.

Creating a New Document from a Template

After you create a template and set all the editable regions needed inside it, you can begin building the Web site with pages generated from the template.

Create a new template-based page by following these steps:

1. **Choose File⇨New to open the New Document dialog box.**

2. Click the Templates tab at the top of the dialog box to select the template by site and template name.

Be sure that the Update Page When Template Changes check box is checked.

3. Choose File⇨Save to save the new template-based file to the local root folder of the managed site.

The file is saved as a regular HTML file based on a Dreamweaver template. As shown in Figure 2-17, template-based pages are quickly identifiable by the yellow highlighted rectangle displaying around the inside of the entire document, topped by a yellow Template: *filename* tab at the top right edge of the page.

Template tab

Figure 2-17:
The
Template
tab in
Design
view.

Book III
Chapter 2

Building Sites with
Templates

4. Add page-specific content to the editable areas of the page.

Add text, graphics, tables, and other elements as you need.

Locked uneditable regions are easily identifiable by the mouse pointer changing into the locked region pointer (see Figure 2-18).

Figure 2-18:
The locked
symbol.

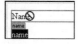

Continue building all the pages for the Web site in a similar fashion until your site is complete, fully tested, and ready for uploading.

Editing Templates and Updating Pages

Whenever you modify and save a template, Dreamweaver not only recognizes that the template has changed, but also gives you the option to automatically update all the documents on the local managed site that were created with that template. If you'd rather selectively update template-based documents, Dreamweaver provides a method for that as well.

Modifying a template and updating all the pages that use it

You can update a template in Dreamweaver whenever you want and then apply the changes to all the files based on that template. For example, suppose that you want to change the name of one of the main navigation links (for example, changing "Contact" to "Order") on all the template-based pages on your site. To make the change, open the template that you used to create the template-based pages and modify the link and any other content that may need changing. When you save the template with these changes, Dreamweaver then updates all the pages created with that template.

To edit a template and update all the pages that use the template, follow these steps:

1. **Open an existing template by double-clicking the template file listed inside the Templates folder in the Files panel.**

You can also select the template from the Templates folder in the Files panel and choose File⇨Open from the Files panel Options menu.

2. **Make any changes to the template.**

As long as the template file is open in the Dreamweaver workspace, you can perform multiple undos from the History panel or choose Edit⇨Undo.

3. **Choose File⇨Save.**

Dreamweaver recognizes any changes made to a template and opens the Update Template Files dialog box (shown in Figure 2-19), which prompts you to let the program automatically update all pages that use the template.

Figure 2-19: Dream-weaver automates the template-based page updating process.

Update Template Files

Update all files based on this template?

page1.html
page2.html
page3.html

Update

Don't Update

4. To update any pages that use this template, click the Update button.

When the update is complete, the Update Template Files dialog box displays a status log to confirm how many files were examined and updated. Dreamweaver actually hard-codes the changes into all the files that use the template. You can now confidently upload all the changed documents to the remote server.

Another automatic feature Dreamweaver performs when saving changes to templates is syntax checking to ensure that any expression or template parameter added in Code view is accurate. If the syntax is bad, Dreamweaver displays an error message with a reference to the line of code containing the error. You can manually check template syntax at any time by choosing Modify⇨Templates⇨Check Template Syntax.

While you can edit regular pages in Contribute, you must edit templates in Dreamweaver. For more information about working with Contribute sites, turn to Book VI.

Selectively updating pages with the most recent version of the template

If you make edits to a template but don't want to apply them to all the pages based on it, such as when you add a template to your site from an external source or edit the template in another program, you can manually update the pages. This is also how you can make modifications to a template before committing to updating all the pages on the site, so long as you click No to the Dreamweaver prompt that asks if you want to update all the files that use that template. You can use two methods to selectively update template-based pages.

To update a single template-based document, follow these steps:

1. Open the template-based document in the workspace window.

2. Choose Modify⇨Templates⇨Update Current Page.

The current page updates to reflect the most recent version of the template file upon which it is based.

3. Choose File⇨Save to save the open page.

You must save the page to save the updates.

You can update multiple template-based documents — an entire site or just the files that are attached to the specified template — at once by following these steps:

Book III
Chapter 2

Building Sites with
Templates

1. **Choose Modify⇨Templates⇨Update Pages.**

The Update Pages dialog box opens.

2. **Choose one of the following options:**

- **Update the entire site:** Select Entire Site from the Look In drop-down list; then select your site from the second drop-down list.

- **Update pages with a specific template:** Select Files that Use from the Look In drop-down list; then select the Dreamweaver template .dwt file that you want to use to perform the update.

3. **Click the Start button to begin the update.**

The Update Pages dialog box performs the update. To see the status log, click the Show Log check box. Updates are immediate.

4. **When you finish your update, click Close to close the dialog box.**

Applying Templates to Pages

You can selectively apply templates to pages open in the Document window with the Assets panel, regardless of whether or not you previously applied the template.

To apply a template to a new, open document from the Assets panel:

✦ Click the Templates button along the left margin of the Assets panel, select the template from the list, and click the Apply button at the bottom of the panel.

✦ Click the Templates button along the left margin of the Assets panel, then drag and drop the template file into the open Document window.

If you want to apply a template to a document that currently uses a different template, follow these steps:

1. **Open the document in the Dreamweaver workspace.**

2. **Choose Modify⇨Templates⇨Apply Template to Page.**

The Select Template dialog box opens.

3. **Choose a site from the list of managed sites and a template from the list of available templates in that site.**

4. **Click the Select button in the dialog box.**

The Inconsistent Region Names dialog box opens.

5. **Map the editable regions from the old template to the new template. In the Name column under Editable Regions, select the old editable region name. Then choose the new region name from the Move Content to New Region drop-down list.**

   This tells Dreamweaver which editable regions in the new template the content from the old template's editable areas should go into. For instance, the old template may have two editable regions called `body` and `head` while the new template has two regions called `main` and `header`. Select and match those regions from the old template to the regions on the new template so the content on the existing page moves to the specified region of the new template.

   When regions in the old and new templates have the same names, content in those editable regions are automatically matched up. If all regions match up, the mapping process happens automatically.

6. **Choose File⇨Save to save the updated page.**

For an alternate method, create a new template-based page, and transfer content (by copying and pasting) from the editable regions on the original file to the editable regions on the new template-based page.

Detaching Templates from Pages

Why would you want to detach a template? You may need a page that looks like the rest of the site but is not controlled by the template, or perhaps a particular page needs to be significantly different from the rest of the site and modifying a template-based page is easier than building the new page from scratch, or you want to quickly remove all the editable regions and other template markup on a page rather than having to selectively remove the restrictive code. Whatever your reason, the detachment process is fairly simple.

To detach a template from a page, follow these steps:

1. **Open the document in the Dreamweaver workspace.**

2. **Choose Modify⇨Templates⇨Detach from Template.**

   All the template-specific markup is removed from the file, making any formerly uneditable areas in the code fully editable again.

3. **Save the file.**

After you detach the template from the page, you can reattach it by choosing Modify⇨Templates⇨Apply Template to Page. Additionally, you can reattach the template by undoing the detachment through the History panel as long as you keep the document open (see Book III, Chapter 4 for more on the

History panel). However, after you save and close the file you have to re-attach the template manually.

Managing Templates

Use the Assets panel for renaming and deleting any of your existing templates. To display the list of templates, click the Templates button along the left margin of the Assets panel (see Figure 2-20).

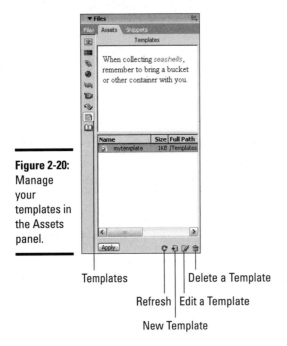

Figure 2-20:
Manage your templates in the Assets panel.

Templates

Refresh | Edit a Template

New Template

Delete a Template

Renaming a template

Should you ever need to rename a template, Dreamweaver can automate the name change across all the files in the managed site.

To rename a template in the Assets panel, follow these steps:

1. **From the Templates listing in the Assets panel, click to select the template name that you want to change.**

Make sure that the template file you're renaming is not open. You can also rename the template from the Files panel.

2. **Click the filename again so the text becomes selectable; then type a new filename.**

   If you accidentally double-click and open the template for editing, try the single-click, pause, single-click method again on the template filename.

3. **Press Enter (Windows) or Return (Mac) to complete the name change.**

   Dreamweaver prompts you to update all the template-based documents that use this file.

4. **Click the Update button to update all the template-based files.**

Deleting a template file

At the end of a project, you may need to delete a template file that wasn't used on the site:

1. **From the templates listing in the Assets panel, click to select the template that you want to delete.**

2. **Click the Delete button at the bottom of the Assets panel.**

   After clicking the button, you're prompted to confirm the deletion.

When deleting files, remember that once they're gone, your files are gone for good. If you think you may need the file in the future, make a backup of the entire managed site before making the deletion.

Documents based on a deleted template do not get automatically detached from it; rather, they keep their existing format, including editable regions. If you need to, you can convert template-based files into regular HTML files by choosing Modify⇨Templates⇨Detach from Template.

**Book III
Chapter 2**

Building Sites with Templates

Chapter 3: Using Library Items and Server-Side Includes

In This Chapter

✔ **Creating library items**

✔ **Managing and editing library items**

✔ **Creating server-side includes (SSIs)**

✔ **Inserting and editing SSIs**

Dreamweaver provides you with two different ways of creating reusable assets for your Web pages: library items and server-side includes. You can add both to documents, templates, and template-based pages, and both can contain any content that normally goes in the body of the page. Here's a closer look at the two methods:

✦ **Library items:** These special files contain content of your choice that you can insert onto multiple Web pages, yet manage the contents of in one location. Once inserted on a page, the library item content gets hard-coded into the HTML surrounded by special Dreamweaver library item comment tags. Any time you edit the library item's contents, all the pages that contain the library files are automatically updated. Library items are great for subnavigation tables, copyright notices, and other common page elements that need frequent editing.

✦ **Server-side include (SSI) files:** Like library items, SSIs are special files containing specific content that you can add to multiple Web pages and update in one centralized location. The main difference from library items, however, is that SSI content isn't hard-coded into the HTML file it's inserted into; instead, SSI files are saved as external HTML files and are then linked — similar to CSS — to a file. When the page is viewed in a browser, the browser finds the external SSI file and displays that content as if it were naturally coded into the page. Use SSIs for sections of Web pages that need frequent or constant editing on larger Web sites, such as a navigation item, daily menu, or class schedule.

This chapter shows you how to create, use, and edit library items and server-side includes.

Introducing Library Items

If you're familiar with Dreamweaver's templates (discussed in Book III, Chapter 2), library items work in a similar way. Whereas templates are the master documents from which you create new documents, *library items* are simply master page elements (such as navigation menus, tables, and images) containing whatever content you desire. You can use them as many times as you want without the need for rewriting the code each time. Library items are typically placed inside templates or used as stand-alone master elements in regular or template-based pages.

To understand more plainly how library items work, think of the original/ duplicate relationship of a rubber stamp. Your rubber stamp has the original design, and when you ink it up, you can stamp it to make as many copies of that stamp's design as you like. Similarly, with library items you create the original library item, save it, and then insert a copy of it when and where you need it on your Web pages.

Creating Library Items

Create library items from any selected content in the body of your page, including text, graphics, forms, tables, media, and JavaScript. If the selected content has images or other linked items, those items must stay in their original locations for the library item to work properly.

When your library items include Dreamweaver JavaScript *behaviors* (which let visitors interact in some way with your Web page), Dreamweaver also copies the element and its *event handler* (an action that specifies when the event occurs, such as `onMouseOver`) to the library item file. Then, when you insert that library item into another document, Dreamweaver automatically adds the necessary JavaScript functions into the `<head>` area of the file so the copied library item containing the behavior works in the new file. By contrast, when hand-coding JavaScript behaviors, be sure to use the Call JavaScript behavior as part of the library item to execute the code; the behavior allows you to set a function or line of script to execute when a particular event happens in the browser. (See Book IV, Chapter 2 for more on behaviors.)

Here are some general guidelines of when to use library items:

✦ Your Web site is small (less than 30 pages).

✦ You manage the site yourself.

✦ You expect to make periodic changes to the library items or you antici- pate the library item content may need altering in the future.

✦ You understand that making edits to the library items requires a rewrit- ing of all the pages on your site that use those library items, which therefore means you must upload all the updated files to your server before site visitors can view those changes.

✦ Your Web host doesn't support server-side includes.

✦ Every bit of processor speed is important to you (pages with SSIs take a little longer to load in a browser than pages containing library items).

Here are some good uses for library items:

✦ Footers

✦ Navigation elements

✦ Parts of your page/site that may require periodic updating and appear on multiple pages, such as product tag lines, sponsorship listings, and contact information.

✦ Copyright notices

One great use for a library item is a copyright notice at the foot of a page, such as: *Copyright 2006. All rights reserved.* It uses the current year now, but come January 1st, you need to update the year. Fortunately when you're ready to make the date change, you need to update only the original library item while Dreamweaver updates all the pages that use the library item with the new code.

Creating a selection-based library item

Follow these steps to create a library item based on content you've created:

1. **In the Files panel, click the Assets tab and then click the Library button in the left margin of the Assets panel.**

The Library options appear in the Assets panel (see Figure 3-1).

2. **In Code or Design view of an open document, select the content you want to convert into a library item.**

Library items can contain text, graphics, links, tables, JavaScript, Flash movies, and other HTML code elements.

In the copyright example, select the copyright sentence in your docu- ment such as: *Copyright 2006. All rights reserved.*

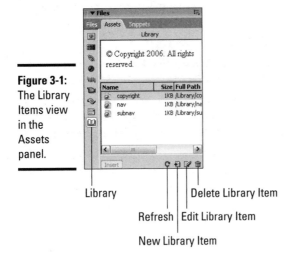

Figure 3-1:
The Library
Items view
in the
Assets
panel.

Library

Refresh | Edit Library Item

Delete Library Item

New Library Item

3. **Click the New Library Item button in the Assets panel.**

   You can also choose Modify➪Library➪Add Object to Library to create a new library item.

   Dreamweaver converts your selected code into a library item with the .lbi file extension, then creates a Library folder and puts your newly created library item there.

   You know your code converted properly to a library item because it displays in your page, in Design and Code views, as a block of code with pale yellow highlighting.

4. **Give your new library item a descriptive name, such as** copyright, **and press Enter (Windows) or Return (Mac).**

   By default, new library items are called untitled.lbi until you rename them in the Assets panel. See the later section, "Renaming library items."

Creating an empty library item

For times when you know you need a library item on your site but don't have the content for it yet — such as when a client still needs to send you approved text — you can create and use an empty library item. You can edit the library item when the content becomes available.

You can create an empty library item for editing at a later time by following these steps:

Changing library highlighting preferences

You can change the highlighting color and the visibility of the highlighting of library items in the Preferences dialog box.

To alter the highlight color, follow these steps:

1. **Choose Edit⇨Preferences (Windows) or Dreamweaver⇨Preferences (Mac) to open the Preferences dialog box.**

2. **Choose the Highlighting category on the left side of the dialog box.**

3. **On the right side of the panel, click the Library Items color box to choose a new** highlight color with the color picker or type the hexadecimal value in the text box.

4. **Click Show to see the highlighted library color in your documents or deselect the Show option to hide the highlighting.**

5. **Click OK.**

To see library item highlight colors in your documents, choose View⇨Visual Aids⇨Invisible Elements. Toggle on and off the display of library item highlighting.

1. **In the Files panel, click the Assets tab and then click the Library button in the left margin of the Assets panel.**

2. **Click the New Library Item button at the bottom of the panel.**

   A new untitled library item is added to the Library folder. Make sure nothing is selected in the Document window before doing so; otherwise, the selected content is converted into a library item. That means if you have a library item selected on the page, it becomes duplicated.

3. **Give your new library item a descriptive name and press Enter (Windows) or Return (Mac).**

   You can now add the library item to your pages and edit the content at any time.

Inserting a Library Item in Your Document

When you insert a library item in a document, the entire contents of that library item are added to the page along with library item markup tags, as shown in the following example:

```
<!-- #BeginLibraryItem "/Library/copyright.lbi" -->&copy; Copyright 2006. All
    rights reserved.<!-- #EndLibraryItem -->
```

Follow these steps to insert a library item on a page:

1. **Place your cursor inside the open document where you want to insert the library item.**

   Setting the insertion point determines the location of the library item. For example, if you want to insert a library item that's a copyright notice, place your cursor at the foot of a page.

2. **Open the Library area of the Assets panel by clicking the Assets tab in the Files panel, and clicking the Library button at the left edge of the panel.**

   The Library button looks like an open book.

3. **Select the library item that you want to insert.**

   The Library area of the Assets panel contains a list of all available library items for the currently managed site. If you have created library items but do not see them in this listing, click the blue Refresh button at the bottom of the Assets panel.

4. **Click the Insert button in the Library area of the Assets panel.**

   You can also drag and drop the library item from the Library area of the Assets panel into your open document.

Notice that when you insert your library item, Dreamweaver writes opening and closing comment tags along with your library item contents, as shown in Figure 3-2.

Figure 3-2:
Highlighting and comment tags appear when inserting library items.

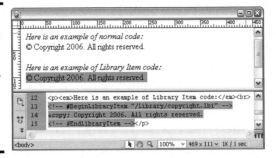

If you want to insert the contents of a library item onto a page without the library item markup, press Ctrl (Windows) or Option (Mac) while dragging the item onto the document from the Assets panel. The content becomes disconnected from the library source so the library item doesn't control the content.

Using library items sounds so easy that you may be wondering why you wouldn't use them. The main complaint about library items is this: Because they're hard-coded into your pages, when you edit them, any pages on your site that contain the library item must be updated with the new code and subsequently uploaded to your server before site visitors can see those changes. When your site has a lot of pages, the time the uploading process takes to complete is a major consideration. This is especially an issue when your site uses the Check In/Check Out system. Furthermore, updating library items alters the Last Modified time of each file, making it more difficult for you to track when a file's unique content was actually last changed.

Editing and Managing Library Items

After you successfully create a library item, you can edit it any time. You can then apply those changes to a single page, the entire site, or all the files that use the library item.

In addition to regular content updates, you may occasionally need to perform other management tasks such as renaming, deleting, detaching, duplicating, or re-creating a library item.

Editing library items

Follow these steps to edit a library item:

Book III
Chapter 3

Using Library Items and Server-Side Includes

1. **In the Files panel, click the Assets tab and click the Library button in the left margin of the Assets panel.**

2. **Select the library item that you want to edit.**

    If you're unsure what the library item is named, look in the preview pane of the Library area of the Assets panel to see a thumbnail of the library item.

3. **Click the Edit button on the bottom of the Library area of the Assets panel to open the library item in the Dreamweaver workspace window.**

    You can also open the library item into its own Document window by selecting the library item in Design or Code view and clicking the Edit button in the Properties inspector.

4. **Edit the library item and save the changes by choosing File➪Save.**

    Because library items are hard-coded into your pages, Dreamweaver prompts you to update all the pages that contain that item.

5. **Click OK if you want Dreamweaver to find all the instances of the original library item code on any pages on your site and update it to match the changes you just made.**

   If you happen to skip this updating prompt, manually perform updates by choosing Modify➪Library and the item you want to update.

Updating documents and sites that use library items

After editing a library item, you may want to manually update the files that use it. You can update a single page from within that document, your entire site, or all the files that use a particular library item.

To update a library item in the open document, choose Modify➪Library➪ Update Current Page.

To update an entire site or all files using a specific library item, follow these steps after you edit the library item:

1. **Choose Modify➪Library➪Update Pages.**

   The Update Pages dialog box opens, as shown in Figure 3-3.

Figure 3-3:
Update library items on an entire site.

2. **Select an option from the Look In drop-down list, depending on what you want to do:**

   • **Update the library item sitewide:** Select Entire Site, and in the right drop-down list, select the name of the site.

   • **Update the library item in all files:** Select Files That Use, and in the right drop-down list, select the library item name.

3. **Check to see that Library Items is checked as an Update option.**

4. **Click the Start button to begin the update process.**

   Select the Show Log check box to view a status log of the update process. There you find a record of the number of files on the site that were examined and updated, plus any files that Dreamweaver was unable to update.

5. **When you finish, click Close.**

Renaming library items

You can easily rename library items in the Library area of the Assets panel of a managed site, and it's recommended you perform your library name changes from within Dreamweaver.

Renaming a library item outside of Dreamweaver breaks the library links to the documents that use them.

To rename a library item, follow these steps:

1. **In the Files panel, click the Assets tab and click the Library button in the left margin of the Assets panel.**

2. **Select the library item you want to rename.**

   If you're unsure of the library item's current name, look in the preview pane of the Library area of the Assets panel to see a thumbnail of the library item.

3. **Click the library item name again, so the text becomes editable, and typing the new name.**

   If you accidentally double-click and open the library item for editing, try the single-click, pause, single-click method again on the library item filename.

4. **After entering the new name, press Enter (Windows) or Return (Mac) to complete the name change.**

   Dreamweaver opens the Update Files dialog box.

5. **Click the Update button.**

   Dreamweaver automatically updates all the documents in the managed site that use this library item. To prevent Dreamweaver from performing the automatic update, click the Don't Update button. For example, you may want to delay if you intend on changing multiple library files on a site.

Book III
Chapter 3

Using Library Items
and Server-Side
Includes

Deleting library items

To help keep your library items organized while developing your site, delete any unused or unnecessary library items from the Library area of the Assets panel by following these steps:

1. **In the Files panel, click the Assets tab and click the Library button in the left margin of the Assets panel.**

2. **Select the library item that you want to delete.**

   If you're unsure of the name of the library item you want to delete, select an item from the list and look in the preview pane to see a thumbnail of the selected item.

3. **To permanently delete the library item from the library, press the Delete key on your keyboard and confirm the deletion.**

   You can also click the Delete button at the bottom of the Assets panel and confirm the deletion.

   This deletion process permanently removes the library item from the library though it doesn't delete instances of that item from the contents of any documents that used it. Therefore, delete your library items with care.

Detaching library items

After you insert a library item into a document, you can't edit an individual instance of it unless you break the link between the library item and the document by detaching it and converting the library item into editable text. Then, when you update the original library item after an instance is detached, the detached instance doesn't update along with the other instances of the library item.

You may want to detach an instance of a library item from its source for many reasons:

✦ You need to modify a significant portion of the library item on a single page.

✦ You've only used the library item on a single page.

✦ You want to insert a library item created for another site. You insert it on a page, detach it to break the links to that other site, and then re-create the link within the currently managed site.

To detach a library item and convert it into editable text, follow these steps:

1. **Select the library item in the document that you want to convert.**

2. **Click the Detach from Original button in the Properties inspector.**

   Dreamweaver alerts you that making the item editable prevents it from receiving updates from the original library item.

3. **Click OK.**

   The selected library item then loses its library item highlighting and markup to become normal, editable text.

To modify library items that contain Dreamweaver behaviors, you must detach the library item from its source to make the behavior editable. After editing the behavior, use the updated content to create a new library item or use it as a replacement for its previous version.

Duplicating library items

To use an existing library item as the basis for creating a new library item, create a duplicate copy with a new name, and then edit the duplicate.

To duplicate an existing library item, follow these steps:

1. **In the Files panel, click the Assets tab and click the Library button. Then, from the list of Library items, select the library item that you want to duplicate.**

2. **To create a duplicate, choose Edit⇨Duplicate from the Options menu in the Assets panel.**

   Dreamweaver inserts the duplicate copy inside the Library folder.

3. **To rename the duplicate copy, select the duplicate library item and enter a new name for the file.**

Re-creating library items

Occasionally, you delete a library item from the Library area of the Assets panel even though instances of it still remain throughout the site. If you want the library item back to control modifications made to all the instances, you must re-create it.

Here's how to re-create a library item:

1. **In an open document, select the instance of the library item that you need to re-create.**

2. **Click the Recreate button in the Properties inspector.**

A new library item is added to the Library area of the Assets panel. If a library item already exists there with the same name, Dreamweaver asks if you want to overwrite the existing file. Click OK to proceed.

A master copy of the re-created library item is inserted into the Library folder.

Understanding Server-Side Includes

If you understand how to create and use library items (as described earlier in the chapter), you can quickly grasp the concept behind server-side includes (SSIs). Like library items, SSIs can be composed of HTML, JavaScript, or graphics. But unlike library items, they have no opening and closing comment tags surrounding the code and the content of the SSI is not hard-coded into your Web page. Rather, a simple line of code is added to your page that points to the external SSI file on your server, like this:

```
<!--#include file="serversideinclude.html" -->
```

Only the reference to, and not the contents of, the SSI file are part of the include instructions.

An SSI is an external HTML file that a server adds to the page it's inserted on when a browser requests that page from the server. The server then processes the include instructions and delivers a document that replaces the SSI statement code with the content of the SSI file.

When making the decision to use SSI, keep these points in mind:

✦ When you preview the file with the include instructions in a browser locally (before testing it on a live server), your browser doesn't *parse* the SSI, in which case you may not see the include content on the page.

To solve this issue, Dreamweaver lets you preview documents in Design view exactly as they'll appear on a server. Furthermore, by checking the Preview Using Temporary File option in the Preview in Browser category of Dreamweaver's Preferences dialog box, you can create a temporary copy of the file for preview and testing that displays the SSI in your local browser by mimicking how the file would behave on a server.

✦ Servers process, or *parse,* pages with SSIs differently than regular HTML documents, and that may put more demand on a server's processor, which in turn could lead to slower page serving for all the pages on your entire site.

✦ The SSI markup syntax must match the type of Web server the files are being displayed on. Some servers are configured to examine all files to see if they have server-side includes, whereas other servers examine only files with the `.shtml`, `.shtm`, or `.inc` file extension.

Your particular server may require that you rename all files containing SSIs with the `.shtml`, `.shtm`, or `.inc` file extension. For example, you may need to rename a file with an SSI named `menu.html` to `menu.shtml` to manifest the include properly. Check with your system administrator or host provider to see whether you're required to change the file extension for documents with SSIs.

The bottom line is that you should test files containing SSIs on a server before publishing them on the Internet, just in case the host server isn't configured to display them properly or you need to modify your code to support them.

Creating and Inserting Server-Side Includes

Like a regular HTML file, a server-side include file (an example of which is shown in Figure 3-4) is composed of the content you want to include on another page, and should be saved with the `.html` or `.htm` file extension. What it shouldn't contain, however, are any `<doctype>`, `<meta>`, or opening or closing `<html>`, `<head>`, `<title>`, or `<body>` tags in the code. This is because the SSI is included on another page that already has those HTML tags. Figure 3-5 demonstrates how an SSI file is included in the code of another document.

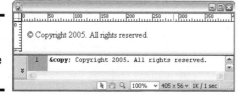

Figure 3-4:
A server-side include file.

Figure 3-5:
A server-side include inside another document.

Here are some general guidelines for when you may want to use server-side includes:

✦ Your Web site is large (more than 30 pages).

✦ Two or more people manage the site from different locations.

✦ You have site content that needs frequent editing.

✦ You are confident your host provider supports SSIs.

✦ Your clients want to update part of the site regularly, and they understand and can write the SSI content in HTML themselves.

✦ You have a client who doesn't have Dreamweaver and can't take advantage of library items.

✦ You love the fact that you only have to upload the SSI files to the server when their content changes, rather than uploading all the files that contain them, as you must do for library items.

✦ Your site is database driven (ASP, JSP, PHP, CFML).

✦ You've tested your server and are confident that the SSIs work.

Here are some good uses for SSIs:

✦ Footers

✦ Copyright notices

✦ Navigation elements

✦ Jump menus

✦ Parts of your page/site that may require periodic updating, such as class schedules, course descriptions, news items, and so on

✦ Parts of your site that require regular updates, such as a menu or event listing

If you're uncertain whether a library item or server-side include is best for your projects, consider this general rule: If the site is small, use library items. If the site is large and needs regular updates to certain parts of the content, your server supports them, and you don't mind the ever-so-slightly slower page opening times, use SSIs.

Creating a server-side include

One fast way to create an SSI file is to first build the content in a normal Dreamweaver HTML file, and then copy the content from that file and paste it into an empty document that doesn't contain any HTML markup.

Presuming you've already created a document with the content for the SSI, follow these instructions to convert that content into a server-side include file:

1. **Open the document that has the content for the SSI file.**

2. **Select the content and choose Edit⇨Copy.**

    The copied content is temporarily placed in your computer's Clipboard. Close that file without saving the changes.

3. **Choose File⇨New to open a new basic HTML document in the Dreamweaver workspace window.**

4. **In Code view, choose Edit⇨Select All to select all the code in the file, and press the Delete or Backspace key on your keyboard.**

    Be sure the entire document is empty of all code before proceeding.

5. **With your cursor still in Code view of the empty file, choose Edit⇨Paste to paste the copied content from the original file.**

6. **Save the new SSI file with an appropriate filename and the `.html` or `.htm` file extension.**

    If you plan on having several SSI files on the same Web site, consider saving all the SSI files into one folder at the site's root level for better organization of the SSI files.

You can now insert the SSI file into another file, as described in the next section.

Inserting a server-side include

Dreamweaver writes the appropriate syntax into your code when you use the built-in SSI command. Insert your server-side include files into regular documents, dynamic documents, templates, or template-based files.

To insert an SSI into a page, follow these steps:

1. **Open the document that you want to add the SSI to.**

2. **Click the cursor where you want the SSI to display.**

    Use either Design or Code view.

3. **Choose Insert⇨Server-Side Include.**

    The Select File dialog box opens.

4. **Browse to and select the SSI `.html` file.**

If you've saved your SSI files into a separate folder, navigate to that folder and select the appropriate SSI file.

5. **Click OK.**

   Dreamweaver adds the appropriate SSI code to your document, as shown in the following example where the SSI file, called `copyright.html`, is located in a folder called `ssi`:

   ```
   <!--#include file="/ssi/copyright.html" -->
   ```

6. **Select the newly inserted SSI in Design view, and then choose File or Virtual as the include type in the Properties inspector.**

   You can choose from two SSI types: File or Virtual. Depending on the type of server you have, you may need to replace the word *file* with *virtual* in the include instructions. Apache servers typically use the Virtual setting (this is the Dreamweaver default), whereas File is the standard for Microsoft Internet Information Server (IIS).

   When the server runs IIS software, ask your host provider or system administrator about installing special software if you include a file in a folder above the current folder in the site root folder hierarchy.

   If your server uses another kind of software besides Apache or IIS, check with your host provider or system administrator for which SSI type to use.

   Dreamweaver immediately displays the include file's content in Design view, such as

   ```
   © Copyright 2006. All rights reserved.
   ```

   while showing include instruction markup in Code view, such as

   ```
   <!--#include file="/ssi/copyright.html" -->
   ```

7. **Save the file that contains the newly inserted SSI with the `.html` or `.shtml` file extension as instructed by your system administrator or host provider.**

   The include file itself doesn't need any particular extension. However, if you want the include file to also include another sub-file, then you need to save the include file as an `.shtml` file (or whatever extension type enables server-side includes on your server).

8. **Upload the SSI files and any documents containing SSI to your remote host server.**

   If you saved the SSI files into a local folder, be sure to upload the same folder structure to the server so the links to the SSI files match.

To change to a different SSI file after inserting one on a page, select the server-side include in the open file and click the folder button next to the Filename field in the Properties inspector to browse for and choose a new SSI file.

Document versus root-relative links

When working with SSIs, their mere existence on some Web servers may require site root-relative linking rather than document-relative linking. In other words, you may need to add a forward slash before the SSI filename such as the following:

Document-Relative:

```
<!--#include file="ssi/serversideinclude.
       html" -->
```

Site Root-Relative:

```
<!--#include
       file="/ssi/serversideinclude.
       html" -->
```

The forward slash at the start of the path, before the folder or filename, tells the browser viewing the site to use the root level as the starting point for locating files on the server.

Speak with your system administrator or host provider to find out if and how they support SSIs before building your pages with them. If you do ultimately choose to use server-side includes, test them on your server to ensure they'll display properly before publishing the entire site.

For further information about relative links and site organization, see Book I, Chapter 2.

The SSIs now render seamlessly in the browser window. If the SSI files do not display in the browser, you need to convert your Web site linking system to use site root-relative linking, as the next section describes.

Editing Server-Side Includes

Edit a server-side include file just as you would any other HTML document by opening the file in the Dreamweaver workspace, making changes, saving it, and uploading the changed SSI file to the host server.

To open the file for editing in the Dreamweaver workspace window, double-click the SSI file from its location in the Files panel. You can also select the SSI content in Design or Code view of the page it's inserted on and click the Edit button in the Properties inspector, or simply double-click the SSI content in Design view.

Within Dreamweaver's Design view, edits to the SSI file appear immediately in the files containing them, but for site visitors to see the changes in a browser window, you must upload the updated SSI file to the host server.

Chapter 4: Creating Code Snippets and History Panel Commands

In This Chapter

✔ **Understanding snippets**

✔ **Using Dreamweaver's snippets**

✔ **Making your own snippets**

✔ **Editing, deleting, and managing snippets**

✔ **Working with the History panel**

✔ **Creating History panel commands**

*I*f you build a lot of Web sites, you know that you'll use certain elements over and over again, but each time you need them, you either have to recall a particular command, or more likely copy and paste the code containing the content you want to reuse. Knowing that is not the most efficient way to work, Dreamweaver created a solution called Code Snippets that, once created, become available to developers across all sites.

Don't confuse snippets with library items or SSIs (which we cover in Book III, Chapter 3). Snippets are intended to be used as either shortcuts for inserting a single instance of content on a page or as a way of quickly modifying selected content in a file.

Similar in theory to Microsoft's macros or Adobe's Actions, Code Snippets are a fantastic way to automate some of your repetitive tasks and make your job easier. They are composed of bits of code and/or content that you can save, edit, use, and reuse as often as you want on any Web site you happen to be working on. Dreamweaver even comes with a great set of prewritten, logically categorized, ready-to-use snippets. You can find them sitting in the Snippets panel (which you open by choosing Window⇨Snippets).

Other terrific timesaving tools are the temporary and permanent custom commands you can create with the Dreamweaver History panel (which you open by choosing Window⇨History). Record and save any series of steps — such as select, bold, deselect — to play again and again at a later time.

In this chapter, you find out how to create, insert, edit, and delete snippets, as well as organize them in folders to share with your workmates. This chapter also covers how to record and play History panel commands.

Understanding What Snippets Do

The best snippets are the ones that save you time or at least limit the work you need to perform so you don't have to retype anything, such as the following:

✦ Code including HTML, JavaScript, ASP, JSP, and even CFML (*ColdFusion Markup Language*).

✦ Text that you use often. For instance, you may like to add a copyright notice such as © *2006 All rights reserved* at the foot of your pages.

✦ Navigation tables with bullets and text that have temporary links already applied to each navigation word so all you need to do after inserting the snippet on your page is type the real navigation names and links.

✦ JavaScript information, such as the Set Text of Status Bar JavaScript behavior, or perhaps opening and closing comment tags.

There are two basic types of snippets:

✦ **Wrap snippets** insert code before and after any selected content on the page, such as adding `<div>` tags with center alignment around a selected line of text, as in:

```
<div align="center">This sentence uses a div align center tag.</div>
```

✦ **Block snippets** simply drop in the snippet content after the insertion point on the page, such as a line of code with JavaScript to display the current date.

Using Dreamweaver's Snippets

Dreamweaver comes with a great set of preset snippets already categorized into files for Navigation, Meta, JavaScript, Headers, Footers, Content Tables, Comments, Accessible, Text, and Form Elements. Open the Snippets panel by choosing Window⇨Snippets to review Dreamweaver's snippets folders, as shown in Figure 4-1.

Each folder includes a list of snippets organized alphabetically by name. To preview each snippet for how it will appear on the page, select it and look in the preview pane of the Snippets panel. To read a description of the snippet and review the code that it uses, click the Edit Snippet button at the bottom of the panel to open the Snippet dialog box.

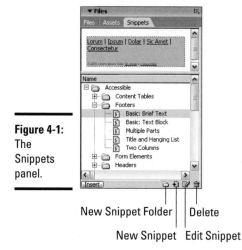

Figure 4-1:
The
Snippets
panel.

New Snippet Folder | Delete

New Snippet | Edit Snippet

To use a block snippet, place an insertion point inside an open document, select the snippet from the Snippets panel, and click the Insert button at the bottom of the panel. You can also drag and drop the snippet from the panel into an open document, as you would an image or any other media file.

To use a wrap snippet, select the content in Design view that the snippet will wrap around, select the snippet in the Snippets panel, and click the Insert button at the bottom of the panel.

You can find several good sites — including the Macromedia Web site — to exchange snippets with other designers and programmers. Search for **Dreamweaver snippets** or **Snippets exchange**. Then, when you download new snippets or create your own, you can file them in any of the existing Dreamweaver snippets folders or create new folders and file them there.

Creating Code Snippets

To create a Code Snippet, you must first begin by knowing what you want to turn into a snippet. Think about what can save you time, such as a snippet to create a time/date stamp, or the types of content you frequently use, such as copyright notices or meta tag information.

Snippets can be as simple or as complex as you need them to be. The following sections show you how to create four types of snippets from scratch: text, JavaScript, wrap, and graphic.

Book III
Chapter 4

Creating Code
Snippets and History
Panel Commands

To download copies of the snippets described in this chapter, visit `www.luckychair.com`.

Creating a text snippet

Say you work with a lot of artists and have a standard copyright notice you want to use regarding their work being displayed online. By creating a code snippet, you never have to type that copyright notice again, save for adding the correct artist name and company information after inserting the snippet into your page.

Follow these steps to insert a text snippet on your Web page:

1. **Choose Window⇨Snippets to launch the Snippets panel.**

2. **Click the New Snippet button (refer to Figure 4-1).**

The Snippet dialog box opens.

3. **Type a name for the snippet in the Name text box.**

Snippet names can't contain characters that are invalid in filenames, such as slashes (/ or \), special characters, or double quotes (").

In Figure 4-2, the snippet is named `Artist Copyright Notice`.

4. **Write a text description for the snippet in the Description text box.**

For a copyright notice, your description may look like this: `Inserts standard copyright statement for artists`.

5. **Select Insert Block as the snippet type.**

The Insert Block type is best for snippets containing content only. By contrast, the Wrap Selection type surrounds or wraps around your selected content, which is especially helpful for applying links, scripts, special formatting, and navigation.

6. **Add the code in the Insert Code text box.**

Here's what to type for the Copyright example:

```
All artwork featured on THIS WEBSITE is copyrighted material and may not
     be reproduced, downloaded, or used in any other format, on any other
     product, without permission from THIS COMPANY and the artist.
```

7. **Pick a preview type: Design or Code.**

The Code preview type shows the code in the preview pane of the Snippets panel. To see how graphics contained in your snippet may appear, choose Design view.

8. **Click OK when you're done.**

Your new snippet appears in the Snippets panel.

Figure 4-2:
Enter your
snippet
details.

To use your new snippet, open an HTML page and in Design view, click anywhere on the page to create an insertion point with your cursor. Select the
new snippet from the Snippets panel and click the Insert button or double-
click the Snippet name to quickly insert the snippet onto your page. The
snippet appears on your page, as shown in Figure 4-3.

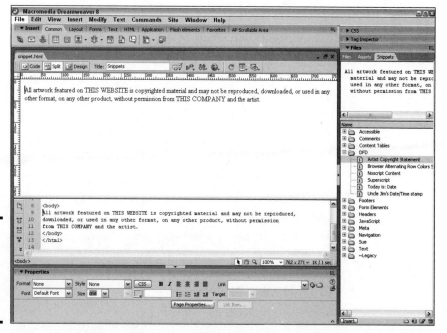

Figure 4-3:
The snippet
shows up
in the
Document
window.

Creating a JavaScript snippet

A lot of great free JavaScripts snippets are available on the Internet for use on a Web page that aren't built into the Dreamweaver interface (turn to Book IV, Chapter 2 to find out about JavaScript). You can find many useful free JavaScripts on the following sites:

```
www.dynamicdrive.com/
www.javascript.com/
www.24fun.com/
javascript.internet.com/
www.javascriptkit.com/cutpastejava.shtml
www.java-scripts.net/
www.javafile.com/
webdeveloper.earthweb.com/webjs/
www.javascriptsearch.com/
```

Regularly used JavaScripts make great Code Snippets. Besides saving you valuable time, one of the greatest advantages to using JavaScript snippets is that you needn't understand the JavaScript code to use them. The following are some great examples of JavaScript that you can easily convert into reusable Code Snippets:

✦ Time/date stamps and clock scripts

✦ Customizable menu navigation scripts

✦ Game scripts

✦ Password-protection scripts

✦ Text and status bar effects scripts

✦ Image effects and slide show scripts

Follow these steps to make a JavaScript snippet:

1. **Open the Snippets panel by choosing Window⇨Snippets.**

2. **Click the New Snippet button at the bottom of the Snippets panel (refer to Figure 4-1).**

   The Snippet dialog box opens.

3. **Type a name for the snippet in the Name text box.**

   Suppose, for example, you want to create a snippet with JavaScript that displays the document's last modified date starting with the words, `This document was last modified on:`. In the Name text box, type something like **This document was last modified on: (Date)** for the name.

4. **Write a text description for the snippet in the Description text box.**

   You may also want to include instructions about how to use the snippet. For example, you can note to insert the snippet in the `<head>` , not the

`<body>` tag and that the snippet is only supported by particular browser versions.

5. Choose Insert Block for the snippet type.

JavaScript is code that modifies the behavior of your content, so you always choose Insert Block as the type rather than Wrap.

6. Insert the code in the Insert Code text box.

The following JavaScript example inserts the current date into your Web page. If using CSS for styling your page, disregard the `<bold>` and `<font>` tags. You can also customize the script to display something else besides `This document was last modified on:` before the date by modifying the line of code that says `document.write("This document was last modified on: ");`. Type this data:

```
<p><font face="arial, helvetica" size="1"><b>
<SCRIPT LANGUAGE="JavaScript">
function initArray() {
this.length = initArray.arguments.length
for (var i = 0; i < this.length; i++)
this[i+1] = initArray.arguments[i] }
var DOWArray = new
     initArray("Sunday","Monday","Tuesday","Wednesday","Thursday",
     "Friday","Saturday");
var MOYArray = new
     initArray("January","February","March","April","May","June","July",
     "August","September","October","November","December");
var LastModDate = new Date(document.lastModified);
document.write("This document was last modified on: ");
document.write(DOWArray[(LastModDate.getDay()+1)],", ");
document.write(MOYArray[(LastModDate.getMonth()+1)]," ");
document.write(LastModDate.getDate(),", ",2006);
document.write(".");
</SCRIPT></b></font></p>
```

The final output looks something like this:

```
This document was last modified on: Thursday, March 16, 2006
```

7. Pick Code as the Preview Type.

The Code preview type shows you the code in the preview pane of the Snippet panel.

8. Click OK when you're done.

To test your new snippet, click anywhere on any open page in Design view to create an insertion point with your cursor and double-click the snippet in the Snippets panel.

When snippets containing JavaScript are inserted on a page, Dreamweaver's Design view may either indicate you have JavaScript code on your page by displaying an invisible element icon, or you may see nothing at all in Design view, though you see the newly inserted code in Code view in both cases.

Browsers, by contrast, display the JavaScript as it's meant to display and function. Therefore, for testing purposes, be sure to press F12 to launch your primary browser or Shift+F12 to launch your secondary browser to see how the JavaScript snippet looks.

TIP

To turn on the yellow script invisible element, choose Edit➪Preferences (Windows) or Dreamweaver➪Preferences (Mac) to launch Dreamweaver's Preferences dialog box. Select Invisible Elements from the Category list on the left and then select the Scripts option. Upon clicking OK, Dreamweaver indicates with the invisible element icon in Design view that you have JavaScript on your page.

Figure 4-4 shows how the icon looks as well as how the snippet actually appears in a browser.

Invisible Element   Snippets preview in browser

Figure 4-4:
Snippets containing JavaScript appear as invisible element icons in Design view, but as fully realized script when viewed in a browser.

Creating a snippet with the wrap option

The wrap option allows you to write opening and closing tags that surround whatever code or content is selected on your page. Wrap snippets are especially helpful for applying links, scripts, special formatting, and navigation. For instance, you may want to create a snippet that quickly adds a link around selected text, such as `<a href="#">link</a>`. To create a snippet with the wrap option, follow these steps:

1. **Open the Snippets panel by choosing Window➪Snippets.**

   The Snippets panel appears.

2. **Click the New Snippets button (refer to Figure 4-1).**

The Snippets dialog box appears.

3. Type a name for the snippet in the Name text box.

Say, for example, that you want to generate a snippet that superscripts text, such as on 42nd Street. In the Name text box, type **Superscript**.

4. Write a text description for the snippet in the Description text box.

In this example, type something like this for the description: **This snippet will Superscript any selected content using the tags.**

5. Choose Wrap Selection as the snippet type.

Use this type because the code in your snippet will surround or wrap around your selected content. When selecting the Wrap Selection type, notice that the dialog box changes from displaying one box for code input to displaying two boxes, as shown in Figure 4-5.

Figure 4-5: Enter your snippet in the Insert Before and Insert After boxes.

6. Add the appropriate code to the Insert Before box.

To create a superscript snippet, type the following:

```
<sup>
```

7. Add the appropriate code to the Insert After box.

To continue creating the superscript snippet, type the following:

```
</sup>
```

8. Pick Code as the Preview Type.

Because wrap snippets typically have no graphics, select Code as the preview type to see code in the preview pane of the Snippet panel.

9. Click OK when you're done.

The wrap snippet is inserted in your Web page (see Figure 4-6).

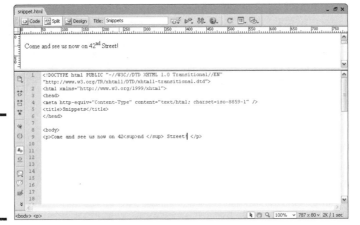

Figure 4-6:
Wrap
snippets
are useful
for super-
scripts.

Applying wrap snippets is a little different than block type snippets because if you want the code to wrap around the content you must select the copy on your page that you want to apply the snippet to *before* you insert the snippet code. Using the 42nd Street example, highlight the nd in Design view first, and then insert the snippet. Because this snippet contains simple HTML tags, Dreamweaver's Design view renders and displays the superscript code for you, without the need to launch a browser to see it. Alternately, you don't have to apply wrap tags to existing text; you could insert the wrap snippet on the page first and then add content between the tags at a later time.

Creating a snippet with graphics

Good uses for graphic snippets include:

✦ **Special symbol graphics:** Create a graphic with a stylized ™ or other symbol in a particular font.

✦ **Animated GIFs:** Design an animated graphic, such as a flashing NEW graphic, to add next to special entries on your site.

✦ **Reusable page elements:** Build reusable elements with For Placement Only (FPO) text and graphics, such as a sidebar subnavigation area.

Snippets with graphics work the same as snippets with text and JavaScript but with one added benefit when you choose Design as the Preview Type in the Snippet dialog box. Like the Design or Code views you see when editing a page in Dreamweaver, the Snippets panel has a little preview pane above the named list of snippets. Selecting Design as the preview type in the Snippet dialog box makes Dreamweaver render the code in the preview pane as it would in Design

Adding keyboard shortcuts to play snippets

You can easily and quickly customize keyboard shortcuts to run any of your snippets with key commands using Dreamweaver's Keyboard Shortcut Editor. You can also create, remove, and edit shortcuts at any time.

To create custom keyboard shortcuts for your snippets, follow these steps:

1. **Choose Edit⇨Keyboard Shortcuts (Windows) or Dreamweaver⇨Keyboard Shortcuts (Mac).**

   The Keyboard Shortcuts dialog box appears.

2. **Create a duplicate of the default Macromedia Standard shortcut set by clicking the Duplicate button. Name your duplicate set.**

   Making a duplicate set ensures that you can always go back to the factory default settings in the future if you need to.

3. **Select Snippets from the Commands drop-down list to see a list of your custom snippets along with the standard snippets.**

4. **Navigate through the list to find the snippet you want to assign a keyboard shortcut to.**

5. **Click the plus (+) button to add a shortcut.**

6. **Place your cursor in the Press Key field and press the combination of shortcut keys.**

   Warning: Be careful not to use a key combination reserved for programs other than Dreamweaver, such as F11 or ⌘+H on a Mac, or Option+R on Windows.

   Be sure to press all the keys at once, such as Ctrl+Alt+Shift+9 (Windows) or ⌘+Opt+Shift+9 (Mac). Dreamweaver displays alerts for any shortcut key combos that are already assigned to another function within the program so you won't accidentally overwrite one of the presets. Feel free, though, to overwrite a preset if you find it useful.

7. **Click OK when done.**

   Your new shortcut works immediately.

To see all the existing keyboard shortcuts at a glance, download the Dreamweaver 8 Keyboard Shortcut Quick Reference PDF for Windows and Mac. Go to www.macromedia.com/support/documentation/en/dreamweaver/ and click the Products Manuals tab.

view (see Figure 4-7). By contrast, if you select Code as the preview type, Dreamweaver shows the code of the snippet in the preview pane.

If you do not see your image rendered in the preview pane in the Snippets panel, you may need to edit your snippet code to use site root-relative linking for the graphic. Simply put, you must add a forward slash (/) before the graphic source folder, like this:

```
ORIGINAL, DOCUMENT-RELATIVE LINK:
<p><img src="images/trademark.gif" width="87" height="87" border="1"></p>


SITE ROOT-RELATIVE LINK:
<p><img src="/images/trademark.gif" width="87" height="87" border="1"></p>
```

Figure 4-7:
The snippet
displays in
the preview
pane of the
Snippets
panel.

You may also need to add the forward slash (/) to any HREF links in your graphic snippets, as in this site root-relative link example:

```
<a href="/about.html">about</a>
```

For a thorough discussion about site root-relative versus document-relative linking, see Book I, Chapter 3 on root level organization.

Working with Snippets

Snippets are easy to edit and delete, and easy to file and manage. You can even share snippets with your coworkers.

Sharing snippets

If you want to share your custom snippets with other members of your work team, you can easily copy them from one computer to another. Here's how to share Code Snippets:

1. **Find and copy them from the Configuration/Snippets folder inside of the Dreamweaver application folder.**

2. **Paste them into a shared folder on your computer/network or e-mail them to your co-workers.**

3. **Have the other team members copy the snippet files to their Configuration/Snippets folders in their Dreamweaver application folders.**

   Once in place, the snippets are ready to use.

You should be able to find your custom snippets in the Macromedia Dreamweaver Configuration folder, but that folder can actually be in a few different places on your computer, depending on your platform. See Danilo Celic's blog entry at `www.communitymx.com/blog/index.cfm?newsid=27` for possible locations on both a Mac and a PC. To see your custom snippets, you may need to try adjusting the Application Data (Windows) or Application Support (Mac) folder properties to view both hidden and read-only files.

If you're interested in a faster method for sharing your custom snippets with others, visit Massimo Foti's Web site at `www.massimocorner.com` where you can download his free Dreamweaver Snippets Import/Export 1.0 Extension. Install the extension with Macromedia's Extension Manager (see Book IV, Chapter 2 for instructions on using the Manager). Once installed, the tool lets you import and export snippets straight from the Snippets panel.

Editing snippets

After you create a snippet, you'll probably rarely need to edit it. However, some snippets may contain specific dates or graphics that need occasional updating or editing. Additionally, you may want to create a new version of an existing snippet. In any case, editing a code snippet is simple and straightforward.

To edit a snippet, follow these steps:

1. **Select the snippet from the Snippets panel and click the Edit Snippet button at the bottom of the panel.**

   The Snippet dialog box appears.

2. **Make any changes to the snippet.**

3. **When finished, click OK and the new changes are ready to use.**

Deleting snippets

To delete a Code Snippet quickly and permanently, select the snippet from the Snippets panel and then either click the Remove button (refer to Figure 4-1) or press the Delete key.

Dreamweaver always displays an alert dialog box asking if you're sure you want to delete that particular snippet, giving you a chance to cancel the command if you change your mind about deleting it.

Managing snippets

One of the cool things about the Snippets panel is that you can create folders to manage your snippets into logical categories. Moving snippets around the Snippets panel, from folder to folder, is as easy as dragging and dropping.

If you want to create a new folder for your snippets, follow these steps:

**Book III
Chapter 4**

**Creating Code
Snippets and History
Panel Commands**

1. **Click the New Snippet Folder button at the bottom of the Snippets panel.**

2. **Type a name for the new folder and then press Enter (Windows) or Return (Mac).**

If you don't name it, the folder is called "untitled" by default, but you can always change the name later.

Rename and delete folders as needed. To delete a folder, select it and click the Delete button at the bottom of the Snippets panel.

Creating History Panel Commands

The History panel is one of those panels that many Dreamweaver users don't take full advantage of. When a document is open in the Dreamweaver workspace, the History panel records all the actions you make in the file up to a certain number of steps (specified in the General category of the Preferences dialog box). Keep in mind that after you save and close the document, the history steps associated with the file go away; when you reopen the file, a new history is created.

Through the History panel, you can take multiple steps backwards with the use of the panel's slider as well as copy and paste steps to use on the current or other open documents. In addition to using the History panel to undo and redo steps, you can also record your own custom actions and save them as reusable, playable commands to automate repetitive actions.

Working with the History Panel

To view the panel, choose Window➪History or press Shift+F10. As you work, notice how the panel records each step you make. For example, when you type text, a typing layer displays the copy you just entered. When you apply bold to your text, an Apply Bold layer appears in the panel. Each action creates a new action layer in the panel, as shown in Figure 4-8.

Figure 4-8:
The History panel.

Record

To undo a single step in your document, drag the slider in the History panel up a layer in the list (or choose Edit⇨Undo). To undo multiple steps, simply drag the slider to the desired step in the History panel or click to the left of the path next to the slider to scroll automatically to that step. After undoing a single step or multiple steps, any subsequent new actions erase and over-write previous actions.

Though it's not advised, you can erase the history list for a document by right-clicking (Windows) or Control+clicking (Mac) the History panel and choosing Clear History. After clearing the history in this manner, you can't undo any steps in your document.

Recording commands

To record and save a command, be sure the panel is open before you per-form the actions you want to save. After you perform the actions, you can record and save them.

Keep these points in mind when recording actions:

✦ Use the arrow keys instead of the mouse to move the insertion point in the document. You can also use the arrow keys plus Shift to make or extend a selection. Mouse movements aren't saved and are identified in the History panel with a black divider line between the steps.

✦ Other actions are also unrepeatable, such as dragging an asset from one place on the page to another. These types of steps display a small red X next to the action layer in the History panel.

Follow these steps to record and save a command:

1. **Open the History panel by choosing Window⇨History.**

Press Shift+F10 to quickly open the panel.

2. **Edit your document.**

The History panel records all your actions as individual steps.

3. **In the History panel, select the step you want to record.**

To select multiple steps, Shift+click to select consecutive steps; Ctrl+click (Windows) or ⌘+click (Mac) to select or deselect non-consecutive steps.

4. **Click the Record button at the bottom of the panel.**

Dreamweaver displays a dialog box indicating that you may have clicked or dragged in the document in some of your steps.

5. **Click Yes to continue or No to cancel the recording process.**

The Save As Command dialog box appears prompting you to enter a name for the new command.

6. Name the new command.

Name your commands using simple descriptive titles, such as `Bold & Italic`.

7. Click OK.

The new command appears by name at the bottom of the Commands menu.

You can also make a temporary command by clicking the Copy Selected Steps to the Clipboard button at the bottom of the panel after selecting a series of steps. The steps are temporarily stored on the Clipboard for easy pasting into any open document in Design view.

New commands are saved as JavaScript or HTML files in the Dreamweaver/Configuration/Commands folder.

Playing commands

Playing a saved command is as easy as choosing it by name from the Commands menu. For example, if you create a Bold & Italic command that bolds and italicizes a selection, select some text on your document and then choose Commands⇨Bold & Italic to play the command, as shown in Figure 4-9.

Commands	Site	Window	Help	
Start Recording				Ctrl+Shift+X
Play Recorded Command				
Edit Command List...				
Get More Commands...				
Apply Source Formatting				
Apply Source Formatting to Selection				
Clean Up XHTML...				
Clean Up Word HTML...				
Add/Remove Netscape Resize Fix...				
Optimize Image in Fireworks...				
Create Web Photo Album...				
Format Table...				
Sort Table...				
Insert Mark of the Web				
Bold Italic				

Figure 4-9: Select the command you created from the Commands menu.

More options are available when playing commands with the History panel. You may repeat the last step, repeat a series of consecutive or touching steps, or repeat a series of nonconsecutive steps:

✦ **Repeat a single step:** Select a step in the History panel and click the Replay button. Or choose Edit⇨Redo (Action).

Recording commands with the Commands menu

Another way to record temporary commands is to use the Commands menu instead of the History panel. Temporary commands stay on the Commands menu and you can play them on any open document as long as you have Dreamweaver open. Temporary commands disappear when you do one of the following:

✔ You close Dreamweaver. The temporary command is erased.

✔ You record a new temporary command. The new command takes the places of the old command.

To record a temporary command:

1. **Choose Commands⇨Start Recording before performing the steps you want to copy.**

   You can also begin the recording process by pressing Ctrl+Shift+X (Windows) or ⌘+Shift+X (Mac).

2. **Perform the steps.**

   Whenever possible, press the arrow keys instead of moving the mouse to reposition the cursor during the recording process.

3. **When finished, choose Commands⇨Stop Recording.**

To play back a temporary command, choose Commands⇨Play Recorded Command.

You can also begin the playback process by pressing Ctrl+Shift+R (Windows) or ⌘+Shift+R (Mac).

To save a temporary command into a permanent command with the History panel:

1. **Choose Commands⇨Play Recorded Command.**

   The command plays and displays a new Run Command step at the bottom of the History panel.

2. **Select the new Run Command step in the History panel and click the Save As Command button.**

   The Save As Command dialog box opens.

3. **Name the command and click OK to save it.**

   The command now appears at the bottom of the Commands menu.

Click the Get More Commands link on the Command menu to launch Macromedia's Dreamweaver Exchange to browse for and download additional commands.

✦ **Repeat a series of consecutive steps:** Select the steps in the History panel and click the Replay button.

To select multiple steps, either drag from one step to another or click the first step and Shift+click the last step. Whichever steps are highlighted are the ones that play.

✦ **Repeat a series of non-consecutive steps:** Select a step in the History panel and Ctrl+click (Windows) or ⌘+click (Mac) to select other steps;

then click the Replay button. Steps replay in the order they appear in the History panel.

✦ **Deselect a selected step**: Ctrl+click (Windows) or ⌘+click (Mac) the step.

You can also copy and paste steps from one open document to another, as each file has its own history of steps. Simply select the steps and click the Copy Steps button in the History panel. Then choose Edit⇨Paste in the new document to paste the steps.

If you paste selected steps into a text editor, Code view, or the Code inspector, you may notice that the pasted information appears as JavaScript, which can be really useful for learning to write your own Dreamweaver scripts. For example, the copied command to insert and resize an image is this:

```
<img src="image23.gif" width="100" height="46" />
```

This line appears in a text editor as a bit of JavaScript like this:

```
dw.getDocumentDOM().insertHTML('<img src=\"image23.gif\">', false);
dw.getDocumentDOM().resizeSelection('100', '46');
```

Renaming and deleting commands

After saving a new command, you can rename or delete it.

To rename a command:

1. **Choose Commands⇨Edit Command List.**

2. **Select the command in the list and enter a new name.**

3. **Click the Close button.**

To delete a command:

1. **Choose Commands⇨Edit Command List.**

2. **Select the command in the list and click the Delete button.**

Clicking the Delete button permanently removes the command from the Commands menu.

3. **Click the Close button.**

Chapter 5: Integrating Dreamweaver with Fireworks

In This Chapter

✓ **Working with Fireworks**

✓ **Setting launch-and-edit preferences**

✓ **Inserting Fireworks images**

✓ **Making changes to your Fireworks images and tables**

✓ **Image optimizing in Fireworks**

✓ **Inserting, pasting, and updating Fireworks HTML**

*D*reamweaver is tightly integrated with Fireworks, a Web image creation, editing, and optimization program from Macromedia. Fireworks lets you create animations, pop-up menus, and *rollover buttons* (buttons that change in appearance when you mouse over them); *optimize* your graphics (reduce the file size while preserving image quality to improve download times in a browser); and export graphics, HTML, and JavaScript code to an HTML editor like Dreamweaver — all without needing to know a lick of code.

When used together, Fireworks and Dreamweaver provide you with a smooth process for editing, optimizing, and exporting graphics into HTML pages. This process, called *roundtrip editing,* enables you to make seamless updates to your Fireworks graphic and HTML files while working in Dreamweaver. The code stays accurate to preserve links and other functionality such as rollover behaviors.

During the roundtrip editing process, Fireworks creates special *Design Notes* about all the graphics and HTML exported to Dreamweaver. The Notes, which are generated during the graphic export process, are sent from Fireworks into Dreamweaver, store references to the Web-ready images (GIF, JPEG, HTML), and enable Dreamweaver to quickly locate them and the Fireworks source files (PNG) they were created from. In addition, the Design Notes often include information about the export process itself, such as the location of JavaScript data within the HTML files and details such as rollover capabilities and hotspots about the graphics inside of table cells.

To be fair, Fireworks is not a prerequisite for creating or designing Web sites, so please don't feel that you must run out and buy Fireworks to successfully build a Web site; it's entirely possible to build an entire Web site without using Fireworks or any of its features. Many designers actually prefer to use other design, illustration, and Web graphic optimization programs, such as Photoshop, Illustrator, and ImageReady to create their Web graphics. What Fireworks is required for, however, are all the features described in this chapter.

This chapter presumes that you already own and know how to use Fireworks but need help using it together with Dreamweaver. Here you find out how to insert Fireworks images, edit images and tables, optimize your images in Fireworks, and add and edit Fireworks HTML in Dreamweaver.

Preparing to Work with Dreamweaver and Fireworks

Before you begin a roundtrip editing process, you must enable a few settings within Fireworks and Dreamweaver to ensure the smoothest possible integration between the programs. Specifically, you must specify your launch-and-edit preferences in Fireworks, and optimize Dreamweaver for working with Fireworks by adding Fireworks as a primary image editor.

Setting Fireworks launch-and-edit preferences

If you use Fireworks to create and edit images, by default Fireworks exports those images from a source PNG (Portable Network Graphics) file. PNG is an image compression file format that allows for the exporting of Web graphics with the highest image quality and a relatively small file size. A source PNG file is a master file that Fireworks uses to generate Web-ready graphics.

When creating graphics in Fireworks, be sure to store the PNG source files in a different place on your computer than the Web graphics generated from them so you don't accidentally alter them.

By default, when you edit a Fireworks image within Dreamweaver, Fireworks launches and automatically reopens the source PNG file. This is the Fireworks default launch-and-edit preference. You could also set the preferences in Fireworks to either have Dreamweaver open and directly edit the inserted graphics (which is not a good choice because Dreamweaver is not an image editing or optimization application) or have Fireworks open and use the inserted Web-ready image for editing instead of the image's source PNG file (which is not good either because the original source PNG always generates better quality Web graphics than an already optimized Web graphic).

You should note that Dreamweaver only recognizes these launch-and-edit preferences when certain conditions apply:

✦ You must specifically open and optimize images that include the right Design Notes path to the source PNG file. You can ensure you're using the right Design Notes path to the source PNG by selecting the Always Use Source PNG option for the launch-and-edit preference (see the next section).

✦ The image can't be a part of a Fireworks table. Fireworks tables use a series of images with the HTML code. You must always open the source PNG file inside Fireworks to edit any of the graphics from within Dreamweaver.

To set Fireworks' launch-and-edit preferences, follow these steps:

1. **Choose Edit⇨Preferences (Windows) or Fireworks⇨Preferences (Mac) to open the Fireworks Preferences dialog box.**

2. **Click the Launch and Edit tab (Windows) or select Launch and Edit from the drop-down list (Mac).**

The Launch and Edit tab is shown in Figure 5-1.

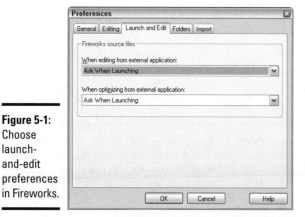

Figure 5-1:
Choose launch-and-edit preferences in Fireworks.

3. **Set the launch-and-edit preference options for editing and optimizing Fireworks images to be exported to external applications such as Dreamweaver. Select one of the following options in each of the drop-down lists:**

• **Always Use Source PNG:** This setting enables Fireworks to open the PNG file defined in Design Notes as the source for the externally placed graphics. When edits are made to the source PNG, all those changes are automatically updated in the exported or placed Web graphic.

- **Never Use Source PNG:** This option tells Fireworks to open the placed graphic for editing, even if a source PNG file is available. Changes to the graphic are permanent and appear in the placed graphic. The source PNG file stays the same.

- **Ask When Launching:** If you want to use both methods intermittently, select this option to choose the PNG file or the placed graphic on a case-by-case basis.

4. **When you finish, click OK to save your changes.**

Optimizing Dreamweaver for use with Fireworks

Make the following changes to optimize Dreamweaver for use with Fireworks.

Enable Design Notes

Verify that the managed site you're creating or using has Design Notes enabled. This is the default site setting in Dreamweaver.

1. **Choose Site➪Manage Sites.**

2. **Select your site and click the Edit button in the Manage Sites dialog box.**

3. **Click the Advanced tab in the Site Definition dialog box.**

4. **Choose Design Notes from the Category list and verify that the Maintain Design Notes option is enabled.**

   If you want to share Design Notes with others on your team, also enable the Upload Design Notes for Sharing option.

Add Fireworks as an image editor

In the Dreamweaver Preferences dialog box, set Fireworks as the primary external image editor for selected graphics files. This enables Fireworks to be the editor that automatically launches for editing your placed graphics files. For example, you may want to launch Fireworks as the primary editor for GIF and PNG files, and another application for editing JPEG files.

To add Fireworks as an image editor, follow these steps:

1. **Choose Edit➪Preferences (Windows) or Dreamweaver➪Preferences (Mac).**

   The Dreamweaver Preferences dialog box appears.

2. **In the File Types/Editors category, as shown in Figure 5-2, click the plus (+) button to add Fireworks (and any other applications you want to include) as an editor for any of the graphic extensions.**

   Dreamweaver doesn't automatically detect that you have Fireworks installed so you must enter the path to the Fireworks application in the Fireworks text box.

3. **To make Fireworks the primary editor for any given extension, select it from the list of editors and click the Make Primary button.**

   For example, after adding Fireworks to the list in Step 2, select it and click the Make Primary button. The Fireworks application name has (Primary) appended to it.

4. **Click OK when you're finished.**

Figure 5-2:
Add
Fireworks
as the
primary
image
editor in
Dream-
weaver's
Preferences.

Save all your Fireworks files in the same site folder

Save all your Fireworks PNG source and Web-ready files in the same Dreamweaver site folder. This ensures that everyone in a workgroup can easily find and edit all the source files for the site.

Export Fireworks image files to the same site folder

Exporting Web graphics from Fireworks into a Dreamweaver site folder ensures that Design Notes are integrated and up-to-date. Fireworks creates a Notes folder for the Design Notes, which Dreamweaver uses to update code and graphics.

Using Fireworks Images in Dreamweaver

When you're ready to insert Fireworks images into your Dreamweaver document, you can do so two ways. The first way is to place exported Fireworks graphics directly into a file by choosing Insert⇨Image in Dreamweaver. The other way is to design images in Fireworks to replace Dreamweaver image placeholders.

Inserting a Fireworks image in a Dreamweaver document

When you've designed, saved, and exported your graphics from Fireworks, you're ready to import those exported graphics into a Dreamweaver document. If you need help creating, saving, and exporting Fireworks graphics, refer to the Fireworks Help files or download a copy of the Fireworks manual from Macromedia at www.macromedia.com/support/documentation/en/fireworks/.

Follow these steps to insert an exported Fireworks image into a Dreamweaver file:

1. **In Dreamweaver, click inside the document where you want the image to go and choose Insert⇨Image.**

   Or, on the Common tab of the Insert bar, click and drag the Image button into the open document.

   The Select Image Source dialog box opens.

2. **Browse to and select the exported Fireworks image and click OK (Windows) or Open (Mac) to complete the insertion.**

   If you select an image from outside the Dreamweaver local site folder, a message appears asking if you want Dreamweaver to copy the file into the root folder of the managed Dreamweaver site. Click Yes.

Now you can easily edit your images in Fireworks using the roundtrip editing feature, as described in "Editing Images in Fireworks Tables," later in the chapter.

Replacing an image placeholder with a Fireworks graphic

In Dreamweaver, you can create *image placeholders* that set aside space for graphics that haven't been created yet. (See Book II, Chapter 3 for details on creating image placeholders.) With roundtrip editing, you can select an individual image placeholder in Dreamweaver and use Fireworks to create a graphic to replace it.

Before beginning the roundtrip editing process, be sure that you specify Fireworks as the image editor for `.png` files (as described in "Optimizing Dreamweaver for Use with Fireworks," earlier in the chapter) and create all the image placeholders in a Dreamweaver document.

Follow these steps to replace a Dreamweaver image placeholder with a Fireworks image:

1. **In your Dreamweaver document, select the image placeholder (see Figure 5-3) that you want to replace.**

2. **Click the Create button in the Properties inspector to launch Fireworks.**

Fireworks opens the selected image placeholder in Editing from Dreamweaver mode.

3. **In Fireworks, design the replacement image.**

Fireworks detects image placeholder settings from Dreamweaver, such as image width and height, alternate text, and image ID, as well as links, text alignment settings, and JavaScript behaviors, and uses these settings as the basis for the replacement graphic. Therefore, you may just see an empty white canvas instead of an exact replica of the placeholder image.

Figure 5-3:
The placeholder image in the Document window.

Links assigned to image placeholders in Dreamweaver are maintained but are not visible inside Fireworks. Therefore, if you add a new link or hotspot from within Fireworks, the original Dreamweaver link is still there. However, if you cut a slice from the image in Fireworks, the Dreamweaver link is deleted when the image gets updated.

4. **When you finish designing the image (see Figure 5-4), click the Done button.**

   Fireworks launches the Save As dialog box, prompting you to save the PNG file.

5. **Browse to and select the root folder of your managed Dreamweaver site as the location to save the PNG file.**

6. **Enter a name in the File Name text box.**

   If you previously named the image in Dreamweaver when creating the image placeholder, the File Name text box is already filled in with that name.

7. **Click the Save button to save the PNG file.**

   The Export dialog box opens.

8. **From the Export dialog box, select the Dreamweaver site folder for the Save In option.**

9. **Enter a name in the Name text box.**

   Again, the PGN filename is in the Name text box.

10. **Choose a graphic type from the Save as Type drop-down list.**

    Select the file type (GIF or JPEG) or the type of file you're exporting, such as HTML and Images, Images Only, or HTML Only.

11. **Click the Save button to save the exported file.**

    The replacement image PNG file is saved, and you return to Dreamweaver, where the exported Web-ready file or Fireworks table has replaced the image placeholder, as shown in Figure 5-5.

Repeat these steps for each Dreamweaver image placeholder you want to replace. If a replacement graphic file needs further editing, select the image in Dreamweaver and click the Edit button in the Properties inspector, as described in the next section, "Editing Images in Fireworks Tables."

Figure 5-4:
Design a replacement image for a placeholder image in Fireworks.

Book III
Chapter 5

Integrating Dreamweaver with Fireworks

Figure 5-5:
The new Fireworks graphic replaces the old placeholder graphic in the Dreamweaver file.

Editing Images in Fireworks Tables

Before editing any images containing Fireworks tables, be sure you've set up Fireworks launch-and-edit preferences and optimized Dreamweaver for use with Fireworks (refer to the "Preparing to Work with Dreamweaver and Fireworks" section, earlier in this chapter).

Then, if you want to edit a Fireworks image in your Dreamweaver document, you can either have Dreamweaver launch Fireworks to edit it there or use the limited image editing tools (crop, resample, brightness and contrast, and sharpen) to edit your image within Dreamweaver.

When editing images or image *slices* (graphics that are cut into smaller pieces) that are part of a Fireworks table, Dreamweaver opens Fireworks automatically, which in turn opens the source PNG file for the entire Fireworks table.

Fireworks *tables* are Fireworks-generated navigation bars, pop-up menus, and sliced images, which have nothing to do with traditional HTML tables.

When editing images that are part of a Fireworks table, you can edit the entire table as long as the `<!--fw table-->` comment tag is visible in the HTML code. That comment gets automatically inserted whenever the source PNG gets exported from Fireworks to a Dreamweaver site using the Dreamweaver Style HTML and Images setting.

To edit Fireworks images placed in Dreamweaver files, follow these steps:

1. **In Dreamweaver, select the image or image slice in the open document that you want to edit.**

The Properties inspector identifies the selected graphic as a Fireworks image or Fireworks table, along with the name of the source PNG file.

2. **Click the Edit button in the Properties inspector to launch Fireworks.**

Fireworks opens the source PNG file for editing (see Figure 5-6). If Fireworks can't find the source PNG file, it prompts you to find it. If the source file is missing, you can use the inserted image as the source for the edits.

3. **In Fireworks, edit the source PNG file.**

4. **When finished, click the Done button.**

Fireworks saves the changes to the PNG file, exports the updated graphic (or HTML with images), and returns to Dreamweaver, where the updated image or table appears in the open document.

Figure 5-6:
The source
PNG file for
the entire
table gets
launched in
Fireworks.

Optimizing Your Images in Fireworks

Before you add Fireworks images to your Dreamweaver document, you should *optimize* those images for use on the Web. By optimizing your images, you reduce the amount of time the user's browser takes to download and display the images. By optimizing images in Fireworks, you can

✦ Reduce the image file size while maintaining image quality

✦ Change the file format of the Web-ready image

✦ Adjust color depth and other format-specific options to control file size

To change settings for Fireworks images placed in Dreamweaver, follow these steps:

1. **In Dreamweaver, select the image you want to optimize from an open document and choose Commands⇨Optimize Image in Fireworks.**

If the placed image in the document has a source PNG file, Fireworks uses that file. However, if that source file cannot be found, Fireworks may prompt you to locate the source PNG file.

Fireworks opens and displays the Optimization dialog box, as shown in Figure 5-7.

Figure 5-7:
Use the
Fireworks
Optimize
Images
dialog box
to change
optimization
settings of
Fireworks
images
placed in
Dream-
weaver files.

2. **On the Options tab, change the optimization settings to support the selected file format:**

- **Format:** Select a file format for the optimized graphic. Choose from GIF, Animated GIF, JPEG, PNG-8, PNG-24, or PNG-32.

- **Palette:** (GIFs and PNGs only) Choose a color palette for the graphic. Options include Adaptive, Web Adaptive, Web 216, Exact, Windows and Macintosh, Grayscale, Black and White, Uniform, and Custom.

- **Loss:** (GIFs only) Add a loss setting to compress GIF files for smaller file sizes. The higher the number, the smaller the file, but the greater the potential loss of image quality.

- **Dither:** (GIFs and PNGs only) Enable the dithering option to control how colors not in the selected palette are approximated using colors within the palette.

- **Transparency:** (GIFs and PNGs only) Choose a transparency setting.

- **Quality:** (JPEGs only) Adjust the quality setting to control the loss of image quality during compression. Higher numbers produce better quality images with larger file sizes.

- **Smoothing:** (JPEGs only) Enable a smoothing setting to blur hard edges in the graphic and reduce file size. Higher numbers reduce file size but can distort the quality of the image.

3. On the File tab, edit the size and area of the graphic file.

To modify the size of the image, adjust the Scale field in percentages or type the exact pixels in the Width and Height fields.

To optimize and export only part of the selected graphic, enter X and Y coordinates relative to the original graphic dimensions.

4. Click the Update button when finished.

The updated image exports with any new settings. Exporting includes updating the placed GIF or JPEG file in Dreamweaver, as well as the source PNG file.

If the image format has changed, Dreamweaver's link checker prompts you to verify the graphic's link references. For instance, if you changed the format of a graphic called `submit.jpg` from JPEG to GIF, click OK and all references to `submit.jpg` are converted to `submit.gif`.

Editing Fireworks Pop-Up Menus

A *pop-up menu* is a navigation menu that temporarily appears in a browser window when the user makes a specific mouse action. If you've created any pop-up menus in Fireworks 8 or later, you can now edit them either directly in Dreamweaver or use Fireworks roundtrip editing. If you created your pop-up menu in earlier versions of Fireworks, you have to edit it in Dreamweaver.

If you make changes to your Fireworks 8 pop-up menus directly in Dreamweaver and then subsequently make changes to them in Fireworks, you lose all your previous edits to the menus except for text changes. To avoid this, always create your menus in Fireworks first and then use Dreamweaver exclusively to customize the menus. However, if you prefer to do the menu editing in Fireworks, do not edit them in Dreamweaver at all and instead exclusively use the roundtrip editing feature.

Roundtrip pop-up menu editing (Fireworks 8 and later)

If you want to edit a pop-up menu that you created with Fireworks 8 or later, you can do roundtrip editing of the pop-up menu:

1. In Dreamweaver, select the graphic in the Fireworks table that contains the Fireworks pop-up menu, and click the Edit button in the Properties inspector.

Fireworks launches and opens the source PNG file for the pop-up menu.

2. **In Fireworks, select the slice in the table that has the pop-up menu you want to edit and choose Modify⇨Pop-up Menu⇨Edit Pop-up Menu**

   The Fireworks Pop-up Menu Editor opens.

3. **Adjust the menu content, appearance, and position.**

4. **When you finish, click the Done button in the Pop-up Menu Editor to close the dialog box, and click the Done button on the Fireworks tool-bar to save the changes to the menu.**

   The edited menu is updated in Dreamweaver.

Pop-up menu editing (Fireworks MX 2004 and earlier)

If you want to edit a pop-up menu you built with Fireworks MX 2004 or earlier, you can't use Fireworks' roundtrip editing. You must use Dreamweaver to edit the menu.

To edit pop-up menus created with Fireworks MX 2004 or earlier, follow these steps:

1. **In Dreamweaver, select the image or hotspot that triggers the pop-up menu.**

2. **In the Behaviors panel (choose Window⇨Behaviors), double-click the Show Pop-up Menu icon from the Actions list.**

   The Show Pop-up Menu dialog box opens where you can edit the menu.

3. **If needed, add, change, or rearrange menu items.**

   For more information about the Pop-up Menu behavior, see Book IV, Chapter 4.

4. **Click OK to save the changes.**

Using Fireworks HTML in Dreamweaver

You can quickly insert Fireworks-generated HTML (including all graphics, formatting, and JavaScript behaviors) into a Dreamweaver document. This roundtrip feature lets you design Web elements in Fireworks and add them to new or existing Dreamweaver files. Or as an alternative, you can simply copy and paste your HTML code from Fireworks to Dreamweaver. Either method allows you to design in Fireworks. For example, you can create a navigation bar with a series of buttons, each of which has JavaScript rollover functionality including a hyperlink to another page.

Inserting Fireworks HTML in a Dreamweaver document

After you design your Web elements in Fireworks, inserting the element into your Web page is a two-step process: You must export the HTML into a managed Dreamweaver site and then insert it on your Dreamweaver page.

Follow these steps to export the Fireworks HTML into Dreamweaver:

1. **Click the Quick Export button and choose Dreamweaver⇨Export HTML from the menu.**

The button looks like a little Fireworks icon with a white arrow behind it pointing to the right and is located in the top-right corner of the Fireworks Document window.

The Export dialog box opens.

2. **Enter a filename for the exported HTML file, choose the Dreamweaver site folder as the destination for the file, and select other options relative to the export command.**

3. **Click the Export button to complete the export process.**

After you export the Fireworks HTML into a Dreamweaver site folder, follow these steps to insert the exported HTML into a Dreamweaver document:

1. **In Dreamweaver, click your cursor inside the document where you want to insert the Fireworks HTML code.**

2. **Choose Insert⇨Image Objects⇨Fireworks HTML.**

You can also click the Insert Fireworks HTML button on the Common tab of the Insert bar.

The Insert Fireworks HTML dialog box appears.

3. **Browse to and select the exported Fireworks HTML file.**

4. **Check the Delete File After Insertion option if you want to delete the original files after the Fireworks HTML is inserted into the Dreamweaver file. Otherwise leave it unchecked.**

If the original Fireworks HTML is on a network drive, however, it's immediately deleted. This setting does not affect source PNG files associated with the HTML.

5. **Click OK.**

Dreamweaver inserts the Fireworks HTML into the Dreamweaver file (see Figure 5-8). This insertion process includes HTML code, graphic images, slices, and JavaScript.

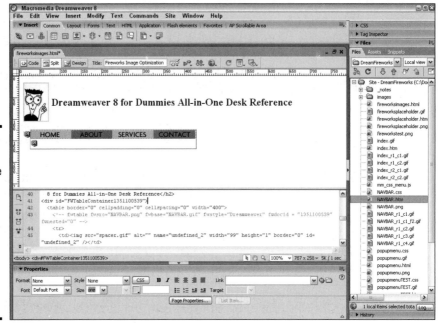

Figure 5-8:
Use the
Insert Image
Objects
Fireworks
command
to quickly
insert
Fireworks
HTML into
a Dream-
weaver file.

Pasting Fireworks HTML in a Dreamweaver document

Rather than using the Insert Fireworks HTML command from the previous section, you can also copy and paste the Fireworks-generated HTML code directly inside a Dreamweaver file.

To copy and paste Fireworks HTML into a Dreamweaver document, follow these steps:

1. **In Fireworks, choose Edit➪Copy HTML Code.**

Fireworks presumes you intend to copy the entire file, so unless you want to copy only a part of the graphic, you don't need to select anything.

The Copy HTML Code Wizard opens.

2. **Use the wizard to walk through the process of exporting Fireworks HTML and images. Click the Next button to proceed through each step in the wizard.**

- **Screen 1:** Select an HTML style for the copied HTML, such as Dreamweaver XHTML.

- **Screen 2:** Enter a base filename for the copied graphic slices. For example, if the graphic is for a logo for ABC company, the base filename might be `abclogo`. Click the Optional HTML settings button to specify additional settings for HTML output.

- **Screen 3:** Click the Browse button to select a destination for the copied HTML code. Typically this is the root folder of your Dreamweaver site.

- **Screen 4:** Click the Finish button. Web-ready images export to the destination folder, and the HTML code copies to your computer's Clipboard.

3. **In Dreamweaver, click your cursor inside the document where you want to paste the HTML code and choose Edit➪Paste Fireworks HTML.**

   The copied Fireworks HTML and any associated JavaScript code are pasted into the Dreamweaver file. At the same time, links to the images inside the pasted code are updated to match the freshly exported Fireworks images in the Dreamweaver site folder.

Updating Fireworks HTML in a Dreamweaver Document

To edit Fireworks HTML files inserted in Dreamweaver documents from within Fireworks and without launching Dreamweaver, try the Fireworks Update HTML command. This command lets you make changes to source PNG files in Fireworks and automatically update exported HTML and image files placed in Dreamweaver, even if Dreamweaver isn't running.

Follow these steps to update any Fireworks HTML you have in your Dreamweaver document:

1. **In Fireworks, open the source PNG file for the Fireworks HTML that you want to edit.**

   Make any edits to the source PNG file that you need.

2. **Choose File➪Save.**

   You must save your changes before moving on to the next step.

3. **Choose File➪Update HTML.**

   In the Locate HTML File dialog box that opens, browse to and select the Dreamweaver folder containing the HTML file that needs updating.

4. **Select the file to be updated and click the Open button.**

   The Update HTML dialog box opens, where you can choose whether to replace images and associated HTML or only update images. Make your selection and click OK.

5. **In the Select Images Folder dialog box, select the folder in the Dreamweaver site where you want to place the updated image files, and click Select (Windows) or Choose (Mac).**

The updated Fireworks HTML and images, including any associated JavaScript code, are saved into the Dreamweaver file.

Should Fireworks be unable to find a matching HTML file to update, you have the option of inserting new HTML into the chosen Dreamweaver file. Any JavaScript associated with the HTML is added into the document code appropriately.

Book IV

Energizing Your Site

By Rich Tennant

"We have no problem funding your Web site, Frank. Of all the chicken farmers operating Web sites, yours has the most impressive cluck-through rates."

Contents at a Glance

Chapter 1: Working with Layers

In This Chapter

✔ **Understanding how layers work**

✔ **Using the Layers panel**

✔ **Setting layer preferences**

✔ **Creating, editing, and managing layers**

✔ **Using CSS with layers**

✔ **Converting layers to tables (and tables to layers)**

*L*ayers are containers for HTML page elements that you can place anywhere on your Web page. Typically tagged with the `<div>` tag, layers can hold any kind of content you'd place elsewhere in the body of a document, such as text, graphics, JavaScript, Flash movies, and more.

Because you can position layers anywhere on a page, including on top of each other, they enable you to create interesting page layouts. In addition, you can make layers visible or hidden, styled and positioned with CSS, animated across the browser window, nested inside one another, and stacked in any order. Combined with JavaScript behaviors, you can manipulate layers in a browser window and provide engaging opportunities for visitor interaction.

Because of their flexibility, layers have become the new solution for many complex Web layouts. While many new browsers support layers, some of the older versions do not, though that's not too much of an issue because these days the ratio of browsers that don't support layers is extremely low. Still, if you need to ensure compatibility with an isolated pool of older browsers, or if you want to cover all eventualities, you could convert your layers into a table-based layout using the Convert command (as described at the end of this chapter), so any browser — even the oldest one — can interpret the content.

This chapter explores all the aspects of using layers in Dreamweaver. Starting with an introduction to layers management with the Layers panel, it also shows you how to set layer attributes, use CSS to style and position layers, and convert layers into a table-based layout and vice versa.

Understanding Layers

Traditionally, Web designers have used table-based page layouts, placing graphics and content inside tables. With tables, the cells are side by side and the content can't overlap. One of the drawbacks of a table-based layout is that content and form are meshed together in one document, which doesn't quite harness the full power of formatting and styling with layers and CSS. The full power of CSS comes when you begin laying out pages with layers and using styles to position and style objects on the page. Tables, by contrast, tend to be more static than layers and offer fewer opportunities for CSS formatting and styling. With layers, when you strip some of the formatting instructions from the HTML and hand them off to a Cascading Style Sheet, not only is the HTML code much cleaner, but the formatting capabilities of CSS enable you to lay out pages without the use of (or with significantly less reliance upon) tables. Tables aren't necessarily a bad thing; they're just being relied on less for formatting than they used to be.

Layers are what the W3C refers to as a *block-level element.* Block-level elements are containers that can hold content (such as images, text, and Flash movies), be any size, and be positioned anywhere on a page when styled with CSS. Furthermore, you can align blocks together on a page to create fairly sophisticated layouts, including layers that overlap! Figure 1-1 shows how you can have multiple layers on a page, each with unique content, positioning, and styles.

Figure 1-1:
Position
layers
anywhere
on a page
with text,
images,
Flash
movies,
and more.

When you draw or insert a layer in Dreamweaver (as described in the next section), CSS style data for the layer's size and positioning is automatically inserted into the head of the open document, and the `<div>` tag is inserted in the code at the insertion point with the layer id value of `Layer1`. Subsequent layers added to the page are given id values of `Layer2`, `Layer3`, `Layer4`, and so forth. To better identify each layer by its contents, however, you can change the id names in the Properties inspector or in the Layers panel after inserting them on the page.

Here's an example of the HTML code after inserting a layer on a page:

```
<!DOCTYPE HTML PUBLIC "-//W3C//DTD HTML 4.01 Transitional//EN"
"http://www.w3.org/TR/html4/loose.dtd">
<html>
<head>
<meta http-equiv="Content-Type" content="text/html; charset=iso-8859-1">
<title>Working with Layers</title>
<style type="text/css">
<!--
#Layer1 {
    position:absolute;
    left:50px;
    top:50px;
    width:400px;
    height:100px;
    z-index:1;
}
-->
</style>
</head>
<body>
  <div id="Layer1"></div>
</body>
</html>
```

Don't confuse layers with the old `<layer>` and `<ilayer>` tags used for positioning, which arrived as a blip on the Netscape 4 radar but quickly went away by Netscape 6 and are no longer supported by any browsers or contained in any W3C standards. Rather, the layers used in Dreamweaver refer to when the `<div>` tag is paired with the id attribute and used as a block-level container for HTML content.

Creating Layers

You can place layers anywhere on the page, nest them inside one another, place content in them, and size them to any rectangular shape. You can add layers to a page by three simple methods: drawing, inserting, and dropping. Use any and all of the methods interchangeably to suit your particular Web design needs in the moment.

Drawing a layer

The most effective way to add a layer to your page is to draw it because it can be drawn anywhere on the page.

To draw a single layer on a page, follow these steps:

1. **On the Layout tab of the Insert bar, click the Draw Layer button.**

2. **In the open Document window, click and drag a rectangular shape on the page in Design view where the new layer should appear.**

The drag can flow in any direction from the insertion point, and remember that the layer size and placement is approximate at this phase (see Figure 1-2).

To draw multiple layers at the same time without having to click the Draw Layer button each time, Ctrl+drag (Windows) or ⌘+drag (Mac) each of the layers. You can continue drawing new layers as long as you press Ctrl (Windows) or ⌘ (Mac).

3. **When the size and placement of the drawn layer is acceptable, release the mouse.**

4. **To add more layers to the page, repeat Steps 1 through 3.**

New layers added to the page are stacked directly on top of one other, each with a unique layer `id` and z-index number for identification and stacking order.

Dreamweaver provides two other ways you can add layers to your page:

✦ **Insert a layer:** Place the cursor in your document where you want to insert the new layer. Choose Insert⇨Layout Objects⇨Layer. The new layer is automatically inserted at the insertion point.

New layers added to the page stack directly on top of one other (unless you've repositioned the insertion point), each with a unique layer `id` and z-index number for identification and stacking order.

✦ **Drop a layer:** On the Layout tab of the Insert bar, click the Draw Layer button, and then drag and drop it into the open Document window.

The new invisible layer is automatically inserted at the default position in the top-left corner of the Document window. Repeat the process to add more layers to the page.

For more precise layout and placement of layers, some people find it helpful to enable the Grid and Snap to Grid features when drawing layers on the page. To find out more about using and customizing the grid, see Book I, Chapter 1.

Figure 1-2:
Draw layers
on the page.

Adding content to layers

Layers can hold most of the kinds of content you'd place in the body of a document, such as text, graphics, JavaScript, flash movies, and more. When you're ready to add content to a layer, place the insertion point inside the layer and either paste information, begin typing, or insert content using any of the options on the Insert menu, Insert bar, or Assets panel.

Creating nested layers

A *nested layer* is a layer that's controlled by, but not necessarily inside of, another layer. More simply, think of nested layers as having an interesting parent-child relationship where the child layer can move or function independently of the parent layer, but when the parent layer moves or hides, the child does too. The HTML code of a nested layer is inside the code of the parent layer, which you can see when you view the source code, even though the nested layer may appear elsewhere on the screen due to absolute positioning. Nested layers can be useful, for example, when creating custom navigation menus or when using layers that need to hide and show at the same time.

Figure 1-3 shows an example of how a nested layer appears in Design view, Code view, and the Layers panel.

Figure 1-3:
Nested
layers are
easy to
identify in
Code view
and in the
Layers
panel, but
may be
difficult to
spot in
Design view.

Before you can create nested layers, make sure that the Nesting preference is enabled in the Preferences dialog box (as described in the next section). Then follow these steps to create a nested layer:

1. **Choose Insert⇨Layout Objects⇨Layer.**

The new invisible layer is automatically inserted at the top of the page.

2. **Place the cursor inside the new layer, and then choose Insert⇨Layout Objects⇨Layer to create a second layer.**

The second layer is nested inside the first layer.

3. **To reposition the nested layer (the second layer) anywhere in the document, select the nested layer in the Layers panel to make it active, and do one of the following:**

 • Press the arrow keys to move the layer.

 • Click a selection handle and drag the layer to its new location.

Setting layer preferences

When inserting layers onto a page, the layers are added using the default dimensions and other attributes as specified in the Layers category of the Preferences dialog box. For example, if Dreamweaver's default layer width and height is set to 200 x 115 pixels, all new layers are added to the page at that default size unless you add a layer to the page by drawing it (see the "Drawing a layer" section earlier in this chapter).

You can edit the default layer size settings at any time by following these steps:

1. **Choose Edit⇨Preferences (Windows) or Dreamweaver⇨Preferences (Mac).**

The Preferences dialog box appears.

2. **Select the Layers category in the left column of the panel to display the layer attributes, as shown in Figure 1-4.**

Figure 1-4: These settings determine the default layer properties of all new layers.

3. **To set the default visibility of the layer (whether the layer will be seen or hidden from view when the page loads in the browser), select an option from the Visibility drop-down list.**

Options include Default (visible), Visible, Hidden, and Inherit.

4. **To set the default pixel width and height for new layers, fill in the Width and Height text boxes.**

5. **To specify a color for the default background color for all new layers, select a color from the Background Color palette or enter a hexadecimal value.**

Be sure to enter the number symbol before the hexadecimal value, as in #FF0000.

6. **To add a default background image for all new layers, click the Browse button next to Background Image to find and select the file.**

7. If you want to create nested layers, select the Nesting check box.

The nesting option enables you to draw a layer inside the bounds of another layer.

To toggle this feature on or off when drawing layers, hold Alt (Windows) or Option (Mac).

8. Select the Netscape 4 Compatibility check box if you want to enable the Netscape 4 compatibility feature.

Dreamweaver automatically adds the following JavaScript code to the head of the current page, which fixes a known browser resizing bug in Netscape 4:

```
<script type="text/JavaScript">
<!--
function MM_reloadPage(init) {  //reloads the window if Nav4 resized
  if (init==true) with (navigator) {if
    ((appName=="Netscape")&&(parseInt(appVersion)==4)) {
    document.MM_pgW=innerWidth; document.MM_pgH=innerHeight;
    onresize=MM_reloadPage; }}
  else if (innerWidth!=document.MM_pgW || innerHeight!=document.MM_pgH)
    location.reload();
}
MM_reloadPage(true);
//-->
</script>
```

If you don't choose this option now, you can choose Command⇨ Add/Remove Netscape Resize Fix later.

9. While still in the Preferences dialog box, select the Invisible Elements category and enable the Anchor Points for Layers option.

When you enable this option, each layer has its own yellow anchor point marker, which can assist greatly in the selection of specific layers in Design view, especially when several layers overlap or have visibility set to hidden.

10. Click OK to close the Preferences dialog box.

Managing Layers with the Layers Panel

The Layers panel is the place to go to select layers, name them, change their *z-index* (stacking order), modify nesting placement, enable overlapping, and edit visibility settings. The Layers panel is grouped with the CSS Styles panel in the CSS panel. To open the Layers panel, choose Window⇨Layers.

The Layers panel lists the layers on a page by visibility setting, name, and z-index number, as shown in Figure 1-5. The sorting order of the list is determined by the z-index. High z-index numbered layers appear at the top of the list while lower z-index numbered layers appear at the bottom of the list.

Figure 1-5:
The Layers panel displays information about all the layers on the page.

Try not to be confused by the default layer names and the z-index numbers. The default layer names are arbitrary (you can rename them to reflect their purpose) and are only meant to assist with identifying layers and applying CSS styles to them. The z-index, however, is used for the ordering or stacking of the layers between the browser and the site visitor. For example, on a page with 12 regular, non-nested layers, each named `Layer1`, `Layer2`, `Layer3`, and so on, where you want `Layer7` to appear on top of the other layers, assign `Layer7` a higher stacking order than 12. When you have nested layers on the page, nested layers often appear on top of parent layers, regardless of the stacking number of the parent. Within a nested group, though, normal z-index ordering applies.

Preventing layer overlap

To prevent layers from overlapping each other as you draw, move, or resize them, enable the Prevent Overlap option. This feature is handy if you plan on using layers for page layout and plan on converting the layers into tables (as described in the "Converting Layers to Tables and Tables to Layers," section later in this chapter), or if you want to add layers to your page that fit right up against one another without any gaps.

Though the Prevent Overlap option doesn't modify existing layer overlaps until you change them manually, it prevents you from drawing new layers on top of or inside another layer. It also prevents existing layers from being moved onto or resized over another layer, and instead helps layers snap into position next to each other.

To prevent layer overlaps, do one of the following:

✦ In the Layers panel, enable the Prevent Overlaps option.

✦ In Design view, choose Modify⇨Arrange⇨Prevent Layer Overlaps.

For most layer creation, layer movement, and layer resizing on a page, the Prevent Overlaps feature works wonderfully. However, some layer actions still allow you to add new layers that do overlap existing layers even with

**Book IV
Chapter 1**

Working with Layers

this option selected. For instance, layers inserted with the Insert menu and positioned with data in the Properties inspector can overlap existing layers in Design view. You can achieve the same effect when editing layer HTML source code directly in Code view.

If you like the way the new overlapping layers look in Design view and in your target browsers, the overlapping layers can be left as they are. However, to remove the new layer overlaps from a page, enable the Prevent Overlaps option first, and then drag the new layers to a new position in Design view. The new layers snap into position next to, and not on top of, adjoining layers.

Naming layers

A layer's name refers to the layer's id. The id is then used to attach CSS and positioning information to the layer. By default, Dreamweaver names layers Layer1, Layer2 and so on, but you can rename them to better identify them from each other.

To edit the name of a layer with the Layers panel, follow these steps:

1. **Double-click the layer name you want to edit.**

   The current name of the layer is highlighted.

2. **Type the new name for the layer. Then press Enter (Windows) or Return (Mac).**

   The new layer name is reflected in the code's <div> tag id attribute as well as in the layer's CSS style info embedded in the head of the document, in the Layers panel, and in the Properties inspector.

Changing the z-index (stacking order)

You can modify the *z-index*, or stacking order, of a layer with either the Layers panel or the Properties inspector. The higher the z-index number, the closer to the top of the list and the closer the layer appears to the visitor in the browser window relative to the other visible layers on the page.

To edit the z-index of a layer on the Layers panel, select a layer by its name and drag it up or down in the list to the new desired position. When moving a layer, a dark line appears between existing layers to assist with layer placement, indicating a safe spot to release the layer. Be alert when moving layers, as the repositioning can affect a layer's nesting and visibility as well as its z-index.

Editing layer visibility

Using the Layers panel in Design view, you can show or hide layers to see how the page displays in a browser window under different conditions. The default visibility status for all layers is to display layers both in Design view and in a browser window.

To set or change a layer's visibility in the Layers panel, click in the eye column next to the layer that you want to alter visibility for:

✦ **Open eye:** Indicates the layer is visible when the page initially displays in a browser.

✦ **Closed eye:** Indicates the layer is hidden, or invisible, when the page initially displays in a browser.

✦ **No eye:** When no eye icon is next to a layer, no visibility is set for the layer and it inherits the parent layer's visibility status. Nested layers inherit parent visibility settings, and non-nested layers inherit the document body's visibility settings (which is visible, unless you have hidden the body with CSS).

Figure 1-6 shows the Layers panel with sample layers set to on (show), off (hide), and none (default).

Figure 1-6:
Use the
Layers panel
to specify
each layer's
visibility
setting.

Show layer

No preference set

Hide layer

 To change all the layers on the page to Visible or Hidden at once, click the eye header icon at the top of the visibility column. The eye header icon works as a toggle button to switch between visible and hidden for all layers. Click once to make all layers visible. Click again to make all layers hidden.

Selecting and Adjusting Layers

Before moving, aligning, resizing, or editing the contents of a layer, you must first select the layer. You know you've selected a layer by its bold blue outline, corner and mid-section border anchor points, and visibility of the selection handle on the layer's top-left corner, as shown in Figure 1-7.

Figure 1-7: Selected layers display with a bold blue outline, anchor points, and a selection handle.

Selection handle

Outline

Anchor point (sizing handle)

Selecting layers

To assist you with selecting the layer, hover your mouse over the layer's edge and a highlight border appears. When you see the highlight border, click the layer's edge to select the entire layer.

TIP

You can change the color of the layer highlighting — or turn the feature off — by modifying the Mouse-Over option in the Highlighting category of the Preferences dialog box. Choose Edit⇨Preferences (Windows) or Dreamweaver⇨Edit (Mac).

You can also select a layer in any of these other ways:

✦ In the Layers panel, click the name of the layer you want to select.

✦ In Design view, do any of the following:

  • Click anywhere inside the layer to make the layer active; then click the layer's selection handle.

  • Ctrl+Shift+click (Windows) or ⌘+Shift+click (Mac) inside a layer.

If you want to select multiple layers, do either of the following:

✦ In Design view, Shift+click the border, selection handle, or inside area of any two or more layers.

✦ In the Layers panel, Shift+click two or more layer names.

With multiple layer selection, the corner and mid-section layer border anchor points turn hollow and the layers are highlighted in blue in the Layers panel.

Resizing and moving layers

Select the layer or layers using any of the selection methods in the previous section before making any adjustments to layers such as resizing, moving, or aligning:

✦ **Resize a layer:** Drag the selected layer's resize handles to the new desired size. You can also adjust the layer's Width and Height sizes in the Properties inspector, or, if using CSS, adjust the size in the layer's CSS through the CSS panel.

✦ **Resize multiple layers at once:** Select two or more layers and enter Width and Height values in the Multiple Layers W and H fields in the Properties inspector.

✦ **Move a selected layer or layers in Design view:** Drag the selection handle. With multiple layers, drag the selection handle of the last selected layer.

You can reposition layers on the page just like graphics and other objects; however, if you've enabled the Prevent Overlaps option, you can't reposition the layer on top of another layer. (See "Preventing layer overlap," earlier in the chapter, for more on this option.)

✦ **Align two or more selected layers:** Choose Modify⇨Arrange and choose an alignment option. Align layers to the left, right, top, or bottom edge of the last selected layer. When aligning nested layers, any child layer moves along with the parent layer, but isn't included in the alignment unless explicitly selected first.

Setting Layer Properties

Layers have properties that, among other things, define their size, position, name, z-index (stacking order), background color, and visibility. Though you can also set a layer's name, visibility status, and z-index in the Layers panel, you can easily adjust all the layer's properties in one go around using the Properties inspector.

Properties are real-time attributes that immediately reflect on the page in Design view when you press Tab or Enter (Windows), or Return (Mac). Therefore, any time you adjust a layer property in the Properties inspector, the Layers panel updates to reflect the new layer settings. This also works in the reverse direction; when you make modifications in the Layers panel, the Properties inspector also instantly updates.

The Properties inspector (shown in Figure 1-8) includes the following layer properties:

✦ **Layer ID** identifies each layer using a unique name or ID. The name you enter is used to attach CSS styles and JavaScript behaviors to the layer. Make sure each layer id is a single word using letters or numbers but without any funky characters, dashes, hyphens, periods, or spaces.

Figure 1-8:
Set
properties
for selected
layers.

✦ **L** and **T** (left and top) are the coordinates or absolution position of the layer relative to the top-left corner of the containing box, which is usually the body of the page, but can sometimes be a parent layer. For example, a setting of `left:100px` and `top:300px` places the layer exactly 100 pixels from the left and 300 pixels from the top of the browser window. Nested layers use these coordinates for absolute positioning relative to the parent layer.

✦ **W** and **H** (width and height) are the size of the layer. By default, layer sizes are specified in pixels. To enter another unit, add the appropriate abbreviation after the number without a space, such as **1in**, **10pt**, or **80%**. Acceptable units include (px) pixels, in (inches), pc (picas), pt (points), mm (millimeters), cm (centimeters), or % (percentage of a parent layer's size).

When the contents of a layer exceed the specified size of the layer and the Overflow setting is set to Visible, the bottom of the layer grows to display all the layer's contents in both Design view and in a browser window. To use the specified width and height instead, adjust the Overflow setting.

✦ **Z-Index** sets the stacking order of the layer. Enter positive or negative numbers. In a browser, the lower numbered layers appear behind the higher numbered layers.

Note: If you select a `<layer>` or `<ilayer>` tag instead of the `<div>` tag, additional options appear in the Properties inspector:

- **Left, Top** specifies the layer's position relative to the layer's parent top, left coordinates.

- **PageX, PageY** uses X and Y coordinates for positioning relative to the page.

- **A/B (Above/Below)** sets the stacking order of the selected layer relative from the first A/B menu to the layer name selected in the second A/B menu.

- **Src** selects another HTML file to display inside the layer. (This feature does not render in Design view, but displays in a browser; press F12 to preview.)

✦ **Vis** determines whether you can see the selected layer on the Web page when the page initially loads in a browser:

- **Default** uses a browser's default layer visibility status, which in most cases is Inherit.

- **Visible** displays the layer and its contents in a browser.

- **Hidden** hides the layer and its contents from view in a browser.

- **Inherit** uses the same visibility setting as a parent layer's visibility. Nested layers inherit parent visibility settings, and non-nested layers inherit the document body's visibility settings, which is always visible.

You can manipulate the visibility feature with JavaScript to hide and show layers when certain events occur, such as an `onMouseOver` event. See Book IV, Chapter 2 to find out more about how to manipulate layers with JavaScript.

✦ **Background Image** adds a background image for the layer. When specified, a background image tiles both vertically and horizontally to fill the entire visible area of the layer.

✦ **Background Color** adds a background color to the layer. Be sure to enter the number symbol before the hexadecimal value, as in #FF0000. When both a background color and background image are set, the background image sits on top of the background color.

✦ **Class** applies a custom style to the layer from an internal or externally linked cascading style sheet.

✦ **Overflow** determines how content that exceeds the specified size of the layer gets handled. This option currently has inconsistent browser support, so be sure to test this feature in all your target browsers to see if it works properly or fails acceptably:

- **Default** displays the layer and its contents in a browser.

- **Visible** expands the layer to fit the size of the contents and display the full layer's contents.

- **Hidden** hides contents that exceed the layer's size from view in a browser.

- **Scroll** adds scroll bars to the specified size of the layer, regardless of whether the contents exceed the specified size.

- **Auto** adds scroll bars to the specified size of the layer only when the contents exceed that size.

✦ **Clip** determines the visible area of a visible layer. Set left, top, right, and bottom coordinates for the visible clipping area on the layer. Numbers are measured in pixels relative to the top-left corner of the layer. You must set the Overflow option to Hidden, Scroll, or Auto for this feature to work properly. Figure 1-9 shows an example of a selected layer with a specified clipping area.

For example, to make a clipping area of 50 x 50 pixels at the top, left edge of the layer, set L to **0**, T to **0**, R to **50**, and B to **50**.

Figure 1-9:
Set a visible rectangular area.

Controlling Layer Style and Positioning with CSS

Dreamweaver 8 is configured to create individual layer styles in an internal style sheet for all the new layers added to your page. These layer styles control all the layer style attributes — for example, the layer's background color — as well as the layer's size and position on the page.

The benefit of using CSS with your layers is that you can

✦ Utilize all the capabilities of CSS with your layers.

✦ Move the CSS information to an external style sheet and link that CSS to all the pages on your site.

✦ Use these individual layer styles to control the look and placement of layers of the same name across multiple pages.

For instance, you may have a layer called Navigation that contains navigation links that go on every page of your site. Should you need to modify any of the properties of the layer (not the layer's content, just its position and style) you could modify the properties for that style through the CSS panel, and all the pages on the site that contain a layer called Navigation are updated with those new properties.

When creating a layer in Dreamweaver 8, two things happen in the code simultaneously:

✦ The layer is added to the code at the insertion point using the `<div>` tag, which gets assigned with a temporary layer `id` value of something like `Layer1` or `Layer2` (rename layers at any time using the Layers panel or Properties inspector).

✦ The layer's size and positioning information gets translated into CSS syntax and is automatically inserted between `<style>` tags into the head of the open document.

Here's an example:

```
<!DOCTYPE HTML PUBLIC "-//W3C//DTD HTML 4.01 Transitional//EN"
"http://www.w3.org/TR/html4/loose.dtd">
<html>
<head>
<meta http-equiv="Content-Type" content="text/html; charset=iso-8859-1">
<title>Working with Layers</title>
<style type="text/css">
<!--
#Layer1 {
    position:absolute;
    left:0px;
    top:0px;
    width:760px;
    height:150px;
    z-index:1;
}
-->
</style>
</head>
<body>
  <div id="Layer1"></div>
</body>
</html>
```

Notice that the layer's style name inside the `<style>` tags displays a number symbol (#) before the layer's `id`, in this case, `#Layer1`. Whenever the number symbol is paired with a layer's `id` as a style name in a style sheet, the style data gets automatically applied (much like a tag redefine style) to the layer with the same `id`. To illustrate, a set of style definitions using the style name `#header` is automatically applied to a layer with the `id="header"` and style definitions using the style name `#closeup` is automatically applied to a layer with the `id="closeup"`.

Ideally, all the style and positioning information for all the content on all the pages on a Web site are in one centralized location, preferably a single external style sheet. Therefore, you need to export the internal CSS style data for layers entered automatically on the page by Dreamweaver to an external style sheet. You can export internal styles two ways:

✦ Cut and paste the internal styles to an external style sheet.

✦ Use the CSS panel export command, which essentially copies the code onto any existing or new CSS, but doesn't remove the internal CSS from the source page. You must manually remove the internal CSS from the page before the external CSS takes control of the layers positioning. (See Book III, Chapter 1 to use the export command.)

**Book IV
Chapter 1**

**Working with
Layers**

After transferring the style sheet positioning data to an external style sheet, continue adding additional styling information, such as the layer's background color, font face, font size, and font color, to the layer style.

To add style information to a layer style, follow these steps:

1. In the CSS Styles panel, select the layer style name and click the Edit Style button (which looks like a pencil) at the bottom of the panel.

The CSS Rule Definition dialog box for the selected layer style opens..

2. Edit or add new layer style definitions in any of the categories in the dialog box.

When you select a category from the listing on the left, the right side of the panel changes to support that category's options. For example, to add a background color, select the Background category and click the Background Color color picker icon to select a hexadecimal value for the background color. See Book III, Chapter 1 for more guidance on picking the appropriate settings in the CSS Rule Definition dialog box.

3. To preview before committing to the style settings, click the Apply button.

4. When you finish making changes, click OK.

The updated style information is added to the style sheet and is displayed in the CSS Styles panel.

In the following style example, part of the style data (from `position` to `visibility`) is used for the layer's positioning and the rest (from `background-color` to `border`) is for layer styling:

```
#Layer1 {
    position:absolute;
    left:157px;
    top:38px;
    width:229px;
    height:279px;
    z-index:1;
    visibility: visible;
    background-color: #FF3366;
    font-family: Arial, Helvetica, sans-serif;
    font-size: 14px;
    font-weight: bold;
    color: #FFFFFF;
    margin: 0px;
    padding-top: 10px;
    padding-right: 0px;
    padding-bottom: 0px;
    padding-left: 10px;
    border: 10px solid #99CC00;
}
```

Controlling Layers with Behaviors

Dreamweaver comes with over 20 pre-written JavaScript behaviors that allow a designer to create interactive sites by controlling or manipulating objects on a Web page. Here are three behaviors that apply directly to layers:

✦ **Drag Layer:** This behavior allows you to provide a visitor with the ability of dragging or moving a layer inside a browser window. Often used for interactive games and puzzles, the behavior allows the following things:

- **Snap-to capability:** Visitors can drag layers in any direction and they snap to a target destination within a specified number of pixels.

- **Handles:** You can define a drag handle somewhere on the layer.

- **Event handlers:** You can assign an event handler to the layer as the trigger for the layer's mobility, such as when a visitor moves the mouse over or clicks the layer.

✦ **Set Text of Layer:** This behavior allows you to replace the contents of an entire layer with new HTML content and formatting, including any JavaScript property, global variable, function call, or other valid expression embedded in the code, when an event is triggered by a visitor's action, such as mousing over the layer.

✦ **Show-Hide Layers:** Use the Show-Hide Layers behavior when you want to control a layer's visibility with user interactivity. For example, you can have a rollover button that, when clicked, reveals a hidden layer. Then, on that layer you can include a link or graphic that, when clicked, hides the layer.

Book IV, Chapter 2 describes each of these behaviors, including how to insert, modify, and remove them.

Converting Layers to Tables and Tables to Layers

Layers, due to their flexibility, have become the new solution for many Web designers who need to create complex page layouts. A tables-based layout is still great when you have a lot of images that need to fit together tightly within a specified area of the page, such as a navigation table or other menu-type item. But a layers-based layout can look like a tables-based layout, plus you have the added control of positioning the layer and styling the layer's content using CSS. Alternatively, you may find it useful to combine the use of tables and layers for your layout.

While now considered less contemporary than a layout that relies almost exclusively on layers, tables are still an acceptable method for page layout because most browsers support tables, whereas layers are not universally supported. If you want the flexibility of layers but need to use tables for your code, consider using layers to design page layouts and then converting the layers into tables before adding content to the page.

The conversion process is very simple and you can toggle an entire page layout from layers to tables and tables to layers. Though you can't use the conversion to convert a single layer or table, keep experimenting until you get your layout perfect.

Be forewarned that the conversion process has two minor shortcomings:

✦ The conversion from layers to a table may create a table with a bunch of empty cells, which you then need to manually merge to simplify the table.

✦ You can't apply the conversion process to templates or template-based pages; you must create the table in a normal file and then convert it into a template. If the layout is simply a component of a template-based page, build the table in a new, blank document first and then paste the finished layout into the template-based page.

When creating a layout using layers, be sure to enable the Prevent Overlaps option to constrain layers from nesting or overlapping (see "Preventing layer overlap," earlier in the chapter). Because table cells can't overlap, the layers that are converted into tables can't overlap either.

Converting layers to a table

To convert a layout using layers to table-based layout, follow these steps:

1. **Create the layers-based layout in a new, blank HTML document and save the file.**

2. **Choose Modify⇨Convert⇨Layers to Table.**

The Convert Layers to Table dialog box opens, shown in Figure 1-10.

Figure 1-10:
Convert a
layers-
based layout
to tables
quickly.

3. **Specify Table Layout and Layout Tool options:**

- **Most Accurate:** This default option makes a table cell for each layer as well as create additional cells when needed to ensure that spacing between the old layers is maintained in the new table layout.

- **Smallest: Collapse Empty Cells:** Select this option to align the edges of layers into columns or rows of table cells when within a specified number of pixels. While this feature creates tables with less empty rows and tables, the layout may not be as precise as the original.

- **Use Transparent GIFs:** Choose this feature to have Dreamweaver add presized transparent GIFs to the bottom row of the table, which forces browsers to display the table using the same column widths. The drawback to this feature is that the table is not easily resized by simply dragging columns. When disabled, the columns are easily resizable, but the table itself may not display the same in all browsers.

- **Center on Page:** By default, the table displays aligned to the left of the browser. Select this option to center the new table on the page using the `align="center"` attribute inside the opening `<table>` tag.

- **Prevent Layer Overlaps:** Pick this option to prevent layers from being drawn, resized, or moved on top of one another.

- **Show Layers Panel:** Select this option to open the Layers panel.

- **Show Grid:** Choose this option to see the grid in Design view. The grid can assist you with the placement of layers on the page.

- **Snap to Grid:** Select this feature make the layers snap to the grid when placing, sizing, and moving layers on the page.

4. **Click OK to complete the conversion.**

If the layout contains overlapping or nested layers, an alert message may appear stating that the file isn't compatible with 3.0 browsers and the conversion is cancelled. When that happens, make adjustments to the layers and try the conversion process again.

Converting tables to layers

To convert a layout using tables to a layers-based layout, follow these steps:

1. **Create the tables-based layout in a new, blank HTML document and save the file.**

Only table cells with content convert into layers; table cells without content or background color disappear from the page layout during the

**Book IV
Chapter 1**

**Working with
Layers**

conversion process. If you don't want this to happen, be sure to add some kind of content to the cells you do want to convert into layers.

Any content on the page that wasn't in a table before is put into its own layer during the conversion.

2. **Choose Modify⇨Convert⇨Tables to Layers.**

The Convert Tables to Layers dialog box opens, as shown in Figure 1-11.

Figure 1-11:
The Convert
Tables to
Layers
dialog box.

3. **Enable Layout Tools options:**

   • **Prevent Layer Overlaps:** This option prevents layers from being drawn, resized, or moved on top of one another.

   • **Show Layers Panel:** Choose this option to open the Layers panel.

   • **Show Grid:** Select this option to see the grid in Design view. The grid can assist you with the placement of layers on the page.

   • **Snap to Grid:** Select this option to make the layers snap to the grid when placing, sizing, and moving layers on the page.

4. **Click OK to complete the conversion.**

Chapter 2: Jazzing Up Pages with JavaScript Behaviors

In This Chapter

✔ **Understanding JavaScript behaviors**

✔ **Using Dreamweaver's default behaviors**

✔ **Changing and deleting behaviors**

✔ **Using the Extension Manager to install third-party behaviors**

*J*avaScript is a scripting language created by Netscape that enables you to create interactive sites when you embed the scripts in your HTML pages. All the newest versions of the major browsers support JavaScript because it is an open-source language, which means anyone can write and use it without having to buy a license.

JavaScript can enhance your Web site and provide many kinds of interactivity for the visitor. For example, with JavaScript you can create rollover buttons and navigation menus; display dates, times, and slide shows; add cookies to a visitor's computer; play games; process forms; and even control browser windows.

Dreamweaver 8 comes with the following commonly used JavaScripts, which it refers to as *behaviors,* ready to insert onto your pages from the Behaviors panel:

Call JavaScript	Change Property
Check Browser	Check Plug-in
Control Shockwave or Flash	Drag Layer
Go to URL	Jump Menu/Go
Open Browser Window	Play Sound
Popup Message	Preload Images
Set Nav Bar Image	Set Text of Frame
Set Text of Layer	Set Text of Status Bar
Set Text of Text Field	Show-Hide Layers
Show Pop-Up Menu	Swap Image
Swap Image Restore	Validate Form

This chapter shows you what behaviors do and how you can insert, modify, or delete them. You also find information about downloading third-party behaviors from Macromedia's Dreamweaver Exchange and installing them using the Macromedia Extension Manager.

Understanding JavaScript Behaviors

JavaScript is a scripting language, not a programming language. Unlike programming languages such as C or VisualBasic, JavaScript is not that difficult to learn. You also shouldn't confuse JavaScript with Java, the object-oriented programming language used for writing applets. Unlike Java and other programming languages, JavaScript doesn't require compilation to run and it's much, much easier to write.

JavaScript includes three main types: client-side JavaScript (CSJS), server-side JavaScript (SSJS), and core JavaScript (CJS). Because server-side and core are more complex, this chapter deals exclusively with Dreamweaver's client-side JavaScript Behaviors. Client-side JavaScript builds on the Core JavaScript commands by adding common functionality useful in a browser situation. For a comprehensive look at JavaScript, check out WikiPedia's entry at `en.wikipedia.org/wiki/Javascript`. If you'd like to try your hand at some JavaScript tutorials, a fine place to begin is at the W3Schools Web site at `www.w3schools.com/js/default.asp`.

Client-side JavaScripts, or *behaviors* as Dreamweaver calls them, run in browsers (not on servers) and are the combination of an event and an action triggered by that event:

✦ **Events** are things that a visitor does to interact with a page (or things that happen to a page without visitor interaction, such as when the page loads in a browser) that triggers an action script that causes something on the page to change. Different events are associated with each page element. For instance, the `onMouseOver` event occurs when visitors move their mouses over a particular element on the page (for example, a graphic) that contains a JavaScript. That event then *triggers,* or tells, the browser to check the page's code to *call,* or put into action, any additional JavaScript based on the event.

✦ **Actions** are the parts of a script that perform specific tasks such as opening another browser window, displaying a message in the browser's status bar, swapping an image in a rollover button, or hiding and showing layers. A great example of a script that uses the `onMouseOver` event to call an action is a rollover button. When you visit a site, you typically see the button graphic in its normal state. However, when you move your cursor over the button, you see a replacement image (called an *over state* image) appear instead of the normal state. In most cases, when you move your mouse off or away from the over state graphic, the normal state graphic reappears.

Though you don't need to master JavaScript to use it, you would certainly benefit from any time spent learning more about it. If you're interested in finding out more about this scripting language, check out *JavaScript For Dummies,* by Emily A. Vander Veer (Wiley).

Adding JavaScript to Your Page

Using the Dreamweaver Behaviors panel and some of the other tools that support JavaScript interactivity, you can add JavaScript to HTML pages in four different ways:

✦ As an internal script in the head of a page between the `<script> </script>` tags, with event functions specified in the body tag when necessary, such as `onLoad="preloadImages();"`.

✦ As an external script file using the `<script src="...">` tag inside the head of an HTML page, similar to linked external Cascading Style Sheets.

✦ As an *event handler* (the event that triggers the JavaScript) inside HTML elements on forms to perform certain functions, such as returning the results of a Celsius to Fahrenheit temperature conversion or calling a JavaScript alert window to pop open.

✦ With the `Javascript: URL` protocol to add functionality to a page for actions such as reloading a page in the browser window, as in this example of a text link:

```
<a href="javascript:history.go(0)">Reload This Page</a>
```

Besides using the Behaviors panel, Dreamweaver also supports the addition of JavaScript behaviors to your pages in a handful of ways, though you may need to alter scripts obtained from outside Dreamweaver to get them to work specifically with your Web site:

✦ Write your own JavaScripts and hand-code them in the Code editor.

✦ Copy and paste JavaScripts into your pages from another source, such as a script you used on another site or copied from a free scripts Web site.

✦ Insert them into your pages as JavaScript snippets. (Book III, Chapter 4 discusses snippets.)

✦ Download, install, and use third-party behaviors (scripts for use in a Dreamweaver site that were developed by anyone other than Macromedia), as described at the end of this chapter.

When hand-coding or copying JavaScript behaviors, be sure you add the code in Code view rather than Design view. You also need to pay close attention to where you place the behavior script, as oftentimes JavaScript contains one to three parts: a script that goes into the head of the page, an event handler that goes into the <body> tag of the page, and some inline script that goes somewhere inside the body area of your page to call and display the script.

For example, take a look at Listing 2-1, which is a date and time script by Jim Stiles (www.jdstiles.com/java/livedate.html). This example requires script inside the <head> and <body> tags as well as between the opening and closing <body> tags.

Listing 2-1   Date and Time Script

```
<html>
<head>
<meta http-equiv="Content-Type" content="text/html; charset=iso-8859-1" />
<title> Time and Date JavaScript</title>
<script type=text/javascript>
<!-- Script by Jim Stiles http://www.jdstiles.com/java/livedate.html -->
<!--
var dayarray=new Array("Sunday","Monday","Tuesday","Wednesday","Thursday",
    "Friday","Saturday")
var montharray=new Array("January","February","March","April","May","June",
    "July","August","September","October","November","December")

function getthedate(){
var mydate=new Date()
var year=mydate.getYear()
if (year < 1000)
year+=1900
var day=mydate.getDay()
var month=mydate.getMonth()
var daym=mydate.getDate()
if (daym<10)
daym="0"+daym
var hours=mydate.getHours()
var minutes=mydate.getMinutes()
var seconds=mydate.getSeconds()
var dn="AM"
if (hours>=12)
dn="PM"
if (hours>12){
hours=hours-12
}
if (hours==0)
hours=12
if (minutes<=9)
minutes="0"+minutes
if (seconds<=9)
seconds="0"+seconds
//change font size here
var cdate="<font color='#000000' face='Arial' size='1'>"+dayarray[day]+",
    "+montharray[month]+" "+daym+", "+year+" "+hours+":"+minutes+":"+seconds+"
    "+dn
```

```
+"</font>"
if (document.all)
document.all.clock.innerHTML=cdate
else
document.write(cdate)
}
if (!document.all)
getthedate()
function goforit(){
if (document.all)
setInterval("getthedate()",1000)
}
-->
</script>
</head>

<body onLoad="goforit()">
<span id="clock"></span><BR>
</body>
</html>
```

When inserted on a page, this script returns the current date and time between the `<span>` tags in the following format:

```
Saturday, March 18, 2006 5:21:21 PM
```

Another thing you may want to consider whenever you add JavaScript behaviors to your pages is to add content between `<noscript>` tags for visitors who view sites with old versions of browsers or with browsers that have the JavaScript turned off, as in the following example:

```
<NOSCRIPT>
This page includes programming that requires a browser that can interpret
    JavaScript, such as Internet Explorer 4.0 and above, Netscape Navigator 4.0
    and above, Safari 1.0 and above, and Firefox 1.0 and above. If you see this
    message you may not have full access to this page's content.
</NOSCRIPT>
```

Place the `<noscript>` tags and contents inside the body of the page where you want the message to display when conditions warrant it. You can find a free snippet of this `<noscript>` tag with text at `www.luckychair.com`.

Using Dreamweaver's Default Behaviors

When you're first starting to work with JavaScript, trying to remember what goes where and when can be complicated. To ease the learning curve, try inserting a behavior with Dreamweaver's Behaviors panel.

Dreamweaver comes with over 20 preinstalled behaviors you can use to embed client-side JavaScript code in your documents. Many of these scripts let visitors interact with content on your pages. The behaviors are typically made up of events combined with actions that trigger those events.

340 *Using Dreamweaver's Default Behaviors*

Behaviors can do all kinds of things. For example, the Open Window behavior can open a page and force the browser window to resize automatically to a predetermined pixel width and height, and the Check Browser behavior can detect which browser and browser version a visitor is using and redirect visitors with specified browser types to another page on the site. (Both of these behaviors are described in detail later in this chapter.)

Using Dreamweaver's Behaviors panel, you can quickly add these scripts to your page. All the behaviors have dialog boxes to guide you through the process of entering in required data for customizing and inserting them. You can even choose the appropriate event handler to trigger the behavior's action, as well as specify that a certain event triggers several actions at once and set the order of those actions.

All of Dreamweaver's behaviors have been written to work in IE 4.0 and later and Netscape 4.0 and later. Many of them also work fine in Netscape 3.0 and later, but most of them don't work properly in IE 3.0. To maintain the best possible cross-browser compatibility, take care when removing or editing the JavaScript code by hand.

Using the Behaviors panel

To open the Behaviors panel, choose Window⇨Behaviors. In Dreamweaver 8, the Behaviors panel is nested with the Attributes panel inside the Tag panel, as shown in Figure 2-1.

The Behaviors panel is active when you have a document open in the Dreamweaver workspace window. To find out more about any previously applied behaviors, select the object or tag with the behavior on the page and any behaviors associated with the object or tag appear in the Behaviors panel listing. When an event includes multiple actions, the actions are triggered in the order they appear in the list.

Click to open Actions menu

Figure 2-1:
The Behaviors panel shows behaviors and events.

▼ Tag <input>	
Attributes Behaviors	
onLoad	Drag Layer
onMouseOver	Set Text of Statu...
onClick	Jump Menu Go

Actions column

Events column

Behaviors are typically attached to tags for text and graphics, but you can also apply them to the `<body>` element, to links, and to form fields.

The Behavior panel's Actions menu (which you open by clicking the Actions [+] button) lists Dreamweaver's preset behaviors. Which behaviors are available or disabled on this menu depends on two factors:

✦ Which object or asset on the page you select prior to clicking the Actions (+) button

✦ Which browser is selected in the Show Events For submenu at the bottom of the Actions menu (see Figure 2-2). The browser you select determines which events are supported and thus which Actions display, as every browser provides different sets of events that can be associated with the actions in this list.

To see a listing of names and descriptions of events by browser, check out the Dreamweaver Support Center at `www.macromedia.com/go/ dreamweaver_support`.

Figure 2-2:
The Show Events For submenu.

You can use the Show Events For submenu to help figure out whether certain browsers support selected behaviors for certain page assets. Try inserting the object on your page and attaching a behavior to it. When events are *grayed out,* or disabled, the specified browser doesn't support them.

Attaching a behavior

Attaching behaviors to objects on your page is fairly easy and requires only a few simple steps. Typically, you select an object or linked text on the page, choose a behavior from the Behaviors panel, complete the dialog box that appears associated with the behavior, and verify that the *event handler* (the event that triggers the action) matches your needs.

To attach a behavior, follow these steps:

1. **Select an object or element on the page, such as a graphic or a text link.**

   When attaching a behavior to the entire page, select the opening `<body>` tag from the Tag selector at the bottom-left corner of the open Document window.

2. **If you're attaching a behavior to text, you need to add a null link. To do so, type the JavaScript null link (`javascript:;`) in the Link text box in the Properties inspector**

   You can't attach a behavior to plain text, but you can attach it to a link. For this reason, if you're attaching a behavior to text, you must add a *null link* (a link that doesn't go anywhere) to the selected text before you can attach the behavior.

   Remember, the null link must contain both the colon and semicolon.

   If you want to remove the underline from linked text but add some other property (for example, a color) so that the behavior is available but the text that triggers the behavior to occur doesn't look like a traditional link, you could add some inline CSS to the link's `<a href>` tag to disable the default link underline and convert the text to another color, like this:

   ```
   <a href="javascript:;" style="text-decoration:none;
       color:#000000;">Example 1</a> </p>
   ```

   Better still would be to create and use a non-underlining class in an external CSS, as many CSS purists frown upon inline styles.

3. **Open the Behaviors panel by choosing Window⇨Behaviors.**

4. **Click the Actions (+) button in the Behaviors panel and select an action from the list.**

The actions that are active in the list support the selected element; any actions that are grayed out are unusable. Either the asset doesn't exist in the document or the target browser specified in the Show Events For submenu doesn't support that action. For example, you can't use the Drag Layer action if no layers are present on the page. All the actions in this list work in 4.0 and later browsers, but some don't work in browsers older than that.

After selecting an action, a dialog box opens with parameters to set and options to select that support the behavior.

5. **Fill in the action's dialog box to specify how you want the behavior to work.**

   Some dialog boxes have multiple tabs with several fields for data entry.

6. **When you finish, click OK.**

   The behavior is inserted into the page, and the default event handler for that behavior appears in the Behavior panel's Events column (the first column in the panel).

7. **If you want to change the event handler, select the current event handler from the Behaviors panel. Then select a different event handler from the Events drop-down menu.**

   If the event handler you want to use is not on the list, try changing the target browser in the Show Events For menu at the bottom of the Behaviors panel Actions menu.

Changing and deleting behaviors

You can modify or delete a behavior at any time. For instance, you can change the event handler, add and remove actions, edit action parameters, and delete attached behaviors.

To change a behavior in Dreamweaver, follow these steps:

1. **Select the asset on the page that has the behavior attached to it.**

2. **In the Behaviors panel, select the associated action you want to change.**

   To open the Behaviors panel, choose Window⇨Behaviors.

3. **Do any of the following to change the behavior:**

   • **Change the order of the actions:** When two or more actions are listed in the Behaviors panel, you can change the order of the actions by selecting an action and clicking the up or down arrows.

- **Edit an action's parameters:** Double-click the action name to launch the action's dialog box and change the action's parameters. You can also launch the dialog box by selecting the behavior's name and pressing Enter (Windows) or Return (Mac).

- **Delete a behavior:** Delete a behavior by selecting it by name and clicking the minus (–) button in the Behaviors panel or pressing the Delete key on your keyboard.

In your code, some behaviors' events may appear in parentheses to indicate links, for example, when you attach some behaviors to an image. In those cases, Dreamweaver automatically wraps the <a> tag around images and defines a null link using the javascript:; syntax in the Properties inspector's Link text field, as with this example:

```
<a href="javascript:;"
    onClick="MM_openBrWindow('welcome.html','','width=300,height=300')"><img
    src="images/logo.gif" width="195" height="200" border="0"></a>
```

In these cases, you can still edit the behavior in the Behaviors panel if you like, or edit the JavaScript behavior in Code view.

Updating old behaviors

For pages with behaviors created in Dreamweaver 1 and 2, and possibly for some behaviors created in Dreamweaver 3 and 4, you have to manually update the behaviors in the current version of Dreamweaver. Fortunately, this process takes a little less time because of help provided by Dreamweaver. When you manually update one instance of a behavior, Dreamweaver automatically updates all other instances of the same behavior. Granted, you still need to update all the old behaviors on every other page on your site, but at least the process goes a little faster with this helpful feature.

Follow these steps to update an old behavior:

1. **Select the asset on the page that has the old behavior attached to it.**

2. **Open the Behaviors panel by choosing Window⇨Behaviors.**

3. **Double-click the action in the Behaviors panel. And in the behavior's dialog box, verify or modify any of the settings.**

   Opening the behavior's dialog box in the newer version of Dreamweaver is how the behavior code gets updated.

4. **Click OK in the behavior's dialog box.**

   Dreamweaver automatically updates any other instances of that behavior on the same page.

Call JavaScript

With the Call JavaScript behavior, you can add your own JavaScript to your page as a custom function or a line of code that gets triggered by a specified event. For example, you could add JavaScript that makes the browser window close when the user clicks a specified button. If you know JavaScript, you can write these JavaScript behaviors yourself, or if you're not as familiar with JavaScript syntax, you can usually find free source code on the large number of JavaScript tutorial and library Web sites, including these:

```
www.w3schools.com/js/default.asp
www.dynamicdrive.com/
www.javascriptkit.com/javatutors/
javascript.internet.com/
```

To add the Call JavaScript behavior to a document, follow these steps:

1. **Select an object or text link on your page.**

2. **Click the Actions (+) button in the Behaviors panel, and choose Call JavaScript.**

The Call JavaScript dialog box opens, as shown in Figure 2-3.

Figure 2-3:
Enter scripts and custom functions.

3. **In the JavaScript box, type your JavaScript or function:**

For example, to make a Close button, you'd enter either of the following scripts, including the parentheses and semicolon:

```
javascript:window.close();
```
or
```
window.close();
```

Dreamweaver writes the JavaScript function to the head of the page for you, which means technically all you really need to type is the function name, such as `closepopup()`.

4. **Click OK to close the dialog box.**

**Book IV
Chapter 2**

Jazzing Up Pages
with JavaScript
Behaviors

5. **Verify that the event handler listed in the Events column of the Behaviors panel is the one you want to use.**

   You can use the Behaviors panel to change the event handler. If the event handler you want to use is not on the list, try changing the target browser in the Show Events For menu at the bottom of the Behaviors panel Actions menu.

Change Property

You can use the Change Property behavior to change an object's properties, such as the background color of a layer, the text contained inside of a `<div>` tag, or the source file of an image. The properties that you can change depend largely on the browser type and version your visitors use when viewing the page. For example, IE 4.0 and up supports many more properties than do IE 3.0, NN 3.0, and NN 4.0.

Because this behavior requires you to type some code in the dialog box it uses, be sure you know HTML and understand JavaScript a little before using it, and test the actions in your target browsers before publishing them.

To use the Change Property behavior on a page, follow these steps:

1. **Select an object on your page.**

   You can modify these objects or tags with this behavior: `layer`, `div`, `span`, `img`, `form`, `input/checkbox`, `input/radio`, `input/text`, `textarea`, `input/password`, and `select`.

2. **Click the Actions (+) button in the Behaviors panel, and select Change Property.**

   The Change Property dialog box opens, as shown in Figure 2-4.

Figure 2-4: Select the object type and specify the property to change.

Change Property		
Type of object: LAYER		OK
Named object: layer "Layer1"		Cancel
Property: ⦿ Select: style.backgroundColor IE4		Help
○ Enter:		
New value: #FF3300		

3. **From the Type of Object menu, choose the object type that matches your selection.**

   For example, to change the background color of a layer, select LAYER from the Type of Object menu, as shown in Figure 2-4.

   The Named Object drop-down list changes to support that selection.

4. **From the Named Object list, choose the object whose properties you want to change.**

   When the Type of Object selected is not found on the page, you see an object not found message on the Named Object menu, such as `*** no FORMs found ***`.

5. **In the Property section, select a property that you want to change from the Select drop-down list, or select the Enter Property radio button and type the property name in the Enter text field.**

   When using the Select Property field to select an action from the Select drop-down list, be sure to also select a browser type and version from the drop-down list to see which properties a specific browser supports (the properties appear in the Select drop-down list).

   For example, in Figure 2-4, we selected the `style.backgroundColor` property and IE4 as the browser type/version.

   Pay close attention to spelling and letter case when typing the JavaScript property name.

6. **In the New Value text field, type the new value for the property.**

   For example, if changing the background color of a layer, type a hexadecimal value preceded by a number symbol (#), like #FF3300.

7. **Click OK to close the dialog box.**

8. **Verify that the event handler listed in the Events column of the Behaviors panel is the one you want to use.**

   Because the property of the object changes when the event occurs, you need to check that the right event is listed with the action in the Behaviors panel. If necessary, change the event handler in the Behaviors panel; if the event handler you want to use is not on the list, try changing the target browser on the Show Events For menu at the bottom of the Behaviors panel Actions menu.

Check Browser

Because you have no control over what browser and browser version visitors will use when viewing your site, a great script to consider using is the Check Browser behavior. This behavior can auto-detect the user's browser and browser version and direct the visitor to an alternate Web page. For instance, you can let everyone viewing the site with IE and Netscape 4.0 and above see the regular home page of your site, but redirect visitors using earlier versions of IE and Netscape to another page with a special message about minimum Web browser requirements for viewing the site.

Here's an example of a special message that could include links to download the latest versions of the most popular browsers:

If you're having problems viewing our Web site...

The browser you are using is either out of date or a version this Web site doesn't support, as this site is designed with standards for the most commonly used, recent Web browsers.

For a better viewing experience, upgrade to one of these browsers:

For Windows: Internet Explorer 5 or greater | Firefox | Opera

For Macintosh: Safari | Firefox | Opera

For Unix/Linux: Firefox | Opera

The Check Browser behavior works best when you add it to the page's opening `<body>` tag. The visitors using browsers with JavaScript disabled still see the content on the default home page. If you don't attach the behavior to the `<body>` tag, be sure to use a null link with an action that specifies the destination link based on the detected browser and version, as in this example:

```
<a href="javascript:;"
    onclick="MM_checkBrowser(4.0,1,2,4.0,1,2,2,'index.html','alternate.html');
    return document.MM_returnValue">Check Browser Compatibility</a>
```

To add the Check Browser action to your page, follow these steps:

1. **Select an object, null text link, or the `<body>` tag on your page.**

   You can select the object or text link in Design view, but if you're attaching the behavior to the `<body>` tag, select it in Code view or in the Tag selector.

   To create a null text link, select the text in the document and type **javascript:;** in the Properties inspector Link text field.

2. **Click the Actions (+) button in the Behaviors panel, and select Check Browser.**

   The Check Browser dialog box opens, as shown in Figure 2-5.

Figure 2-5:
The Check
Browser
behavior
can send a
visitor to a
page you
specify.

3. **Review the dialog box options to decide how to divide site visitors by browser version and type.**

   You can divide site visitors by browser brand, browser version, or both. For instance, you may want to send all visitors using Mac IE 5 to one page and everyone else to another page.

4. **Specify a minimum browser version in the Netscape Navigator and Internet Explorer fields.**

   By default both are set to 4.0, but you can change them to earlier or later versions, depending on the complexity of your site and known browser compatibility issues.

5. **In the drop-down lists next to the Netscape Navigator and Internet Explorer fields, select options for each of the Or later and Otherwise conditions.**

   For instance, if the browser detected is Netscape 4.0 or later, you must decide what page the visitor will see. The options include Stay on This Page, Go to URL, or Go to Alternate URL.

6. **From the Other Browsers drop-down list, specify what you want to happen when the detected browser is not IE or Netscape.**

   Set this option for other popular browser such as Safari, Opera, and Firefox, or text-based browsers such as Lynx. Options in this menu include Stay on This Page, Go to URL, or Go to Alternate URL. If you're not sure which option to use, select Stay on This Page.

7. **In both the URL and Alt URL fields, enter a URL including path and filename.**

   When entering a remote URL, be sure to type the **http://** prefix before the www address, as in `http://www.macromedia.com`.

8. **Click OK to close the dialog box.**

9. **Verify that the event handler listed in the Events column of the Behaviors panel is the one you want to use.**

The default event handler for the Check Browser behavior is onLoad, but you can change the event handler in the Behaviors panel.

Because this behavior is best for checking browser versions, aim to select an event handler that works in IE and Netscape browsers that are version 3.0 and later. If the event handler you want to use is not on the list, try changing the target browser in the Show Events For menu at the bottom of the Behaviors panel Actions menu.

Check Plug-In

The Check Plug-in behavior checks to see if the user's computer has the necessary plug-ins installed to successfully view your page. If the user has the necessary plug-ins, the Check Plug-in behavior displays the current page; if the user doesn't have the required plug-in, it can send the visitor to an alternate page. For example, you may have created a Shockwave movie for your site that requires the latest free Shockwave player. Use the Check Plug-in behavior to detect whether the right Flash player is installed and, if it is not, send visitors to a page telling them how to find and install the required plug-in.

Internet Explorer can't interpret JavaScript for plug-in detection. As a workaround in Windows, when you select Flash or Director, Dreamweaver writes the VBScript to your page that auto-detects those plug-ins in IE. Unfortunately, IE on the Mac has no workaround. By contrast, Netscape Navigator always detects plug-ins on both Mac and Win.

To add the Check Plug-in behavior to your page, follow these steps:

1. **Select an object on your page.**

2. **Click the Actions (+) button in the Behaviors panel, and select Check Plugin.**

The Check Plugin dialog box opens, as shown in Figure 2-6.

3. **Select a plug-in type from the Select drop-down list, or type the plug-in name in the Enter text field.**

Plug-in options include Flash, Shockwave, LiveAudio, QuickTime, and Windows Media Player. When typing the plug-in name in the text field, the spelling and letter case must be accurate for this behavior to work.

To find out more about plug-ins, see the Netscape About Plug-ins page: On Windows, open Netscape and choose Help⇨About Plug-ins. On a Mac, open Netscape and choose About Plug-ins from the Apple menu.

Figure 2-6:
This behavior detects if visitors have the right plug-ins installed.

4. **Enter a URL in both the If Found and Otherwise Go To URL fields.**

Typically, the If Found URL is the page to go to when the plug-in is installed on the visitor's computer, and the Otherwise URL is the page to go to if the plug-in is not installed. When you want visitors without the plug-in to stay on the current page, leave the Otherwise URL field blank.

When either of the URLs are remote (not on your Web site), be sure to type the **http://** prefix before the www in the Web address, as in `http://www.macromedia.com`.

5. **Enable the Always Go to First URL option if Detection Is Not Possible option for visitors using Internet Explorer.**

When you enable this option, the visitor is sent to the URL in the If Found text field; when you leave this option disabled, the visitor is sent to the Otherwise URL.

If you're not sure whether to enable or disable this option, I recommend enabling this feature so that IE visitors lacking the plug-in get prompted by their browsers to download and install it before viewing the page.

6. **Click OK to close the dialog box.**

7. **Verify that the event handler listed in the Events column of the Behaviors panel is the one you want to use.**

The default event handler for this behavior is `onFocus`. You can change the event handler in the Behaviors panel. If the event handler you want to use is not on the list, try changing the target browser in the Show Events For menu at the bottom of the Behaviors panel Actions menu.

Control Shockwave or Flash

After you insert a Shockwave or Flash movie (SWF file) on your page (see Book II, Chapter 5 for details on inserting media files), you can assign the Control Shockwave or Flash behavior to an object (such as a graphic) to play, rewind, go to a frame, or stop the movie.

Follow these steps to install the Control Shockwave or Flash behavior:

1. **Insert the Shockwave or Flash movie to your page.**

To insert the movie, choose Insert⇨Media⇨Shockwave or Insert⇨Media⇨Flash.

2. **Select the Shockwave or Flash movie in the document and enter a name for it in the Properties inspector.**

The Name field is in the top-left corner of the Properties inspector next to the movie icon. The movie must have a name to use this behavior.

3. **Select the object on the page that controls the movie.**

For instance, select a graphic on the page that stops the movie.

4. **Click the Actions (+) button in the Behaviors panel, and select Control Shockwave or Flash.**

The Control Shockwave or Flash dialog box opens, where you can select the appropriate movie and assign an action to the selected object (see Figure 2-7).

Figure 2-7:
Select an
action.

5. **From the Movie menu, select the Shockwave or Flash movie that the new behavior controls.**

The menu lists all the names of any Shockwave or Flash SWF files found on the page. More specifically, the listing includes any files that are coded in the `object` or `embed` tags on the page and have file extensions ending with: `.swf`, `.dir`, `.spl`, or `.dcr`.

6. **Choose an action for the object selected in Step 3.**

Select Play, Rewind, Stop, or Go to Frame. For the Go to Frame option, enter the frame number in the adjoining text field.

7. **Click OK to close the dialog box.**

8. **Verify that the event handler listed in the Events column of the Behaviors panel is the one you want to use.**

You can change the event handler in the Behaviors panel. If the event handler you want to use is not on the list, try changing the target browser in the Show Events For menu at the bottom of the Behaviors panel Actions menu.

Drag Layer

If you're using layers on your site and want to add some interesting viewer interactivity, consider adding the Drag Layer behavior to allow site visitors to move and reposition layers in the browser window. This is a great behavior for creating interactive games, puzzles, movable navigation layers, and other user interface controls.

The Drag Layer behavior enables your Web page visitors to drag layers up, down, left, right, and diagonally on the screen. Among other things, you can also set a target destination for the layer (think puzzles) and whether or not to snap the layer to the target within a specified number of pixels.

Like all behaviors, the action must be called before the behavior can be used, so you need to choose the right event handler. For this reason, you must attach this behavior to the `<body>` tag and use the `onLoad` event handler to trigger the event. This ensures the layer is ready for dragging the minute the page finishes loading in the browser.

Alternatively, you could attach the behavior to a link inside the layer that takes up the entire layer size (such as a linked image) paired with the `onMouseOver` event handler. You have to first apply the behavior to the `<body>` tag so that Dreamweaver can add all the JavaScript to the page that defines the drag layer function. Then you move by hand the `onload` script line from the `<body>` tag to the new link location in the code. The last thing you do is change the event handler in the Behaviors panel, as in the following code:

From this:

```
<body onload="MM_dragLayer('Layer1','',0,0,0,0,true,false,-1,-1,-1,-
    1,false,false,0,'',false,'')">
<div id="Layer1">
  <p><a href="http://www.dummies.com"><img src=" images/dummies.gif"
    name="dummies" width="50" height="80" border="0" id="dummies"/></a></p>
</div>
</body>
```

To this:

```
<body>
<div id="Layer1">
  <p><a href="http://www.dummies.com"><img src=" images/dummies.gif"
    name="dummies" width="50" height="80" border="0" id="dummies"
    onmouseover="MM_dragLayer('Layer1','',0,0,0,0,true,false,-1,-1,-1,-
    1,false,false,0,'',false,'')"/></a></p>
</div>
</body>
```

To attach the Drag Layer behavior to a layer on your page, follow these steps:

1. **Draw a layer on the page.**

Choose Insert➪Layer. Or click the Draw Layer button on the Insert bar and draw a layer in an open document in Design view.

See Book IV, Chapter 1 for the skinny on layers.

2. **Select the opening <body> tag with the Tag selector (which is located in the bottom-left corner of the Document window).**

3. **Click the Actions (+) button in the Behaviors panel, and select Drag Layer.**

The Drag Layer dialog box opens, as shown in Figure 2-8. The dialog box has two tabs: Basic and Advanced. Each tab allows you to enter specific parameters for this behavior.

Figure 2-8: Specify a drop target position and whether to constrain the layer's movement.

4. **On the Basic tab, select the layer to be dragged from the Layer menu.**

Layers are listed alphabetically by name to help you identify them quickly. If you forgot to name your layers, cancel out of the dialog box, select and name the layer(s), and reopen the Drag Layer dialog box.

5. **From the Movement menu, choose Unconstrained or Constrained.**

Select Unconstrained for free-form movement, as with puzzles and games, or choose Constrained for movements that need to be controlled, as with sliders or other movable elements.

6. For constrained movements, type pixel values for the Up, Down, Left, and Right parameters.

The pixel coordinates are relative to the layer's original position, and you can enter positive, negative, and 0 values in any of the fields. For example, if you want to constrain movement of the layer to the left and right only, enter positive pixel values in the Left and Right boxes and 0s in the Up and Down boxes.

7. In the Top and Left Drop Target fields, type pixel values for the desired finish position of the layer, relative to the top-left corner of the browser window.

The target is considered reached when the layer's top and left positioning values match the drop target's top and left coordinates.

To get the selected layer's current top and left coordinates, click the Get Current Position button. This sometimes helps when you're trying guesstimate pixel values for the drop target position relative to the current position.

8. If you want the layer to snap to the drop target coordinates when the visitor drags it within a specified range, enter a pixel value for the range in the Snap if Within text box.

The bigger the number, the easier the visitor can drag the layer to the drop target.

9. Select the Advanced tab to enter additional parameters and call JavaScript for the dragged layer:

- **Drag Handle:** By default the Entire Layer option is selected, which means the whole layer acts as a drag handle. If you want a specific part of the layer to be used as a drag handle, select the Area Within Layer option and enter the Top and Left coordinate values and a Width and Height in pixels for the drag handle.

- **While Dragging:** When the Bring Layer to Front option is enabled, you can select Leave on Top or Restore Z-Index to alter the stacking order of the layer while dragging it.

- **Call JavaScript:** Type JavaScript code or a function name in the Call JavaScript text field. This feature requires an understanding of JavaScript and how to collect data about the layer as it's being dragged. The JavaScript code repeats while the layer is being dragged.

- **When Dropped:** Type additional JavaScript code or a function name in this Call JavaScript field to call actions when the layer is dropped or reaches its target destination.

- **Only if Snapped:** When enabled, the When Dropped Call JavaScript executes only when the dragged layer reaches the drop target.

10. **Click OK to close the dialog box.**

11. **Verify that the event handler listed in the Events column of the Behaviors panel is the one you want to use.**

The default event handler for this behavior is `onLoad`. The `onClick` and `onMouseDown` event handlers don't work well with this behavior. If you need to, change the event handler in the Behaviors panel. If the event handler you want to use is not on the list, try changing the target browser in the Show Events For menu at the bottom of the Behaviors panel Actions menu.

Go to URL

Add the Go to URL behavior to insert JavaScript that opens a new page in the same browser window or in a specified frame. Use this behavior in combination with other behaviors so that the link information gets placed inside the JavaScript rather than in the Properties inspector (for instance, when you add a link to a graphic that has multiple rollover behaviors). When working with frames, this action is particularly useful because you can set the action to change the contents of multiple frames with one click. (For more on frames, see Book IV, Chapter 3.)

To add the Go to URL action to your page, follow these steps:

1. **Select an image, object, or text link on your page.**

This image, object, or text becomes the link that triggers the action.

2. **Click the Actions (+) button in the Behaviors panel, and select Go to URL.**

The Go to URL dialog box, shown in Figure 2-9, opens displaying a list of windows and/or frame names.

Figure 2-9:
Select
the main
window or
individual
frames.

3. **In the Open In text field, select a window or frame as the target destination for the URL.**

   For example, if you're using the behavior to open a page in the same window, the Open In field lists only Main Window as the target destination. When working with framesets, the frame names are listed, such as topFrame, mainFrame, and leftFrame, along with Main Window.

   Try not to name your frames top, blank, self, or parent, as these filenames may conflict with the reserved frame target names (_top, _blank, _self, or _parent) and create strange results in different browsers.

4. **In the URL field, type the path and filename of the document to be opened, or click the Browse button to find and select the file.**

   If the page you want to open is not on your site, be sure to include the **http://** prefix before the www in the Web address.

5. **If changing URLs in multiple frames, repeat Steps 3 and 4 to select frames and URLs.**

   For example, to open two URLs with one event using frames, you can select mainFrame and type **welcome.html** in the URL field to open welcome.html in the mainFrame, and select leftFrame and type **navigation.html** in the URL field to open navigation.html in the leftFrame.

6. **Click OK to close the dialog box.**

7. **Verify that the event handler listed in the Events column of the Behaviors panel is the one you want to use.**

   The default event handler for the Go to URL behavior is onClick. You can change the event handler in the Behaviors panel. If the event handler you want to use is not on the list, try changing the target browser in the Show Events For menu at the bottom of the Behaviors panel Actions menu.

Jump Menu/Jump Menu Go

A jump menu is a pop-up menu of links that automatically opens another page in the browser when an item on the menu is selected. The Jump Menu behavior simply controls the structure and content of the menu links. The links on the menu can be to files on your Web site, pages on other Web sites, links to graphics, e-mail addresses, PDFs, Word documents, PowerPoint files, or any other kind of file that a browser can open.

Creating a jump menu

To add a jump menu to your page, follow these steps:

1. **Insert a jump menu by choosing Insert⇨Form Objects⇨Jump Menu.**

   You can also click the Jump Menu button on the Forms tab of the Insert bar. The Insert Jump Menu dialog box opens, shown in Figure 2-10.

Figure 2-10:
Create jump menus quickly with the Insert Jump Menu dialog box.

2. **Click the plus (+) button above the Menu Items text field to add an item to the menu and complete the fields:**

   • **Text:** Type a name for the menu item.

   • **When selected, go to URL:** Type the path and filename that identifies the jump to URL destination.

   When creating a menu *header* for the first entry in the jump menu, such as *Select a State* or *Choose One,* add a null JavaScript link to the URL field, like this: `javascript:void(0)`. The null link prevents the page containing the jump menu from doing anything to the page if that option is selected. If you don't specify a destination, the script uses the menu text as the filename and tries to jump to a Web page with that name.

3. **Repeat Step 2 for each additional item on the list. Click the up and down arrows to sort and reposition list items.**

   For example, you may want to reposition the menu items to be listed alphabetically. To sort, select an item and click the up or down button.

4. **In the lower half of the dialog box, complete the remaining fields, and enable or disable the other menu options:**

   • **Open URLs In:** Select Main Window, or when working with framesets or multiple windows, select any of the other window or frame names from the list.

- **Menu Name:** When the page has only one menu, the default menu name available for selection is called menu1.

- **Insert Go Button After Menu:** Enable this option to add a Go button after the jump menu, which means the visitor must select an item from the menu and click the Go button to jump to the destination URL. Leave this option disabled to have the jump menu control the automatic jump to the target destination.

  You must remove the onChange Jump Menu behavior from the menu object in the Behaviors panel after adding the Go button to get the button to work properly.

- **Select First Item After URL Change:** Enable this option to have the menu revert to the first item in the list after every selection. This is particularly useful if you have created a menu header at the top of the list, such as Choose a Country or Quantity.

5. **Click OK to close the dialog box.**

6. **Verify that the event handler listed in the Events column of the Behaviors panel is the one you want to use.**

The default event handler for the Jump Menu behavior is onChange and the default event handler for the Jump Menu Go behavior is onClick. You can change the event handlers in the Behaviors panel. If the event handler you want to use is not on the list, try changing the target browser in the Show Events For menu at the bottom of the Behaviors panel Actions menu.

Dreamweaver adds the jump menu to your page along with the proper JavaScript to control the behavior. If you add the Go button to your menu, the jump menu is included in the Behaviors panel with the Jump Menu behavior and button and Jump Menu Go behavior.

Editing the Jump Menu behavior

If you need to edit the menu after adding it to a page, you can reopen the Insert Jump Menu dialog box through the Behaviors panel. Follow these steps:

1. **Select the jump menu on the open document and make sure the Behaviors panel is open.**

2. **Double-click the Jump Menu icon in the Actions column in the Behaviors panel.**

The Insert Jump Menu dialog box opens (refer to Figure 2-10).

3. **Make changes to the menu as you need.**

You can add new entries, rearrange entries, edit or remove existing entries, and specify target windows for the target URLs in any of the entries.

4. **Click OK to close the dialog box.**

Adding and removing a Go button

You can do two other things with the Jump Menu or Jump Menu Go behavior:

✦ Add a Go button if you originally created the jump menu without it. Adding a Go button to a jump menu is a good idea when working in framesets, as it allows visitors to reselect menu options that they already have selected.

✦ Remove the Go button if you've added it originally and no longer want it there.

Follow these steps to add a Go button to your jump menu:

1. Place your cursor to the right of the jump menu in the open document and add a button to the page by clicking the Button icon on the Forms tab of the Insert bar.

You can also insert a button by choosing Insert⇨Form⇨Button.

2. With the button still selected, select None from the Action drop-down list in the Properties inspector.

The button action is changed and the label changes from Submit to Button.

3. In the Label field in the Properties inspector, type Go.

The button's label changes from Button to Go.

4. With the button still selected, click the Actions (+) button in the Behaviors panel, and select Jump Menu Go.

5. Select the jump menu that you want the new Go button associated with.

6. Click OK to close the dialog box.

The Jump Menu Go button now has the Jump Menu Go behavior attached to it with the onClick event handler, but you need to modify the behavior associated with the jump menu before the Go button can work properly.

7. Select the jump menu, and in the Behaviors panel, select the onChange Jump Menu behavior and click the minus (–) button.

The Jump Menu onChange behavior is removed from the jump menu and the target URL is transferred to the Go button.

Follow these steps to remove the Go button from your jump menu:

1. Select the Jump Menu Go button on the open document.

2. In the Behaviors panel, select the Jump Menu Go behavior and click the minus (–) Actions button.

Dreamweaver removes any JavaScript from the code on your page associated with this behavior.

3. **With the Go button still selected, press the Delete key to delete the button from the page.**

   The jump menu now needs a behavior so it can work properly, as presumably you'd already deleted the `onChange` behavior associated with the menu when you added the Go button to the menu initially.

4. **Select the jump menu and from the Behaviors panel, choose the Jump Menu behavior.**

   The behavior picks up all the existing items in the list and assigns the correct event handler (`onChange`) to the menu.

Open Browser Window

The Open Browser Window behavior lets you open any URL in a new browser window on top of the current browser window. You can also set some of the new window's properties, such as its name, width, and height, and whether or not certain features appear on the new window, such as the status bar, menu bar, and scroll bars.

For instance, if you sell energy bars, you may want to have the product's nutritional information open in a new browser window when a visitor clicks a text link. With the Open Browser Window behavior, you can have the new browser window open to a specific size with no resize handles, scroll bars, menu bar, status bar, navigation bar, or location bar, such as the example in Figure 2-11.

Figure 2-11: The Open Browser Window behavior opens a new browser window.

By default, none of the new window attributes are enabled in the Open Browser Window dialog box, which means you must enter the URL to display and enable any features that you want for your new window. As long as you enter at least one attribute, the new window won't resemble the parent window's attributes and instead has only the attributes you specify. However, if you don't enter any window attributes other than the URL, the new window opens at the same size and with the same attributes as the parent window.

Before you learn how to use this behavior, keep in mind that pop-up windows are often over- and improperly used and abused. Some people even consider new browser windows a form of Internet pollution! For that reason alone, try to use this feature sparingly for specific purposes, such as showing a detailed image of a product you're selling or to display another document in a separate window from the rest of your site. In fact, you may want to add a warning message near the link that clicking the link opens a new window.

To add the Open Browser Window action to your page, follow these steps:

1. **Select an image or text on your page.**

This object or text becomes the link that triggers the action to open a new browser window.

When using text to open the new window, be sure to add a *null link* (a link that doesn't go anywhere) to the selected text before assigning the behavior. To create a null link, select the text and type `javascript:;` in the Link text box in the Properties inspector. Type carefully; the null link must contain both the colon and semicolon as shown above.

2. **Click the Actions (+) button in the Behaviors panel, and select Open Browser Window.**

The Open Browser Window dialog box opens (see Figure 2-12), displaying a text field to add the URL of the page to be opened and a set of new window attribute options.

Figure 2-12: Set target URL and browser window attributes.

Open Browser Window		
URL to display: ingredients.html Browse...		OK
Window width: 440 Window height: 440		Cancel
Attributes: ☐ Navigation toolbar ☐ Menu bar		Help
☐ Location toolbar ☑ Scrollbars as needed		
☐ Status bar ☐ Resize handles		
Window name: ingredients		

3. **Next to URL to Display, click the Browse button to select a local file or type the URL that you want to open in the new browser window.**

    When entering a remote URL, you need to type the **http://** prefix before the www address, as in http://www.macromedia.com.

4. **Specify new window attributes:**

    - **Window Width** and **Window Height:** Enter a number in pixels to set the size of the new window.

    - **Navigation Toolbar:** This window toolbar has browser navigation buttons including the Back, Home, and Reload buttons.

    - **Location Toolbar:** This toolbar shows browser options including the current URL or location of the visitor.

    - **Status Bar:** The status bar is located at the bottom-left edge of the browser window and displays such information as the URL, special messages, and page loading times.

    - **Menu Bar:** This part of the browser window (Windows) or desktop (Mac) has menu options for your applications such as File, Edit, View, and so on. When you disable this option in Windows, the visitor can only close or minimize the new window. On a Mac, the menu bar stays at the top of the desktop regardless of the Menu Bar setting.

    - **Scrollbars As Needed:** Enable this option to view scroll bars on the new browser window when the content in that window exceeds the visible size of the window. When you disable this option, any content that extends beyond the size of the window is hidden.

    - **Resize Handles:** This option enables or disables resize handles from appearing in the bottom-right corner of the window. When enabled, the visitor can click and drag the handles to resize the window. If disabled, the window size is fixed and cannot be changed.

    - **Window Name:** Enter a name or ID for the new window in this field. Names help target the new window with links, apply CSS styles to the window contents, and control the window using other JavaScript behaviors. Make sure the window name doesn't include any special characters, spaces, or punctuation, and is written in lowercase letters.

5. **Click OK to close the dialog box.**

6. **Verify that the event handler listed in the Events column of the Behaviors panel is the one you want to use.**

    The default event handler for the Open Browser Window behavior is onClick. You can change the event handler in the Behaviors panel; if the event handler you want is not on the list, try changing the target browser on the Show Events For menu at the bottom of the Behaviors panel Actions menu.

Though it's not part of the Dreamweaver dialog box for this behavior, you can hand-code additional information to specify the location of the new window when it opens, relative to the top-left corner of the parent browser window. In the code directly after the width and height dimensions, add top and left pixel coordinates separated by commas and no spaces, as in this example:

```
<a href="javascript:;"
    onclick="MM_openBrWindow('index.html','Details','width=300,height=300,
    top=500,left=300')">View Details</a>
```

Play Sound

Though playing sounds is not the most sophisticated way to enhance a Web site, you can easily drop in sound or sound effects on your page using the Play Sound behavior. For instance, you may want to play a sound when the cursor mouses over a particular image on the page or play a clip of music every time the page loads or reloads.

One of the main issues with playing sound files on the Internet is that different browsers handle sounds in different ways, and because you have no control over a visitor's platform, browser, and browser version, this can create a variety of user experiences. Furthermore, some browsers need plug-ins to play sounds, while others automatically launch sound applications to play them. Check out Book II, Chapter 5 if you're interested in reading more about the debate on linking versus embedding sounds.

To use the Play Sound behavior to add sound to a page, follow these steps:

1. **Select an object or text link on your page that you want to attach the sound file to.**

2. **Click the Actions (+) button in the Behaviors panel and select Play Sound.**

The Play Sound dialog box opens, as shown in Figure 2-13.

Figure 2-13: The Play Sound dialog box.

Play Sound			☒
Play sound:		Browse...	OK
			Cancel
			Help

3. **In the Play Sound text field, type the path and filename of the sound file, or click the Browse button to find and select one.**

The most common sound files are: `.mp3`, `.qt`, `.qtm`, `.mov`, QuickTime, `.ra`, `.ram`, `.rpm`, Real Audio, `.wav`, `.midi`, `.mid`, and `.aif`.

4. **Click OK to close the dialog box.**

5. **Verify that the event handler listed in the Events column of the Behaviors panel is the one you want to use.**

The default event handler for the Play Sound behavior is `onClick`, though you can change the event handler in the Behaviors panel. If the event handler you want to use is not on the list, try changing the target browser in the Show Events For menu at the bottom of the Behaviors panel Actions menu.

Popup Message

The Popup Message behavior opens a JavaScript alert window with your specific text message. Because it's a text-only script, the look of the alert window is totally controlled by the site visitor's browser, which means you can't format the text message in any way. The only thing in common as a layout feature between the different browsers, in fact, is that along with your message they all display an OK button for the user to click to acknowledge seeing the message.

For this reason, this type of alert message is best used when you don't care how the message is formatted and need to communicate something to the visitor rather than needing the visitor to interact with the site in some way. If you really need to control how the message looks, use the Open Browser Window behavior (described earlier in the chapter) to display your message instead.

On the plus side, these JavaScript alert messages can have any JavaScript property, global variable, function call, or other valid expression embedded inside the text as long as it's embedded inside braces (`{}`). For example, to have visitors open a box that displays the current date, you'd type the following script into the behavior dialog box: `Today is {new Date()}`.

Once added to the page, the behavior's JavaScript in the code takes on the following syntax:

```
<p onclick="MM_popupMsg('Today is '+(new Date())+'')">Click here for today's
    date.</p>
```

When a viewer clicks the link, the script returns a box that looks like the example in Figure 2-15.

To add a pop-up message to your page, follow these steps:

1. **Select a word, phrase, image, or other object on your page.**

2. **Click the Actions (+) button in the Behaviors panel and select Popup Message.**

The Popup Message dialog box appears, shown in Figure 2-14.

Figure 2-14:
Create
JavaScript
alert
messages.

3. **Type your text message, including any additional JavaScript expressions.**

Using the same example, which gives the visitor the option of viewing the current date by clicking a text link, you'd type the following into the Popup Message dialog box:

```
Today is {new Date()}.
```

To have a brace display as part of the alert, type it with a backslash before the brace, like this (\{).

4. **Click OK to close the text message dialog box.**

5. **Verify that the event handler listed in the Events column of the Behaviors panel is the one you want to use.**

The default event handler for the Popup Message is onClick. You can change the event handler in the Behaviors panel, and if the event handler you want to use is not on the list, try changing the target browser in the Show Events For menu at the bottom of the Behaviors panel Actions menu.

Figure 2-15 shows how Today is {new Date()}. appears in an alert window.

Figure 2-15:
An alert
window.

Preload Images

The Preload Images behavior preloads specified images into the browser's cache so that they're ready for viewing when called by the browser. The preload process is invisible to the site visitor and helps ensure a seamless visitor experience with the Web site. Use this behavior for the times that you want to preload images that are not on the page when the page initially loads in the browser or for images on the page that are not associated with the Swap Image behavior.

Follow these steps to add the Preload Images action to your page:

1. **Select an object or text link on your page.**

2. **Click the Actions (+) button in the Behaviors panel, and select Preload Images.**

   The Preload Images dialog box opens (see Figure 2-16).

Figure 2-16: Preload as many images as you like.

3. **In the Image Source field, type the path and filename of the image you want to preload or click the Browse button to find and select an image.**

4. **Click the plus (+) button to add the image name to the Preload Images listing.**

5. **Repeat Steps 3 and 4 to add more images to the Preload list.**

   To remove an image from the listing, select the image from the list and click the minus (–) button.

6. **Click OK to close the Preload Images dialog box.**

7. **Verify that the event handler listed in the Events column of the Behaviors panel is the one you want to use.**

   The default event handler for the Preload Images behavior is `onLoad`. You can change the event handler in the Behaviors panel. If an event handler you want to use is not on the list, try changing the target browser in the Show Events For menu at the bottom of the Behaviors panel Actions menu.

Set Nav Bar Image

The Set Nav Bar Image behavior lets you convert any graphic into a navigation bar image or alter the way existing navigation bar images display on the page. If you haven't created a navigation bar with images yet, check out Book II, Chapter 3 before proceeding

To edit an image with the Set Nav Bar Image behavior, follow these steps:

1. **Select an image on an existing navigation bar for editing.**

To use the Set Nav Bar Image behavior to convert a plain image into a navigation bar image, select that image, select the Set Nav Bar Image behavior from the Actions menu in the Behaviors panel, and complete the Set Nav Bar Image dialog box.

2. **In the Actions column in the Behaviors panel, double-click the Set Nav Bar Image action connected with the selected image.**

The Set Nav Bar Image dialog box opens (shown in Figure 2-17).

Figure 2-17: Use this behavior to convert any graphic into a nav bar image.

3. **Edit the Basic tab dialog box options as needed.**

You can add or change the Up, Over, Down, and Over While Down state images, as well as their URLs and window destination targets.

4. **Click OK when you finish making changes.**

To edit several images at once for a navigation bar button, follow these steps:

1. **Select an image in the navigation bar that you need to edit.**

2. **In the Actions column in the Behaviors panel, double-click the Set Nav Bar Image action related with the image.**

The Set Nav Bar Image dialog box opens.

3. Select the Advanced tab.

Figure 2-18 shows the Advanced tab.

Figure 2-18: Create an action to change multiple images.

4. From the When Element Is Displaying menu, choose an image state:

- **Over Image or Over While Down Image:** Pick this option to change how another image displays when the user clicks the selected image.

- **Down Image:** Pick this option to change how another image displays when the user moves the mouse over the selected image.

5. From the Also Set Image text box, select the graphic that will change when the user moves the mouse over or clicks the selected image.

6. In the To Image File text box, browse for or type the path and filename of the image to be displayed.

7. If applicable, in the If Down, To Image File text box, browse for or type the path and filename of the image to be displayed.

This option is presented only when you select the Over Image or Over While Down Image option for the When Element Is Displaying choice in Step 3.

8. Click OK to close the dialog box.

Set Text of Frame

The Set Text of Frame behavior works exclusively with framesets and allows you to replace text or HTML content in a frame with a specified action. What's more, the HTML replacement content can include any JavaScript property, global variable, function call, or other valid expression embedded inside the text as long as it's embedded inside braces ({ }). To have a brace display, type it with a backslash, like this (\{).

Book IV Chapter 2

Jazzing Up Pages with JavaScript Behaviors

By allowing you to change the content on a page inside a frame, this behavior is an alternative to opening another page in a frame. For example, you may want to change the text inside a frame containing a graphic that, when moused over, changes to display a special message to the visitor or identifies the URL of the page inside the frame.

With this behavior, most of the frame's formatting is lost, but you can retain the background and text colors if you want. If you need to control more than text content, you may want to open a new page in the frame instead.

To begin using this behavior, you must start with a frameset (see Book IV, Chapter 3). You can use any of Dreamweaver's preset framesets when you're creating a new document: Choose File⇨New, and then in the New Document window, select the Framesets category. Or choose Modify⇨Frameset⇨Split Frame and select any option to create a quick and simple frameset on an existing open document.

To add the Set Text of Frame action to your page, follow these steps:

1. **Select an object or text link on your page to attach the behavior to.**

The object can be in any of the frames in the frameset.

2. **Click the Actions (+) button in the Behaviors panel, and choose Set Text⇨Set Text of Frame.**

The Set Text of Frame dialog box opens, shown in Figure 2-19, where you can enter in the new HTML content for the page.

Figure 2-19:
Enter
replacement
HTML
content for
a targeted
frame.

3. **From the Frame menu, select the target frame.**

The target frame is the frame that will display the replacement content.

4. **In the New HTML text box, type or paste the replacement HTML content for the targeted frame.**

To copy the existing `<body>` content of the selected target frame into the text box, click the Get Current HTML button.

To use the same background color of the current frame's page with the new text, enable the Preserve Background Color check box.

5. **Click OK to close the dialog box.**

6. **Verify that the event handler listed in the Events column of the Behaviors panel is the one you want to use.**

   You can change the event handler in the Behaviors panel. If the event handler you want to use is not on the list, change the target browser in the Show Events For menu at the bottom of the Behaviors panel Actions menu.

Set Text of Layer

The Set Text of Layer behavior replaces existing HTML content and formatting of a layer with new HTML content and formatting. The new HTML content can have any JavaScript property, global variable, function call, or other valid expression embedded inside the text as long as it's embedded inside braces ({ }). You can even have a brace display in the content by adding a backslash before it, like this (\ {).

By allowing you to change the content inside a layer, this behavior is an alternative to hiding the current layer and showing another layer with different content. For example, you could change the text inside the current layer from a message that tells visitors to click there for details to a message containing those details.

To begin using this behavior, you must start with at least one layer on the page. To add a layer to your page, choose Insert⇨Layer, or click the Layer button on the Layout tab of the Insert bar and draw a layer anywhere in an open document. You may also want to name all your layers with the Properties inspector before attaching this behavior to help identify them easier (Book IV, Chapter 1 discusses layers in detail).

To attach the Set Text of Layer action to a page, follow these steps:

1. **Select an object on your page.**

2. **Click the Actions (+) button in the Behaviors panel, and choose Set Text⇨Set Text of Layer.**

   The Set Text of Layer dialog box opens (see Figure 2-20).

3. **From the Layer menu, select the target layer.**

   The target layer is the layer where the new content will be displayed.

Figure 2-20:
Change the
text on a
layer.

4. **In the New HTML text box, type or paste the replacement HTML content for the targeted layer.**

   Enter any HTML including valid JavaScript and formatting code. When no formatting is entered with the new HTML text, the original text color and background color of the layer will be applied to the new text content.

5. **Click OK to close the dialog box.**

6. **Verify that the event handler listed in the Events column of the Behaviors panel is the one you want to use.**

   If the event handler is not right, you can change it in the Behaviors panel. If the event handler you want to use is not on the list, change the target browser in the Show Events For menu at the bottom of the Behaviors panel Actions menu.

Set Text of Status Bar

Use the Set Text of Status Bar action to add a text message to the browser window's status bar (at the bottom-left corner of the window) when the visitor interacts with the page in a specified way. For example, you can have the status bar display a message about a particular link or image on the page when the visitor mouses over that link or graphic (On Sale through July 31st, 2006!) or list the title of the given page (Contact Us) rather than its URL, which appears by default.

While adding a message to the status bar can be an interesting way to enhance a site visitor's experience of a page, many visitors don't know to look in this area for messages or may even have the status bar disabled. Also, because the status bar displays useful information from the browser, replacing it with your own text can be seen as rude to some visitors.

For these reasons, using this behavior for optional information messages rather than important ones is for the best. Therefore, for the important messages, consider using the Popup Message, Open Browser Window, or Show-Hide Layers behaviors, all of which are also described in this chapter.

Also, just like the Popup Message behavior, you can have any JavaScript property, global variable, function call, or other valid expression embedded inside the status bar text as long as it's embedded inside braces ({ }).

To add the Set Text of Status Bar action to your page, follow these steps:

1. **Select an object or text link on your page.**

This is the object or text link that triggers the action.

2. **Click the Actions (+) button in the Behaviors panel, and choose Set Text⇨Set Text of Status Bar.**

The Set Text of Status Bar dialog box opens (see Figure 2-21).

Figure 2-21:
Add a
custom
message.

3. **Type your text message including any additional JavaScript expressions.**

For example, to display the URL for the visited page when mousing over a specified object or text link using a JavaScript function, type the following code:

```
The URL for this page is {window.location}.
```

Try to keep your message short because many browsers that support this behavior may truncate longer messages.

4. **Click OK to close the dialog box.**

5. **Verify that the event handler listed in the Events column of the Behaviors panel is the one you want to use.**

The default event handler for the Set Text of Status Bar behavior is onMouseOver, but you can change it in the Behaviors panel. If the event handler you want to use is not on the list, try changing the target browser on the Show Events For menu at the bottom of the Behaviors panel Actions menu.

Set Text of Text Field

This handy behavior replaces the existing content of a text field on a form with specified new content. For example, you may want to enter sample text so a visitor knows the type of content they're expected to type in the field.

The new HTML content can have any JavaScript property, global variable, function call, or other valid expression embedded inside the text as long as it's embedded inside braces ({ }). You can even have a brace display by adding a backslash before it, like this (\ {).

To begin using this behavior, you must start with at least one text field on a form on the page. To add a text field to your page, choose Insert⇨Form Objects⇨Text Field or click the Text Field button on the Forms tab of the Insert bar to insert a text field at the insertion point on an open document. If prompted to add the Form Tag, click Yes. When the page has multiple text fields, it's also helpful to name all the form fields to better identify them before attaching this behavior.

Follow these steps to use the Set Text of Text Field behavior:

1. **Select a text field in a form on the open document.**

2. **Click the Actions (+) button in the Behaviors panel, and choose Set Text⇨Set Text of Text Field.**

   The Set Text of Text Field dialog box opens, as shown in Figure 2-22.

Figure 2-22: Add example text into a form field.

3. **From the Text Field menu, select the target text field.**

   The target text field is where the new content displays.

4. **In the New Text text box, type or paste the replacement text.**

5. **Click OK to close the dialog box.**

6. **Verify that the event handler listed in the Events column of the Behaviors panel is the one you want to use.**

   The default event handler is onMouseOver. If you don't like the event handler, you can change it in the Behaviors panel. If the event handler you want to use is not on the list, try changing the target browser in the Show Events For menu at the bottom of the Behaviors panel Actions menu.

Show-Hide Layers

When one or more layers are present on your page, you can control a layer's *visibility* (whether it's shown or hidden) with the Show-Hide Layers behavior. You can also use this behavior to restore a layer's visibility to its default setting.

The Show-Hide Layers behavior is great for hiding and showing information as a visitor interacts with objects on your Web page. For example, you may have an online photo gallery page with a series of thumbnail images and an area to display close-up images. With the Show-Hide Layers behavior, when the visitor slides the mouse over one of the thumbnail images, a layer with a close-up image is shown, and when the visitor's mouse moves off the thumbnail, the close-up layer is hidden.

Before using this behavior, you must have at least one layer on the page. To add a layer to your page, choose Insert⇨Layer, or click the Layer button on the Layout tab of the Insert bar and draw a layer anywhere in an open document. You may also want to name all your layers with the Properties inspector before attaching this behavior to objects on your page to help identify them easier. (Book IV, Chapter 1 describes layers in detail.)

Follow these steps to use the Show-Hide Layers behavior on your page:

1. **Select any object on your page except a layer.**

2. **Click the Actions (+) button in the Behaviors panel, and select Show-Hide Layers.**

The Show-Hide Layers dialog box opens (see Figure 2-23). If the behavior is not available in the list of actions, you may need to select a different object on your page, like the <body> tag or a link (<a> tag).

Figure 2-23:
Alter a layer's visibility in the browser.

3. **From the Named Layers menu, choose the layer that you want to change the visibility for.**

4. **Edit the layer's visibility status by clicking any of the following buttons:**

   • **Show:** Shows the selected layer.

   • **Hide:** Hides the selected layer.

   • **Default:** Restores a layer's default visibility.

5. **Repeat Steps 3 and 4 for each additional layer that you want to modify.**

   A single event handler controls all the layers selected here.

6. **Click OK to close the dialog box.**

7. **Verify that the event handler listed in the Events column of the Behaviors panel is the one you want to use.**

   You can always change the event handler in the Behaviors panel. If the event handler you want to use is not on the list, try changing the target browser in the Show Events For menu at the bottom of the Behaviors panel Actions menu.

Be aware that some browsers support layers differently than others. Netscape, for instance, often collapses layers to fit the content of the layer. To stop browsers from altering layers, try setting layer clip parameters or adding images or text to the layer to hold the layer open to the size you want it to be (see Book IV, Chapter 1 for more information on setting layer clip parameters).

Another cool use of this behavior is to make a preload layer by creating a layer that covers the rest of the page as the page loads. Your visitors are engaged with other content, such as a Flash move, while the main content loads. Then, when the content finishes loading, the preload layer gets hidden.

Follow these steps to make a preload layer with the Show-Hide Layers behavior:

1. **Create a layer on your page in the size you need that will cover the page's main content while it loads.**

   To add a layer to your page, click the Layer button on the Layout tab of the Insert bar and draw a layer anywhere in an open document.

2. **Name the new layer** preload **or something similar in the Properties inspector or in the Layers panel to help easily identify the layer when attaching the behavior.**

3. **In the Layers panel, select the preload layer and drag it to the top of the list of layers.**

   The layer needs to be at the top of the z-index (stacking order) for the behavior to work properly.

4. With the preload layer selected, edit the layer's background color to match the rest of the page.

Use the color picker in the Properties inspector to set the layer background color.

5. To add HTML content to the preload layer, click inside the layer and type or paste the content.

As an example, on the preload layer you may want to play a flash SWF file, display an animated GIF, or show a `Please wait. . .page loading` type of message.

6. On the Tag selector at the bottom of the open document window, select the `<body>` tag, click the Actions (+) button in the Behaviors panel, and select Show-Hide Layers.

The Show-Hide Layers dialog box opens.

7. Select the preload layer from the Named Layers listing and click the Hide button.

8. Click OK to close the dialog box.

9. Verify that the event handler next to the Show-Hide Layers behavior says `onLoad`.

If not, change the event handler to `onLoad` in the Properties inspector.

Show Pop-Up Menu

One of the most useful enhancements to Dreamweaver since Dreamweaver MX is the addition of the Show Pop-Up Menu behavior. With this behavior, you can create and edit a *pop-up menu* (a menu that appears temporarily when the user moves the mouse over an object) and specify parameters such as the font face, font color, background color, position, and direction. You can also use this behavior to modify a more advanced Fireworks pop-up menu. (For specific instructions on editing Fireworks menus, refer to Book II, Chapter 5.)

The Show Pop-Up Menu behavior is made up of several pieces of JavaScript including scripts in the head and body areas of the page and an externally linked javascript file called `mm_menu.js`. You must upload the external JavaScript file to the server along with the page containing the pop-up menu for the menu to function properly.

To add a pop-up menu on your page, follow these steps:

1. **Select an object or text link to attach the menu to.**

For example, if the pop-up menu will be a submenu of a main menu item, select the main menu item graphic. This graphic serves as the trigger for the pop-up menu.

2. **Click the Actions (+) button in the Behaviors panel and select Show Pop-up Menu.**

The Show Pop-up Menu dialog box opens with the Contents tab selected, as shown in Figure 2-24.

3. **Add, sort, and remove menu items from the Contents tab:**

- **Text:** Type a label for the menu item.

- **Link:** Enter the filename or complete URL of the target page. Or click the Folder icon to find and select a file.

- **Target:** Select a target window or frame for the target URL. If the frame name you want to target is not showing, you probably forgot to name the frame. In that case, close the dialog box and name the frame before continuing.

Figure 2-24:
Create pop-up menus easily with the Show Pop-up Menu dialog box.

- **Move Item Up/Move Item Down:** To change the order of the menu items, select an item and click the up or down arrows to reposition the selected item to a new location in the list.

- **Indent/Outdent:** To indent a menu item and create a new submenu, select any item but the first menu item in the list and click the indent button. To remove the indent, select the indented menu item and click the outdent button.

- **Add Item:** Click the plus (+) button to add a menu item to the menu list. Successfully added menu items are listed by name, link, and target.

- **Remove Item:** To remove an item from the list, select the item and click the minus (–) button.

4. **Click the Appearance tab to set the look of the menu item up and over states:**

   - **Menu:** Select Vertical Menu or Horizontal Menu from the menu at the top of the Appearance tab.

   - **Font:** Choose a font set. Select the Edit Font List option to create your own font set; just try to pick fonts for the custom list that visitors are likely to have.

   - **Size:** Select a size, in pixels, for the menu font.

   - **Bold/Italic:** Toggle the Bold or Italic styles on or off.

   - **Left/Center/Right Align:** Select an alignment option for the menu item text by clicking the Left, Center, or Right Align icons.

   - **Up State/Over State:** Select hexadecimal values for the Text and Cell colors of the menu items by clicking all four of the color picker icons. The preview area shows an approximation of how the color selections will look on the pop-up menu.

5. **Click the Advanced tab to customize the formatting attributes for the menu cells:**

   - **Cell Width:** The width is set automatically to match the width of the longest menu item's contents. To override this setting, select the Automatic option and then select Pixels to activate the Cell Width text box. Type the pixel value for the cell width.

   - **Cell Height:** Like the width, the cell height is also set automatically to match the width of the tallest menu item. To override this setting, select Automatic and then select Pixels to activate the Cell Height text box. Type the pixel value for the cell height.

   - **Cell Padding:** Enter a value in pixels to set the space between the cell edges and the cell contents. To remove space completely, enter **0**.

**Book IV
Chapter 2**

Jazzing Up Pages
with JavaScript
Behaviors

- **Cell Spacing:** Enter a value in pixels to set the space between the cells. To remove space completely, enter **0**.

- **Text Indent:** Enter a value in pixels to set the indentation of the cell contents. To remove space completely, enter **0**.

- **Menu Delay:** The default menu delay setting is 1000 ms or 1 second. The delay controls the time the menu takes to disappear after a visitor mouses off the menu. You can increase or decrease the delay value.

- **Pop-up Borders:** Select this option to add borders around all the menu items. Deselect the check box if you do not want borders to display.

- **Border Width:** Enter a value in pixels for a border width. This option is only active when you enable the Pop-up Borders option.

- **Border Color/Shadow/Highlight:** Select hexadecimal values for the border, border shadow, and border highlight colors of the menu items by clicking all three of the color picker icons. The preview area shows an approximation of how the border color will look on the pop-up menu. The Shadow and Highlight colors aren't visible until the menu displays in a browser window.

6. **Click the Position tab to determine where the menu displays relative to the trigger object.**

   - **Menu Position:** To set the position of the menu relative to the trigger object, click one of the buttons (Bottom Right Corner of Trigger, Below and at Left Edge of Trigger, Top and at Left Edge of Trigger, or Above Right Corner of Trigger) or type pixel values into the X/Y coordinate text boxes.

   - **X/Y Coordinates:** To create a custom location for the menu position, or to edit the placement of one of the present menu positions, enter values in pixels for the X and Y coordinates of the menu relative to the top-left corner of the trigger object.

   - **Hide menu on onMouseOut event:** Enable this option to hide the menu when the visitor moves the mouse off the menu. This option is enabled by default, as visitors are now used to menus disappearing after mousing off. To leave the menu displayed after a visitor mouses away from the menu, deselect this option.

7. **Click OK to close the dialog box.**

8. **Verify that the event handler listed in the Events column of the Behaviors panel is the one you want to use.**

   The default event handler for the Popup Message is `onClick`. If you want a different event handler, change it in the Behaviors panel. If the event handler you want to use is not on the list, change the target browser in the Show Events For menu at the bottom of the Behaviors panel Actions menu.

After you add the menu to the page, the Behaviors panel displays a set of two actions to represent the pop-up menu: Hide Pop-up Menu and Show Pop-up Menu.

To see the pop-up menu after inserting it on the page, launch the page in a browser and move the cursor over the object on the page that triggers the menu to appear.

To edit the pop-up menu at any time, do the following:

1. **Select the object on the page that has the Show Pop-up Menu action attached to it.**

2. **In the Behaviors panel, double-click the Show Pop-up Menu action.**

   The Show Pop-op Menu dialog box opens.

3. **Edit the menu as you need, and when finished, click OK to close the dialog box.**

This behavior has a known bug that occasionally prevents you from changing the cell width and height pixel dimensions on the Advanced tab of the Show Pop-up Menu dialog box. If you find that you can't adjust these settings, try adjusting the code. You find the width and height numbers written in red text (shown here in bold) in the mmLoadMenus script inside the head of your page, as in this partial example of the script:

```
<script type="text/JavaScript">
<!--
function mmLoadMenus() {
  if (window.mm_menu_0105144808_0) return;
        window.mm_menu_0105144808_0 = new
Menu("root",100,23,"Verdana, Arial, Helvetica, sans-
    serif",10,"#4777AC","#FCFBFA","#FFFFFF","#4777AC","left","middle",3,0,1000,-
    5,7,true,true,true,0,false,false);
```

Swap Image

With the swap image behavior, you can assign a rollover button script to any graphic on the page. When the user moves the cursor over the graphic, the JavaScript tells the user's browser to display a new graphic (the *over state* graphic) in its place. You also have the option to preload images and restore the graphic to its original state with the MouseOut event. You can even assign rollover graphics to several graphics on the page with one event handler, such as changing a button graphic and an image graphic at the same time when the visitor places the mouse over the button graphic.

The script calls an action that changes the image listed in the `src` attribute of the `<img>` tag. The two things you need to do in advance of using this behavior is to name the normal state image in the Name field in the Properties inspector and ensure that the over state image has the same width and height dimensions as the normal state graphic for a smooth mouseover effect.

To add the Swap Image behavior to your page, follow these steps:

1. **Select an image on your page.**

If you need to insert an image, click the Image button on the Insert bar or choose Insert⇨Image.

2. **In the Properties inspector, type a name for the image in the Name field.**

If you forget to name your images, you can still use the Swap Image action, but it may be hard to assign the behavior to the correct image when your page has multiple unnamed images.

3. **If assigning the same rollover action to multiple graphics on your page, repeat Steps 1 and 2 until all the graphics are in place.**

In other words, if you know you want images 2 and 3 to change when image 1 is moused over, insert and name images 2 and 3.

4. **Select the image on the page you want to attach the behavior to, click the Actions (+) button in the Behaviors panel, and select Swap Image.**

The Swap Image dialog box appears displaying a list of named (and unnamed) images on the page (see Figure 2-25).

Figure 2-25: Add the Swap Images behavior to named images on your page.

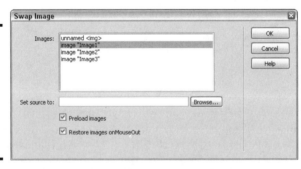

5. **Select a named image from the list that you want to assign a rollover graphic to and click the Browse button to select the over state graphic for that image.**

If you know the path and filename, you can type it in the Set Source To text field rather than browsing for it.

6. **Repeat Steps 4 and 5 to create multiple rollover actions at once.**

   This would be, say, if you want to change both a photo and a button graphic with one mouseover event.

7. **Select the Preload Images and Swap Image Restore options.**

   By default both options are enabled, which are recommended settings:

   - **Preload Images:** This setting adds JavaScript to the head area of the page that tells the visitor's browser to preload the rollover graphics when the page loads so that the user experiences no delay in viewing the rollover effect. Leave this option enabled, as images that aren't preloaded could create problems for displaying the page in a browser.

   - **Swap Image Restore:** This option adds JavaScript to the page that tells the browser to restore the over state image to the normal state image when the site visitor moves the mouse cursor away from the rollover image graphic.

Figure 2-26 shows an example of how you can use the Swap Image behavior to create multiple over states for a single mouse event. When a visitor mouses over a main navigation button, like the one for reptiles, the navigation button over state graphic appears along with a graphic of a lizard and a graphic containing text about reptiles.

Figure 2-26:
Create dynamic rollover graphic effects.

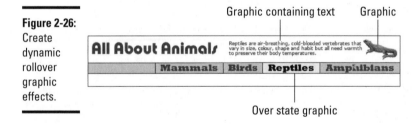

Graphic containing text Graphic

Over state graphic

Swap Image Restore

The Swap Image Restore action restores a swapped image to its original state. Because the Swap Image Restore action gets added automatically when you use the Swap Image behavior and leaves the Restore option enabled, you'll probably never need to manually add the Swap Image Restore action.

On the blue moon occasion when you need to use it, simply select the behavior from the Actions menu in the Behavior panel and click OK in the Swap Image Restore dialog box. Dreamweaver adds the appropriate JavaScript to your page to restore the last set of swapped images to their original source graphics.

Validate Form

The Validate Form action verifies whether the visitor has accurately completed a form, and when inaccurate displays a JavaScript alert window with an error message. To use this behavior turn to Book II, Chapter 7, which is entirely devoted to creating forms.

Using Third-Party Behaviors

Dreamweaver is an *extensible* program, which means that you can enhance its functionality by installing object, command, behavior, and other extensions that perform various functions. You can find a ton of these third-party extensions at the Macromedia Exchange Web site and by searching for the terms **Dreamweaver Extensions** in your favorite browser.

When you find extensions you want to try, you can download them and use the Macromedia Extension Manager to install them on your computer. The Extension Manager is a stand-alone application that installs, manages, and uninstalls extensions in Dreamweaver and other Macromedia programs. Dreamweaver installs the Extension Manager as part of the Dreamweaver software installation process.

Visiting the Macromedia Exchange Web site

Over a thousand extensions are available in the Dreamweaver Exchange section of Adobe's Macromedia Exchange Web site. Among them, you'll find extension to insert form fields, format tables, create navigation menus, and e-commerce shopping carts. Many of the extensions are offered for free to registered members. Others are available as either shareware requiring small fees or as fully supported software extensions for those willing to pay full price.

Adobe has its Macromedia Dreamweaver extensions grouped into several categories including: Accessibility, App Servers, Browsers, DHTML/Layers, Extension Development, Fireworks, Flash Media, Learning, Navigation, Productivity, Rich Media, Scripting, Security, Style/Format, Tables, Text, Commerce, Content, and Web Analysis.

In addition to listing the platform availability (Windows, Mac, or both) for each of the extensions, you'll also find such helpful statistics as the number of recorded downloads, a rating based on 5-star rating system, the Dreamweaver product version compatibility (8, MX, MX 2004), and the date the extension was released. You'll also find links to a variety of discussion groups and user reviews on the site to help you make the best decision about which extensions to download.

To download and install extensions from the Macromedia Dreamweaver Exchange Web site, follow these steps:

1. **Open the Dreamweaver Exchange Web site by choosing Help⇨ Dreamweaver Exchange.**

The Dreamweaver Exchange opens in your primary Web browser, presuming you have a live Internet connection.

2. **Look around the various categories or search for extensions related to specific functions you're interested in.**

3. **When you find a behavior you want, download or save it.**

When accessing extensions on the exchange, browsers often give you the option of downloading and installing the extension directly from the source or saving the extension file to your local computer.

When you opt to save the file to your computer, Macromedia recommends that you save the extensions to a Downloaded Extensions folder within the Dreamweaver application folder on your computer so you can manage all the extensions in one location. Another option is to download them to your desktop, but move them to another folder after installation for archiving purposes.

Using the Extension Manager

Using the Extension Manager is really easy. To launch the application, choose Help⇨Manage Extensions. If for some reason you do not have the application installed on your computer, visit the Adobe Macromedia site at `www.macromedia.com/exchange/em_download/` to download a copy of the latest version of the application.

To install, manage, and uninstall extensions with the Extension Manager, follow these steps:

1. **From the Extension Manager's main menu, choose File⇨Install Extension to install the new extension.**

Some extensions install immediately, while others launch the Extension Manager application panel and display the Macromedia disclaimer. If this happens, skip to Step 4. Otherwise, continue to Step 2.

2. **In the Extension Manager, select the Macromedia application into which you want to install the extension (for example, Dreamweaver or Flash).**

This step is especially important when you have multiple Macromedia products or multiple versions of the same product installed on the computer. When you upgrade your application, the extensions are installed into the newest or currently running version.

Book IV Chapter 2

Jazzing Up Pages with JavaScript Behaviors

3. **Choose File⇨Install Extension.**

   The Select Extension to Install dialog box opens. Browse to and select an extension file with the `.mxp` file extension and click the Install button.

4. **Read the Macromedia extensions disclaimer that appears including any extension license information.**

   You must accept the terms of the disclaimer and license to complete the installation.

5. **If prompted to replace any existing files, click Yes or Yes to All to accept the version of the extension being installed.**

   If you click No, the current version of that file is kept. If you click Cancel the installation stops without replacing or installing any new files.

   If the installation is good, you see a message that the extension was installed successfully: The *XYZ* extension has successfully been installed.

   Note: Some extensions require you to close and restart Dreamweaver before taking effect.

Figure 2-27 shows how newly installed extensions appear in the list of Installed Extensions in the Extension Manager.

Figure 2-27: The Extension Manager lists all installed extensions as well as extension details including version, type, and author.

Chapter 3: Designing Pages with Frames

In This Chapter

✔ **Understanding frames**

✔ **Creating frames and framesets**

✔ **Modifying frame and frameset properties**

✔ **Targeting frames with links**

✔ **Adding noframes content**

✔ **Creating floating frames**

*B*ack in the early days of the Internet, the most common use of frames was to ease navigation and reduce page loading wait times for site visitors using dialup modem connections. The idea behind frames is this: The browser window is divided into several panes, or *frames,* that each display different HTML pages, independent of the content in the other frames. Furthermore, by specifying the target frame, you can control which frame opens the new page when a user clicks a link.

Suppose, for instance, a user visits a Web site comprised of a three part frameset with company information in the top frame, some navigation buttons in the left frame, and information pertinent to the Web site's products or services, such as contact information, in the main frame. With this type of frameset, a visitor can click a link in the navigation frame, and the linked page opens in the main frame of the frameset.

Today many people visiting Web sites have high-speed connections, such as DSL, cable, T-1, or broadband. With these faster types of Internet access, frames are not as necessary as they once were. Nevertheless, they're still used widely enough that you should know how to use them, and we think you'll find many practical contemporary uses for them, such as creating Web photo galleries and adding inline frames for displaying one page's content in a smaller area on another page.

This chapter provides you with an overview of frames, including how to create and modify framesets, set attributes for frames and framesets, set the target attribute to display pages in specific frames, add noframes content for visitors using browsers without frame support, and insert floating frames on a page.

Understanding Frames

Frames enable you to divide a browser window into multiple panes, which are called *frames*. Each frame contains a unique Web page that displays independently of the pages in the other frames in the browser window. Then, with regular HTML, you can control the contents of each framed area separately. For example, when a visitor clicks a link, you can have some frames on the page remain static while the content in another other frame changes.

In the code, a page that defines the frame divisions or layout is called a *frameset*. The frameset itself doesn't display any content in the browser window (except when you use the <noframes> tag, as described at the end of this chapter). Rather, the frameset provides formatting and layout instructions to the browser on how to display the pages *inside* the frames. In other words, the frameset is merely a container in which other documents display.

You can use frames to format your entire Web site or just a particular section or page of a site. When using frames as the layout format for your entire Web site, you typically save the frameset file as index.html so the page loads in the browser window when people visit the URL. When the frameset page loads, the browser collects and displays the pages inside the individual frames.

You can divide frames vertically and horizontally into as many frame rows and columns as you need to achieve your layout. For example, in Figure 3-1, the browser window is divided into three frames with static company information in the top frame, static navigation buttons in the left frame, and general information in the main frame. When a visitor clicks a link in the navigation area, a new page displays in the main frame.

In the code, <frameset> tags replace the <body> tags, and the <frame> tags further define divisions in the frameset, as in the following sample code:

```
<frameset rows="80,*" cols="*" frameborder="NO" border="0" framespacing="0">
  <frame src="top.html" name="topFrame" scrolling="NO" noresize title="topFrame">
  <frameset cols="80,*" frameborder="NO" border="0" framespacing="0">
    <frame src="left.html" name="leftFrame" scrolling="NO" noresize
    title="leftFrame">
    <frame src="main.html" name="mainFrame" title="mainFrame">
  </frameset>
</frameset>
```

When you create new frames, rows are created top to bottom, and columns are created left to right. The smallest frameset division can contain either two rows or two columns. However, you can nest a frameset within a frame of another frameset, to any level of nesting, for some highly complex page display effects.

Top frame   Main frame

Figure 3-1:
Create
framesets
with as
simple or
complex a
layout as
necessary.

Left frame

After you divide your page into a frameset, specify the frameset and the
frame parameters and attributes in the Properties inspector, just as you do
with text and graphics. For instance, you can set the width and height of
frames, the number of rows and columns in the frameset, the source page
for a frame along with the source page margin width and height, a name or
ID of a frame for targeting purposes, a border width and border color,
whether the frame has scroll bars, and whether a visitor can resize it.

There are both good and bad things about framesets; frames are great
because

✦ You can display multiple pages in one browser window.

✦ You can use them for displaying Web gallery images, including thumb-
nails and close-up images.

✦ The browser does not need to reload graphics for each page, which
speeds up page display.

✦ Each page in a frame can have its own set of scroll bars, which means a visitor can scroll in one frame of the browser while referring to the unmoving area of another frame of the browser.

✦ You can use several JavaScript behaviors with frames, such as the Set Text of Frame, Go to URL, and Insert Jump Menu options. These behaviors allow you to modify content of a page in a frame without opening a new page in the frame, create a link to another page in particular frame, and open a new page in a particular frame of the frameset using a jump menu. For details on each of these and other scripts, check out Book IV, Chapter 2.

Frames are not so good because

✦ Visitors can't bookmark individual pages within framesets. The URL of the frameset page (usually `index.html`) doesn't change at all as the visitor navigates through the site and visitors can't save individual configuration of pages in frames.

✦ You need to define the `<target>` tag so new pages open in the correct frame.

✦ Visitors with disabilities may have difficulty navigating the frames.

✦ Designing framesets can get very confusing.

✦ Precisely aligning elements between frames is more difficult than aligning elements on regular unframed pages.

✦ You're likely to create errors with links and targets.

✦ Most site visitors don't like frames, especially badly crafted framesets. (One alternative is to build a frameless version of the site and let visitors pick which version they want to visit, but that's double the work and nowadays unnecessary — especially when using Dreamweaver templates for including consistent navigation on every page of the site.)

Creating Frames and Framesets

Before creating framesets in Dreamweaver, you need to do two things to customize your work environment and improve the display of the frameset document in Design view:

✦ **Open the Frames panel.** The Frames panel, shown in Figure 3-2, displays all the frames in a frameset document and can assist you with selecting the frame elements during the frameset building process. To open the Frames panel, choose Window⇨Frames.

Figure 3-2:
Be sure to
open the
Frames
panel before
working
with frames.

✦ **Enable the Frame Border visual aids.** When you have this feature enabled, the open document displays frame borders and divider bars, as shown in Figure 3-3. To enable Frame Border visual aids, choose View➪Visual Aids➪Frame Borders.

Frame borders

Figure 3-3:
Turn on the
Frame
Border
visual aids.

Divider bars

The W3C recognized frames as of the HTML 4.0 doctype, and because browsers need to know what they're looking at, Dreamweaver automatically inserts the appropriate doctype when creating frames. This ensures that the browsers interpret the file accurately. However, if you're hand-coding or inheriting a frameset from another source (as with a Web site redesign project, for instance), be sure to add the following doctype to the master frameset file, above the opening <HTML> tag:

```
<!DOCTYPE HTML PUBLIC "-//W3C//DTD HTML 4.01 Frameset//EN"
    "http://www.w3.org/TR/html4/frameset.dtd">
```

Building framesets is a somewhat complex process and you need to set them up carefully to display correctly in browsers. For that reason, try following these general steps whenever building framesets:

1. **Create the frameset and select the files that you want to appear in each frame.**

   See the following section for details.

2. **Save the frameset and all the files in each frame, and name each of the frames for later targeting with links.**

   See "Saving Frames and Framesets," later in the chapter.

3. **Set the properties for the frameset and the individual frames in the Properties inspector to achieve the look you want.**

   See the later section "Setting Frame Properties with the Properties Inspector."

4. **Set the target attribute for all the links on all the pages to display in the frames of the frameset so they'll accurately display where you intend them to.**

   For details, see "Targeting Frames with Links."

In the next few sections, you find out how to create a frameset and select files for the frames.

Using predefined framesets to create a new file

When you need a simple frameset with two to three frames, consider using one of Dreamweaver's predefined framesets. To create a new document with one of the predefined framesets, follow these steps:

1. **Choose File⇨New to open the New Document window, shown in Figure 3-4.**

2. **Select the Framesets category and choose a predefined frameset from the Framesets list.**

   If you're not sure which frameset to choose, select any frameset in the Frameset list and a preview and description of that preset appears on the right.

3. **Click the Create button.**

   The new frameset appears in the Document window.

   Note: If the Frame Tag Accessibility Attributes dialog box opens, select a frame in the frameset from the Frame menu and add a title for that frame. Repeat this process until all the frames in the frameset have titles and then click OK. Or to bypass accessibility tags, click the Cancel button.

Figure 3-4:
Choose a
predefined
frameset
from the
Frameset
category.

Displaying a file in a predefined frameset

Another way of using the predefined framesets is to convert an existing open document into a file displaying inside a frameset. To display a file inside a predefined frameset, follow these steps:

1. **Open the file you want to display inside a frame in a frameset.**

2. **Place an insertion point somewhere inside the file.**

3. **Choose a predefined frameset from the Frames menu on the Layout tab of the Insert bar.**

When you're trying to decide which frameset to choose, look at the thumbnail images that appear next to the predefined frameset options, as shown in Figure 3-5. The frame in blue indicates where your document appears if you select the predefined frameset. The white areas represent the frames that open in the frameset, where you can display other documents.

Note: If you've enabled the Frame Accessibility features in the Preferences dialog box, the Frame Tag Accessibility Attributes dialog box, shown in Figure 3-6, opens.

Select a frame in the frameset from the Frame menu and add a title for that frame. Repeat this process until all the frames in the frameset have titles.

To bypass this feature, click the Cancel button and Dreamweaver creates the frameset without the associated accessibility tags and attributes in the code.

Figure 3-5:
Use the
Frames
menu on the
Layout tab
of the
Insert bar to
convert a
blank page
into a
predefined
frameset.

Figure 3-6:
The
Frame Tag
Accessibility
Attributes
dialog box.

Creating custom framesets

You can create a custom frameset in Dreamweaver by splitting an existing, blank Document window into frames. To design a custom frameset from a blank, open document, do either of the following:

✦ Choose Modify➪Frameset, and choose a splitting option from the sub-menu, such as Split Frame Left or Split Frame Down.

✦ Enable the Frame Border visual aids, and then manually drag a frame border into the open document in Design view to split the frame into a frameset. The frame borders are the thin gray bars located on the top and left edges of the Document window between the ruler and the content area of the page.

To further customize and refine the frameset with additional frames, continue splitting frames by these methods or the other techniques available in Dreamweaver, as described in the next section.

Adding, Removing, and Resizing Frames

Before adding, removing, or resizing frames, enable the Frame Border visual aids and open the Frames panel, as described in "Creating Frames and Framesets," earlier in the chapter. Visual aids enable you to see the frame borders and frame divisions so that you can modify divisions on a frameset, and the Frames panel assists you with selecting and naming the frames.

Adding frames

To add frame divisions, do any of the following:

✦ **Divide a frame or set of frames vertically or horizontally:** In Design view, drag a frame border from the top or left ruler edge of the window to the middle of the page.

✦ **Divide a frame vertically or horizontally but do not split any existing frames:** Ctrl+drag (Windows) or ⌘+drag (Mac) when dragging a new frame border.

✦ **Split a frame into four parts:** In Design view, drag a frame border from a corner to the middle of the frame. Begin dragging when the cursor turns into a hand.

✦ **Split a frame with a border that doesn't touch the edge of the master frameset:** In Design view, Alt+drag (Windows) or Option+drag (Mac) to drag a new frame border from an existing frame border.

✦ **Divide the frame that contains the insertion point:** Choose Modify⇨ Frameset and then a split option.

Though they're super easy to split, you can't easily merge frames the way you can with table cells. Try, therefore, to have a clear idea of the frameset layout you need before building it. For instance, when you need a frameset with three frames, split the page into two frames first, and then split one of the two frames into a third frame.

Removing frames

To remove a frame division, do either of the following in Design view:

✦ Drag a frame border off the side of the page onto the ruler bar.

✦ Drag a frame border onto the border of a parent frame or frameset.

Because you can't completely remove framesets by dragging, you must delete the file or modify the code. For instance, after you remove all the frame borders from a page, the code still displays a frame doctype, `<frame>`, and `<noframes>` tags, as in the following:

```
<!DOCTYPE HTML PUBLIC "-//W3C//DTD HTML 4.01 Frameset//EN"
    "http://www.w3.org/TR/html4/frameset.dtd">
<html xmlns="http://www.w3.org/1999/xhtml">
<head>
<meta http-equiv="Content-Type" content="text/html; charset=ISO-8859-1">
<title>Untitled Document</title>
</head>
<frame src="file:///C/Project Files/Project ABC/Untitled-1">
<noframes><body>
</body></noframes>
</html>
```

As you can see, the doctype still identifies the file as a page using framesets, and the `<frame>` and `<noframes>` tags identify the content as sitting inside a frame structure. If you want to use the page as a regular HTML file, you can modify the code to reflect the doctype and tags of a normal HTML or XHTML document, but creating a new document by choosing File⇨New is much faster.

Resizing a frame

To resize a frame, do either of the following:

✦ In Design view, drag the frame borders inside the Document window to the size you want.

✦ Select a frame or frameset in the Frames panel and set the exact sizes for the frames in pixels or percentages, or choose the Relative size setting in the Properties inspector.

Nested Framesets

Nested framesets occur when a frameset sits inside another frameset. Nesting is very common, found in even the simplest of framesets. You can nest as many framesets as you need to achieve your layout. The three-part Web site shown in Figure 3-7 is an example of a frameset containing two nested framesets. The main window is divided into two rows, top and bottom, and the bottom row is further split into two columns, left and right. The entire bottom row is the first nested frameset inside of the master frameset. In the right column of the bottom row, another nested frameset is split into two columns.

Figure 3-7:
Build framesets with nested framesets for more complex page layouts.

You can create nested framesets two ways:

✦ Define the inner frameset in the same file as the outer frameset or in a separate file of its own. In other words, you can use Dreamweaver's frame-splitting tools to create the complex structure of the frameset all in the same master frameset file.

✦ Open a separate, external frameset page inside one of the frames of the frameset using the Open in Frame command (as described in the next section).

Because framesets can get very complicated very fast — especially when you start targeted linking — you may do better nesting with the first method.

Fortunately, when you use the frame-splitting tools Dreamweaver provides, you can virtually forget about having to oversee the complexity of nesting details because Dreamweaver handles the coding for you.

Opening Pages in a Frame

After creating the layout for your frameset, you can add new page content to any blank untitled documents in the frameset, or even better, open an existing page within an empty frame.

**Book IV
Chapter 3**

**Designing Pages
with Frames**

To open an existing page in a frame, follow these steps:

1. **In a saved frameset, place your cursor anywhere inside the frame where you want to open your page (see Figure 3-8).**

Figure 3-8:
Place your cursor inside the empty frame.

If you haven't saved and titled the master frameset yet, do so before proceeding by selecting the outer frameset in the Files panel and choosing File⇨Save Frameset or Save Frameset As. Once saved, give the frameset a title by typing one in the Title field on the document toolbar.

2. **Choose File⇨Open in Frame.**

Do *not* select the Open option! You want the fourth option down in the list, Open in Frame, which comes after New, Open, and Open Recent, as shown in Figure 3-9.

Figure 3-9:
Select the Open in Frame option.

The Select HTML File dialog box opens.

3. **Browse to and select the HTML file you want to open in that frame or type the path and filename of the page you want to open. Click OK (Windows) or Choose (Mac).**

   The selected page appears inside the frame on the frameset, as shown in Figure 3-10.

Figure 3-10: The selected page appears inside the frame of the frameset.

If at any time you want to change the page that is currently open in the frameset, select the frame in the Frames panel and edit the Src field in the Properties inspector to select another document.

Saving Frames and Framesets

When you save them properly, all the files inside a frameset display accurately in a browser. Therefore, after creating a frameset, you must save both the frameset document and all the individual files in each of the frames. You can save all the frames and framesets at once by using the Save All Frames command. Or, if you prefer, save the frameset and individual frame documents one at a time.

Saving all the files in the frameset

To save a frameset and all files opened in all the frames at once, follow these steps:

1. **Choose File⇨Save All.**

   All the files associated with the frameset are saved including the frameset document and all the files opened in each of the frames.

   The Save As dialog box appears, as shown in Figure 3-11.

2. **Dreamweaver prompts you to save and name each file. Each time the Save As dialog box appears, look at the page in Design view to identify the frame you're saving and then enter a filename and click Save.**

The frame with a dark border surrounding it is the frame you're saving. Figure 3-11 shows an example of how the border surrounds the frame.

Figure 3-11: In Design view, a dark border appears around the frame being saved when you're saving a frameset and its files.

This border designates which frame you're saving.

If you choose File⇔Open in Frame to open existing files inside all your frames, you only need to name and save the frameset file.

Saving only the frameset file

To save only the frameset, follow these steps:

1. **In the Frames panel or in the Document window, select the frameset.**

You can select the frameset with either of the following methods:

- In the Document window, click in the border between any two frames in the frameset.

- In the Frames panel, click the master frameset border that surrounds the entire frameset. You can tell you've selected the frameset when the Frames panel displays a black border around the outermost frameset.

2. To save the selected frameset, choose File⇨Save Frameset.

Saving an individual file in a frame

To save a file opened inside a frame:

1. Click inside the frame that contains the file you want to save.

2. To save the selected file, choose File⇨Save Frame.

Titling a Frameset

One of the most often overlooked parts of a frameset is the frameset title. The title for the frameset page appears in the title bar at the top of an open browser window. If left unaltered, the title bar reads Untitled Document, which is unhelpful to site visitors and may be perceived as unprofessional, so be sure to title the frameset file!

Follow these steps to name your frameset file:

1. Select the frameset by any of the following methods:

- In the Document window, click in the border between any two frames in the frameset.

- In the Frames panel, click the master frameset border that surrounds the entire frameset. You can tell it's selected when the Frames panel displays a black border around the outermost frameset.

2. Type a title for the file in the Title text box on the Document toolbar, as shown in Figure 3-12.

**Book IV
Chapter 3**

**Designing Pages
with Frames**

Enter title here

Figure 3-12:
Add a title to
the frameset
document.

Setting the Background Color of a File in a Frame

For simple frameset designs in which documents contain only text and perhaps a graphic or two, you can easily set the background color of a page displaying in a frame. For more complex layouts, however, use Cascading Style Sheets to set the background color of a page (see Book III, Chapter 1).

Follow these steps to change the background color of a file in a frame:

1. **In Design view, click inside the frame where you want to change the background color of the page.**

2. **Choose Modify⇨Page Properties.**

You can also click the Page Properties button in the Properties inspector.

The Page Properties dialog box opens.

3. **Click the Background Color color picker icon to choose a color for the page background, or type the hexadecimal value including the number symbol (#) in the Background color text box, such as #003300.**

4. **Click OK to close the dialog box.**

Setting Frame Properties with the Properties Inspector

The properties and attributes in the Properties inspector control different viewable parts of the frame or frameset that display in a browser window, such as adding a frame border in a particular size and color or setting row and column values. Tables 3-1 and 3-2 show the attributes for framesets and frames.

Table 3-1	Frameset Attributes
Frameset Attributes	*Used For*
`cols="50,25%,*"`	Sets the number and size of columns (each column separated with a comma). An asterisk (*) represents a value equal to the remaining space in a browser window after frames with pixel or percentage space are allocated.
`rows="23,23,23,23"`	Sets the number and size of rows.
`border="1"`	Sets the frame border in pixels for IE.
`frameborder="5"`	Sets the frame border in pixels for Netscape.
`framespacing="5"`	Sets the frame spacing in pixels for Netscape.

Table 3-2		Frame Attributes
Frame Attributes	*Value*	*Used For*
`frameborder="0"`	0 or 1	Enter **0** or **No** to hide, **1** or **Yes** to show a border between frames.
`framespacing="5"`	0 – 100	Sets the frames spacing in pixels for Netscape.
`marginwidth=""`	0 – 100	When set to 0, the frame displays flush with the left and right edge of the frame.
`marginheight=""`	0 – 100	If set to 5, a 5-pixel-wide space is between the window and the top of the frame.
`name=""`	Any name	Assign a name to your frames so you can use them as targets with the `<a>` tag.
`noresize`	None	Disallow the user to resize the frame.
`scrolling=""`	Auto/on/off	Decide whether to include the scroll bars on the right side of each frame. The auto setting displays scroll bars only when content in the frame exceeds the frame size.
`src=""`	Filename.html	Set the filename and its location on your hard drive (or the server hard drive) to display in the frame. Remember that servers use UNIX, which makes filenames case sensitive.

The next two sections show you how to specify properties for frames and framesets.

Setting frameset properties

Follow these steps to set frameset properties with the Properties inspector:

1. **Select a frameset by either of the following methods:**

- In the Document window, click in the border between any two frames in the frameset.

- In the Frames panel, click the frameset border. You can tell you've selected the frameset by the thick black border surrounding it.

2. **In the Properties inspector, check to see if the expander arrow (in the lower-right corner) is pointing up or down. If the arrow points down, click it to reveal all the properties, as shown in Figure 3-13.**

3. **In the Properties inspector, enter information to set the attributes for the frameset.**

**Book IV
Chapter 3**

**Designing Pages
with Frames**

Figure 3-13:
The Properties inspector showing all the frameset properties.

Here's a rundown of the options in the Properties inspector:

✦ **Borders:** Determine if borders display around the frames in a browser window. Choose Yes to display the borders, No to hide borders, or Default to use a browser's default border setting.

✦ **Border Width:** Set the width of the border to any size in pixels. If you've selected No from the Borders drop-down list, leave this field blank.

✦ **Border Color:** Use the color picker icon or type a hexadecimal value including the number symbol (#) before it, such as #999999, to set the color of the border for the selected frameset.

✦ **Row/Col Selection:** To set the frame size of any particular frame in a selected frameset, select a frameset in the Frames panel. Click one of the tabs (left or right for columns, top or bottom for rows) on the Row/Col Selection area of the Properties inspector and enter a height or width value in the adjoining Row/Col Value text box.

✦ **Units:** Determine the size of the selected Row/Col:

• **Pixels:** Sets the size of the selected row or column to a fixed pixel width or height. Choose this option for frames you want to remain a fixed size, as with a navigation frame. Frames with pixel values are allocated space before frames using percents and relative sizes.

• **Percent:** Sets the selected row or column to a percentage of the total width and height of the frameset. Percentages are allocated space after frames set with pixels but before frames set with relative values.

• **Relative:** Sets the row or column to be as large or small as the remaining space available in a browser window after frames sized with pixels and percentages. Any number you've entered in the Value field is replaced with an asterisk (*) in the code to represent the relative value. You can also enter a number in the Value field with the Relative setting, such as 3*, which displays in the code as `<frameset rows="23,3*,*">`. In this example, the 3* is 200 percent bigger than 1*.

Setting frame properties

To set frame properties with the Properties inspector, follow these steps:

1. **Select a frame in a frameset document by either of the following methods:**

- In the Frames panel, click anywhere inside the frame's border. You can tell a frame is selected when a thin black line outlines it.

- In the Document window in Design view, Alt+click (Windows) or Shift+Option+click (Mac) a frame in the frameset.

2. **In the Properties inspector, check to see if the expander arrow is pointing up or down. If the arrow is pointing down, click it to reveal all the frame properties.**

Figure 3-14 shows all the properties of a frame.

Figure 3-14:
The Properties inspector showing all the frame properties.

3. **In the Properties inspector, enter information to set the options for the frame.**

You can change the following properties for a frame:

✦ **Frame Name:** Get in the habit of naming all your frames as you create them. The name of the frame is absolutely necessary if you want to target a frame and open a new page inside it. Name your frames with a single word that starts with a letter and does not contain any funky characters, dashes, periods, or spaces (though you can use an underscore, as in `left_frame`). Try not to use words that are common in HTML and JavaScript such as `top` or `parent`, but instead use descriptive terms such as `left`, `main`, or `nav`.

✦ **Src:** This path and filename of the document displays inside the selected frame. Click the folder icon to browse for and select the file, or if you know the path and filename, type it directly into the Src text box.

✦ **Scroll:** Decide whether scroll bars appear on the frame. The Default value does not turn the scroll bars on or off, but instead tells the page to adopt the default scroll bar settings of the browser displaying it. Most browsers use the Auto setting as the default, meaning the frame displays scroll bars when the contents of a frame exceed the display area in the browser. You can also select No for never, or Yes for always.

✦ **No Resize:** Stop users from dragging any visible frame borders and changing the size of the frame in the browser window. It does not affect your ability to modify frame sizes in Dreamweaver.

✦ **Borders:** To view or hide borders around the selected frame in a browser window, select Yes, No, or Default. The Default setting for most browsers is to show the borders unless the parent frameset has borders set to No. To truly hide all borders from displaying, choose No for the frameset and all the frames that share the border. If you have doubt about the visibility or invisibility of the border, test the page in several browsers and alter the settings until you get the effect you want.

✦ **Border Color:** Use the color picker or type a hexadecimal value in this field to set the color of the borders for the frame. The color you specify overrides the color of the parent frameset border. Be warned that the logic of frame borders is very complex and may not make immediate sense. One simple solution is to use the same border color throughout the frameset. Remember to add the number symbol before the hexadecimal value, as in #FF0033.

✦ **Margin Width:** Set the width of the space between the frame borders and the content by entering pixels here. This setting is a frame, not a page, attribute.

✦ **Margin Height:** Set the height of the space between the frame borders and the content by entering pixels here. This setting is a frame, not a page, attribute.

Frame Accessibility Settings

To work with Frame Accessibility settings in Dreamweaver, you can either enable the settings in the Accessibility category of the Preferences dialog box so that you always add accessibility tags as you create the frameset, or set accessibility values for frames and framesets after you create the frames.

Setting accessibility preferences

To enable Frame Accessibility settings in Preferences, follow these steps:

1. **Open the Preferences dialog box by choosing Edit⇨Preferences (Windows) or Dreamweaver⇨Preferences (Mac).**

2. **Select the Accessibility category on the left side of the dialog box.**

3. **Enable the Frames option as shown in Figure 3-15.**

Figure 3-15: Alter the Dream- weaver Accessibility preferences.

Adding or editing accessibility settings to a frame with the Tag Editor

To set accessibility values for an individual frame, follow these steps:

1. **In the Frames panel, click a frame to select it.**

2. **Choose Modify⇨Edit Tag to open the Tag Editor.**

3. **Select Style Sheet/Accessibility from the Category list to display a list of frame accessibility options.**

4. **Enter accessibility values and click OK to close the dialog box.**

   The values are added to the document code.

Targeting Frames with Links

How do you specify which frame should display the linked page when a visitor clicks a link? With the `target` attribute of the `<link>` tag, of course. With framesets, you can use the default `_top` or `_parent` target attribute, or if you happen to name the frames when building the frameset, you can also use the frame names as target destinations for your linked files.

To illustrate, suppose you have a frameset that has the standard two rows with the bottom row split into two columns (see Figure 3-16). Logically, you can name the top frame `topFrame`, the left frame `leftFrame`, and the right frame `mainFrame` (because that's where the bulk of your new content is). When you place navigation links in the left frame, you can add the `target` attribute equal to `mainFrame` so that the linked page opens in the main frame of the frameset, as in this line of code:

```
<a href="techniques.html" target="mainFrame">Fishin' Techniques</a>
```

So, for example, in Figure 3-16, if the user clicks any of the navigation links in the left frame (Fishin' Facts, Fishin' Techniques, and so on), a new page opens in the main frame.

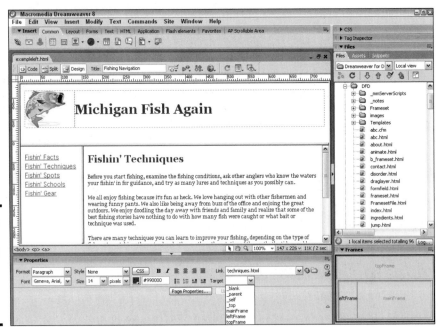

Figure 3-16:
Select the target of the frame you want the linked page to load in.

Target a specific frame when setting links with these steps:

1. **In Design view, select the text or object that you want to convert into a targeted link.**

2. In the Link text box in the Properties inspector, select the file to link to.

Type the path and filename, click the folder icon to browse and select the file, or drag the Point-to-File icon onto the file in the Files panel.

3. In the Target menu in the Properties inspector, choose the frame or window where you want the linked file to display:

- **_blank:** Opens the linked file in a brand new browser window above, or on top of, the existing parent window.

- **_parent:** Opens the linked file inside the parent frameset of the frame where the link appears, replacing the frameset with the content of the linked file.

- **_self:** Opens the linked file inside the same frame the link exists in and replaces the previous content. This option is the default for all links unless another setting overrides it.

- **_top:** Removes any and all framesets and opens the linked file inside the main browser window.

- **(Frame_Name):** When you name all the frames, the frame names appear in this list and you can select one as the target frame. You must be editing the document within the frameset structure to view the frame names. Otherwise, when editing files in their own windows, type the target frame name in the Target field in the Properties inspector.

When linking to a page outside of your Web site while using frames, use the `target="_blank"` or `target="_top"` option. This forces the page to open in a new window or remove the master frameset while making it clear to visitors that the link is a separate entity from your site.

Adding Noframes Content

In HTML, elements that are not understood by a browser are ignored. This means, for example, that if the user's browser doesn't support frames, nothing displays on the page unless you add content inside `<noframes>` tags. Place these tags after the closing `<frameset>` tag on the master frameset and nest them with the `<body>` tag so the content displays in the body area of the page when the frames content doesn't display.

In Listing 3-1, if the frames content doesn't display in the user's browser window, a message displays explaining that the browser doesn't support frames.

Listing 3-1:   Using the Noframes Tag to Display a Message

```
<frameset rows="80,*" cols="*" frameborder="NO" border="0" framespacing="0">
  <frame src="top.html" name="topFrame" scrolling="NO"
  noresize title="topFrame">
  <frameset rows="*" cols="150,*" frameborder="NO" border="0"
  framespacing="0">
    <frame src="left.html" name="leftFrame" scrolling="NO"
    noresize title="leftFrame">
    <frame src="main.html" name="mainFrame"
    title="mainFrame">
  </frameset>
</frameset>
<noframes><body>
Your browser does not support frames. We encourage you to upgrade your browser to
    a version that provides frame support so you can fully experience the
    content provided here:
For Windows:  Internet Explorer 5 or greater | Firefox | Opera
For Macintosh:  Safari | Firefox | Opera
For Unix/Linux:  Firefox | Opera
You might also find it helpful to view the <a href="noFramesIndex.html">
    frameless</a>version of our site. </body></noframes>
```

The noframes content is coded as part of the frameset syntax and only displays in browsers that either don't support frames or have frames disabled.

To add or edit noframes content, follow these steps:

1. **Choose Modify⇨Frameset⇨Edit NoFrames Content.**

A blank window and the words NoFrames Content replaces any content previously displaying in Design view (see Figure 3-17).

Figure 3-17: Use the Edit NoFrames Content command to edit noframes content.

2. **In the Document window, type or paste the noframes content, the same way you would for a regular HTML page.**

Or enter code by choosing Window⇨Code Inspector. When the Code inspector opens, add the HTML content between the <body> and <noframes> tags.

3. **Choose Modify⇨Frameset⇨Edit NoFrames Content to return to Design view of the frameset file.**

Whatever you write for your specific noframes content, try to include both a message about upgrading to a browser that supports framesets (with links to those download pages!) and some kind of acknowledgement of the visitor's use of an old browser or a browser with disabled frames. Because the main point of a Web site is to provide information to all site visitors, treat the noframes content as another opportunity to communicate positively with site visitors.

Creating Floating Frames

Floating frames, or *inline frames,* are framesets or pages embedded inside the body of another page using the `<iframe>` tag. Normally, frames have to stick to the sides of the browser window. However, floating frames can sit anywhere inside a browser window.

When would you want to use floating frames? To display multiple pages in a bookmarkable page, such as a Web photo gallery with clickable thumbnail graphics and close-up images. Or perhaps for those times you want to display a lot of content in a small, scrollable area within another page — for example, a long user agreement — rather than having the visitor scroll down a long page of content.

Floating frame structure is fairly simple. Unlike the `<frameset>` tags that require `<frame>` tags to identify the source of the content in each frame, the floating frame code uses the single opening and closing `<iframe>` tags that include the size of the floating frame and the source file that displays inside it:

```
<iframe width="300" height="150" src="iframefile.html align="left"> </iframe>
```

To add a floating frame to your page you could, of course, hand-code it. If you want to use Dreamweaver's interface, however, follow these steps:

1. **Place your cursor inside the file where you want the floating frame to appear.**

2. **Choose Insert⇨Tag.**

   The Tag Chooser dialog box opens.

3. **Click to expand the HTML Tags folder and select Page Elements on the left side of the dialog box; then select iframe from the list on the right, as Figure 3-18 shows.**

Floating frames in older browsers

Originally recognized only by IE 3.0, floating frames are now widely supported by IE 3.0 and up, Netscape 6.0 and up, Opera, and other popular browsers. For older browsers, the contents inside the iframes don't display on the page. Some tutorials on iframes may instruct you to add a `<frame>` tag with the same document source as your iframe in between the `<iframe>` tags to account for older browsers, like this:

```
<iframe width="300" height="150" src="iframefile.html align="left" frameborder="2"
        hspace="5" vspace="5" scrolling="auto" name="contactlist"> <frame
        src="iframefile.html"> </iframe>
```

While not a perfect solution, it may improve the display of your iframe content on the page in older browsers.

Another option worth considering is to add a browser detection script to the page with the iframe where older browsers are redirected to another page that includes the content of the iframe source file. Check out Book IV, Chapter 2 to find out how you can add a browser detection script to your page.

4. **Click the Insert button.**

The Tag Editor–iframe dialog box opens.

Figure 3-18: Dreamweaver's Tag Chooser lets you select specific tags.

5. **Complete the dialog box with the attributes you want.**

Floating frames have attributes similar to framesets and frames that you need to specify if you want to override the default browser settings. Use these attribute settings to visually differentiate (or not) the floating frame content from the rest of the content on the page.

Figure 3-19 shows the fields completed with sample content. Here's a rundown of the options in the dialog box:

Figure 3-19:
Set
`<iframe>`
tag
attributes
easily using
Dream-
weaver's
Tag Editor.

- **Source:** Type the URL of the file to display in the floating frame.

- **Name:** Give the frame a name so you can use it for targeting. As long as you name the floating frame in the code, you can target the iframe just like a frame within the frameset. For example, if you name an iframe `contactlist`, you can specify that name as a target for a link:

```
<iframe width="300" height="150" src="iframefile.html align="left"
    frameborder="2" hspace="5" vspace="5" scrolling="auto"
    name="contactlist"> </iframe>
<a href="contactlist.html" target="contactlist">See our Contact List</a>
```

- **Width and Height:** Set the width and height sizes using fixed pixels or percentages relative to the visitor's browser and monitor resolution settings.

- **Margin Width and Height:** To adjust the margin space surrounding the floating frame, use the `hspace` (left/right) and `vspace` (top/bottom) attributes, as in the following example:

```
<iframe width="300" height="150" src="iframefile.html align="left"
    frameborder="2" hspace="5" vspace="5"> </iframe>
```

- **Alignment:** Align the iframe relative to the horizontal sides of the browser with the `align` attribute of `left`, `center`, or `right`.

- **Scrolling:** To add or remove scroll bars on the iframe, include the `scrolling` attribute in your iframe code. Use `scrolling ="no"` to remove scroll bars, `scrolling="yes"` to always include scroll bars, and `scrolling="auto"` to add scroll bars as needed:

```
<iframe width="300" height="150" src="iframefile.html align="left"
    frameborder="2" hspace="5" vspace="5" scrolling="auto"> </iframe>
```

- **Show Borders:** Decide whether or not to include frame borders on the floating frame, which by default displays if you don't change this setting. When you enable the Show Borders option, the `frameborder` attribute is absent and the browser displays a simple border. By contrast, when you disable the Show Borders option, the `frameborder` attribute is set to `0` and the floating frame appears borderless.

6. **(Optional) Complete the fields in the Browser Specific, Style Sheet/ Accessibility, and Alternate Content categories of the Tag Editor.**

   For example, you may want to add alternate content between the opening and closing `<iframe>` tags for older browsers:

```
<iframe width="300" height="150" src="iframefile.html align="left"
    frameborder="2" hspace="5" vspace="5" scrolling="auto"> Alternate
    content for older browsers. </iframe>
```

Additionally, though it's not part of the Tag Editor, you can add (by hand-coding) the `long description` attribute with a URL of a page containing a long description of the contents inside the floating frame:

```
<iframe width="300" height="150" src="iframefile.html align="left"
    frameborder="2" hspace="5" vspace="5" scrolling="auto"
    name="contactlist" longdesc="iframefiledescription.html"> </iframe>
```

7. **Click OK to close the Tag Editor.**

   The iframe code is added to your page.

8. **Click the Close button to close the Tag Chooser.**

For even more precise placement of the floating frame on your page, you can envelope the `<iframe>` tags with floating `<div>` layer tags and use Cascading Style Sheets to create a style that positions it. Here's an example:

```
<div id="floatingframe"><iframe width="300" height="150" src="iframefile.html
    align="left"> </iframe></div>
```

Your CSS looks something like this:

```
<style type="text/css">
#floatingframe {
position:absolute;
left: 100px;
top: 100px;
width: 300px;
height: 150px;
z-index: 5;
}
</style>
```

Though Dreamweaver can't display the iframe content in Design view, it shows an appropriately sized gray iframe placeholder box on the page, as shown in Figure 3-20. The placeholder box represents the width and height of the iframe embedded in the source code. To view the iframe content as you intend it to appear to visitors, open the page in a browser window.

Figure 3-20:
Dream-
weaver
displays
iframe
placeholder
boxes in
Design
view.

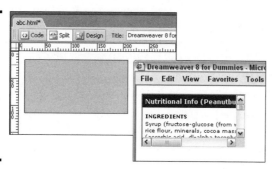

Chapter 4: Introducing Timelines

In This Chapter

✔ Animating layers with timelines

✔ Creating complex animation paths

✔ Adding behaviors to timeline animations

✔ Working with multiple timelines

*B*elieve it or not, you can create simple animation effects in Dreamweaver using layers and JavaScript behaviors! For instance, you could create an animation that moved a graphic across the page or have an image appear and then disappear from an edge of the browser window.

Similar in concept to creating keyframe-based animations in Flash, Dreamweaver's DHTML timelines modify the properties of a layer over time to animate it, without the need for inserting any plug-ins, Java applets, or ActiveX controls. DHTML, or *Dynamic HTML*, changes the layer's style and positioning properties in a browser window (4.0 or higher) with the use of JavaScript.

Use timelines to create animations by changing the layer's position, size, z-index (stacking order), or visibility over a time continuum in a browser window. You can have the movement triggered automatically when the page loads, or you can require some kind of interaction by the site visitor before the movement begins. In addition, you can modify the contents of a layer. For instance, a timeline can display a new image at specific times as the visitor views the page.

Using the Timelines Panel

To begin creating a timeline animation, open the Timelines panel by choosing Window➪Timelines. The panel displays a timeline with individual keyframes to indicate how a layer changes over time. Figure 4-1 identifies each essential part of the Timelines panel, which are described in the following list:

+ **Timeline drop-down list** identifies the timeline on the page you're modifying. When only a single timeline exists on the page, this menu displays only one option. By default, timelines are named numerically such as `Timeline1` and `Timeline2`. However, you can change the names by typing the new name in the Timeline drop-down list.

Timeline drop-down list

Rewind   Frame numbers

Back   Play   Behaviors channel

Figure 4-1:
Create layer
animations.

Keyframes   Animation bar   Animation channel

Playback head

✦ **Timeline Playback Options** previews the timeline animation in the Dreamweaver workspace. Here's a rundown:

   • **Rewind** takes the playback head all the way to the first frame in the timeline.

   • **Back** takes the playback head backward one frame at a time. To play the animation backward, click and hold the Back button.

   • **Play** takes the playback head forward one frame at a time. To play the animation forward, click and hold the Play button.

   • **Autoplay** forces the animation to play automatically when the page opens in a browser window. When enabled, Dreamweaver adds the `onload="MM_timelinePlay('LayerName')"` code to the page's opening `<body>` tag.

   • **Loop** tells the timeline animation to play continuously as long as the browser window has the page opened, going back to the beginning of the animation and replaying each time it reaches the end.

   When enabled, Dreamweaver adds the Go To Timeline Frame behavior to the Behaviors channel of the Timelines panel right after the last frame of the animation. After it's inserted, you can edit the behavior's parameters in the Go To Timeline Frame dialog box, shown in Figure 4-2. Do so by double-clicking the behavior marker in the Behaviors channel or the Go To Timeline Frame behavior in the Behaviors panel.

✦ **Behaviors Channel** displays any behaviors associated with the timeline that is carried out at a particular point in time.

Figure 4-2:
Customize
a timeline
animation's
looping
behavior.

✦ **Frame Numbers** identify the order of each frame by number. The frame number identified between the play and back buttons at the top of the Timelines panel is the current frame. In the Fps field, specify the number of frames per second. By default, the Fps field is set to 15 frames, a speed that most browsers handle well. Another contributing factor to how an animation is perceived in a browser is the user's computer processor speed. Faster frame rates may work well in some browsers on some computers but not in others, so be sure to test the animation in all the target browsers if you increase the Fps number.

✦ **Playback Head** identifies the current frame of the animation on the timeline and in the Document window.

✦ **Animation Channels** are numbered along the left vertical edge of the Timelines panel and represent each layer or image being animated.

✦ **Keyframes** are the frames marked with a small circle inside the Animation channel where specific properties for the object on the timeline change, such as the position of a layer or the source of an image.

✦ **Animation Bar** indicates the length of the animation from start to end point. Each bar controls its own object, and though animations can't overlap, multiple bars can be represented on a single row or animation channel.

Animating Layers in a Timeline

You can animate both images and layers along a timeline animation path. An *animation path* is the line the object in the animation follows across or around the page throughout the length of the animation.

When you drag an image onto the timeline, you can change the image's source but not its position. By contrast, when you drag a layer onto the timeline, you can animate not only the layer, but the contents of the layer as well. Because you can insert any content into a layer, you can add an image to virtually any content along a timeline animation path. Combined with behaviors, you can use timeline animations to do the following:

✦ Move a layer along a timeline animation path, such as making an image of a bumble bee bumble continuously along a circular path.

✦ Alter a layer's visibility, size, and stacking order at any point along the timeline animation path. For instance, you may want to have a layer appear from off screen, move to its final position and stay open for a minute, and then disappear.

✦ Change the source file of an image in a layer at any point along the time-line animation path, such as rotating through a set of four different images displaying on a layer every fifteen seconds.

Dreamweaver places the timeline code as an `MM_initTimelines` function inside a `<script>` tag in the head of the page. Given that the code is written in JavaScript, the script must remain completely intact for the animation to work properly. This includes the script location, name, and syntax as it appears in the code on the page.

For best animation performance, consider the following guidelines:

✦ **Simplicity:** Make your animations as simple as possible so they can play smoothly in the most recent versions of browsers. For truly complex animations, use a program dedicated to creating animations, such as Macromedia Flash.

✦ **Smoothness:** The longer the animation, the smoother the playback in a browser. Create extended animations by dragging the end keyframe on the animation bar out to the right and increasing the number of frames per second (fps) to between 15 and 25.

✦ **File Size and Speed:** To avoid slow or sluggish animations, don't animate super large graphic images, and especially avoid large bitmap files. Try instead to animate only parts of an image to show movement, such as animating only the legs of a giant running chicken.

Creating a simple timeline animation

The most basic form of animation is a simple timeline animation along a single straight or curved path. Use this type of animation to make an image fly onto the page, loop around, and disappear, or make an image gently zigzag from side to side within a specified area of the page. You could also make an image, such as a company logo, suddenly glide into the page, move into position, and stop.

To create a simple animation, you need to have layers added to your page. Turn to Book IV, Chapter 1 to find out more about creating and working with layers.

To create a simple layer timeline animation, open your document and follow these steps:

1. **Choose Window⇨Timelines to open the Timelines panel.**

2. **Select the layer in your open document that you want to animate.**

To select a layer, click anywhere inside the layer to make the layer active and then click the layer's selection handle. The layer's selection handles are visible in Figure 4-3.

3. **To add the layer to the timeline, choose Modify⇨Timeline⇨Add Object to Timeline.**

You can also click the layer's selection handle and drag the layer onto one of the animation bars in the Timelines panel.

The layer appears by name as an animation bar in an animation channel in the Timelines panel. If this layer is the first on the timeline, the layer appears in the first channel. Subsequent layers are placed beneath previous layers on the timeline, unless you manually drag it into new positions.

Selection handle

Figure 4-3: A selected layer displays the layer selection handle at the corners and mid-segment resize anchor points.

Note that the animation bar displays a keyframe at both the start and end of the bar. The first frame of the animation can begin anywhere along the timeline, and the last frame can end anywhere on the timeline to the right of the first frame.

4. **Select the keyframe at the end of the animation bar.**

5. **Click the layer by its selection handle and reposition it to the location in the Document window where it should be at the end of the animation.**

   A straight path is created for the animation from the starting keyframe to the ending keyframe and a straight path line appears in Design view indicating the connection between the layer's start and end positions (see Figure 4-4).

   If you want the animation to end off the page, enter positive and negative positioning values for the layer, such as **560px** and **–100px** in the Left (L) and Top (T) text fields in the Properties inspector.

   If you want the animation to begin off the page, select the starting keyframe of the layer's animation bar in the Timelines panel and enter negative positioning values for the layer, such as **50px** and **50px** in the Left (L) and Top (T) text fields in the Properties inspector.

Figure 4-4:
The animation path spans from the starting keyframe layer position to the ending keyframe layer position.

6. **To curve the path line, Ctrl+click (Windows) or ⌘+click (Mac) anywhere in the middle of the layer's animation bar to add a keyframe; then select the layer by its selection handle and move it to a new position.**

   A curved path line gives the illusion of a more natural, organic path of movement. After you add another keyframe and reposition the layer it's attached to, the path becomes curved by sloping smoothly from keyframe to keyframe.

   Repeat this step until you achieve the curvy path. For more complex paths, follow the steps in the next section.

7. **To preview the animation in Design view, press and hold the Play button in the Timelines panel.**

   For best preview results, however, press F12 to launch the page in a target browser.

Creating a timeline with a complex path

For complex paths that move in a sophisticated manner around a large area of the page, a more efficient method than inserting a zillion keyframes and repositioning the layers at each point in the animation is to record the manual dragging of a layer along a path and have Dreamweaver create all the keyframes for your recorded movement.

For instance, if you have an animated GIF of a wing-flapping bluebird that you wanted to make "fly" onto the page, loop, and then land on top of a tree branch graphic, you could place the animated GIF on a layer, record the movement of the layer you want the bird to take, and then end the recording when the bird layer is positioned above the branch graphic.

To make a timeline animation that moves along a complex path, follow these steps:

1. **Place the layer in the document in the location where you want the animation to begin.**

   To begin the animation slightly off the page, be sure to enter negative positioning values for the layer, such as **–50px** and **–50px,** in the Left (L) and Top (T) text fields in the Properties inspector.

2. **Select the layer and choose Modify⇨Timeline⇨Record Path of Layer.**

3. **Drag the layer around the Document window by its selection handle to create the new complex path, and when finished, release the layer where you want the animation to end.**

While dragging the layer, a dotted line appears to track the flow of the complex path. After your release the layer, the dotted line is converted into a solid path line in the Document window, and a new animation bar for the layer is added to the Timelines panel with all the keyframes necessary to follow the recorded path! Figure 4-5 shows an example of what a complex path line looks like in both Design view and in the Timelines panel.

Figure 4-5:
Create complex animation paths with the Record Path of Layer command.

4. **To preview the animation in Design view, press and hold the Play button in the Timelines panel.**

   For best preview results, however, launch the page in a target browser.

Adding Behaviors to a Timeline Animation

You can add behaviors to an animation at any point or keyframe in the animation timeline. When the playback head reaches that frame in the timeline, it triggers the behavior. For example, you may want to open another page in the browser window when the animation reaches the end keyframe, or perhaps you want to hide the layer after the animation has looped three times.

(For a complete description of how to use behaviors with layers and other objects, check out Book IV, Chapter 2.)

Follow these steps to add a behavior to the timeline:

1. **Select the frame on the timeline's Behaviors channel where you want to attach the behavior to the timeline.**

For instance, to add a behavior to frame 35, you'd click the Behaviors channel at frame 35, as shown in Figure 4-6.

You can also select the Behaviors channel by selecting the layer at the point on the timeline you want to add the behavior to and choosing Modify⇨Timeline⇨Add Behavior to Timeline.

Figure 4-6:
Select a
frame.

2. **Click the Actions (+) button in the Behaviors panel and select a behavior from the list.**

After selecting a behavior, the selected behavior's dialog box opens, which you complete to customize the action that supports the behavior. Turn to Book IV, Chapter 2 to complete the behavior you selected.

Editing the Animated Layer's Properties or Image Source

After you place a layer on a timeline, you can then customize it by changing an image inserted on the layer or modifying layer properties, such as the layer size, stacking order, and visibility.

Changing the image source

One cool thing you can do with an image inserted on a layer that's been animated is swap the current image with another image at a specified point along the animation path. You might do this to create visual interest for viewers while they're looking at the content on your page, and if the animation is on a loop, you could even have the animation rotate through a series of images.

If you want to change the image source, follow these steps:

***1.* In the Timelines panel, select the keyframe you want to change or create a new keyframe on the animation bar where you want the image source change to occur.**

To create a new keyframe, choose Modify⇨Timeline⇨Add Keyframe.

***2.* Click in a frame on the timeline's Behaviors channel above the keyframe you want to change.**

***3.* Click the Actions (+) button in the Behaviors panel and select the Swap Image behavior from the list.**

Complete the Swap Image behavior dialog box (see Book IV, Chapter 2) to provide the source information of the replacement image.

The new image replaces the previous image automatically when the playback head reaches the keyframe with the Swap Image behavior.

***4.* To view the animation with the new changes, click and hold the Play button.**

For best preview results, launch the page in a target browser.

Alternatively, consider using the Show-Hide Layers behavior to hide a layer with one image and show a layer with another image. In addition to allowing you to use differently sized images, the Show-Hide Layer behavior creates smoother animations than either editing the source file directly in the Properties inspector or using the Swap Images behavior.

Altering the layer size

By altering a layer's size you can create an unlimited number of interesting animation effects on your page, such as hiding or revealing content that lies below the animated layer.

Follow these steps to change the layer size:

***1.* In the Timelines panel, select the keyframe you want to change or create a new keyframe on the animation bar where you want the layer size change to occur.**

To create a new keyframe, choose Modify⇨Timeline⇨Add Keyframe.

***2.* Adjust the layer size by dragging the selected layer's resize handles.**

If your keyframe is at the start or end of an animation, the layer size grows (or shrinks) in a one-way direction, relative to the layer's previous size. However, when the keyframe is in the middle of an animation, the layer size change occurs twice: once between the layer size at the starting keyframe and the change layer size keyframe, and again between the layer size of the change layer size keyframe and the ending keyframe.

3. **To view the animation with the new changes, click and hold the Play button.**

    For best preview results, launch the page in a target browser.

Changing the layer stacking order (z-index)

By changing the stacking order of a layer within an animation, you can make the layer look as though it's disappeared behind or sliding on top of another layer on the page. For example, you could create an animation of a rabbit (on one layer) that looks like it is hiding behind a top hat (on another layer), or an animation that shows a hat (on one layer) blowing into the page and landing on top of a rabbit's head (on another layer).

Follow these steps to change the layer stacking order:

1. **In the Timelines panel, select the keyframe you want to change or create a new keyframe on the animation bar where you want the layer stacking order change to occur.**

    To create a new keyframe, choose Modify⇨Timeline⇨Add Keyframe.

2. **Click in the frame on the timeline's Behaviors channel above the keyframe you want to change.**

3. **Add the Change Property behavior in the Behaviors panel.**

    This enables you to edit a layer's z-index.

4. **Select the layer and choose the style.zIndex option. Enter the new value in the New Value text field, as shown in Figure 4-7.**

5. **To view the animation with the new changes, click and hold the Play button.**

    For best preview results, launch the page in a target browser.

Figure 4-7:
Change the
z-index of a
layer.

In addition to modifying the layer's z-index with the Change Property behavior, you can also modify the layer's visibility, background color, background image, clipping area, height and width, and top and left positions. If you're modifying the visibility of the layer, be sure all the layers have the appropriate starting visibility status (visible, hidden, or inherit) set in the Layers panel. For more on setting layer visibility, see Book IV, Chapter 1.

Adjusting a Timeline

Established timelines are not set in stone, which means you can further edit them to create even more interesting animation effects. Timeline modifications include adjusting the number of frames, repositioning keyframes, looping, and adjusting the start and end times of an animation.

To adjust a timeline, do any of the following in any order and combination:

✦ **Set a timeline animation to play continuously:** Enable the Loop option at the top of the Timelines panel.

✦ **Play a timeline automatically when the page loads:** Enable the Autoplay option at the top of the Timelines panel.

✦ **Move the start time of an animation:** Select the first keyframe marker on the layer's animation bar and drag it to the left or right on the animation channel.

✦ **Adjust the length of an animation:** To make the animation play longer or shorter, drag the end keyframe marker to the left or right on the timeline. Keyframes between the start and end of the animation automatically reposition so that the animation plays relatively the same as it did before, only for a longer or shorter duration. To increase or decrease the animation length without moving the keyframes, press Ctrl (Windows) or ⌘ (Mac) while dragging the end keyframe marker.

✦ **Reposition a keyframe on a timeline:** Select the keyframe marker on the timeline and drag it to the left or right into a new position.

✦ **Add or remove frames to all the layers on a timeline:** Do either of the following:

• Choose Modify⇨Timeline⇨Add Frame.

• Choose Modify⇨Timeline⇨Remove Frame.

✦ **Add or remove keyframes on a timeline:** Do either of the following:

• Choose Modify⇨Timeline⇨Add Keyframe.

• Choose Modify⇨Timeline⇨Remove Keyframe.

✦ **Add a selected layer to a frame on a timeline:** Set the position of the playback head on the timeline and choose Modify➪Timeline➪Add Object to Timeline.

✦ **Remove a selected animation bar from a timeline:** Press the Delete key.

✦ **Adjust the location of an animation path in the document:** Select the animation bar and then drag the layer by its handle into its new position. Dreamweaver automatically updates the code to adjust for the new path coordinates and keyframe positions.

✦ **Reposition an animation along the timeline:** Select the layer's animation bar and move it along the animation channel to its new position. To reposition multiple animations at once, press Shift to select the animation bars before sliding them on the timeline to a new position.

Copying and Pasting a Timeline Animation

You can use any of the timeline animations you create elsewhere by copying and pasting. You can paste animation bars onto the same timeline or another timeline within the same document, as well as onto any timeline of another document.

Follow these steps to copy and paste animations:

1. **Click an animation bar in the timeline to select it.**

For multiple selections, hold Shift while clicking to select each additional animation bar.

2. **Choose Edit➪Copy to make a copy of the selection.**

If you want to relocate the animation bars, choose Edit➪Cut.

3. **Before pasting the animation bar, do one of the following:**

• Within the same document, select another timeline from the Timeline drop-down list and position the playback head where you're going to paste the animation bar.

• Within the same document, position the playback head where you want the animation bar.

• Within another document, select a timeline from the Timeline drop-down list and position the playback head where you want the animation bar.

4. **Choose Edit➪Paste to insert the animation into the timeline.**

Because you place an object only in one place at a time and because any image can only have a single source at a time, you can't place the animation bars for the same object into an overlapping position on the timeline. Therefore, any time you potentially cause an overlap, Dreamweaver adjusts the pasted content into the next nearest non-overlapping animation frame.

When pasting animations into a new document, the copied animations are pasted as layers along with their contents and entire animation sequence. This includes the layer's ID or name. Thus, if the copied layer name already exists in the new document, the paste command applies the animation to the existing layer of the same name in the new file. For example, if you copy a layer named bunny in page1.html to page2.html where you already have a layer with that name, the copied animation is applied to the second animation in page2.html.

As a massive timesaver, you can apply pasted animations to other existing layers in a file by choosing Edit⊃Change Object. Then in the Change Object dialog box that appears (shown in Figure 4-8), select a different object to animate. For instance, if you paste an animation layer copied from Timeline1 called Spin to Timeline2 but you need the animation to apply to the layer called Propeller, choose Edit⊃Change Object after pasting the animation and select Propeller from the Change Object dialog box.

Figure 4-8:
Select an object.

Working with Multiple Timelines

When creating timeline animations, all the layers on the timeline are treated as a single animation, which means that certain things such as looping and autoplay apply to the entire animation rather than any one component of the timeline. To solve this predicament, Dreamweaver is configured to allow multiple timelines to exist on a single page, each with its own animation path and set of behaviors. With multiple timelines, you gain more control over each animated layer on your document. For instance, you may want to have separate animations that play when visitors place their cursors over each of the site's navigation buttons.

To work with multiple timelines, do the following:

✦ **Add a new timeline:** Choose Modify➪Timeline➪Add Timeline.

✦ **Permanently remove a timeline:** (This also removes all the timeline's animations.) Choose Modify➪Timeline➪Remove Timeline.

✦ **Rename a timeline:** Choose Modify➪Timeline➪Rename Timeline. Alternatively, you can type a new name in the Timeline drop-down list.

✦ **View a different timeline:** To see a particular timeline in the Timelines panel, select the desired timeline from the Timeline drop-down list.

Chapter 5: Making Your Pages XHTML Compliant

In This Chapter

✔ Understanding the benefits of XHTML

✔ Dreamweaver's automatic XHTML code compliance

✔ Making documents XHTML compliant

✔ Migrating a page or site from HTML to XHTML

✔ Performing XHTML validation

XHTML *(eXtensible HyperText Markup Language)* is a form of HTML coding that extends document functionality by conforming to more strict *eXtensible Markup Language* (XML) rules. XML, a markup language used to represent complex object relationships, is used by many Web applications and services.

XHTML is not just a cleaner and stricter version of HTML; you can also view, edit, and validate XHTML pages with standard XML tools. Plus, XHTML works wonderfully in combination with Cascading Style Sheets (CSS).

In 2000, the W3C proposed that XHTML be the new language for building Web pages, and in 2002, XHTML became an accepted standard, whereby all new browsers should contain built-in XHTML support. Using XHTML also ensures the forward and backward compatibility of your Web files. In other words, XHTML is the future of Web development. This chapter gives you the basics you need to get started.

Understanding the Benefits of Using XHTML with Dreamweaver

The biggest benefit of using XHTML with Dreamweaver is that Dreamweaver makes the transition virtually painless. Dreamweaver provides you with the option of choosing XHTML as the primary markup language. When you select this option, the program automatically inserts the appropriate `doctype` tag on the page and writes XHTML-compliant code. Furthermore, you can easily convert a page from HTML to XHTML using Dreamweaver's Convert command, and have Dreamweaver perform code validation to ensure the code is XHTML-compliant prior to publishing your pages online.

Creating XHTML-compliant documents in Dreamweaver is easy to do and provides both immediate and long-term benefits, including the following:

✦ **Simple transition to advanced technology:** Because the Web is moving toward XML, the simple transition to XHTML enables you to take advantage of this new technology for your Web sites.

✦ **Cleaner code:** With its strict guidelines, XHTML provides for cleaner and more uniform coding. Cleaner code means more accurate rendering in browsers.

✦ **Improved accessibility:** Users can view XHTML files on many different media types, including Braille displays, screen readers, wireless devices, and other specialized Web environments that provide wider access of information and improved accessibility for people with disabilities.

The key to XHTML is the concept of *extensibility.* XHTML combines HTML's ability to define the way content displays with XML's ability to describe how content functions. Because XHTML is an application of XML, any language with an XML parser can parse XHTML. For programmers, this means you can reuse any content you write in XHTML. *That's* extensibility.

Getting the Basics of XHTML Syntax

Before you can fully appreciate the benefits of XHTML, you have to know some important regulations. Check out the following sections for more information.

Discovering the strict rules you can't live without

XHTML is written with a very strict set of rules. You must adhere to all of the following rules:

✦ Specify a `doctype` tag before the opening `<html>` tag.

✦ Write all tags and attributes in lowercase.

✦ Surround all attribute values with double quotes (`"like this"`), as in `<p align="center">`.

✦ Assign a value to all attributes, as with `<input checked="checked">`.

✦ Replace attribute values containing special HTML characters such as &, <, and >, with entity representations; for example, `"&"`, `">"`, and `"<"`.

✦ Replace the `id` attribute with the `name` attribute when attaching attributes to elements in all circumstances, with the exception of form input elements such as `<select>` or `<input>`.

✦ Close all tags without inner content with `/>`, including non-container tags such as `br`, `hr`, and `img`. For instance, the XHTML shorthand version of `<br></br>` is `<br />`.

✦ Remove all special coding, such as inline style sheets and inline JavaScript, from the XHTML document and store it in separate `.css` and `.js` files, with references in the head to those external files:

```
<link rel="stylesheet" type="text/css" ref="my_style.css" />
<script language="JavaScript" src="my_javascript.js"></script>
```

✦ Use CSS for text formatting in XHTML documents. XHTML doesn't support the `<font>` tag.

Taking advantage of strict and transitional rules

One key feature that sets XHTML apart from HTML is its use of markup that conforms to and takes advantage of XML rules used in Web applications and services. These rules, specified in the `doctype`, can be strict or transitional. Strict rules are better at automating data processing than transitional rules are, but both work great on plain static Web pages.

XHTML files have three parts: the `doctype`, which states the *DTD* (document type definition); the `<head>`; and the `<body>`. The `<doctype>` tag defines the syntactic constraints allowed the code as well as the usage and meaning of those constraints. The `<head>` and `<body>` areas are just like regular HTML files, with a few additional syntax rule changes in the code, such as properly closing and nesting tags (see the previous section for more information).

You can set the DTD definition to *strict, transitional,* or *frameset.* Here are some sample DTD definitions for each type, along with descriptions:

✦ **Strict:** Use this DTD with Cascading Style Sheets:

```
<!DOCTYPE html
PUBLIC "-//W3C//DTD XHTML 1.0 Strict//EN"
"http://www.w3.org/TR/xhtml1/DTD/xhtml1-strict.dtd">
```

✦ **Transitional:** Choose the Transitional DTD with HTML and CSS. For example, you can add the `bgcolor` attribute to the `<body>` tag when you want to ensure your pages render accurately in older browsers that don't support CSS:

```
<!DOCTYPE html
PUBLIC "-//W3C//DTD XHTML 1.0 Transitional//EN"
"http://www.w3.org/TR/xhtml1/DTD/xhtml1-transitional.dtd">
```

✦ **Frameset:** Use this DTD with frames:

```
<!DOCTYPE html
PUBLIC "-//W3C//DTD XHTML 1.0 Frameset//EN"
"http://www.w3.org/TR/xhtml1/DTD/xhtml1-frameset.dtd">
```

To find out more about XHTML 1.0, visit the World Wide Web Consortium (W3C) Web site, where you find information about XHTML 1.0 specification (`www.w3c.org/TR/xhtml1/`), DTD definitions (`www.w3.org/TR/xhtml1/dtds.html`), and free online tools for markup validation of published Web sites (`http://validator.w3.org/`) and unpublished local files (`http://validator.w3.org/file-upload.html`).

Handling Dreamweaver's Automatic XHTML Code Compliance Tools

Inside the New Document window, Dreamweaver gives you the option of selecting an XHTML Document Type (DTD) for generating and cleaning up your XHTML code:

✦ XHTML 1.0 Transitional.

✦ XHTML 1.0 Strict.

✦ XHTML 1.1.

✦ XHTML Mobile 1.0.

✦ XHTML 1.0 Frameset. (This option is not selectable when creating new HTML pages. Instead, the DTD automatically gets added to your code when creating pages using frames.)

Each of these DTDs renders XHTML-compliant code. If you're unsure what which DTD to use, select XHTML 1.0 Transitional.

After you select a DTD, Dreamweaver writes code that automatically meets XHTML requirements. Table 5-1 provides an overview of those requirements.

Table 5-1	Dreamweaver XHTML Compliance
XHTML Code Requirements	*Dreamweaver Automatically Writes XHTML Compliant Code*
The page must contain a doctype declaration above the opening HTML or XHTML tag and must include one of the three document type definition (DTD) files for XHTML (strict, transitional, or frameset).	For regular, noframe XHTML documents, the doctype gets added to the file: `<!DOCTYPE html PUBLIC "-//W3C//DTD XHTML 1.0 Transitional//EN" "http://www.w3.org/TR/xhtml1/DTD/xhtml1-transitional.dtd">`

XHTML Code Requirements	Dreamweaver Automatically Writes XHTML Compliant Code
	For XHTML files with framesets: `<!DOCTYPE html PUBLIC "-//W3C//DTD XHTML 1.0 Frameset//EN" "http://www.w3.org/TR/xhtml1/DTD/xhtml1-frameset.dtd">`
The page's root element must be HTML and it must designate the XHTML namespace. The namespace is an attribute of the HTML tag that defines the document as XML.	Dreamweaver adds the `html` root element and namespace attribute to the file: `<html xmlns="http://www.w3.org/1999/xhtml">`
All XHTML files must have `head`, `title`, and `body` elements, and all framesets must have `head`, `title`, and `frameset` elements.	All XHTML files include the `head`, `title`, and `body` elements, and all frameset XHTML files, include the `head`, `title`, and `frameset elements`.
Any included script or style element in the code must have a `type` attribute. For example, the `type` attribute of the `stylesheet` element is `text/css`.	Dreamweaver automatically adds the `type` and `language` attributes in `script` elements, and the `type` attribute in `style` elements for all newly generated code, and adds them, if missing, when cleaning up XHTML.
All element and attribute names must be coded in lowercase.	Dreamweaver makes sure that all element and attribute names are in lowercase for all newly generated XHTML code, and converts text to lowercase when cleaning up XHTML with the Clean Up XHTML command.
All `area` and `img` elements must have the `alt` attribute.	Dreamweaver automatically adds these attributes to newly generated code and inserts them if missing when cleaning up XHTML. Missing `alt` attributes are also part of validation reports.
Elements must use proper nesting: `<p><b>This is incorrect.</p></b>` `<p><b>This is correct.</b></p>`	Dreamweaver automatically writes properly nested code, and can fix bad nesting from code generated outside Dreamweaver with the Clean Up XHTML command.
All elements must have closing tags, unless specifically declared in the DTD as empty.	Dreamweaver adds closing tags to all newly generated code and adds missing closing tags when cleaning up XHTML.

(continued)

Book IV Chapter 5

Making Your Pages XHTML Compliant

Table 5-1 *(continued)*

XHTML Code Requirements	*Dreamweaver Automatically Writes XHTML Compliant Code*
All empty elements must have closing tags or have opening tags ending with `/>`. This includes non-container tags such as ` `, `<hr>`, and `<img>`. For instance, ` ` would no longer be valid, but ` </br>` and ` ` are both valid and acceptable formats. This requirement applies to the following empty elements: `area`, `base`, `basefont`, `br`, `col`, `frame`, `hr`, `img`, `input`, `isindex`, `link`, `meta`, and `param`. The preferred method for backward-compatibility in non-XML-enabled browsers is to add a space before the `/>` when closing non-container tags, as in `<hr />`, not `<hr/>`.	Dreamweaver adds the appropriate space before the closing slash (" /") to all empty elements and noncontainer tags both when generating new code and cleaning up XHTML.
All attributes with no value must be assigned a value, as with `<input checked="checked">`. The old minimized format, `<input checked>`, is not valid. This requirement applies to the following attributes: `checked`, `compact`, `declare`, `defer`, `disabled`, `ismap`, `multiple`, `noresize`, `noshade`, `nowrap`, `readonly`, and `selected`.	Dreamweaver adds the correct attribute-value pairs in newly generated code and corrects them when cleaning up XHTML. ***Note:*** This feature is for browsers that support HTML 4 and above. For older browsers, these Boolean attributes may not display accurately.
All attribute values must be surrounded by double (`" "`) quotes: `<p align="center">`.	Dreamweaver adds quotation marks around all attribute values for newly generated code, and adds missing quote marks as needed when cleaning up XHTML.
The `id` attribute must replace or be included, in addition to the `name` attribute, when attaching attributes to elements in all circumstances, with the exception of form input elements like `<select>` or `<input>`. This requirement applies to the following elements: `a`, `applet`, `form`, `frame`, `iframe`, `img`, and `map`. For example, `<a name="FAQ1">FAQ Answer 1</a>` is not valid because it lacks the `id` attribute. The correct form includes both `id` and `name` attributes: `<a name="FAQ1" id="FAQ1">FAQ Answer 1</a>`.	Dreamweaver automatically adds both the `name` and `id` attributes to the same value, when the `name` attribute is entered in the Properties Inspector, when generating new code, and when cleaning up XHTML.

XHTML Code Requirements	Dreamweaver Automatically Writes XHTML Compliant Code
Attributes with enumerated type values must be coded in lowercase. The enumerated type value is a value that can be chosen from a list of possible values, as with the OL attribute, which allows values for type equal to Number, Roman Small, Roman Larger, Alphabet Small, and Alphabet Larger (1, I, i, A, and a).	Dreamweaver automatically writes these enumerated type values in lowercase for new code and adjusts the case when cleaning up XHTML.

Making Sure Your Documents Follow XHTML Syntax

Dreamweaver's preferences allow you to set the default DTD for your files. If you set the default DTD to XHTML 1.0 Transitional, for example, then every time you create a new Dreamweaver document, it's XHTML compliant (see the upcoming section). Furthermore, if you're working with existing HTML files, you can tell Dreamweaver to convert the HTML code to XHTML-compliant markup using Dreamweaver's Convert XHTML command.

Creating a new XHTML document with Dreamweaver

Each time you create a new document, you can choose to have Dreamweaver write XHTML code instead of HTML code. Here's what you need to do:

1. **Choose File➪New.**

The New Document window opens.

2. **Choose a page category and type.**

For XHTML files, select the Basic, Dynamic, or Template page category and choose a file type from the center pane. For example, you could select the Basic Page category and the Basic Page HTML type.

3. **Select an XHTML document type from the Document Type (DTD) drop-down list.**

Choose XHTML 1.0 Transitional, XHTML 1.0 Strict, XHTML 1.1, or XHTML 1.0 Mobile as the DTD. If you're creating a frameset, the appropriate XHTML Frameset DTD is automatically inserted into your frameset page when you select any of the XHTML DTD types.

4. **Click Create.**

The new document opens in the Dreamweaver workspace window and any content you add to your page automatically conforms to XHTML rules.

**Book IV
Chapter 5**

**Making Your Pages
XHTML Compliant**

Telling Dreamweaver to create XHTML-compliant files all the time

You can set up Dreamweaver to create XHTML-compliant files by default in the Preferences dialog box. Follow these steps:

1. **Choose Edit➪Preferences (Windows) or Dreamweaver➪Preferences (Mac).**

   The Preferences dialog box appears.

2. **Select the New Document category (shown in Figure 5-1) and choose a DTD from the Default Document Type (DTD) drop-down list.**

Figure 5-1:
Set the default document type definition to XHTML.

Choose from XHTML 1.0 Transitional, XHTML 1.0 Strict, XHTML 1.1, or XHTML Mobile 1.0. If you're creating a frameset, the appropriate XHTML Frameset DTD automatically is inserted into your frameset page when you select any of the XHTML DTD types.

If you're unsure of which option to select, choose XHTML 1.0 Transitional, which is a little less strict than XHTML 1.0 Strict.

3. **Click OK.**

Dreamweaver is now set up to write XHTML-compliant code for all new documents.

Transforming HTML document code into XHTML

Choose Commands➪Clean Up XHTML to have Dreamweaver get rid of HTML inconsistencies and make sure your documents are XHTML ready.

Dreamweaver does everything it needs to do — automatically — to instantly convert tag attributes to all lowercase, fix syntax errors, and add or report missing required tag attributes, such as images with missing `alt` attributes. For more detailed information on cleaning up your code with the Clean Up HTML/XHTML command, see Book V, Chapter 2.

Converting existing HTML files to XHTML

If you want to turn your existing HTML documents into XHTML documents, we could give you a set of complicated steps, but why should we? The reality is that Dreamweaver makes this task so painfully simple that you may actually wonder if you've missed something. Simply open an HTML document in the Dreamweaver workspace window and perform one of the following tasks:

✦ If your HTML file doesn't use frames, choose File➪Convert and select an XHTML DTD type.

✦ If your HTML file uses frames, select the frameset, choose File➪Convert, and choose XHTML 1.0 Frameset. Then place your cursor inside a document in any of the frames in the frameset, choose File➪Convert, and select an XHTML DTD type. The HTML code inside the frameset converts from HTML to XHTML. Repeat this process for each document that appears inside a frame in the frameset.

Note: While it doesn't really matter if you mix and match DTDs, you should probably pick one type and stick with it for the entire frameset. If you're unsure which DTD to choose for the pages that are displayed inside the frames of your frameset, use XHTML 1.0 Transitional.

Making sure your HTML file can be converted to XHTML

Though we wish it weren't true, some HTML files can't be converted to XHTML and not all files can be made XHTML-compliant. For example, some template-based files written in HTML can't be converted to XHTML because the converted file must be in the same language as the template file.

The best way to determine whether you can convert one of your HTML files to XHTML is to test it. After converting the file, try entering a few line breaks to the code. If the code looks like `<br />`, the conversion was a success. To ensure that your code is fully compliant after the conversion, however, choose Commands➪Clean Up XHTML to perform XHTML validation on all your documents. Check out Book V, Chapter 2 for more information about this useful tool.

Book IV
Chapter 5

Making Your Pages
XHTML Compliant

Validating Your XHTML

Dreamweaver has a built-in tool for validating your XHTML code. The tool looks for any and all tag or syntax code errors and lets you know what it thinks you should do by displaying a convenient report. In addition to XHTML, this tool also validates HTML, XML, JavaServer Pages (JSP), ColdFusion Markup Language (CFML), and Wireless Markup Language (WML). For step-by-step instructions on validating your XHTML, as well as other tips on using Reports to test your site before publishing, Book V, Chapter 1 covers everything you need to know about validating XHTML.

Book V

Publishing Your Site

The 5th Wave   By Rich Tennant

"This is a 'dot-com' company, Stacey. Risk taking is a given. If you're not comfortable running with scissors, cleaning your ear with a darning needle, or swimming right after a big meal, this might not be the place for you."

Contents at a Glance

Chapter 1: Using Reports to Test Your Site before Publishing

In This Chapter

✓ **Previewing your site before you publish it**

✓ **Validating your code**

✓ **Testing your pages with the Results panel**

✓ **Checking and fixing broken links**

*B*efore you launch your Web site on the Internet, you need to spend some time reviewing your site content to address accessibility issues, spelling errors, broken links, orphaned files, and code syntax problems. The benefits of following some general testing guidelines are endless. Nothing is worse than a site that doesn't work as it should. That's why this chapter gives you expert advice on performing browser compatibility checks, shows you how to test your pages with browser page previews, and helps you adjust download times.

Happily, Dreamweaver comes with several tools that help you tinker your site until everything's perfect. First of all, you can use the powerful HTML and Workflow reports. These tools enable to you review your page content and make important improvements before publishing. In addition, the Results panel has several site evaluation tools that you can run to stream-line testing and fixing problems on your pages. This chapter shows you how to use the Results panel to search code, validate tags, test pages for poten-tial problems in specified target browsers, fix links, use the FTP log, and run a Server Debug report. You can also use the Preferences dialog box to deter-mine page-loading times for the best viewing experience.

Testing Your Site

You've put all the work into getting your site together, and now all you want to do is publish the darn thing. Well, not so fast. You have to go through the essential testing phase before the site goes live.

In fact, you should test your site and fix problems throughout the entire Web site building process, but if you've waited until now, that's okay too.

All your site's pages should look good and function as you intend them to in all the browsers you're targeting. That means you have to verify the accuracy of your links and check download times for your larger files. Running reports can be a crucial part of this process; you can run several built-in reports from Dreamweaver's Results panel to make sure that all the code is right on the money.

Following general testing guidelines

Your main goal, ultimately, is to try to build a Web site that users enjoy viewing and navigating. If you follow these few simple guidelines, you're well on your way:

✦ **Preview your pages in as many browsers and browser versions as possible, on both Macs and PCs, to ensure browser compatibility.** You need to verify that the pages work the way you intend them to — or fail in a way that's acceptable to you — so make sure that you really spend some time previewing just about every combination of browser version and hardware you can think of. Your Web pages should look good in browsers that both support and don't support JavaScript, layers, CSS, and plug-ins.

For super-old browsers that fail unacceptably, you may want to use the Check Browser behavior to redirect visitors to another page. See Book IV, Chapter 2 to find out more about the Check Browser behavior.

✦ **Check your links — both internally and externally — and fix any that are broken or don't work as you intended.** The Link Check report tests links and identifies any that are broken, external, and orphaned. See the "Checking and Fixing Links" section, later in this chapter, for more details.

✦ **Check the file sizes of all your Web pages and pay attention to their download times.** When pages have a lot of content, especially when they include large graphic files, some or all the page content may not load until all the data finishes loading. Consider adding text outside a content-heavy table so some content is viewable while the rest of the page is downloading.

✦ **Run reports on your site.** Always test for potential errors and common coding omissions or mistakes such as missing Alt text, untitled files, and redundant or improperly nested tags. (See the "Searching Your Code for Tags and Attributes" section, later in this chapter).

✦ **Validate all your tags.** Validating tags is the best way to ensure that your code syntax meets compliance standards. If you find any broken or missing information, fix it now. (See the "Validating Your Code" section later in this chapter.)

After you publish the site, continue to update and check the site regularly for possible errors, such as broken links, problematic code, JavaScript and

CSS usage, and browser incompatibilities. For specific issues, visit the Dreamweaver discussion forums on the Macromedia Web site at www.macromedia.com/go/dreamweaver_newsgroup. You can find discussion strings related to common browser and platform issues as well as technical notes and helpful tips from other Dreamweaver users.

Previewing your pages in a browser

Dreamweaver 8 writes code that supports industry standards and best practices, such as the use of advanced CSS, RSS and XML feeds, and accessibility requirements. The main graphical browsers — Internet Explorer, Netscape, Firefox, Opera, and Safari — support Cascading Style Sheets. Of course, just because the main browsers should support these features doesn't mean that they automatically will. The only way to know for sure is to check for compatibility issues.

When fashioning a Web site, determining your target audience for the site in advance is very helpful. If you know your target, you can figure out what browsers users are likely to have. For example, if you're building an intranet site for employees who all use new PC computers running the latest version of Internet Explorer, the need to test the site on other browsers isn't as critical. If you're building a site selling widgets on the Internet, it's essential to test a variety of operating systems and as many browsers and browser versions as possible.

You should also use the Target Browser Check report to assist you with the testing of your site in multiple browsers. This test checks the code in your files and reports tags, attributes, and CSS values and properties that are unsupported by your target browsers without altering any of the code. You can find out how to run the Target Browser Check report and use all the report features in the section, "Testing Your Pages with Target Browser Check," later in this chapter.

Setting the primary and secondary browsers

Dreamweaver enables you to specify two different browsers as the primary and secondary browsers that launch for page previews when you press F12. To specify the primary and secondary preview browsers, follow these steps:

1. **Choose File⇨Preview in Browser⇨Edit Browser List.**

You can also launch the preferences by choosing Edit⇨Preferences (Windows) or Dreamweaver⇨Preferences (Mac).

The Preferences dialog box opens, as shown in Figure 1-1.

2. **Select the Preview in Browser category from the Category list on the left side of the dialog box and choose a browser from the browser list on the right.**

Figure 1-1:
Add
browsers
and set
primary and
secondary
browser
options.

3. **To add a browser to the list of browsers, click the plus (+) button and enter information about the browser in the Add Browser dialog box that appears.**

   Type the browser name and version in the Name field, such as IE 6.0. In the Application field, browse to and select the browser's application file. Click OK when you finish. The new browser appears in the browser listing.

   Add as many browsers as you like to this list. Although you can only select two browsers as the primary and secondary browsers for launching with a keyboard shortcut, you can preview your page with any of the browsers installed on your computer, as described in the next section.

4. **To delete a browser from the list of browsers, select the browser you want to delete and click the minus (–) button.**

   Deleted browser names immediately disappear from the list.

5. **Select a browser from the list and click to add a check mark next to Primary Browser to set the primary browser.**

6. **Select another browser from the list and add a check mark next to Secondary Browser to set the secondary browser.**

   Now you can press F12 (Windows) or Option+F12 (Mac) and your open document launches in the primary browser; pressing Ctrl+F12 (Windows) and ⌘+F12 (Mac) launches your open file in the secondary browser.

7. **Enable or disable the Preview Using Temporary File option.**

   When enabled, this option tells your computer to create a temporary copy of the file in the browser window for previewing and server debugging. When this option is disabled, the document may not display accurately in the browser; however, you can make updates and changes directly to the file.

Previewing pages in multiple browsers

When you design pages in Dreamweaver, Design view provides you with a general idea of how your page will look in a browser window. What Design view can't do, however, is display some dynamic features, such as JavaScript, or the very subtle HTML display differences between browsers. The only way to see exactly how a page will look to visitors is to preview pages in individual browsers. In fact, you should test all the pages on your site on as many browsers as possible and on both the Mac and Windows platforms.

You can preview and test your pages in more than one browser at a time. To set which browsers you want Dreamweaver to test, check out the previous section, "Setting the primary and secondary browsers." Then follow these simple steps:

1. **To preview your page in your primary browser, press F12 (Windows) or Option+F12 (Mac).**

   The document launches in the specified primary browser.

2. **To preview your page in your secondary browser, press Ctrl+F12 (Windows) or ⌘+F12 (Mac).**

   The document launches in the specified secondary browser.

3. **To preview the file in a third (or fourth) browser, choose File⇨Preview in Browser to select any of the browsers from the Preview list.**

4. **Verify the links, dynamic content, and layout of the page.**

   Check all your JavaScript behaviors, links, plug-ins, ActiveX controls, and any other media files installed on the page.

If some content on your page doesn't display accurately in one or more of your target browsers, you have more work ahead of you. For example, your page may need adjustments to some JavaScript behaviors, CSS, or some other features on the page.

If you're testing your page with Internet Explorer on a computer running Windows XP with Server Pack 2, the browser may display a message that some content on the page has been restricted. You can fix this problem by inserting the Mark of the Web code as described in the aptly named sidebar, "Inserting the Mark of the Web."

Setting download times and size

Dreamweaver provides you with important download times and size data to help you control the way visitors with varying connection speeds experience your pages.

Inserting the Mark of the Web

If you have Windows XP Service Pack 2 installed on your PC, you may have problems previewing local Dreamweaver files with active content and scripts (such as Flash movies or client-side JavaScript behaviors) in Internet Explorer. You can easily determine whether Internet Explorer is having problems with your content if a pale-yellow security message bar at the top of the browser window appears saying the file's active content has been restricted, as shown in the figure.

Right-click the security message bar and choose Allow Blocked Content to run the content or scripts in the Local Machine zone. For better protection, add the Mark of the Web code to your pages for testing purposes, and then remove it before publishing.

One of the reasons Internet Explorer added this feature was to protect local machines from hackers and attackers that use the Local Machine zone. The Mark of the Web instructs the browser to run the active content on the page in the Internet zone instead in the Local Machine zone.

To insert the Mark of the Web to view active content in Internet Explorer running Windows XP Service Pack 2, follow these steps:

1. **Open your document in the Dreamweaver workspace.**

2. **Choose Commands⌐Insert Mark of the Web.**

The following line of generic code is automatically inserted into the head of your code:

```
<!-- saved from url=(0014)about:internet
     -->
```

If you want to include the code in your published projects, you should customize the URL by having it point to your domain name. You also need to modify the number, such as (0028), to match the number of characters in your domain name starting with the h in http and ending with the last letter of your domain name, as with the m of .com in the following example:

```
<!-- saved from url=(0028)http://www.
          yourdomainURL.com -->
```

If you don't want to include the code in your published projects, you can easily remove the code through Dreamweaver.

To remove the Mark of the Web code, do one of the following:

✔ Select and delete the code directly from Code view

✔ Choose Commands⇨Remove Mark of the Web

Note: This command is compatible with the Windows versions of Dreamweaver MX, Dreamweaver MX 2004, and Dreamweaver 8.

To find out more about this feature, see the TeachNote 19578 on the Macromedia Web site at www.macromedia.com/go/19578.

Dreamweaver calculates the file size of an open document by counting up the K (kilobytes) of all text and linked objects, such as images and Flash movies, and then provides a download time estimate based on the default connection speed (kilobits per second, or Kbps) you've entered in the Status Bar preferences. You can use this information to determine whether to modify the page to improve its load time.

The average time visitors connecting at 56Kbps are willing to wait for a page to display without feedback is eight seconds. Thus, your goal should be to get all your pages up and working in less than eight seconds. If your page weighs in at higher than 30K, you may want to consider reducing the number of objects or assets on the page (for example, using CSS rollovers instead of graphic rollovers).

By default, the connection speed in the Status Bar preferences is set to 56K, but you can change this setting to another speed. For example, when designing a site for an intranet on a T-1 (1500Kbps speed) circuit, you can change the preference to 1500 kilobits per second. Believe it or not, Macromedia reports that the average connection speed in the United States is still only 28.8K! Therefore, you may want to edit the connection speed to display download time and size for 28.8 kilobits per second.

To set the download time and size preferences, follow these steps:

1. **Choose Edit⇨Preferences (Windows) or Dreamweaver⇨Preferences (Mac).**

   The Preferences dialog box opens.

2. **Click the Status Bar category on the left side of the dialog box.**

   Status Bar preference options appear on the right side of the dialog box, as shown in Figure 1-2.

Figure 1-2:
Choose a connection speed in the Status Bar preferences.

3. **Select a connection speed from the Connection Speed drop-down list at the bottom of the dialog box.**

   Dreamweaver uses the speed you select to calculate the download time of your page.

Examining the Results Panel

Dreamweaver reports enable you to quickly find, test, and fix the content on your Web pages from one convenient location: the Results panel. To view the Results panel, choose Window⇨Results or press F7.

The Results panel, shown in Figure 1-3, has several tabs that provide access to the following report types:

✦ **Search:** Search your code for your tags and attributes.

✦ **Validation:** Validate your code.

✦ **Target Browser Check:** Test your page with a targeted browser.

✦ **Link Checker:** Check and fix links.

✦ **Site Reports:** Run Workflow and HTML reports.

✦ **FTP Log:** View file transfer activity.

✦ **Server Debug:** Debug a ColdFusion application.

A green Play icon (a triangular icon reminiscent of a Play button in a media player) appears in every tab view. Clicking the Play icon launches the reports related to the active tab.

The following sections discuss how you can use the Results panel to view reports and fix problems throughout your site.

Searching Your Code for Tags and Attributes

If any of the reports identify problems in your code, you may want to globally change those problems throughout your entire Web site. You can use the Search tab of the Results panel to open Dreamweaver's Find and Replace dialog box. The Find and Replace tool enables you to search for specific text, tags, and attributes in text or source code on a document, selected files, a specific folder, or all the files inside a defined site. Once found, you can replace that text, tag, code, or content with new information.

Stop

Play

Figure 1-3:
The Results
panel.

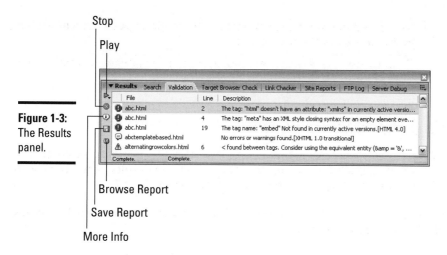

Browse Report

Save Report

More Info

Turn to Book II, Chapter 2 to find out how to search for specific tags and
attributes, search for text in specific tags, save and reuse search strings, and
search using regular expressions.

Validating Your Code

The Validation panel checks HTML or XHTML code in the current document,
entire current local site, or selected files in the site for tag, syntax, and other
common formatting errors in many languages such as HTML, XHTML,
JavaServer Pages (JSP), ColdFusion Markup Language (CFML), XML, and
Wireless Markup Language (WML). It then displays the results in the
Validation panel (see Figure 1-4).

Running the Validation panel

To validate your tags, follow these steps:

1. **On the Validation tab of the Results panel, click the green Validate
    button (looks like a play button) and select a validation option from
    the menu.**

    You can choose to validate the current page only, the entire local site, or
    selected files (from the Files panel) on the site.

    You can also validate code for a single page by choosing File⇨Check
    Page⇨Validate markup. If your page uses XHTML or XML, however,
    choose File⇨Check Page⇨Validate as XML instead.

The validation results display on the Validation tab of the Results panel and includes messages about errors and warnings as well as a list of all the syntax and tag errors Dreamweaver detected (see Figure 1-4).

Results display as errors, warnings, or messages. See the "Testing Your Pages with Target Browser Check" section later in this chapter for details about each of these result types.

If the report finds no code errors, Dreamweaver displays a `No errors or warning` message. Congratulations!

Figure 1-4:
The
Validation
panel.

File	Line	Description
layers.html	90	The tag name: "ilayer" Not found in currently active versions.[XHTML 1.0 tra...
layers.html	96	Quotation mark found between tags, HTML documents should not contain th...
layers.html	96	Quotation mark found between tags, HTML documents should not contain th...

Complete.   Complete.

2. **To fix an error, warning, or message in the results listing, double-click the error, warning, or message in the list.**

The document with the error opens in the Document window and the error is highlighted, ready for you to fix it. If you want, you can correct these changes directly in the document code, and rerun the validation report to ensure the changes are compliant.

To find out more about any of the errors in the list, right-click (Windows) or Control+click (Mac) the error message in the list and select More Info from the context menu. The complete error message appears in its own pop-up window. This feature works for all results listed in the Validation, Target Browser Check, and Site Reports tabs of the Results panel.

3. **(Optional) Click the Save Report button to save the report as an XML file.**

The Save Report button looks like a disk and can be found on the left edge of the Results panel (refer to Figure 1-3).

4. **Click the Browse Report button to see and print the report from a browser window.**

The Browse Report button looks like a tiny picture of the earth and can be found on the left edge of the Results panel (refer to Figure 1-3).

Setting Validator preferences

The Validator not only quickly finds syntax problems in your code, but you can also customize it in Dreamweaver's Preferences to check for specific tag-based languages or problems in the code. Remember, however, that these preferences settings are ignored if your file contains a specific doctype.

To set Dreamweaver's Validator preferences, follow these steps:

1. **Choose Edit⇨Preferences (Windows) or Dreamweaver⇨Preferences (Mac) to open the Preferences dialog box.**

2. **Choose the Validator category to view the Validator preferences (see Figure 1-5).**

Figure 1-5:
Customize
the
Validator
preferences.

3. **Select a doctype for Dreamweaver to validate against when no doctype is specified in the file.**

You can select only one doctype at a time. For example, you can select XHTML 1.0 Transitional, but not also HTML 4.0.

4. **Click the Options button to set specific validator options.**

The Display options enable you to set the type of errors or warnings included in the Results panel. By default, all options are selected and are universal for all doctypes.

You can also have the Validator check for quotes or entries in text. Both options are selected by default. Leaving the Quotes in Text option enabled tells Dreamweaver to include warnings about quotation marks in the document text. You should use the " entity instead. Leaving the Entities in Text option enabled tells Dreamweaver to find certain characters in the text and convert them to their entity equivalents, such as & instead of &.

5. **Click OK to close the Validator Options box, and click OK again to close the Preferences dialog box.**

   Changes to the Validator Preferences go into effect immediately, but you can modify them at any time.

Testing Your Pages with Target Browser Check

The Target Browser Check tests your HTML files for any tags or attributes that are deprecated (such as <b>, <i>, <center>, or <font>) or are unsupported by the target browsers on your computer (such as the height attribute of the <table> tag in Firefox 1.0, Netscape Navigator 7.0, Netscape Navigator 8.0, Safari 1.0, and Safari 2.0). This is much different than simply previewing your page in a browser, as described earlier in this chapter, which only shows you how the page would look in a particular browser.

You can run the Target Browser Check report on the current document, the entire local site, or selected files (from the Files panel) of a site. After making corrections to the files on your site, you can run the report again to ensure your changes haven't caused any other browser issues.

Before you run the Target Browser Check report, set the target browsers for the report, as described in the next section, so error results are returned for the browsers you want.

Setting the target browsers for the Target Browser Check

You can target several browsers for the Target Browser Check to test code against, regardless of whether you have all the browsers installed on your computer. For example, if you're working on a PC platform, you can still test for Internet Explorer 5.2 on a Mac.

To set the target browsers for the Target Browser Check, follow these steps:

1. **Open the Results panel, click the Check Target Browsers tab and press the green Check Target Browsers button and select Settings.**

   The Target Browsers dialog box appears, as shown in Figure 1-6.

Figure 1-6:
Choose
several
browsers
and
browser
versions in
the Target
Browsers
dialog box.

2. **Add a check mark next to each browser against which you want to verify code in the Target Browser Check report.**

3. **Next to each selected browser, choose a minimum browser version against which you want to verify the code.**

   For example, to verify code against Safari, put a check mark next to Safari and choose either 1.0 or 2.0 as the browser version.

   At a minimum, you should consider checking Internet Explorer 5.0, Netscape 6.0, Safari 1.0, and Firefox 1.0.

   For the latest information about trends in browser usage, operating systems, and screen resolution, visit the w3schools.com Web site at www.w3schools.com/browsers/browsers_stats.asp.

4. **When you finish, click OK to close the dialog box and save your changes.**

   Once set, these browsers are included in the Target Browser Check report results.

Using the Target Browser Check panel

To run a Target Browser Check report, follow these steps:

1. **Open the Results panel, click the Check Target Browsers tab, and click the green Check Target Browsers button to select the Check Target Browsers For option for this report.**

   You can run this report against the code in the current document, the entire local site, or selected files in the site.

2. **The report runs and returns the results in the Results panel.**

   If the report takes a long time to generate and you want to stop it before it's complete, click the Cancel icon, which appears on the left edge of the Target Browser Check panel.

The Target Browser Check report defines three levels of problems: *errors, warnings,* and *informational messages,* each easily identifiable by an icon next to the filename that contains the potential problem, as shown in Figure 1-7.

✦ **Errors:** These messages, displayed with a red polygon and a white exclamation mark, identify code problems that may cause display issues in a particular browser or issues with unsupported tags that may potentially cause an unknown problem. A typical error alert about the `id` attribute looks like this: `The id attribute of the Object tag is not supported. [Netscape Navigator 6.0].`

✦ **Warnings:** Code identified with a yellow triangle and a white exclamation mark is a warning. This code won't display correctly in a specified browser, but it probably won't cause additional or serious display issues. The following message about the `<object>` tag is a typical warning: `The title attribute of the OBJECT tag is not supported. [Safari 1.0, Safari 2.0].`

✦ **Messages:** A particular browser doesn't support code identified with an informational message (a white word balloon). But it probably doesn't have any visible effect altering the display of the page in the browser. The message is an FYI and not anything you have to worry about or respond to. For example, ignored tag attributes such as this `<html xmlns="http://www.w3.org/1999/xhtml">` HTML tag give rise to a benign `The xmlns attribute of the HTML tag is not supported, but it has no detrimental effect. [Netscape Navigator 6.0, Netscape Navigator 7.0]` informational message.

Informational messages

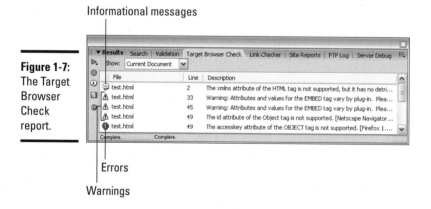

Figure 1-7:
The Target Browser Check report.

Errors

Warnings

You can perform other tasks in the Target Browser Check panel, including the following:

✦ **View long error messages:** Longer error messages may be truncated in the Results panel. To see the complete long error messages, click the More Info button on the left side of the panel. A Description dialog box appears showing the full error message and the browsers and browser versions that don't support the code.

✦ **Jump to code:** Double-click the error message in the Results panel. Problematic code is highlighted in the open file in Code view. This trick helps speed up the correction process!

✦ **Jump to next or previous error:** Click Next Error or Previous Error from the Target Browser Check menu on the Document toolbar. This is just another useful way to jump directly to any code that may be problematic and speeds up the process of fixing any errors in the code by hand.

✦ **Fix errors:** Make changes directly in Code view or in the Target Browser Check panel. You can find out how to fix errors in the next section, "Viewing and fixing errors."

✦ **Toggle between document and site report views:** Select Current Document or Site Report from the Show menu at the top of the Target Browser Check panel.

✦ **Save a Report:** Click the Save Report button on the left edge of the panel and save the report in the location of your choice with the `.doc`, `.txt`. or `.html` file extension.

✦ **View a report in a browser:** To see a copy of the report in a browser, click the Browse Report button on the left edge of the panel.

✦ **Ignore specific errors:** Right-click (Windows) or Control+click (Mac) any of the red underlined tags or attributes in Code view and select Ignore Error from the context menu. The errors you ignore are converted into warnings. From then on, Dreamweaver stops displaying that error type with the red wavy underline in Code view for all documents.

✦ **Edit the Ignored Errors list:** Choose Edit Ignored Errors List from the context menu in the Target Browser Check panel. The `Exceptions.xml` file opens, and you can manually make changes to the exceptions listing.

Viewing and fixing errors

You can easily see the errors in the code of a document identified in the results of a Target Browser Check. Double-click any of the errors in the results listing to open that document in the Dreamweaver workspace in Code or Split view; anywhere you see a wavy red underline in the code is where Dreamweaver has identified potentially problematic code that may cause an error in one or more of your specified the target browsers. If Dreamweaver doesn't identify any errors, you don't see any wavy red underlines in the code; instead, you see the No Errors button on the Document toolbar to the right of the Title text box where the Target Browser Check button displayed before.

You need to analyze errors in Code view to find out the best way to resolve them. Here are some tips:

✦ **Hover the cursor over red-underlined code:** To find out which target browsers don't support a particular red underlined tag or attribute in the code, hover the cursor over any of the red underlined code in Code view. An error tip appears, displaying relevant error information, including browser and version types.

✦ **Right-click (Windows) or Control+click (Mac) red-underlined code:** In Code view, you can access other target browser check commands by right-clicking (Windows) or Control+clicking (Mac) any of the red underlined tags or attributes in the code. Select an option from the context-sensitive menu that appears. For example, to see a report for the entire open document, select Show All Errors from the context-sensitive menu. The Results panel displays errors, warnings, and messages.

Only target browser errors, and not warnings and messages, display in Code view of an open file. Therefore, if you want to see all potential code issues, including the warnings and information messages, run a manual check on the entire document or site and review the results in the Results panel.

If you want, you can disable the automatic document verification feature by deselecting the Auto-Check On Open option from the Target Browser Check menu on the Document toolbar.

The Target Browser Check report doesn't check the accuracy of any scripts contained in the code or validate your syntax. It evaluates any markup that specified target browsers may not support by using an editable text file called `browser profiles` that specifies which tags particular browsers support. For information about editing the text file, to change the existing browser profile, or add a new profile, visit the Macromedia Support Center and look for a "Customizing Dreamweaver" heading. You can find the Support Center at `www.macromedia.com/go/dreamweaver_support`.

Checking and Fixing Links

The Link Checker panel identifies broken internal, external, and broken links on your pages. *Broken links* are often associated with the wrong filename or contain typos, and *orphaned files* are files on a defined site that are not being linked to on the site and can be safely removed from the site listing. However, because Dreamweaver only verifies local files within a defined site, it displays — but can't verify — *external links*.

The Link Checker panel is accessible from the Results panel. Simply select the Link Checker tab in the Results panel.

By identifying and listing all the links in one location, you can quickly verify them and make manual corrections as needed. In fact, you can fix all these links right in the Link Checker panel by selecting and editing the links listed by the report or by opening the files in question and fixing the errors on the page in Code view or with the Properties inspector.

To run a report to identify broken links, orphaned files, and external links, follow these steps:

1. **Open the Results panel, click the Link Checker tab, and press the green Check Links button to select a Check Links option for this report.**

You can run this report against the code in the current document, the entire local site, or selected files in the site.

The Results panel lists the results.

2. **Select a report results type from the Show menu to view the results of each report in the Link Checker panel.**

Your options include Broken Links, External Links, or Orphaned Files.

To fix broken links, follow Steps 3 through 7.

External links are listed for your information, but you can't test them through the panel. To test these links for accuracy you must launch the page in a browser and click the link by hand. You can, however, modify spelling errors in external links in the Link Checker panel.

You can safely delete orphaned files from the Link Checker panel or by selecting and deleting files from the Files panel. Deleting an orphaned file permanently removes the file from your computer. If you think you may need the orphaned file sometime in the future, however, make a backup of the site before deleting the orphans or simply move the orphaned files to a location outside the managed site.

3. **To fix a broken link, select Broken Links from the Show menu in the Link Checker panel and select a broken link from the results list under the Broken Links column (see Figure 1-8).**

Figure 1-8:
Select a broken link to correct it in the Link Checker panel.

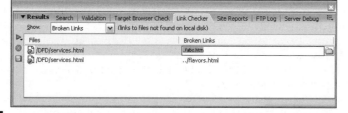

A folder button appears to the right of the selected link.

4. **Click the folder button to browse to and select a new file to update the link, or type the correct URL or filename over the existing broken link information.**

   To correct a broken link with the Properties inspector, open the file by double-clicking the link's source page from the Files column of the Results listing. The broken link in the opened file is highlighted in Design view and Code view, and the broken link displays in the Link field in the Properties inspector. Correct the link in the Properties inspector, and save and close the file. To verify the broken link is now correct, rerun the Link Check report.

   When fixing a broken link to an image from within the document the image is contained in, be sure to click the Refresh button next to the image W and H labels in the Properties inspector so the corrected image uses its actual size, rather than the old image width and height dimensions. The W and H labels are displayed as bold characters when the new image dimensions need refreshing and as normal type when the W and H dimensions match the selected image.

5. **Press Enter (Windows) or Return (Mac) to accept the new link.**

   When multiple instances of the same broken link appear throughout the list, Dreamweaver asks whether you want to apply the same change to the other instances. Click Yes to update all instances or No to update only the current instance.

   If you've enabled the Check In/Check Out system, you need to check out the files before modifying them. If Dreamweaver can't locate any particular file associated with a broken link, a warning message indicates that the file was not found. Any broken links associated with the missing file remain broken.

6. **Repeat Steps 3 through 5 for each broken link.**

7. **Click the Save Report button on the left side of the panel to save a copy of the report.**

   You can also choose Options⇨Save Results. Save your reports with the .doc, .txt, or .html file extension.

When you fix links by following these steps, the links are automatically removed from the Results list on the Link Checker panel. If you fix a link but it still appears in the list, Dreamweaver didn't recognize your corrections. Perhaps the new filename you've added is wrong. Try fixing the link from the Reports panel, saving the open file, and rerunning the Link Check report.

Handling Workflow and HTML Reports

The Site Reports panel provides quick access to the Reports dialog box, from which you can select and run a variety of Workflow and HTML reports. Consider using these reports to begin your site clean up prior to site launch.

Launching reports

The Workflow reports are great if you're working on a major site with a group of people. The sole function of the reports is to help team members work together more effectively. As long as you've defined a remote site connection in the managed site, these reports can provide important statistics on Design Notes, file modification dates, and file checkout status. For example, you can run a report to see which team members have files checked out or which files contain Design Notes. The Design Notes report can even contain specific name and value parameters, such as `Author=Sue`, for more specific search results. (Design Notes are described in detail in Book VI, Chapter 1.)

The HTML reports are a must for all Web sites, big and small. These reports identify problems in your code that could bloat file sizes, cause slower page viewing times, and even prevent your pages from displaying properly. HTML reports include data about missing Alt text, removable empty tags, untitled documents, nested font tags that can be combined, redundant nested tags, and accessibility issues.

You can run both Workflow and HTML reports simultaneously through the Reports dialog box; follow these steps:

***1.* Choose Site⇨Reports.**

The Reports dialog box opens, as shown in Figure 1-9.

Figure 1-9:
Select
individual
Workflow
and HTML
Reports
from the
Reports
dialog box.

To run an accessibility-only report, choose File⇨Check Page⇨Check Accessibility. The accessibility report results appear on the Site Reports tab of the Results panel.

2. **Choose an option from the Report On drop-down list.**

   Choose the option that matches your specific needs. For example, if you want to check just the current page, select Current Document; to check the whole site, choose Entire Current Local Site; if you want to check some, but not all, the pages on the site, choose Selected Files in Site or Folder.

3. **Select categories from the Workflow options:**

   • **Checked Out By:** This option generates a report of all files checked out by a specific person.

   • **Design Notes:** This report creates a list of Design Notes for either a set of selected files or the entire Web site.

   • **Recently Modified:** This option makes a list of files that have been created or modified within a specific number of days or within a chosen range of dates.

4. **Click the Report Settings button.**

   When you enable any of the Workflow reports, you should also select each report and click the Report Settings button at the bottom of the dialog box to choose customized options for each specific report. For example, to search for all the files checked out by Lee, select the Checked Out By category, click the Report Settings button, and type the name **Lee** in the Checked Out By dialog box.

   • **Checked Out By:** Enter the name of the team member this report searches for, such as **Jane Smith**.

   • **Design Notes:** Enter names and value pairs and choose comparison values from the corresponding menus, such as **status is draft**.

   • **Recently Modified:** Enter data for the report to search for files that were created or modified within a specific number of days or a range of dates, as in **Files Created or Modified in the Last 7 Days**.

5. **Select categories from the HTML Reports options:**

   • **Combinable Nested Font Tags:** This report option shows a list of any nested font tags that could be combined to make the code cleaner. For example, `<font size="5"><font color="#CC0000">big red text</font></font>` would be cleaned up as `<font size="5" color="#CC0000">big red text</font>`.

   • **Accessibility:** This option creates a report listing any code that does not comply with the Section 508 accessibility guidelines of the 1998 Rehabilitation Act.

- **Missing Alt Text:** Select this option to show a list of all `<img>` tags missing alternate text attributes. This attribute displays in browsers that are set to download image files manually or in place of images in text-only browsers, and to be read by screen reader software.

- **Redundant Nested Tags:** This setting lists any redundant tags that could be removed for cleaner code. For example, in the sentence `<b>Monkeys like to eat <b>bananas</b> and cake.</b>`, the `<b>` tags surrounding the word `bananas` are redundant.

- **Removable Empty Tags:** Choose this option to see a list of tags without content inside of them, as in `<span></span>` or `<font size="1"></font>`, but not `<i>kitten</i>`.

- **Untitled Documents:** Choose this option to find any untitled documents on your site as well as files with default, missing, or duplicate title tags.

6. **Click the Run button to generate the report.**

   Some report options may require that you save any unsaved open files or choose a specific folder or site prior to displaying report results. The results themselves display on the Site Reports tab of the Results panel (see Figure 1-10).

Figure 1-10:
Site reports results are listed in the Site Reports area of the Results panel.

Saving reports as XML files

You can save your report results as an XML file for later importing to a database, spreadsheet, or template instance for printing or for display in a browser window. Because report data is essentially temporary information that reflects the current state of a document, folder, site, or selected files, saving report results may be very useful if your company or client's company likes to archive the report data.

To save and use a report, follow these steps:

1. **Run your report.**

2. **Before saving the report, you can view code, sort, or review report data by any of the following methods:**

   - **View Code:** To view and edit any code in a document listed in the report, double-click a line in the report to open the document in the Document window. The document opens in either Code or Split view.

   - **Sort:** To sort report data, click the column heading above the category. You can sort by filename, description, or line number.

   - **Review:** To review a description of any of the problems listed on the report, select a line in the report and click the More Info button, which appears on the left edge of the panel. The description information displays in the Reference panel.

3. **Click the Save Report button.**

   The Save As dialog box appears. The default filename for your saved report is ResultsReport.xml. You can change the filename to anything you like, as long as you keep the file type as XML.

   When you finish reviewing report data, choose Commands➪Clean Up HTML/XHTML to automatically fix the HTML errors.

Viewing File Transfer Activity with the FTP Log

The FTP Log panel displays FTP file transfer activity for all the times you use the Get, Put, Check In, and Check Out commands in the Files panel. This log activity is very helpful when you're troubleshooting connection errors or documenting transfer process information.

To save FTP log information, select all the content in the FTP Log panel; right-click (Windows) or Control+click (Mac) and choose the Select All option. Then copy and paste the data into another file, such as a Microsoft Word document, a text file, or HTML file.

Debugging a ColdFusion Application (Windows)

Choose the Server Debug panel to see helpful information that can assist you with debugging a ColdFusion application in Windows without having to exit Dreamweaver.

If you don't see any data in this panel, you must first assign a testing server to the site definition to specify where to process dynamic pages. The testing server can be your local machine, or a staging, development, or production server. To set the testing server, open the Site Definition dialog box for the defined site, click the Advanced tab, and choose the Testing Server category. From there, you can enter the necessary information to identify the testing server. For more information on setting up a testing server, see Book VII, Chapter 1.

If you work on a Mac, press ⌘+F12 to open any ColdFusion pages in a separate browser window. From there, you can find errors at the bottom of the page.

Before beginning the debugging process, you may need to enable certain features in ColdFusion Administrator. For example, when using ColdFusion MX 7.0 and above, Dreamweaver automatically enables debugging, but if you're running ColdFusion MX 6.1 or earlier, you must enable debugging settings manually. See Dreamweaver's ColdFusion documentation for assistance with these settings by choosing Help➪Using ColdFusion.

If you're testing your pages in Internet Explorer, consider enabling Internet Explorer to refresh page data each time the page displays so that the browser displays the most recent data available. In Internet Explorer, choose Tools➪ Internet Options and click the General tab. Click the Settings button in the Temporary Internet Files area. The Settings dialog box appears, where you select the Every Visit to Page option.

To run the Server Debug report on a ColdFusion page, follow these steps:

1. **Open the ColdFusion page in the Document window.**

2. **Click the Preview/Server Debug in Browser button on the Document toolbar.**

The page is requested from the ColdFusion server and appears on an internal Internet Explorer browser. Any errors and their possible causes appear at the bottom of the page.

At the same time, the Server Debug panel also displays information to assist with the debugging process. For example, the report may list SQL queries, server variables, and an execution time summary.

3. **To expand the Exceptions category on the Server Debug panel, if one appears, click the plus (+) button.**

The Exceptions category appears only when the server finds problems with the page. Expanding the category reveals a more detailed list of information about each problem.

4. **To fix any problems listed in the Location column of the Server Debug panel, click the page URL to open the page.**

The page opens and the code in question is highlighted in Code view so that you can edit it. You may be prompted to locate the document on your own if Dreamweaver can't automatically locate it for you.

5. **Fix errors and save the files to the server; then click the Preview/Server Debug in Browser button again.**

   The browser gathers the latest information from your page and the server and renders the page again in an internal browser. The Server Debug panel also updates to show you any remaining or new potential problems. After all the problems are addressed, the Exceptions category disappears from the panel.

6. **Exit the debugging mode by choosing View⇨Design or View⇨Code.**

Chapter 2: Keeping Your Code Clean

In This Chapter

✔ **Changing code preferences**

✔ **Removing irrelevant code with the Clean Up Word HTML/XHTML command**

✔ **Applying source formatting to your pages**

✔ **Running a spell check**

✔ **Updating links sitewide**

*W*henever you build and edit Web pages in Dreamweaver — especially if you're hand-coding or pasting content — some of the markup may get crowded with redundant elements and unnecessary or unwanted code. You need to remove those extra bits of code from all the pages on the site whether you do that in advance (by setting preferences), during page creation (by selecting paste and import options), or as a final code cleanup (with Dreamweaver's HTML/XHTML Clean Up, spell check, and other code reporting tools) when the site is complete.

Why? Actually, for a few reasons. For one thing, that extra code adds to the overall file size that can impact page-loading times in a browser. For another thing, badly formatted code may confuse some browsers, causing the information on your pages to display less accurately than you intended. Even more important perhaps is the fact that some code errors can prevent browsers from displaying the HTML or XHTML entirely. If these issues aren't enough to convince you to clean up your code before publishing, you've been warned. At least think about keeping your code as clean and error free as possible as a reflection of your professionalism. After all, anyone can look at your Web site code by simply doing a View Source.

So how do you go about cleaning up your Web site code without having to review the code in each file, line by line? Fortunately, the answer can be as simple as running a few quick commands in Dreamweaver. First, set up some of Dreamweaver's preferences to avoid some of the issues in advance. If you've already created your site, you should still set up Dreamweaver's preferences so any new documents you create use these settings.

After Dreamweaver's preferences are set, you should perform the following tasks, in roughly the following order, to make sure that your code is error free and clear of miscellaneous junk: Run Dreamweaver's spell checker, use the appropriate commands to remove unnecessary code pasted from other programs, apply source formatting to your pages if it's missing, and, finally change links across the site.

Eliminating Formatting Issues Before They Occur

The developers at Dreamweaver understand that previously applied formatting can be a killer to your code. Imagine this scenario: You're designing a new site. Your client, who is very eager to "help" you, sends you a bunch of content for the Web as text documents created with a program like Microsoft Word. (Alternatively, the file could come from other word processor software or as Microsoft HTML files.) No matter how the files start out, if they're filled with a lot of fancy formatting (from italics to complicated styles) and structural additions (such as automatic bullet lists and tables), you need to transform them *before* you put them into Dreamweaver.

Although the text may start out well formatted and well organized in the original client-provided file, the second you copy and paste the content into Dreamweaver without first setting Dreamweaver's Copy/Paste preferences, some of the formatting data may get translated into inline HTML formatting tags and be included with the text along the way. For example, a styled sentence pasted from Microsoft Word might look something like this:

```
<p><strong><span style="font-family:'Comic Sans MS'; font-size:20pt;
    color:#3366FF; ">Let's all do the Scrambled-Egg Dance</span></strong></p>
```

You can — and probably should — replace most of that Word-generated HTML formatting code with CSS formatting markup. In addition to creating and applying a style sheet, you need to remove the HTML formatting code from the page, either by hand or using the Find and Replace tool. When you remove everything that could end up being a problem (the Word-generated HTML formatting), your sentence looks more like this:

```
<p><strong>Let's all do the Scrambled-Egg Dance</strong></p>
```

Ultimately, the best defense against bad code is a good offensive strategy. The following sections list some preferences and settings that you can put into place before you even start building a site. If you use these tools now, getting your pages cleaned up before publishing is that much easier.

Setting Copy and Paste preferences

To help solve some of this transfer of undesired code, Dreamweaver 8 allows you to set Copy/Paste preferences for pasted data from Microsoft Word and other word processing programs. To change the Copy/Paste preferences, follow these steps:

1. **Choose Edit⇨Preferences (Windows) or Dreamweaver⇨Preferences (Mac).**

The Preferences dialog box opens.

2. **Select the Copy/Paste category on the left.**

On the right side of the dialog box you see some Copy/Paste options (see Figure 2-1):

- **Text only:** Not surprisingly, this option is the simplest and gives you the greatest control.

- **Text with Structure:** Dreamweaver's definition of *structure* is any formatting that affects the overall appearance of paragraphs, lists, or tables. It's not concerned with individual font formatting.

- **Text with Structure Plus Basic Formatting:** Dreamweaver's definition of *basic formatting* is stuff like **boldface,** *italics,* and underlining.

- **Text with Structure Plus Full Formatting:** Dreamweaver defines *full formatting* as formatting that affects not just the basics but also individual styles.

- **Retain Line Breaks:** This option keeps any line breaks from the source when the content is pasted.

- **Clean Up Word Paragraph Spacing:** Use this option to remove extra space between paragraphs when content is pasted.

Figure 2-1:
Set your
Copy/Paste
preferences
to auto-
matically
remove
unwanted
markup
from copied
text.

TIP

If you're unsure which options to select, choose Text with Structure Plus Basic Formatting with both Retain Line Breaks and Clean Up Word Paragraph Spacing enabled. Basic formatting tags like `<strong>` and `<em>` are more effective markup for accessibility than creating styles that use bold and italic, as screen readers modify intonation for content inside these tags.

3. Click OK to close the Preferences dialog box.

New preference settings take effect immediately. You can always come back and modify these preferences later, should the need arise.

Using the Paste Special command

The *Paste Special* command enables you to control how much (and what kind of) formatting is moved from the original file to your Dreamweaver file each time you perform a paste.

When you use the regular Paste option for copied content, your paste includes all the formatting contained in the source content. However, when you copy a list of items from a Word document that's been formatted with a special font, font color, font size, bold and italics, and alignment and want to paste it into your Dreamweaver file *without* the font but yet retaining the list structure, bold, and italic settings, use the Paste Special option.

When you use Edit⇨Paste Special instead of the regular Paste command, the Paste Special dialog box, shown in Figure 2-2, opens so you can select a Paste preference for the copied content you're about to paste. The options in the dialog box are the same choices in the Preferences dialog box (refer to the previous section, "Setting Copy and Paste preferences," for information about your options). The default setting in the Paste Special dialog box matches the setting you choose in the Copy/Paste preferences, but you can override that default option on a case by case basis using the Paste Special command.

Figure 2-2:
Select Paste
Preferences
from the
Paste
Special
dialog box.

Cleaning Up Word HTML

Microsoft Word has a feature that enables users to convert documents into Microsoft HTML files that are viewable in a browser window. Not a bad option, really. Unfortunately, in versions of Word 97 and later, Microsoft adds extra markup for the purpose of displaying the content in a browser window and leaves in extra formatting data only necessary for the display of the page as a document. All this extra code adds to the overall file size and may affect the speed the page loads in a browser.

You can easily remove the extra markup (such as redundant or unnecessary nested tags, as well as Word-specific markup) with the Clean Up Word HTML command. Using this handy tool is a good way to keep file sizes as small as possible, and cleaning up the code is essential if you plan on using style sheets.

As a precaution, always try to retain a backup copy of the original Word (.doc) and especially Word HTML (.html) files before performing the clean up, because the Word HTML file may not reopen in Word after the clean up.

Follow these steps to clean up an HTML file generated by Word 97 or later:

1. **Open the Microsoft HTML file in the Dreamweaver workspace window.**

To see the Microsoft markup in the code before it gets removed, switch to Code or Split view by choosing View⇨Code or View⇨Code and Design.

2. **Choose Commands⇨Clean Up Word HTML.**

The Clean Up Word HTML dialog box, shown in Figure 2-3, appears.

Figure 2-3:
Use the default settings in the Clean Up Word HTML dialog box for the best Word HTML cleanup results.

Dreamweaver attempts to auto-detect the version of Word the file was generated in. If the file version is undetectable, you can choose the proper version from the Clean Up HTML From drop-down list.

3. Select any cleanup options that you want.

The default settings are to have Dreamweaver check for and fix everything it possibly can.

We recommend that you keep the default settings on the Basic tab intact. These options are pretty crucial to stripping all the Microsoft markup from the document. If anything, you may want to tinker with the options even more (you can do so by clicking the Detailed tab):

- **Remove All Word Specific Markup:** This setting removes all Microsoft Word-specific HTML, metadata, and link tags, XML markup, and other style markup.

- **Clean Up CSS:** Use this setting to remove all Word-specific CSS, especially any inline styles that match parent styles in the markup. The options here also zap style attributes that start with `mso`, styles applied to table rows and cells, and any declarations that are not CSS.

- **Clean Up `<font>` Tags:** Choose this setting to remove HTML font tags and convert the entire body text to size 2 HTML text.

- **Fix Invalidly Nested Tags:** This option deletes font markup tags that Word inserted outside heading and paragraph (block-level) tags.

- **Set Background Color:** Select a hexadecimal color to use as the background color for the page. When a background color is not specified for the page, the default color is gray. Dreamweaver automatically suggests you set the default color to the hexadecimal value for white, though you may enter another color value here instead.

An even better option, however, is to deselect this option and add a background color to your pages with CSS.

- **Apply Source Formatting:** This option applies the source formatting options you chose in the `SourceFormat.txt` file and the Code Format category of Dreamweaver's Preferences to the page. For more on this feature, see the "Introducing your Code Category preferences" and "Applying Source Formatting" sections later in this chapter.

- **Show Log On Completion:** Select this option to view a log of changes performed during the clean up. Definitely turn this feature on so you can see how much Dreamweaver has improved the file!

4. Click OK.

Dreamweaver performs the clean up with the selected settings.

Checking Your Spelling, Grammar, and Readability

When it comes time to proofread your copy for spelling and grammatical errors, much of the responsibility sits with you. Although Dreamweaver offers a spell checking feature, you have to remember to run the spell check prior to publishing your Web site. And, although the spell checker may catch some of your spelling errors, it won't alert you to poorly chosen words, *homophones* (words that sound the same but have vastly different meanings, such as *sight* and *site*), words used out of context, or other common grammatical errors that can have an impact on meaning (such as *it's* instead of *its*).

REMEMBER

The best way to make sure that everything makes sense is to use your eyes. No mechanical tool can substitute for taking the time to read (and reread) your site content. In fact, you should have at least two other people assist you in checking your site for spelling, grammar, and readability.

Before you recruit your coworkers, friends, clients, and family members to join in on the spell checking fun, use the Dreamweaver Check Spelling command, which isolates common spelling errors in text while ignoring HTML tags and attribute values in the code.

Follow these steps to check and correct spelling:

1. **In Dreamweaver, open the document to be spell checked.**

2. **Choose Text⊅Check Spelling or press Shift+F7.**

The Check Spelling dialog box, shown in Figure 2-4, appears if Dreamweaver finds a word or words that are not recognized. If Dreamweaver finds no errors, you may see a recommendation that you begin a new spell check from the start of the document. Otherwise, you're presented with a Spelling Check Completed alert box.

Figure 2-4:
Use the Check Spelling dialog box to ignore or change unrecognized words.

3. Choose an option to handle each unrecognized word:

- **Ignore** ignores the current instance of an unrecognized word.

- **Ignore All** ignores all instances of an unrecognized word.

- **Change** replaces the unrecognized word with a selected suggestion or text typed in the Change To text box.

- **Change All** replaces all instances of the unrecognized word with the selected suggestion or text typed in the Change To text box.

- **Add to Personal** adds the unrecognized word to the personal dictionary, which appends the default or substitute language dictionary.

If you accidentally click Ignore All or Select All for the wrong thing, errors can occur where previously there were none. Checking each found item on an individual basis is always a good idea.

The Dreamweaver spell checker uses the U.S. English spelling dictionary by default, but you can choose other dictionaries from the Spelling Dictionary drop-down list in the General category of Dreamweaver's Preferences.

Getting Your HTML and XHTML Code Consistent

Most Web designers speak a few markup dialects, such as XHTML and HTML. Like most multilingual individuals, you may lapse into a hybrid language that (unfortunately) only you understand (we figure it's the markup equivalent of *Spanglish*). Or maybe you're translating something from HTML to XHTML. In either case, winding up with some inconsistent tags, unneeded comments, and redundant or unnecessary tags in your code sometimes happens to the best of us. To do general HTML cleanup work on your files, such as removing empty container or redundant nested tags, run the Clean Up HTML/XHTML command on any open document.

Dreamweaver auto-detects the doctype of the document open in the workspace window and displays the HTML or XHTML Clean Up command on the Commands menu to match the doctype it detects. For example, if the doctype is HTML, the Clean Up HTML command appears on the Commands menu; if the doctype is XHTML, the Clean Up XHTML command appears instead.

When your file uses XHTML markup instead of HTML, this command performs all the XHTML cleanup tasks, plus it instantly converts all the tag attributes to lowercase, fixes XHTML syntax errors, and adds or reports any required tag attributes that are missing, such as images with missing `<alt>` tags.

To clean up HTML/XHTML code, follow these steps:

1. **Open the document. For HTML documents, choose Commands➪Clean Up HTML. For XHTML documents, choose Commands➪Clean Up XHTML.**

The Clean Up HTML/XHTML dialog box opens, as shown in Figure 2-5.

Figure 2-5:
Choose
options to
clean up
your text
from the
Clean Up
HTML/
XHTML
dialog box.

2. **Choose any combination of cleanup options:**

- **Empty Container Tags:** This option removes tags without content inside of them, as in `<i></i>` or `<font size="2"></font>`, but not `<i>hello</i>`.

- **Redundant Nested Tags:** Clean up any redundant tags with this setting. For example, in the sentence `<b>Blue frogs hop on <b>green</b> lily pads.</b>`, the `<b>` tags surrounding the word green are redundant.

- **Non-Dreamweaver HTML Comments:** This option removes any comments in the code that Dreamweaver didn't automatically insert. For instance, a comment tag to define the beginning of image slices in the code like `<!-- ImageReady Slices (filename.psd) -->` or a comment tag from you to another member of your work group, like `<!-- Phil, insert the Peanut Data table here -->` would be removed, but code to identify a Dreamweaver-editable area like this `<!-- #BeginEditable "doctitle" -->` would not.

- **Dreamweaver Special Markup:** Use this option to remove the special markup tags that Dreamweaver uses to automatically update templates and library items. Removing this special markup detaches the document from its original source, as with a template-based file and its source template file.

- **Specific Tag(s):** To remove specific markup from the code, type the tag in the Specific Tag text box. To remove multiple tags at the same time, separate tags with commas, as in `span,font`.

- **Combine Nested <font> Tags When Possible:** This option combines any nested font tags when they could be joined to do the same task. For example, `<font size="2"><font color="#006699"> little blue Thomas train</font></font>` would be cleaned up as `<font size="2" color="#006699"> little blue Thomas train</font>`.

- **Show Log On Completion:** Check this box to have an alert box with details about the clean up display at the end of the clean up process. Leave this option enabled to see how much your file is improved.

3. Click OK to start the cleanup process.

If you left the Show Log On Completion check box enabled, a Clean Up Summary alert window opens when the cleanup process is finished, listing details about the clean up. You may see messages such as `XHTML syntax fixed` or `12 comment(s) removed`.

Reviewing Source Formatting and Making Changes

Dreamweaver has done a wonderful job coloring and organizing the coding environment to assist you with reviewing and editing your code. For instance, style information is color coded to differentiate between the style or selector name, the style property, value, and separators between them in the declaration, and the opening and closing style tags. And take a look at the code for any table on a page; the `<table>`, `<tr>`, and `<td>` tags are in one color (green), the values (like a color value of `#99CCFF`) for any properties in the table are in another color (blue), and any content placed inside a table cell is yet another color (black).

Dreamweaver provides the flexibility of allowing you to customize the coding preferences if you ever want to change them. That means, for example, if you're trying to isolate specific tags in the code, you could change the color of those tags.

In fact, you can set Dreamweaver preferences to specify code formatting, editing, coloring, viewing, and hinting options. All coding preferences apply to both new documents and new content on existing documents created in Dreamweaver.

Setting code formatting preferences

To customize your Dreamweaver coding environment, follow these steps:

1. **Choose Edit⇨Preferences (Windows) or Dreamweaver⇨Preferences.**

   The Dreamweaver Preferences dialog box appears.

2. **Choose a code category on the left and edit the preferences for that category as needed.**

   A description of each code category and its preferences settings is listed in the following section.

3. **Click OK to save the new settings.**

Introducing your Code Category preferences

Though it may appear you have more preferences than you know what to do with, take a quick look at the following options to see if you want to adjust anything to improve your coding environment:

✦ **Code Coloring:** Change the default code colors for different document types, which means you can use one set of colors for HTML code and another set of colors for PHP code. After you select a document type, click the Edit Coloring Scheme button. You can modify the code text and background colors, along with Bold, Italic, or Underline styles, for specific code elements such as form tags, JavaScript elements, CSS elements, and library items (see Figure 2-6). For example, if you wanted your image tags to stand out you'd select the HTML Image Tags style and change the text color, background color, and perhaps apply bold and underline, too.

Figure 2-6:
Edit the coloring scheme for different document types.

✦ **Code Format:** Set code formatting preferences such as default indent and tab size, default attribute and tag case, and centering tag options, as shown in Figure 2-7:

• **Indent:** This option indents Dreamweaver-generated code (though not for any code you hand-code) according to the number of spaces or tabs set in the With field and drop-down list.

• **Tab Size:** This option sets the character width of each tab character in Code view. For instance, if set to 5, each tab displays as a blank space equal to five characters wide. This measure also affects the indent size when you've selected Tabs from the With drop-down list.

• **Automatic Wrapping:** Enable this option to have the code automatically wrap in Code view, with the insertion of a line break character, when it reaches the number of characters set in the After Column field. This is different than the Wrap option, which virtually wraps the code when it reaches the edge of the window in Code view but doesn't actually add line break characters.

• **Line Break Type:** This preference identifies the type of remote server hosting your site. Choose Windows, Macintosh, or Unix to ensure the line breaks in your code appear correctly when viewed on the remote server. This option only applies to binary transfer mode when connected with FTP; the ASCII transfer mode is ignored. However, when downloading files in ASCII mode, the line breaks are automatically set to match the computer's OS, and when uploading in ASCII mode, the line breaks are automatically set to CR LF (Windows).

• **Default Tag Case/Default Attribute Case:** These two settings control whether your code uses uppercase or lowercase for tags and attributes in Design view. These settings have no control over editing in Code view or over existing document attributes, unless you select one or both of the Override Case Of options.

• **Override Case Of: Tags and Attributes:** Turn on one or both of these options to have Dreamweaver enforce the case rules set for the Default Tag Case and Default Attribute Case at all times. This automatically converts code in existing files as well as enforces case rules for content added to new files.

Because the Web is moving more toward XHTML compliance and XHTML requires lowercase letters for the coding of tags and attributes, it's best to set Default Tag Case and Default Attribute Case to lowercase and enable Override Case of settings for both tags and attributes.

• **Centering:** This feature allows you to choose whether to use the `<div align="center">` versus the `<center>` tag for centering elements on the page. Though both of these options are being deprecated as of HTML 4.01 in favor of using CSS for centering text, both options are still valid for XHTML 1.0 Transitional (but not XHTML 1.0 Strict) coding.

Figure 2-7:
Set Code
Format
preferences
for normal
coding and
use with the
Apply
Source
Formatting
command.

✦ **Code Hints:** Decide how Dreamweaver's code hint preferences display in
  Code view and in the Quick Tag Editor. Here are your options:

  • **Close Tags:** Choose to have Dreamweaver automatically insert clos-
    ing tags after typing "</", add closing tags after entering the opening
    tag's angle bracket (>), or never insert closing tags.

  • **Enable Code Hints:** Choose to see code hints when typing in Code
    view. Use the code hint delay slider to adjust the number of seconds
    to wait before the hints are shown.

  • **Menus:** Choose this option to select from a list of menus what kind of
    code hints display.

✦ **Code Rewriting:** Select how Dreamweaver rewrites or fixes invalid code.
  These settings can rewrite code when opening files, copying and pasting
  form data, and entering link URLs and attributes in Dreamweaver. They
  won't, however, change code when you're editing HTML or scripts in
  Code view. When you have this feature disabled, Dreamweaver shows
  the invalid markup for HTML that it would have rewritten in the
  Document window.

  • **Fix Invalidly Nested and Unclosed Tags:** This setting reorders improp-
    erly nested tags as well as inserting any missing quote marks or clos-
    ing brackets. For example, `<strong><em>Monkey!</strong></em>`
    would be rewritten as `<strong><em>Monkey!</em></strong>`, and
    `<div <img src="images/logo.gif"></div>` would be rewritten as
    `<div><img src="images/logo.gif"></div>`.

  • **Rename Form Items When Pasting:** When pasting elements from
    other documents, this default setting makes sure that the page has
    no form objects with the same name. For example, if one text field is
    named `textfield`, the next would be named `textfield2`, and so on.

- **Remove Extra Closing Tags:** This setting deletes any extra closing tags that don't have opening tag mates.

- **Warn When Fixing or Removing Tags:** Enable this setting to see a summary of invalid HTML markup that Dreamweaver couldn't fix. The summary identifies the source of the problem by using line and column numbers so that you can easily find and fix the error.

- **Never Rewrite Code: In Files with Extensions:** Enable or disable Dreamweaver from rewriting code in files with particular filename extensions, like `.css` or `.shtml`. This setting is particularly handy when adding third-party tags to your code.

The next four options do not apply to existing code or new URLs typed in Code view but do apply to all new coding added to documents in Design view and through the Properties inspector:

- **Encode <, >, &, and " in Attribute Values Using &:** Because attribute values entered or edited in Dreamweaver must have legal characters, the default setting makes sure that entered data conforms to those standards.

- **Do Not Encode Special Characters:** Stop Dreamweaver from adjusting URLs that use nonlegal characters.

- **Encode Special Characters in URL Using &#:** This setting makes sure that URLs use only legal characters by using special encoding.

- **Encode Special Characters in URL Using %:** Like the previous setting, this option makes sure that URLs have only legal characters, but uses a different encoding method for special characters. This option works well with older browsers, but doesn't work so well with some characters in other languages.

Applying Source Formatting

You can use the Code Format coding preferences listed in the previous section for the creation of new Dreamweaver files and additions to existing documents. You can't, however, use them on HTML files that you created before these preferences were set. To do that, you'd essentially be reformatting the old code. If you want to change the original code, therefore, you must *apply source formatting*. Applying source formatting means using the Code Format settings you customized in the previous section to reformat the code in an existing HTML file.

You can apply source formatting to an entire document or to a particular selection on a page.

Applying source formatting to a complete file

To apply source formatting to an existing file, follow these steps:

1. **Open the file in Dreamweaver.**

2. **Choose Commands⇨Apply Source Formatting.**

Dreamweaver immediately applies all existing and any new coding preferences to the page code.

3. **Save the file by choosing File⇨Save.**

Applying source formatting to a selection of a file

To apply source formatting to a selection of an existing file, follow these steps:

1. **Open the file in Dreamweaver and select the content in Design view that you want to modify with the new coding preferences.**

Selected content must be *contiguous* (touching). There is no option for selecting multiple, non-touching areas of your document. If you need to apply source formatting to several sections of a page, repeat these steps for each section.

2. **Choose Commands⇨Apply Source Formatting to Selection.**

Dreamweaver immediately applies any new coding preferences to the selected page code.

3. **Save the updated file by choosing File⇨Save.**

Changing Links Sitewide

In a managed site, whenever you rename or move a file, Dreamweaver offers to automatically update those links for you. You can also manually change links throughout your site at any time. (To discover more about links in general, see Book II, Chapter 4. To find out how to check and fix links with Dreamweaver's Check Links report, see Book V, Chapter 1.)

The Change Link Sitewide feature enables you to change individual text, e-mail, FTP, null, and script links from one setting to another. For example, you may have a text link, such as "This Month's Newsletter," that needs to point to a new HTML file each month, such as `/newsletters/september.html` this month and `/newsletters/october.html` next month. Likewise, if you need to change an e-mail address across all the pages on a Web site (such as changing `mailto:info@dummies.com` to `mailto:orders@dummies.com`), you can use this command to do it.

Follow these steps to change a link throughout your site:

***1.* In the Files panel, select a file from the Local view listing.**

If you're changing an e-mail address, FTP, script, or null link, you can skip this step.

***2.* Choose Site⇨Change Link Sitewide.**

Or choose Site⇨Change Link Sitewide from the Files panel Options menu.

The Change Link Sitewide dialog box appears, as shown in Figure 2-8.

Figure 2-8:
Change
individual
links
sitewide.

Change Link Sitewide	
Change all links to:	OK
home.html	Cancel
Into links to:	
index.html	Help

***3.* Enter the current and new link information in the Change All Links To and Into Links To text fields, respectively.**

For changing filenames, enter the old filename and new filename in the appropriate text fields. For any other type of link, enter the complete old and new text of the link you want to change. For instance, to replace one e-mail address with another, type **mailto:info@example.com** for the old address and **mailto:contact@example.com** for the new address.

***4.* Click OK.**

Dreamweaver updates all instances of that link with the new link information. Any path associated with the former link remains intact, regardless of whether the path is site root-relative or document-relative.

After the change is made, the file with the old filename becomes an orphan with no files on the managed site pointing to it. You can safely delete it from the local site folder without any fear of creating broken links. When uploading the updated pages to the remote server, don't forget to manually delete the same orphaned file from the remote server so that site visitors see the changed links.

Chapter 3: Preparing to Publish Your Files

In This Chapter

✔ Setting up a remote connection

✔ Choosing a remote access type

✔ Cloaking files and folders

*I*n Book V, Chapter 1, you discover how to run Workflow and HTML reports to check for coding errors on your pages. Then, in Book V, Chapter 2, you find out how easy cleaning up your code is when you use the Clean Up and Spell Checking commands. The next step to take before you publish your site is to set up a remote connection for your site. (We cover the final step, actually transferring your files, in Book V, Chapter 4.)

The *remote connection* defines the folder or destination where you're publishing your files. The remote folder can be on a testing server or production server, or any other type of server for storing your published files.

In this chapter, we show you how to create a remote connection for uploading and downloading files. You also find out how to cloak file types and folders to make sure that specified files aren't included in sitewide operations like uploading, report generation, and changing links.

Creating a Remote Connection

Before you set up a remote connection, you need to create a managed site. If you still need to set up a proper structure for your site, turn to Book I, Chapter 3 to find out about general Web site structure, document-relative and site root-relative paths, and how to create a managed site in Dreamweaver.

Setting up a remote connection requires you to create a *remote folder*. This folder is the location where you store a copy of the Web site's files, separate from the local version. You need this copy in place (and in a remote location) so that you can test, produce, deploy, and collaborate on the site.

If you plan on running the Web server on your local computer, you don't need to specify a remote folder; as long as the local folder points to the system running your Web server, Dreamweaver automatically uses the local folder (specified in the Local Info category) as the remote folder.

Setting up a remote folder

You can connect and access the remote folder using any of several methods. This section focuses on using the Advanced tab of the Site Definition dialog box to enter all your remote folder information.

To set up a remote folder, follow these steps:

1. Choose Site⇨Manage Sites.

Or choose Sites⇨Manage Sites from the Files panel Options menu.

The Manage Sites dialog box appears.

2. Select a site from the Dreamweaver site listing.

If you don't see any sites listed, you must create a new *managed site* before proceeding (see Book I, Chapter 3).

3. Click the Edit button.

The Site Definition dialog box appears.

4. Click the Advanced tab, if it's not already showing.

The Advanced site definition options enable you to enter specific information about your managed site.

5. Click the Remote Info category, and then from the Access menu, select one of the access types for uploading and downloading files to the remote site folder on the Web server.

A *remote access type* is simply the means to transfer files from your local computer to a remote location.

The option that's best for you depends on how large the team of Web developers working on the site is, as well as the existing technology you already have in place:

- **None:** Select this option if you won't be uploading the site to a server. You can also select this option to remove prior access settings.

- **FTP:** Choose this option if you'll be using File Transfer Protocol (FTP) to connect to your Web server. Where prompted, enter host name, username, host directory (if any), and password information, as well as firewall, server compatibility, or secure/passive FTP settings. This option presumes you've already registered your domain name (with a company like Network Solutions) and secured a hosting plan for your domain with a reputable host provider (check out the top 10 list at www.webhostinginspector.com/).

To connect and disconnect to a remote folder with FTP, all you need to do is click the Connect to Remote Host button in the Files panel.

- **Local/Network:** Select this option if you'll be running a Web server on your local computer or accessing a local area network (LAN) folder. Click the folder next to the Remote Folder text field to browse for and select the folder to which you want to send the remote site files. You don't need to manually connect and disconnect to a remote folder with network access, because you're always connected if you choose this type of access. You may, however, want to click the Refresh button in the Files panel often so that you can see the latest version of your remote files.

- **WebDAV (Web-based Distributed Authoring and Versioning):** Use this access method if you connect to a server that supports the WebDAV protocol, such as a Microsoft Internet Information Server (IIS) 5.0 or an Apache Web server with the right configuration settings. Enter the URL for the WebDAV server, username, and password before testing the connection.

- **RDS (Rapid Development Services):** Use this setting to connect to your Web server using RDS. The remote folder must be on a computer running ColdFusion. Enter the host name for the server, the port number, and the remote root folder, username, and password.

- **Microsoft Visual SourceSafe:** This is a Windows-only setting. Select this access method if you connect to your Web server using Microsoft Visual SourceSafe for Windows and have Microsoft Visual SourceSafe client Version 6 installed on the local computer. Specify the Microsoft Visual SourceSafe database, a Microsoft Visual SourceSafe project, username, and password.

After you make your selection, the appropriate options for that access type appear below the Access menu. For instance, if you select FTP, you see text fields for inputting FTP access information, such as host URL, username, and password.

To find out how to set each of the access types, see the following section, "Configuring a remote access type."

6. **Click OK to save the entered information.**

Dreamweaver saves remote information settings and closes the Site Definition dialog box. Dreamweaver knows that it needs to create, or be ready to create, a connection to the specified remote server.

Configuring a remote access type

Your development environment determines which remote access type you choose, as well as where the remote folder resides. The following sections show you how to select category options for each of the remote access types available.

For each of these remote access types, these options also appear:

✦ **Maintain Synchronization Information:** Choose to synchronize local and remote files automatically. This option is enabled by default so you must deselect it if you don't want Dreamweaver to synchronize your files. (We recommend keeping the option enabled if you want Dreamweaver to automate the synchronization process — Dreamweaver's synchronization tools are very useful. For details on the entire synchronization process, read Book V, Chapter 4.)

✦ **Automatically Upload Files to Server on Save:** Most developers leave this option disabled so they can test locally before publishing the updated files to the remote server. When enabled, Dreamweaver uploads files to the remote site whenever files are saved locally.

✦ **Enable File Check In and Check Out:** When enabled, three additional fields appear. These fields are the Check Out Files When Opening field, the Check Out Name field, and Email Address field of the main person using the current workstation. Unless you work in a group setting (see Book VI, Chapter 1), leave this option disabled.

✦ **Refresh Remote File List Automatically:** Choose to have the Files panel refresh automatically when you add and delete files.

This option can slow down the process of copying files to the remote server. If you want to copy files quickly, disable this option and click the Files panel Refresh button to manually refresh.

FTP

One of the most common methods of accessing a Web server is by using File Transfer Protocol (FTP). This is a good catchall remote access option, and the most common protocol used for transferring files. This section covers how to use Dreamweaver's built-in FTP client for transferring files, but you could also transfer your files using any of the more common stand-alone FTP client applications (see Book VII, Chapter 2).

Access the Site Definition dialog box and follow these steps to enter information in the Remote Info category (see Figure 3-1):

1. **Enter the FTP host name where you will upload your files in the FTP Host field.**

The FTP host name is the full Internet name of the server, such as `ftp. macromedia.com` or `www.mysampleURL.com`. Don't enter any additional text such as the protocol name before the host name. You can also enter the IP address if you have it. If you do not know this information, contact your host provider or system administrator.

Figure 3-1:
The FTP
remote
access type.

2. In the Host Directory field, enter the address of the host directory provided by your service provider.

The host directory is the location on the remote site where the files that will be visible to the Internet public are stored.

Not all servers require this information, so if you don't know it, leave this text field empty or speak with your host provider or system administrator before continuing. Some servers use a directory called public_html or www, or use your username. To see if you have a directory as part of your hosting plan, establish an FTP connection without one to see whether the Remote view lists any host directory folders, such as public_html. If you see a directory folder, make a note of it and complete this step later.

3. Enter the login or username and password you're using to connect to the FTP server in the Login and Password fields.

When you sign up for FTP, your host provider gives you this information. If you don't know your username and password, contact your host provider or system administrator.

Keep your username and password confidential.

4. Click the Test button to test your connection.

If your FTP host name, host directory, username, and password information are valid, Dreamweaver displays an alert message that says the connection was a success. If the connection fails, an error message appears telling you that a connection could not be established. If that happens, check the spelling and accuracy of all the information you've entered, paying special attention to character case and spelling, and try again.

By default, Dreamweaver saves your FTP login information and password.

5. If you prefer to enter your password each time you log in to your remote folder using FTP, deselect the Save check box to the right of the Password text box.

6. (Optional) Enable the Use Passive FTP option if your firewall configuration requires it.

Passive FTP uses the local software to set up the connection, rather than relying on the remote server to create the connection. For more information about whether you should use this option, contact your host provider or system administrator, and see the Macromedia TechNote 15220 at www.macromedia.com/go/15220.

7. Enable the Use Firewall option when connecting to a remote server from behind a firewall.

If you're unsure whether you need to enable this option, speak with your system administrator.

If you need to edit the firewall host or port information, click the Firewall Settings button. The Preferences dialog box opens with the Site category options showing (see Figure 3-2), where you can modify, among other things, the FTP connection, transfer, and hosting preferences:

Figure 3-2:
Modify the FTP connection settings.

- **Always Show:** When using Dreamweaver for FTP, adjust these settings to determine which site (local or remote) is shown by default in the Files panel. You can also choose which pane in the expanded Files panel (left or right) displays local and remote files. Dreamweaver's default is to always show local files on the right, which happens to be the opposite of most stand-alone FTP client applications.

- **Dependent Files:** Enable one or both of these options to have Dreamweaver display a prompt when transferring dependent files (such as images, PDFs, CSS, and so on) that the browser needs when displaying the pages being uploaded. Both options are enabled by default, so we recommend you leave these settings as they are.

- **FTP Connection:** Set the disconnect time after a period of idleness, such as 30 minutes.

- **FTP Time Out:** Set the number of seconds it takes for Dreamweaver to attempt making a connection with the server. If there's no response after the time specified, a warning alert displays.

- **FTP Transfer Options:** Use this setting to have Dreamweaver use a default option after the number of seconds specified to display a dialog box during the file transfer when there's no user response.

- **Firewall Host:** Enter the address of the proxy servers through which you connect to remote servers when using a firewall. Leave this field blank if you don't use a firewall.

- **Firewall Port:** If you do use a firewall host to connect to a remote server, enter the port number here. Otherwise, leave this field set to 21, the default number for FTP.

- **Put Options: Save Files Before Putting:** Enable this feature to have unsaved files automatically save before you upload them to the server.

- **Manage Sites:** Click this button to launch the Manage Sites dialog box to create new sites or edit the settings on an existing site.

8. **(Optional) Enable the Use Secure FTP (SFTP) option if you need to connect with SFTP for secure authentication.**

   SFTP uses public keys and encryption to create a secure connection with the testing server running an SFTP server.

9. **(Optional) Click the Server Compatibility button if you're having difficulty making a successful connection with the server:**

   - **Use FTP Performance Optimization:** Deselect this option if you're having trouble connecting to the server with Dreamweaver.

   - **Use Alternative FTP Move Method:** Enable this option if you're getting errors when rollbacks are enabled or when moving files.

10. **Click OK to save these settings and exit the Site Definition dialog box.**

Local/Network

Use the Local/Network access type when you're running a Web server on your local computer or accessing a network folder.

One of the benefits of this configuration is that you're always online. Access the Site Definition dialog box, and then in the Remote Info category, follow these steps to complete the always-connected Local/Network access configuration:

1. **Next to the Remote Folder text field, click the folder button to browse to and select the remote folder that contains your remote site files.**

On a local machine running a Web server, this folder is probably located on the Web server, as shown in Figure 3-3. If your computer is running on a network, the folder is the one on the network that stores the remote site files.

Figure 3-3:
Select the Local/Network access type to create an always-on connection.

2. **Click OK to save these settings and exit the Site Definition dialog box.**

WebDAV

Use WebDAV, or *Web-based Distributed Authoring and Versioning,* as your access method if you're connecting to a server that supports the WebDAV protocol. Microsoft Internet Information Server (IIS) 5.0 and Apache Web servers with the right configuration settings are the only servers that should use this remote access setup. If you're not sure whether your server falls into this category, it probably doesn't.

To set up your configuration, first access the Site Definition dialog box. In the Remote Info category, follow these steps:

1. Type the full URL that points to the directory on the WebDAV server you want to connect to, as shown in Figure 3-4.

The URL includes protocol, port, and directory, like this: `http://webdav.mydomain.net/mySiteName`.

Figure 3-4: Enter the connected server's URL including protocol, port, and directory for WebDAV access.

2. Type your login and password in the text fields provided.

The login and password are used only for server authentication.

3. Click the Test button to test the connection.

If the full URL, username, and password information are valid, Dreamweaver displays an alert message that the connection was a success. If the connection fails, an error message appears. Check the spelling, pay attention to character case, and review the accuracy of the URL before you try again.

4. **Click the Save option to store your password for future sessions.**

5. **Click OK to save these settings and exit the Site Definition dialog box.**

RDS

Use the RDS remote access setting to connect to a Web server running ColdFusion with Rapid Development Services (RDS). If you're not sure whether your server is running ColdFusion with RDS, it probably isn't. To set up your configuration, first access the Site Definition dialog box. In the Remote Info category, follow these steps:

1. **Select RDS as the access type and click the Settings button.**

The Configure RDS Server dialog box appears, as shown in Figure 3-5.

Figure 3-5:
Select RDS when connecting to a server running ColdFusion with RDS.

2. **In the Configure RDS Server dialog box, complete all the fields:**

- **Host Name:** Type the name of the host computer where the Web server is installed. Often, the host name appears as an IP address or URL.

- **Port:** Enter the port number you want to use to connect to the remote location. By default, Dreamweaver enters port 80. If you have no reason to change this setting, then don't.

- **Full Host Directory:** Enter the local path of the root remote folder, as in `C:\inetpub\wwwroot\myFullHostDirectory\`.

- **Username** and **Password:** Enter a username and password for the RDS. If you don't see these fields, you've already set the username and password in the ColdFusion Administrator.

- **Save:** By default these settings are automatically saved. To enter these settings manually each time you connect, deselect the Save option.

3. **Click OK to close this dialog box.**

You return to the Site Definition dialog box.

4. **Click OK to save these settings and exit the Site Definition dialog box.**

Microsoft Visual SourceSafe

Use the Microsoft Visual SourceSafe option (which is a Windows-only access method) when you're connecting to a Web server using Microsoft Visual SourceSafe for Windows and have Microsoft Visual SourceSafe Client Version 6 installed on the local computer. If you're not sure whether your server is running this application, it probably isn't. To set up your configuration, first access the Site Definition dialog box. In the Remote Info category, follow these steps:

1. **Select Microsoft Visual SourceSafe as the access type and click the Settings button.**

The Open Microsoft Visual SourceSafe Database dialog box appears, as shown in Figure 3-6.

Figure 3-6:
Select Microsoft Visual SourceSafe when connecting to a Microsoft Visual SourceSafe database.

2. **In the Open Microsoft Visual SourceSafe Database dialog box, complete all the fields to configure the database:**

   - **Database Path:** Type the full file path to the Microsoft Visual SourceSafe database or click the Browse button to browse for and select the database. The selected file becomes the `srcsafe.ini` file that launches Microsoft Visual SourceSafe.

   - **Project:** Type the project within the Microsoft Visual SourceSafe database to be used as the remote site's root directory.

   - **Username** and **Password:** Enter a username and password for the database.

   - **Save:** By default these settings are automatically saved. To enter these settings manually each time you connect, deselect the Save option.

3. **Click OK to close this dialog box and return to the Site Definition dialog box.**

4. **Click OK to save these settings and exit the Site Definition dialog box.**

Cloaking Your Files and Folders

Cloaking is a Dreamweaver feature that enables you to exclude specified folders and file types from sitewide operations such as uploading, report generation, and changing links. For example, if you transfer files to a remote server using the Get and Put or Check In/Check Out systems, cloaking shields some of those files from being uploaded to or checked out from the remote server.

When else does cloaking come in handy? Well, it definitely helps if you have some files on your site that you don't want to transfer to the server. If some files aren't being changed or updated, or if some files really don't need to be on the server, then you have no real reason to keep transferring them, right? Say you're running a busy design services Web site that requires weekly and sometimes daily updates. If you don't want to upload the same white papers and graphic files every day, you can cloak .pdf, .gif, and .jpg file types in the Cloaking category of the Site Definition dialog box. Those files on that site would then be excluded from the file transfer process until such time as you changed the cloaking information again.

You need to know a few things about cloaking:

✦ **Dreamweaver, by default, enables cloaking for each managed site.** This means you can cloak and/or uncloak individual files and folders through the Files panel. You can disable the setting if you need to with the Cloaking category of the Site Definition dialog box.

✦ **When cloaking is enabled, you can further set Dreamweaver to automatically exclude files with specific file suffixes.** For example, if you wanted to exclude all `.png` files and all `.fla` files from sitewide operations, you could.

✦ **Dreamweaver saves and uses the cloaking settings entered in the Cloaking category of the Site Definition dialog box for each managed site.** You don't need to reenter these settings every time you view a particular site.

You can cloak folders, files, and file types when conducting the following sitewide procedures:

✦ Transferring files with the Get/Put or Check In/Check Out system.

✦ Synchronizing a local site with a remote site.

✦ Creating sitewide reports.

✦ Updating templates and library items.

Dreamweaver excludes cloaked templates and library items from Get/Put operations but don't exclude them from batch operations, as that might cause synchronization issues between them and their instances.

✦ Changing the contents in the Asset panel.

✦ Finding newer local and remote files.

✦ Changing or checking links.

Enabling and disabling cloaking options

To disable or enable cloaking and specify file types to exclude for any managed site, follow these steps:

1. **Choose Site⇨Manage Sites to open the Manage Sites dialog box.**

2. **Select a site from the site listing and click the Edit button.**

The Site Definition dialog box opens with the Advanced tab showing (click the Advanced tab if the Basic tab is showing).

3. **Select the Cloaking category from the left side of the Advanced tab.**

The Cloaking settings appear, and the Enable Cloaking option is set by default. To disable this feature, deselect this check box.

If you disable the cloaking feature, all previously cloaked files become uncloaked. When you enable the feature again, all prior cloaking settings are restored.

4. **(Optional) Add a check mark to the Cloak Files Ending With check box.**

If you want to cloak files that end with certain suffixes, continue with Step 5. Otherwise skip to Step 6.

5. **In the text box below the Cloak Files Ending With check box, enter the file types you want excluded from site operations.**

The file types can be any pattern at the end of a filename; you're not limited to merely entering file extensions. For example, you can cloak all files with the `.txt` extension or all files and folders that end with `_bak`.

As you can see in Figure 3-7, you can even specify multiple file patterns by separating each pattern with a single space. Do not use colons, commas, or semicolons to separate your parameters, as doing so causes errors.

Figure 3-7: Enter cloaking file extensions to exclude certain files and folders.

In the Files panel, you can easily identify cloaked files because a red diagonal line appears through the icon associated with the cloaked file. When you disable or otherwise change the cloaking setting so that the file is no longer cloaked, the red line disappears.

6. **Click OK to exit the Site Definition dialog box.**

Cloaking individual folders

Though you can't cloak the root folder of a managed site (because that would mean the entire site would be excluded from sitewide operations), you can cloak any of the site's other folders.

To cloak individual folders on a site, follow these steps:

1. **Select a folder, or multiple folders, in the Files panel.**

The selected folders can be cloaked or uncloaked, and when multiple folders have been selected, you may uncloak them all at the same time.

2. **Right-click (Windows) or Control+click (Mac) one of the selected folders, choose Cloaking from the context menu, and select Cloak, Uncloak, or Uncloak All.**

You can also access these Cloaking options from the Options menu in the Files panel. Because the default setting for all sites is to have cloaking enabled, depending on which folder(s) you have selected, you can choose to uncloak individual folders, to cloak specified folders, or to uncloak all selected folders at the same time.

In the Files panel, folders that are cloaked have a diagonal red line through the folder icon next to the folder name. Folders that aren't cloaked appear without a red line through them.

Take caution when using the Uncloak All feature. Although enabling this option uncloaks folders, it doesn't really disable the cloaking system itself. What's worse, there is no efficient way to re-cloak previously cloaked files and folders. You have to select the files and folders by hand.

Uncloaking previously cloaked file types

If you change your mind after cloaking specified file types, you can easily uncloak them. Follow these steps to do so:

1. **Right-click (Windows) or Control+click (Mac) in the Files panel and choose Cloaking⇨Settings from the context menu.**

The Site Definition dialog box opens to the Advanced tab with the Cloaking category selected.

2. **To uncloak previously cloaked files, do any of the following:**

• Delete the file patterns in the text box below the Cloak Files Ending check box.

• Disable the Cloak Files Ending With check box. This action leaves the file patterns previously entered into the text field, but temporarily disables the cloaking action.

3. Click OK to exit the Site Definition dialog box.

After you exit the Site Definition dialog box, any red diagonal lines appearing through the file icons of any previously cloaked files in the Files panel disappear, leaving the files uncloaked.

You can also right-click (Windows) or Control+click (Mac) any file or folder in the Files panel and choose Cloaking➪Uncloak All. This option removes all prior cloaking settings, including any file endings entered in the Cloaking category of the Site Definition dialog box. You *can't* undo this action, so be sure you really want to uncloak.

Chapter 4: Publishing Your Web Pages

In This Chapter

✔ Understanding file transferring

✔ Putting and getting files with the Files panel

✔ Synchronizing local and remote files

The final step of publishing your site is getting your files online. Luckily, with Dreamweaver's built-in FTP features, you can quickly transfer your Web site files to a remote server.

During the transfer process, Dreamweaver can verify that both your local and remote file and folder structures match one another and even identify which files are newer on either the local or remote site to help you stream-line the publishing process. You can also use the handy Synchronize Files command to copy updated files between local and remote sites, if neces-sary, and to decide whether to delete any files on the destination site that don't have corresponding files on the starting site.

You can always manually transfer individual files and folders at any time, but having Dreamweaver synchronize your files totally ensures that both locations have the most recent versions of all the files at all times.

This chapter walks you through the file transfer process as well as explains *background transfers*. We show you how to use the Files panel for *uploading* files (putting them online) and *downloading* files (getting them from the Internet to your computer), and how to use the Synchronize Files command to synchronize your local and remote files.

Understanding File Transfer Basics

A typical work process involves designing, building, and testing a local ver-sion of your Web site before publishing it on the Internet. After you finish all those tasks, you need to establish a connection with the remote server (as described in Book V, Chapter 3) and send an exact copy of the local files to the server location so that anyone on the Internet can see them.

If, after putting your files online, you need to make changes to your site, you can make your modifications to the local version of the files, and then upload them to the server to overwrite the older versions of the files.

Most file transfers go in one direction: You *put,* or upload, files to the server. However, you can both put and *get* (download) from the remote server at the same time. For instance, you may occasionally need to get a copy of the remote site for your local archive or a new workstation, or to restore an old or corrupted version of a file.

When you transfer your files from local to remote, all the default read and write privileges of the original file are maintained with the transfer. However, when you get files with the Check In/Check Out feature turned on, the copies sent to your local site are marked with read-only privileges so you can't alter them and other team members can still access those files for check out. See Book VI, Chapter 1 for more about the Check In/Check Out feature.

Transferring dependent files

When you transfer files, you upload *copies* of the files rather than the original files themselves. The process may only take a matter of seconds, depending on the file size and the number of extra things that appear on the page or are linked to it, such as graphics, PDFs, style sheets, library items, and JavaScript files, which may or may not need to be uploaded with the file.

By default, Dreamweaver asks whether you want to include any *dependent files* — the page's graphics, movies, style sheets, for example — during a transfer, to which you can choose Yes or No. If the prompt doesn't appear, you can force it by holding Alt (Windows) or Option (Mac) when you click the Get, Put, Check In, and Check Out buttons.

Also, because Dreamweaver treats library items as dependents, which could cause report errors when those files are *put* on some servers, consider cloaking the library items to prevent them from transferring automatically. To find out how to cloak library items, see Book V, Chapter 3.

Working during file transfers

During your file transfers (no matter your transfer method), Dreamweaver enables you to continue doing any non-server-related work, such as editing text, adding images, creating style sheets, attaching JavaScript behaviors, and running reports. Dreamweaver calls these *background file transfers*.

We discuss the technology you use for file transfers in Book V, Chapter 3, so if you're curious about using your LAN versus an FTP connection to upload files, skip back to that chapter and get reading.

You do have a few file transfer limitations, however, which means Dreamweaver can't perform some server-related tasks simultaneously. Server-related work that you *can't* do during file transfers includes the following:

✦ Additional file transfers, checking files in and out, and undoing checkouts

✦ Creating database connections and bindings

✦ Previewing live data or inserting a Web service

✦ Deleting or saving files and folders on a remote server

✦ Opening, dragging, or inserting images on files on a remote server

✦ Copying, cutting, and pasting files on a remote server

✦ Refreshing Dreamweaver's Remote view in the Files panel

✦ Previewing files in a browser on a testing server

✦ Automatically putting (uploading) files to the remote server when saving

Putting Files on and Getting Files from the Remote Server

The *Get* and *Put* commands are fantastic collaboration tools, although you can put them to good use even if you fly solo in your Dreamweaver endeavors. The Get and Put commands enable you to transfer files from your local computer to your remote host location without checking files in and out of the site. That means you can even put a version of a file you're editing onto the server as you continue working on that file.

If you use Dreamweaver as part of a team, you must enable Design Notes and use the Check In/Check Out feature. Even if you work alone, you can still enable the Check In/Check Out system. For instance, though you're one person, you may work at two locations and choose to check in files to help keep track of their location and check out status. Turn to Book VI, Chapter 1 to find out more about these features.

The Put and Get commands are accessible through the Files panel, where you can upload and download files from your local machine to the remote server:

✦ **Get** copies files from the remote site to your local machine.

✦ **Put** places local files onto the remote site.

Examining the Files panel transfer options

You can transfer files to and from your local machine and a remote server with the Files panel in either the collapsed or expanded view, though you may prefer to use the expanded view to see a list of all the files on both the local and remote sites at the same time.

In collapsed mode, the top of the Files panel has a simple row of buttons to assist you with transferring files to and from a remote server, as shown in Figure 4-1:

Figure 4-1:
Transfer files to and from a remote server through the Files panel.

◆ **Site Management Menu:** Choose the site you need to transfer files for from this list. This menu appears in both the collapsed and expanded views and lists all the *managed sites* you've created in Dreamweaver. For more details on creating a managed site, see Book I, Chapter 3.

◆ **Site View:** When the Files panel is collapsed, use this menu to toggle between the four site views (Local, Remote, Testing Server, and Site Map). In the expanded view, this menu disappears and three other buttons (Site Files, Testing Server, Site Map) are shown in its place:

• **Local:** Select this view to see the file structure of the local site in the Files panel. You can also use this view to see both local and remote sites with the Files panel split into two panes. In the expanded view, this option is presented as a button.

• **Remote:** Select this view to see the file structure of the remote site. You must set up a remote site in advance for you to see the remote site files. For details on setting up a remote site, see Book V, Chapter 3.

- **Testing Server:** This view shows a directory listing of the testing server only in normal view, or both the testing server and local site files in the expanded view. You must set up a testing server in advance for you to see the testing server site. In the expanded view, this option is presented as a button. For details on setting up a testing server, see Book VII, Chapter 1.

- **Site Map:** This view shows a graphic map of the site based on how the files are linked together. In the expanded view, this option is presented as a button. For site map details, see Book VI, Chapter 1.

✦ **Connect/Disconnect:** Connect/disconnect to the remote site with FTP, SFTP, RDS, WebDAV, and Microsoft Visual SourceSafe. With FTP connections, Dreamweaver disconnects from a remote site if it has no activity for over 30 minutes. To increase or decrease this time, choose Edit⇨Preferences (Windows) or Dreamweaver⇨Preferences (Mac) and enter a new number in the Site category of the Preferences dialog box.

✦ **Refresh:** Manually refresh both the local and the remote file listings. To have your local file lists refresh automatically, enable the Refresh option in the Local Info category of the Site Definition dialog box.

✦ **View Site FTP Log:** This button only appears in the expanded Files panel after the initial FTP transfer. Click this button to launch the Results panel where you can view the FTP log that contains a record of the site's FTP file transfer activity. See the "Viewing the FTP and background file activity logs" section later in this chapter.

✦ **Get File(s):** Get copies of files and folders selected in the Files panel from the remote server to your local site. Any existing files on the local site become overwritten during the Get process.

✦ **Put Files(s):** Put copies of files and folders selected in the Files panel from the local site to the remote or testing server.

✦ **Check Out Files:** This option is only available when you're using the Check In/Check Out system (which is described in Book VI, Chapter 1). Click this button to get a copy of a selected file from the remote server to your local site. If the file already exists on the local site, this process overwrites the local version of the file. After the file copies, the file on the server is marked as checked out and a small green check mark icon appears next to the filename in the Files panel.

✦ **Check In Files:** This option is only available when you're using the Check In/Check Out system. Click this button to put a copy of a selected file from the local site to the remote server. After the file copies, the server version file is marked as Checked In and the local site file has a small lock icon next to the filename as an indication of the local file's read-only status.

✦ **Expand/Collapse:** This button toggles the Files panel between the collapsed view and the expanded view. In the collapsed view, the Files panel displays the Local, Remote, Map, or Testing Server views. In the expanded view, you can view a directory listing of files in both the local and remote or testing server sites. By default, the local site appears in the right pane, but you can modify this setting in the Site category of Dreamweaver's Preferences.

✦ **Synchronize:** This button only appears in the expanded view and allows you to launch the synchronization command. For details about the synchronization process read the section, "Keeping Your Local and Remote Site Files Up to Date" later in this chapter.

In expanded mode, the Files panel expands into two panes for displaying both local and remote files and a complete row of buttons appear at the top of the panel to assist you with transferring files to and from a remote server, as shown in Figure 4-2.

Putting files on a remote server

To put files on the remote server, follow these steps:

1. **In the Files panel, select the files you want to upload.**

Use either Local view or Remote view to select your files. If you're attempting to upload only local files that are more recent than their remote counterparts, see the "Keeping Your Local and Remote Site Files Up to Date" section later in this chapter.

2. **Click the Put Files button at the top of the Files panel (refer to Figure 4-1).**

You can also right-click (Windows) or Control+click (Mac) the file in the Files panel and choose Put from the context menu.

If you attempt to transfer a file (or multiple files, for that matter) that you've edited but haven't yet saved, a dialog box may appear (depending on your setting), prompting you to save the files prior to copying them to the remote destination. See Book V, Chapter 3 for more information on setting these preferences.

3. **If prompted to save unsaved open files, click the Yes button to save the files or the No button to put the most recent version of the files on the remote server while leaving the unsaved files open in the Dreamweaver workspace.**

The Dependent Files dialog box opens if the transferred files contain any dependents.

4. **Click the Yes button to upload dependent files, or No to bypass this upload feature.**

For example, if the remote site already contains most or all the dependent files (such as images and style sheets), you don't need to upload them again.

Site Map

Testing Server | Get Files

Site Files | Put Files

View Site FTP Log | Check Out Files

Refresh | Check In Files

Connect/Disconnect | Synchronize

Site Management | Expand/Collapse

Figure 4-2:
View both
local and
remote files.

Remote view | Local view

The file transfer begins immediately — too fast, perhaps, for you to even review the Transfer Status dialog box. If you do see the status dialog box, however, and you need to cancel the transfer, you can click the Cancel button if you're quick enough.

Getting files from a remote server

To get files from the remote or testing server onto your local site using the Files panel, follow these steps:

1. **In the Files panel, select the files to download.**

Although you're more likely to select files from the Remote view, you can also select the files from Local view.

If you want to get only remote files that have been recently changed, you're better off with the Synchronize command as described in the section, "Keeping Your Local and Remote Site Files Up to Date" later in this chapter.

2. **Click the Get Files button at the top of the Files panel.**

   Or right-click (Windows) or Control+click (Mac) the file in the Files panel and choose Get from the context menu.

   The Dependent Files dialog box opens if you've enabled this setting in the Site category of the Preferences dialog box (see Book V, Chapter 3).

3. **Click the Yes button to download any dependent files, or click No to bypass this feature, or Cancel to stop the transfer.**

   If the local site already contains most or all the dependent files, don't bother downloading them again.

   The file transfer begins immediately. When using Check In/Check Out in a collaborative situation, Dreamweaver transfers a copy of each file to the local site, and then marks it as read-only until you check it in again. When you have Check In/Check Out disabled, copies to the local site have the default read and write privileges.

When you get files from the server, you're not actually removing them from the server. The files are copied, and those copies are transferred to your local computer.

Viewing the FTP and background file activity logs

When you transfer files in either direction — whether you're getting or putting files — Dreamweaver keeps two logs of the file and transfer activity. The logs include operations and outcomes such as whether the transfer was a success or failure, in case you need to troubleshoot connection errors or want to keep a record of the transfer process.

Each log records and stores data in different ways and in different locations:

✦ **Background File Activity Log:** This log only appears during a background file transfer but you can access it at any time subsequent to the first transfer. This log records details about the transfer, including start and finish times, the name of the files being transferred, and the number of files successfully updated. To view this log, click the Log button at the bottom of the Files panel. The Background File Activity dialog box opens, as shown in Figure 4-3. You can save this log as a text file by clicking the Save Log button in the dialog box.

✦ **FTP Log:** This log keeps a running record of all file FTP transfer activity. You can access it through the Results panel at any time subsequent to the first transfer. To view the FTP log, open the Results panel (choose Window➪Results) and click the FTP Log tab, as shown in the example in Figure 4-4. You can save the content on this log by selecting all the content and right-clicking (Windows) or Control+clicking (Mac), and then pasting it into any text editor or other application and saving the file with the appropriate file extension.

Figure 4-3:
The
Background
File Activity
dialog box.

Figure 4-4:
The FTP log
in the
Results
panel.

Keeping Your Local and Remote Site Files Up to Date

After you establish a remote connection and create a mirror copy of your local site on the remote server, you can use Dreamweaver's Synchronize Files command to synchronize the files between the two locations. Synchronization isn't exactly the same thing as transferring files; it's mainly a cleanup/housekeeping feature, useful mostly for making sure that existing (not new) files on both your local and remote sites are up to date.

You can set the synchronization settings a variety of ways. Specify, if you like, that the entire site gets synchronized, or override that option by selecting individual files to ignore, put, get, or delete during the synchronization. At the end of the synchronization process, Dreamweaver provides confirmation of the updated files.

Viewing the newest files without synchronization

Before you begin synching files, you may find viewing all your Web site files by date helpful. The idea is to see which files are newer in both locations *before* you synchronize.

To select the newest files that haven't been synchronized, do one of the following:

✦ In the Files panel, right-click (Windows) or Control+click (Mac) anywhere in the listing area and choose Select➪Newer Local or Select➪Newer Remote.

✦ Choose Edit➪Select Newer Local or Edit➪Select Newer Remote from the Files panel Options menu.

You can also search for recently modified files without synchronization by choosing Edit➪Select Recently Modified. When you make this selection, the Select Recently Modified dialog box shown in Figure 4-5 appears, where you can choose to view files created or modified within a specified number of days or view files created within a specified range of dates.

Figure 4-5:
View files in Local or Remote view that were created or modified recently.

The new or recently modified files are selected and appear with gray highlighting behind them (as shown in Figure 4-6) in the Files panel for easy identification, making them easy to update with the synchronization command, which is explained in the following section.

Figure 4-6:
Recently modified files highlighted in the Files panel.

Synchronizing your files

When you're ready to synchronize your files, follow these steps:

1. From the Files panel, choose a site from the Managed Site drop-down list.

If you haven't managed a site in Dreamweaver yet, see Book I, Chapter 3.

If you want to synchronize specific files or folders in the site, select them in the Files panel before proceeding.

2. Choose Site⇨Synchronize Sitewide from the main menu.

The Synchronize Files dialog box, shown in Figure 4-7, appears.

Figure 4-7:
The
Synchronize
Files dialog
box.

3. Choose an option from the Synchronize drop-down list:

- **Entire Managed Site:** Select this option to synchronize all the files on the selected managed site.

- **Selected Local Files Only:** Use this option when you need to synchronize selected files from a managed site (the option says Selected Remote Files Only when your most recent file selection was done in the Remote view of the Files panel).

4. Choose an option from the Direction drop-down list:

- **Put Newer Files to Remote:** Upload any files from the local site that have been updated since the last upload, plus any new files that don't appear on the remote server yet.

- **Get Newer Files from Remote:** Download remote files that have been updated since the last download, plus any new files that don't appear on the local site yet.

- **Get and Put Newer Files:** Put the most recent versions of all the files, including any missing files, on both local and remote sites.

5. Select or deselect the Delete Remote Files Not on Local Drive option.

Select this option to have Dreamweaver remove files on the destination site when originals don't exist. For example, if you delete a local file prior to transferring, this option also deletes the deleted file's counterpart from the remote site.

6. Click the Preview button.

Before committing to the synchronization process, you must review a list of all the files that are updating in the Synchronize dialog box shown in Figure 4-8.

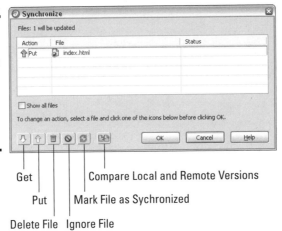

Figure 4-8:
The Synchronize dialog box shows the files being synchronized.

Get

Put

Delete File   Ignore File

Mark File as Sychronized

Compare Local and Remote Versions

If you want, you can change the action associated with each file (Get, Put, Delete, and Ignore). To change any of the actions associated with the files, select a file and click the appropriate button at the bottom of the dialog box.

7. Click OK to begin the synchronization.

If all the files are already in sync, Dreamweaver displays a message that politely notifies you that the synchronization isn't necessary. Otherwise, the synchronization process runs. When it's done, Dreamweaver returns to the Files panel.

TECHNICAL STUFF

Using diff tools (if you have 'em)

One of the actions in the Synchronization dialog box is to compare local and remote versions of the files with a third-party tool *before* the synchronization process. These tools, also called *diff tools,* can compare code between two versions of the same file so that you can merge changes between the files before the transfer process.

This option requires the installation of a third-party comparison/merging application and the specification of that application in the File Compare category of the Preferences dialog box. For details about Macromedia recommended file comparison tools, visit the Macromedia Web site at `www.macromedia.com/go/dw8_compare_util`.

Book VI

Working Collaboratively

The 5th Wave   By Rich Tennant

"Ooo-wait! That's perfect for the clinic's home page. Just stretch it out a little further... little more..."

Contents at a Glance

Chapter 1: Working Efficiently with a Team

In This Chapter

↙ **Enabling and using Design Notes**

↙ **Using the Check In/Check Out feature**

↙ **Customizing File View Columns**

↙ **Working in Site Map Layout mode**

Most likely you're not working alone. The larger the Web site, the greater the odds that you're getting help from other people. Most Web sites these days require a team — someone who works on the dynamic aspect, a JavaScript expert, and yet more people who work on the HTML and the graphics. And of course, you, who pulls all these aspects together into one cohesive Web site.

How do you keep track of who's working on what at a certain time? Team members overwriting files or two members working simultaneously on the same file are what nightmares are made of.

Dreamweaver comes to your rescue. It includes several features to keep you in tune with your other team members, such as Design Notes and the Check In/Check Out feature. And if you customize the columns in the Files panel, you can see at a glance the status of each page in the Web site. Furthermore, you can see and manage all your files in Site Map Layout mode to assist you with defining and refining your Web site's structure. We discuss all these features — and how you can use all of them to work efficiently with your team — in this chapter.

Attaching Design Notes to Your Files

Dreamweaver's Design Notes are reminder notes that you can create and attach to individual files on a site to help you and your team with site file management. You can attach Design Notes to documents, templates, images, Flash movies, ActiveX controls, and applets. The Design Notes data itself is stored in a separate linked file that allows for shared access and retrieval. This tool is a must if you're working collaboratively on site design and management.

Design Notes come in two flavors:

+ **Notes you create:** The Design Notes feature is especially helpful if you're exchanging files within a design team or workgroup. For example, you may have a monthly newsletter that gets updated to a site on the first day of each month. With Design Notes, you can add comments about file transfer data, archived file locations, and other information related to the uploading of the newest newsletter. You may also want to use Design Notes for storing sensitive data such as marketing strategy guidelines or pricing arrangements.

+ **Notes that are created for you automatically:** Macromedia's Fireworks and Flash programs integrate and update Design Notes all on their own (whether you want them or not) so that you can use them later in Dreamweaver sites with the same site-root path. When you open files in either of those programs and export them to another file format, the Design Notes feature launches (behind the scenes) to store data about the original source file, such as filename, type, and location. For instance, when opening the `fatcat.png` file in Fireworks and exporting it as `fatcat.gif`, Fireworks creates a Design Note called `fatcat.gif.mno` that includes the name of the original `.png` file and the absolute location where it is stored:

```
fw_source="file:///LocalDisk/sites/assets/orig/fatcat.png"
```

In Dreamweaver, when the graphic is imported from Fireworks, the Design Notes automatically copy to the site. Then, if you need to edit the graphic in Fireworks, Fireworks can use those Design Notes to quickly locate the original `.png` file and open it for editing, all the while adding any new data to the Design Notes.

Enabling and disabling Design Notes

By default, Design Notes are enabled for each managed site, but you can change them in the Design Notes category of the Site Definition dialog box. Follow these steps:

1. **Choose Site⇨Manage Sites to open the Manage Sites dialog box.**

2. **Select a site from the site listing and click the Edit button.**

The Site Definition dialog box opens. Click the Advanced tab if it's not showing.

3. **Select the Design Notes category.**

The Design Notes category options appear, as shown in Figure 1-1. As you can see, both the Maintain Design Notes and Upload Design Notes for Sharing options are enabled by default. To disable these features, deselect the check boxes.

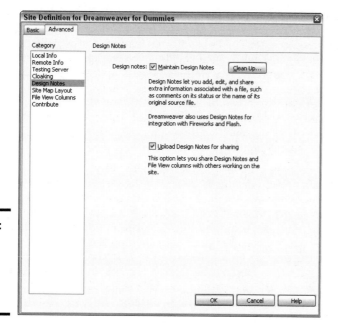

Figure 1-1:
Enable or
disable
Design
Notes for
your site.

4. **Enable or disable the Upload Design Notes for Sharing option.**

- **Enable:** If you want Dreamweaver to upload the Design Notes associated with files on the site along with the rest of your files when it transfers files to the remote server, leave the Upload Design Notes for Sharing option enabled.

- **Disable:** To keep Design Notes locally and not have Dreamweaver upload them to the remote site when files are transferred, disable this option.

5. **Click OK to exit the Site Definition dialog box.**

Removing Design Notes

Design Notes, when enabled, do increase the file transfer time slightly, so if you're working alone and do not use this feature, you may want to disable and remove them completely.

To disable and permanently remove Design Notes, follow these steps:

1. **Deselect the Maintain Design Notes option in the Design Notes category of the Site Definition dialog box (see the previous section).**

2. **Click the Clean Up button to delete all the Design Notes from your local computer.**

3. **To proceed, click the Yes button.**

Dreamweaver deletes all the Design Notes on the local computer.

You can't undo this step, so be sure this is something you really want to do before clicking the Yes button!

Click the No button if you have a change of heart and want to leave Design Notes as they are.

4. **Click OK to exit the Site Definition dialog box.**

Adding Design Notes to a file

Add your own Design Notes to individual files, folders, or templates on your site every time you modify the content and want to communicate with other members of the team about it. When you add Design Notes to a template, they attach only to the template and aren't copied to any template-based documents. That way, individual template-based files can each have their own individual Design Notes! You can also attach Design Notes to graphics, Flash movies, ActiveX controls, applets, and Shockwave objects.

To add Design Notes to a file, follow these steps:

1. **Open the file you want to add the Design Notes to and choose File⇨ Design Notes.**

   Or right-click (Windows) or Control+click (Mac) a closed file in the Files panel and choose Design Notes from the context menu.

   If you want to add Design Notes to a file that's located on a remote site, you must check out the file first (see the next section "Checking Files In and Out," to find out more about using the Check In/Check Out feature). Then you can add the Design Notes to the local version of the file.

   The Design Notes dialog box opens.

2. **On the Basic Info tab, fill in the following fields to create your Design Notes:**

   • **Status:** Select a status for the file from the Status menu. The status reflects the document's current condition, relative to it being finalized and ready for publication. Dreamweaver presents you with eight status settings to select from: Draft, Revision1, Revision2, Revision3, Alpha, Beta, Final, and Needs Attention. To create your own custom status setting, move on to Step 3.

- **Date:** To insert the current date in your Design Notes, click the Date icon above the Notes field.

- **Notes:** Type your Design Notes in the text field.

3. **On the All Info tab, click the plus (+) button to add new *key/value pairs,* which you can use as custom status settings and search criteria for Design Notes reports:**

- **Keys:** Enter a word in the Name field to identify the first part of the note information, such as **Author** or **Status**.

- **Values:** Enter a word or two in the Value field to represent the attribute for the associated key, such as **Sue** or **Draft6**.

Each *key* must have a *value* and can be composed of any words — as customized as you need — to assist you. For example, create custom status definitions, such as *Status=Draft6* or a key/value pair to refine a Design Note report, such as *Author=Sue, V=2.b,* or *Revision=4/15/06,* as shown in Figure 1-2.

Figure 1-2:
Enter key/
value pairs
in the All
Info tab of
the Design
Notes
dialog box.

To delete an existing key/value pair, select it from the list and click the minus (–) button.

4. **Click OK to close the Design Notes dialog box.**

Design Notes for each file are saved in a _notes folder on your site. The individual Design Notes files are named after the document they're attached to and have the .mno file extension. For instance, if the main filename is contact.html, the corresponding Design Notes file is _notes/contact.html.mno.

Viewing and editing Design Notes

After you add Design Notes to a file, you can view, edit, and add additional information to them at any time. To see which files have Design Notes attached to them, view the Files panel in expanded mode by clicking the expand/collapse button at the top of the Files panel. Look for a Design Notes icon (it looks like a little cartoon speech bubble) next to the filename in the Notes column, as shown in Figure 1-3.

Figure 1-3:
Files with Design Notes display a Design Notes icon next to the filename.

Design Notes icon

> *TIP*
>
> If you're having trouble seeing the Design Notes icon in the Files panel, you may need to adjust the Design Notes icon setting in the Site Definition dialog box. Turn to the "Defining File View Columns" section for details.

Checking Files In and Out

When working as a member of a collaborative team, using the Check In/Check Out Files feature is a must. The beauty of the system is that you must check in and check out files not only from the remote site but from the shared local site as well — so no two people can work on the same file at the same time. This single innovation goes a long way toward maintaining the integrity of a Web site.

Dreamweaver uses a simple icon system next to filenames within the Files panel to help keep track of all the files and their check in/check out status. When a file is checked out, Dreamweaver shows the person's name and a red check mark next to the checked out file. When a file is checked back in, a green check mark appears. After checking a file back in, the local copy of the file becomes read-only and a little lock icon appears next to the filename. The remote files, however, can't be turned into read-only versions after check-out. That means that if anyone transfers files to the remote server with a program other than Dreamweaver, the remote files can be overwritten. To help prevent this from accidentally happening when using other programs, a `.lck` file usually appears next to the checked out file as a sort of visual indication of the file's checked out status.

To enable the Check In/Check Out system, do the following:

1. **Choose Site⇨Manage Sites to launch the Manage Sites dialog box.**

2. **Select the site and click the Edit button to open the Site Definition dialog box.**

3. **Click the Advanced Tab.**

4. **Select Remote Info from the Category list. On the right side of the dialog box, at the bottom, is the Check In/Check Out information (see Figure 1-4).**

Figure 1-4:
Enable the
Check In/
Out feature.

Note: If the Check In/Check Out options aren't displaying, check to see that you've selected an access type and configured it. (Turn to Book V, Chapter 3 if you still need to do this.) You must enter remote information before enabling Check In/Check Out.

5. **Check the Enable File Check In and Check Out box.**

If you're using FTP, enter a checkout name and e-mail address. The e-mail address you enter here becomes a clickable link in the Files panel when the file is checked out. If you want, you can place check marks next to the other options so that files can be automatically checked out and uploaded when they're saved.

6. **Click OK to save your settings and close the Site Definition dialog box.**

The Check In/Check Out settings work immediately and can be modified or disabled at any time. To begin checking files into and out of a remote folder in the Files panel, follow these steps:

1. **Select the files you want to check in or out.**

2. **Click the Check In or Check Out buttons at the top of the Files panel toolbar.**

Expand the Files panel for a view of both local and remote files.

3. **Click Yes or No as appropriate when prompted to include dependent files, such as graphics or CSS files.**

When a remote file is checked out, its counterpart in the local file listing in the Files panel appears with a little lock icon next to it, as shown in Figure 1-5. The lock is virtual, however, and you can remove its locked status if needed.

Check In

Check Out

Figure 1-5:
A lock icon appears next to local files when checked out.

Locked file

To manually unlock a file, select the file in the Files panel and right-click (Windows) or Control+click (Mac) and select Turn Off Read Only for a regular site, or Undo Check Out for a Contribute site. If prompted, click Yes to confirm that you want to unlock the file.

Defining File View Columns

In the expanded Files panel, Dreamweaver displays all the file and folder details in columns next to each of the filenames. Using the File View Columns category of the Site Definition dialog box, you can tailor which file and folder details display by modifying the default column settings and adding customized columns. Here are a few of the things you can do to change the File View Columns:

✦ Add new custom columns (up to ten custom columns).

✦ Delete custom columns.

✦ Rename custom columns.

✦ Hide columns.

   You can't hide the filename column.

✦ Realign and reorder columns.

✦ Set column sharing options with users connected to a site.

✦ Attach Design Notes to custom columns.

Customizing File View Columns

Each member of your team can customize their computer to view the contents of the expanded Files panel to suit their specific needs. You can add, edit, remove, hide, and show Dreamweaver's built-in columns, as well as add personal customized columns associated with your Design Notes on your own computer or to be shared with the entire work team!

To add, edit, or delete File View Columns in the Files panel, follow these steps:

1. **Choose Site⇨Manage Sites to open the Manage Sites dialog box.**

2. **Select a site from the site listing and click the Edit button.**

   The Site Definition dialog box appears. If the Advanced tab isn't showing, click the Advanced tab.

3. **Select the File View Columns category.**

   The File View Columns category options display, as shown in Figure 1-6.

4. **To hide any of the built-in categories, select the category and deselect the Options: Show check box.**

   Categories marked with Hide in the Show column are hidden from view in the Files panel.

Figure 1-6:
Customize
the Files
panel by
adjusting
settings in
the File
View
Columns
category.

5. **To add a new custom column, click the plus (+) button.**

   Enter the name of the new column in the Column Name text box, select a Design Notes value from the Associate with Design Note drop-down list or type your own, select an alignment option for the custom column, and decide to make the custom column visible (Show) or hidden (Hide). Custom columns are marked as Personal in the Type column.

6. **To remove a custom column, select the column from the list and click the minus (–) button.**

   Deletion is immediate and undoable, and does not come with a confirmation message, so take special care when deleting columns.

7. **To share a custom column, select the column from the list and select the Show and the Share with All Users of This Site check boxes.**

   This option enables all users connected to the site to view and share the column. Shared columns are marked as Shared in the Type column.

8. **Click the up and down arrows to reorder any of the columns (except for the Name column, which is always first).**

   For example, if you want the Size column to be next to the Name column, select the Size column and click the up arrow button once to reposition the Size column next to the Name column.

9. **Click OK to exit the Site Definition dialog box.**

Sorting columns

After customizing columns, return to the expanded Files panel to sort column data by any of the column headings. Click a heading once to sort all the file data by that column. Click the same heading a second time to reverse the order of the sort from ascending to descending or vice-versa.

Using Site Map Layout

If you're interested in viewing and managing the files in your local site folder in a more graphical way, use Dreamweaver's Site Map Layout mode to see the files as a visual map of linked file icons. If you find problems with your site map organization, turn to Book I, Chapter 2 to find out more about Web site design.

The site map is a good tool to use for laying out site structure because it displays your files as page icons, up to two levels deep, along with any links found in the page source code. You can save maps as .bmp or .png files for printing and editing with an image editor.

Setting a home page and viewing the site map

Before you can view your Web site as a site map, you must define a home page for the site. The home page can be any page on the site; you probably should use the index.html page, but you don't have to. Whatever page you select, it should be a page that is somewhat central to your site, unless you don't mind being disorganized.

To set the home page, right-click (Windows) or Control+click (Mac) the page that you want to become the Site Map home page and choose Set as Home Page from the context menu.

To see the site map, do one of the following:

✦ **In the collapsed Files panel:** Select Map View from the Site View drop-down list on the top-right side of the panel.

✦ **In the expanded Files panel:** Click the Site Map button and from the drop-down menu, select Map Only or Map and Files. The Map and Files option displays in dual panel mode with the site map on one side and the Files panel showing the local site files on the other side, while the Map Only option shows a single pane with just the Map icons.

The Site Map Layout mode displays two levels of icons and shows links along with the filename or page title of each file. Click the plus and minus buttons next to filenames to view pages linked below the current level. Figure 1-7 shows an example of a site map layout.

Figure 1-7: Use Site Map Layout mode as an alternate way of viewing your site.

A broken link.   A locked file.   Someone else has the file checked out.

You have the file checked out.   An e-mail link.

The site map uses colors and icons to indicate the following file attributes:

✦ **A green check mark next to a file:** You have the file checked out.

✦ **A red check mark next to a file:** Another person has checked out the file.

✦ **Red text:** A broken or problematic link.

✦ **Blue text with a globe icon next to it:** Either the file is located on another site or the page contains a script or e-mail link.

✦ **A lock icon next to a file:** The file is either read-only (Windows) or locked (Mac).

When viewing your site in Site Map Layout mode, you can add new and existing pages to the site, edit page titles, select and open pages for editing, and create new links between pages on the site.

Linking and adding a page to a site

You can link brand-new pages or existing pages to a site using the Site Map Layout mode.

To link and add a new page to a site, follow these steps:

1. **Select a file in the site map.**

2. **Right-click (Windows) or Control+click (Mac) and choose Link to New File from the context menu.**

The Link to New File dialog box opens.

3. **Type a filename, title, and text for the new link.**

4. **Click OK.**

The new file displays on the site map, saved into the same location as the selected file. The new file inherits any hidden attributes of the selected file.

To link and add existing pages to a site, do either of the following:

✦ Right-click (Windows) or Control+click (Mac) a file in the site map, choose Link to Existing File from the context menu, and browse to and select the file that you're adding to the site.

✦ Drag and drop a file from Windows Explorer or Macintosh Finder onto a file in the site map. The new file is added to the site along with a link to the file you dragged it to.

Linking files in the site map

You can easily create links between files on the site map when viewing your files in Site Map Layout mode. New links are placed at the bottom of selected files below any existing links. Follow these steps to create file links using the Point-to-File icon in the Map and Files view:

1. **In the expanded Files panel, click the Site Map button and choose Map and Files from its drop-down list.**

2. **Select an HTML file from the site map.**

As you select a file from the site map, the Point-to-File icon appears to the right of the file icon.

3. **Drag the Point-to-File icon next to the selected file on the site map to another file on the site map or to a file in the Site Files view.**

Figure 1-8 shows how to drag and release the Point-to-File icon on top of the file you want to create a link to.

4. **Release the mouse button.**

Dreamweaver adds a link with the name of the newly linked file at the bottom of the selected file.

Site Map

Figure 1-8:
Create links
between
files using
the Site
Map
Layout's
Point-to-
File icon.

Point-to-File icon

Editing page titles and filenames in site map layout

To edit the filenames and titles of your files while working in site map layout, follow these steps:

1. **Choose whether to modify the page titles or filenames and modify the Site Map view as needed:**

   To change the filename of a selected file, skip to Step 2.

   To change the page title, you must first modify the Site Map view to see page titles instead of filenames for all the files (see the "Customizing the site map layout" section coming up).

   Choose View⇨Site Map Options⇨Show Page Titles to toggle back and forth between page titles and filenames.

2. **Select a file in the site map and click either the filename or page title to make it editable. Type the new filename or page title.**

   Or select the file and choose File⇨Rename to highlight the filename or page title, and then type the new name or title.

3. **Press Enter (Windows) or Return (Mac) to set the name or title change.**

   Title changes take effect immediately. For filename changes, Dreamweaver automatically prompts you to update any links to filenames that have changed. For example, if you change `info.html` to `contactus.html`, any links to `info.html` on the site update to link to `contactus.html`.

Additional features in site map layout

You can select multiple pages, open pages to edit in the Document window, and refresh the site map.

To select multiple pages, do any of the following:

✔ Click and drag a marquee around the pages you want to select.

✔ Shift+click to select multiple pages that sit next to each other.

✔ Ctrl+click (Windows) or ⌘+click (Mac) to select multiple pages that do not necessarily sit next to each other.

To open pages for editing in the Document window, do either of these:

✔ Right-click (Windows) or Control+click (Mac) a file and choose Open from the context menu.

✔ Double-click the filename or icon.

To refresh the site map at any time:

1. **Click anywhere inside the site map to deselect any selected files.**

2. **Click the Refresh button in the Files panel.**

Marking and unmarking files in site map layout

By default, site map layout shields you from viewing hidden files and dependent files, such as graphics and other assets. The main reason for the exclusion is to help keep the layout mode clean and easy to use. You can, however, edit the site map to hide or show specific hidden and dependent files by marking or unmarking files as hidden and then choosing to hide or show marked files.

To mark a file as hidden on the site map, follow these steps:

1. **Select a file or files in the site map.**

2. **Right-click (Windows) or Control+click (Mac) and choose Show/Hide Link from the context menu.**

To unmark a file as hidden on the site map, select a file or files in the site map and do any of the following:

✦ Right-click (Windows) or Control+click (Mac) in the site map and choose Show/Hide Link from the context menu.

✦ In the collapsed Files panel, choose View⇨Show/Hide Link from the Options menu.

Files marked as hidden, and any links associated with hidden files, disappear from the site map unless you choose to display hidden files. When you display marked files, the page icon and link appear but the filenames are shown in italics.

Hiding and showing files in site map layout

To hide or show files marked as hidden on the site map, do either of the following:

✦ In the collapsed Files panel, choose View⇨Layout from the Options menu. The Site Definition dialog box opens. Put a check mark next to the Display Files Marked as Hidden option.

✦ In the collapsed Files panel, choose View⇨Show Files Marked as Hidden from the Options menu.

To show hidden and dependent files on the site map, do either of the following:

✦ In the collapsed Files panel, choose View⇨Layout from the Options menu. The Site Definition dialog box opens, where you select the Display Dependent Files option.

✦ In the collapsed Files panel, choose View⇨Show Dependent Files.

Customizing the site map layout

You can do several things to customize the layout of the site map. Using the Site Map Layout category on the Advanced tab of the Site Definition dialog box, you can select a home page, decide how many columns wide you want the site map to be, choose whether to display the hidden and dependent files, and opt to show the filename or page title by default below each page icon. Follow these steps to customize your layout:

1. **Choose Site⇨Manage Sites to open the Manage Sites dialog box.**

2. **Select a site from the site listing and click the Edit button.**

The Site Definition dialog box opens with the Advanced tab showing. If the dialog box opens with the Basic tab showing, click the Advanced tab.

3. **Select the Site Map Layout category.**

The Site Map Layout category options appear, as shown in Figure 1-9.

4. **Fill in the fields in the dialog box:**

• **Home Page:** Change the home page (Dreamweaver chooses the `index.html` page by default; you can choose any page).

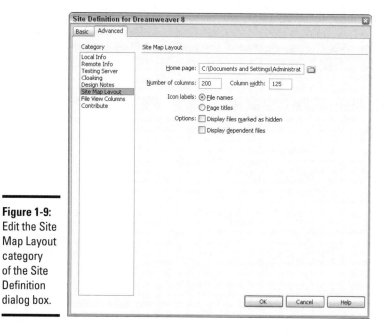

Book VI
Chapter 1

Working Efficiently
with a Team

Figure 1-9:
Edit the Site
Map Layout
category
of the Site
Definition
dialog box.

- **Number of Columns:** Change the number of columns and modify column widths. Type a number here to specify the number of page icons to display in each row on the site map, such as 30. Enter a number in pixels for the width of each column, such as 100 pixels.

- **Icon Labels:** Add icon labels. Choose an option here to have all page icon labels display as either filenames or page titles.

- **Display Files Marked as Hidden:** Enable or disable this option to show or hide your site's HTML files marked as hidden on the site map. When this option is selected, hidden filename labels and links display in italics.

- **Display Dependent Files:** Choose to see or hide all the dependent files, such as images and Cascading Style Sheet files, on the site map layout.

5. **Click OK to save these settings and exit the Site Definition dialog box.**

Saving the site map as a graphic file

Having a graphic of the site map can assist you and your client or team make important decisions about the layout and functionality of the Web site. You can save the site map as a .bmp or .png graphic image for printing and viewing in an image editor.

To create a graphic image of the site map, follow these steps:

1. **With the Map View selected in the collapsed Files panel, choose File⇨ Save Site Map from the Options menu.**

The Save Site Map dialog box opens.

2. **In the File Name text field, type a name for the graphic.**

3. **Select .bmp or .png from the File Type menu.**

4. **Browse to and select a location to save the file.**

5. **Click the Save button.**

Chapter 2: Setting Up and Connecting to a Contribute Site

In This Chapter

✔ **Building a site for Contribute users**

✔ **Connecting to a Contribute site**

✔ **Transferring files to and from a Contribute site**

✔ **Setting server file and folder permissions**

✔ **Understanding and using Contribute special files**

*I*n 2003, Macromedia developed a great little software program called Contribute (the current version is Contribute 3) that, for under $200 per user, enables nontechnical people to edit some of the content on their Dreamweaver-created Web sites. With Contribute, even your least technical clients or office mates can edit and update pages on the site without any fear of breaking or ruining the site.

The program is as easy to use as Microsoft Word and comes with a fantastic instructional tutorial. Contribute has its own built-in Web browser with FTP access which anables you to navigate and download a copy of any existing page on your Web site to your local computer. From there, you can make any edits you want and publish them back to the remote server.

For example, from Contribute you can download a local copy of a Web page on your site, modify it locally, and upload the changed page to the Web site, thereby overwriting what was previously online. If you're working with several people in a workgroup, all members can use Contribute to edit pages on a Web site as long as they have copies of Contribute installed on their computers. Of course, one person has to act as the *site administrator*. Typically that person is either the Web designer who builds the site in Dreamweaver or the Contribute workgroup manager. And because you have to have one Big Cheese, Contribute comes with tools that enable you to create and administer Web sites that are optimized for seamless editing and updating. We explain some of these tools in this chapter and in Book VI, Chapter 3.

In this chapter, you also discover the important differences between building a site in Dreamweaver for Contribute users and building regular Dreamweaver sites. Then you make a Contribute-compatible site connection, use Dreamweaver to administer the site to do things like set file and folder permissions for users, and transfer the Contribute site files to the remote server.

Understanding Contribute Best Practices

A Contribute site really isn't much different from other Web sites you build in Dreamweaver, but you do have to keep a few considerations in mind when you plan and build a site for Contribute users. For example, Contribute is intended to bring the technical elite and the technical novice together so that they can build and maintain an excellent site. That means laying out a logical yet simple site plan that multiple users can understand and use, which is where the Site Map Layout mode comes in handy (see Book VI, Chapter 1).

The Contribute software was very appropriately named. The program not only empowers users to contribute to the Web site in meaningful ways, but it also prevents users from making catastrophic changes that could cripple the site's essential functions (or worse).

Setting up Dreamweaver to work with Contribute is essential. You need to make sure that Contribute users can get in, do what they need to do, and get out — without mucking up the site infrastructure and processes. Here are a few things you should remember to do:

✦ **When you create a new managed site, don't forget to enable Contribute settings.** To access Contribute settings, click the Advanced tab in the Site Definition dialog box.

✦ **Build a Dreamweaver template-driven Web site with specified editable content areas.** Although you don't have to do this, doing so makes the site easier for novices to use when editing and creating new pages in Contribute. For example, you may want to specify one editable area on the template for the main text area of the page, another area for page headers, and another for graphics.

✦ **Make site navigation as simple as possible.** See the section "Leaving a Trail of Bread Crumbs for Contribute Users," later in this chapter.

✦ **Use Dreamweaver to create a style sheet and apply styles to the pages on the Contribute site.** Although you can apply styles (but not create them) with Contribute, it's often faster and easier to do CSS stuff in Dreamweaver.

If Contribute users are using Microsoft Word to write and format site content, consider naming styles after Word style names so Contribute can map the styles when a user copies and pastes data from a Word file into a Contribute file.

✦ **Hide some styles to prevent Contribute users from changing them.** To hide a particular style from Contribute users, edit the style name in Code view so that it starts with `mmhide_`. For instance, if you have a style that makes text bold and 36 pixels called `Bold36`, rename the style to `mmhide_Bold36`.

✦ **Set up read and write file and folder permissions on the server for Contribute users.** Setting up permissions designates what Contribute users can and cannot access and edit on the site after it's published.

✦ **Group similar items together, don't go crazy with folder nesting, and include index pages to each folder that contain links to all the other pages within the folder.** To modify or create new pages, Contribute users must be able to navigate to existing site files through Contribute's browser interface. Once your folders are set up, be sure to encourage users to save new pages they create on the site into the appropriate folders.

✦ **Create a Contribute-compatible site connection and test it in preparation for uploading the files to the remote server.** That way, you know in advance that everything is functioning when you hand off the basic site maintenance tasks to Contribute users later.

Book VI Chapter 2

Setting Up and Connecting to a Contribute Site

Making a Dreamweaver Site Connection Compatible with Contribute

Before building a Contribute site, you need to create a managed site in Dreamweaver so the program knows where on your local machine you're housing all the files you create for the new Contribute site.

You also need to enable Contribute compatibility within Dreamweaver through the Manage Sites dialog box. One of the great benefits of enabling Contribute compatibility is that Dreamweaver automatically saves a version of each file when it's opened. That way if a user ever needs to revert to a previous version of that file, he or she can *roll back* to that version easily. See Book VI, Chapter 3 for more details about the rollback process.

Before you can use Contribute, you need to create a new managed site in Dreamweaver. See Book I, Chapter 3 for details.

After you've defined your site, follow these steps in Dreamweaver to enable site compatibility with Contribute:

1. **From the main menu or from the Options menu in the Files panel, choose Site⇨Manage Sites.**

   The Manage Sites dialog box opens.

2. **Select the site you want to make compatible with Contribute and click the Edit button.**

3. **Choose the Advanced tab in the Site Definition dialog box.**

4. **Click the Contribute category near the bottom of the Category list.**

   The dialog box displays the Enable Contribute Compatibility option, as shown in Figure 2-1.

Figure 2-1:
Enable your site for Contribute compatibility.

5. **Click the Enable Contribute Compatibility check box.**

   Dreamweaver may alert you that you need to select a remote access method (see Book V, Chapter 3), or enable Check In/Out and Design Notes (see Book VI, Chapter 1) prior to enabling the Enable Contribute Compatibility option.

6. **Click OK to accept all the settings in the Site Definition box.**

7. **Click the Done button to close the Manage Sites dialog box.**

After you enable site compatibility with Contribute, you can successfully administer the site with Dreamweaver. You can set up and test the server connection, set server and folder permissions for Contribute users, and transfer files to the remote server, all from within Dreamweaver.

You create the Contribute site just as you do any other site, including having a local and remote copy of all the files. The main difference between a regular site and a Contribute site is that you set up the Contribute site in Dreamweaver so that users can log into the remote site, download pages, modify pages, and upload those pages back to the remote server with Contribute.

**Book VI
Chapter 2**

**Setting Up and
Connecting to a
Contribute Site**

Using Dreamweaver to Administer a Contribute Site

Before you can administer a Contribute site from Dreamweaver, you must also have a copy of Contribute software installed on your computer. After you have both software programs installed on the same computer, you can use Dreamweaver to launch Contribute for site administration tasks such as:

✦ Changing the administrative settings for the Contribute site

✦ Setting up Contribute users with individual *connection keys* (the electronic version of a password that enables them to access the remote server to download, modify, and upload pages on the Web site)

✦ Setting and changing permissions to Contribute roles, which determine the level of access any one Contribute user has on a Web site

One of the great benefits to being a Contribute administrator is that you can assign user roles for each Contribute user and set file and folder permissions for each one. None of these roles and permissions settings affect the Dreamweaver Administrator, however. The Dreamweaver administrator (that's you) is the master of all.

Follow these steps to administer a Contribute site in Dreamweaver:

1. **Select the Contribute category in the Site Definition dialog box.**

   If you're not sure how to do this, follow Steps 1 through 4 in the preceding section.

2. Click the Administer Site in Contribute button (shown in Figure 2-2).

This button appears only after you enable Contribute compatibility as outlined in the preceding section.

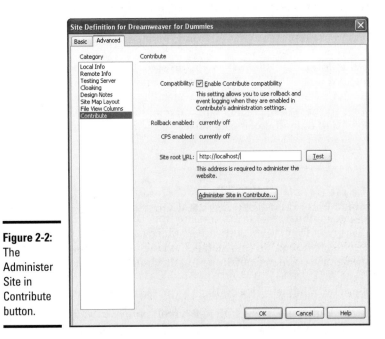

Figure 2-2:
The
Administer
Site in
Contribute
button.

3. In the dialog box that appears (shown in Figure 2-3), select a method for editing and click the Yes button to become the Web site's Contribute Administrator.

Figure 2-3:
Assign
yourself as
the Web
site's
Contribute
Admini-
strator.

Your computer launches Contribute (if it's not already open), and the Contribute Administer Website dialog box appears (see Figure 2-4).

Figure 2-4:
Configure
settings
for the
Contribute
site.

4. **In the Contribute Administer Website dialog box, you can perform the following tasks:**

   • To change administrative settings, select the Administration category to enter a contact e-mail address, set the Administrator password, or remove administrative settings for this site.

   • To edit role settings, select the Users and Roles category and edit or remove existing roles and create new roles.

   • To send connection keys (Contribute site access information) to users, select the Contribute user's name from the list of connected users and click the Send Connection Key button.

   You should, at minimum, set the Administrator password. Additional settings in the Contribute Administer Website dialog box are entirely up to you.

   Note: This book focuses on using Dreamweaver. If you need more detailed support on Contribute, such as setting up administrative settings, connection keys, and user roles, read the Contribute Help files on Macromedia's LiveDocs Web site at

   ```
   http://livedocs.macromedia.com/contribute/311/deploying_en/wwhelp/
        wwhimpl/js/html/wwhelp.htm?href=00000048.htm
   ```

5. **Click OK to accept all the settings in the Administer Website dialog box.**

6. **Click OK to close the Site Definition dialog box.**

7. **Click Done to close the Manage Sites dialog box.**

Making the Most of Templates

Remember when you were just starting out in your career as a Web designer? If not, start reflecting. When you conceive of a Web site for Contribute users, the design can be as elaborate as your imagination can fathom, but you need to ensure that the design has content areas that are easy to edit from the Contribute user's (read novice's) perspective.

Although using templates is by no means required, building a Web site from a Dreamweaver template is one of the best ways to create and manage a site for Contribute users. We recommend that you use a master template in Dreamweaver to build all the pages on the site. That way, you can create editable areas within the template to define what content (including text, graphics, tables, and more) Contribute users can edit. You (as Administrator) still maintain the look and feel of the site, which means you can easily update the layout at a later time, should you need to. See Book III, Chapter 2 to find more about templates.

After you create the templates and build the site in Dreamweaver, you can upload the templates, along with the site files, to the server to make them available to Contribute users. As long as the site root folder for each user's profile matches the site root folder you define for the site in Dreamweaver, the templates appear in Contribute's New Page dialog box when users create a new page.

If you choose not to build the Contribute site using Dreamweaver templates, you could instead designate any page on the site as a Contribute template, from which users can create new pages. For simplicity's sake, we refer to these Contribute-Administrator-designated-template pages as *Contribute templates*.

The main difference between the two template types is that Dreamweaver templates can have editable areas and locked areas, whereas Contribute templates are completely editable. We recommend you use Dreamweaver templates because you have much more control over the integrity of any new pages that are created.

To create a (fully editable) Contribute template, follow these steps:

1. **In Dreamweaver, select the Contribute category in the Site Definition dialog box.**

   If you're not sure how to do this, follow Steps 1 through 4 in the earlier section "Making a Dreamweaver Site Connection Compatible with Contribute."

2. **Click the Administer Site in Contribute button.**

This button appears only after you enable Contribute compatibility (as described in the earlier section "Making a Dreamweaver Site Connection Compatible with Contribute").

If you created an Administrator password when configuring Dreamweaver to administer a Contribute site, the Administrator Password dialog box opens.

3. **Enter an Administrator password if prompted and click OK.**

Your computer launches Contribute (if it's not already open), and the Contribute Administer Website dialog box appears (refer to Figure 2-4).

4. **Select the Administrator role in the Users and Roles category and click the Edit Role Settings button.**

The Edit Administrator Settings dialog box opens.

5. **Choose the New Pages category (shown in Figure 2-5).**

Book VI
Chapter 2

Setting Up and
Connecting to a
Contribute Site

Figure 2-5:
Create new
Contribute
templates
from any
existing file.

6. **Enable the Create a New Page by Copying a Page from This List check box, click the Add button, and select a page on the site to use as a Contribute template.**

7. **Click OK to close the Edit Administrator Settings dialog box.**

8. **Click Close to close the Contribute Administer Website dialog box.**

Now Contribute users can use pages in this list as a starting point for creating new pages.

Leaving a Trail of Bread Crumbs for Contribute Users

When you build a site for Contribute users, try to create a site structure that is easy to navigate. Here are some basic site-organization tips:

✦ **If you're building a small site, organize content in a logical manner by having all the files reside at the root level.** To keep things simple, don't go too crazy with nested folders. You want Contribute users to be able to easily find where they're supposed to be. Book VI, Chapter 1 covers Site Map Layout mode and can help you envision the layout for your Contribute site.

✦ **If you're building a larger site, or if your small site necessitates a folder structure, use folders to organize similar Web pages.** When using subfolders to organize content, make sure that each folder has a main page with the filename `index.html` that contains links to all the other pages within that folder. Then the main page opens automatically in a browser when the URL specifies that folder name, and Contribute users can easily navigate to and open any of the pages in that folder for editing.

For example, if a company provides ten services and needs a separate Web page for each service, organizing all ten services' HTML files inside a Services folder is a logical file management solution. Then the URL, when displayed in a browser, would look something like `http://www.mysamplesite.com/services/`.

Using folders may make Contribute editing go faster than when you use a flat document structure, especially when a lot of editing is going on. With folders, the different versions of files are contained in separate directories, making editing go a little faster.

✦ **If you have server-side includes for HTML content, such as footers or navigation tables, create a simple HTML page with links to all the include files on the site.** Contribute users can then use that HTML page to navigate to and edit the include files.

Connecting to a Contribute Site

In Dreamweaver you can treat a Contribute site just like any other site by connecting to a remote server and editing pages as needed.

That being said, although you can connect to a remote site in several different ways, not all of them are compatible with Contribute. Specifically, the following connections have restrictions:

✦ **Your local computer acts as the Web server:** To share your connection with Contribute users, you need to set up the site with FTP or a network connection instead of using the local folder path.

✦ **You're using WebDAV or Microsoft Visual SourceSafe:** You're out of luck. These connection options aren't compatible with Contribute.

✦ **You're using an RDS (Rapid Development Services) connection:** You can achieve Contribute compatibility, but you need to customize your connection prior to sharing with Contribute users.

When you enable the site for use with Contribute, Dreamweaver creates a site root URL for the Contribute site based on other information about the site. Unfortunately, this information is not always accurate, so you may need to test the connection manually. To see whether your connection is accurate, open the Dreamweaver Site Definition dialog box, and in the Contribute category, click the Test button. Dreamweaver notifies you if the connection is good or lets you know if the connection needs troubleshooting. If it's good, you're ready to transfer files. For troubleshooting help, see "Troubleshooting a Contribute Site in Dreamweaver," later in the chapter.

Transferring files to and from a Contribute site from within Dreamweaver

Just as Dreamweaver has its Check In/Out system, Contribute uses its own method of file transfer to help prevent multiple users from accessing and editing the same file at the same time. In Contribute, users download and open a draft of a page, edit it, and then publish it to the remote server. (Your Contribute users can learn how to do that by taking the cool Contribute tutorial that comes with Contribute.)

As Contribute Administrator, you can use Dreamweaver to transfer files to the remote server instead of uploading and downloading files from within Contribute. Just be sure to always use the Check In/Check Out commands as discussed in Book VI, Chapter 1 when transferring files to a Contribute site from within Dreamweaver.

If you accidentally use Dreamweaver's Get/Put commands instead of Check In/Check Out when transferring files to the remote server, they may accidentally overwrite changes another Contribute user has made to a file. As a failsafe, Dreamweaver gives you a warning if someone else checks out a file.

To aid with the Check In/Out process, Dreamweaver makes automatic backups of all Contribute site files upon check in and puts them in the _baks folder along with your name and a date stamp in a Design Notes file.

Turn to Book V, Chapter 4 to find out how to transfer files from a local site to the remote server.

Setting Contribute file and folder permissions

As the Contribute Administrator, you can set unique file and folder permissions for every Contribute user in a group. These permissions are attached to each user's role rather than to the files and folders. While enforced on Contribute users, these permissions don't affect the files when edited from within Dreamweaver.

For example, a Contribute user with read-only permission to a folder can't write to that folder. The same goes for read access to dependent files.

If a Contribute user doesn't have permission to access an images folder, those images appear as broken image icons when viewing the file for editing purposes in Contribute. Because templates reside in a Templates subfolder at the root level of the site, you need to be aware of read and write permissions so that Contribute users can create new files from templates as needed.

Additionally, Contribute doesn't have any way to manage read-write privileges assigned to files and folders; those must be managed directly on the remote server through Dreamweaver.

Understanding Contribute Special Files

Contribute creates a bunch of *special files* to assist with the administration and editing process of your Contribute Web site. These special files are not viewable by site visitors, and they don't need to be edited or updated by you. They just exist in the background on the remote server to help Dreamweaver manage Contribute files for all the users making changes to pages on the site. These files include

✦ Backup files for old or rollback versions of files in the Contribute-generated _baks folder

✦ Contribute site management files with the .csi file extension that are saved in the Contribute-generated _mm folder

✦ Design Notes files with metadata about the files (see Book VI, Chapter 1 to find more about Design Notes)

✦ Temporary files with the .tmp extension created for previewing purposes within Contribute

✦ Temporary locked (read-only) files to show Contribute users when those files are opened elsewhere

When Contribute creates all these special administrative files, they are automatically updated and uploaded to the publicly accessible remote server for the Web site. If you don't want to see these Contribute files on your server (specifically the _mm and _baks folders), you can create what's called a *staging server* (or *production server*) as a place for Contribute users to work on the site before publishing them to the remote server. After users complete any changes to their pages, those site files can be copied from the staging server to the production server without the special files. To discover how to add another level of security that blocks folders beginning with an underscore from being copied to the production server, search for **Website security** and **Staging Servers and Contribute** in Contribute Help.

Troubleshooting a Contribute Site in Dreamweaver

If you have a problem with a Contribute site in Dreamweaver, most likely it has something to do with the connection or the administration tools. Fortunately, both are fairly easy to troubleshoot. Of course, this book gives only a large-scale view of Contribute, so if your problem falls beyond the information offered here, you should search the Contribute Help files for more information.

Fixing connection problems

You can figure out whether you have a connection problem fairly easily because Dreamweaver enables you to test the remote connection with the root URL any time. All you need to do is click a button related to site administration for Contribute. If the URL is incorrect, Dreamweaver displays an error message.

You can manually check the connection at any time by following these steps in Dreamweaver:

1. **Open the Contribute category on the Advanced tab of the Site Definition dialog box.**

   If you're not sure how to do this, follow Steps 1 through 4 in the earlier section "Making a Dreamweaver Site Connection Compatible with Contribute."

2. **Copy and paste the Site Root URL from the dialog box into a browser to see whether the URL is valid. If it's not, check the spelling and syntax to correct the URL.**

3. **Select Remote Info from the Category list.**

   The right side of the dialog box now displays the Remote Info details.

4. **Click the Test button to test the connection.**

   When the connection is good, Dreamweaver displays an alert message that says it successfully connected with the remote server. When the connection is bad, you see an error message indicating what may be wrong with the connection, such as `Your login or password is incorrect.`

   If you're sure the URL is right but you still get an error message, speak to your system administrator or host provider; the problem is probably server related.

Checking the _mm folder

If the Contribute administration tools aren't working right, the problem may lie in the _mm folder, which should contain a shared settings site-management file with a long funny name and the `.csi` file extension.

The first thing you need to do is to verify that the read and write permissions are enabled on the server. If they aren't, enable them and try using the administration tools again. If they are enabled, you may need to re-establish a connection as administrator, which re-creates or replaces a missing or corrupted shared-settings file in the _mm folder.

If you're still having problems, follow these steps:

1. **Check the _mm folder in the Contribute site from within Dreamweaver to make sure that it contains a shared-settings file with the `.csi` extension.**

   The file has an odd filename like `cthubff3ce10d8490f3d1.csi`.

   This folder and this file are necessary for proper site administration.

2. **If the file is missing or possibly corrupted, you may need to create a new site connection within Dreamweaver and attempt to become the Site Administrator again.**

   The _mm folder and shared settings file are automatically created when you become the Contribute Administrator. If they are missing or corrupted, re-establishing yourself as the site administrator creates new files.

If the problem persists, search for **Troubleshooting** in Contribute's Help files for more information.

Chapter 3: Managing a Contribute Site

In This Chapter

✔ **Using the rollback feature**

✔ **Editing remote files**

✔ **Making templates available to Contribute users**

✔ **Gaining access to files that are checked out**

✔ **Using Dreamweaver to update templates and CSS**

Managing a Contribute site using Dreamweaver is easy and is not much different from creating and managing a non-Contribute site. A key benefit of managing the site using Dreamweaver instead of Contribute, however, is that Dreamweaver automatically does some file management tasks for you that Contribute simply can't do.

Contribute users can, for example, browse to a page on their site, download a copy of it; edit the text, images, links, and tables on it (if they have been granted permission to do so by the Administrator); save the file; and then send it back to the server, which instantly displays the updated page.

Contribute users can't, however, do some of the more complex site-management and page-editing tasks, such as editing or creating new styles in a CSS, renaming and moving files, or making global changes to the site's layout by editing a Dreamweaver template. The Contribute Site Administrator in Dreamweaver must do these things.

In the previous chapter, we show you how to create and set up a Contribute site. This chapter deals with file management. If you're ready to manage a Contribute site, we presume that you have already done the following things:

✦ Installed Contribute and Dreamweaver on the same local computer.

✦ Connected to the Contribute site with Dreamweaver. In the Dreamweaver Site Definition dialog box, you have to enter the Contribute site's Local Site and Remote Site information. You must include a local root folder and a site root URL on the server.

✦ Tested the site's connectivity by making sure that the root URL works.

✦ Enabled Contribute compatibility in Dreamweaver. You should also turn on Design Notes and the Check In/Check Out feature (as described in Book VI, Chapter 1).

✦ Clicked the Administer Site in Contribute button in the Dreamweaver Site Definition dialog box to provide administration details for the site and for Contribute users as required.

✦ Designed, built, and uploaded a Contribute site to the remote server.

If you haven't done all these things, flip back to Book VI, Chapter 2 before continuing.

Managing Contribute Files Using Dreamweaver

As the Dreamweaver Administrator, you can perform certain high-level tasks that Contribute users can't. Table 3-1 contains a list of general tasks that can be performed in one or both programs. These management tasks include *rolling back* to older versions of files; editing, deleting, moving, and renaming files; giving Contribute users access to templates even though they don't have root folder access; and unlocking locked files on the remote server.

Table 3-1	Web Site Management Tasks	
Contribute Site Management Tasks	*Dreamweaver Administrator*	*Contribute User*
Connect to the Web site on the remote server	Yes	Yes
Set up Contribute users and define user roles	Yes	No
Check in/check out files	Yes	Yes, as part of the Edit/Publish process
Edit files	Yes	Yes
Move and rename files	Yes	No
Delete files	Yes	Yes, but only if Administrator has enabled this option for the user
Create new pages	Yes	Yes
Create new Dreamweaver template-based pages	Yes	Yes, but only if Administrator has granted permission to the Templates folder on the remote server
Convert files with FlashPaper	Yes	Yes
Roll back files	Yes	Yes, but only if Administrator has enabled this option for the user

Contribute Site Management Tasks	Dreamweaver Administrator	Contribute User
Administer a Web site	Yes	Yes, but only if Administrator has enabled this option for the site
Create Contribute templates	Yes	Yes, but this is typically allowed for only one person
Create Dreamweaver templates	Yes	No
Access Dreamweaver templates	Yes	No
Modify Dreamweaver templates	Yes	No
Create, edit, delete external CSS linked to pages	Yes	No
Enable event log in	Yes	No
Unlock locked files on the remote server	Yes	No
Create Design Notes	Yes	No

Be benevolent with your power. Give your Contribute users the right access to the right tools, and you may be surprised to discover that you create less work for yourself.

Rolling back your files

You have probably enabled compatibility between Dreamweaver and Contribute by now. If you haven't, open the Site Definition dialog box in Dreamweaver, as explained in Book VI, Chapter 2.

The next step is to log in to the Contribute site through Dreamweaver as the Administrator. When the Administer Website dialog box opens, select the Rollbacks category and select the Enable Rollbacks feature, as shown in Figure 3-1. The default number of file versions to keep for rollback purposes is three, but you can increase or decrease the number if you like.

After that you need to enable the rollback feature within Contribute. To do so, choose Edit➪Administer Website and select the name of the Contribute site. The Administer Website dialog box opens, which looks exactly like the dialog box that opens from within Dreamweaver. Select the Rollbacks category and select the Enable Rollbacks feature and then click the Close button to close the dialog box.

With rollback turned on, Dreamweaver automatically saves every version of a file (up to the number specified in the Rollbacks category, which is typically three versions) as it gets edited. If you need to revert to a previous version of a file, no problem; each version is stored with the date and editor's name for easy retrieval. You can use a previous version to roll back to and overwrite any mistakes that were made on the most recent version.

Figure 3-1:
Enable the
Rollback
feature.

You may think that the rollback feature is a function you'd never need, but trust us when we tell you it can come in handy some day. The more Contribute users working on a site, the greater the likelihood of the need to roll back files.

To roll back a file in Dreamweaver, follow these steps:

1. **In the Files panel, right-click (Windows) or Control+click (Mac) the filename that you want to roll back.**

2. **From the context menu that appears, choose Roll Back Page.**

   The Roll Back Page dialog box appears displaying a list of versions of the file you can select and roll back to, as shown in Figure 3-2.

Figure 3-2:
Select a
version of
a file to roll
back.

3. **Select the version of the file you want to roll back to.**

   When there are no prior versions, the dialog box displays a message that you can't roll back to a previous version of the selected file.

4. **Click the Roll Back button to roll back to the selected version, or the Cancel button to exit the dialog box.**

The rollback version replaces the newest version of the file.

Making changes to Contribute files

Contribute users can do some tasks, such as edit and republish existing files, create new pages based on existing pages, and create brand-new pages to add to a Contribute site. They can't, however, delete, move, and rename files, and do some file editing tasks on a remote Contribute site. The site Administrator must perform these tasks through Dreamweaver.

Keep in mind the following points when making changes to Contribute files:

✦ **Editing files:** Use the Check In/Check Out feature (instead of Get and Put) to check out the file to which you want to make changes, make the changes, save the file, and check it back in.

   We discuss editing templates and style sheets later in this chapter, in the section, "Using Dreamweaver to Edit a Contribute Site."

✦ **Moving and renaming files:** On the surface, moving a file from one location on the remote server to another, or even renaming a file, works the same in a Contribute site as it does in a Dreamweaver site. But Dreamweaver tracks and saves these changes in the _baks folder, and modifies the filename or location in all the previous versions of the file. That way, if you need to roll back to a previous version, the file location or name change stays intact. Pretty smart, huh?

   We strongly recommend that if you have to move or rename a file, you do so from within Dreamweaver.

✦ **Deleting files:** If you're using Dreamweaver to delete a file, Dreamweaver asks whether you want to fully delete all previous versions of that file at the same time. If you say yes, they all disappear forever. If you say no, Dreamweaver saves a copy of the current version as a new version of the file in the _baks folder on the remote server for future restoration using the Roll Back Page command.

To delete a file on a remote Contribute site using Dreamweaver, follow these steps:

1. **In the Remote pane of the Files panel, select the file you want to delete and press the Delete key on your keyboard.**

A Confirmation dialog box opens for you to confirm the deletion.

2. **If you want to also delete any rollback versions of the selected file, enable the Delete Rollback Versions option.**

Deselect the Delete Rollback Versions option to keep previous versions of the selected file online, including a copy of the version you're deleting.

3. **Click Yes to delete the selected file.**

You can't undo this action! Deleted files are permanently removed from the server and are irretrievable.

Enabling Contribute users to use templates

When you set up folder and file permissions for users on the Contribute site through Dreamweaver's Administer Website dialog box, be sure to give Contribute users read access to any files and folders on the remote server. Such folders include root-level files, images subfolders, and perhaps read access to the Templates folder if you want Contribute users to create template-based files from Dreamweaver-generated templates. You can grant file and folder permissions to users through the Folder/File Access category of the Edit Role Settings dialog box, shown in Figure 3-3.

Figure 3-3:
Set file and folder permissions for Contribute users.

If you're weary of granting users permission to the Templates folder, you could allow them to use Dreamweaver templates by copying the entire Template folder from the main site's root folder to the Contribute site's remote root folder through the Files panel.

Thereafter, whenever the Dreamweaver templates are updated on the main site through Dreamweaver, you must remember to copy the updated templates to the Template folder on the remote Contribute site. Copying the updated templates to the Contribute site is the only way to overwrite the older files so that users can access them.

Unlocking a checked out file

When you enable the Check In/Check Out feature, it may sometimes appear (by the presence of a lock next to the file on the user's computer) that a remote file is checked out when it really isn't. That means the file isn't really locked, but in order for any users to access the file, the lock needs to be removed. As Administrator, you have that power.

Before you unlock the file through Dreamweaver, be sure the file's not really checked out by a Contribute user. If the file is unlocked when it really is checked out, that would grant file access to multiple users with the potential of creating multiple versions of the file at once!

To manually unlock a file in a Contribute site that appears to be checked out, select the file in Dreamweaver's Files panel and right-click (Windows) or Control+click (Mac) it and select Undo Check Out. If prompted, click Yes to confirm that you indeed want to unlock the file. To find out more about the Check In/Check Out feature, see Book VI, Chapter 1.

Using Dreamweaver to Edit a Contribute Site

Some things *you* — as Administrator — can do in both Dreamweaver and Contribute. And some tasks you should perform only in Dreamweaver. Make any robust changes to a Contribute site, such as modifying a template or CSS, in Dreamweaver to maintain the integrity of the site's design.

Updating templates in a Contribute site

Contribute users can't change Dreamweaver templates, and that's a good thing because they're typically not Web designers. If a template needs editing, you need to do it in Dreamweaver. What part of a template might you need to edit? Perhaps you need to remove a navigation button from the layout or edit some text that appears on every page. Or maybe you need to overhaul the site design, with all new graphics, while keeping the overall content intact.

If you remove or rename an editable region from a template, Contribute users may not know what to do with the content from the old editable region. To avoid confusion, try to make changes to the templates before or after normal business hours and be sure to have Contribute users close down and relaunch their Contribute programs prior to making any new changes to the site. Contribute users can only get new remote server information to their local computers by closing and relaunching Contribute.

To edit a Dreamweaver template used in a Contribute site, follow these steps:

1. **In Dreamweaver, open, edit, and save the Contribute site template.**

Find out more about templates in Book III, Chapter 2.

2. **Tell the Contribute users about the change so that they can close and restart their Contribute programs.**

Restarting Contribute enables Contribute users to access the site with the most recent documents and templates.

Editing style sheets in a Contribute site

Making sure that the look and feel of a site stays under tight control is important in any Web design scenario. Contribute users aren't allowed to change the contents of style sheets, which means that you don't have to worry about style sheets being messed up by anyone but you and any other Dreamweaver users on the team.

As with any site using style sheets, when you delete a style, the tag to apply that style to a particular word, sentence, or paragraph still resides in the code of the Web pages. The discrepancy may confuse your Contribute users. To quickly remove or rename style tags from an entire site, use Dreamweaver's Find and Replace tool (see Book II, Chapter 2).

Also, let the Contribute users know about any changes you make to the CSS during work hours, because they can't see changes to any pages they're currently editing until they publish the page back to the site.

Follow these steps to edit a style in a Contribute site through Dreamweaver:

1. **Use Dreamweaver's style-sheet editing tools.**

You have a variety of options. You can use the CSS Styles panel, the Attributes panel, or edit the CSS code by hand. See Book III, Chapter 1 for everything you wanted to know about using CSS in Dreamweaver but were afraid to ask.

2. **Tell the Contribute users about the change so that they can publish and re-edit pages with the newest version of the style sheet.**

Better yet, tell users to restart Contribute so they can access all the site pages and assets with the most recent versions of everything.

Book VII

Building Web Applications

The 5th Wave   By Rich Tennant

FREELANCER NED WILLIS CONSULTS
WITH A MEMBER OF HIS TECHNICAL STAFF

©RICHTENNANT

"...and that's pretty much all there is to converting a document to an HTML file."

Contents at a Glance

Chapter 1: Building Web Applications

In This Chapter

✔ **Choosing a database**

✔ **Selecting a Web application platform**

✔ **Installing an application server**

✔ **Analyzing your choices for Web and application servers**

✔ **Defining the Testing Server settings in Dreamweaver**

*W*eb-based applications allow you to present dynamic Web pages that come alive because the user can interact with them. You can customize what information displays on-screen based on the user's input and then store that input in a database. This allows you to build applications such as a user forum, a guestbook, or a recipe collection and sharing site. Your possibilities are endless.

The first challenge when planning how to build applications from Web pages is picking a set of tools to use. Because you're building Web pages that are intelligent about content delivery, you need to stop thinking of Web sites as only HTML files that work whether you access them from a directory on your computer or through the World Wide Web. If you try to directly access pages that contain application logic, you'll end up seeing the code without it being translated by the Web platform and the application server.

This chapter gives you the lowdown on designing your database and choosing the right database application. Additionally, you find out what Web application platforms and application servers are and how to choose the right ones for your needs. We also touch on various languages, such as ASP, JSP, and ColdFusion, that work hand-in-hand with the application server when generating your dynamic Web pages.

Introducing Databases

A *database* is a collection of data organized in such a way that you can quickly add, retreive, or modify the information. For example, Amazon.com and Monster.com use enormous databases that enable users to search and navigate the immense amounts of data on their sites. Creating your own database is nothing more than putting data into a logical system that stores and retrieves related information.

The information in a database is organized into tables. Each table has multiple *fields* (or *columns*) and individual records in *rows.* For example, take a look at Table 1-1, the Employees table.

Table 1-1		Employees	
EmployeeID	*FirstName*	*LastName*	*Department*
697882	Jane	Smith	Accounting
598066	Joseph	Taylor	Sales
596072	Larry	Walters	Sales

At the top of the Employees table are the column (field) names: EmployeeID, FirstName, LastName, and Department. The three subsequent rows contain the individual records.

To extract your data correctly, you need to set up the relationships between pieces of data properly. Data has three kinds of relationships:

✦ **One-to-one:** In a one-to-one relationship, each item is related to one and only one other item. In the Employees table, the Employee ID and the name of the employee have a one-to-one relationship. Each employee has one and only one ID number, and each ID number can belong to one and only one employee.

✦ **One-to-many:** A one-to-many relationship has *keys* (unique identifiers) from one table that appear multiple times in another table. Say you have a Department table along with an Employees table. The Employees table has a one-to-many relationship with the Department table. A department (such as Accounting) can have many employees, but each employee can work in only one department.

✦ **Many-to-many:** A many-to-many relationship means that two tables each have multiple keys from another table.

Your data should also conform to *normalization* rules (a series of progressively strict rules to help you build a well-designed database):

✦ **First normal form:** For your database to be in first normal form, it must satisfy two requirements. First, every table must not have repeating columns that contain the same kind of data, and secondly, all columns must contain only one value.

✦ **Second normal form:** Stricter than the first normal form, the second normal form requires that each field be based specifically on the key.

✦ **Third normal form:** The third normal form expands on the second normal form by allowing no other column in the table except for the key column to define any other column.

If you're interested in delving deeper into the subject of databases, we recommend that you check out *Database Development For Dummies* by Allen G. Taylor (Wiley).

Choosing a Database

You have many database choices. Any of these databases work well with Dreamweaver:

✦ **Microsoft Access (www.microsoft.com/access):** If you're just getting started, consider using Access. It's good for establishing a small, simple database when you're not too concerned about performance. It's also bundled with Microsoft Office, so it isn't very expensive (you may even already have it installed).

✦ **Microsoft SQL Server Express Edition (http://msdn.microsoft.com/sql/express/):** A free, lighter-duty edition of SQL Server, this database is a good choice if you don't need the enterprise features that SQL Server offers.

✦ **MySQL (www.mysql.com/):** MySQL is a good choice if you're creating a small site. It's available for free and runs on Windows, Mac OS X, and Linux.

✦ **Microsoft SQL Server (www.microsoft.com/sql/):** SQL Server is more complicated to set up and run than other database choices, but it offers a large cornucopia of procedures that Access doesn't and has the power to handle a large quantity of requests from users of your Web site.

After you choose the right database for your needs, consult your database system's documentation for details on how to create the database. Book VII, Chapters 2 through 6, gives you the details on setting up PHP, ASP, ASP.NET, JSP, and ColdFusion database connections in Dreamweaver.

Choosing a Web Application Platform

Web application platforms (or *Web servers*) are programs that run on your computer or on a server that takes requests for a Web page and deliver the page to a Web browser over a network, such as the Internet. Without the Web platform, people couldn't get to the sites you create and publish in Dreamweaver.

Dreamweaver 8 allows you to create pages and sites that can display in a variety of Web services that are available on the Internet. Web services allow a Web site to integrate logic and content from a remote server using a standard interface. The server may provide the Web service free of charge or as a paid service. The Web site that calls the Web service is called a *consumer,* and the Web service is called the *publisher*. The consumer may pass information to the Web service, which affects the data that's returned. The returned data is usually HTML that's integrated into the consumer's dynamic Web pages. This can be as simple as a publisher providing a service that takes a zip code and returns its state.

Additionally, Dreamweaver 8 supports the creation of Web-based sites or other applications that use an *application server.* The application server supports the processing of your Web pages as the Web platform serves them up. It acts as a helper to the Web server for processing the code that's part of the pages. See Figure 1-1 for a look at how your pages are processed. The languages Dreamweaver supports for the application server are PHP, Macromedia ColdFusion MX, ASP, ASP.NET, and Java Server Pages (JSP). Each of these languages corresponds to a Dreamweaver document type.

Figure 1-1:
The steps of processing a Web application page request.

If you're already familiar with one of these languages, then choose that one. If they're all new to you, PHP and ASP are very popular choices. You can find plenty of help and sample code on the Web for both of them. (See "Adding an Application Server," later in this chapter.)

However, before you can develop Web services, you need to choose the underlying server technology. The two popular choices are Microsoft Internet Information Services (IIS) and Apache. If you've already worked with one, then go ahead and stick with it because you'll have less to learn.

The choice may not even be yours. If you're using a Web hosting service to publish your Web pages, you need to determine which type of Web platform your Web hosting service uses. Your ISP usually has a How To page that describes which operating system and Web platform it uses to host your Web pages. Generally speaking, if it provides *shell access,* it uses a Unix-based OS, so you can assume it's running Apache; however, if it offers only FTP access to files, it's probably using a Windows OS and IIS.

If you're still in the process of selecting a hosting company for your Web sites, or if you want to test your Web application pages on your computer without uploading them to a remote server, compare the pros and cons of using the IIS Web platform versus the Apache Web platform, as described next.

Microsoft IIS

IIS (Internet Information Services) is a good choice if you're planning to develop pages with ASP or ASP.NET models because IIS has built-in support for handling those development languages. If you choose ASP.NET, download the ASP.NET framework from Microsoft. Don't be put off by the word *framework;* Microsoft really just means *development kit.* It's available at `www.asp.net`.

Book VII
Chapter 1

Building Web
Applications

For all versions of Windows, make sure that you run Windows Update (it's available from the Tools menu of Internet Explorer). It updates all Microsoft software on your computer, including IIS. In fact, this task is important to do to minimize the risk of picking up nasty viruses from the Internet. Computer maintenance, such as consistently installing your Microsoft patches and running Ad-Aware (`www.lavasoftusa.com/software/adaware/`) to make sure that your system isn't compromised, is important, so do it. Another program to help clean your system and purge it of unwanted parasites is SpyBot S&D, which you can download at `www.safer-networking.org/`.

Which version of Windows you're running determines which version of IIS you can run. To verify that IIS is installed on your computer, follow these steps:

1. **Choose Start⇨Control Panel⇨Add/Remove Programs or choose Start⇨ Control Panel and double-click the Add/Remove Programs icon.**

   The same dialog box that you've probably used to remove software opens.

2. **In the Add or Remove Programs window, click the Add/Remove Windows Components button.**

   This step tells Windows that you want to change which Microsoft components (including IIS) are installed.

   The Windows Components Wizard opens.

3. **Click the Internet Information Services check box, as shown in Figure 1-2.**

   Windows tells you approximately how much space you need to install IIS. If the check box was already checked, that means IIS is already installed, and you can stop.

Figure 1-2:
Verifying that IIS is installed on your Windows computer.

4. **Click Next.**

   You may need your Windows Installer CD-ROM to install IIS, so make sure it's somewhere handy.

5. **Follow the on-screen prompts to finish installing IIS and then click OK.**

The default directory for IIS-stored Web pages is `C:\Inetpub\wwwroot`. This is often called the *Web root folder*.

Follow these steps to access configuration settings for IIS. This may be useful when troubleshooting problems in the future.

1. **Choose Start⇨Control Panel and open Administrative Tools.**

   The Administrative Tools menu is found in the Performance and Maintenance category for XP and contains options for changing the configuration of your Windows operating system.

Windows 2000 doesn't have categories, so you immediately see the Administrative Tools folder in the Control Panel.

2. **Double-click Internet Services Manager.**

The Internet Information Services window displays a tree structure that shows the options you can change, as shown in Figure 1-3.

Figure 1-3:
Configuring
IIS from the
Internet
Information
Services
config-
uration
window.

If you like having more than one choice, you'll be happy to hear that IIS isn't your only Web platform option. Apache, described next, is another option for you to consider.

Apache

The Apache Web platform is the most popular one for Web usage. It's an *open-source* product, so it's free to download and use. Apache works well with the PHP Application Server model as well as with JSP. You need to install it separately from a downloadable installer file if you're using Windows.

You can download Apache for Windows from `http://httpd.apache.org`. Download the prepackaged Microsoft Installer (MSI) files with names similar to `apache_2.0.55-win32-x86-no_ssl.msi`. The `win32` in the filename indicates that it is meant for Windows.

If you're using Windows XP, make sure you've run Windows Update before installation to avoid any problems when running Apache.

Mac OS X

If you're using Mac OS X and you want to run your Web application files locally, your choice for a Web platform is quite simple. IIS doesn't run on the Mac, but Apache does. In fact, your Mac already comes with Apache installed.

To enable it, you simply pop over to your System Preferences tool, as described in the following steps:

1. **From the Apple menu, choose System Preferences.**

The System Preferences application in Mac OS X controls the configuration of your system, including optional components such as Apache.

2. **Click the Sharing icon.**

The Sharing panel (shown in Figure 1-4) tells OS X which services your computer provides, including Apache and file sharing.

Figure 1-4:
The Sharing panel in Mac OS X.

3. **If the Personal Web Sharing check box isn't already checked, then check it.**

Apple doesn't come right out and call it *Apache* in the setup; instead, it's called *Personal Web Sharing* or just *Web Sharing.*

4. **Click the Start button on the same screen.**

You're all set to start using Apache.

The Mac is set up to support multiple users on a single machine, so the Web root for Apache depends on your Mac *short username.* (You can find out your short username by going to System Preferences, selecting Accounts, and clicking the Edit User button. In the Accounts dialog box, you'll see the Short Name field.) For example, if your short name is `jonp`, the default Web root is `http://127.0.0.1/~jonp/`. The short name must come after the tilde (~) character, and the last slash must be present for the address to work.

You may have noticed the special IP address of `127.0.0.1`. This address is called the *localhost address.* It always points to the local computer. Typically, computers have two IP addresses: the public one, such as `128.34.34.34`, and the localhost host address, `127.0.0.1`. In order for Web users at large to access your Web pages, they must reference the external address.

Hosted ISP sites

Specifically, Dreamweaver allows you to perform the following Web service development tasks:

✦ Select Web services available on the Internet.

✦ Generate a Web service proxy that allows the Web page to communicate with the Web service publisher.

The *proxy,* also known as an *abstraction class,* contains the fields, methods, and properties of the Web service and makes them available to the locally hosted page. When you generate a proxy for your page, Dreamweaver lets you view it in the Components panel (choose Window➪Components to open the panel).

Before you create a Web page that uses a Web service, you must be familiar with the underlying server technology of the application and the programming constructs the application requires.

Dreamweaver lets you author Web pages that can access Web services and use the functionality the services provide. In addition, you can create and publish Web services for deployment using Macromedia ColdFusion MX.

Adding an Application Server

After you select a Web platform (as described in the first part of the chapter), you're ready to add an application server. Some of the Web platforms come essentially prebuilt with some application server functionality. For example, IIS comes with support for ASP processing. By and large, though, you need to do some software installation for the application server.

PHP

PHP stands for *PHP: Hypertext Preprocessor.* It's an open-source programming language that is well adapted to creating Web applications. It works well with many databases, including the popular open-source database MySQL.

It supports all major operating systems, including Windows, Mac OS X, and Linux. It integrates with either IIS or Apache to form a PHP Application Server. For Apache, it's loaded as an Apache Module. For IIS, it's loaded as an ISAPI add-on.

Windows setup

Installing PHP for use with IIS is fairly easy with the automatic installation available from the PHP site. Download PHP from www.php.net. Get the automatic installation package under Windows Binaries; it's an executable (.exe) file. Be sure to use a download mirror that's close to where you live.

After you download the file, follow these steps to install PHP:

1. **Double-click the .exe file.**

2. **Click Next to install.**

3. **Agree to the license terms by clicking I Agree.**

4. **Select the Standard Install radio button and click Next.**

The standard install uses default values for many of the settings. You can use the defaults without problems.

5. **Click Next to accept the default installation directory of c:\PHP.**

6. **(Optional) Enter values for the Mail Configuration.**

You can also leave the default values.

These are the same settings you selected when you configured your e-mail client.

7. **Select Microsoft IIS 4 or higher from the list of HTTP servers if you installed IIS, or select Apache if you installed the Apache Web server.**

8. **Click Next.**

9. **To begin the installation, click Next again.**

10. **Click OK in the IIS Has Been Configured dialog box.**

This dialog box only appears if you didn't select IIS as your HTTP server.

11. **Click OK in the Installation Complete dialog box.**

If you're using Windows NT, follow the directions in the dialog box; otherwise the installation is complete.

Mac OS X setup

Mac OS X includes the files necessary to run PHP, but those files require manual editing that's quite tedious for most users. To enable PHP support for Mac OS X without messing around with your system files, visit www.entropy.ch/software/macosx/php and then follow these steps:

1. **Download an installer file for Mac OS X based on the version of Mac OS X you're running.**

Packages are available for both PHP4 and PHP5. Go ahead and select PHP5.

2. **The Mac installer file is a .dmg disk image. Double-click the .dmg file.**

The Mac mounts the disk image and displays a drive icon with the files.

3. **When you see the installer package, double-click it and follow the directions.**

That was pretty simple. Congratulations, you've successfully installed the PHP application server for your Mac.

ASP

Active Server Pages (ASP) is Microsoft's original entry into the Web application world. ASP is designed to work with the IIS Web platform. Dreamweaver supports building ASP code that can stand alone or be modified outside of Dreamweaver, if you feel so inclined.

ASP aims to make Web application development as easy as possible by grouping common tasks together into objects. These objects include Application, ASPError, Request, Response, Server, and Session objects. The ASPError, for example, provides functions for handling errors.

Most ASP pages use VBScript as the programming language, with JavaScript being a close second. Dreamweaver knows what code to put in regardless of which one you choose. If you're not sure, go with VBScript.

Support for ASP is built into IIS. To put it another way, if you've installed IIS and run Windows Update, you're ready to begin using the ASP application server, too.

ASP.NET

ASP.NET, despite its name being similar to ASP, is really a complete rewrite of the ASP development platform to conform to the Microsoft .NET style. The .NET style attempts to make developing a Web application as easy as developing a non-Web-based application.

Support for ASP.NET is integrated with IIS, but you must make sure you've installed the .NET framework from Microsoft. To get started with ASP.NET, download the Visual Web Developer 2005 Express Edition from Microsoft at `http://msdn.microsoft.com/vstudio/express/vwd`.

JSP

Java Sever Pages (JSP) use the Java language and processor to deliver Web-based applications written in Java. JSP pages are different from other pages because they're compiled into byte code by the JSP compiler. These compiled JSP pages are called *servlets*.

Apache Jakarta Tomcat is the servlet container that's used for both the Java Servlet and JSP technologies. Apache Jakarta Tomcat is an open-source application that helps develop large-scale, high-traffic Web applications.

Jakarta Tomcat is available from `http://tomcat.apache.org`. If you're using Windows, download the core Windows Executable installer. For Mac OS X, visit `http://developer.apple.com/internet/java/tomcat1.html` for instructions on installing the Mac OS X binaries of Tomcat.

Other commerical JSP Application Severs include the following:

+ Macromedia JRun

+ Sun ONE Application Server

+ IBM WebSphere

+ BEA WebLogic

Most commercial distributions include a 30-day trial period if you're interested in how they compare to each other, as opposed to buying one without test-driving it.

ColdFusion

When you think of ColdFusion, you may think of some over-hyped boundless energy from atoms fusing together, but that's not the only ColdFusion out there. ColdFusion also refers to a Web application development language that has syntax similar to HTML markup. ColdFusion allows people familiar with tag-based languages such as HTML to easily learn ColdFusion.

ColdFusion was originally developed by Allaire and has since been acquired by the makers of Dreamweaver. The similarity to HTML tags comes at a price; ColdFusion doesn't support developing anything but Web applications.

Considering Web/Application Server Combinations

Although each of the Web platforms and application servers described in this chapter does essentially the same thing, processing Web application pages that have code in them differs slightly because of where all additional files are located and the URL to access these files.

The Web root folder for your application varies depending on the Web platform you choose and what your ISP dictates as the Web root. You want to create a directory in your Web root folder for each Web application you build.

Table 1-2 lists the default Web root folder and base URLs for each combination of Web platforms and application servers.

Table 1-2	Default Web Root and Base URLs	
Web Server	*Default Web Root*	*Default Base URL*
Apache on Windows	`C:\apache\htdocs`	`http://localhost/`
Apache on Mac OS X	`/Users/UserName/Sites`	`http://localhost/~UserName/`
IIS	`C:\Inetpub\wwwroot`	`http://localhost/`
ColdFusion	`C:\CfusionMX7\wwwroot`	`http://localhost:8500/`
Jakarta Tomcat on Windows	`C:\jakarta-tomcat-4.x.x\webapps\ROOT\`	`http://localhost:8080/`

For Apache on Mac OS X, the username is the short Macintosh username.

You can verify that you have the correct Web root setup by placing a sample file in the Web root directory and then navigating your browser to the base URL. An example of a test file is a file called `index.html` that contains the following:

```
<html>
<body>
Hello!
</body>
</html>
```

If you're running IIS and place the file in `C:\Inetpub\wwwroot`, for example, you can access it from your Web browser at `http://localhost/index.html`.

Setting Up the Testing Server in Dreamweaver

The Testing Server category in the Advanced Site Definition dialog box tells Dreamweaver how to process the Web application pages locally while you're developing them. Often, you simply use a local directory if you're using a server technology that your local Web platform can process, such as IIS and ASP.

Here's how to set up the Testing Server category:

1. **Choose Site⇨Manage Site.**

   The Manage Site dialog box appears.

2. **Select your site from the list and click the Edit button.**

   If you need to create a site from scratch, see Book I, Chapter 3.

3. **Click the Advanced tab and select the Testing Server category.**

   The Advanced Site Definition options for entering testing server preferences for your managed site appear. You need to enter this information in order for your site's dynamic data to process correctly.

4. **Click the Testing Server category on the left side of the Site Definition dialog box.**

   This screen starts out with only two drop-down lists, for the server model and the remote access type, as shown in Figure 1-5.

5. **Pick the server technology from the Server Model drop-down list.**

   Your choices are

   - ASP JavaScript
   - ASP VBScript
   - ASP.NET C#
   - ASP.NET VB
   - ColdFusion
   - JSP
   - PHP

   For this example, we picked ASP JavaScript, as shown in Figure 1-6.

Figure 1-5:
Fill in the
Testing
Server
category for
your site.

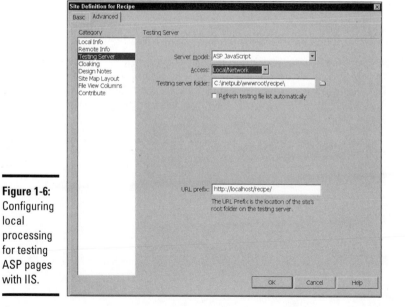

Figure 1-6:
Configuring
local
processing
for testing
ASP pages
with IIS.

6. **Select how to get your files from your local computer to your remote site from the Access drop-down list.**

   Your selections include

   • None

   • FTP

   • Local/Network

   • WebDAV

   For the example, we picked Local/Network.

7. **In the URL Prefix field, enter the URL path that your testing server uses to publish the pages.**

   If this is on your local machine, it looks like `http://localhost/recipe_test`. If it's on a remote server, it looks like `http://example.com/recipe_test`.

   Dreamweaver assumes, by default, that both the Web server and application server are running on the same system. Therefore, if you specify a remote location (see Book V, Chapter 3), Dreamweaver assumes that the testing server is the same URL. If you don't enter a remote category, Dreamweaver makes sure that the default testing server matches the local folder.

8. **Click OK to save your changes and begin using the new site.**

You can also use a directory on your server for testing the Web application pages. This choice is good if you haven't set up an application server on your local computer or if you're using a computer that doesn't work well with the code you're developing, for example, using ASP on a Mac.

Chapter 2: Configuring Database Connections for PHP

In This Chapter

✔ **Connecting to a MySQL database**

✔ **Adding a database connection**

✔ **Editing or deleting a database connection**

*I*f you've decided to go the open-source route and use PHP as your application server language and MySQL for your database, this chapter is for you. (If you haven't set up PHP, see Book VII, Chapter 1 for details.) We recommend having your database, MySQL, PHP, and Dreamweaver 8 all reside on the same local server. That way, you don't risk damaging any information on the publicly visible production server. If you see a glitch, you can fix it immediately, as opposed to correcting the file and then FTPing it to the production server. As an aside, you also know exactly what's installed locally because, most likely, you did it yourself.

If you're not comfortable working with a local copy of PHP and MySQL, you can certainly use a remote server. Also, if you're using an older computer and are concerned it may not have enough umph to process everything, you can take the remote route.

Whether your MySQL database resides on a local drive or with your ISP, this chapter shows you how to connect to it and create a dynamic Web page with PHP, which allows your site to interact with Dreamweaver. Additionally, you find out how to set up a MySQL database connection and add, edit, or delete a connection.

Gathering What You Need to Connect to a MySQL Database

Connecting to a MySQL database in Dreamweaver is easy. You need three pieces of information to make a connection from PHP to MySQL:

✦ Host name or IP address of the MySQL server

✦ Username and password with authority to access your database

✦ Name of the database to which you're trying to connect

In addition to the preceding information, you need a File Transfer Protocol (FTP) account at your ISP to transfer your files and directories. After you have an FTP login, you upload your HTML and PHP files by using an FTP client.

One FTP client is your DOS prompt, available by choosing Start⇨Programs⇨ Accessories⇨Command Prompt (Windows) or Macintosh HD⇨Applications⇨ Utilities⇨Terminal (Mac). Type **ftp** and then the server address and you're ready to use `mput` * and `mget` * to transfer files, as shown in Figure 2-1. The `m` in these commands stands for multiple file, and the asterisk is a wildcard that says to transfer every file.

Figure 2-1:
DOS prompt
to run FTP.

Using a graphical program may be easier than using DOS, which is text-based. Here are a few that we recommend:

✦ **SmartFTP:** SmartFTP features an Explorer-like, customizable interface and supports drag-and-drop functions (see Figure 2-2). A cool thing about SmartFTP is that you can resume broken downloads in the event you lose your connection. You can get this Windows-based FTP program from `www.smartftp.com/download`.

✦ **Fetch:** Fetch is for Macintosh users. Fetch 5.0 interfaces with Mac OS X 10.2.4 or later, including Tiger (see Figure 2-3). You can use Fetch to publish a Web site at a Web hosting provider, which is your primary goal. But it also does many other things, such as rename, move, delete, and change the permissions of files on a Web server in order to maintain a Web site.

Additionally, Fetch is compatible with a wide range of FTP and SFTP servers, from mainframes and high-end servers to Macintosh, Unix, and Windows. You can retrieve Fetch from `http://fetchsoftworks.com`.

Figure 2-2:
The
SmartFTP
interface.

**Book VII
Chapter 2**

**Configuring
Database
Connections for PHP**

Figure 2-3:
The Fetch
interface.

✦ **Cyberduck:** Cyberduck is a free, open-source FTP browser client for the Mac. It supports Mac OS X features such as storing passwords in your keychain and a dashboard if you're using a version of Mac OS X that includes the dashboard (see Figure 2-4). The latest version requires OS X 10.3, but older versions are available that support OS X 10.2. You can get Cyberduck from `http://cyberduck.ch/`.

Figure 2-4:
The
Cyberduck
interface.

+ **CuteFTP:** An easy-to-use FTP client for Windows is CuteFTP (see Figure 2-5), which has been around a long time. The Professional edition provides simple tools for tackling the complex challenges of data transfer and management. CuteFTP has become very corporate; it has a lot more security features because its market share is directed at proprietary information like government compliance with HIPAA and the Sarbanes-Oxley (SOX) Act.

   However, it's still easy to use, which is one reason CuteFTP has the luxury of a non-techie crowd following. To see how CuteFTP looks on your desktop, visit www.cuteftp.com.

All graphical FTP programs, which excludes the DOS window, allow dragging and dropping of your files, which is easy and convenient. All the programs display several panes and status displays so you know what the software is doing at all times.

These applications are meant to transfer files, but they have a robustness that you can use in other arenas as well, depending on how much of the software's capability you want to learn.

**Book VII
Chapter 2**

Configuring
Database
Connections for PHP

Figure 2-5:
The
CuteFTP
interface.

Adding a PHP Database Connection

To create a database connection in PHP to access a MySQL database, you need to create a new dynamic PHP page. The database connection enables Dreamweaver to interact with the database using database connections through PHP. Dreamweaver automatically adds code that's specific to your dynamic page type to your new dynamic page when creating a database connection.

Creating a new dynamic PHP page

To create a new dynamic PHP page in Dreamweaver, follow these steps:

1. **Choose File⇨New.**

The New Document window opens.

2. **Click the General tab.**

A Category list appears.

3. **Select Dynamic Page from the Category list.**

A list of dynamic page types appears to the right of the Category column, under the Dynamic Page heading.

4. Select PHP from the Dynamic Page list.

5. Select a Document Type (DTD) from the drop-down list.

This setting makes your page XHTML compliant. Select the default, XHTML 1.0 Transitional.

6. Click Create.

A new dynamic PHP page is created.

Creating the database connection for PHP

After you create a new dynamic PHP page (as described in the preceding steps), you can connect to the database. Connect to your MySQL database by following these steps:

1. Choose Window⇨Application to open the Application panel.

If the Application panel is not expanded, click the small triangle in the panel's title bar until it points down.

2. Click the Databases tab of the Application panel.

The Databases panel opens (see Figure 2-6).

Figure 2-6:
The Databases panel before defining a database connection.

3. Click the plus (+) button, and from the drop-down list that appears, select MySQL Connection.

The MySQL Connection dialog box opens, as shown in Figure 2-7.

Figure 2-7:
The MySQL Connection dialog box.

4. **Enter a name for the database connection in the Connection Name field.**

Dreamweaver uses this name to reference your database connection. The name can contain only letters, numbers, and underscores.

5. **Enter the host name or IP address of the database server in the MySQL Server field.**

This may be a host name or IP address. If the MySQL server resides on the same system as the Web or application server, you need to reference it locally with the host name **localhost**.

6. **Enter the username for the database in the User Name field.**

The server's administrator provides this information.

7. **Enter the corresponding password in the Password field.**

8. **Click the Select button.**

If your settings are correct to this point, the Select Database dialog box opens, as shown in Figure 2-8. If you receive an error that the MySQL module isn't loaded, verify that your Apache PHP configuration is set to load the MySQL module for PHP 5 (PHP 4 includes this by default). If you receive an Access Denied error, double-check the login credentials for your MySQL database.

Figure 2-8:
The Select
Database
dialog box.

9. **Select your database from the list and then click OK.**

The Select Database dialog box closes, and the name of the database you selected appears in the Database field of the MySQL Connection dialog box.

10. **Click the Test button to confirm that your connection is set up properly.**

An alert box tells you whether the connection was successful.

11. **Click OK to close the alert box.**

12. **Click OK to close the MySQL Connection dialog box.**

Dreamweaver creates the database connection.

Editing a PHP Database Connection

Just in case you change the password for your database connection or the address of your database server changes, you need to know how to update your MySQL database connection settings.

To edit a MySQL database connection in PHP, follow these steps:

1. **Click the Databases tab of the Application panel.**

2. **Right-click (Windows) or Control+click (Mac) the database connection you want to edit.**

A list of options appears, as shown in Figure 2-9.

Figure 2-9: Right-click the database connection you want to edit or delete.

3. **Select Edit Connection.**

The MySQL Connection dialog box opens.

4. **Edit the connection properties as necessary.**

5. **Click the Test button to confirm your connection is properly set up.**

An alert box tells you whether the connection was successful.

6. **Click OK to close the alert box.**

7. **Click OK to close the MySQL Connection dialog box.**

Dreamweaver saves your changes to the database connection.

Deleting a PHP Database Connection

To delete a MySQL database connection in PHP, follow these steps:

1. **Open the Databases tab of the Application panel.**

2. **Right-click (Windows) or Control+click (Mac) the database connection you want to delete.**

A list of options appears.

3. **Choose Delete Connection.**

An alert box appears to confirm your deletion.

4. **Click Yes.**

The database connection is deleted and removed from the list of connections on the Databases tab in the Application panel.

Deleting the database connection deletes a PHP file that Dreamweaver created in a Connections directory in your local directory. The directory itself remains. You can delete this directory if you want to keep your directory uncluttered.

Chapter 3: Configuring ASP Database Connections

In This Chapter

✔ **Gathering database connection information**

✔ **Adding a database connection**

✔ **Connecting to a remote database**

✔ **Editing or deleting a database connection**

*I*n this chapter, we show you how to set up a database connection in ASP (Active Server Pages) using Dreamweaver. You find out how to add, edit, and delete a database connection and connect to a remote database.

Gathering Database Connection Information

You can easily overcome the complexities of connecting to a database from ASP if you have the right information about your database. To make a connection in ASP to a database, here's what you need to know:

✦ The type of database you're connecting to (for example, SQL Server or Oracle)

✦ The host name of the database server, or the IP address if no host name is available

✦ The username and password to access your database

✦ The name of the database to which you are trying to connect, or the Data Source Name (DSN)

Adding an ASP Database Connection

Dreamweaver offers two ways to connect to a database in ASP:

✦ **Data Source Name (DSN):** The DSN is a setting configured on your application server that contains the information needed to connect to your database. ASP then connects through the DSN instead of connecting directly from ASP. The advantage of using a DSN is that it's simpler than setting up the OLE DB driver, described next.

✦ **Custom connection string:** To set up a custom connection string, you enter information about your database server, and ASP uses that information to connect directly to your database. Connecting directly to a database requires ASP to run a small program called a *driver,* which enables ASP to speak directly with your database. Because this *OLE DB* driver talks directly to the database, it's faster than other drivers but requires extra steps (such as downloading and installing the driver).

OLE DB drivers are available for download from the provider of the database. For example, Microsoft supplies Access and SQL Server OLE DB drivers as part of its MDAC download at `http://msdn.microsoft.com/data/mdac/downloads/`. To download OLE DB drivers for Oracle databases, visit `www.oracle.com/technology/software/tech/windows/ole_db/index.html`. These packages come with installers that guide you through the process of installing the OLE DB driver on your computer.

Before you can create an ASP database connection, you have to create a new dynamic ASP page. Creating a new dynamic ASP page enables Dreamweaver to interact with the database using database connections through ASP.

Creating a new dynamic ASP page

To create a new dynamic ASP page, follow these steps:

1. **Choose File➪New.**

   The New Document window appears.

2. **On the General tab, select Dynamic Page from the Category list.**

   A list of dynamic page types appears to the right of the Category list in the Dynamic Page list.

3. **Select ASP VBScript or ASP JavaScript from the Dynamic Page list.**

   This selection is based on the type of scripting enabled on your server.

4. **Select a document type definition (DTD) from the drop-down list.**

   This setting makes your page XHTML-compliant. Select the default option, which is XHTML 1.0 Transitional.

5. **Click Create.**

   A new dynamic ASP page is created.

After you create a new dynamic ASP page, you can establish the database connection.

You also need a valid testing server setup, either on your local computer or a remote server. See Book I, Chapter 3 for more information.

Connecting with a Data Source Name (DSN)

To create a database connection in ASP through a DSN, follow these steps:

1. Open the Databases panel.

Choose Window⇨Database to open the panel. If the panel is not expanded, click the small triangle in the panel's title bar until it points downward.

2. Click the plus (+) button; in the drop-down list that appears, select Data Source Name (DSN).

The Data Source Name (DSN) dialog box opens, as shown in Figure 3-1.

Figure 3-1:
Enter the information about your database's DSN.

3. Enter a name for the new database connection in the Connection Name field.

Dreamweaver uses this name to reference your database connection. The name can contain only letters, numbers, and the underscore character: No other characters are permitted.

4. Enter the username for the database in the User Name field.

The server's administrator should provide this information.

5. Enter the corresponding password in the Password field.

The password goes with the username from the previous step.

6. Click the DSN button.

The Select ODBC DSN dialog box appears, as shown in Figure 3-2.

7. Select the Data Source Name (DSN) of your database from the Select ODBC DSN list, and then click OK.

The Select ODBC DSN dialog box closes, and the name of the selected DSN appears in the Data Source Name (DSN) field of the Data Source Name (DSN) dialog box.

Figure 3-2:
Select your
database
DSN from
the list.

8. **In the Dreamweaver Should Connect area, select the Using DSN on Testing Server radio button.**

Selecting this option tells Dreamweaver to connect to your database using a DSN created on the testing server.

9. **Click the Test button to confirm your settings.**

An alert box tells you whether the connection was made successfully. The two most common causes of an error are an incorrect username and password. Try connecting to the database using the client that's supplied with the database. This verifies that you have the correct user, password, and database names.

10. **Click OK to close the alert box, and then click OK once more to close the Data Source Name (DSN) dialog box.**

The database connection is created, and it's listed on the Databases panel.

Connecting with a custom connection string

To create a database connection in ASP through a custom connection string, follow these steps:

1. **Open the Databases panel.**

Choose Window⇨Application to open the panel. If the panel is not expanded, click the small triangle in the panel's title bar until it points downward.

2. **Click the plus (+) button and then select Custom Connection String from the drop-down list that appears.**

The Custom Connection String dialog box opens, as shown in Figure 3-3.

Figure 3-3:
Enter the
custom
connection
string for
your
database.

Custom Connection String

Connection name: asp_sql

Connection string: Provider=SQLOLEDB;Server=WIN2K-ASP\MSSQL;Database=

Dreamweaver should connect: ⊙ Using driver on testing server
○ Using driver on this machine

OK Cancel Advanced... Test Help

3. **Enter a name for the database connection in the Connection Name field.**

Dreamweaver uses this name to reference your database connection. The name can only contain letters, numbers, and the underscore character: No other characters are permitted.

4. **Enter a connection string for your database in the Connection String field.**

For example, suppose that you want to connect to a database named Thor on a SQL server named Poseidon, with the username dbadmin and a password of pass. The connection string would look like this:

```
Provider=SQLOLEDB;
Server=Poseidon;
Database=Thor;
UID=dbadmin;PWD=pass
```

To connect to Oracle, you use the same connection string as in the previous example, except you use the following Provider value:

```
Provider=OraOLEDB;
```

To connect to an Access database file, the connection string may look like this:

```
Driver={Microsoft Access Driver (*.mdb)};
DBQ=D:\Inetpub\wwwroot\data\myaccessdb.mdb
```

DBQ= specifies the path to the Access database file on the hosting server where it resides. Although this connection string lacks some of the fields, it's still a complete, valid, connection string. Because we didn't specify the provider, Dreamweaver defaults to the ODBC driver.

5. **Select the Using Driver on Testing Server radio button in the Dreamweaver Should Connect area.**

This option tells Dreamweaver to connect to your database using the driver installed on the testing server.

6. **Click the Test button to confirm your settings.**

An alert box tells you whether the connection was successful.

Book VII Chapter 3 — Configuring ASP Database Connections

7. Click OK in the alert box.

The alert box closes, and the Custom Connection String dialog box appears.

8. Click OK to close the Custom Connection String dialog box.

Dreamweaver creates the new database connection and lists it on the Databases panel.

Connecting to a Remote Database without a DSN

More than likely, you're planning to host your site with a commercial ISP or hosting provider. If your ISP provides a DSN, then connecting to the database works the same as in the preceding steps. However, many hosting providers don't provide a DSN to connect to a remote ODBC database, so you may have to specify the ODBC connection details without a DSN.

To set up a custom connection string to access a remote database, you need to know the *physical path* to your database file.

Understanding physical paths and virtual paths

When you upload your pages to a Web server using Dreamweaver, they're placed in a folder on the Web server just like when you copy files from one place to another on your own computer. For example, if you upload your pages to a Web server running Microsoft IIS, your files may be placed in the following directory:

```
D:\Inetpub\wwwroot\
```

If your home page file was named `home.htm`, the *physical path* to your home page would be

```
D:\Inetpub\wwwroot\home.htm
```

When you use your Web browser to visit a Web site, however, you don't type the physical path. Instead, you enter the URL:

```
http://mywebsite.foo/home.htm
```

This URL helps you access the `home.htm` page. The piece of the URL that follows the Web site name is the *virtual path*. In this example, the virtual path is `home.htm`.

When a Web site is configured on a Web server, the server is instructed to point all requests for a particular virtual path to a corresponding physical path. In the preceding example, all requests for pages located at `http://mywebsite.foo/michele` are transparently fulfilled with the files in the physical path: `D:\Inetpub\wwwroot\michele`.

Finding the database's physical path when you know the virtual path

If you need to know the physical path to your database, but only have the virtual path, you're in luck. The ASP method MapPath allows you to feed a virtual path and get back the corresponding physical path. Follow these steps to use MapPath to retrieve a physical path:

1. **Choose File⇨New.**

The New Document window opens.

2. **On the General tab, select Dynamic Page from the Category list.**

3. **Select ASP VBScript or ASP JavaScript from the Dynamic Page list.**

This selection is based on the type of scripting enabled on your server.

4. **Select a document type definition (DTD) from the drop-down list.**

This setting makes your page XHTML-compliant. Select the default option, which is XHTML 1.0 Transitional.

5. **Click Create.**

A new dynamic ASP page is created.

6. **Choose View⇨Code to switch to Code view.**

The Document window displays the code for your page.

7. **Enter the following code into the page's HTML between the `<body>` tags:**

```
<% Response.Write(Server.MapPath("/virtualpath/fileinpath")) %>
```

Replace `virtualpath` with the site's virtual path, and replace `fileinpath` with the name of a file in the directory. If you're just looking for the physical path of the site's root directory, simply enter a forward slash (/) in the quotes.

8. **Choose View⇨Design to switch to Design view.**

The Document window displays your page with the code hidden.

9. **Choose View⇨Live Data.**

Dreamweaver displays the physical path, which corresponds with the virtual path you entered in the ASP code snippet.

**Book VII
Chapter 3**

Configuring ASP
Database
Connections

Connecting to a remote database with a virtual path

Using a virtual path to connect to your file-based database actually calls a command on your remote server to look up the physical path. The command string used is determined by your ASP server's scripting language, either VBScript or JavaScript. You need to create a custom connection string to connect to the remote database without using a DSN.

For VBScript, your custom connection string looks like this:

```
"Driver={Microsoft Access Driver (*.mdb)};DBQ=" &
    Server.MapPath("/virtualpath/databasefile.mdb")
```

For JavaScript, your custom connection string looks like this:

```
"Driver={Microsoft Access Driver (*.mdb)};DBQ=" +
    Server.MapPath("/virtualpath/databasefile.mdb")
```

In either case, replace `virtualpath` with the site's virtual path, and replace `databasefile.mdb` with the name of the database file in the directory.

To prevent a user from downloading your entire database, always place your .mdb database files in a directory that isn't in your Web root.

To set up a database connection using the custom connection string, follow the steps in "Connecting with a custom connection string," earlier in this chapter. In Step 4, use the custom connection string you just created.

Editing an ASP Database Connection

Sometimes after setting up a database connection, some of the connection details may change. For example, the server that hosts the database could change, or you might select a new password for the database. To edit an ASP database connection in Dreamweaver to reflect these changes, follow these steps:

1. **In the Databases panel, right-click (Windows) or Control+click (Mac) the database connection you want to edit and choose Edit Connection from the drop-down list that appears, as shown in Figure 3-4.**

The Custom Connection String or Data Source Name dialog box opens, depending on which type of connection you're editing.

2. **Edit the connection properties as necessary.**

3. **Click the Test button to confirm your settings.**

An alert box tells you whether the connection was made successfully.

Figure 3-4:
Right-
click the
database
connection
you want
to edit.

4. **Click OK to close the alert box, and click OK once more to close the connection dialog box.**

   Dreamweaver saves your changes to the database connection.

Deleting an ASP Database Connection

To delete an ASP database connection in Dreamweaver, follow these steps:

1. **On the Databases panel, right-click (Windows) or Control+click (Mac) the database connection you want to delete and choose Delete Connection from the drop-down list that appears.**

   An alert box appears to confirm the deletion.

2. **Click Yes to confirm the deletion.**

   The database connection is deleted and removed from the list of connections on the Databases panel.

Chapter 4: Configuring ASP.NET Database Connections

In This Chapter

✔ **Gathering database connection information**

✔ **Adding a database connection**

✔ **Editing or deleting a database connection**

Dreamweaver supports several languages: PHP, ASP, ASP.NET, JSP, and ColdFusion. In this chapter, we show you how to set up a database connection in ASP.NET using Dreamweaver. You find out how to add, edit, and delete a database connection.

Collecting Database Connection Information

The best way to simplify connecting to a database from ASP.NET is by gathering the necessary information about your database. To make a connection in ASP.NET to a database, here's what you need to know:

- ✦ Type of database you are connecting to (for example, SQL Server, Access, Oracle)

- ✦ Host name of the database server, or the IP address if no host name is available

- ✦ Username and password to access your database

- ✦ Name of the database to which you are trying to connect; in the case of a file-based database such as Access, the location of the database file

Adding an ASP.NET Database Connection

Dreamweaver offers two ways to connect to a database in ASP.NET:

- ✦ **OLE DB connection:** With this method, you enter the information about your database server, and ASP.NET uses that information to connect directly to your database. Connecting directly to a database requires

ASP.NET to run a driver program to be able to speak directly with your specific type of database. Because the *OLE DB* driver talks directly to the database, it's faster than other drivers but requires extra steps (such as downloading and installing the driver).

OLE DB drivers are available for download from the provider of the database. For example, Microsoft supplies Access and SQL Server OLE DB drivers as part of its MDAC download at `http://msdn.microsoft.com/data/mdac/downloads/`. To download OLE DB drivers for Oracle databases, visit `http://www.oracle.com/technology/software/tech/windows/ole_db/index.html`. These packages come with installers that guide you through the process of installing the OLE DB driver on your computer.

✦ **SQL Server connection:** This setting is specific to connecting with MS SQL Server databases and won't work with any other type of database. The SQL Server connection option is nearly identical to the OLE DB connection option for MS SQL Server, except that you don't have to give Dreamweaver a `Provider` value in the SQL Server connection option.

Go ahead and create a SQL Server connection if using SQL Server; otherwise create an OLE DB database connection. Before you create an ASP.NET database connection, you must first create a new dynamic ASP.NET page. Creating a new dynamic ASP.NET page enables Dreamweaver to interact with the database using database connections through ASP.NET.

Creating a new dynamic ASP.NET page

To create new dynamic ASP.NET page, follow these steps:

1. **Choose File⇨New.**

   The New Document window opens.

2. **On the General tab, select Dynamic Page from the Category list.**

   A list of dynamic page types appears to the right of the Category list in the Dynamic Page list.

3. **Select ASP.NET C# or ASP.NET VBScript from the Dynamic Page list.**

   This selection is based on the type of scripting enabled on your server.

4. **Select a document type definition (DTD) from the drop-down list.**

   This setting makes your page XHTML-compliant. Select the default option, which is XHTML 1.0 Transitional.

5. **Click Create.**

   A new dynamic ASP.NET page is created.

After you create a new dynamic ASP.NET page, you can establish the database connection. You can create an OLE DB connection using either the templates or data link properties, which we cover in the next section. An alternative to connect to a SQL Server database is through the method provided in the Microsoft .NET Framework, which we discuss later in the chapter in the section titled, "Building a SQL Server connection."

Building an OLE DB connection

Because it's a common choice, the SQL Server database connection has its own connection type. You can create a SQL Server database connection by using OLE DB as well. Which one you use makes no difference, but you need to use OLE DB if you're connecting to a database other than SQL Server.

Using templates

To use a template to create an OLE DB connection in ASP.NET, follow these steps:

1. **Open the Databases panel.**

   If the Application panel isn't expanded, click the small triangle in the panel's title bar until it points downward.

2. **Click the plus (+) button, and select OLE DB Connection from the drop-down list.**

   The OLE DB Connection dialog box opens, as shown in Figure 4-1.

**Book VII
Chapter 4**

Configuring
ASP.NET Database
Connections

Figure 4-1:
Create an
OLE DB
connection
from a
template.

3. **Enter a name for the database connection in the Connection Name field.**

Dreamweaver uses this name to reference your database connection. The name can only contain letters, numbers, or an underscore: No other characters are permitted.

4. **Click the Templates button.**

The Connection String Template dialog box appears, as shown in Figure 4-2.

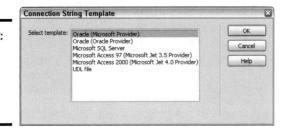

Figure 4-2:
Select a template for your database type.

5. **Select your database type from the Select Template list and then click OK.**

The Connection String Template dialog box closes, and the template for the database type you selected appears in the Connection String text box in the OLE DB Connection dialog box.

You can skip Steps 6 and 7 if you selected the UDL file template.

6. **Enter the user ID for the database by replacing the [*username*] text with the username provided to access your database.**

Do not include the square brackets when entering the username. Remember to end the line with a semicolon. Most ISPs with hosted databases provide a page for you to view your database username and password. If not, contact the person that supports the database for the username and password.

7. **Enter the password for the database by replacing the text [*password*] with the password provided to access your database.**

Do not include the square brackets when entering the password, and be sure the line ends with a semicolon. The UDL file template doesn't require this step.

8. **Modify the remainder of the template values using the settings detailed in Table 4-1.**

Table 4-1 provides you with details on the values to enter for each connection string template.

Table 4-1		OLE DB Connection Settings
Template Name	*Database Type*	*Properties*

Oracle (Microsoft Provider)	Oracle	`Provider=MSDAORA;`
		`Data Source=[`*`OracleInstanceName`*`];`
		`User ID=[`*`username`*`];`
		`Password=[`*`password`*`];`

Oracle (Oracle Provider)	Oracle	`Provider=OraOLEDB.Oracle;`
		`User ID=[`*`username`*`];`
		`Password=[`*`password`*`];`
		`Data Source=[`*`OracleInstanceName`*`];`

Microsoft SQL Server	Microsoft SQL Server	`Provider=SQLOLEDB.1;`
		`Persist Security Info=False;`
		`Data Source=[`*`serverName`*`];`
		`Initial Catalog=[`*`databaseName`*`];`
		`User ID=[`*`username`*`];`
		`Password=[`*`password`*`];`

Microsoft Access 97 (Microsoft Jet 3.5 Provider)	Microsoft Access	`Provider=Microsoft.Jet.OLEDB.3.5;`
		`Data Source=[`*`databaseName`*`];`
		`User ID=[`*`username`*`];`
		`Password=[`*`password`*`];`

Microsoft Access 2000 (Microsoft Jet 4.0 Provider)	Microsoft Access	`Provider=Microsoft.Jet.OLEDB.4.0;`
		`Data Source=[`*`databaseName`*`];`
		`User ID=[`*`username`*`];`
		`Password=[`*`password`*`];`

UDL file		`File Name=[`*`filename`*`]`

9. **Click the Test button to confirm that your connection is properly set up.**

An alert box informs you whether the connection was successful. The two most common causes of an error are incorrect usernames and passwords. Try connecting to the database using the client that's supplied with the database. This verifies that you have the correct user, password, and database names.

10. **Click OK to close the alert box, and then click OK to close the OLE DB Connection dialog box.**

The database connection is created.

Using data link properties

To enter data link properties to create an OLE DB connection in ASP.NET, follow these steps:

1. **In the Databases panel, click the plus (+) button, and select OLE DB Connection from the drop-down list.**

2. **Click the Build button in the OLE DB Connection dialog box that appears.**

The Data Link Properties dialog box appears.

3. **On the Provider tab, select the appropriate Microsoft OLE DB Provider for your database type.**

Most applications use a provider beginning with "Microsoft OLE DB Provider for."

4. **On the Connection tab, shown in Figure 4-3, enter the connection information for your database.**

The database server administrator provides this information.

Figure 4-3:
Using
data link
properties
to build a
database
connection.

5. **Click the Test Connection button to confirm that your connection is properly set up.**

An alert box tells you whether the connection was successful.

6. **Click OK to close the alert box, and then click OK to close the OLE DB Connection dialog box.**

You are connected to the database.

Building a SQL Server connection

To create a .NET SQL Server database connection in ASP.NET, follow these steps:

1. **In the Databases panel, click the plus (+) button and select SQL Server Connection from the drop-down list that appears.**

The SQL Server Connection dialog box opens, as shown in Figure 4-4.

Figure 4-4:
Building the connection string for your SQL database.

2. **Enter a name for the database connection in the Connection Name field.**

Dreamweaver uses this name to reference your database connection. The name can only consist of letters, numbers, or an underscore: No other characters are allowed.

3. **In the Connection String field, build a connection string for your database.**

For example, to connect to a database named Thor on a SQL server named Poseidon, with the username dbadmin and a password of pass, the connection string would be

```
Persist Security Info=False;
Data Source=Poseidon;
Initial Catalog=Thor;
User ID=dbadmin;
Password=pass;
```

The Persist Security Info parameter tells the ASP.NET functions to forget the password after using it to login instead of keeping it in memory.

4. **Click the Test button to confirm that your connection is properly set up.**

An alert box tells you whether the connection was successful.

5. **Click OK to close the alert box, and then click OK to close the SQL Server Connection dialog box.**

The database connection is created.

Editing an ASP.NET Database Connection

Nothing is ever perfect, so at some point, you're going to want to edit an ASP.NET database connection in Dreamweaver. This can happen if the database moves to a different server or you change your password. To edit a connection, follow these steps:

1. **In the Databases panel, right-click (Windows) or Control+click (Mac) the database connection you want to edit and choose Edit Connection from the drop-down list that appears, as shown in Figure 4-5.**

Figure 4-5: Right-click the database connection you want to edit or delete.

The OLE DB Connection or SQL Server Connection dialog box appears, depending on which database connection type you're editing.

2. Edit the connection properties as necessary.

3. Click the Test button to confirm that your connection is set up properly.

4. Click OK to close the alert box that appears, and then click OK to close the connection dialog box.

The connection has been edited.

Deleting an ASP.NET Database Connection

To delete an ASP.NET database connection in Dreamweaver, follow these steps:

1. In the Databases panel, right-click (Windows) or Control+click (Mac) the database connection you want to delete and choose Delete Connection from the drop-down list that appears.

An alert box appears to confirm that you want to delete the selected connection.

2. Click Yes to close the alert box.

The database connection is deleted and removed from the list of connections in the Databases panel.

Chapter 5: Configuring JSP Database Connections

In This Chapter

✔ **Gathering database connection information**

✔ **Adding a database connection**

✔ **Connecting to a remote database**

✔ **Editing or deleting a database connection**

This chapter shows you how to create a database connection for your JSP pages and edit or delete the connection after you create it. You also find out what you need to know about the option settings that you're likely to use for this connection.

Gathering Database Connection Information

Dreamweaver enables you to connect to a variety of databases by modifying the database driver and *connection string* (URL) for each type of database. Before you can set up a connection to your database, make sure that you have the following information on hand:

✦ The location of the database server as a host name or an IP address. If the database resides on the same machine as the application server, this could be localhost.

✦ The database username.

✦ The database password.

✦ The name of the database instance. Because a database can host several distinct groups of tables, the instance provides a way to indicate which set of tables to use.

You need to download the Java JDBC driver from the supplier's Web site, which is the database vendor, such as Oracle or IBM. If you don't download the driver, you receive a Java error that the connection method is missing when you try to connect to the database.

Adding a JSP Database Connection

JSP pages use a standard interface for connecting to databases called Java Database Connectivity (JDBC) drivers. The JDBC driver for your database translates the information traveling between your JSP program and your database, enabling the two to communicate with one another.

Dreamweaver offers six different drivers for connecting to a database in JSP through JDBC, as well as an option for creating a custom JDBC connection. Here are Dreamweaver's built-in JSP database connection types:

✦ Custom JDBC Connection

✦ IBM DB2 App Driver (DB2)

✦ IBM DB2 Net Driver (DB2)

✦ MySQL Driver (MySQL)

✦ Oracle Thin Driver (Oracle)

✦ Inet Driver (SQLServer)

✦ Sun JDBC-ODBC Driver (ODBC Database)

For the first option, Custom JDBC Connection, you enter all the necessary information to create the custom database connection. For the rest of the database types, Dreamweaver fills in the appropriate driver name and provides a URL template that you can replace with the information for your database. Table 5-1 shows the driver and URL fields for Dreamweaver's database connection types.

Table 5-1   Database Connection Types and Their Respective Drivers and URLs

Database	Driver	Connection URL
Custom JDBC Connection	Custom	Custom
IBM DB2 App Driver (DB2)	COM.ibm.db2.jdbc.app. DB2Driver	jdbc:db2:[*database name*]
IBM DB2 Net Driver (DB2)	COM.ibm.db2.jdbc.net. DB2Driver	jdbc:db2://[*host name*]: [*server port*]/[*database name*]
MySQL Driver (MySQL)	org.gjt.mm.mysql.Driver	jdbc:mysql://[*host name*]/ [*database name*]
Oracle Thin Driver (Oracle)	oracle.jdbc.driver. OracleDriver	jdbc:oracle:thin:@[*host name*]:[*port*]:[sid]

Database	Driver	Connection URL
Inet Driver (SQLServer)	com.inet.tds.TdsDriver	jdbc:inetdae:[*host name*]: [*port*]?*database*=[*database*]
Sun JDBC-ODBC Driver (ODBC Database)	sun.jdbc.odbc. JdbcOdbcDriver	jdbc:odbc:[*odbc dsn*]

When you create a JSP connection to your database, replace the [`host name`] and [`database name`] shown in Table 5-1 with your database's values. For example, if you're creating a connection to a local MySQL database named `test`, use the following connection URL:

```
jdbc:mysql://127.0.0.1/test
```

Java Runtime Environment Installation

You must have the Java Runtime Environment (JRE) installed to use a JDBC driver. Visit Sun's site at `http://java.sun.com/j2se/index.jsp` if you haven't installed the JRE.

If you're deploying your code to a remote server, you also need to have the JDBC driver installed, or your application won't work when you upload it.

Installing the JDBC Driver

Although Dreamweaver includes everything you need to use the Java JDBC driver classes for several databases, it doesn't include the code for the JDBC drivers.

To install the appropriate JDBC driver for your database, follow these steps:

1. **Download the Java `.jar` file for your database.**

Java packages are distributed as `.jar` files. See Table 5-2 to find out where to download the file you need.

2. **Copy the Java `.jar` file to `C:/program files/macromedia/ Dreamweaver/configuration/JDBCDrivers`.**

The name of the .jar file may not exactly match the class that's supplied in the file. For example, the name of the MySQL .jar file is `mysql-connector-java-3.1.12-bin.jar`.

3. **Restart Dreamweaver.**

After you install the database driver, you can create a dynamic page and the database connection in JSP, as described in the next section.

Table 5-2	JDBC Database Driver Download Locations	
Database	*Driver*	*Web Site*
IBM DB2 App/Net Driver	COM.ibm.db2.jdbc.app. DB2Driver	`www-306.ibm.com/ software/data/db2/ udb/ad/v8/java/`
MySQL Driver Connector/J	org.gjt.mm.mysql.Driver	`www.mysql.com/ products/ connector/j/`
Oracle Thin Driver	oracle.jdbc.driver.OracleDriver	`www.oracle.com/ technology/software/ tech/java/sqlj_jdbc/ htdocs/jdbc_10201. html`
Inet Driver (i-net Gate)	com.inet.tds.TdsDriver	`www.inetsoftware.de/ Download.htm`
Sun JDBC-ODBC Driver	sun.jdbc.odbc.JdbcOdbcDriver	Included with Dreamweaver

Creating a new dynamic JSP page

Because pages that work with a database are dynamic, Dreamweaver requires you to create a dynamic page before you can add a database connection.

Follow these steps to create a new dynamic JSP page:

1. **Choose File⇨New.**

   The New Document window appears.

2. **On the General tab, select Dynamic Page from the Category list.**

3. **Select JSP from the Dynamic Page list, as shown in Figure 5-1.**

   Dreamweaver now includes JSP code whenever code segments are needed.

4. **Select a document type definition from the Document Type (DTD) drop-down list.**

   Accept the default XHTML 1.0 Transitional setting to create an XHTML-compliant page.

5. **Click Create.**

   Your new dynamic JSP page is ready to use.

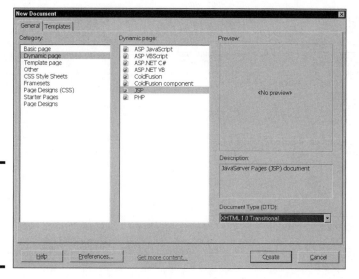

Figure 5-1:
The New
Document
window for
an XHTML
JSP page.

Dreamweaver allows you to add a database connection now that the dynamic JSP page exists.

Connecting to a database

**Book VII
Chapter 5**

Configuring JSP
Database
Connections

After you create a dynamic JSP page (as described in the previous section), follow these steps to create a database connection in JSP:

1. **Open the Databases panel.**

   Expand the Application panel, if it's not already expanded, and then click the small triangle in the panel's title bar until it points downward.

2. **Click the plus (+) button and select a database connection type from the drop-down list.**

   You can choose from the database types listed in Table 5-1. After you make a selection, a connection dialog box named for the type of connection appears. The Driver and URL fields are prefilled for all the standard database driver types (see Figure 5-2, which shows the MySQL driver). The fields in the custom connection dialog box, shown in Figure 5-3, are all blank.

3. **Enter a database connection name in the Connection Name field.**

   Dreamweaver uses this name to reference your database connection. The name can have letters, numbers, or an underscore: No other characters are allowed.

Figure 5-2:
The MySQL
Driver
(MySQL)
database
connection
dialog box.

Figure 5-3:
Enter the
custom
JDBC
connection
for your
database.

4. Enter the JDBC database driver in the Driver field.

The field is prepopulated for every database type except the Custom
JDBC Database. If you're setting up a custom connection, you can
usually find the Java class name in the driver's documentation. The
class name tells Dreamweaver what Java code to call to access the
database. For example, using the MySQL driver, the class name is
`org.gjt.mm.mysql.Driver`.

If you're using a JDBC driver, you should have already downloaded it. If
you click the Test button and you get a `Class not found` alert, you need
to download the class. See Table 5-2 for a list of download locations.

**5. In the URL field, replace the bracketed values with the information
for your database. If you're creating a custom connection, refer to the
documentation that came with your JDBC driver for the format of this
connection string.**

The URL field contains all the information required to log in to the database in one long string. For example, for the MySQL driver, it lists the
following URL:

```
jdbc:mysql://[hostname]/[database name]
```

In this example, replace the bracketed values `[hostname]` and
`[database name]` with the information for your database.

6. Enter the database username in the User Name field.

The server's administrator should provide this information.

7. Enter the database password in the Password field.

The password goes with the username from the previous step.

8. Choose the Using Driver On This Machine radio button.

This setting determines if the local machine or the remote application server's driver is used to connect to the database. If you're using a Macintosh, you can ignore this setting: Macs always use the remote application server to connect.

9. Click the Test button to confirm that your connection is set up correctly.

A dialog box confirms a successful connection or displays an error message if it couldn't connect.

If you received a `Class was not found` error message when you clicked the Test button, you don't have the driver installed for that type of database. Download the Java package that corresponds to the type of database driver. Table 5-2 lists where to find each driver on the Internet.

10. Click OK in the Connection Test dialog box.

The dialog box closes.

11. Click OK.

Dreamweaver creates the database, and the database connection dialog box closes.

JDBC allows you to create an ODBC database connection with the Sun JDBC-ODBC driver using a Data Source Name (DSN). See Book VII, Chapter 3 for more information on using DSNs. You need to make sure that you've set up the DSN before you use it.

Browsing a database

Once you can connect through JDBC to a database, you can use the Dreamweaver Databases panel to browse the tables and even the data in each table. To browse the tables, simply expand the entries in the Databases panel beginning with the Tables entry.

Editing a JSP Database Connection

Sometimes you need to go back to your database connection and make a change. Here's how to edit the JSP database connection in Dreamweaver:

1. **Open the Databases panel.**

2. **Right-click (Windows) or Control+click (Mac) the database connection you want to edit and select Edit Connection from the list that appears (as shown in Figure 5-4).**

The database connection dialog box opens.

Figure 5-4:
Right-click the database connection to edit.

3. **Edit the connection properties as necessary.**

4. **Click the Test button to confirm that your connection is set up correctly.**

5. **Click OK to close the alert box.**

6. **Click OK to close the database connection dialog box.**

Dreamweaver saves the changes to your database connection.

Deleting a JSP Database Connection

Deleting database connections in Dreamweaver is similar to editing them. To delete a JSP database connection in Dreamweaver, follow these steps:

1. **Open the Databases panel.**

2. **Right-click (Windows) or Control+click (Mac) the database connection you want to delete and select Delete Connection from the list that appears.**

An alert box appears to confirm your deletion.

3. **Click Yes to close the alert box and delete the connection.**

The database connection is deleted and removed from the list of connections on the Databases panel.

Chapter 6: Configuring ColdFusion Database Connections

In This Chapter

✔ **Pulling together database connection information**

✔ **Understanding how ColdFusion connects to databases**

✔ **Adding a database connection**

✔ **Editing or deleting a database connection**

ColdFusion is a server-side extension created by Allaire. It uses the `.cfm` extension as opposed to the `.html` extension. Some examples of ColdFusion applications include event registration, catalog searches, directories, calendars, and even interactive training. ColdFusion applications are moderately complex; they execute on the Web server as CGI scripts. In this chapter, we explain how to set up a database connection in ColdFusion using Dreamweaver. You find out how to add, edit, and delete a database connection.

Pulling Together Database Connection Information

ColdFusion is by far one of the most complex Web application development platforms available. ColdFusion is highly flexible in its ability to connect to different types of data sources, especially databases. Although ColdFusion supports a wide array of database types, some key pieces of information to create a connection to a database are common among all the database types. To make a connection to a database in ColdFusion, you need to know the following information:

✦ Type of database you are connecting to (for example, SQL Server, Oracle, Access, and so on)

✦ Host name of the database server, or IP address if no host name is available

✦ Username and password to access your database

✦ Name or file location of the database to which you are trying to connect

Understanding How ColdFusion Connects to Databases

ColdFusion is designed to connect to databases at the server level, which means a database connection must be set up on the ColdFusion server itself. This task traditionally requires a ColdFusion administrator's assistance. After the connection is set up, your ColdFusion application can use it. This connection differs from other Web application platforms in that many other Web applications' database connections are created from within your Web application and don't require prior setup on the application server.

ColdFusion uses Java Database Connectivity (JDBC) to connect with databases. If you're unable to find an appropriate database driver included with ColdFusion, you can enter the JDBC driver information directly. See Book VII, Chapter 5 for details on downloading and installing JDBC drivers.

Although the design of how ColdFusion connects to databases has stayed consistent, ColdFusion MX 7 provides greater flexibility in configuring database connections than the previous version. It enables you to create ColdFusion database connections within Dreamweaver 8 directly on the ColdFusion server.

Adding a ColdFusion Database Connection

You can connect ColdFusion to a database a couple different ways, depending on which version of ColdFusion you're running. If you're running ColdFusion MX 7, you can set up the database connection within Dreamweaver 8. However, if you're using ColdFusion version 6.0 or earlier, you must use the ColdFusion Administration Web site on the ColdFusion server to configure your database connection.

Before you create a ColdFusion database connection, you must first create a new ColdFusion document and specify an RDS login. Creating the new ColdFusion document tells Dreamweaver the platform of the connection you're trying to set up, and ensures you have the correct document type to use the new database connection. The RDS login tells Dreamweaver how to communicate with the ColdFusion server to publish files.

Creating a new ColdFusion document

To create a new ColdFusion document, perform the following steps:

1. **Choose File⇨New.**

The New Document window opens.

2. **On the General tab, select Dynamic Page from the Category list.**

3. **Select ColdFusion from the Dynamic Page list.**

This selection is based on the type of scripting enabled on your server.

4. **Select a document type definition from the Document Type (DTD) drop-down list.**

   This setting makes your page XHTML-compliant. We recommend selecting the default option, XHTML 1.0 Transitional.

5. **Click Create.**

   A new ColdFusion document is created.

Now that you have created a new ColdFusion document, you can establish a database connection for Dreamweaver to use.

Specifying RDS login information

Prior to setting up the first database connection for a Dreamweaver site, you must specify a Remote Development Services (RDS) password for the ColdFusion server. This password allows Dreamweaver to interact directly with the ColdFusion server to exchange database connection information. If you haven't already entered the RDS password, a checklist appears in the Databases panel, as shown in Figure 6-1. If you installed the ColdFusion server, use the password from the installation; otherwise contact the administrator of the ColdFusion server.

Modify Data Sources

Figure 6-1: A checklist for using ColdFusion database connections.

To set up the RDS connection, do the following:

1. **Open the Databases panel.**

   If the Application panel is not expanded, click the small triangle in the panel's title bar until it points downward.

   A checklist appears in the panel.

2. **Click the RDS Login link in the fourth step of the checklist.**

A Login to ColdFusion Remote Development Services (RDS) dialog box appears.

3. Enter the RDS password for your ColdFusion server.

The ColdFusion server administrator provides the password.

4. Click OK to close the dialog box.

A list of existing database connections appears in the Databases panel.

Configuring a database connection with the ColdFusion Administrator

If you're using ColdFusion versions prior to ColdFusion MX 7, you must use the ColdFusion Administrator to create the database connection. This method works on all versions of ColdFusion, including the current one. The biggest advantage to configuring through Dreamweaver is not having to open up a separate browser window to access the administration pages.

To create a database connection in ColdFusion, follow these steps:

1. Open the Databases panel.

If the Application panel is not expanded, click the small triangle in the panel's title bar until it points downward.

2. Click the Modify Data Sources button (which looks like a yellow cylinder with a pencil; refer to Figure 6-1).

Dreamweaver opens a new Web browser window with the Administrator Login page of the ColdFusion server, shown in Figure 6-2.

3. Enter the ColdFusion Administrator password in the text box next to the Login button.

The ColdFusion server administrator must provide this password.

4. Click the Login button.

After you submit the password, your Web browser is redirected to the ColdFusion Administrator Web console. The page should read Data & Services > Datasources at the top. If it doesn't, select the Data Sources option under the Data & Services heading on the menu, as shown in Figure 6-3.

5. Enter a name for the database connection in the Data Source Name field.

ColdFusion uses this name to reference your database connection. The name can be made up of letters, numbers, or the underscore character only. Additionally, you can't use the names *service*, *jms_provider*, *comp*, or *jms* — these are reserved by ColdFusion.

Figure 6-2:
The login page for the ColdFusion Administrator console.

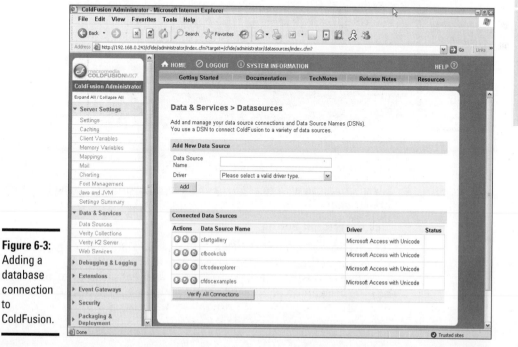

Figure 6-3:
Adding a database connection to ColdFusion.

 6. **Select the appropriate database driver type from the Driver drop-down list.**

If you're unsure which selection is best for your database, consult your database provider for specific details.

 7. **Click the Add button.**

You are directed to the next step of the creation process, as shown in Figure 6-4.

Figure 6-4:
The Add Datasource page for a MySQL connection.

 8. **Enter your database connection information.**

This information includes the username, password, server name, and database name.

 9. **Click the Submit button.**

You are directed back to the Data & Services > Datasources page. If your connection settings contain any errors, ColdFusion displays the errors in red text at the top of the page. A green success message at the top of the page indicates a successful configuration.

In either case, the connection is created. If an error still exists, the connection appears with a yellow background, and the error details show in the Data Source Name column in the Connected Data Sources table. The error details disappear after you fix the error.

10. **Click Logout to close your session in the ColdFusion Administrator console.**

Sometimes the Logout button isn't visible, depending on your server-specific configuration. If no Logout button is available, close the window.

Your new database connection appears in the Dreamweaver Databases panel. If the connection doesn't appear immediately, click the Refresh button to update Dreamweaver's list of available connections.

Configuring a database connection in Dreamweaver 8 (ColdFusion MX 7)

This method only works if you're using both Dreamweaver 8 and ColdFusion MX 7.

To create a database connection in ColdFusion MX 7 through the Dreamweaver 8 interface, do the following:

1. **Open the Databases panel.**

If the Application panel isn't expanded, click the small triangle in the panel's title bar until it points downward.

2. **Click the plus (+) button and select the appropriate database connection type from the drop-down list.**

If you're unsure which selection is best for your database, consult your database provider for specific details.

A dialog box appears for the database connection type you selected, similar to Figure 6-5.

Figure 6-5:
Adding a
SQL Server
connec-
tion to
ColdFusion
through
Dream-
weaver.

3. **Enter the connection information for your database.**

   This information includes username, password, server name, and database name.

4. **Click the Test button to confirm that your connection is set up correctly.**

   An alert box tells you whether the connection was successful.

5. **Click OK to close the alert box, and click OK again to close the database server connection dialog box.**

   The database connection is created on the ColdFusion server.

Editing a ColdFusion Database Connection

You can edit a ColdFusion database connection in one of two ways. One method is through the ColdFusion Administrator Web console, which works for all versions of ColdFusion. The other method requires both Dreamweaver 8 and ColdFusion MX 7, and allows editing of a connection through the Dreamweaver interface.

Using Dreamweaver 8 (ColdFusion MX 7)

This method only works if you're using both Dreamweaver 8 and ColdFusion MX 7. To edit a database connection on ColdFusion MX 7 through the Dreamweaver 8 interface, do the following:

1. **In the Databases panel, right-click (Windows) or Control+click (Mac) the database connection you want to edit and select Edit Connection from the list that appears, as shown in Figure 6-6.**

   The connection dialog box opens.

Figure 6-6:
Right-click the database connection you want to edit.

2. **Edit the connection properties as necessary.**

3. **Click the Test button to confirm that your connection is set up correctly.**

An alert box tells you the connection was successful.

4. **Click OK to close the alert box.**

The alert box closes, and you return to the connection dialog box.

5. **Click OK to close the connection dialog box.**

Dreamweaver saves the changes to your database connection.

Using the ColdFusion Administrator (All versions of ColdFusion)

This method works for all versions of ColdFusion and Dreamweaver. To edit a ColdFusion database connection in Dreamweaver through the ColdFusion Administrator Web console, do the following:

1. **In the Databases panel, right-click (Windows) or Control+click (Mac) the database connection to edit, and select Modify Data Sources.**

Dreamweaver opens a new Web browser window with the Administrator Login page of the ColdFusion server.

2. **Enter the ColdFusion Administrator password in the text box and click the Login button.**

The ColdFusion server administrator must provide this password.

After you submit the password, your Web browser redirects to the ColdFusion Administrator Web console. The page should read Data & Services > Datasources at the top. If it doesn't, select the Data Sources option from the menu on the left side of the screen.

3. **Select the database connection you want to edit by clicking its name in the Connected Data Sources table.**

You're redirected to a page showing the selected database connection's settings.

4. **Edit the connection information for your database.**

This information includes username, password, server name, and database name.

5. **Click the Submit button.**

ColdFusion tests your connection. If an error occurs, an error message in red text appears at the top of the page. If the connection is set up properly, a green success message is displayed.

In either case, the connection is created. If an error still exists, the connection appears with a yellow background, and the error details show in the Data Source Name column in the Connected Data Sources table until the error is fixed.

6. **Click Logout to close your session in the ColdFusion Administrator console.**

    If no Logout button is available, simply close the window.

Deleting a ColdFusion Database Connection

To delete a ColdFusion database connection in Dreamweaver, follow these steps:

1. **In the Databases panel, right-click (Windows) or Control+click (Mac) the database connection you want to delete and select Modify Data Sources from the list that appears.**

    Dreamweaver opens a new Web browser window with the Administrator Login page of the ColdFusion server (refer to Figure 6-2).

2. **Enter the ColdFusion Administrator password in the text box and click the Login button.**

    The ColdFusion server administrator must provide this password.

    The password is submitted, and your Web browser redirects to the Data & Services > Datasources page of the ColdFusion Administrator Web console (refer to Figure 6-3).

3. **Select the database connection you want to delete by clicking the red circle icon to the left of the connection's name in the Connected Data Sources table.**

    A dialog box appears, confirming that you want to delete the selected data source.

4. **Click OK.**

    The dialog box closes and the Data & Services > Datasources page updates. The deleted connection no longer appears in the Connected Data Sources table.

5. **Click Logout to close your session in the ColdFusion Administrator console.**

    If no Logout button is available, simply close the window.

Chapter 7: Dealing with Database Issues

In This Chapter

✔ **Database connection troubleshooting**

✔ **Resolving permission problems**

✔ **Addressing error messages**

✔ **Avoiding database errors**

The majority of error messages that you may experience when working with a database involve connectivity. These errors principally break down like this:

✦ Invalid host, username, or password

✦ The driver files are missing

✦ A file's permission settings prevent reading a file-based database such as Access

✦ The remote host doesn't support the database driver you're using

Within the database, errors you can encounter include

✦ Attempting to insert a duplicate record into a database with a unique constraint

✦ Creating a table that already exists

✦ Not having proper database access rights within the database, including read, modify, and create permissions

✦ Attempting to insert data that is different than the data type of a column

✦ Misspelling a table or column name

✦ Not including the same number of values as table columns

This chapter shows you how to troubleshoot database problems and resolve permissions issues.

Troubleshooting Basic Database Access

Depending on the type of database you're using, you can troubleshoot a database problem in several ways. First, ping the database to verify connectivity. Then if that's successful, validate your settings for username, password, and host name, making sure they're correct. The following sections give you the details on how to do these troubleshooting tasks.

Verifying contact with the database server

If your database is on a remote server, you should start your troubleshooting by verifying that your computer can reach the database server. The following steps show how to use the `ping` command to verify connectivity:

1. **Open a command prompt on the Mac or PC.**

To reach the command prompt on a PC, choose Start⇨Run, enter **cmd** in the Run dialog box that appears, and click OK.

To reach the command prompt on a Mac, start the Terminal application by choosing Applications⇨Utilities.

2. **On the command line, enter** `ping` [*host name*] **where** [*host name*] **is the name of the database server.**

For example, if your database is on a host called `db.krautgrrl.com`, you'd enter the following command:

```
ping db.krautgrrl.com
```

3. **Analyze the output from ping to determine whether it was successful.**

If the ping attempt is successful, you see output like this:

```
Pinging krautgrrl.com [24.94.201.11] with 32 bytes of
    data:

Reply from 24.94.201.11: bytes=32 time<10ms TTL=64
Reply from 24.94.201.11: bytes=32 time<10ms TTL=64
```

Unsuccessful output looks like this:

```
Pinging 12.3.2.4 with 32 bytes of data:
Request timed out.
Request timed out.
```

4. **Press Ctrl+C (Windows) or ⌘+click (Mac) to stop executing the** `ping` **command.**

If your ping was unsuccessful, make sure you have the right information for your host name, are connected to your network correctly, and that the database server isn't down for maintenance.

Validating your database username and password

After verifying contact with the database server (as described in the previous section), the next step is to make sure that your username and password are correct. To eliminate any possible driver issues with Dreamweaver, use your database client to test this information. Each particular database has a different protocol.

MySQL databases

For MySQL, use the `mysql` command-line client to verify the username and password. Specify your database connection information like this:

```
mysql -u[username] -p[password] -h[host name]
```

Figure 7-1 shows a successful database login to a MySQL database.

Figure 7-1: Connecting to a MySQL database.

```
C:\WINNT\system32\telnet.exe
jon@krautserver:~$ mysql -u root -p
Enter password:
Welcome to the MySQL monitor.  Commands end with ; or \g.
Your MySQL connection id is 942 to server version: 4.1.11-Debian_4-log

Type 'help;' or '\h' for help. Type '\c' to clear the buffer.

mysql>
```

Access and SQL Server

For Access or SQL Server databases, try connecting from Access or SQL Server through ODBC. For both Access and SQL Server, make sure that you have your DSN set up correctly. Also make sure that the remote server has the DSN set up. See the "Problematic Permissions: IIS and File-Based Databases" section for more information on accessing the DSN definition through the Windows Control Panel.

Oracle

For Oracle, use the `sqlplus` command-line tool to verify the username and password. Specify your connection information as follows:

```
sqlplus [username]/[password]@[db_descriptor]
```

The syntax is `sqlplus username@database`. Oracle also provides a utility called `tnsping` that attempts to ping the database server based on its Oracle database descriptor.

For example, in Figure 7-2, we called `sqlplus` from the command line. In this case, `sqlplus` prompted for a username and password. After entering the correct username and password, we were able to successfully log in.

Figure 7-2:
Using
`sqlplus` to
successfully
connect to a
database.

```
C:\WINNT\system32\cmd.exe - sqlplus                          _ □ ×
C:\>sqlplus

SQL×Plus: Release 10.2.0.1.0 - Beta on Fri Jan 13 09:37:13 2006

Copyright (c) 1982, 2005, Oracle.  All rights reserved.

Enter user-name: scott
Enter password:

Connected to:
Oracle Database 10g Express Edition Release 10.2.0.1.0 - Beta

SQL>
```

IBM Universal Database

Before you test your username and password, make sure you have the DB2 Runtime Client and the ODBC to DB2 driver installed. For the IBM client, verify your login using the Command Center. To test connectivity from the Command Center, follow these steps:

1. **Start the Command Center by choosing Start⇨Programs⇨db2⇨ Command Line Tools⇨Command Center.**

   The Command Center launches. If this folder isn't in your Program Files list, then you don't have the client installed.

2. **Click the Scripts tab.**

3. **Enter a simple query, such as the following, into the Query field:**

```
connect to sample;
```

4. **Click the Execute icon at the top left.**

Oracle names

Your Oracle database may require access through an Oracle names file called `tnsnames.ora`. You can use the Oracle Network Configuration tool to set up this file, or the Oracle database administrator may supply it. To verify that your Oracle names configuration is correct, use the Oracle command `tnsping`.

The `tnsping` command takes the name of your database as an argument and pings the database server that the configuration points to. If there's a problem resolving the name or reaching the server through the network, you receive an error message. If not, you know that your naming files are configured correctly and that the database is available over the network.

If you're able to execute your query without an error, you know that your database details are correct.

Problematic Permissions: IIS and File-Based Databases

Although file permissions are necessary to keep your computer and servers secure, they can thwart your development process when you're working with a Web server and a database, both of which execute with limited permissions to help keep systems secure. The unfortunate reality is that you'll probably run into a permission problem or two when developing and deploying your database-driven Web sites. Permissions apply to both directories and individual files, including database files. When access permission prevents your Web server from reading the database file, you get error messages that don't always clearly point to the problem. Also, verifying that permissions are set correctly on more than one computer can be time-consuming.

IIS permission problems are likely to rear their ugly heads when you publish your site or attempt to use Live Data view on a dynamic page. (See Book IX, Chapter 1 for more on Live Data view.) The same problems can happen whether you're running Windows 2000 or XP; however, the Windows administrative tools you can use to fix them vary slightly.

IIS usually runs as the limited access account on Windows called `IUSR_ [computer name]`. For example, if your computer name is `server`, your limited access account name is `IUSR_server`. IIS may take on increased permissions for a Web page if the page allows a user to log in to a specific account. In that case, you still need to be sure that the login account allows access to the database file.

The default for users who don't log in is `IUSR_[computer name]` unless it's been changed.

You receive an error message if the Web server and database driver can't read the database file as the `IUSR_server` user. Both the database file and the directory containing the database file must have read and write permissions. If the path to the database file uses a share name, regardless of whether the share is on the local computer or a remote computer, make sure that the file share has the proper permission to access the database file as `IUSR_[computer name]`.

Windows XP tends to have fewer permissions problems than NT or 2000 but the same general steps apply if you run into trouble. To check or change the database file permissions within Windows 2000 and XP, follow these steps:

1. **Log in as an Administrator.**

   Windows won't allow you to make changes if you don't have the Administrator privilege. If you don't have this, you need to log out and log back in with the Administrator account.

2. **Open the folder that contains your database file.**

   You specified this directory when creating the database.

   To find out where the file is located, check the ODBC data sources from the Windows Control Panel's Data Source (ODBC) program. It's located in the Administrative tools folder.

3. **Right-click (Windows) or Control+click (Mac) the database file and select Properties.**

   The filename usually has the `.mdb` extension.

4. **Click the Security tab.**

   If you're still using the older FAT32 file system, this tab doesn't appear, and you don't have to worry about the file permissions because they aren't supported. Figure 7-3 shows the permission for an Access database file with a location of: `C:\db1.mdb`. If you're on Windows XP and the Security tab is not visible, follow the directions at `http://support.microsoft.com/kb/307874/` to enable the tab.

Figure 7-3: The Security tab of the file's Properties dialog box.

5. **Verify that either the `IUSR_[computer name]` or the special user Everyone is listed in the Name column. If either account is listed, skip ahead to Step 10. Otherwise, proceed to the next step to add the `IUSR_[computer name]` account.**

The user Everyone means that any user, including the `IUSR_[computer name]` user, receives the permission granted to it.

6. Click the Add button to open the Users, Computer, or Groups dialog box.

7. Select your computer name from the list.

Don't worry if it's grayed out. That just means your computer name is the only choice because you're not part of a Windows domain.

8. Select `IUSR_[computer name]` from the list of names.

For example, select `IUSR_JOE` if your computer name is `Joe`.

9. Click Add and then click OK.

You return to the file's Properties dialog box.

10. While `IUSR_[computer name]` is highlighted, click the Allow check box for Full Control in the Permissions section.

Clicking Full Control is a shortcut for clicking all the other permission check boxes. This ensures that the file can be used by the Web application.

11. Click OK.

The file's permissions are set to allow access.

Repeat these steps for the directory that contains the database file.

If you want to restrict Web users from browsing the folder that contains your database file, if it's within your Web root folder you can clear the Read permission for the database folder. This still allows your application to read the file (because it already knows where the file's located), but prevents users from browsing the directory. Of course, placing the database file outside of the Web root folder automatically means the file can't be viewed through the browser.

**Book VII
Chapter 7**

**Dealing with
Database Issues**

Troubleshooting Microsoft Error Messages

When working with IIS and a file-driven database such as Access or SQL Server, a common set of errors can crop up. They involve the interaction between the Web server and the database when requesting dynamic pages. In this section, we look at these common error messages:

✦ 80004005: Couldn't use '(*unknown*)'; file already in use. (Another variation is 80004005: Microsoft Jet database engine cannot open the file (*unknown*).)

+ 80040e07: Data type mismatch in criteria expression.

+ 80040e10: Too few parameters.

+ 80040e14: Syntax error in `INSERT INTO` statement.

+ 80040e21: ODBC error on Insert or Update.

+ 800a0bcd: Either BOF or EOF is true.

For each of these errors, the following sections summarize the root cause and the action you need to take to fix it.

80004005: Data Source Name Not Found

Another variation is "80004005: Microsoft Jet database engine cannot open the file (*unknown*)". This error generally means that you can't access the database file either because of permissions or because another process is already using the file. Verify that you've set the permissions correctly and that you don't have the database open in another program such as Access. See Microsoft's page for more troubleshooting tips at `http://support.microsoft.com/kb/306345/EN-US/`.

80040e07: Data type mismatch in criteria expression

This error means that you've attempted to enter a value into a database column that isn't the correct type and can't be converted automatically (for example, inserting a string like `midwest` into a number column). The solution is to supply the correct type of data or change the column's data type.

80040e10: Too few parameters

This error indicates that one of the columns you've specified to add data to doesn't exist in the database. To fix this error, check the spelling of your commands and fields. Verify that each column exists. Create a new column in the table to match the data you're trying to insert if it doesn't already exist.

80040e14: Syntax error in INSERT INTO statement

This error may indicate that you've used an invalid character in the name of a table or column. Spaces and special characters such as punctuation symbols aren't permitted. Also, in an Oracle database, you can see this error when using the `distinct` keyword in a `select` statement. See `http://support.microsoft.com/default.aspx?scid=kb;EN-US;238164` for patch instructions.

80040e21: ODBC error on Insert or Update

This error indicates that the field you're inserting into isn't large enough to hold the value you're inserting. For example, if you have a string column with a length of five characters and attempt to insert `Tuesday`, you get this error. To correct the error, either increase the size of the column or reduce the size of the string you're inserting.

800a0bcd: Either BOF or EOF is true

You're attempting to display an element from a recordset that doesn't exist in the database table. To resolve this error, verify that each element of your recordset has a corresponding column in the database table using the Server Behaviors tool for the deployments. The Server Behaviors panel allows you to expand your recordset; click the plus button to reveal the fields of the recordset.

Troubleshooting JSP Database Connections

The most common error you are likely to encounter when working with a Java Database Connection (JDBC) database is that the JDBC driver isn't loaded on your machine or your server. If this happens, you receive an error ending in `class not found`. Search the database vendor's Web site for the JDBC driver. Dreamweaver is not capable of including them all because literally hundreds of JDBC drivers are available. After installing the driver, restart Dreamweaver so it can detect the presence of the driver. (See Book VII, Chapter 5 for more on setting up JSP database connections.)

**Book VII
Chapter 7**

**Dealing with
Database Issues**

Identifying Problems within the Database

When working with database data, sometimes you may accidentally ask the database to do something it can't do, or something that you don't have permission to do. For each of these scenarios, you encounter an error, regardless of which database you're using:

✦ Creating an object that already exists always causes an error unless your database supports a `replace` keyword. It's a good idea to *drop* (delete) objects such as tables before creating them to avoid creation errors.

✦ Inserting a row with a key that's already been used causes an error. To avoid this problem, either create the table without a unique requirement (if that's okay with your data) or check that the value you're trying to insert doesn't already exist in the table. You can use a simple `select` statement to do this.

✦ Misspelled table or column names cause problems. Use the database object browser to check all your column and table names before using them.

✦ Data type and size problems can also creep up in your pages. Always validate the database column type before inserting data into it. Each development model provides functions for checking the length and type of data for a variable. A little checking before your page goes live (and before your users get creative with entering data) can prevent annoying errors.

General Troubleshooting

In general, testing your queries outside of Dreamweaver is a great way to make sure that you can connect to your database and that your SQL queries are correct. If your query works with the database client, you can focus on the code that is creating and executing the query. A *query* tells the database the information you're looking for. We discuss queries in detail in Book IX, Chapter 2.

Verify permission on the database file if you're using a file-based database on both your local computer and the server or with your ISP account. You must also verify that the Web server is set to execute whichever type of code you've chosen as your dynamic site type. In general, make sure that a simple dynamic page is executable before attempting database operations. If the file is executable, you see a blank page or whatever test code you place in the file. If it isn't executable, you likely see the contents of the file with any processing.

Book VIII

Making Pages Dynamic

The 5th Wave   By Rich Tennant

"I hope you're doing something online. An indie band like yours shouldn't just be playing street corners."

Contents at a Glance

Chapter 1: Preparing Dynamic Content Sources

In This Chapter

✔ **Exploring your database in Dreamweaver**

✔ **Creating parameters for your form data**

✔ **Adding URL parameters to Web page requests**

✔ **Keeping track of users with session variables**

✔ **Using a database as your data source**

A dynamic Web site has content that regenerates every time a user visits or reloads the site. For example, the JavaScript that displays the time at the bottom of the www.krautgrrl.com Web site is dynamic content. If you go to the Web site and click the Reload button several times, you'll notice that the time changes. You can choose from a variety of languages to make a dynamic Web site, including PHP.

When you're preparing dynamic content sources, as described in this chapter, you're actually creating code and working with variables and sessions that help you manage your Web site more efficiently. A *data source* is a source of information from which you can extract data to display in your dynamic Web pages. This data can come from several sources in Dreamweaver:

✦ A form submission from another Web page

✦ URL parameters that are part of the Web page request

✦ A session variable that you set on another Web page

✦ A database table column

✦ Other advanced sources, such as JavaBeans properties

Before you can use a data source in your dynamic Web pages, you need to define it by using the Dreamweaver Bindings panel. This chapter shows you how to define several data sources — form parameters, URL parameters, session variables, and databases — and make them available for use in your dynamic Web pages.

This chapter also explains how to use the Databases panel to navigate your database and make sure that you're using the right column names.

Exploring Your Database in the Databases Panel

The Databases panel lists the tables and fields for an active database connection. After connecting to your database, you can view its structure and data within the Dreamweaver Databases panel, which displays your database in a tree-like structure. You can view a database table much more easily in Dreamweaver than you can by working directly through a command-line SQL client, using commands like `describe [table_name]`.

To explore your database visually in the Databases panel, follow these steps:

1. **Open the Databases panel by choosing Window⇨Databases.**

   This panel displays all the database connections defined for your site (see Figure 1-1). Any databases with a properly configured connection display with a plus sign before them. You can explore only an accessible database.

   If no database appears in the panel, you have to create a database connection, which you find out how to do in Book VII.

2. **Click the plus (+) sign before the database to view the object types associated with that database.**

   The tree view expands to show these database object types:

   - **Stored Procedures:** A *stored procedure* is code that is stored within the database itself. Because the stored procedure runs directly on the database server, it can be faster at complex analysis of database data. Stored procedures can also be useful for validating data.

   - **Tables:** Database tables are discussed in Book VII, Chapter 1.

   - **Views:** *Views* are tables that are based on a database query. They are read-only.

Figure 1-1:
The Databases panel for a sample database connection called `test`.

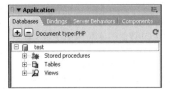

3. **Click the plus (+) sign before a database category — Stored Procedures, Tables, or Views — to see what your database contains for that category.**

4. **Click the name of the object to expand the details again.**

You see different information, depending on which database category you select in Step 3:

- **Stored Procedures:** Listing the stored procedure's parameters and return values.

- **Tables:** Lists the table's columns and those columns' data types (see Figure 1-2).

- **Views:** Lists the view's columns and those columns' data types.

Figure 1-2:
The Databases panel showing the columns of a table.

For database tables, you can view the data in the table by right-clicking (Windows) or Control+clicking (Mac) the table name in the Databases panel and selecting View Data from the context menu. A window appears that lists the table data.

Defining Form Parameters

The whole point of dynamic Web pages is to not return the same page each time a page is requested. One tool that's used to mix up what's returned is a form parameter. When you add a form to your page (as described in Book II, Chapter 7), you need to keep track of how you submit your form data to the server. You have two methods to choose from:

✦ The POST method, which sends parameters in the body of the request

✦ The GET method, which places the data in the URL as parameters

You can use either GET or POST methods, but you need to be consistent about which you use between the page that submits the values and the page that processes them. You need the type of request when you tell Dreamweaver about your form input. You also need to know the field names listed in the Field Properties dialog box because you need to create a form parameter for each of these fields. To view the field name, select the form field with the Properties inspector open.

To add a data source for a form field, follow these steps:

1. **Create a new dynamic page and add a form, or open an existing page that contains a form element.**

See Book II, Chapter 7 for the lowdown on creating forms.

2. **If you don't already have the Bindings panel displayed, choose Window⟳Bindings.**

Before you create any bindings, you see the Dynamic Page setup check-list in the Bindings panel.

3. **Click the plus (+) button, and from the list that appears, select the appropriate form item for your dynamic page type.**

Options appear on the list based on your dynamic page type. Table 1-1 lists the option names to select for each page type.

Table 1-1	Add a Binding Menu Form Item Name Based on the Dynamic Page Type
Dynamic Page Type	*Menu Item Name*
ASP	Request Variable > Request.Form
ColdFusion	Form Variable
JSP	Request Variable
PHP	Form Variable

The Form Variable dialog box displays, as shown in Figure 1-3.

Figure 1-3:
The Form
Variable
dialog box
for a form
field called
username.

4. Enter the name of the form variable in the dialog box and click OK.

The form parameter name is normally the name of the HTML form field or object that the parameter uses to obtain its value. For example, if the field on your form is labeled Username, enter **username** in the dialog box.

The form parameter appears in the Bindings panel, as shown in Figure 1-4.

Figure 1-4:
The Bindings panel after adding a `username` form field binding.

After you define the form parameter as a data source, you can insert the parameter in your document by selecting it in the Bindings panel. See Book VIII, Chapter 3 for details.

Defining URL Parameters

URL parameters are a simple way of passing information to the Web server as part of the Web page request. When the Web server receives the request, the URL parameter is included in that request. This allows dynamic pages to be generated based on a specific parameter from a prior page. In the URL, a question mark (?) separates the Web site location from the parameters. Here's an example:

```
http://www.example.com/?username=jon&password=test
```

In this example, the Web site is `http://www.example.com`. The two parameters are `username` (which has a value of `jon`) and `password` (which has a value of `test`). An equal sign (=) separates each parameter from its value. If more than one parameter exists, as in this example, an ampersand (&) separates the parameters. Passing these values to the server is important because it allows the server to determine if the username and password are valid. Username and password validity determines access to subsequent pages.

When a server processes a Web page request that contains URL parameters, the server makes those parameter values available to the dynamic page before returning the page to the Web browser, where the user sees the updated page displayed.

Dreamweaver uses URL parameters automatically when you submit a form by using the `HTTP GET` method. The `GET` method specifies that the parameters are appended to the URL when the page request is sent to the Web server. URL parameters are also frequently used to pass a value to the Web server, such as an action to take, when the user clicks a link. For example, you may have a URL parameter called `action` that takes the values `insert`, `update`, and `delete` based on the action that the link indicates. You can pass more than one URL parameter at a time to a Web site.

To define a data source binding for a URL parameter, follow these steps:

1. **Create a new dynamic page or open an existing dynamic page.**

2. **If you don't already have the Bindings panel displayed, choose Window⇨Bindings.**

Before you create any bindings, you see the Dynamic Page setup checklist in the Bindings panel.

3. **Click the plus (+) button and select the URL item for your dynamic page type from the list that appears.**

Dreamweaver uses different names for this field based on your dynamic page type. Table 1-2 lists the appropriate URL item for your page type.

Table 1-2	Add a Binding Menu for URL Parameters Based on the Dynamic Page Type
Dynamic Page Type	*URL Item Name*
ASP	Request Variable > Request.QueryString
ColdFusion	URL Variable
JSP	Request Variable
PHP	URL Variable

The URL Variable dialog box appears, as shown in Figure 1-5.

4. **Enter the name of the URL variable in the dialog box and click OK.**

The URL parameter name is normally the name of the HTML form field or the object used to obtain its value.

Figure 1-5 shows the new binding called `search`.

Figure 1-5:
The URL
Variable
dialog box
for a form
field called
`search`.

The form parameter appears in the Bindings panel (shown in Figure 1-6).

Figure 1-6:
The Bindings
panel after
adding a
`search`
URL binding.

After you define the URL as a data source, you can insert the URL in your document from the Bindings panel. See Book VIII, Chapter 3 for details.

Defining Session Variables

Session variables store information that the user enters and make that information available to any page during the user's visit, or *session.* For example, if a user logs in to the Web site, a session variable saves that authentication information, making it available to every page on the Web site throughout the user's visit. Without a session variable, the user has to reenter the login information every time he or she visits a new page on the site.

The session variable remains in effect until the user ends the session or a timeout period expires. Because the session is tracked on the server, the information stored in session variables is also stored on the Web server. Only a small unique identifier, called a *cookie,* is stored on the Web browser's computer.

You have to use Code view to add a session variable to a page. Follow these steps to define the session variable in the page and add it to the Bindings panel:

1. **Create a new dynamic page or open an existing page that contains a session variable.**

2. **If you don't already have the Bindings panel displayed, choose Window⇨Bindings.**

3. **Click the plus (+) button and select Session Variable from the list that appears.**

Unlike the other binding types, Dreamweaver uses the name *Session Variable* on this list for every dynamic page type.

The Session Variable dialog box displays.

4. **Enter the name of the session variable in the dialog box and click OK.**

Figure 1-7 shows the new binding called `first_name`.

Figure 1-7:
The Session Variable dialog box for a form field called `first_name`.

The session variable appears in the Bindings panel (shown in Figure 1-8).

Figure 1-8:
The Bindings panel after adding a `first_name` session variable binding.

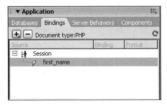

After you define the session variable as a data source, you can insert your session variable in your document from the Bindings panel. See Book VIII, Chapter 3 for details.

Using a Database as Your Data Source

If you want to use a database as a data source for your dynamic Web site, you build a *query* to gather specific data from the database to use in your page. For example, you might build a query to retrieve all the information about a user before presenting the page so the user can update the data. The data that results from that query is called a *recordset*. After you create a recordset, you can display information from your database in your page.

Understanding recordsets

The recordset lets Dreamweaver process more than one piece of data in a dynamic page. The other data sources that we cover in this chapter (form parameters, URL parameters, and session variables) work with a single piece of data. Because recordsets are the results of database queries, they can contain more than just a single piece of data. This allows displaying an entire list of results on a page.

Recordsets contain one or more results. Each result has one or more columns. Working with recordsets can be complex because of the variable number of results. To make accessing the data for a recordset as fast as possible, the database server stores the results in its memory.

You can create database queries using a graphical table linking tool or by using the standard database language called Structured Query Language (SQL). SQL provides a standard format for specifying how information in a database is linked together and then filtered. SQL is specifically designed to describe the relationships between data and how to filter matching rows. Dreamweaver includes a simple-query building tool called SQL Builder to help build simple queries.

Microsoft's ASP.NET coding platform calls a recordset a *dataset.* Despite the different names, they're really the same thing. When working with ASP.NET document types, you can think of the terms recordset and dataset as interchangeable wherever you run into them.

Book VIII
Chapter 1

Preparing Dynamic
Content Sources

Defining a recordset

Although you build the queries for a recordset with SQL, Dreamweaver enables you to create a recordset without writing a SQL query. It lets you select fields graphically from a table and column listing.

Before you can define a recordset, you need to establish a database connection in Dreamweaver. See Book VII for details on setting up a database connection.

To define a simple recordset in Dreamweaver, follow these steps:

1. **Create a new dynamic page or open an existing page.**

2. **In the Bindings panel, click the plus (+) button and select Recordset (Query) from the list that appears.**

   The Recordset dialog box opens. Depending on your dynamic page type, the dialog box may look slightly different.

   If you want to write your own SQL queries for a recordset, use the Advanced Recordset dialog box. You can open this version of the dialog box by clicking the Advanced button in the Recordset dialog box.

3. **In the Name field, enter a name for your recordset.**

   Remember to use only letters, numbers, and underscores for names to be sure that the name is compatible with your dynamic page type. In the example in Figure 1-9, we accepted the default name *Recordset1*.

4. **Select a database connection from the Connection drop-down list.**

   In the example, we selected the phptest connection.

5. **Select the database table from the Table drop-down list.**

   The database table serves as a foundation for retrieving data for a database query. The Columns field updates to display the columns in your selected table. By default, all the columns are included in the recordset.

   In the example shown in Figure 1-9, we selected the logins table.

6. **If you want to specify which columns to include, choose the Selected radio button and select the desired columns.**

   If you choose the Selected radio button, you can select multiple columns that you want to include from the Columns listing by Ctrl+clicking (Windows) or ⌘+clicking (Mac) them.

7. **(Optional) If you want to filter the records, do the following:**

- **In the first Filter drop-down list:** Select a table column to filter. You can compare the database field against one of the previously defined bindings to limit the results of the query.

- **In the second list:** Select a conditional expression (such as =, <, or >) with which to compare the data from the column that you select in the first drop-down list.

- **In the third list:** Select the data source for comparison. Your choices include any previously bound values, such as username, first_name, or search.

- **In the fourth list:** Enter a value to compare to the database column.

For example, Figure 1-9 shows the Recordset dialog box comparing a column value (username) and a URL parameter.

Figure 1-9:
The Recordset dialog box is set to compare the database column value against the URL parameter.

8. **If you want to sort the records, select the table column that you want to sort by from the first Sort drop-down list. In the second drop-down list, specify whether you want the records sorted in ascending or descending order.**

9. **Click the Test button to verify that the query works correctly.**

   Dreamweaver executes your query and displays the rows in the Test SQL Statement window. Figure 1-10 displays the matching rows for the recordset.

   If your query uses a filter, Dreamweaver displays the Test Value dialog box and prompts you to enter a value to use in the filter before executing the Test query. Enter a filter value typical of what you expect your query to encounter when it's executed as part of the Web page, and then click OK.

Figure 1-10:
The
Test SQL
Statement
window
displays two
`logins`
records.

10. **If the test returns the records that you expect, click OK.**

The recordset now appears in the Bindings panel, as Figure 1-11 shows.

Figure 1-11:
The Bindings
panel
reflects
the new
recordset,
`Logins`
`Record`
`set.`

Chapter 2: Using Dynamic Content in Your Web Pages

In This Chapter

✔ Adding dynamic content to your page

✔ Formatting dynamic content

✔ Showing multiple records from a recordset

✔ Navigating through your records

✔ Showing and hiding regions of your page

To make dynamic pages as flexible as possible and yet still organized, Dreamweaver places all *bindings* (references) to external data before you use it in your dynamic page. Once the data is bound, you can select the exact format to display it in. You can even hide portions of pages depending on the values of bindings. After you master these concepts, you're ready to build complex dynamic Web pages.

Displaying and Formatting Dynamic Content

When you want to insert dynamic text on your page, your key tools are the Bindings panel and the Server Behaviors panel. To insert dynamic text, open the Bindings panel (choose Window➪Bindings), locate the item that you want to use, and drag the item to your page. Then, if you want to format the new dynamic text, you can use the Server Behaviors panel (choose Window➪ Server Behaviors). The following sections describe in more detail how to add, format, and test dynamic content.

Before you can add dynamic text to your pages, you need to establish a database connection (as described in Book VII) and define a data source (as described in Book VIII, Chapter 1).

Adding dynamic text

To insert dynamic text on your page, follow these steps:

1. **In your document, place your cursor where you want to insert the dynamic text.**

2. **In the Bindings panel, locate the data source that you want to use.**

You can choose from any existing data sources, such as recordsets, URL parameters, form parameters, and session variables. (See Book VIII, Chapter 1 for more on these data sources.)

3. **Drag the data source to your document.**

The dynamic text appears on your page, enclosed by curly brackets {}. For example, if you add a URL parameter named `username` to your page, it looks like this in the Document window:

```
{URL.username}
```

This dynamic text entry is also added to the Server Behaviors panel, as shown in Figure 2-1.

Dynamic text placeholder   Dynamic text listing

Figure 2-1:
The dynamic text place-holder in the Document window and the dynamic text listing in the Server Behaviors panel.

Formatting your dynamic content

After you get dynamic text on your page, you can modify how it appears. For example, if you're displaying a numeric field as money, you generally want it to appear in a format like $2.43. It doesn't look very professional to say that something costs $1.1 or $1.154. Fortunately, you can optionally modify the display format of server behavior dynamic text fields.

The formatting options that Dreamweaver provides for dynamic data display depend upon what dynamic page type you're using. In general, you can find functions that change the case (upper or lower) of strings, format numbers, and format dates and times.

To change the formatting of dynamic text, follow these steps:

1. **In the Server Behaviors panel, double-click the dynamic text that you want to format.**

The Dynamic Text dialog box appears with your dynamic text already selected.

2. **Select the appropriate formatting option from the Format drop-down list.**

For example, if you want to capitalize the first letter of each word, select the AlphaCase-Capitalize option, as Figure 2-2 shows. Or if you want to format a numeric field so that it shows dollars and cents, select Currency – 2 Decimal Places.

You can download more formats for dynamic text by selecting Edit Format List at the bottom of the Format drop-down list.

3. **You can safely leave the Code field alone.**

The Code field tells you the actual code that Dreamweaver is using to produce the dynamic text. It's populated automatically when you select a data source.

Figure 2-2:
Format your parameter in the Dynamic Text dialog box.

4. **Click OK to close the Dynamic Text dialog box.**

Dreamweaver applies the formatting that you select in Step 2 to your text.

Testing your dynamic text

If you think that you have your page the way that you want it, the next step is to test it out. You can test the page by using Dreamweaver's Preview in Browser command or Live Data view (both are described in Book VIII, Chapter 3). Live Data view is a little easier to use because it gives you a dialog box for entering parameter values. For example, you can enter URL parameter values in this dialog box instead of having to manually add them to the URL like this:

```
http://127.0.0.1/url_case.php?username=jon%20phillips
```

To use Live Data view to test your dynamic text, open your document and follow these steps:

1. **Choose View⇨Live Data Settings.**

The Live Data Settings window appears.

2. **Click the plus (+) button to add a new entry to the URL Request list.**

3. **Enter the name of the URL parameter in the Name column.**

The name must match the name of the parameter from the URL. For example, we entered **username** to match the name of the URL parameter in Figure 2-3.

4. **Enter a sample value in the Value field and then click OK.**

For our example, we entered **jon phillips**, as shown in Figure 2-3. We selected text that starts with lowercase letters so that we can check that the formatting is actually doing something. This value simulates an actual value sent to your script when it runs. To find out how to format dynamic content, see the earlier section, "Formatting your dynamic content."

Figure 2-3:
The URL parameter username set to a testing value of jon phillips.

5. Choose View⇨Live Data.

Your Document window updates to show the processing of the page's dynamic content. For example, in Figure 2-4, the URL parameter `username` is replaced with `Jon Phillips`. Notice that the first letter of each word is capitalized in Figure 2-4, so the formatting works.

Dynamic text

Figure 2-4:
The value
`Jon`
`Phillips`
replaces
the URL
parameter
placeholder.

Working with Database Recordsets

You can display database recordsets much like you display simple dynamic data (as described in the earlier sections of this chapter) when you're working with a recordset that has one row in its results. You can even use the Dynamic Text server behavior to display a field from a recordset. (If you have more than one row in your recordset, the behavior shows just the first row.)

Things get a bit more complex when your recordset has several rows that you want to include. The dynamic page must be able to apply formatting for each row in a recordset. Dreamweaver lets you specify the format for your results, gives you navigation tools, and uses HTML tables to display the recordsets neatly.

Repeating regions on your page

The Repeat Region server behavior lets you display multiple records from a single recordset on the same page. Select an area, or *region,* of the page that you want to repeat and specify the number of times that you want to repeat it. The Repeat Region server behavior then populates the contents of each repeated region with values from the recordset.

To add a repeat region to your page, follow these steps:

1. **Select the content on the page that you want to repeat.**

For example, we're working with a recordset that's defined to return all the entries from the login table, which has two fields: a username and a plain text password. In Figure 2-5, the two dynamic text fields appear highlighted: `Recordset1.username` and `Recordset1.password`.

Figure 2-5:
The Document window displays dynamic text placeholders for the username and password fields.

2. **In the Server Behaviors panel, click the plus (+) button and select Repeat Region from the drop-down list that appears.**

The Repeat Region dialog box appears, as shown in Figure 2-6.

Figure 2-6:
The Repeat Region dialog box for `Record set1`.

3. **From the Recordset drop-down list, select the recordset that you want to use.**

4. **In the Show area, select the number of records that you want to show on the page.**

The default displays ten records, but you can pick a different number. You can also display all records by clicking the All Records radio button. In our example, we selected two records.

5. **Click OK to close the Repeat Region dialog box.**

   A gray box appears around the repeating fields with the text *Repeat* on a tab. A repeat region (`Recordset`) also shows up in the Server Behaviors listing.

   To view invisible elements on your page, choose View➪Visual Aides➪ Invisible Elements.

6. **Choose View➪Live Data to view the page with actual data from the database.**

   Figure 2-7 shows that the two records in this result cause the repeated region to appear twice.

   Fields that appear highlighted in Live Data view are dynamic text. In other words, the text disappears when you turn off Live Data view. (See Book VIII, Chapter 3 for more on Live Data view.)

Figure 2-7: The Live Data view shows the data from the `Recordset` database.

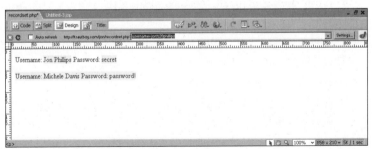

Username: Jon Phillips Password: secret

Username: Michele Davis Password: password!

Repeating regions in HTML tables

To make your data easier to read, you can integrate an HTML table and a repeating region. The bulk of these steps work the same as the last example but the dynamic text is placed into a table row:

1. **Open a new dynamic page and create a recordset or open an existing page with a defined recordset.**

   You can use the default recordset name of `Recordset1`.

2. **Insert a table by choosing Insert➪Table.**

3. **Enter the number of rows and columns you want in the Rows and Columns fields.**

   The defaults are fine for the other settings.

Book VIII
Chapter 2

Using Dynamic
Content in Your
Web Pages

4. Click OK.

The table appears in the Document window (see Figure 2-8).

Figure 2-8:
The table
that
holds the
recordset.

5. Enter the name of the field in the first column of the table heading.

This text displays in the header of the table and describes the contents of the column. In Figure 2-9, we entered **Username**.

6. Enter the name of the second field in the second column of the table heading.

In our example in Figure 2-9, we entered **Password**.

7. Select the first column of the table's second row.

This is where you'll place the dynamic text.

8. Open the Server Behaviors panel by choosing Window⇨Server Behaviors.

9. Click the plus (+) button and choose Dynamic Text.

The Dynamic Text dialog box appears.

10. Expand the recordset.

All the database table columns display.

11. Select the column from Step 7.

You can leave format and code alone because you just want to display these fields as they are in the database.

12. Click OK.

Your dynamic field appears on your page enclosed by curly brackets {} (in our example, it's `Recordset1.username`). The dynamic text (in our example, `Recordset1.username`) entry is added to the Server Behaviors list.

13. **Select the second column of the second table row.**

14. **Repeat Steps 7 through 12 to add the second field.**

15. **Select the rows in the table with both dynamic text fields.**

16. **Click the plus (+) sign in the Server Behaviors panel and choose Repeat Region.**

The Repeat Region dialog box appears.

17. **Click OK.**

The default displays ten records but you can pick a different number or display all records by selecting the All Records radio button.

A gray box appears around the repeating fields with the text *Repeat* on a tab. The repeat region (`Recordset1`) also shows up in the Server Behaviors listing.

Figure 2-9 shows the repeated regions defined on the table row.

Figure 2-9:
The repeat region for `Record set1`.

18. **Choose View➪Live Data to view the actual data from the database.**

Figure 2-10 shows that the two records in this result cause the repeated region to display twice.

Figure 2-10:
The Live Data mode view shows the data from the database `Recordset` presented in an HTML table.

Adding a recordset navigation bar

Dreamweaver provides paging functions in the Server Behaviors panel for the Web user to go to the first page, last page, next page, and previous page of multi-page repeating regions. You can associate these behaviors with text or with images that you select on the page itself, such as the forward and backward arrows.

When applying a Navigation server behavior to a dynamic Web page, you can display only one recordset on the page because you can't specify to which recordset the navigation applies.

To help users keep track of which record they're viewing in a multi-page recordset, you can add a Record Count server behavior. You can display the total number of records, the first record on a page, and the last record on a page.

Before you can add a Recordset Navigation server behavior, you must have a Repeat Region server behavior on your page (as described in the previous section). Although you can individually add a Navigation server behavior to your page, the easiest way to build navigation for a recordset is to use a navigation bar.

Follow these steps to add the navigation bar to your page:

1. **In the Document window, place the pointer where you want to insert the navigation bar.**

2. **Choose Insert⇨Application Objects⇨Recordset Paging⇨Recordset Navigation Bar.**

   The Recordset Navigation Bar dialog box appears.

3. **Select the recordset that you want to control from the Recordset drop-down list.**

   Leave the default selected to Text or select Images to include icons instead of text to indicate the navigation.

4. **Click OK.**

   The navigation bar appears on your page, as shown in Figure 2-11.

Showing and hiding regions on your page

The Show Region server behavior lets you show or hide areas of your document based on certain conditions. For example, a page that displays personal information about users should only be visible by the site administrator. Here's a rundown of the six Show Region server behaviors:

+ Show If Recordset Is Empty

+ Show If Recordset Is Not Empty

+ Show If First Page

+ Show If Not First Page

+ Show If Last Page

+ Show If Not Last Page

For example, the Show If Not First Page and Show If Not Last Page server behaviors let you display previous and next links only when you have a next or previous page that you can jump to.

To apply one of the server behaviors to your page, open your document and follow these steps:

1. **In Design view, select the region that you want to show or hide.**

To select the region, drag the pointer while clicking the mouse.

2. **In the Server Behaviors panel, click the plus (+) button and then select an option from the Show Region submenu that appears.**

You can choose from the six Show Region server behaviors.

3. **In the dialog box that corresponds to the type of region you're showing, select the recordset that you want to apply the server behavior to.**

4. **Click OK.**

The server behavior is applied to the selected region.

Figure 2-11: Dreamweaver has added a new navigation bar to your page.

Navigation bar

Book VIII
Chapter 2

Using Dynamic
Content in Your
Web Pages

Adding Dynamic Form Elements to Your Page

In the same way that you use the Bindings panel to insert dynamic text on your Web page (as described at the beginning of the chapter), you can integrate dynamic text into form elements. Dreamweaver supports using dynamic data for all the major form elements, including text boxes, check boxes, radio selections, and menus.

To insert a dynamic form element on your page, follow these steps:

1. **Insert a form on your page.**

See Book II, Chapter 7 for the lowdown on creating forms.

2. **Choose Insert⇨Form and select a form object of the same type as the dynamic object.**

For example, if you're adding a dynamic check box to a form, you must have a check box element already on that form.

The form object appears on the page.

3. **In the Server Behaviors panel, click the plus (+) button and select a dynamic form type from the Form Elements menu.**

Figure 2-12 shows the Dynamic CheckBox dialog box.

4. **In the Check If field, select the binding to verify against the value in the Equal To field to determine if the check box is checked by default.**

5. **Click OK.**

The check box now gets its default value from the defined comparison.

Figure 2-12:
Enter a value that will determine if a check box is checked.

Chapter 3: Previewing and Testing Your Dynamic Pages

In This Chapter

✔ Testing your dynamic pages by using Live Data mode

✔ Previewing your dynamic pages in a Web browser

*W*riting dynamic pages is great, but if you can't test them or publish them, how do you know if they're usable? In this chapter, you find out how to preview and test your dynamic pages by using the Live Data mode or a Web browser.

For your pages to work, you must transfer your files to the remote folder. See Book V, Chapter 4 for details on publishing your site.

Viewing Live Data in Your Dynamic Web Pages

A great way to test the functionality of your dynamic Web site is to use Dreamweaver's Live Data mode. When you use the Live Data mode while developing a page in Dreamweaver, Dreamweaver connects to your Web server, pulls the dynamic data for the page from the database, and then uses that data to replace the dynamic data placeholders on your page.

For details on adding dynamic data to your page, see Book VIII, Chapter 2.

In order for the Live Data mode to work correctly, you must simulate any input that usually comes from the user. You also need any supporting files such as server-side includes so the Web server can execute the dynamic code without errors.

Understanding how Live Data mode works

Here are the specific tasks that Dreamweaver performs when you use the Live Data mode:

1. Transfers your dynamic page to the server temporarily.

2. Requests the page from the server.

3. The Web server executes the dynamic page code that may contain calls to database functions.

4. Integrates the page request results into the page and displays them in Design view.

5. Deletes the temporary file from the server.

Figure 3-1 shows how a Web page looks with placeholders. Figure 3-2 shows how the same Web page looks with Live Data mode.

In order for Live Data mode to work properly, Dreamweaver has to know how to get the page that you're previewing to the server and how to request that page from the server, specifically the URL path. These paths are set up as part of your testing server (see Book VII, Chapter 1).

TIP

You can manually refresh your Live Data page by clicking the Refresh button. You may find refreshing your Live Data page useful if you've changed any data in the database. You can see how those changes affect your page.

Figure 3-1:
This page contains placeholders for fields in an employee database when not in Live Data mode.

Figure 3-2:
Live Data
mode
replaces the
placeholders
with actual
data from
the data-
base.

Uploading dependent files to the testing server

Some dynamic Web pages rely on dependent files to work properly.
Dependent files are files that your Web page references and a browser
loads when it displays the page. If a dependent file is missing, your page may
generate an error or there may be images missing when the browser displays the page. Dependent files can include

✦ **Code files:** These files include JSP `.jar` classes, ASP `.asp` files, and
   ColdFusion `.cfm` files.

✦ **CSS files:** The files include style sheet details such as how different
   classes of text appear. See Book III, Chapter 1 for more information.

✦ **Image files:** Such as JPG or GIF files. Depending on your image tags, you
   may not need to have the images on the testing server. Missing images
   won't cause your page to fail to load.

✦ **Server-side includes:** Code that is included from a file as the dynamic
   Web page code executes. An include statement is replaced by the contents of the included file when the page is processed on the Web server.

Dreamweaver doesn't know which dependent files to send to the testing server, so you need to upload the appropriate files manually. Follow these steps to upload your dependent files to the testing server:

1. **Open the Files panel to see the files for your site.**

The Files panel displays files for each portion of your site, including the local, remote, and testing servers.

2. **Click the Expand/Collapse button, as Figure 3-3 shows.**

Expand/Collapse button

Figure 3-3:
The Expand/
Collapse
button.

The expanded view displays two file views at the same time. By default, the local files always appear on the right half of the screen.

3. **Click the Testing Server button (see Figure 3-4).**

The file view on the left displays the Testing Server files, as shown in Figure 3-4.

4. **Select the dependent files from the Local Files list.**

You can select multiple files by holding the Ctrl (Windows) or ⌘ (Mac) key while clicking the files.

5. **To upload the dependent files to the testing server, click the Put Files button (which you can see in Figure 3-4).**

The files display in the Testing Server file list, and your dynamic page code can now access them during Live Data viewing.

Testing Server button

Testing Server files   Put Files button   Local files

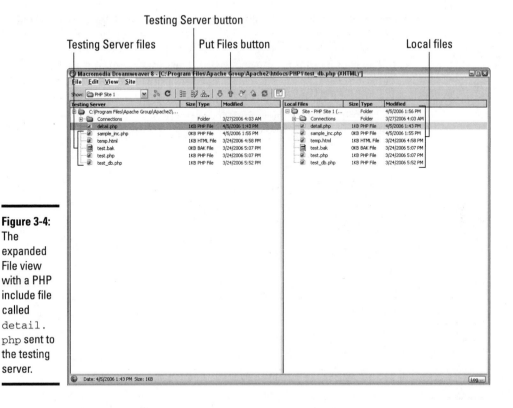

Figure 3-4:
The expanded File view with a PHP include file called `detail. php` sent to the testing server.

Figure 3-4 shows the testing server with the `detail.php` dependent file. The `detail.php` file supplies the code to view more detailed information about a record selected from the list.

Providing parameters for user input

Sometimes your dynamic page code generates different output based on the user's input, such as a username or a value that indicates a database row (such as a user ID). If your dynamic page code processes user input results, such as a form submission, you may need to update the Live Data settings to supply the value (simulate the user's input). If you don't update the Live Update settings, your page may issue a warning that it can't find any data to display. Follow these steps to add parameters for user input:

1. **Choose View➪Live Data Settings.**

The Live Data Settings dialog box appears with an empty list of parameters.

2. **To simulate the user input for each parameter, click the plus (+) button.**

An empty row appears in the Name and Value columns.

3. **In the Name column, enter the name of the parameter, and in the Value column, enter the value that you want to send to your dynamic Web page for that parameter.**

For example, if you have a parameter called `user_id` and want to send the value `testing`, you enter fields like the ones in Figure 3-5. This tells your dynamic page to retrieve data for the `testing` user.

Figure 3-5:
The Live Data Settings dialog box for a sample parameter called `user_id`.

4. **From the Method drop-down list, select a form submission method.**

Your form submits its results by using either a GET or a POST method; select that same method from the Method drop-down list. See Book II, Chapter 7 for details on the GET and POST methods.

5. **(Optional) Set session variables in the Initialization Script text area.**

See Book VIII, Chapter 3 for the lowdown on session variables.

6. **Click OK.**

Your page uses the value in the parameter when updating its Live Data mode.

Troubleshooting problems in Live Data mode

Sometimes your Live Data mode may not work right the first time. If your view doesn't work as planned, troubleshooting suggestions can help you figure out the problem.

The most common problem that you may encounter in Live Data mode happens when you have missing dependent files. Here are some troubleshooting tips to try to resolve this problem:

✦ In the Files panel, verify that every file your script needs, including any database-related files, is present in the Testing Server file listing.

✦ In the Testing Server category of the Site Definition dialog box, verify that your testing server folder points to a location on your testing server that can process the dynamic files (is within the document root of the Web server). Open the Site Definition dialog box by choosing Site➪Manage Sites, choosing your site, and clicking the Edit button.

Verify that the URL prefix maps to the Web address that matches the testing server folder.

Table 3-1 shows some example folders and their corresponding URLs.

Table 3-1	Typical Paths and URLs	
Web Server	*Folder*	*URL*
IIS on Windows	`C:\Inetpub\wwwroot\testapp\`	`http://localhost/testapp`
Apache on Windows	`C:\Program Files\Apache Group\Apache2\htdocs\testapp`	`http://localhost/testapp`
Apache on Linux	`~jon/testapp`	`http://example.com/~jon/testapp`

If you want to make sure that your testing server folder and URL agree outside of Dreamweaver, place a simple HTML file in your testing server folder. For example, you can use `index.htm` with these contents:

```
<html><title>Untitled
    Document</title><body>Hello!</body></html>
```

You can then verify the URL by pasting the URL prefix plus `index.htm` into your browser's address bar. You should see a page with `Hello!`. If you don't, double-check your paths because you have a problem somewhere.

✦ Verify the directory's permissions to be sure that the Web server can read it. If you're using Windows, verify that the folder permissions allow the Web server to execute and read the directory. See Book VII, Chapter 7.

Working on dynamic pages without Live Data

If you temporarily can't access your testing server or you simply like to work without Live Data, you can still work on your dynamic page. Dreamweaver uses placeholders to represent where actual data would appear if you were in Live Data mode. These placeholders appear surrounded by curly brackets { and } to set them apart from the rest of your page.

Previewing a Dynamic Web Page in Your Browser

You may find using Live Data mode great for testing your dynamic pages, but Live Data doesn't completely represent the way that your page looks in a browser. It can't go through multiple pages of results from the database. You may want to use your Web browser to preview a page when troubleshooting a problem because the browser can return a specific error message. For example, you may get an error that you couldn't connect to the database or perhaps you have an unmatched quote somewhere in your page.

To preview a Web page in your local Web browser, open the page in Dreamweaver and press F12. You don't need to copy any files to a temporary folder on the testing server because Dreamweaver can do this copying for you automatically, or your browser can use the files in the local folder.

Follow these steps to tell Dreamweaver that you want to use a temporary copy of your files when previewing with your browser:

1. **Choose Edit⇨Preferences to open the Dreamweaver Preferences dialog box.**

The Dreamweaver Preferences dialog box appears.

2. **Click the Preview in Browser category.**

The option for previewing appears, as shown in Figure 3-6.

Figure 3-6:
The Preview in Browser category from the Preferences dialog box.

3. **Select the Preview Using Temporary File check box.**

   This option tells Dreamweaver to create a temporary copy of the file when previewing the page in a browser.

   You can also use this dialog box if you want to change the default browser that you use for previewing your pages. See Book V, Chapter 1 for details.

4. **Click OK.**

   Now the browser uses a temporary file when previewing your page.

The same requirements for dependent files that apply to Live Data also apply to the browser-based preview: Make sure that you specify in the Files panel all the files that you need to display your page. (See the section "Uploading dependent files to the testing server," earlier in this chapter, for details.)

Figure 3-7 shows a browser preview for a PHP page that includes the `phpinfo()` command to display information about the PHP environment.

If you get a dialog box asking if you want to update the copy of the file on the testing server, click OK.

Figure 3-7: Using a browser preview of a PHP page in the Firefox browser.

Chapter 4: Building Dynamic Forms

In This Chapter

✔ **Understanding dynamic forms**

✔ **Inserting dynamic form elements**

✔ **Making form objects dynamic**

*Y*ou can build dynamic forms using HTML markup, Java, or JavaScript. Dreamweaver 8 also allows you to create ASP.NET Web forms. Dynamic forms are an important technology to understand because most large companies use them on portions of their Web sites. For example, the human resources portion of a large corporate Web site often contains a form that users can fill out to update their contact and withholding information. Typically, a database provides the default values for dynamic forms and is also the repository of any changes that result from the form submission.

Making forms dynamic allows users to update information because the existing values come up as the defaults when the form displays. You must start with a regular form and its elements before making the default values dynamic. We show you how to make text boxes, check boxes, radio buttons, and lists/menus dynamic in this chapter.

Inserting Dynamic Form Elements

The elements that actually make up a form can be supplied with dynamic data. To create a dynamic form, you must define a source for the dynamic data first by creating a binding. The binding tells Dreamweaver what dynamic information your program can reference. These sources can be anything from URL parameters to values for a database recordset.

For more detailed information on the form objects (text fields, check boxes, radio button, lists, and menus) described in the following sections, refer to Book II, Chapter 7.

Text fields

Text fields allow you to capture information from the Web user in a free-form format. In other words, readers can input whatever they like, instead of having to select from a set number of choices provided by the form. Dynamic text fields are very useful when users are updating their information as the current values become the defaults for the update screen. To make a text field dynamic, follow these steps:

1. **Select a text field in a form on your page.**

See Book II, Chapter 7 for the lowdown on creating forms and text fields.

Figure 4-1 shows an example of an inserted text field.

Figure 4-1:
An inserted text field in a form.

2. **In the Properties inspector, click the Dynamic (lightning bolt) button next to the Init Val field.**

The Dynamic Data dialog box appears, as shown in Figure 4-2. It lists the available data sources in the Field area.

Figure 4-2:
You can select a URL parameter in the Dynamic Data dialog box.

3. **In the Field area, select the data source that will supply the default value for the text field.**

For example, in Figure 4-2, we selected the `username` URL parameter. This data source provides the initial value for the text field on the page.

Click the plus sign next to the category of the field (such as Recordset) to expand it before selecting a data source. Leave the Format set to None to display the text exactly as it is in the source.

A recordset can be used as the data source for the dynamic value, but if the recordset returns more than one row, only the first value is used.

4. **Click OK.**

Figure 4-3 displays the placeholder that's created for the dynamic text on the page; in this case, *URL.username*

Placeholder

Figure 4-3:
The dynamic text place-holder for a URL param-eter in a text field.

Check boxes

An HTML check box allows a user to select more than one value from a list of check box values. Dynamic check boxes have their default state of checked or not checked set by the value of a binding. Use bindings for tasks such as defaulting the check box values to their current settings for an update screen.

To make a check box dynamic, follow these steps:

1. **Select a check box in a form on your page.**

See Book II, Chapter 7 for the lowdown on creating forms and check boxes.

2. **In the Properties inspector, click the Dynamic (lightning bolt) button.**

The Dynamic CheckBox dialog box appears. The default value for the CheckBox drop-down list is the current check box.

3. **Click the Dynamic (lightning bolt) button next to the Check If field.**

The Dynamic Data dialog box appears, displaying the available data sources (refer to Figure 4-2).

4. **Select the data source field to use for the default value comparison. Click OK.**

If the Check If value is the same as the Equal To value, then the check box is checked by default.

For example, we selected the `username` recordset field.

Expand the category of the field (such as Recordset, URL, and so on) and then select a data source.

After you click OK, you return to the Dynamic CheckBox dialog box and Dreamweaver automatically fills in the Check If field.

5. **In the Equal To field, enter the value the field must have for the check box to be selected.**

For example, if the username field is *Admin,* the Admin check box is selected by default. Figure 4-4 shows the completed Dynamic CheckBox dialog box.

Figure 4-4:
The Dynamic CheckBox dialog box for comparing the Recordset field username to Admin.

6. **Click OK.**

Figure 4-5 displays the placeholder that's created for the dynamic check box on your page.

Now when you use Live Data view (see Book VIII, Chapter 3) or preview the page in a browser (press F12), the check box appears selected or deselected, based on the value from the data source you selected in Step 4.

You can repeat the same process for each check box in the same group.

Figure 4-5:
The Admin check box after adding a dynamic value.

Radio buttons

Use HTML radio buttons when you want users to select only one choice from a set of options. Radio buttons are typically used in groups (for example, AM or PM when selecting a time). Making a group of radio buttons dynamic means the default value can come from a binding.

To make the default selection dynamic for a group of radio buttons, follow these steps:

1. **In a form on your page, click any of the radio buttons in a radio button group.**

This selects all the radio buttons in the group so you can view its properties.

See Book II, Chapter 7 for the lowdown on creating forms and radio buttons.

2. **In the Properties inspector, click the Dynamic (lightning bolt) button.**

The Dynamic Radio Group dialog box appears, as shown in Figure 4-6.

Figure 4-6:
The Dynamic Radio Group dialog box as it first appears.

3. **Click the Dynamic (lightning bolt) button next to the Select Value Equal To field.**

The Dynamic Data dialog box appears, displaying the available data sources (refer to Figure 4-2).

4. **Choose a data source field to use for the default selection value. The Select Value Equal To field is compared to the checked value for each radio group button to determine the default selection.**

You need to expand the category of the field, such as URL, before selecting a data source. In this example, we selected the `language` URL parameter. The radio group only preselects a radio button if its value matches the value in this field. Dreamweaver automatically fills in the Select Value Equal To field after you select a binding.

5. **Click OK.**

You return to the Dynamic Radio Group dialog box.

6. **Click OK.**

Now when you use Live Data view (see Book VIII, Chapter 3) or preview the page in a browser (press F12), a radio button is selected based on the value from the data source you selected in Step 4.

You need only apply the dynamic formatting once per radio group because a radio group can have only one value at a time selected.

Lists and menus

An HTML form menu or list provides a convenient way for a user to select one or more items from the drop-down menu or list. It also dictates that only supplied values can be selected (unlike text fields where the user can enter anything). You can insert the menu as either a drop-down list or as a scrollable list, which is also called a *list menu*. A list or menu could be used to select which categories you're interested in receiving. Dynamic lists and menus make updating that list simpler by using your current selection values as defaults when updating.

To set the default dynamic values for a menu or list, follow these steps:

1. **Select the menu or list in a form on your page.**

See Book II, Chapter 7 for the lowdown on creating forms, menus and lists.

2. **In the Properties inspector, click the Dynamic (lightning bolt) button.**

The Dynamic List/Menu dialog box opens.

3. **Click the Dynamic (lightning bolt) button to the right of the Select Value Equal To field.**

The Dynamic Data dialog box appears (refer to Figure 4-2).

4. **Select the data source field (binding) for the Select Value Equal To field.**

If the field is equal to one of the values for the menu/list, that item is selected by default.

Click the plus sign next to the category of the field, such as Recordset, to expand it before selecting a data source.

5. **Click OK.**

You return to the Dynamic List/Menu dialog box. The Select Value Equal To field is filled in automatically.

6. **(Optional) To define additional menu/list items from a database table, enter the column names for the items' value and the label.**

This allows you to dynamically generate the entire menu as opposed to manually enter each item value and label pair. Figure 4-7 displays the Dynamic List/Menu dialog box just before you accept the changes.

Figure 4-7:
The Dynamic List/Menu dialog box with the default selection generated from a URL parameter.

7. **Click OK.**

When you use Live Data view (see Book VIII, Chapter 3) or preview the page in a browser (press F12), the items on the dynamic menu or menus are generated and selected based on the data source value you selected in Step 4.

Chapter 5: Advanced Dynamic Data Presentation

In This Chapter

✔ **Working with ColdFusion components**

✔ **Adding Web services to your site**

✔ **Putting custom server behaviors to work**

ColdFusion allows you to add complex dynamic functionality to your pages without worrying about how the component does its magic. Then, Web services allow you to use a remote server to process portions of your Web page. You can use Web services to do something as simple as returning a weather temperature based on the input of a ZIP Code without your site needing to know how to perform the calculation itself, just how to access the server. Additionally, you can customize Dreamweaver's tools for inserting code into your dynamic sites.

Using ColdFusion Components

ColdFusion Components (CFCs) are bits of ColdFusion code that you can use over and over again in your site. Think of CFCs as storage containers that keep your ColdFusion code organized and accessible. CFCs provide access to many more features than you'd have if you simply included ColdFusion code from a file. Here are some of those features and benefits:

✦ **Documentation:** CFCs automatically generate documentation.

✦ **Extendibility:** You can add code to CFCs.

✦ **Security:** You can limit access to portions of the code.

✦ **Speed:** CFCs are faster than other code because they're compiled.

In order to use CFCs, you have to use Macromedia ColdFusion MX or newer. Although CFCs were introduced in earlier versions of ColdFusion, they didn't become refined enough for use by Dreamweaver until the MX release. You can download trial and developer additions from www.macromedia.com.

By creating a CFC for code that you use throughout your site, you can reduce the amount of work you need to do to maintain the site. If you need to change that code, you only need to make the change in one spot, and the code updates throughout the site.

If you're using ColdFusion and create a Pricing component that has a Shipping Charge component, the component takes the price as an argument and returns said shipping charge. For example, an argument of 32.80 for the cost of items returns 6 for the shipping charge. You need to insert a special tag on the shopping cart page and the checkout page in order to use the function.

In order to use ColdFusion components, you either need to install Macromedia ColdFusion on your local computer or have access to a Remote Development Server (RDS) connection. You have to also specify the testing server URL prefix in the the Site Definition dialog box that Dreamweaver uses to display pages after transferring those images to the server. You also have to feel comfortable working directly with ColdFusion code.

Dreamweaver lets you build and use CFCs in your ColdFusion pages, as the following sections describe.

Building Web pages that use ColdFusion components

Dreamweaver comes with preinstalled ColdFusion components, which you can find in the Components panel (choose Window➪Components). When you select a CFC, Dreamweaver places the code to run the CFC into your page so that you have a solid starting point from which you can modify the code.

To include a ColdFusion component call in your dynamic Web page, follow these steps:

1. **Open a new dynamic page of the document type ColdFusion.**

You can also open an existing ColdFusion page to run a ColdFusion Component function.

2. **Switch to Code view to see the ColdFusion Components added to your page.**

Unlike server behaviors, ColdFusion Components don't appear in Design view. Work directly with Code view to see the added Component code.

3. **In the Components panel, select CF Components from the drop-down list.**

Dreamweaver lists the component packages in the Components panel, as shown in Figure 5-1.

Figure 5-1:
The Components panel for a page that uses a connection to a ColdFusion MX 7 Server.

4. Click the plus (+) button to expand a components package.

The component files (functions) within that package are listed (see Figure 5-2). The functions end with parentheses ().

Figure 5-2:
The Components panel listing the functions of a component.

5. Select the function that you want to invoke from your page and then drag that function to the point in the code where you want to place it.

The code from the function is inserted in the Document window. You use the `<cfinvoke>` tag to call ColdFusion Components, as shown in Figure 5-3.

You can also insert code by right-clicking (Windows) or Control+clicking (Mac) the function name and selecting Insert Code. Or you can click the Insert Code button on the Components toolbar.

Book VIII
Chapter 5

Advanced Dynamic Data Presentation

Figure 5-3:
Invoking the
`getTrip`
`Details`
function
in the
Document
window.

6. **If your function needs parameters, you can add them to the function-invoking tag by using the format** `parameter="value"`.

For example, to add the `username` parameter with a value of `Jon Phillips`, use this code:

```
username="Jon Phillips"
```

7. **Choose File⇨Save to save your changes.**

You now have your changes saved to the local folder.

8. **To see your code in action, choose File⇨Preview in the Browser⇨browser.**

Because the site contains dynamic code, you can't see the output without the ColdFusion server processing it.

Creating ColdFusion components

Although you can certainly create your ColdFusion components the old-fashioned way — by writing them entirely in ColdFusion code — you probably want to make the process much easier on yourself by letting Dreamweaver help you.

Depending upon the component, you may have to complete some code by hand.

To create a ColdFusion component in Dreamweaver, follow these steps:

1. **Create a new ColdFusion page or open an existing one.**

2. **In the Components panel, select CF Components from the drop-down list.**

The available components appear in the main portion of the panel.

3. **Click the plus (+) button.**

The Create Component dialog box appears, as shown in Figure 5-4.

Figure 5-4:
The Create Component dialog box's Component section.

4. **Fill in the following fields in the Component section:**

   • **Display Name:** Enter a descriptive name for your component.

   • **Name:** Enter a filename for your component in the Name field. The name follows general naming rules — only letters, numbers, and underscores. Don't add the .cfc file extension to the name.

   • **Hint:** Enter a brief description of what your component does. This field automatically appears in the documentation for your component.

   • **Extends:** You can leave this field blank. Use this field to base your component on an existing component.

   • **Component Directory:** Click the Browse button to specify where you want to save the component. Select a directory by using the Web application root folder, usually C:\Inetpub\wwwroot, or a subfolder.

5. **To define properties (variables for the component), select Properties from the Section list. Click the plus (+) button to add properties:**

   • **Display Name:** Enter a descriptive name for your property.

   • **Name:** Enter a name for your property in the Name field. The name follows general naming rules — only letters, numbers, and underscores.

   • **Hint:** Enter a brief description of what your property stores. This field automatically appears in the documentation for your component.

   • **Type:** Select the type of data your property stores.

**Book VIII
Chapter 5**

**Advanced Dynamic
Data Presentation**

6. **To define a function, select Functions from the Section list on the left side of the dialog box.**

7. **Click the plus (+) button and then fill in the following fields, which are shown in Figure 5-5:**

Figure 5-5:
The Create
Component
dialog box's
Functions
section.

- **Name:** Enter a descriptive name for your function.

- **Display Name:** Enter the same name that you enter in the Name field. This display name gives you the option to make a longer, more descriptive, version of the name.

- **Hint:** Enter a summary of what your function does. This summary appears in the automatic documentation for your component.

- **Access:** Select an access type from the drop-down list. Selecting Remote makes your function available as a Web service.

- **Return Type:** Select a return type from the drop-down list. All the ColdFusion data types appear in the list.

   You can leave the Roles text box blank, and the Output check box deselected.

8. **To define an argument for your function, select Arguments from the Section list on the left side of the dialog box.**

9. **Select the function from the Available Functions drop-down list.**

   Each function can have as many arguments as you want.

10. **Click the plus (+) button and then fill in the following fields, which are shown in Figure 5-6:**

Figure 5-6:
The Create Component dialog box's Arguments section.

- **Name, Display Name, Hint, and Type:** You can enter these fields as you do in the Functions section (see Step 7).

- **Required:** If you need the argument when calling the function, click the Required check box.

- **Default Value:** To supply a default value, enter it in the Default Value field. The function uses this value if calling code doesn't supply a value when calling the function.

11. **Click OK to close the dialog box.**

Dreamweaver creates the component as a `.cfc` file and saves it in the directory that you specify in Step 4.

To ensure that Dreamweaver can use your custom component, upload the `.cfc` file to your remote server.

To remove a component, delete the `.cfc` file from your RDS server. Dreamweaver only lists components it finds on the RDS testing server.

Adding Web Services to Your Pages

Web services enable your Web site to access a distributed application (the code processes over the Internet). If you use Web services, part of the processing on your dynamic page actually executes on another Web server through Web services. The Web site that connects to the distributed application is called the *consumer*. Dreamweaver supports creating Web consumer pages in ColdFusion MX, ASP.NET, and JSP dynamic page types. Web services can be useful for integrating information that would otherwise be unavailable to you, such as the current weather for a specific location.

Dreamweaver lets you select Web services on the Internet through Web service proxies. A *Web service proxy* describes the fields, methods (functions), and properties (variables) that are available from a Web service. The proxy lets local pages use the functionality of the Web service. The Web services appear in the Dreamweaver Components panel (choose Window⇨Components).

To add a Web service to your dynamic page, follow these steps:

1. **Open the ColdFusion, JSP, or ASP.NET document to which you want to add the Web service.**

2. **From the drop-down list in the Components panel, select Web Services.**

Available components appear in the main portion of the panel.

3. **Click the plus (+) button.**

The Add Using WSDL dialog box appears, as shown in Figure 5-7. The Component section is the default section. Web Services Description Language (WSDL) is a standard format for describing Web services.

Figure 5-7:
The Add
Using WSDL
dialog box.

4. **Enter the URL of the WSDL site that you want to try out.**

If you want to browse a list of sites for sources of Web services, click the globe icon and select a site. The site then opens in your Web browser. Make sure to pick an example that matches your dynamic document type. When you find a Web service that you want to use, enter the URL of its WSDL file in the URL of the WSDL File text box.

For example, suppose that you want to try the Hungarian proverbs generator from the xMethods site (and who wouldn't?). To do so, enter **http://phenotypical.com/proverbs.cfc?wsdl** into the URL of the WSDL field.

5. **Leave the Proxy Generator set to ColdFusion MX and click OK.**

The Proxy Generator translates the proxy definition into dynamic code of the type for your dynamic page. The Web service appears in the Components panel. For example, Figure 5-8 shows the Hungarian Proverbs Web service listed in the Components panel.

Figure 5-8:
The
Components
panel
shows the
new Web
service.

6. Drag the Web service from the Components panel to the body section of the Document window in Code view.

A `<cfinvoke>` tag is inserted to your page, which references the remote Web service.

7. After the `</cfinvoke>` tag, enter the following code:

```
<CFDUMP VAR="#aDocument#">
```

The results of the Web service execution that were returned in the ColdFusion `aDocument` variable display. The Document window looks like Figure 5-9.

Figure 5-9:
The
Document
window
with the
code to
invoke
the Web
service.

8. Choose File➪Preview in Browser➪*browser* **to test out the code.**

The browser output looks like Figure 5-10.

Figure 5-10:
The Hungarian Proverb processed on the remote server but displayed through the local server.

9. **If you want to bind a return value to a visual element (such as a dynamic text field), switch to Design view and place a visual element on the page that can accept data binding.**

10. **Switch back to Code view and enter the appropriate code to bind the returned value to the visual element.**

When creating Web services, refer to the Web service provider's documentation for the proper syntax to both request the service and display the returned values to the page.

When you upload Web pages to a production server, Dreamweaver automatically copies the pages, the proxy, and any necessary libraries to the Web server.

Creating Custom Server Behaviors

Server behaviors are blocks of code that send a request to the server and then receive data in return. They're different from JavaScript behaviors (which you can read about in Book IV, Chapter 2), which consist of JavaScript code that the user's browser executes.

Dreamweaver provides many server behaviors in the Server Behaviors panel (choose Windows⊅Server Behaviors), but you can add more. You can use Macromedia Exchange (at www.macromedia.com/cfusion/exchange/index.cfm) to add packages of server behaviors. You can also create your own server behaviors by using the Server Behavior Builder.

If you're planning to create your own server behavior, first check the Exchange site to see if the server behavior that you want to create already exists.

TIP

Conditional code block execution

Sometimes, you may have a chunk of code that you don't always want to execute. For example, you want the code to display an error message only after an error.

To specify that you want a code block to execute based on a condition, you can use this syntax:

```
<@ if (condition1) @>
    codeblockif
[<@ elseif (condition2) @>
    codeblockifelse]
[<@ else @>
    codeblockelse]
<@ endif @>
```

Here's a closer look at this syntax:

✔ Replace `condition1` and `condition2` with any JavaScript expression that evaluates to true or false.

✔ Replace the labels that start with `codeblock` with the code that you want to run for that condition.

✔ You absolutely need only the `if` portion (the brackets [and] represent optional parts).

✔ You can have more than one `elseif` portion of a statement.

✔ The `else` portion executes only if none of the other conditions is true.

To create a custom server behavior, you have to

✦ Write the code that performs the action of the server behavior.

✦ Specify where to place the code within the HTML page.

✦ Determine parameters and prompts (prompting the developer for details about how the code works when it's used in your page) for them.

With the Server Behavior Builder, you enter the code block that you want the custom server behavior to insert into a page. You can use any runtime code valid for your server model. For example, if you choose ColdFusion as the document type for your custom server behavior, you have to write ColdFusion code running on a ColdFusion application server. After you build the custom server behavior, you can access it from the Server Behaviors panel.

To create your own custom server behavior with the Server Behavior Builder, follow these steps:

1. **In the Server Behaviors panel, click the plus (+) button and then select New Server Behavior from the list that appears.**

The New Server Behavior dialog box appears, as shown in Figure 5-11.

**Book VIII
Chapter 5**

**Advanced Dynamic
Data Presentation**

Figure 5-11:
You can use the New Server Behavior dialog box to create a new server behavior.

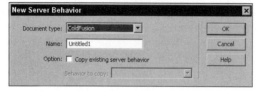

2. **Select from the drop-down list the document type to which you want to add this server behavior.**

3. **Enter a name for your server behavior in the Name field.**

   The name can use only letters, numbers, and underscores.

4. **Deselect the Copy Existing Server Behavior check box if it's selected.**

   You can, of course, select this check box to copy an existing server behavior.

5. **Click OK.**

   The Server Behavior Builder dialog box appears.

6. **Click the plus (+) button.**

   The Create a New Code Block dialog box appears.

7. **Enter the name of your block in the Name field and then click OK.**

   The name is added to the code block list. The other fields in the dialog box prefilled with data and are no longer grayed out, as shown in Figure 5-12.

Figure 5-12:
The Server Behavior Builder dialog box after adding a code block.

8. **Enter the code to perform your action in the Code Block text area.**

You can create the code blocks directly within the Server Behavior Builder, or you can copy and paste the code from other sources. Each code block that you create in the Server Behavior Builder must be a single tag or script block. If you need to insert multiple tag blocks, split them into separate code blocks.

9. **If you want to include runtime parameters in a code block, select the point in the code block where you want to insert the parameter. Otherwise, skip ahead to Step 13.**

To include parameters in your code that you supply when you include the stored procedure in a page during the page's design, you first need to mark where the parameters go in your code by using the following format:

```
@@parameter_name@@
```

10. **Click the Insert Parameters in Code Block button.**

The Insert Parameters in Code Block dialog box appears, as shown in Figure 5-13.

Figure 5-13:
This dialog box contains a field for the parameter name.

11. **Enter the name in the Parameter Name field and click OK.**

The usual naming rules apply.

After you click OK, the parameter name placeholder appears in the code at the point that you select in Step 10.

12. **(Optional) Repeat Steps 9 through 11 to add more parameters.**

13. **From the Insert Code drop-down list, select a location where you want to embed the code block.**

The Insert Code drop-down list lets you select where to place the code relative to the document, including

- Above the <html> Tag
- Below the <html> Tag

- Relative to a Specific Tag

- Relative to the Selection (the point in the current page that's selected)

The Relative to Selection position applies if the page designer doesn't specify a tag to position the code block against.

14. Select the relative position versus the selection of the code from the Relative Position drop-down list.

Depending on which selection you make for the Insert Code selection in Step 13, you see a different listing of relative locations in the Relative Position drop-down list. For example, if you select Above the <html> Tag, you get the following options:

- The Beginning of the File

- Just Before the Recordsets

- Just After the Recordsets

- Just Above the <html> Tag

- Custom Position

Because selecting the After the <html> Tag for Insert code rules out placing the code at the beginning of the file, you don't have that code placement as an option for that selection.

The Custom Position applies if the designer specifies a tag to position the code block against.

15. To create additional code blocks, repeat Steps 6 through 14.

Remember that you can have only one block of code in the Code Block text area. You can create more code blocks within the server behaviors if you need them.

16. Click Next.

The Generate Behavior dialog box appears.

17. Click OK.

Your server behavior displays in the Server Behaviors panel.

Book IX

Developing Applications Rapidly

Contents at a Glance

Chapter 1: Building Master and Detail Pages

In This Chapter

✔ Developing master and detail pages at the same time

✔ Building your master and detail pages separately

✔ Putting together master and detail pages for ASP.NET

✔ Making sure your master and detail pages work

You can use Dreamweaver to build master and detail Web pages, which are a popular way to display information on your Web site. A *master page* displays a list of records and corresponding links for each record. A user can click a link to see further information about a record on its associated *detail page*.

Depending on your programming language, you can either build the set of master and detail pages all in one operation, or you can separately build the master pages and then the detail pages. You can find out more about both methods in this chapter.

The examples in this chapter use a simple Employee table, which you can see in Table 1-1. The first value, the `employee_id`, is a special field called a *key*. It always has a unique value. Therefore, if you query for a record in a table by using the key, you always get only the row that you're looking for because no two rows have the same key.

Table 1-1	The Employee Table
Column Name	Type of Data
employee_id	Integer
first_name	50 Character String
last_name	50 Character String
aAddress1	75 Character String
aAddress2	75 Character String
cCity	50 Character String
sState	50 Character String

(continued)

Table 1-1 *(continued)*	
zZip	5 Character String
pPhone	14 Character String
department_id	Integer

Building Master and Detail Pages in One Operation (PHP, ASP, JSP, ColdFusion)

For PHP, ASP, JSP, and ColdFusion, you can build sets of master and detail pages all in one operation. You can use the same method for all these languages. Creating both the master and detail pages at the same time is generally easier, but Dreamweaver gives you the flexibility of creating them separately, too.

For ASP.NET, you need to build the master and detail pages separately (as described in the section "Developing Master and Detail Pages for ASP.NET," later in this chapter). You can't build these pages at the same time in one operation for ASP.NET.

To create a master and detail page set for PHP, ASP, JSP, or ColdFusion, follow these steps:

1. **Create a new or open an existing PHP, ASP, JSP, or ColdFusion page.**

   A blank page opens in Dreamweaver; this page becomes your master page in the language that you selected.

2. **Define a recordset for the page.**

   For the lowdown on creating a recordset, check out Book VIII, Chapter 1.

   The recordset provides the data that's displayed on both the master and detail pages. Make sure that you include all the table columns that you need to create your master page, including the unique key (the record ID column) for each record and all the table columns that you need to create your detail page. Typically, you show more columns on the detail page than on the master page.

   For the example in this chapter, we created an Employee recordset and included all the columns in the Employee table (see Table 1-1).

3. **Save your changes to the master page.**

   The new recordset appears in the Bindings panel, and a small yellow code indicator is inserted in the Document window, as shown in Figure 1-1. This page allows a listing of employees to display on the master page, which provides links to detail pages with more data than the master page.

Code indicator   New recordset

Figure 1-1:
The
Document
window
with a
recordset
defined.

4. Choose Insert➪Application Objects➪Master Detail Page Set to insert the master and detail pages all in one operation.

The Insert Master-Detail Page Set dialog box appears. You specify the properties for the master page in the top half of this dialog box and the properties for the detail page in the lower half.

5. From the Recordset drop-down list, select the recordset that you want to use for the master page.

For our example, we selected Employee_Recordset.

After you select a recordset, Dreamweaver fills in the rest of the fields with the columns from the recordset.

6. In the Master Page Fields area, select which records you want to appear on the master page.

Click the plus (+) button to add a field, and click the minus (–) button to remove a field. In Figure 1-2, we selected the `first_name` and `last_name` fields. These fields will appear on the master page in a table format.

Typically, fewer fields appear on the master page than the detail page.

7. From the Link to Detail From drop-down list, select the field in the recordset that you want to serve as the link to the detail page.

For example, we selected the `last_name` field to serve as the link to the detail page for each record.

8. **From the Pass Unique Key drop-down list, select which field contains the values that you want to pass on to the detail page so it can identify the records.**

Typically, you select the key field that ends in ID. This key field tells the detail page which record to display for the user. For our example, we selected the `employee_id` field.

9. **Specify the number of records that you want to show at one time on the master page.**

In the example, we chose to show 10 records at a time.

10. **In the Detail Page Name text box, enter a name for the detail page or click the Browse button to select an existing file.**

For the example, we entered `detail.php`. Dreamweaver will automatically use this name when it creates the detail page.

11. **In the Detail Page Fields area, select which records you want to appear on the master page.**

Click the plus (+) button and minus (–) button to change the fields that appear on the detail page.

Typically, more fields appear on the detail page than the master page. For the example, we selected all the fields listed in Table 1-1.

Figure 1-2 shows the configuration of the Insert Master-Detail Page Set dialog box based on the example values.

Figure 1-2:
The Insert Master-Detail Page Set dialog box for the `Employee_Recordset`.

12. **Click OK.**

Dreamweaver creates the master and detail pages and includes dynamic content and server behaviors in both.

The Document window contains the automatically generated objects (a repeated region, navigation objects, record, counter, and link to the detail page), as shown in Figure 1-3.

Figure 1-3:
This
Document
window has
a repeated
region,
navigation
objects,
record
counter, and
link to the
detail page.

13. **Modify the design of the master and detail pages.**

You can modify your dynamic fields just like you'd edit any other object.

When you finish designing the pages, you're ready to view them in a browser. See the section "Testing Your Master and Detail Pages," later in this chapter, for details.

Developing Master and Detail Pages Block by Block

You can develop a master page block by block for PHP, ASP, JSP, and ColdFusion. While you usually create the master and detail pages at the same time, you can create them block by block to have complete control over the placement of the blocks.

Creating the master page

To create a dynamic master page, follow these steps:

1. **Create a page and define a recordset.**

   Turn to Book VIII, Chapter 1 to find out how to define a recordset.

   The Recordset dialog box varies slightly between dynamic page types. Specifically, ColdFusion calls the database connection a data source and includes optional Username and Password fields for the database. The dialog box also has a button to access ColdFusion components. The rest of the dialog box works exactly the same as the dialog box for other development code types.

2. **In the Document window, place the insertion point where you want the records to appear on the page.**

3. **Choose Insert➪Application Objects➪Dynamic Data➪Dynamic Table.**

   The Dynamic Table dialog box opens, as shown in Figure 1-4.

Figure 1-4: The Dynamic Table dialog box for the Employee Recordset.

4. **From the Recordset drop-down list, select the name of the recordset that you want to appear on the master page.**

   For the example, we selected the EmployeeRecordset.

5. **Specify the number of records that you want to show at one time on the master page.**

   In the example, we wanted to show 10 records at a time.

6. **(Optional) Specify border, cell padding, and cell spacing.**

7. **Click OK to close the dialog box.**

   The master page is created.

If you don't want users to see some of the columns on the master page (such as the Record ID column, which describes the record to display but is not useful for the end user), delete the column from the table by following these steps:

1. **In Design view, click anywhere on the master page.**

2. **Put the pointer near the top of the Record ID column so that the column's entries are outlined in red. Then click to select the column.**

3. **Click the Delete button to delete the column from the table.**

Generally, fewer records appear on the master page than the detail page.

Setting up links to open a detail page

After you create the master page (as the preceding section describes), you need to create links that open the detail page and communicate which record the user selected so that only the detail for that record displays.

To set up links to open a detail page, follow these steps:

1. **Open the master page in the Document window.**

2. **In the table, select the placeholder for the dynamic content on which you want to create a link.**

3. **In the Properties inspector, click the folder button next to the Link field.**

The Select File dialog box appears (see Figure 1-5).

Figure 1-5:
Use the
Select File
dialog box
to configure
which page
to link to
and which
parameters
to send.

4. **Browse to and select the detail page.**

5. **Click the Parameters button to the right of the URL field.**

   The Parameters dialog box opens.

6. **Click the plus (+) button to add a parameter.**

   This parameter tells the detail page which row to display. Select the key value column as this parameter.

7. **In the Name column, enter the column name.**

   For the Employee table (Table 1-1) example, the key field is `employee_id`, as shown in Figure 1-6.

Figure 1-6:
Configuring the URL parameter and its recordset.

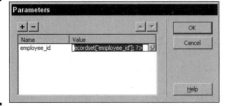

8. **Click in the Value column and then click the Dynamic (lightning bolt) button.**

   The Dynamic Data dialog box displays. This is where you select the column from the recordset.

9. **Expand the recordset, click the key field, and then click OK.**

   In this case, the key field is `employee_id`.

   After you click OK, the Parameters dialog box displays the new parameter and the code that places it into the page dynamically, as shown in Figure 1-6.

10. **Click OK to close the Parameters dialog box.**

    The URL field in the Select File dialog box is pre-populated with the new parameter.

    Each dynamic page type has different code that appears because each programming language uses a slightly different syntax to display a URL variable dynamically. Fortunately, because Dreamweaver is generating the code for you, you don't need to know the syntax differences.

11. **Click OK to close the Select File dialog box.**

    You return to the Document window. The name of the detail page appears in the Link field in the Properties inspector. The placeholder for the dynamic content is now a link.

12. **Save your changes to the master page.**

You now have a complete master page.

Read on to find out how make the detail page.

Building detail pages

To create a detail page for PHP, ASP, JSP, and ColdFusion page types, follow these steps:

1. **Create a new or open an existing PHP, ASP, JSP, or ColdFusion page.**

2. **In the Bindings panel, click the plus (+) button and select Recordset (Query) from the menu that appears.**

The simple Recordset dialog box appears.

If you want to write your own SQL statements, click the Advanced button to display the advanced Recordset dialog box.

3. **In the Name text box, enter a name for your recordset.**

You can use only letters, numbers, and underscores in the name.

4. **Select a database connection for obtaining the data that you want to display.**

5. **Select a table name for obtaining the data that you want to display.**

After you select a table name, the database columns appear in the Columns list. For example, Figure 1-7 shows the columns for the Employee table (see Table 1-1).

Figure 1-7:
The Recordset dialog box after selecting a database table.

Depending on your dynamic page type, the Recordset dialog box may appear slightly different from the one in Figure 1-7. ColdFusion, in particular, calls the Connection field a data source and includes the Username and Password fields for the database. However, these differences don't change the following steps.

6. **Select which columns will provide the record data to display.**

   To use all columns, select All; otherwise, choose Selected and Ctrl+click (Windows) or ⌘+click (Mac) in the list to indicate which columns you want to use.

   Typically, your detail page uses more columns than your master page. You want the recordset for your detail page to contain at least one column (generally the record ID column) that matches the column that you use for the master page.

7. **Complete the Filter sections as follows:**

   - **The first Filter field:** Select the database column name that contains values to match against the URL parameter. You use the filter to find and display the record specified by the URL parameter passed from the master page.

   - **The second Filter field:** Select the equals (=) symbol, if it's not already selected. This requires the fields to be equal, which they must be to display only the record that is detailed.

   - **The third Filter field:** Select the URL parameter.

   - **The fourth Filter field:** Enter the name of the URL parameter that you want the master page to pass to the detail page.

   The recordset now returns only the data for the employee who's been selected on the master page.

8. **Click the Test button.**

   The Test Value dialog box appears.

9. **Enter a value in the Test Value field and click OK.**

   This value represents which detail record displays. This test helps you check that the detail page brings back the data you expect.

   A table displaying data from the recordset appears.

10. **Click OK.**

    The Test SQL Statement window closes.

11. **In the Recordset dialog box, click OK.**

    Figure 1-8 shows the recordset in the Bindings panel of the detail page.

Figure 1-8:
The
Employee
Recordset
appears in
the Bindings
panel.

12. **To bind the columns in the recordset to the detail page, select the columns in the Bindings panel and drag those columns onto the detail page.**

Your detail page can now process requests from the master page. Figure 1-9 shows the Document window after adding fields from the recordset.

Figure 1-9:
The
Document
window
after
dragging
several
fields from
the
recordset
onto it.

See the section "Testing Your Master and Detail Pages," later in this chapter, to find out how to preview your master and detail pages in a browser.

Developing Master and Detail Pages for ASP.NET

For ASP.NET, you can use the DataSet Web control to specify table columns and the DataGrid Web control to list the database records to display on the master page. The Web controls provide an easy way to display database data with controls for paging between multiple pages of records.

You need to define a database connection for the site before you create the master page. See Book VII for details.

Creating a master page

To create an ASP.NET master page, follow these steps:

1. **Create a new or open an existing ASP.NET page in Dreamweaver.**

2. **In the Bindings panel, click the plus (+) button and select DataSet (Query) from the menu that appears.**

The DataSet dialog box appears.

3. **Complete the DataSet dialog box and then click OK.**

Make sure to include all table columns that you need to create your master page, including the unique key (Record ID column) for each record.

A dataset is essentially the same thing as a recordset; see Book VIII, Chapter 1 for more information on recordsets.

The new dataset appears in the Binding panel.

4. **In the Server Behaviors panel, click the plus (+) button and select DataGrid from the menu that appears.**

The DataGrid dialog box opens.

5. **Select the dataset source from the DataSet drop-down list and click OK.**

You can leave the default column type as Simple Data Field. The DataGrid dialog box for our example looks like Figure 1-10.

Figure 1-10: The DataGrid dialog box has the `Employee_Dataset` selected.

Figure 1-11 shows the DataGrid object created for the example.

Figure 1-11:
The
Document
window
with the
DataGrid
object.

Creating links that open the detail page

After you create the ASP.NET master page (as described in the preceding section), you need to create links that open the detail page and communicate which record the user selected. To open an ASP.NET detail page and display the specified record, follow these steps:

1. **Open the master page in the Document window.**

2. **In the Server Behaviors panel, double-click DataGrid.**

The DataGrid dialog box appears.

3. **In the Columns list, select the column that you want to serve as the link to the detail page.**

You can use any field that identifies the record for expanding the detail of the record.

4. **Click the Change Column Type button.**

5. **Select Hyperlink from the pop-up menu.**

The Hyperlink Column dialog box appears.

6. **In the Hyperlink Text section, specify the text that you want to display in the hyperlink column.**

Here are your choices:

- **Static Text:** Select this radio button if you want to use a generic description for this column. Enter text for the link, such as **Details**.

- **Data Field:** Select this radio button if you want to add text for a link based on a hyperlink column. Then from the drop-down list, select a data field in your dataset. In the example, we selected the `last_name` column, as shown in Figure 1-12.

- **Format String:** This field is automatically generated and shows the format of the URL text.

Figure 1-12:
This Hyperlink Column dialog box uses the `first_name` as the parameter and `detail_net.asp` as the page.

7. **In the Linked Page section, specify the URL for the hyperlink column text.**

   Here are your choices:

   - **Static Text:** Select this radio button if you want to use a generic link for this column. Enter the URL for the link, such as **Details.aspx**.

   - **Data Field:** Select this radio button if you want to add a link for data displayed in the hyperlink column. Then from the drop-down list, select a data field in your dataset. In the example, we selected the `first_name` column, as shown in Figure 1-12.

   - **Format String:** This field is automatically generated and shows the format of the URL link.

   The URL opens the detail page and uniquely identifies the record to display on the detail page.

8. **In the Linked Page section, click the Browse button next to the Format String box.**

9. **Locate and select which detail page you want to display.**

Note the following when selecting your link page:

- When you select a detail page, Dreamweaver adds information to the URL that specifies a parameter to use to identify the record.

- Dreamweaver automatically names this parameter based on your database field name, but you can change the name to something else if you want to.

- In any case, be sure to note the name of this URL parameter because you need that name when you create the detail page (which you can read about in the following section, "Creating a detail page").

- Dreamweaver uses a {0} placeholder to indicate where it places the value of the unique identifier when someone accesses the page.

10. **Click OK to close the Hyperlink Column dialog box.**

Figure 1-13 shows the updated DataGrid dialog box for the example.

Figure 1-13:
The DataGrid dialog box displays the `last_name` column as a Hyperlink type.

11. **Click OK.**

The DataGrid dialog box closes. The DataGrid on your page is updated.

Creating a detail page

After you create a master page for ASP.NET (as described in the two previous sections), you need to create a detail page to display the record. To do so, you need to define a dataset for the record and bind its columns to the detail page.

When creating the detail page, you need to know the database column name that you want to reference and the URL parameter that the master page uses to find and display that column's record on the detail page. If you don't remember the URL parameter name, open the master page, go to the Bindings panel, and look under the DataSet listing.

To create an ASP.NET detail page, create a new ASP.NET page in Dreamweaver and follow Steps 2 through 12 in the earlier section, "Building detail pages." Note that although the earlier steps show you how to fill out the Recordset dialog box, the steps are the same for the DataSet dialog box, which you fill out when creating an ASP.NET detail page.

Testing Your Master and Detail Pages

After you create a master and detail page set, you need to test those pages. Follow these steps to preview the pages in a browser:

1. **Open the master page.**

2. **Choose File➪Preview in Browser➪*Your browser type*.**

3. **When Dreamweaver asks you if it's okay to copy the file to the testing site, click OK.**

Your browser launches with your master page (see Figure 1-14).

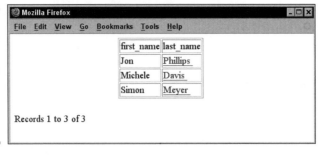

Figure 1-14: The browser displays the master page that uses the data from the database.

4. **Click a hyperlink to view the associated detail page for that record.**

In the employee example, the linked field is the employee's last name. When you click a link, the browser page changes to expand the record and display the detail page, as shown in Figure 1-15.

Figure 1-15:
The browser
displays the
detail page
that uses
the testing
employee
data.

Be sure that both your master page and detail page transfer to the testing server. If not, when you click a link in the master page, you get a `Page not found` error message.

Chapter 2: Creating Search and Results Pages

In This Chapter

✔ Developing search and results pages for most language types

✔ Developing search and results pages for ASP.NET

You can use Dreamweaver to build *search pages,* which allow users to search your database, and *results pages,* which display the search results. Search pages are frequently used with dynamic database-driven Web pages to provide a shortcut to the information the user is looking for. For example, online stores usually give you the ability to search their products.

A basic search page contains a form with a search field and a submit button. Users enter search parameters in the form and click the submit button. The results page then receives the search parameters, searches the database for records that meet the search criteria, builds a recordset to hold the records it finds, and then displays the contents of the recordset for the users.

With the exception of ASP.NET, all the dynamic page code types use identical steps to create search and results pages. ASP.NET uses a slightly different process and allows you to combine search and results pages.

If you allow just one search parameter, Dreamweaver can create the recordset for you with a filter. However, if you have more than one search parameter, you need to work directly with a SQL statement and send a parameter to it. This chapter shows you how to build search and results pages for a single search parameter.

Developing Search and Results Pages for PHP, JSP, ASP, and ColdFusion

The following sections give you the skinny on developing search and results pages for PHP, JSP, ASP, and ColdFusion.

Creating the search page

At a minimum, search pages consist of a form text field and a Submit button. The following steps show you how to create a basic search page:

1. **Create a new or open an existing PHP, JSP, ASP, or ColdFusion document.**

2. **Insert a form by choosing Insert⇨Form⇨Form.**

An empty form displays in the Document window. The form's boundaries display as thin red lines.

If the form isn't visible, enable Invisible Elements by choosing View⇨Visual Aids⇨Invisible Elements.

3. **Add a text area search field by choosing Insert⇨Form⇨Text Field.**

The Input Tag Accessibility Attributes dialog box displays.

You can also add other form objects to limit searches. The downside is that the more objects you add, the more complex your search query becomes.

4. **Enter** Search **in the Label field and then click OK to close the dialog box.**

This tells the user that the text area is a search field.

5. **Choose Insert⇨Form⇨Button to add a Submit button to your form.**

6. **Click OK to close the Input Tag Accessibility Attributes dialog box.**

You really don't need to label this button because its meaning is straightforward. The form should now look like Figure 2-1, which has all the basic elements that are required to request a search.

7. **Select the form by clicking the `form` tag in the Tag selector.**

This selects the form element so that you can modify its properties.

8. **In the Action field in the Properties inspector, enter a filename for the results page (the page that will process the database search request), or click the Folder button to select a file.**

You create this file when defining the results page, as described in the next section. For example, we entered `results.php`, as shown in Figure 2-2.

9. **Select POST from the Method drop-down list.**

You can also use GET for submitting the data to the results page. For more on the GET and POST methods, see Book II, Chapter 7.

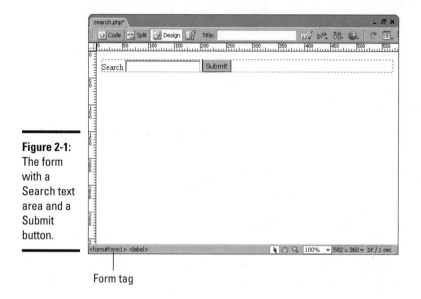

Figure 2-1:
The form
with a
Search text
area and a
Submit
button.

Form tag

Figure 2-2:
The
Properties
inspector
for a form.

You have now completed the search page. After the user fills out the form and clicks the Submit button, the information is passed on to the results page as a *form parameter*. Read on to find out how to create the results page.

Building the results page

The complexity of building your results page is directly related to the number of search parameters users can specify. If you allow only one search parameter, you don't have to modify the SQL query when building the results page. This is the type of search that we describe in this chapter.

The results page receives the search parameters from the form, plugs that data into a recordset filter, and then displays the results from the recordset on the page. The search page can optionally link to another page to expand details for a search result. For example, searching a catalog of products produces a list of matching products. If you then click on one of the products, you see the full detail page for just that product.

In the following sections, you find out how to build the recordset that holds the results as well as the page that displays those results.

Building the recordset

To create the recordset that performs the search in the results page, follow these steps:

1. **Create a new or open an existing PHP, JSP, ASP, or ColdFusion document.**

2. **In the Bindings panel, click the plus (+) button and then select Recordset from the drop-down list that appears.**

   The Recordset dialog box displays. You need to create a recordset to query the database with the search parameters.

3. **Enter the name of the recordset in the Name field.**

   Choose a name that describes the recordset data. For example, we entered **SearchRecordset** (see Figure 2-3), which indicates that the recordset relates to a search.

4. **From the Connection drop-down list, select a connection to the database you want the user to search.**

   You must have an active database connection to create the recordset. See Book VII for details on setting up a database connection.

   Depending on your dynamic page type, the Recordset dialog box may appear slightly different than Figure 2-3. For example, ColdFusion calls the Connection field a data source and includes optional Username and Password fields for the database. However, these differences don't change the following steps.

5. **In the Table drop-down list, select the database table to be searched.**

   For example, we selected the employee table, as shown in Figure 2-3. The Columns list updates after you select a table.

6. **If you want to include only some of the table's columns in the recordset, click the Selected radio button and then select the columns to include.**

   Select the columns you'll display by Ctrl+clicking (Windows) or ⌘+clicking (Mac) them from the Columns list.

   In Figure 2-3, we selected the `first_name`, `last_name`, and `address1` columns.

7. **To create a database filter, complete the fields in the Filter area as follows:**

- For the first Filter field, select the database column you want to search. For example, to search the `last_name` column of the employee table, we selected `last_name`.

- For the second Filter field, select how to filter your results: Contains, Begins With, Ends With, or Numeric Comparisons. Depending on your search, you can leave the default.

- For the third Filter field, select Form Variable if your form uses the `POST` method, or URL Parameter if it uses the `GET` method. For example, we selected Form Variable because the HTML form on the search page uses the `POST` method.

- For the fourth Filter field, enter the name of the search field from the search page. Be sure to use the form field name that's listed in the Properties inspector.

Dreamweaver uses the conditions you specify to filter the search results. If a record doesn't meet the conditions that you've specified, the record is excluded from the recordset. For example, if there are records for employees with the last names `Phillips` and `Davis` searching on the last name field for names containing `il` returns only the record for `Phillips`.

Figure 2-3 shows the completed Recordset dialog box for the example. This recordset returns records that contain the search parameter in the last name. For example, if you can only remember that a name contains the letters `il` you could use this recordset to find the name.

Figure 2-3:
The Recordset dialog box configured to search the last name field of the employee table.

8. **Click the Test button to execute the query and verify that it returns the data you expected.**

   The Test Value dialog box displays.

9. **In the Test Value field, enter a value that represents which record to display and then click OK.**

   The Test SQL Statement window appears, displaying data from the recordset.

10. **To change the order of the results, select a database column to sort by and choose Ascending or Descending from the Sort drop-down menu in the Recordset dialog box.**

    This only changes the order in which the records are returned.

11. **Click OK to close the Test SQL Statement window.**

    You return to the Recordset dialog box.

12. **If the test produced the correct results, click OK to close the Recordset dialog box.**

    If your test didn't produce the results you wanted, check the filtering parameters versus the actual data in the database table.

    The recordset is added to the Bindings panel list.

After you close the Recordset dialog box, Dreamweaver inserts the code that performs a search based on the search parameter passed from the search page. Only records that match the search criteria become part of the recordset. This code is hidden when you're working on the page in Design view, but you can see it by highlighting the recordset in the Bindings panel.

Displaying the results

After you create a recordset that holds the search results, you need to display the data for the user on the results page. Dreamweaver provides several tools for displaying recordsets, but the easiest is the dynamic table.

To create a dynamic table that displays results, follow these steps:

1. **Place the insertion point where you want the records displayed on the page. Then choose Insert⇨Application Objects⇨Dynamic Data⇨Dynamic Table.**

   Be sure to insert the table after the yellow code blocks because they must execute first to generate the recordset. The Dynamic Table dialog box opens.

2. **From the Recordset drop-down list, select the recordset you created in the preceding section.**

   For example, we selected the SearchRecordset, as shown in Figure 2-4.

Figure 2-4:
The
Dynamic
Table dialog
box for the
`Search`
`Recordset`.

3. Specify how many records to show at one time on the results page.

Optionally, specify which border, cell padding, and cell spacing to use.

4. Click OK to close the dialog box.

Dreamweaver inserts a dynamic table that displays the search results. Figure 2-5 shows the dynamic table for the example.

New objects created

Figure 2-5:
The
Document
window
contains the
dynamic
table, and
the Server
Behaviors
panel
reflects the
new objects
that the
dynamic
table
created.

Dynamic table

Creating an ASP.NET Search and Results Page

With ASP.NET, you can combine the search page and the results page into one page. In the following sections, you find out how to create a page that searches your database and displays the results in a DataGrid.

Creating the search form

To build an ASP.NET search page, you need, at a minimum, a form with a search field for users to enter their search criteria and a Search button that they can click to update the page with the search results.

To create the search form, follow these steps:

1. **Create an ASP.NET document.**

2. **Insert a form by choosing Insert⇨Form⇨Form.**

An empty form displays in the Document window. The form's boundaries display as thin red lines.

If the form isn't visible, enable Invisible Elements by choosing View⇨Visual Aids⇨Invisible Elements.

3. **Select the form by clicking on the boundary.**

The Properties inspector shows the form properties.

4. **In the Properties inspector, make sure the method is set to POST.**

You don't need to specify an action. ASP.NET automatically processes the data using the same page.

5. **Add a text area search input to the form by choosing Insert⇨ASP.NET Objects⇨asp:TextBox.**

You can also insert other types of form objects, such as asp:CheckBox, asp:RadioButton, asp:ListBox, and asp:DropDownList, from the same menu.

The asp:TextBox dialog box opens.

6. **In the ID field, enter the name to use to reference the field's value.**

The name should reflect the type of search data stored in the form object. For example, we entered **SearchText**, as shown in Figure 2-6.

7. **Select SingleLine from the Text Mode drop-down list.**

This creates a single line text box needed for searching. You can add other form objects to limit searches. However, the more objects you add, the more complex your search query becomes.

8. Enter default text in the Text field.

This places default text into the text box such as `Enter search here`. The asp:TextBox dialog box for the example looks like Figure 2-6.

Figure 2-6:
The asp:TextBox dialog box configured to display a one-line text box called `Search Text`.

9. Click OK.

The text field appears in the form on your page.

10. Move the insertion point where you want to place the Search button.

It can go anywhere you want on the form. For the example, we wanted to place the button to the right of the text field.

11. Choose Insert⇨ASP.NET Objects⇨asp:Button.

Dreamweaver adds a Search button to the form. The user clicks this button to submit the search data.

The asp:Button dialog box appears.

12. Enter a name for the button in the ID field.

For example, we entered **Search Button**.

13. Enter Search in the Text field.

This text is the name of the button that appears when the form loads, letting users know that they need to click it to perform the search.

14. Click OK.

The button appears on the form (see Figure 2-7).

Now that the search form is complete, the next step is to create a dataset to do the actual searching when the user clicks the Search button.

Figure 2-7:
The form
with the
Search
button to the
right of the
text area.

Creating the dataset to hold the results

The dataset must read the search parameter from the form and then search the database. Define the dataset using these steps:

1. **Follow Steps 2 through 6 in the earlier section "Building the recordset."**

   While the earlier section shows how to build a recordset, you can follow the same steps for a dataset.

2. **To create a dataset filter, complete the fields in the Filter area as follows:**

   - For the first Filter field, select the database column name that contains values to search against the form variable. The filter is used to find and display the records specified by the form variable parameter. For example, if the search parameter searches last names, enter **last_name**.

   - For the second Filter field, select how to filter your results: Contains, Begins With, Ends With, or Numeric Comparisons.

     Now any field matches the filter if it contains the search string.

   - For the third Filter field, select Form Variable if the form uses the POST method, or URL Parameter if it uses the URL parameter.

   - For the last Filter field, enter the name of the form parameter to be passed by the search page. This contains the actual search string from the POST form submission. In the example, the search string is **SearchText**.

Figure 2-8 shows the DataSet dialog box using the employee table example data.

Figure 2-8:
The DataSet
dialog box
set to filter
based
on the
Search
Text form
variable.

3. **Click OK.**

The new dataset appears in the Bindings panel list, as shown in Figure 2-9.

Figure 2-9:
The new
dataset
appears in
the Bindings
panel.

After you define the dataset, Dreamweaver inserts the server code that executes the search in your dynamic page. The next step is to create a DataGrid to display the results from the search.

Adding a DataGrid to display results

To display the search results in a DataGrid:

1. **Place the insertion point where you want the DataGrid to appear.**

You must place the DataGrid in the same form as the search field. ASP.NET generates processing errors if two forms are on a page.

2. **In the Server Behaviors panel, click the plus (+) button and select DataGrid from the menu.**

   The DataGrid dialog box appears.

3. **In the ID field, enter a name for the DataGrid.**

   The name must be made up of only letters, numbers, and underscores. For example, we entered **SearchDataGrid**, as shown in Figure 2-10.

4. **From the DataSet drop-down list, select the dataset that you created in the preceding section.**

   For example, we selected the SearchDataSet value.

5. **You can leave the default column type of Simple Data Field to display data.**

   Other types include hyperlinks to jump to other pages, such as detail pages, and buttons for operations such as updating and deleting the record.

   The DataGrid dialog box for the example looks like Figure 2-10.

Figure 2-10:
The DataGrid dialog box with the `Search DataSet` selected.

6. **Click OK.**

   Your page is now complete. The same page displays the search form and the results, as shown in Figure 2-11. The only downside to this approach is that the empty DataGrid appears at the bottom of the page before any searches are submitted.

Figure 2-11:
The
Document
window
with the
SearchData
Grid.

Testing Your Search and Results Pages

After you create your search and results pages, it's a good idea to test them
to make sure they work properly as described in the following steps for all
dynamic page types:

1. **Open the search page.**

2. **Choose File⇨Preview in Browser⇨*Your browser type.***

3. **If Dreamweaver asks you if it's okay to copy the file over, click OK to
copy files to your testing site.**

Your browser launches with your search page (see Figure 2-12).

4. **Enter a search term in the Search field.**

Figure 2-12:
The browser
displaying
the search
page to
search
for il.

5. **Click the Submit button.**

The browser page changes to the results page, as shown in Figure 2-13.

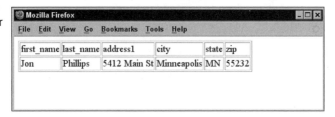

Figure 2-13:
The browser displaying the results page with last names containing `il`.

Be sure that both search and details pages transfer to the testing server. If they don't, you get a `Page Not Found` error when you click a link in the search page.

If you encounter MySQL errors when viewing the results page, you may need to comment out the following line in the PHP code using Code view.

```
//mysql_free_result($SearchRecordset);
```

The problem is that Dreamweaver frees the resultset before displaying it.

ASP.NET System Requirements

In order to get output that works with ASP.NET, keep in mind these system requirements:

✔ Make sure you have the latest version of Microsoft's database software component, which is called MDAC. MDAC is available from Microsoft's site at `http://msdn.microsoft.com/data/mdac/downloads/default.aspx`. Download and install the most recent version available.

✔ Install the .NET Framework to allow IIS to process .NET files. Download it from Microsoft at `http://msdn.microsoft.com/netframework/downloads/updates/default.aspx`.

✔ Upload the `DreamweaverCtrls.dll` Dreamweaver .NET component file. To publish this file on your test or remote server, click the blue up arrow in the Components panel. This places the file in the bin directory of your Web root. Without this file, Dreamweaver-generated code produces errors.

Regardless of which language you choose, if you run into an error, don't panic. Searching for the error with Google or checking the Dreamweaver knowledgebase usually turns up a solution in short order.

Chapter 3: Building Record Insert Pages

In This Chapter

✔ Developing a record insert page in one step

✔ Putting together a record insert page a piece at a time

✔ Making sure your record insert page works

*A*t some point in the process of building your Web application, you may need to include a *record insert page,* which is a page that allows users to insert records into the database. Every record insert page must have

◆ A database connection

◆ A database table to model the insert fields after

◆ A form that collects data

◆ A submit button

When designing the record insert page, you typically arrange the fields on the form in a table and include labels to identify each field. When users open the record insert page in their Web browsers, they just fill in the form fields. When they finish, they click the submit button, and the record is added to the database. A typical use for an insert page is a new member registration page. Another possible use is adding new products to an online catalog.

Dreamweaver gives you two methods to add data to a database table from a dynamic Web page. You can do it all in one step by using the Insert Record dialog box. Dreamweaver also supports creating a record insert page by adding the server behaviors a block at a time. We describe both methods in this chapter, as well as show you how to test your completed record insert page.

Creating the Record Insert Page in One Operation

You can add the basic building blocks of a record insert page in a single operation by using the Record Insertion Form application object. The application object adds an HTML form and an Insert Record server behavior to the page.

You must have an active database connection before you can build a record insert page. See Book VII for details on setting up a database connection.

To build the record insert page with the Record Insertion Form application object, follow these steps:

1. Create a new or open an existing document.

2. Choose Insert⇨Application Objects⇨Insert Record⇨Record Insertion Form Wizard.

The Insert Record Insertion Form dialog box appears as shown in Figure 3-1.

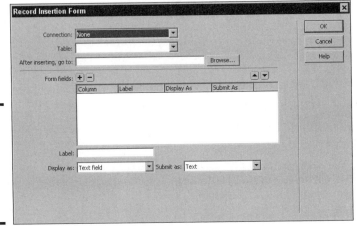

Figure 3-1:
The Record Insertion Form dialog box as it first appears.

3. Select the database connection from the Connection drop-down list.

For example, we selected the phptest connection (see Figure 3-2).

The database connection field varies slightly between the different dynamic document types. For example, ColdFusion includes a Username and Password field.

4. From the Table drop-down list, select the database table that you want to insert the record into.

For example, we selected the Employee table in Figure 3-2.

After you select a table, Dreamweaver updates the Form Fields section with the columns in the table.

5. In the After Inserting, Go To text box, enter the page that you want to go to after the record is added. Or click the Browse button to select a file.

For example, we selected the success.php page in Figure 3-2. This page can just say the insert was successful.

For the ASP.NET dynamic page type, you can also specify a page that you want to go to upon failure or display a debugging page. The rest of the dialog box works the same with ASP.NET as the other page types.

6. **To remove unwanted columns from the record insert page, select the columns that you want to remove in the Form Fields section and click the minus (–) button.**

    The Form Fields section lists the columns that appear on the record insert page. In these fields, the user can enter data before submitting the insert request.

    For the Employee table example, the employee_id field gets removed because it's an auto-generated key field. Removing this field eliminates the risk of the user entering a duplicate key value.

7. **If you're happy with the default settings in the Form Fields section, skip to Step 8. However, if you want to make changes to how a field appears on the record insert page, select the field from the list and fill in the following fields:**

    - **Label:** In this text box, change the Label field to a more descriptive label for the contents of the database field. For example, you can give the first_name field a friendlier label, such as First Name.

    - **Display As:** Select a form type from the Display As drop-down list. The default setting is Text Field. The Display As list includes all the basic form types, including check boxes, menus, and radio buttons. If you select one of the types that requires additional configuration — such as radio groups — a configuration dialog box appears.

    - **Submit As:** From this drop-down list, select the data format that you want to place in the database field. The choices include Text, Numeric, Double, Date, Checkbox Y/N, Checkbox 1/0, and Checkbox -1,0. The data format that you choose here needs to match the database column's type.

    - **Default Value:** Specify a default value for any field by entering that value in this field. Or to specify a dynamic data source for the default value, click the Dynamic (lightning bolt) button and select a binding. This process works the same as specifying a dynamic source for a regular form object.

    Figure 3-2 shows the Record Insertion Form dialog box for the Employee table example.

8. **If you want to change the order in which the fields display in the form, select a field and click the up or down arrow.**

    You need to order table fields together with similar fields (for example, you'll probably want to group all the address fields together).

9. **Click OK to close the dialog box.**

Figure 3-2:
The Record
Insertion
Form dialog
box after
configuring
an insertion
for the
`employee`
database
table.

Dreamweaver automatically adds the form and the submit button to
your page. Figure 3-3 shows the example form in the Document window
along with a submit button labeled Insert Record.

Figure 3-3:
The
Document
window
with the
insertion
form.

You can modify the appearance of the form by using the usual Dreamweaver functions for changing fonts, colors, and alignment. The form elements must stay within the boundaries of the form. To continue working on your form elements, see Book II, Chapter 7.

Click the Insert Record entry in the Server Behaviors panel to edit the server behavior (such as adding additional columns to the insert) in the Record Insertion Form dialog box (refer to Figure 3-1).

Building a Record Insert Page Block by Block

You can add the basic building blocks of an insert page separately by using the form tools and the Server Behaviors panel. While creating your Record Insert page is faster using the Record Insertion dialog box, building block by block allows complete control over placement of blocks on your page.

When creating an insert page manually, you create a form for the user to enter the data and then add an Insert Record server behavior to process the form submission, as the following sections describe.

Adding the form

To add the HTML form, follow these steps:

1. **Create a new page dynamic page.**

2. **Insert a form by choosing Insert⇨Form⇨Form.**

An empty form appears in the Document window, as shown in Figure 3-4. The form's boundaries appear as thin red lines.

If you can't see the form, enable invisible elements by choosing View⇨ Visual Aids⇨Invisible Elements.

3. **To select the form, click the form's boundaries or click the `<form>` tag in the bottom-left corner of the Document window.**

Selecting the form lets you modify that form's properties.

4. **In the Properties inspector, enter a name for the form in the Form Name field.**

You probably want to use something descriptive, such as Insert. Don't set the Action or Method fields because the Insert Record server behavior sets these fields for you.

Figure 3-4:
The
Document
window
has the
empty form
element that
can hold the
insert fields.

5. Add a text area input by choosing Insert➪Form➪Text Field.

You can also add other form objects, depending on the type of data that you want to insert into the database table. See Book II, Chapter 7 for more on the different form objects.

6. In the Input Tag Accessibility Attributes dialog box, enter a description of the column in the Label field and then click OK.

This dialog box appears only if you've enabled accessibility features in Dreamweaver Preferences. This label tells the user which column the text area applies to. For example, the Employee table's first column is first_name, so you can enter **First Name** as the description of that column.

After you click OK, the text area appears to the left of the field on the form.

7. Press Enter (Windows) or Return (Mac) to enter a new line to place the element on a separate line.

You can also use a table element to align your fields (see Book II, Chapter 7).

8. Select the text field and then, in the Properties inspector, change the TextField name to the name of the database column.

For example, we changed the name to **first_name**. This change makes associating the fields in the Insert Record server behavior easier because they match the column names.

9. **For each column that you allow the user to add data to, repeat Steps 5 through 8.**

   For the Employee table example, we added fields for first name, last name, street address, city, state, and zip.

10. **Insert a submit button on the page by choosing Insert⇨Form⇨Button.**

    If the Input Tag Accessibility Attributes dialog box appears, leave the Label field empty and then click Cancel.

    The submit button appears on the form. You don't need to add a label.

11. **If you want to change the button name, follow these steps:**

    1. **Select the submit button.**

    2. **In the Properties inspector, enter the new button name in the Button Name and Value fields.**

    For example, we changed the button name to **Insert** so that the name tells the user what the button does.

    The example form looks like Figure 3-5.

Figure 3-5:
The form with a text area and a submit button — all the basic elements that you need to insert a record.

Adding the Insert Record server behavior

You have to add the Insert Record server behavior to your page so that it can process the data in the form submission.

You must have an active database connection before you can add the Insert Record server behavior. See Book VII for details on setting up a database connection.

To add the Insert Record server behavior, follow these steps:

1. **In the Server Behaviors panel, click the plus (+) button and select Insert Records from the drop-down menu that appears.**

   The Insert Record dialog box appears on-screen.

2. **Select your form from the Submit Values From drop-down list.**

3. **From the Connection drop-down list, select a database connection that contains the table that you want to insert data into.**

4. **From the Insert Table drop-down list, select the database table that you want to insert a record into.**

   The database columns appear in the Columns section, as shown in Figure 3-6.

Figure 3-6:
The Insert Record dialog box can pick which fields supply values from the form to the database table for the Employee table.

Depending on your dynamic page type, the Insert Record dialog box may appear slightly different. For example, ColdFusion calls the Connection field a data source and includes options for Username and Password database fields. However, these differences don't change the following steps.

5. **If you want to modify the associated database column or data type of a field, select the column from the column list and then modify the following fields in the dialog box:**

- **Value:** Select the form field from the Value drop-down list. Each form field appears in the list.

- **Submit As:** Select the data type from the Submit As drop-down list. The data type that you select here should mirror the database column data type. The types include text, integer, date, and check box formats.

Dreamweaver automatically links the form fields that have the same name as the database field.

6. **For each field that you need to change, repeat Step 5.**

7. **In the After Inserting, Go To text field, enter the page that you want to go to after inserting the record. Or click the Browse button and select a file.**

   For our example, we choose the success.php page, as shown in Figure 3-7.

Figure 3-7:
The Insert Record dialog box set to display success. php after a successful record insert.

For the ASP.NET dynamic page type, you have a choice also for the On Failure, Go To text box and a Display Debugging Information check box. You fill in these fields to display debugging information or redirect a user if the record insert fails. The rest of the dialog box works the same as the other document types.

8. **Click OK.**

   Dreamweaver adds the server behavior to the page. You now have a complete page. Users can fill out the fields on the page and then click the submit button.

You can make any visual changes to the form by using Dreamweaver's tools for changing fonts, colors, and placement.

Testing Your Record Insert Page

After you create a record insert page (which you can read about in the "Building a Record Insert Page Block by Block" section, earlier in this chapter), you probably want to test your page. Follow these steps to do so:

1. **Open the record insert page.**

2. **Choose File⇨Preview in Browser⇨*Your browser type*.**

3. **When Dreamweaver asks you if it's okay to copy files to your testing site, click OK.**

Your browser launches and displays the record insert page.

4. **Enter some sample data into the fields.**

Figure 3-8 shows some test data for the Employee table.

Figure 3-8:
Enter sample data in the insert page.

5. **Click the Insert button.**

The browser opens the success page, as shown in Figure 3-9.

Figure 3-9:
The browser displays the success page.

Be sure that both your insert page and success page transfer to the testing server. If not, when you click the button on the insert page, you get a `Page Not Found` error message.

The success page in our example simply contains the text `Inserted Successfully`.

To be sure that the insert really worked, follow these steps:

1. **Use your search page or expand the recordset from the Bindings panel.**

See Book X, Chapter 2 for details on setting up a search page.

2. **Right-click (Windows) or Control+click (Mac) the table on the page.**

3. **Choose View Data.**

The View Data dialog box appears, shown in Figure 3-10.

Figure 3-10:
The View Data dialog box shows the new test data as part of the Employee table.

In the dialog box, you can see that the data was inserted correctly into the table.

Chapter 4: Developing Record Update and Delete Pages

In This Chapter

✓ Creating record update pages

✓ Trying out your record update page

✓ Deleting records by using delete pages

✓ Putting your delete page to the test

---

*T*he record update and delete operations are the last two database functions commonly used in dynamic database sites. For example, suppose that your employees can view their employee data online. Over time, they may want to change their employment details, or an administrator may need to delete an employee record all together. Therefore, you need to give users the ability to update and delete records, which is what this chapter talks about.

Building an Update Page

Before users can update a record, they need to be able to search for the record that they want to update. Therefore, you need to create a search page and a results page. (See Book IX, Chapter 3 for more on search and results pages.) Additionally, you need to create an update page that enables users to enter the data for updating the record. Here's a closer look at the three pages that you need to create:

✦ **Search page:** This page allows the user to search for a record that he or she wants to update. For example, in the case of an employee record, the search page simply searches the employee that's logged in because employees can't modify other employee information.

✦ **Results page:** This page displays the record in a form. The form defaults to the values currently in the database (before the update) and has an update button.

✦ **Update page:** This page performs the update and tells the user when an update is successful.

Here's how the update process works:

1. The user enters search criteria in the form on the search page and then clicks the submit button.

2. The browser displays the results of the search on the results page.

3. The user selects a record to update on the results page and clicks the submit button.

4. The browser displays the update page.

The first step in the update process is to create a search and results page set. If you haven't already created these pages, check out Book IX, Chapter 3 for details. Then read the following sections for details on building the update page.

Creating links that open the update page

After you create the search and results pages, you need to create links on the results page to open the update page and display the selected record in an HTML form.

Open your results page and follow these steps to add update links:

1. **Select the placeholder for the dynamic content on which you want to create a link.**

For example, we selected the last name field to use as the link field, as shown in Figure 4-1. The field placeholder appears as `{SearchRecordset. last_name}`.

Figure 4-1:
The
Document
window for
the results
page with
the `last_
name` field
selected.

2. **In the Action field of the Properties inspector, enter the name of the update page (the page that you want to perform the update operation).**

For example, we entered `update.php` for the update page. For other language types, use the appropriate file extension (such as `.asp`) rather than `.php`.

Defining the URL parameter to pass to the update page

After you add an update link to the results page (which you can read about in the preceding section), you want to modify that link so it passes the identity of the record that the user wants to update. To define the URL parameter that identifies which record to update, follow these steps:

1. **In the Properties inspector, click the folder button to the right of the Link field.**

2. **Select the page that performs an update.**

You can either enter a name for a new file such as `update.php` or select an existing page.

3. **Click the Parameters button.**

The Parameters dialog box appears.

4. **Enter the key field from your database record in the Name column.**

The *key field* is a field that always has a unique value. For example, we entered `employee_id` because this field contains a unique ID for each employee.

5. **Click the Value column to the right of the Name.**

The box is highlighted.

6. **Click the Dynamic (lightning bolt) button to the right of the highlighted box.**

The Dynamic Data dialog box appears, as shown in Figure 4-2.

7. **Select the key field from the recordset and then click OK.**

For example, we selected `employee_id`, as shown in Figure 4-2.

After you click OK, the Values field in the Parameters dialog box updates to contain the URL parameter.

8. **Click OK to close the Parameters dialog box.**

Figure 4-2:
The
Dynamic
Data dialog
box with
`employee_`
`id` selected.

The Select File dialog box appears with an updated value in the URL field. The value in this field varies depending on your dynamic page type. Figure 4-3 shows the results for a PHP page.

Figure 4-3:
The updated
URL field
in the
Select File
dialog box.

9. **Click OK to close the Select File dialog box.**

The Document window shows the new link.

10. **Save the results page.**

The results page is now complete.

Putting the update page together

The update page must read the URL parameter from the results page and store it in a recordset. The recordset provides the default values for the form that enables users to change values. The following sections show how to create the recordset and the form.

Creating the recordset to store the URL parameter

To create the recordset, follow these steps:

1. **Create a new dynamic page.**

   You must have an active database connection to create the recordset. See Book VII for details on creating a database connection.

2. **In the Bindings panel, click the plus (+) button and select Recordset (Query) from the menu that appears.**

   The Recordset dialog box appears.

3. **Enter the name of the recordset in the Name field.**

   Use a name that describes the recordset data. For example, we entered `UpdateRecordset` to indicate that the recordset relates to an update.

4. **Select a database connection from the Connection drop-down list.**

   Depending on your dynamic page type, the Recordset dialog box may appear slightly different. ColdFusion, in particular, calls the Connection field a data source and includes optional Username and Password fields for the database. However, these differences don't change the following steps.

5. **In the Table drop-down list, select the database table that you want to update.**

   After you select a table, the Columns list shows the columns in that table.

6. **Click the Selected radio button to include only some of the columns from the table.**

   Although clicking All works okay if you're not going to allow users to update all the fields in the table, it's best not to include all the fields in the result set.

7. **In the Columns list, select the columns that you want to update.**

   To select multiple columns, Ctrl+click (Windows) or ⌘+click (Mac).

8. **Configure the Filter area so that the database column is compared against the URL parameter from the results page:**

   - From the first list, select the key column. For example, we selected `employee_id`, which is the key column for the Employee table.

- From the second list, select the equals sign (=). This selection limits the result set to only the record that you want to update. You can update only one record at a time.

- From the third list, select URL Parameter.

- From the fourth list, enter the name of the URL parameter defined in the results page. For example, we entered `employee_id`, the same name as the database key column name.

If your form's field has a different name in the Properties inspector, then use that name as the parameter name.

The new recordset retrieves the information needed to update the specific records that the user has selected to update. When the update page is requested, it uses the record ID parameter sent to the page to filter the recordset. The Recordset dialog box for the example looks like Figure 4-4.

Figure 4-4:
The Recordset dialog box configured to select only the row to update based on the URL Parameter from the results page.

9. **Click OK.**

The recordset is added to the Bindings panel list. Now when the user selects a record on the results page, the update page builds a recordset containing only the selected record.

Adding a form to the update page

After creating the recordset for the update page (which you can read about in the preceding section), you need to create the form that will enable the user to modify the record data. Dreamweaver can do the work for you with the Record Update application object. This application object automatically creates the form in the Document window and adds the appropriate server behaviors to allow updates.

Follow these steps to add an HTML form to your update page:

1. Choose Insert⇨Application Objects⇨Update Record⇨Record Update Form Wizard.

The Update Record Form dialog box appears.

Only one application object can exist on the same page. You can't have an update application object and a delete application object on the same page.

2. Select the database connection from the Connection drop-down list.

3. Select the database table that you want to update from the Table to Update drop-down list.

4. From the Select Record From drop-down list, select the recordset that you created, as described in the preceding section.

This list should default to the recordset that you created in the preceding section. In our example, we called it `UpdateRecordset`.

5. From the Unique Key Column drop-down list, select a key column to identify the record in the database table.

For example, we selected `employee_id`. Leave the Numeric check box selected if the key fields are numeric.

6. In the After Updating, Go To text box, enter the page that you want to open after the record is updated. Or click the Browse button to select a file.

For example, we selected a page called `success.php`, which simply displays an `Update successful` message. You can create the page before or after entering the file name for it.

By default, Dreamweaver includes all the columns of the table in the form on the update page.

7. To remove unwanted columns from the update page, select the columns in the Form Fields section and click the minus (–) button.

The Form Fields section lists the columns in which the user can enter data before submitting the update request. For our example, the `employee_id` field is manually removed because it's an auto-generated key field. Removing this field eliminates the risk of the user changing the key value to a duplicate value.

8. If you're happy with the default settings in the Form Fields section, skip to Step 10. However, if you want to make changes to how a field will display on the update page, select the field from the list and fill in the following fields in the dialog box:

- **Label:** Enter a descriptive label for each database field. This label will appear on the form next to the field. By default, Dreamweaver uses the column name as the label. So, for example, rather than use the default label of `first_name`, you could change it to First Name, which is a little friendlier.

- **Display As:** Select a form type for the field. The Display As list includes all the basic form types, including check boxes, radio buttons, and menus. If you select one of the types that needs additional configuration, such as radio groups, a configuration dialog box appears.

- **Submit As:** Select the data format for the database field. The *data format* is the type of data that the database column is expecting. The default matches the current datatype in the database. Your choices include Text, Numeric, Double, Date, Checkbox Y/N, Checkbox 1/0, and Checkbox -1,0.

- **Default Value:** Specify a default value for the field. The value that you enter in the Default Value field is the initial value that appears in the form for the particular field. If you don't enter a value here, Dreamweaver uses the current value from the database for the initial value.

  If you want, you can change the dynamic data source for the default value by clicking the Dynamic (lightning bolt) button and selecting a binding. The value defaults to the value from the recordset. If the data type is a menu, radio group, or check box, another dialog box opens to configure the choices available to the user. For example, a check box has a setting to determine if it should be automatically checked when the update page opens.

9. **Repeat Step 8 for each field that you want to modify in the Form Field list.**

The dialog box for the example looks like Figure 4-5.

Figure 4-5: The Record Update Form dialog box after configuring an update for the `employee` database table.

10. **If you want to change the order in which the fields appear in the form, select a field and click the up or down arrows.**

Table fields should be grouped with similar fields together (for example, address fields should all be placed together).

11. **Click OK to close the Record Update Form dialog box.**

The new form appears as a basic table on your update page. Figure 4-6 shows the form created for the example. You can modify the appearance of form objects as you can any other object in Dreamweaver, but remember to not move them outside the form's boundaries. (See Book II, Chapter 7 for more on form objects.)

Figure 4-6:
The Document window with the update form and Server Behaviors panel.

Testing Your Update Page

You can test your results page by previewing it in a browser:

1. **Open the update results page.**

2. **Choose File⇨Preview in Browser⇨*Your browser type*.**

3. **When Dreamweaver asks if it's okay to copy the files to your testing site, click OK.**

Your browser opens a page that contains a list of records that you can update. For example, Figure 4-7 lists all the employee records that we can update.

Figure 4-7:
The
browser
displays the
rows that
can be
updated.

4. Select a record to update by clicking the link for that record.

The browser opens the update page for that record. For example, we clicked the Davis link (for Michele Davis) on the results page, and the browser displayed the update page with the record for Michele Davis, as shown in Figure 4-8.

Figure 4-8:
The
browser
displays the
update page
with current
values as
defaults.

Be sure that both your search results page and update page transfer to the testing server. If both don't transfer, when you click a link in the update results page, you get a `Page Not Found` error message.

5. Enter a new value for one of the fields on the update page.

For example, we changed the phone number for Michele Davis to 952-111-1212, as shown in Figure 4-9.

6. Click Update Record.

Your changes are saved to the database, and the success page appears in the browser. If it's not successful, verify that your URL parameters match for sending in the key value to update.

To verify the update was saved, you can navigate back to the update results page to verify the new value.

Figure 4-9:
The phone
number is
changed
before
clicking the
Update
Record
button.

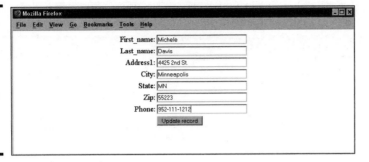

Building Pages to Delete a Record

The typical process for deleting records from a database consists of a few steps. First, users select which record to delete. After they select a record, a confirmation page opens, asking them to confirm the delete request to prevent deleting a record accidentally. Finally, a page opens that indicates the record was successfully deleted from the database.

In order for users to be able to delete a record, they first need to be able to find that record in the database. Therefore, you need to create a search page and results page that enable users to search for the record. See Book IX, Chapter 2 for details.

The following sections detail how to build the pages that allow a user to delete a record from the database.

Creating delete links to open the confirmation page

After you create a search page and results page, you need to create links on the results page that users can click to open a *confirmation page,* which is a page that asks them to confirm the deletion.

To create the links to the confirmation page, open the results page and follow these steps:

1. **Select the last column in the results repeated region.**

   Check out Figure 4-10 to see the column that you want to select.

2. **Choose Insert⇨Table Objects⇨Table⇨Insert Columns To The Right.**

   An empty column appears at the end of the table. The empty column is very skinny.

Selected column

Figure 4-10:
The last
column in
the results
table is
selected.

3. **Select the new column's lower cell, which is part of the repeated region.**

4. **Type** Delete **or insert an image that represents a delete action.**

5. **Select the text you just entered to apply a link to the text.**

6. **In the Properties inspector, enter the name of the confirmation page in the Link field.**

   A good choice for the name is confirm.php. Substitute the appropriate file extension for your dynamic page type.

Defining the URL parameter to pass to the confirmation page

After you create a delete link that opens the confirmation page (which you can read about in the preceding section), you want to modify that link so it passes the identity of the record that the user wants to delete. To define the URL parameter that identifies which record to delete, follow these steps:

1. **Follow Steps 1 through 6 in the "Defining the URL parameter to pass to the update page" section, earlier in this chapter.**

2. **Click the plus (+) button to add another parameter.**

   An empty row appears in the list.

3. **Enter the name of a column that describes which record is about to be deleted on the confirmation page.**

For the Employee table example, a good choice is the last name field. The confirmation page could use the database key to look up the entire row and display it, but that process would give you more code than you really need to confirm the deletion. Figure 4-11 shows the two parameters for the Employee table.

Figure 4-11:
The
Parameters
dialog box
with the key
field and a
descriptive
field.

4. **Click OK to close the Parameters dialog box.**

   The Select File dialog box appears with an updated value in the URL field. The value in this field varies depending on your dynamic page type.

5. **Click OK to close the Select File dialog box.**

   The Document window shows the new link.

6. **Save the results page.**

   The results page is complete. The delete link now appears on the page, as shown in Figure 4-12.

New Delete link

Figure 4-12:
The
Document
window
with the
new Delete
link.

Building the confirmation page

The Confirmation page simply displays enough information to identify the record that's about to be deleted. This page consists of a form with a confirmation button.

To create a page that confirms the record deletion, you need to send two parameters to the confirmation page:

✦ The record ID

✦ A field to display the name of that record

This page saves you from having to create another recordset with a filter to look up information that's already been retrieved from the database.

Follow these steps to create the confirmation page:

1. **Create a new dynamic document and insert a form.**

See Book II, Chapter 7 for details on creating forms.

2. **In the Bindings panel, click the plus (+) button and select URL Parameter from the list that appears.**

The URL Variables dialog box appears.

3. **In the Name field, enter the name of the database column that is the key.**

For the example, we entered **employee_id** because we need to create a binding for the URL parameter `employee_id`.

4. **Click OK.**

The binding is created.

5. **Repeat Steps 3 and 4 for the other parameter.**

For the example, we also created a `last_name` parameter.

6. **Choose Insert⇨Form⇨Hidden Field to add a hidden field to store the record ID.**

The user doesn't need to see the `employee_id`, but that ID has to be part of the form submission.

7. **In the Properties inspector, enter the name of the variable in the HiddenField text box.**

For example, we entered **employee_id** for the Employee table, as shown in Figure 4-13.

8. **Click the Dynamic (lightning bolt) button next to the Value field.**

The Dynamic Data dialog box appears.

9. **Select the type of binding (URL Parameter, for example) from the bindings list.**

For the example, we selected the `employee_id` URL parameter. You can leave the other fields set to their defaults.

10. **Click OK to close the Dynamic Data dialog box.**

In the Properties inspector, Dreamweaver updates the Value field with dynamic code to place the URL parameter into the hidden form field, as shown in Figure 4-13.

Hidden field   Dynamic placeholder

Figure 4-13:
The form with the hidden parameter.

11. **Click in the hidden field in the form and type** Really delete the record for, **as shown in Figure 4-14.**

This text tells users they're about to delete a record.

12. **Insert dynamic text to display the last name by selecting Dynamic Text from the plus (+) menu of the Server Behaviors panel.**

The Dynamic Text dialog box appears.

13. **Select the `employee_id` URL Parameter from the list and then click OK.**

If you're using a different column as the key, select that parameter instead.

Figure 4-14 shows the dynamic text placeholder in the form.

14. **Choose Insert⇨Form⇨Button to add a submit button to your form.**

The Input Tag Accessibility Attributes dialog box appears.

15. **Click OK to close the dialog box.**

You don't really need to label this button because its meaning is straight-forward.

16. **Select the button that you inserted in Step 14.**

17. **In the Properties inspector, change** Submit **to** Delete **in the Button Name and Value fields.**

The button's text changes to Delete, as shown in Figure 4-14.

Figure 4-14:
The complete page with the Delete button defined.

18. **Save the page.**

Use the name that you selected when creating the Delete link (see "Creating delete links to open the confirmation page," earlier in this chapter). Our example uses `confirm.php`.

The page isn't complete yet because it can't actually process the deletion. You need to add logic to delete the record, as described in the following section.

Adding logic to delete the record

Dreamweaver adds the logic to perform the database delete with the Delete Record server behavior. To add this behavior to the HTML form, follow these steps:

1. **In the Server Behaviors panel, click the plus (+) button and select Delete Record from the menu that appears.**

The Delete Record dialog box appears.

2. **Select Primary Key Value from the First Check If Variable Is Defined drop-down list.**

3. **Select the database connection from the Connection drop-down list.**

This field may appear differently depending on your dynamic page code type.

4. **Select the table that you want to delete from the Table drop-down list.**

5. **Select the primary key column from the Primary Key Column drop-down list.**

We left the Numeric check box checked in our example because the `employee_id` record is a numeric field.

6. **Select Form Variable from the Primary Key Value drop-down list.**

Form Variable is the hidden field value from the form submission.

7. **In the text field next to the Primary Key Value drop-down list, enter the name of the variable that contains the key value.**

Again, we entered **employee_id** for the example.

8. **In the After Deleting, Go To text box, enter the page that you want to open after deleting the record.**

We entered `success.php` for the example. You can make this page as simple as the statement `Deleted Successfully`. The Delete Record dialog box for the example looks like Figure 4-15.

Figure 4-15:
The Delete
Record
dialog box
set to delete
an entry
in the
employee
table.

9. **Click OK to close the dialog box.**

Dreamweaver adds the new server behavior to the page.

The deletion pages are complete.

Testing Your Delete Page

To test your delete page by opening it in a browser, follow these steps:

1. **Open the delete results page.**

This page allows the user to select a record that he or she wants to delete.

2. **Choose File⇨Preview in Browser⇨*Your browser type.***

3. **If Dreamweaver asks you if it's okay to copy files to your testing site, click OK.**

Your browser opens and displays a list of records that you can delete. For example, Figure 4-16 lists the employee records that we can delete.

Figure 4-16: The browser displaying the rows that can be deleted.

Mozilla Firefox						
first_name	last_name	address1	city	state	zip	
Jon	Phillips	5412 Main St	Minneapolis	MN	55232	Delete
Michele	Davis	4425 2nd St.	Minneapolis	MN	55223	Delete
Simon	Meyer	3023 Wall St.	New York	NY	00002	Delete
Matt	Wagner	2332 Ocenside Dr	San Francisco	CA	90124	Delete

4. **Click the Delete link next to the row that you want to delete.**

The browser page displays the delete confirmation page. Figure 4-17 shows the delete confirmation page for the example.

Be sure that both your delete results page and confirmation page transfer to the testing server. If both of them don't transfer, when you click a link in the delete results page, you get a `Page Not Found` error message.

5. **Click the Delete button.**

Figure 4-17:
The deletion
confirmation
page
shows the
employee
name of
Wagner.

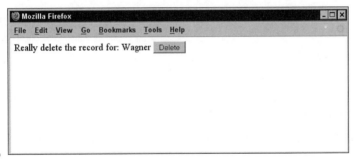

The browser displays the success page.

To verify the record deletion, you can navigate back to the delete results page to make sure the record doesn't appear on that page anymore.

Chapter 5: Using Advanced Data Manipulation Tools

In This Chapter

✔ Calling ASP command objects

✔ Calling JSP prepared statements

✔ Working with database stored procedures

Dreamweaver supports several methods for mixing code into the database. Standard database queries can select information in the database and change it, but those queries can't do any complex conditional logic. That's where advanced data manipulation takes over. Using tools such as stored procedures enables you to store and execute more powerful code in the database.

You can call database manipulation objects — including ASP command objects, JSP prepared statements, and stored procedures — from your dynamic pages. The objects available depend on the code type for your page and the database that you use.

Note: Some databases don't support stored procedures or have added support only recently. For example, Access doesn't support stored procedures, and Dreamweaver doesn't support stored procedures for MySQL.

In this chapter, you can find out how to build pages that use ASP command objects, JSP prepared statements, and stored procedures. These are all essentially the same way to store and execute code in the database, just tailored to their particular database.

ASP Command Objects

An *ASP command object* provides a container for executing SQL statements or calling stored procedures on the server. (See the "Stored Procedures (JSP, ASP, ASP.NET, and ColdFusion)" section, later in this chapter.) You can use command objects in your pages to modify data in your database or even create database objects by using the appropriate SQL commands. A command object can return a recordset or insert, update, or delete records in a database.

To create the command object that calls a stored procedure, follow these steps:

1. **Open an ASP page to which you want to add a command.**

   The page must have an active database connection. See Book VII for details on setting up a database connection.

2. **In the Server Behaviors panel, click the plus (+) button and select Command from the list that appears.**

   The Command dialog box opens.

3. **Enter a name for the command in the Name field.**

   We suggest choosing a name that describes what the command does. For example, we entered **DeleteCommand**, as shown in Figure 5-2.

4. **Select the database connection from the Connection drop-down list.**

5. **Select the editing operation that you want to perform from the Type drop-down list.**

   Your choices include Insert, Update, Delete, and Stored Procedure. For example, in Figure 5-1, we selected Delete because we want to delete information in a database table.

6. **In the Database Items area, select the database table, view, or stored procedure that you want to edit.**

   Click the plus (+) sign to expand the Tables category, which displays a list of table names.

7. **Click the Delete button.**

   Depending on the type you chose, the button may be a Procedure button for stored procedures, a Column button for inserts, or a Where button for updates.

   Dreamweaver automatically builds the SQL statement based on what editing operation you're performing and then displays it in the SQL window. In our example, we wanted to delete information from the Employee table, so Dreamweaver inserted the following SQL statement after we clicked the Delete button:

   ```
   DELETE FROM employee
   WHERE
   ```

8. **To use a variable in the SQL statement, add it manually to the SQL.**

   For example, in Figure 5-1, we added a `var_employee_id` variable.

After the variables have been added to the SQL, you can add the variable to the Variables list (which defines the value of the variable) by clicking the plus (+) button.

9. If you need to define any variables, click the plus (+) button in the Variables area and then enter the variable name.

An empty row is created in the list. Manually enter the values. Use the same name as the variable in the SQL. For example, we entered **var_employee_id**. Enter the values directly into the list.

The Run-Time Value field updates with the code to produce the value. For example, `Request.QueryString("employee_id")` produces the value of the `employee_id` variable. Figure 5-1 shows the dialog box set to delete a record from the Employee table.

Figure 5-1:
The Command dialog box set to delete a record from the Employee table, using a variable to hold the key value.

10. Click OK.

Dreamweaver adds the ASP and SQL code to your page to create and execute the ASP command.

The example command that we created deletes the database record that a URL parameter passes to it. This parameter comes from a form submission. If you want to see the code that was created, look at the document in Code view. Including a confirmation page before doing a delete is good practice; see Book IX, Chapter 4 for details on building the delete form and confirmation page.

In order to save processing time, you can set a command object to be *compiled* (sometimes called *prepared*) on the server. You can use the compiled version over and over without needing to recompile it (which is faster). By default, Dreamweaver sets the Prepared property of the command object to `true`, as in the following VBScript:

```
mycommand.Prepared = true
```

However, you can change the default setting if you want. To do so, in Code view, set the Prepared property of the command object to `false`:

```
mycommand.Prepared = false
```

JSP Prepared Statements

JSP provides a similar framework to ASP for building compiled queries, which it refers to as *prepared statements*. Like ASP objects, JSP prepared statements are reusable and contain an SQL statement that can be assigned variable values. Those values are plugged in when the SQL statement is called. The prepared statement can insert, update, delete, or return a record-set. Because you can compile the prepared statement after it's in the database, you can then call it many times. This easy access saves processing time for the database server.

Dreamweaver enables you to create prepared statements without writing any Java code. If you want to see the code that Dreamweaver generates for you, you can switch to Code view in the Document window.

To create the prepared statement that deletes a record, follow these steps:

1. **Open a JSP dynamic page that has an active database connection.**
2. **In the Server Behaviors panel, click the plus (+) button and select Prepared (Insert, Update, Delete) from the list that appears.**

   The Prepared (Insert, Update, Delete) dialog box appears.
3. **Follow Steps 3 through 10 in the preceding section.**

   Figure 5-2 shows the completed dialog box for deleting information from a table. A record is deleted from the employee table that matches the key value from a form parameter called `employee_id`.

Figure 5-2:
The
Prepared
(Insert,
Update,
Delete)
dialog box
looks very
similar to
the ASP
Command
dialog box.

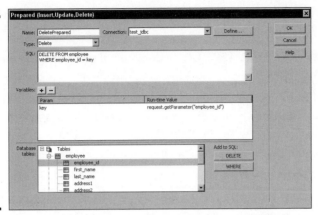

4. **Click OK to close the dialog box.**

   Dreamweaver adds the code to your page that creates and executes the
   JSP command.

Dreamweaver places the JSP code to create the prepared statement into the
page. You can see the code by switching to Code view in the Document
window. The code is now ready for use. For the example that we used in the
previous steps, the JSP code deletes the database records that match the
key value in the `employee_id` form parameter.

Stored Procedures (JSP, ASP, ASP.NET, and ColdFusion)

A *stored procedure* is a block of SQL code that resides inside the database,
and it can do more complex tasks than plain SQL. Stored procedures can call
other stored procedures and perform basic logical evaluations — TRUE,
FALSE, AND, OR, NOT, and XOR (*eXclusive OR*).

A stored procedure can also return more than one value, which makes
returning a whole set of data possible. Because it's more powerful, it's typically used to enforce business rules such as matching values for accounting
transactions in the database. Stored procedures can insert, update, and
delete data, as well as modify database objects, such as tables.

Microsoft Access databases don't support stored procedures. MySQL has
support for stored procedures, but Dreamweaver doesn't currently support
them for MySQL.

To add a stored procedure to a JSP, ASP, ASP.NET, or ColdFusion page, follow these steps:

1. **Open a JSP, ASP, ASP.NET, or ColdFusion page that has an open database connection.**

See Book VII for details on setting up a database connection.

2. **In the Bindings panel, click the plus (+) button and select Stored Procedure from the list that appears.**

For a JSP page type, the menu item is Callable (Stored Procedure).

The Stored Procedure dialog box appears, as shown in Figure 5-3.

Figure 5-3:
The Stored Procedure dialog box for a ColdFusion site.

For a JSP site, the dialog box looks different but collects the same type of information.

3. **In the Data Source drop-down list, select a connection to the database that contains the stored procedure.**

If you're using a ColdFusion dynamic page type, you can enter the username and password for the data source.

4. **From the Procedures drop-down list, select the stored procedure that you want to use.**

Dreamweaver automatically updates the Parameters list with the parameters for the stored procedure that you select.

5. **To make changes to a parameter, select the parameter and click the Edit button. Otherwise, skip to Step 8.**

The empty row appears in the Variable list of the Callable (Stored Procedure) dialog box for a JSP site, as shown in Figure 5-4.

Figure 5-4:
The Callable
(Stored
Procedure)
dialog box
with a blank
line created
in the
Variables
list.

6. **Fill in the following fields in the Edit Stored Procedure dialog box:**

   - Select the parameter's direction from the Direction drop-down list. The direction specifies if the parameter can send or receive information to and from the procedure. The direction can be input, output, or both.

   - Select the variable's data type from the SQL Type drop-down list.

   - Enter a return variable. A return variable allows sending a value back to the calling code.

   - Enter a runtime value. A runtime value allows sending a value to the procedure when it's executed.

   - Enter a test value. A value here can be used when testing your procedure.

7. **Click OK.**

   The Stored Procedure dialog box appears again.

8. **To add a variable, click the plus (+) button.**

   An empty row is created in the list. Each return value from the stored procedure must have a variable. You can remove variables by clicking the minus (–) button.

9. **If the stored procedure returns a recordset, select the Returns Recordset Named check box and enter the name of the recordset.**

   A stored procedure returns a recordset if one is present after expanding the stored procedure parameters (variables).

10. **If the stored procedure returns a status code, click the Returns Status Code Named check box and enter the name of the status code variable.**

    If a return value can be returned, it shows up while expanding the stored procedure definition.

11. **If you're using ASP.NET, fill in these fields: On Success, Go To and On Failure, Go To.**

For example, you can enter `success.aspx` and `failure.aspx`.

12. **Click OK.**

Dreamweaver creates the code on the page that calls the stored procedure.

To use the stored procedure, you need to collect any parameters from the user, usually with a form that contains input fields. (See Book II, Chapter 7 for more on creating forms.) If the stored procedure returns a recordset, you also need to add a server behavior to display the data from the recordset. See Book VIII, Chapter 2 for details on displaying a recordset.

Chapter 6: Restricting Site Access

In This Chapter

✔ **Building pages to restrict site access**

✔ **Building login pages**

✔ **Building a page only authorized users can access**

*A*t some point in the process of building your Web site, you'll want to consider restricting access to parts of your Web site. Restricting access means that you can grant or deny access to users based on criteria you've determined. For example, you can do this based on the user's network address, e-mail address, or age limitations. Think of access control as you would locking the doors of your home, or only letting people into business or school if they have key cards.

Dreamweaver enables you to control access to your Web site in a variety of ways — for example:

✦ Build a registration page for a user to register when first visiting your Web site

✦ Build a login page requiring a user to log in to access pages on your Web site

✦ Build a page that limits access to authorized users only, such as an administrator or a registered user

We describe each of these topics in detail in this chapter.

Building a Registration Page

A registration page requires users to register with your Web site. A user can choose a username and password during the registration process. This is in order to access features that are otherwise unavailable. Dreamweaver comes with a sample page design of a basic registration page, or you can design your own.

Registration pages are great for online communities such as blogs to allow only one person to post and chat as the same user. Other visitors can't post as them. You can restrict problem users from accessing the site.

If you want to use Dreamweaver's registration page design (shown in Figure 6-1), choose File⇨New to open the New Document window. Then select Page Designs from the Category list, select UI: Register (Basic) from the Page Designs list, and click Create.

If you prefer to create your own customized registration page, follow these steps:

1. **Set up a database table to store login information about your site users.**

2. **Create an HTML form for a user to choose a username and password (and any other personal information you want to maintain).**

3. **Add an Insert Record server behavior to update the database table of site users with the new user's login information.**

4. **Use the Check New User server behavior to make sure a new user name entered isn't already taken by another user.**

We cover each of these steps in detail in the following sections.

Figure 6-1:
The Dream-
weaver
Basic
registration
page
created
from the
template.

Setting up a database table for login data

You need to set up a database table to store login information that users enter on the registration page. When creating the database table, include columns for username, password, and any other personal information you want to maintain, such as birthdate, gender, and e-mail address. Include an access privilege column if you want to control users' page access. This column contains a value that represents the level of access the user is allowed such as guest, user, moderator, or administrator. A default privilege is usually assigned with only an administrator having the authority to change the user's privilege level.

You also need to establish a connection to the database. See Book VII for details.

Adding an HTML form to the registration page

The first step in designing the registration page is to create a new page and add an HTML form to it so that a user can choose a username and password. To design the page, follow these steps:

1. **Create a new dynamic page and add a form to it.**

See Book II, Chapter 7 for details on adding forms to your pages.

2. **Click the `<form>` tag at the bottom of the Document window to select the form.**

3. **In the Properties inspector, enter a name for your HTML form in the Form Name box.**

For example, we entered the name **registerForm**. Entering a name for your form is important so you can reference that form later.

4. **For each text field you want to add, choose Insert⇨Form⇨Text Field.**

The Input Tag Accessibility Attributes dialog box displays. Enter labels for each field to tell users what the fields represent. We suggest entering **User Name**, **Password**, and **Re-enter Password** at the very least. You can line up the form objects by placing them inside an HTML table. (See Book II, Chapter 6 for more on tables.)

Notice that Figure 6-2 adds the minimum text fields required for a registration form, which is also the Login page.

At a minimum, you need to store the username and password in your database table. If you want to maintain access privileges, you also need a column for that.

5. **To add a submit button to the page, choose Insert⇨Form⇨Button.**

The Input Tag Accessibility Attributes dialog box appears.

6. **Click OK to close the dialog box.**

The Submit button appears on the form (see Figure 6-3).

Figure 6-2:
The form
with text
fields for the
username
and
password.

Figure 6-3:
Submit
button
added to
form.

Adding an Insert Record server behavior to update the database table

After you add the form to your registration page (as described in the preceding section), the next step is to add an Insert Record server behavior, which updates the database table of Web site users.

The steps required to add an Insert Record server behavior to your registration page vary depending on your programming language, as detailed in the following sections.

ASP.NET, ColdFusion, or PHP

To add an Insert Record server behavior to your registration page in ASP.NET, ColdFusion, or PHP, follow these steps:

1. **In the Server Behaviors panel, click the plus (+) button and select Insert Record.**

Figure 6-4 shows the Insert Record dialog box before you assign any values to the fields.

Figure 6-4:
The Insert Record dialog box as it first appears.

2. **Enter the following information in the Insert Record dialog box:**

- **Submit Values From:** Select the form used on the registration page.
- **Connection or Data Source (ColdFusion):** Select a database connection.
- **Username** and **Password** (ColdFusion only): Enter your username and password if you have them.

- **Insert Table:** Select the name of the database table into which you want to insert the record.

  After selecting a table, the Columns list automatically updates to reflect the columns in the table.

3. **For each form object in your form, provide the following information:**

- **Columns:** Select a database column to insert the record in. For example, we selected the username field, as shown in Figure 6-5.

- **Value:** Select a form object to insert the record. For example, we selected textfield, which is the form object for the username field.

- **Submit As:** Select the type of data your database table expects for the selected column, such as text, numeric, or Boolean values. We selected Text in Figure 6-5.

Figure 6-5 also shows the password database column associated with textfield2.

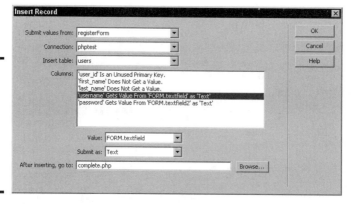

Figure 6-5: The completed Insert Record dialog box for a PHP page.

4. **In the After Inserting, Go To text box, enter the filename of the page to open after the record has been inserted in the database. Or click the Browse button to select the file.**

5. **(ASP.NET only) Enter the page to redirect to if the insert fails in the On Failure, Go To field.**

6. **Click OK to close the dialog box.**

ASP and JSP

To add an Insert Record server behavior to your ASP or JSP registration page, follow these steps:

1. **In the Server Behaviors panel, click the plus (+) button and select Insert Record.**

The Insert Record dialog box appears.

2. **Enter information in the Insert Record dialog box:**

- **Connection:** Select a database connection.

- **Insert into Table:** Select the name of the database table into which you want to insert the record.

- **After Inserting, Go To:** Enter the filename of the page to open after the record has been inserted in the database. Or click the Browse button to select the file.

- **Get Values From:** Select the HTML form in which users enter the registration data.

3. **For each form object in your form, do the following:**

- **Form Elements:** Select a form object from the Form Elements list.

- **Column:** Select a database column in which you want to insert the record.

- **Submit As:** Select the type of data your database table expects for the selected column, such as text, numeric, or Boolean values.

For example, in Figure 6-6 we selected the textfield2 form object in the Form Elements list, chose the password column from the table, and selected the Text data type.

4. **Click OK to close the dialog box.**

Figure 6-6:
The Insert
Record
dialog box
for an ASP
or JSP
page.

Adding the Check New User server behavior to ensure the user name is unique

After you add the Insert Record server behavior to your registration page, as described in the previous sections, the final step is to add the Check New User server behavior. This server behavior ensures that the chosen username is unique and not already taken by someone else. To ensure that usernames are unique, follow these steps:

1. **In the Server Behaviors panel, click the plus (+) button and select User Authentication⇨Check New Username.**

The Check New Username dialog box opens.

2. **From the Username Field drop-down list, select the form text field in which visitors enter a username.**

3. **In the If Already Exists, Go To box, enter a page name to open if the chosen username is already taken.**

Figure 6-7 shows the Check New Username dialog box, which validates that the username in the textField form field isn't already in the database. If it already exists, the user is sent to `taken.php`. The taken page usually informs the user that the username is already taken and that to try variations on the username (such as adding numbers to the end).

4. **Click OK.**

Your registration page is now complete.

Figure 6-7:
The Check New User-name dialog box links the username field and specifies the page to open in case of a conflict.

Building a Login Page

A login page enables registered users to log in to a Web site. Dreamweaver comes with a sample page design of a login page, or you can design your own.

Here's how the login process works:

1. **The user enters a username and password on the login page and then clicks the Submit button.**

2. **The Log In server behavior compares the values the user entered against the values in the database table that stores login information for your registered users.**

3. **If the values match, the browser opens your Web site's home page (or a similar page), and if the values don't match, it opens a page that explains that the login process was not successful.**

If you want to use Dreamweaver's Login page design (shown in Figure 6-8), choose File➪New to open the New Document window. Then select Page Designs from the Category list, select UI: Login from the Page Designs list, and click Create.

Figure 6-8:
Dream-
weaver's
built-in
login page.

The following sections show you how to complete these steps to build your own login page.

Setting up a database table

If you set up a registration page, as described earlier in the chapter, you've already created this table. See the "Setting up a database table for login data" section for details.

Creating the HTML form on the login page

If you want to design your own login page, first you need to create a new page and add an HTML form with a username text box, a password text box, and a submit button. This process is similar to the process of adding a form to a registration page. Follow the steps in the earlier section, "Adding an HTML form to the registration page," to add a username field and a password field to your login page. Figure 6-9 shows an example of a completed HTML form with username and password text boxes and a submit button.

Figure 6-9: The Document window with your form after you add the Username and Password fields.

Adding a Log In User server behavior to the page

After adding a form to your login page (as described in the preceding section), the final step is to add the Log In User server behavior, which checks to make sure the user entered a valid username and password.

To add the Log In User server behavior to your login page, open the page and follow these steps:

1. **In the Server Behaviors panel, click the plus (+) sign and choose User Authentication⇨Log In User.**

The Log In User dialog box displays.

2. **In the Get Input From Form field, select the form used on the login page.**

3. **In the Username Field and Password Field text boxes, select the appropriate form fields.**

For example, in Figure 6-10, we selected textfield and textfield2, respectively.

4. **For ColdFusion only, enter your username and password.**

5. **In the Table drop-down list, select the database table that you will check the form fields against.**

For example, we selected the users table in Figure 6-10.

6. **From the Username Column and Password Column drop-down lists, specify the table columns for username and password.**

For example, the users table that we selected in Step 5 contains username and password columns, so we selected those columns.

7. **In the If Login Success, Go To text box, enter the name of the page to open if the user successfully logs in.**

Or you can click the Browse button and select the page.

If users try to review a restricted page before logging in, you can send them back to the restricted page after they've successfully logged in. If you want to do this, select the Go to Previous URL check box.

8. **In the If Login Fails, Go To text box, enter the name of the page to open if the user is unable to log in.**

Or you can click the Browse button and select the page.

9. **Indicate whether you want to grant access to this page based just on username and password, or based on authorization level as well.**

Having multiple authentication levels provides more flexibility for segregated access to information but also comes at the cost of added complexity (and time administering your user's levels and categorizing information). Most people can get by without setting up multiple access levels to their sites.

10. **Click OK.**

Your login page is now complete.

Figure 6-10:
The Log In
User server
behavior
sends
users to
`main.php`
for a
successful
login or
`denied.php` for a
failed login.

Restricting Access to Authorized Users Only

If you have a Web page that you don't want all users to be able to view, you can restrict access to it. To do this, you add the Restrict Access to Page server behavior to the page so that only authorized users can view the page. If an unauthorized user attempts to open the restricted page, the user is redirected to another page.

Here are a few examples of when restricted access may be useful:

✦ You have a page that you only want users with Administrator privileges to be able to view.

✦ You want to make sure that users log in before they can view a specific page.

✦ You want to review newly registered users before allowing them to access members-only pages.

Although Dreamweaver doesn't provide the authentication server behavior for ASP.NET, you can use the ASP authentication server behaviors and run them on the same Web site.

To restrict access to a page, you need to do the following tasks:

✦ Add Restrict Access to a Page server behavior to that page.

✦ If you want to use authorization levels to further restrict page access, you need to add a column to your users database table to maintain information about which access privileges each user is entitled to.

Restricting access to a page

Follow these steps to restrict access to a page:

1. **Open the page you want to restrict access to.**

2. **In the Server Behaviors panel, click the plus (+) sign and select User Authentication⇨Restrict Access to Page.**

   The Restrict Access to Page dialog box opens.

3. **In the Restrict Based On area, select one of the following options:**

   • **Username and Password:** Select this option if you only want users with a valid username and password to access the restricted page. Use it when you aren't concerned about access levels (or just aren't using them).

   • **Username, Password, and Access Level:** Select this option if you only want users with specific access privileges to be able to view the page. Specify one or more authorization levels for the page — for example, Administrator.

     To select more than one level (for example, Administrator, Guest, and Member), Ctrl+click (Windows) or ⌘+click (Mac).

4. **In the If Access Denied, Go To text box, enter the name of the page to open if an unauthorized user attempts to open the restricted page.**

   The Restrict Access to Page dialog box in Figure 6-11 requires a username and password to view the page.

5. **Click OK.**

   Dreamweaver adds a server behavior to the page ensuring that only authorized users can access the page.

Figure 6-11:
The Restrict Access to Page dialog box configured to send users to `denied.php` if they aren't logged on.

```
Restrict Access To Page                                        [x]
                                                    ┌──────────┐
  Restrict based on: ⊙ Username and password        │    OK    │
                                                    ├──────────┤
                     ○ Username, password, and      │  Cancel  │
                       access level                 ├──────────┤
                       Select level(s):  test       │   Help   │
                                        Define...    └──────────┘

  If access denied, go to: denied.php      Browse...
```

Index

M

Q

BUSINESS, CAREERS & PERSONAL FINANCE

Grant Writing

0-7645-5307-0

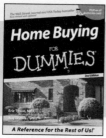

Home Buying

0-7645-5331-3 *†

Also available:
- Accounting For Dummies †
  0-7645-5314-3
- Business Plans Kit For Dummies †
  0-7645-5365-8
- Cover Letters For Dummies
  0-7645-5224-4
- Frugal Living For Dummies
  0-7645-5403-4
- Leadership For Dummies
  0-7645-5176-0
- Managing For Dummies
  0-7645-1771-6

- Marketing For Dummies
  0-7645-5600-2
- Personal Finance For Dummies *
  0-7645-2590-5
- Project Management For Dummies
  0-7645-5283-X
- Resumes For Dummies †
  0-7645-5471-9
- Selling For Dummies
  0-7645-5363-1
- Small Business Kit For Dummies *†
  0-7645-5093-4

HOME & BUSINESS COMPUTER BASICS

Windows XP

0-7645-4074-2

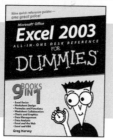

Excel 2003

0-7645-3758-X

Also available:
- ACT! 6 For Dummies
  0-7645-2645-6
- iLife '04 All-in-One Desk Reference For Dummies
  0-7645-7347-0
- iPAQ For Dummies
  0-7645-6769-1
- Mac OS X Panther Timesaving Techniques For Dummies
  0-7645-5812-9
- Macs For Dummies
  0-7645-5656-8

- Microsoft Money 2004 For Dummies
  0-7645-4195-1
- Office 2003 All-in-One Desk Reference For Dummies
  0-7645-3883-7
- Outlook 2003 For Dummies
  0-7645-3759-8
- PCs For Dummies
  0-7645-4074-2
- TiVo For Dummies
  0-7645-6923-6
- Upgrading and Fixing PCs For Dummies
  0-7645-1665-5
- Windows XP Timesaving Techniques For Dummies
  0-7645-3748-2

FOOD, HOME, GARDEN, HOBBIES, MUSIC & PETS

Feng Shui

0-7645-5295-3

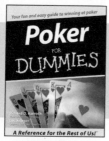

Poker

0-7645-5232-5

Also available:
- Bass Guitar For Dummies
  0-7645-2487-9
- Diabetes Cookbook For Dummies
  0-7645-5230-9
- Gardening For Dummies *
  0-7645-5130-2
- Guitar For Dummies
  0-7645-5106-X
- Holiday Decorating For Dummies
  0-7645-2570-0
- Home Improvement All-in-One For Dummies
  0-7645-5680-0

- Knitting For Dummies
  0-7645-5395-X
- Piano For Dummies
  0-7645-5105-1
- Puppies For Dummies
  0-7645-5255-4
- Scrapbooking For Dummies
  0-7645-7208-3
- Senior Dogs For Dummies
  0-7645-5818-8
- Singing For Dummies
  0-7645-2475-5
- 30-Minute Meals For Dummies
  0-7645-2589-1

INTERNET & DIGITAL MEDIA

Digital Photography

0-7645-1664-7

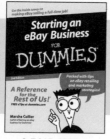

Starting an eBay Business

0-7645-6924-4

Also available:
- 2005 Online Shopping Directory For Dummies
  0-7645-7495-7
- CD & DVD Recording For Dummies
  0-7645-5956-7
- eBay For Dummies
  0-7645-5654-1
- Fighting Spam For Dummies
  0-7645-5965-6
- Genealogy Online For Dummies
  0-7645-5964-8
- Google For Dummies
  0-7645-4420-9

- Home Recording For Musicians For Dummies
  0-7645-1634-5
- The Internet For Dummies
  0-7645-4173-0
- iPod & iTunes For Dummies
  0-7645-7772-7
- Preventing Identity Theft For Dummies
  0-7645-7336-5
- Pro Tools All-in-One Desk Reference For Dummies
  0-7645-5714-9
- Roxio Easy Media Creator For Dummies
  0-7645-7131-1

* Separate Canadian edition also available
† Separate U.K. edition also available

SPORTS, FITNESS, PARENTING, RELIGION & SPIRITUALITY

0-7645-5146-9

0-7645-5418-2

Also available:

- Adoption For Dummies
  0-7645-5488-3
- Basketball For Dummies
  0-7645-5248-1
- The Bible For Dummies
  0-7645-5296-1
- Buddhism For Dummies
  0-7645-5359-3
- Catholicism For Dummies
  0-7645-5391-7
- Hockey For Dummies
  0-7645-5228-7

- Judaism For Dummies
  0-7645-5299-6
- Martial Arts For Dummies
  0-7645-5358-5
- Pilates For Dummies
  0-7645-5397-6
- Religion For Dummies
  0-7645-5264-3
- Teaching Kids to Read For Dummies
  0-7645-4043-2
- Weight Training For Dummies
  0-7645-5168-X
- Yoga For Dummies
  0-7645-5117-5

TRAVEL

0-7645-5438-7

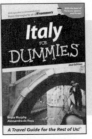
0-7645-5453-0

Also available:

- Alaska For Dummies
  0-7645-1761-9
- Arizona For Dummies
  0-7645-6938-4
- Cancún and the Yucatán For Dummies
  0-7645-2437-2
- Cruise Vacations For Dummies
  0-7645-6941-4
- Europe For Dummies
  0-7645-5456-5
- Ireland For Dummies
  0-7645-5455-7

- Las Vegas For Dummies
  0-7645-5448-4
- London For Dummies
  0-7645-4277-X
- New York City For Dummies
  0-7645-6945-7
- Paris For Dummies
  0-7645-5494-8
- RV Vacations For Dummies
  0-7645-5443-3
- Walt Disney World & Orlando For Dummies
  0-7645-6943-0

GRAPHICS, DESIGN & WEB DEVELOPMENT

0-7645-4345-8

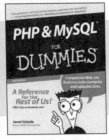
0-7645-5589-8

Also available:

- Adobe Acrobat 6 PDF For Dummies
  0-7645-3760-1
- Building a Web Site For Dummies
  0-7645-7144-3
- Dreamweaver MX 2004 For Dummies
  0-7645-4342-3
- FrontPage 2003 For Dummies
  0-7645-3882-9
- HTML 4 For Dummies
  0-7645-1995-6
- Illustrator CS For Dummies
  0-7645-4084-X

- Macromedia Flash MX 2004 For Dummies
  0-7645-4358-X
- Photoshop 7 All-in-One Desk Reference For Dummies
  0-7645-1667-1
- Photoshop CS Timesaving Techniques For Dummies
  0-7645-6782-9
- PHP 5 For Dummies
  0-7645-4166-8
- PowerPoint 2003 For Dummies
  0-7645-3908-6
- QuarkXPress 6 For Dummies
  0-7645-2593-X

NETWORKING, SECURITY, PROGRAMMING & DATABASES

0-7645-6852-3

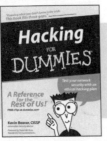
0-7645-5784-X

Also available:

- A+ Certification For Dummies
  0-7645-4187-0
- Access 2003 All-in-One Desk Reference For Dummies
  0-7645-3988-4
- Beginning Programming For Dummies
  0-7645-4997-9
- C For Dummies
  0-7645-7068-4
- Firewalls For Dummies
  0-7645-4048-3
- Home Networking For Dummies
  0-7645-42796

- Network Security For Dummies
  0-7645-1679-5
- Networking For Dummies
  0-7645-1677-9
- TCP/IP For Dummies
  0-7645-1760-0
- VBA For Dummies
  0-7645-3989-2
- Wireless All In-One Desk Reference For Dummies
  0-7645-7496-5
- Wireless Home Networking For Dummies
  0-7645-3910-8